I0137912

Discovering Christ In Ephesians

Discovering Christ

In Ephesians

Donald S. Fortner

Go *publications*

Go Publications
2 The Bridles, Seascale, Cumbria, CA20 1QG, ENGLAND.

ISBN 978-1-908475-31-2

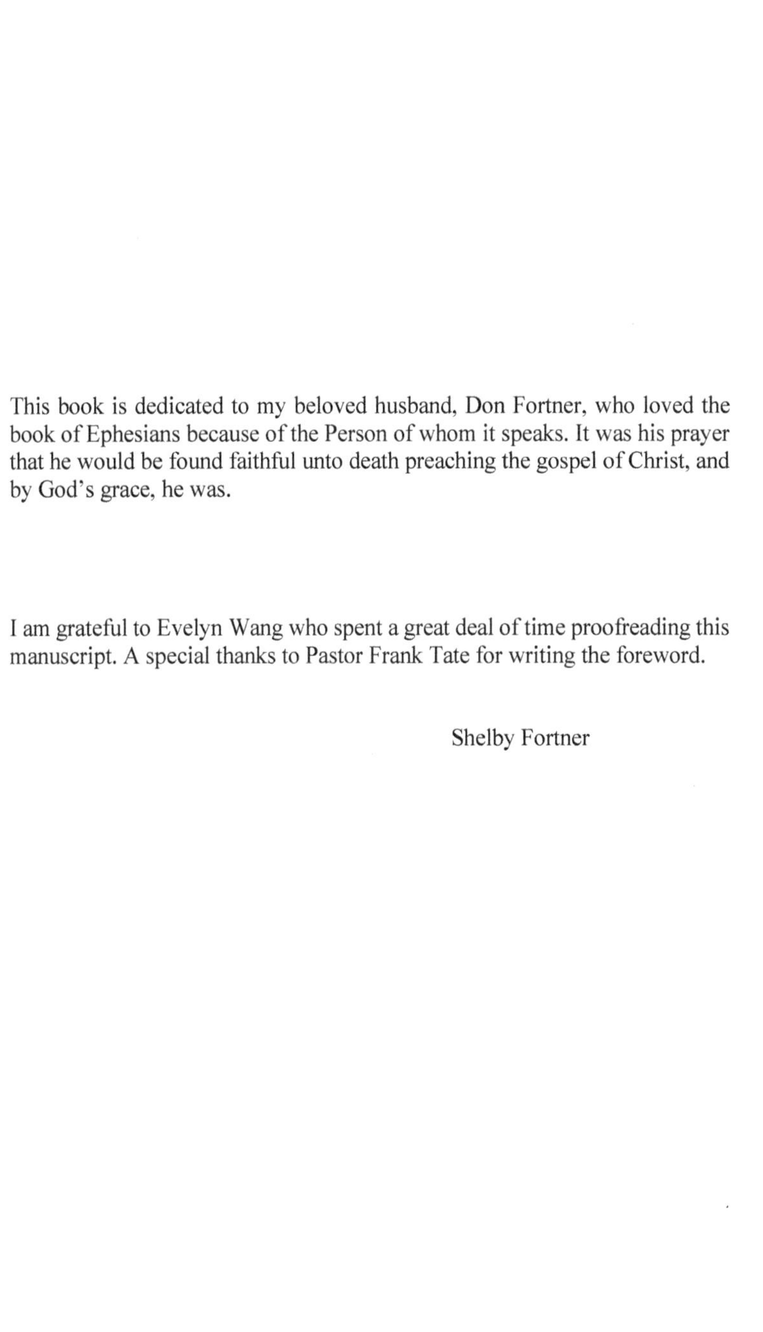

This book is dedicated to my beloved husband, Don Fortner, who loved the book of Ephesians because of the Person of whom it speaks. It was his prayer that he would be found faithful unto death preaching the gospel of Christ, and by God's grace, he was.

I am grateful to Evelyn Wang who spent a great deal of time proofreading this manuscript. A special thanks to Pastor Frank Tate for writing the foreword.

Shelby Fortner

Table of Contents

Foreword

I first heard Don Fortner preach in 1976. I heard him preach many times after that until the Lord called him home in 2020. During all that time, I never heard Don's message change even a little bit. His message was always salvation for sinners through the substitutionary, successful sacrifice of the Lord Jesus Christ for His elect people. Don boldly denounced any hope in the flesh. He consistently pointed out the foolishness of trusting salvation to any work that sinful man can do. He tried to always leave sinners nowhere to trust except Christ alone.

There was an urgency to Don's preaching that I appreciated. One Wednesday evening, before He preached to our congregation at Hurricane Road Grace Church, I told the folks there that night that Don's preaching was always doctrinally sound but the thing that made Don's preaching so special to my heart was that while Don preached the truth, I could tell he cared whether or not I believed on Christ. I said that I wanted to listen to a man preach Christ who cared whether or not I came to Christ. As I was saying that, Don's big booming voice came from behind me saying, "And I want you to come RIGHT NOW!"

You will find that attitude all through this commentary on Paul's letter to the church at Ephesus. In each chapter, Don takes the reader straight to Christ. He shows us how every spiritual blessing is all in Christ. He shows us that Christ has accomplished all of salvation for His people. He shows us Christ is all a sinner needs. He shows us the glory of Christ in all things. He shows us that Christ is the only subject of the gospel. He shows us that the believer's walk is directed by looking to and following Christ our Saviour.

I believe you will receive a blessing if you read this commentary seeking Christ. Throughout the whole book, Don is pointing us to Christ and he is telling us one more time. "Come to Christ and come to Christ RIGHT NOW!"

Pastor Frank Tate,
Hurricane Road Grace Church
Catlettsburg, Kentucky

Introduction

In almost 52 years of preaching, my late husband, Don Fortner, probably preached more messages from the book of Ephesians than any other book of the Bible. In thinking of an introduction for his commentary, 'Discovering Christ in Ephesians,' I felt there could not be a better way to begin than to use Don's own words when he first introduced his series of messages from this book.

Before he began his message, Don said, 'I haven't preached through the book of Ephesians since I was 27 years old. I have three volumes of notes on this epistle, from the series I preached 37 years ago. But I do not intend to simply repeat to you what I preached long ago. Tonight, I will begin anew. The title of my message is Ephesians: "To The Praise Of His Glory".' As he began the series, he gave an overview of the book, taking as his text Ephesians 1:1-6:24. When he introduced his message, Don said, 'Paul's letter to the Ephesians is one of my favourite portions of Scripture. I would not exalt one portion of Scripture above another. Yet, there are some portions more specifically suited to constant meditation and study than others. For example, I know very few people who have memorised or spent much time studying the first chapter of Numbers, which records the numbering of the children of Israel in their genealogies. Though those genealogies are very important, they are not exactly designed for daily meditation.'

'The book of Ephesians is different. Here we are brought immediately into the council chambers of the Triune God, caused to think about electing love, blood atonement, effectual grace, and preserving mercy, and made to worship before the august throne of our Triune, covenant-keeping God, our Father in heaven, our beloved Saviour, and our divine Comforter.

'This is an illustrious book, setting forth solid truths of the faith. It deals most clearly with the heavenly and soul comforting doctrines of grace; divine predestination, eternal election, substitutionary redemption, peace and pardon by the blood of Christ, conversion by the effectual working of the Holy Spirit, and salvation by the free-grace of God in opposition to human works. It also gives instruction concerning the nature and usefulness of the gospel ministry and the gifts qualifying men for the ministry. The epistle is concluded by demonstrating the effects of the gospel in the hearts and lives of God's people, and gives solemn instruction concerning the duties of Christians in all areas of life.

Before getting into his message, Don said, 'We will skip along the surface of these deep, deep waters, like one of those birds you see, swooping down here and there for an invigorating dip in the cool water, a refreshing drink, or a tasty morsel of meat. We will stroll along the shore, picking up the most obvious nuggets of gold. Before you wade into these waters, as you pull your shoes and socks off and roll your britches' legs up, let me tell you why Paul's letter to the Ephesians is such a delightfully precious portion of Holy Scripture and why it is such a constant source of meditation'. Don gave the following reasons why he loved this book.

Speaks of Christ

'I love this book because of the Person of whom it speaks. When I open the book of Ephesians, no matter where I am reading, no matter where I sit down, no matter where I walk in this treasure house, I feel as if I am immediately in the presence of our Lord Jesus Christ. At least fifty-five times in Ephesians, the Holy Ghost reminds us that everything we have from God, everything we are by grace, and everything we hope to enjoy in glory is in Christ! In Christ God has given us all that he can give and all that we can enjoy. He has given us himself.

The Ephesians

'I love to muse upon the things written in these pages because of the people to whom this book was written – The Ephesians. The city of Ephesus was the capital of Asia Minor, a province of the Roman Empire. It was a large, wealthy, metropolitan city flourishing with the riches of trade and commerce. It was called, 'The Light of Asia'. It was filled with brilliant men of much wisdom and learning, and people of great wealth. Tradesmen, scholars, philosophers and orators flocked to Ephesus. It was famous because of the magnificent temple to the goddess Diana. From the history we have in the book of Acts it is clear that the people in Ephesus were engulfed by superstition. Idolatry and satanic crafts of many kinds abounded.

'Ephesus was the envy of the world in its day. People thought it had everything a man could want. They had gods galore yet was a godless society. They were altogether without the knowledge of God and had no room for the true God. Like the society in which we live, idolatrous, man-centred religion walked hand in hand with superstition, immorality, lasciviousness and utter decadence. It openly promoted every moral perversity imaginable.

'Yet, from among these hell-bent pagans the Lord God was pleased to raise up a people, objects of his everlasting love to whom he revealed his gospel and made known his grace. Paul first came to Ephesus for a brief visit after leaving Corinth. Later he returned and ministered to the saints for about three years. A growing church was established in the midst of this idolatrous and wicked city before Paul was driven from them by persecution.

'It was to this congregation that this epistle is addressed. It appears to be one of Paul's prison epistles, written about the same time as were the epistles to the Philippians, Colossians and Philemon. It was probably written around the year 59 A.D., but not for the church at Ephesus alone. This precious portion of Holy Scripture was inspired and written for the church of God in all ages.

Heavenly places

'I love the book of Ephesians because it brings me into "heavenly places". The words "heavenly places" are found nowhere else in the Bible except in the book of Ephesians where the Holy Spirit inspired Paul to use this term five times. This term, "heavenly places" refers to heavenly things, heavenly words, heavenly doctrines, heavenly promises, heavenly possessions and heavenly experiences belonging to God's elect in Christ.

Grace

'And I love this blessed book of Ephesians because it talks so much about grace, God's free, sovereign, saving grace in Christ. When we open the book of Ephesians we immediately open a door that brings us into an indescribable treasure-house of grace. All grace is ours in Christ by divine purpose, to use for our own comfort and peace and for one another's good; to enable us to enjoy the glory of our great God and Saviour, the Lord Jesus Christ.

'Everything in this epistle is profoundly delightful and wonderfully sublime. The things written upon the pages of this book are things that could never have been written except by the inspiration of God the Holy Spirit. And that which is written here cannot be understood by any mortal, unless God the Holy Spirit teach him.'

After telling of his love for the book of Ephesians, as he began his study in this blessed book, Don said, 'All right, you've got your shoes and socks off and your britches legs rolled up. Now, let's go wading for a little while. Wherever you see a diamond or nugget of gold, if you care to pick it up and put it in your pocket you are free to do so. If you see an inviting deep pool, just dive in. Everything here in this treasure filled ocean is yours if you are in Christ.'

Chapter 1

God's Messenger And His Message

Paul, an apostle of Jesus Christ by the will of God, to the saints which are at Ephesus, and to the faithful in Christ Jesus: Grace *be* to you, and peace, from God our Father, and *from* the Lord Jesus Christ.

(Ephesians 1:1, 2)

Paul's purpose in writing this epistle was to lay a solid foundation of doctrine for the church at Ephesus and the church universal. He knew that in time false teachers would arise in the church and spread corrupt doctrines, doing great harm to the church and destroying the souls of men. This letter was designed to establish us in gospel doctrine so we might not be carried away with the devices of Satan.

That a gospel church was established in Ephesus is itself a matter of great wonder. Ephesus was a place of enormous wealth, luxury and learning, but it was given over to idolatry and the debauchery that always follows idolatry. The Ephesians erected an extravagant temple for the worship of the dunghill goddess Diana. Yet, among the Ephesians, there were many of the Lord's hidden ones; a people chosen of God and redeemed by the precious blood of Christ, who must be called. So, at the appointed time the Lord God sent the Apostle Paul to that pagan city to preach the gospel. In accordance with his covenant promises God sent his Spirit to gather out Christ's redeemed ones in that place to show forth his praise (Jeremiah 32:37, 38; Ezekiel 34:12; 36:24). Many believed on the Lord Jesus and a gospel church was established (Acts 19). It was to that church this epistle was written.

You will perhaps be surprised in reading the book of Ephesians to realise there are no personal references to the church at Ephesus. This is astonishing as Paul spent more of his ministry here than in any other single place. He came to Ephesus on his third missionary journey and preached the gospel for over three years (Acts 18-20). Many were converted by the grace of God. The gospel church in Ephesus quickly became a lighthouse for truth, from which the gospel of God's free and sovereign grace in Christ went forth into all the world. When he finally left the city, it was because he was forced to do so. His preaching caused a riot and he left with his life in great danger. His ministry in Ephesus was full of personal encounters that might have been helpful to others. Why, then, are all personal references left out of the letter? It is because this letter was not just to the Ephesian church. It was addressed to the church in every age and locality, 'to the faithful in Christ Jesus', to be obeyed by all believers as though Paul had written to each of us personally.

As was his custom, Paul began his letter to the Ephesians with a gracious salutation and introduction to the saints at Ephesus. 'Paul, an apostle of Jesus Christ by the will of God, to the saints which are at Ephesus, and to the faithful in Christ Jesus.' These two introductory verses are often skimmed over very lightly but they are full of instruction. Here Paul affirms his authority over the churches as an apostle of Jesus Christ. He describes his calling and power in that office as being 'by the will of God'. He tells us the general scope of his ministry was to the saints and kingdom of Christ. The purpose of his ministry was to make known unto men, by the power of God, the grace, peace and salvation we have from God through Jesus Christ the Lord.

God's messenger

This epistle begins by Paul identifying himself as a messenger of Jesus Christ, 'Paul, an apostle of Jesus Christ, by the will of God'. Who is God's messenger? We have preachers galore. You can find one on every street corner. We have preachers everywhere claiming to be God's messenger. So how do we know which ones are God's messengers and which ones are not his messengers? God the Holy Spirit makes clear distinctions for us in this Book. We will be wise to pay attention.

Paul also gives his name and apostolic authority to confirm the authenticity of his epistle. He does not call himself 'the apostle', but 'an apostle of Jesus Christ'. He was one among many. Every true servant of God recognises he is but 'a voice', 'a servant of Jesus Christ', just one among many, labouring together for Christ.

Nor did Paul thrust himself into the office or seek it in any way. He was 'an apostle of Jesus Christ, by the will of God'. He declared, 'Necessity is laid upon me; yea, woe is unto me, if I preach not the gospel' (1 Corinthians 9:16). His labours, sacrifices and sufferings were patiently endured because of that necessity. He did not engage in this work that he might obtain a livelihood, or secure an honourable name but because God had called him to the work and put him in it. 'No man taketh this honour unto himself.' Yet, he who is called of God does not shrink from the responsibilities and sacrifices demanded by the 'necessity' God puts upon him. The church desperately needs servants of God today, messengers of Jesus Christ, sent by the will of God. We need men 'called of God' to preach the everlasting gospel of his free and sovereign grace in Christ. Men constrained by the love of Christ and not by the love of money. Men who labour not for gain, but for the glory of God. Men who do not fleece the sheep, but feed them. Men who are sent into the field to work, not men who seek attention!

A man sent 'By the will of God'

First, understand this about God's messenger. That man who is called of God to preach the gospel is a man called, gifted and sent 'by the will of God'. He is a sent man. The man who puts himself into the ministry, who labours from any motive other than the will of God and the glory of God, cannot preach the gospel. He may proclaim truth, but he cannot preach the gospel. He may preach many things pleasing to the ear, but he cannot preach the gospel in the power of God. 'How shall they preach, except they be sent?' (Romans 10:15).

The man who bears God's message to God's people must be sent of him. The prophets of old were sent of God. Those who were not sent of God, had no message from God. The apostles were sent out to preach the gospel of the kingdom, in the power of God, by Christ. Even our Lord Jesus himself as 'the Messenger of the Covenant', was sent of God. It is to him, as the Lord of the harvest, we are directed to pray that he will send labourers into his field.

Paul's confession was that he was an apostle 'by the will of God'. He confessed there was nothing in him which made him worthy of the ministry. Like all men, he was corrupt by nature. He had been a blasphemer and a persecutor. Before Paul could be a messenger for Christ to men, he had to be born-again. He had been called to life 'by the will of God'. He was chosen to be God's child in eternity. He was redeemed by Christ's blood at Calvary. He was called by God's Spirit on the Damascus road by a personal, powerful and particular call.

Paul was full of amazement at God's grace in calling such a sinner and making him the messenger of Christ. He said, 'Unto me, who am less than the least of all saints, is this grace given, that I should preach among the Gentiles the unsearchable riches of Christ' (Ephesians 3:8). 'But we have this treasure in earthen vessels, that the excellency of the power may be of God, and not of us' (2 Corinthians 4:7). Paul confessed he was now God's servant only by 'the will of God'. God had eternally chosen him for the work he was to do. His call came from God alone.

Paul was a servant of Jesus Christ

Second, God's messenger is his servant. We cannot do better when we look for a model of a gospel preacher than the Apostle Paul. In Romans we have another example of the way Paul describes himself and all who truly preach the gospel. 'Paul, a servant of Jesus Christ, called to be an apostle, separated unto the gospel of God' (Romans 1:1).

The man who truly preaches the gospel is a servant of Jesus Christ. Gospel preachers are willing, voluntary bond-slaves of the Son of God. Paul did not call himself, 'Rev. Paul', 'Dr Paul', 'Father Paul', or 'Pope Paul' but 'Paul, a servant of Jesus Christ'. This man counted it his highest honour to be a servant of Christ. He was one servant among many and he was just a servant.

It is no light matter for a man to take upon himself the title of 'the servant of Jesus Christ'. Such a title implies that a man has been called of God to be his ambassador in the world. It is the greatest honour on earth to be called the servant of Jesus Christ. Those who are truly God's servants have an awesome responsibility and they are equal to their task only as they have been called 'by the will of God'. As God's servant stands before men with the Word of God, he is the messenger of Christ and must be received as such.

What is the call to the ministry? God gives his servants a desire to serve the souls of men. He gives his servants understanding in the Word of God. He gives his servants ability to communicate the things of God to men. He gives his servants the ability to lead men.

Called to be an apostle

Gospel preachers are called and gifted of God to be his messengers. A gospel preacher is a man with a message, a message from God, a message burning in his soul which he must deliver. He is a man with a messianic call, a messianic purpose, and a messianic mandate. If you ever run across a man with a mandate from God, or a man who even thinks he has a mandate from God, you will not have to wonder about it. You will know it. He will fit no mould, bow to no pressure, surrender no ground, make no compromise. Why should he? He has a mandate from God! That makes him utterly uncontrollable by anyone except God who sent him.

Paul claimed to be a messenger of Jesus Christ. As such he claimed to bear the message of the King to his kingdom. He was the apostle God appointed to take the place of Judas. He was born out of due time. He had the signs, wonders and miracles which affirmed his office. As the apostle of Christ, Paul had authority over the churches and they were bound under God to receive his instruction.

If a man is God's messenger he is aware of his commission from God in heaven. His commission is not to be a social worker but a messenger of Christ (John 20:21). Those who preach the gospel, though they are the servants of men, yet they have but one Master. It is God who determines their place of service. It is God who gives them the message needed on any occasion. It is God to whom they give account.

Separated unto the gospel

I will tell you something else about that man who truly preaches the gospel. He is a servant of Jesus Christ, a divinely called messenger of Jesus Christ and he is 'separated unto the gospel'. God's servants do not take this business of being God's servants lightly. They are men separated unto the gospel by God's decree, God's call, God's gifts, God's placement and by their own, ever-increasing devotion and determination (Romans 1:9-17).

Paul was not only called by God to do the work of the ministry but he was qualified to be the servant of God by his will and grace. He was a man filled with the Holy Spirit. He was a man humbled by the realisation of the momentous task set before him and his own insufficiency to accomplish it (2 Corinthians 2:16); but he was a man bold and fearless before men.

We also know that Paul was a man given to the study of the Scriptures, constant in labour, fervent in prayer and full of love. He was a self-sacrificing man whose heart was set upon heaven. That man who preaches the gospel of Christ is like Abraham's servant who was sent to get a bride for his son Isaac. He will not be distracted from his work by pleasure or pressure. He is 'separated unto the gospel'.

His authority

In every epistle addressed to a specific assembly or person the apostle Paul began by setting forth his authority as God's servant. He did this so the saints might be assured he spoke not of himself but as the ambassador of God. Therefore, the churches were obliged to render obedience to him. To reject him was to reject God.

The Word of God has much to say concerning the authority of those who are sent forth as God's servants. In our day, when men rebel against authority of every kind, people have come to look upon the minister of Christ as one who may make suggestions to the church but not have any authority in the church. Most people suppose their pastors are to be dictated to and governed by the church.

What does the Word of God say about the authority of the ministry? I do not suggest pastors are in absolute, dictatorial authority over men but in the Scriptures their office is that of a spiritual ruler. In Hebrews 13:7 we read a command to the church, 'Remember them which have the rule over you, who have spoken unto you the word of God: whose faith follow, considering the end of their conversation'. Again, in verse 17, the saints are commanded, 'Obey them that have the rule over you, and submit yourselves: for they watch for your souls, as they that must give account, that they may do it with joy, and not with grief: for that is unprofitable for you'. In Titus 2:15, Paul admonishes the servant of God to 'speak, and exhort, and rebuke with all authority. Let no man despise thee'. In 1 Timothy 3:5, the rule of a pastor in the church is compared to the rule of a father in his home. 'For if a man know not how to rule his own house, how shall he take care of the church of God?'

Pastors have authority as God's representatives to rule the church with the Word of God. Otherwise, the minister becomes a mere speaker who makes suggestions to the congregation which they may, or may not, choose to obey. And in the church, every man does that which is right in his own eyes. When an assembly of believers calls a man to become their pastor, they recognise the gifts of God in him and agree to submit themselves to him as God's servant among them, qualified to be their ruler. Like a wife in her marriage vows agrees, of her own desire, to submit to her husband's authority in the Lord, so the church agrees, when they call a pastor, willingly to submit to the oversight of God's servant. James Montgomery poetically described the manner in which a minister is to be received:

Come as a shepherd, guard, and keep
This fold from hell, and earth, and sin:
Nourish the lambs, feed the sheep,
The wounded heal, the lost bring in.

Come as a teacher sent from God,
Charged His whole counsel to declare:
Lift over our ranks the prophet's rod,
While we uphold thy hands in prayer.

When God calls a man to the work of the gospel he qualifies him for the work with the necessary gifts and graces. He empowers him with authority of heaven to watch over the souls of men. The servant of God must rule the church of God with love, patience, and tenderness. He must rule by the Word of God. He must rule faithfully and freely. He must rule with boldness and he must rule by example.

His desire

In verse 2, God's messenger expresses the desire of his heart for God's elect. A faithful pastor's heart is incessantly anxious for the people trusted to his care, constantly desiring and seeking the everlasting welfare of their souls. As a faithful father seeks the good of his family the faithful servant of God seeks the good of God's family and devotes himself to it.

Look at what Paul here expresses as the desire of his heart for the people of God whom he dearly loved. Remember he is writing by the inspiration of God the Holy Spirit. That means he is telling us the incessant desire of God's heart for his people. God's desire is his determination. 'Grace be to you, and peace, from God our Father, and from the Lord Jesus Christ'.

This sentence is an inspired pronouncement of grace and peace upon every believing sinner for time and eternity! Grace will be the constant gift of God our Father upon us in boundless abundance, and the constant result of that grace will be ever increasing peace from the Lord Jesus Christ.

When God the Holy Spirit puts the grace of God in us he gives us faith in and peace from the Lord Jesus Christ who is our Peace. With every fresh experience of grace, we are given ever-increasing peace, 'peace that passeth understanding'. Peace in our conscience by the blood of Christ. Peace in our heart by confidence in Christ. Peace with one another as we are increasingly united to one another in Christ. Soon, the perfect peace of eternal glory in the presence of Christ.

The servant of Christ has primarily three areas of concern. These three things are the goals which every true gospel minister sets for his life.

First, it is the desire of Christ's servant to glorify God. Every decision a minister makes must be governed by the question, 'How is God to be most honoured?' In every sermon a minister must strive to give no honour to man but to honour God. The man who desires the office of a bishop desires a good work but his desire must be for God's glory. A minister of the gospel must be willing to sacrifice many family joys and comforts for God's glory. He is first God's servant, then a husband. He is first God's servant, then a father. He is first God's servant, then a citizen.

Second, it is the desire of Christ's servant to win men to Christ. His heart is in travail for the souls of men. His desire is to do men good. Therefore, he does not make merchandise of their souls. He tells them the truth about sin. He tells them the truth about justice. He tells them the truth about salvation.

Third, it is the desire of Christ's servant to serve Christ's kingdom. The servant of Christ is a shepherd, a friend, a teacher to the saints. He is a watchman in Israel.

To the saints ... to the faithful in Christ Jesus

I admire the way Paul speaks of God's people in Ephesians 1:1, 'Paul, an apostle of Jesus Christ by the will of God, to the saints which are at Ephesus, and to the faithful in Christ Jesus'. He calls them 'saints' because he always looked upon them as God's chosen people, a people separated from the world and made holy by his free grace in Christ; sanctified by his grace.

Because all who trust Christ are saints and a holy people in him, they are to be looked upon by us as saints. As those who being precious and honourable in God's sight, holy and without blame before him, are to be esteemed better than ourselves (c.f. Philippians 2:3).

Then, the inspired apostle addresses God's saints as those who are 'the faithful'. He thereby makes it clear that he is not addressing just the saints at Ephesus, but all the faithful wherever they are found. 'The faithful' are those who have God-given faith in Christ. They trust Christ with all their heart, to the saving of their soul. The faithful look to him alone for all grace and salvation, venture on him, rely on him, and trust him for eternal life and salvation. Their faith in Christ makes them faithful and true to him whose name is Faithful and True. They are faithful to his cause, his gospel, his church, his people, and faithful in the totality of their lives.

The message

That man who is called, gifted and sent of God to preach the gospel has a message to deliver, a message that burns like fire in his bones, a message he must deliver. Bro. Scott Richardson described preaching better than I have ever heard it described when he said, 'Preaching is getting a message from God's heart, to my heart, to your heart'. No man can do that but if God the Holy Spirit speaks through a man, that is exactly what happens.

The man who is sent of God has a message from God to deliver. The old prophets spoke of it as 'the burden of the word of the Lord'. Insofar as its doctrinal content is concerned the message is always the same (1 Corinthians 2:2; Isaiah 40:1-31; 2 Timothy 1:9-11). It is always a message of comfort to the hearts of

God's elect (Isaiah 40:1, 2) 'Comfort ye, comfort ye my people, saith your God. Speak ye comfortably to Jerusalem, and cry unto her, that her warfare is accomplished, that her iniquity is pardoned: for she hath received of the Lord's hand double for all her sins' (Isaiah 40:1, 2).

God's servants have a message of grace and peace to men through Jesus Christ. They tell perishing sinners of the free, eternal, undeserved, sovereign grace of God which flows freely to men ruined by the fall and is given to all sinners who go to Christ in repentance and faith (John 6:37; 1 Timothy 1:15). The one central message of God's servant is the substitutionary work of Jesus Christ. God's servants proclaim a message of God's absolute sovereignty (Ephesians 1:4-14).

'What shall I cry?' All God's servants who are sent to preach the gospel see eye to eye. They all preach the same message. They announce redemption accomplished! They preach, 'All flesh is grass!' They declare, 'Behold your God! Omnipotent, holy, sovereign and gracious!'

Chapter 2

Blessing For Blessing

Blessed *be* the God and Father of our Lord Jesus Christ, who hath blessed us with all spiritual blessings in heavenly *places* in Christ.

Ephesians 1:3

Paul took up his pen to write to the Church at Ephesus but no sooner had he began his letter with the gracious salutation of verses 1 and 2 than he erupts with praises to God in verse 3, 'Blessed be the God and Father of our Lord Jesus Christ, who hath blessed us with all spiritual blessings in heavenly places in Christ'. Robert Hawker suggests that, 'his heart was so full, in the contemplation of the divine love, that, like bottles ready to burst, he could no longer contain'. 'Behold, my belly is as wine which hath no vent; it is ready to burst like new bottles' (Job 32:19).

Jesus is God

First, this statement sets before us the deity, the eternal Godhead of our blessed Saviour. Paul is celebrating the praise of the three persons of the undivided God: Father, Son and Holy Ghost. As he does, the Holy Ghost declares again that Jesus the Man is God our Saviour. If the Son is equally to be blessed with the Father it is because he is equal with the Father and one with him. How precious! He who is our Saviour, the Lord Jesus Christ, is himself God. Take from us this sweet truth, and you take from us the mediatorial office of our Redeemer and our hope perishes. There is no sweeter portion of divine truth and no gift more precious than the knowledge that our Saviour is both God the eternal Son and our Mediator, Jehovah's Servant, who said, 'I must work the works of him that sent me'.

But why is God the Father here called 'the God and Father of our Lord Jesus Christ'? He is the Father of Christ, the God-man, our Mediator, who was foreordained before the foundation of the world to his work and office as the Mediator (1 Peter 1:20) when the Father made the covenant of grace with him, who is the Surety of the covenant.

He is the Father of Christ as both God and man. In his eternal deity our Saviour is the Son of God, 'the only begotten of the Father', by glorious and eternal generation, the eternally begotten Son. As a man, our Saviour is that 'holy thing' that is called the Son of the Highest (Luke 1:35). The Firstborn from the dead is the Firstborn, the Firstborn Son in the family of God.

Bless God

Second, the apostle calls upon us to bless God. 'Blessed be the God and Father of our Lord Jesus Christ'. The Greek word translated 'blessed' is the word from which we get our English word 'eulogise'. It means to speak well of and praise highly. 'Bless the Lord, O my soul', cries the Psalmist, 'and forget not all his benefits'. Paul is saying, 'Speak well of God and praise him highly'. Prayer arises from our sense of need. Praise arises from our sense of God's boundless goodness and infinite grace, the goodness of his being and the grace he bestows.

God has blessed us. That is to say, God has highly esteemed us and highly spoken of us in Christ from everlasting. Therefore, let us bless him. Let us make it our business to bless the Lord.

Bless God when you are sitting in his house hearing his Word. Then go on blessing God until your last mortal breath. Enter into heaven's eternal glory blessing God. Throughout our lives, here and hereafter, let us bless him who gave us our life. Let it be our delight to bless him who gives us all our delights.

How can we bless God? Without a doubt, the less is blessed of the Greater. Can the Greater be blessed by the less? Yes, we are to bless God but in a indescribably lesser way. God blesses us with all spiritual blessings but we cannot increase his blessedness. He needs nothing from us and if he did, we could not give it. 'If I were hungry', the Lord God declares, 'I would not tell thee: for the world is mine, and the fulness thereof'.

God is all-sufficient within himself and never dependent upon his creatures. He is infinitely blessed already. We cannot add to his blessedness. When he blesses us, he gives us a blessedness we never had before, but when we bless him, we cannot, by any degree, increase his absolutely infinite blessedness. David said, 'My goodness extendeth not to thee'.

Gratitude and praise

How, then, do we bless God? We bless God by our heartfelt gratitude to him and our expressions of that gratitude. We say with David, 'Bless the Lord, O my soul'. We say with Paul, 'Blessed be the God and Father of our Lord Jesus Christ'. We bless God by praising him, extolling him, desiring all honour for him, ascribing all good to him, magnifying and lauding his holy name. Let us do it. Sit still and let your heart be silent before the Lord. No language can ever express the gratitude we have for him who has blessed us with all spiritual blessings in Christ Jesus. Praise him in your heart, praise him in your speech. Break the silence. Speak of his glory. Invite others to cry with you, 'Hallelujah!' 'Praise Jehovah!' 'Ascribe ye greatness unto our God.' Oh, that all flesh would magnify the Lord with us (Psalm 34:1-8).

Heartfelt assent

We bless God by our heartfelt assent to all the blessedness that is ascribed to him. After hearing how great he is, how glorious he is, how happy he is, we bless him by saying, 'Amen; so let it be! So would we have it! Let him be great, glorious, and blessed, beyond all conception. Let God be all that God is!' We bless God when we say, concerning the whole of his character, 'Amen. This God is our God forever and ever.' Let him be just what this Book says he is. I would not have him be anything less.

Sternly just, he will not spare the guilty. Amen, blessed be his name! Infinitely gracious, ready to forgive. Amen, so let it be! Everywhere present, always omniscient. Amen, we wish him to be! Eternally the same, unchanging in his truth, his promise, his nature. We say, 'Amen. We are thankful and bless him for it.'

Our God is just such a God as we want him to be and we worship, trust, love, and adore him for all that he is. He is God indeed. Every attribute of his being is a diadem of beauty in our eyes. We rejoice in the fact that Jehovah is God. Therefore, we bless him in humble adoration.

Spread his praise

Let us bless the Lord our God by spreading his praise. 'Sing unto the LORD a new song, *and* his praise from the end of the earth, ye that go down to the sea, and all that is therein; the isles, and the inhabitants thereof. Let the wilderness and the cities thereof lift up *their voice,* the villages *that* Kedar doth inhabit: let the inhabitants of the rock sing, let them shout from the top of the mountains. Let them give glory unto the LORD, and declare his praise in the islands. The LORD shall go forth as a mighty man, he shall stir up jealousy like a man of war: he shall cry, yea, roar; he shall prevail against his enemies' (Isaiah 42:10-13).

We bless God by proclaiming his gospel and seeking others to bless him. Surely, if there is joy in heaven over one sinner who repents, we are in the best and most practical way blessing God when we labour to bring sinners to Christ Jesus. Nothing so highly honours him as the salvation of his elect. Nothing so highly honours our God as faith in Christ. Let us make it our business to spread his praise through all the earth.

Serve his children

If you would like to honour a man, if you really want to honour a man, honour his children; do good to his sons and daughters. If you wish to bless God, if we really desire to honour our God, there is no better way to do so than by doing good to his children. When they are sick, visit them. When they are downcast, comfort them. When they are in need, help them. When they are opposed, stand at their side. When they are spoken against, speak for them. When someone exposes some evil thing about them, extol something good in them.

You cannot bless the feet without blessing the Head. When you have refreshed the feet, you have refreshed the Head. Our Saviour says, 'Inasmuch as ye have done it unto one of the least of these my brethren, ye have done it unto me' (Matthew 25:40). If they are naked and you clothe them, if they are sick and you visit them, if they are hungry and you feed them, you bless and honour God their Father, Christ their Saviour, and the Spirit their Comforter.

I can add nothing to the happiness and blessedness of my God. But I can add to your happiness. I can add to your blessedness. O Spirit of God, make me to be a blessing to your people.

> Out in the highways and byways of life,
> Many are weary and sad. —
> Carry the sunshine where darkness is rife,
> And make the sorrowing glad.
> Make me a blessing, Make me a blessing,
> Out of my life may Jesus shine
> Make me a blessing, O Saviour, I pray,
> Make me a blessing to someone today.

Blessed of God

Third, this verse declares that blessedness with which the Lord our God has blessed us in Christ. 'Who hath blessed us with all spiritual blessings in heavenly places in Christ.' With those words the Apostle gives us reason to bless our God.

The God and Father of our Lord Jesus Christ 'hath blessed us', past tense, all at once, all together at one time in the eternal past. We bless God by desiring his praise, honour and glory. He has blessed us by commanding blessedness upon us.

He 'hath blessed us with all spiritual blessings'. Those to whom the Almighty gives one spiritual blessing are given all spiritual blessings eternally and forever! Those to whom God has given Christ are given all things in Christ; all the blessings of grace, all the blessings of salvation, all the blessings of time, all the blessings of providence, all the blessings of heavenly glory.

He 'hath blessed us with all spiritual blessings in heavenly places'. The word 'places' is in italics because it was added by our translators. Perhaps the word would be best read, 'heavenlies' or 'heaven glories' or 'heavenly things'.

However it is translated, Paul's meaning is that God blessed us with all spiritual blessings in heaven before the world was made. God our Father, who blessed us is in heaven. Christ our Saviour, in whom we are blessed, is in heaven. All these blessings shall at last bring us to heaven where we shall forever enjoy them perfectly and fully.

'Spiritual blessings' are blessings pertaining to heavenly things. They are absolutely secure, blessings that can never decay or be taken away! This blessedness bestowed upon us originated in heaven and brings us to heaven. It is a blessedness that makes us fit for heaven.

In Christ

God 'hath blessed us with all spiritual blessings in heavenly *places* in Christ'. What blessed words these are 'in Christ'. Everything is in Christ. If we have not yet learned that Jesus Christ and him crucified is the foundation, essence, and fulness of all divine truth; if we have not yet learned that the message of the Bible and the hope of the gospel is Christ and him crucified, then we have read the Word of God with no profit to our souls, our religion is a vain show and we are yet without hope before God. What knowledge we have of this sacred Book will only add to our condemnation in the day of judgment.

Without Christ and him crucified we have no forgiveness of sin, no comfort in trouble, no strength in trial, no atonement, peace or reconciliation with God, no hope in death, no access to God, no door of entrance into heaven!

'Christ is all.' Without Christ we are nothing, we have nothing, we can do nothing (1 Corinthians 1:30, 31). All God has for guilty sinners is in Christ, only in Christ (John 3:35, 36; Colossians 2:9, 10).

The love of God is in Christ. The mercy of God is in Christ. The grace of God is in Christ. Without Christ there is no mercy, love and grace but only wrath, judgment and condemnation.

When the flood came, there was no mercy and deliverance anywhere but in the ark. That ark was Christ! When the man-slayer fled from the avenger of blood he found no safety until he entered the city of refuge. That city of refuge was Christ![1] God said to Israel, 'I will meet with thee' … (upon) 'the mercy-seat, from between the two cherubims' (Exodus 25:22). Christ is our Mercy-Seat. God meets sinners nowhere else but in Christ!

Among the untold millions of the redeemed in heaven there shall not be found a single voice that shall not sing the praises of Christ, the Lamb of God. There ransomed sinners sing, 'Thou art worthy, … for thou wast slain, and hast redeemed us to God by thy blood' (Revelation 5:9). To him alone every knee shall bow. To him every tongue shall confess.

Every blessing of life and grace is ours only in Christ. In this first chapter of Paul's letter to the Ephesians, he uses the words 'in Christ', or their equivalent, fourteen times. He means for us to understand that all grace, all salvation, all blessedness is 'in Christ'. All that the Triune God has done for us, all he gives to sinners, and all he requires of sinners is in Christ; all spiritual blessings, all covenant mercies; election, predestination, adoption, redemption, forgiveness, acceptance, truth and knowledge and the eternal inheritance of God's saints.

Christ is all blessedness and all blessings are in him. He is not one blessing among many but all blessings in one! All blessedness is in Christ. All the blessings wherewith God blessed us were conferred upon us in Christ. He, by his merit, purchased them for us as the Lamb slain from the foundation of the world. He, as our Head and Advocate, as our Mediator and Surety, as our Representative and Forerunner, has received them in our name. And, by virtue of our union with him, we have them by right!

---

[1] When the man-slayer fled for refuge, he found no safety until he was in the city. He might know everything there was to know about the city; its size, its gates, its walls, its beauty, but he was not safe until he was in the city. Now hear me well. You may know everything there is to know about Christ, you may know about him; his Person, his work, his doctrine, you may even fight for and defend these things, but no blessing of grace is yours until you are found in Christ by faith.

Behold the transcendent bounty and liberality of our heavenly Father. He has more than one blessing for his children, he has all spiritual and heavenly blessings for them. Grace on earth and glory in heaven, grace to enable us to glorify him upon the earth and glory as the reward of grace with himself in heaven!

Christ the blessing

All blessings are in Christ but that is not all. Christ is the Blessing! Where Christ is not there is no blessedness, only cursedness. I see Christ's hand and Christ's blessing in the mercy he bestows upon me but this makes the blessing sweetest. Christ himself is the Blessing! He gives me light and he is my Light! He gives me life and he is my Life! Christ gives me salvation. That is wonderful but this is better. Christ is my salvation!

'The LORD is my portion, saith my soul; therefore will I hope in him' (Lamentations 3:24). This is our lot and portion forever! Rejoice! 'Blessed be the God and Father of our Lord Jesus Christ, who hath blessed us with all spiritual blessings in heavenly places in Christ.'

Chapter 3

God's Election: The Source And Cause Of All Blessedness

According as he hath chosen us in him before the foundation of the world, that we should be holy and without blame before him in love.

(Ephesians 1:4)

The Apostle Paul has exhorted us to bless and praise God because he has graciously blessed us in Christ. He has chosen us to be his sons, sent his Son to redeem us from our sins and given us an eternal inheritance in Christ. Now in Ephesians 1:4, Paul brings us to the origin and source of all these spiritual blessings. He shows us that God's choice and election of his people to salvation is the cause of everything he does for us in Christ. That is clearly the doctrine of God the Holy Ghost in Ephesians and the doctrine of the whole Book of God regarding God's election. In order to exclude all merit from man and to show that all goodness and grace comes to us from God alone, the Apostle teaches us that all of the blessings of God in Christ come to us according to His election of us before the foundation of the world.

In Psalm 65:4, the Psalmist David says, 'Blessed *is the man whom* thou choosest, and causest to approach *unto thee, that* he may dwell in thy courts: we shall be satisfied with the goodness of thy house, *even* of thy holy temple'. Here election is spoken of as being in the present tense, though it was done before the world began, because this great work of grace is known and experienced in time.

No one knows his election until he has been effectually called by the Holy Spirit to life and faith in Christ.

Notice the progression of grace running through this verse of Scripture. 'Blessed is the man whom thou choosest.' That is election. God chose to save some in eternity and those he chose to save in eternity he graciously cuts out from the rest of mankind in time, like a rancher cutting his cattle out of the many roaming the open range. They were his cattle before. He simply rounds them up at the appointed time.

'And causest to approach unto thee'. This refers to irresistible, saving grace, the effectual call of God the Holy Spirit. Election both precedes and is the source and cause of this call. Now look at the next line.

'That he may dwell in thy courts.' Sinners chosen and called by grace are caused to dwell, not to visit, but to dwell in the courts of Divine worship. Those who are chosen and called by the grace of God to life and faith in Christ are kept and preserved by that same grace unto eternal glory.

Moreover, election is the source and cause of the everlasting happiness and satisfaction of God's saints in heaven. 'We shall be satisfied with the goodness of thy house, even of thy holy temple.' The house and temple of God in the Old Testament were typical of and representations of Christ and heaven, of God's salvation and our everlasting nearness to and worship of him. This is true blessedness; this blessedness rises from and is effectually caused by God's election of his people unto salvation in Christ before the world began.

No wonder David sang, 'O the blessedness of the man whom thou choosest and causest to approach unto thee'. No wonder God's election was so much on his mind and heart. It was the thought of God's election that made him leap and dance before the ark of God (2 Samuel 6:21). It was the fact of his election by God unto salvation and eternal life in Christ that sustained his heart and rejoiced his soul as he lay upon his deathbed (2 Samuel 23:5). Indeed, this is a doctrine full of joy and comfort to every child of God.

Some chosen

'According as he hath chosen us in him before the foundation of the world.' God chose some to salvation and eternal life in Christ before the world began. There are some who will tell you, 'The Bible does not teach the doctrine of election'. Those who make such foolish statements have either never read the Scriptures or have totally forgotten what they read or else they are out and out liars. Election is taught everywhere in the Bible.

God's Election:
The Source And Cause Of All Blessedness

The Scriptures speak of 'elect angels', an 'elect nation', an 'elect lady', and 'elect churches'. God chose some angels and passed by others. Of the first two men born in the world, Cain and Abel, he chose one and passed by the other. He chose Noah and his family and left the rest of the world to perish. He chose Abram but no one else in his father's house. He chose Jacob but not his brother, Esau. God chose Israel, the smallest of all nations, to be the nation to whom he would reveal himself. All other nations were left in utter darkness. He chose Joseph but not Pharaoh. No one can, with any measure of integrity, teach that the Word of God does not teach the doctrine of election. That is too obvious to even discuss.

However, the question of importance is this: does the Bible teach the election of some to salvation to the exclusion of others? Does the Bible teach that God chose some, not all the sons and daughters of Adam, to be the heirs of grace and glory in Christ? Indeed it does. The Apostle Paul, among others, thoroughly and frequently taught the doctrine of election. Here are just a few texts where this blessed doctrine is clearly taught.

> So the last shall be first, and the first last: for many be called, but few chosen (Matthew 20:16).
>
> For many are called, but few *are* chosen (Matthew 22:14).
>
> Ye have not chosen me, but I have chosen you, and ordained you, that ye should go and bring forth fruit, and *that* your fruit should remain: that whatsoever ye shall ask of the Father in my name, he may give it you (John 15:16).
>
> (For *the children* being not yet born, neither having done any good or evil, that the purpose of God according to election might stand, not of works, but of him that calleth;) It was said unto her, The elder shall serve the younger. As it is written, Jacob have I loved, but Esau have I hated. What shall we say then? *Is there* unrighteousness with God? God forbid. For he saith to Moses, I will have mercy on whom I will have mercy, and I will have compassion on whom I will have compassion. So then *it is* not of him that willeth, nor of him that runneth, but of God that showeth mercy. For the scripture saith unto Pharaoh, Even for this same purpose have I raised thee up, that I might show my power in thee, and that my name might be declared throughout all the earth. Therefore hath he mercy on whom he will *have mercy,* and whom he will he hardeneth (Romans 9:11-18).
>
> Even so then at this present time also there is a remnant according to the election of grace. And if by grace, then *is it* no more of works: otherwise

> grace is no more grace. But if *it be* of works, then is it no more grace: otherwise work is no more work. What then? Israel hath not obtained that which he seeketh for; but the election hath obtained it, and the rest were blinded (Romans 11:5-7).

There is absolutely no question about the fact that the Bible clearly and distinctly teaches the doctrine of election. God chose to save some and passed by others. Really, the only question to be answered is, 'What does the Bible teach about election'?

God's purpose

The purpose of God in all things is the salvation of his elect.

> And we know that all things work together for good to them that love God, to them who are the called according to *his* purpose. For whom he did foreknow, he also did predestinate *to be* conformed to the image of his Son, that he might be the firstborn among many brethren. Moreover whom he did predestinate, them he also called: and whom he called, them he also justified: and whom he justified, them he also glorified (Romans 8:28-30).

We recognise, of course, that the Word of God teaches the doctrine of God's glorious, sovereign predestination. Like election, it is a truth so plainly revealed in Holy Scripture that it simply cannot be denied by honest men. For that matter I cannot imagine why anyone would want to deny it.

Predestination is the all-inclusive purpose of God by which he sovereignly determined all things that come to pass in time for the salvation of his elect. In other words, everything that has been, now is and hereafter shall be was purposed by God in eternity and is brought to pass by God in time for the salvation of that great multitude whose names were inscribed in the Lamb's Book of Life in sovereign election before the world began.

God chose some to salvation and the purpose of God in all things is the salvation of all the chosen, whom he loved with an everlasting love.

Purpose accomplished

'According as he hath chosen us in him before the foundation of the world.' The purpose of God shall be accomplished. All that God has purposed, God will perform. The Bible never talks about God purposing what he does not perform, or trying to do what he does not do, or willing that which he never actually brings to pass, or of him in any way trying to prevent anything that does come to pass. God almighty does not try. He does! He does not wish. He accomplishes! He does not plan. He purposes!

Men talk about God's plan because men can do nothing but plan. God does not talk like that. God talks about his purpose. His purpose of grace is much more than some imaginary 'plan of salvation'. A plan may be interrupted, hindered, altered, or utterly rejected. That is not God's purpose of grace. God's purpose is the eternal determination of his Being to save the people of his love, whom he chose to salvation before the world began. That purpose cannot be frustrated, altered, or even hindered to any degree. Not even the rebellion of Lucifer or the fall of Adam hindered God's purpose of grace. Oh, no! Those events were just part of that which was and is necessary to accomplish God's sovereign purpose of grace according to election (Isaiah 14:24, 26, 27; 46:9-11, 13; Romans 9:11).

Election in Christ

'Blessed *be* the God and Father of our Lord Jesus Christ, who hath blessed us with all spiritual blessings in heavenly places in Christ. According as he hath chosen us in him before the foundation of the world, that we should be holy and without blame before him in love: Having predestinated us unto the adoption of children by Jesus Christ to himself, according to the good pleasure of his will, To the praise of the glory of his grace, wherein he hath made us accepted in the beloved. In whom we have redemption through his blood, the forgiveness of sins, according to the riches of his grace.' Election is in Christ. Here Paul silences the many arguments whereby men try to pervert the doctrine of election. Everything God does for, gives to, and requires from sinners is in Christ. God does nothing for us, requires nothing from us and gives nothing to us apart from Christ. Paul shows us three things in these verses concerning our election.

First, election took place in eternity before the worlds were made. God's love for us did not begin yesterday. It is from everlasting to everlasting. He chose us in Christ before time began. He inscribed our names in the Book of Life from the foundation of the world.

Second, our eternal election in Christ is the source and cause of all the other benefits and blessings of grace. Apart from election there are no blessings of grace here or glory hereafter, but for the elect all the blessings and blessedness of grace and glory are sure. God's blessings of grace and glory flow to sinners 'according as he hath chosen us in him before the foundation of the world'. Adoption, acceptance with God, redemption and forgiveness, regeneration, preservation, resurrection and the heavenly glory of the inheritance awaiting us, all are ours, all are sure to all the elect, all are according to the election of grace! All the chosen shall obtain all these things according to the purpose of God.

Everywhere today people talk about the fact that Christ came into the world but few have any idea who he is or why he came. Very few indeed realise that the Son of God came here to save his people from their sins, the people chosen by and given to him by God the Father (Matthew 1:21).

> 'Twas not to make Jehovah's love
> Towards the sinner flame,
> That Jesus, from His throne above,
> A suffering man became.
>
> 'Twas not the death which He endured,
> Nor all the pangs He bore,
> That God's eternal love procured,
> For God was love before.
>
> He loved the world of His elect
> With love surpassing thought;
> Nor will His mercy e'er neglect
> The souls so dearly bought!'
>
> John Kent

Third, election is for the glory of God. Here is the reason why God chose to save sinners, why he chose some unto eternal life and why he saves us in a manner that demonstrates both his supreme sovereignty and his glorious grace. It is, as Paul here declares, 'That we should be to the praise of his glory'.

Unto salvation

God's election of sinners in Christ is unto salvation (2 Thessalonians 2:13, 14; 1 Peter 1:2). Without question the Bible teaches eternal salvation. There is a sense in which all who are saved in time were saved from eternity. The Word of God declares that all God's elect were in Christ; redeemed, accepted, justified, sanctified and glorified from eternity in the mind, purpose and decree of God (Romans 8:28-30; Ephesians 1:4-6). However, do not ever think of election as salvation. Election by itself is not salvation. Election by itself saves no one. Election is unto salvation. Here are seven things said in 2 Thessalonians 2:13, 14 and 1 Peter 1:2 about God's election:

1. Election is a cause for great thanksgiving and praise to God.

2. Election is according to the foreknowledge of God, according to everlasting love and sovereign foreordination. The word translated 'foreknowledge' in 1 Peter 1:2 is the exact same word translated '*foreordain*' in verse twenty.

3. Election is a personal, distinguishing work of grace. 'God hath from the beginning chosen you.'

4. Election is unto salvation. I realise there is a sense in which some are elected to specific service in the kingdom of God from eternity. Not all are prophets, apostles, evangelists, pastors, teachers and deacons. Those who are, if they hold their offices in faithfulness, were chosen to their work by God. However, the biblical doctrine of election is not election to service but election unto salvation.

5. We were chosen to be saved in a manner consistent with and honouring to the holiness, justice and truth of God. Peter tells us that we were chosen by God 'unto obedience and sprinkling of the blood of Jesus Christ'. That is to say, no one, not even the elect, could ever be saved apart from the obedience and death of Christ by which redemption was accomplished.

6. We were chosen to salvation through the sanctification of the Spirit. In other words, no one can ever be saved who is not born again, regenerated and sanctified by God the Holy Spirit, election and predestination notwithstanding.

7. We were chosen to salvation through the belief of the truth. Not only has God ordained who will be saved he has also ordained the means by which they shall be saved. The means he has ordained is the hearing of faith. Those who were chosen of God in eternity and redeemed by Christ at Calvary must be regenerated and called by the Holy Spirit through the preaching of the gospel.

Unconditional election

God's eternal choice of his people to salvation in Christ was an unconditional election of grace (2 Timothy 1:9). God did not choose us, and he does not save us, because of our works. His choice of us was not based upon foreseen merit or our foreseen choice of Christ or our foreseen faith in him. Our only merit before God is Christ. Our choice of him is the result of his choosing us. Our faith in him is the fruit and result of his election.

Effectual election

God's electing grace is always effectual. That means it gets the job done! All who were chosen in eternity will be called and saved in time by the irresistible power and grace of God in the gospel. 'Who hath saved us, and called us with an holy calling, not according to our works, but according to his own purpose and grace, which was given us in Christ Jesus before the world began, But is now made manifest by the appearing of our Saviour Jesus Christ, who hath abolished death, and hath brought life and immortality to light through the gospel' (2 Timothy 1:9, 10).

Do you now find yourself trusting the Lord Jesus Christ as your only, all-sufficient Lord and Saviour? If you do, if you truly trust the Son of God, it is because, 'God hath from the beginning chosen you to salvation!'

Let every child of God give praise honour, and glory to him forever for his free, electing love and favour, sovereignly and graciously bestowed upon us from eternity in Christ. He who chose us redeemed us, he called us, gave us life and faith in Christ, and he will keep us unto eternal glory by his grace.

'Not unto us, O LORD, not unto us, but unto thy name give glory, for thy mercy, and for thy truth's sake' (Psalm 115:1).

Chapter 4

Eternal Grace

Blessed *be* the God and Father of our Lord Jesus Christ, who hath blessed us with all spiritual blessings in heavenly *places* in Christ: According as he hath chosen us in him before the foundation of the world, that we should be holy and without blame before him in love: Having predestinated us unto the adoption of children by Jesus Christ to himself, according to the good pleasure of his will, To the praise of the glory of his grace, wherein he hath made us accepted in the beloved.

(Ephesians 1:3-6)

In Ephesians 1:3-6, the Spirit of God tells us by the Apostle Paul exactly how we were saved by God's matchless grace in Christ long before the world's foundation was laid. He tells us it was all accomplished in eternity, 'to the praise of the glory of his grace'.

In these verses of Inspiration we are taught to bless, praise, honour and extol the God of all grace for his eternal works of grace. Paul begins by telling us that the God and Father of our Lord Jesus Christ 'hath blessed us with all spiritual blessings in heavenly places in Christ'. In verses 4 to 6 he tells us how he did it.

The time

In Ephesians 1:4, the Holy Spirit tells us that the time of our election was 'before the foundation of the world'. Election was done in eternity. Our names were written in the Lamb's Book of Life from the foundation of the world (Revelation 17:8). Christ is the Lamb of God slain from the foundation of the world (1 Peter 1:20;

Revelation 13:8). The kingdom prepared for us, which we shall receive in the world to come, was prepared for us from the foundation of the world (Matthew 25:34). Indeed, all God's works for us were finished from the foundation of the world (Hebrews 4:3). As John Gill stated, 'No new will, or act of will, can arise in God, or any decree be made by him, which was not from eternity'. All of these things plainly tell us that the election of our souls was a free, unconditional act of God's sovereign love (Jeremiah 31:3; Romans 9:13-16).

How we rejoice to hear our Saviour say, 'Ye have not chosen me, but I have chosen you, and ordained you'. We bow before him and say, 'Amen'. Josiah Conder said it well when he wrote,

'Tis not that I did choose Thee,
For Lord, that could not be;
This heart would still refuse Thee,
Hadst Thou not chosen me.
Thou from the sin that stained me
Hast cleansed and set me free;
Of old Thou hast ordained me,
That I should live to Thee.

'Twas sovereign mercy called me
And taught my opening mind;
The world had else enthralled me,
To heavenly glories blind.
My heart owns none before Thee,
For Thy rich grace I thirst;
This knowing, if I love Thee,
Thou must have loved me first.

Holy and blameless

The Lord God chose us in Christ before the foundation of the world, 'that we should be holy and without blame before him'. God's choice of us in Christ was for this purpose, 'that we should be holy and without blame before him'.

The Lord God has always viewed his people as a perfectly holy people, altogether without blame in Christ. This is the only view our Father has of us, the only view he ever had of us, the only view he shall ever have of us and the only view he constantly has of us. He sees us in Christ, holy and without blame, justified and glorified in him. In Christ there can be no change.

Yes, when we sinned and fell in our father Adam, we became polluted, just like all other people. We were born with Adam's fallen, depraved, corrupt nature, just like all other people. But that which we experience in time, in this present state, does not and cannot, in any way, alter what God did for us in eternity. Our fall in Adam did not, and could not, destroy the holiness and blamelessness given to us in Christ in eternity. Yet, what was done in eternity must be accomplished in time. We were chosen in eternity that we might be made holy and without blame:

1. In redemption by imputed righteousness – by his one offering of himself, our blessed Saviour redeemed us from all iniquity and 'perfected forever them that are sanctified'.

2. In regeneration by imparted righteousness – in the new birth, the Holy Spirit puts a new, righteous, holy and unblameable nature in the chosen, redeemed sinner, imparting to us the righteous, sinless nature of Christ (Colossians 1:27; 2 Peter 1:4). Paul calls this new nature 'the new man, which after God is created in righteousness and true holiness' (Ephesians 4:24). John says this new man that is born of God is 'his seed … and he cannot sin, because he is born of God'. Christ in you can no more do evil than Christ incarnate could do evil on this earth, 'because as he is so are we in this world' (1 John 3:9; 4:17).

In the resurrection by glorious righteousness – when in the resurrection we are finally brought home to glory by Christ we will still be found in him, holy and without blame, before God. Our all-glorious Saviour will present us to himself a glorious Church, not having spot or wrinkle or any such thing, but holy and without blemish before the Triune God (Ephesians 2:7; 5:25-27; Jude 1:24, 25).

In love

It is difficult to say whether the last two words of verse 4, 'in love', should be read at the end of verse 4 or the beginning of verse 5. Both ways are true and both ways are precious. 'According as he hath chosen us in him before the foundation of the world, that we should be holy and without blame before him in love'. 'In love having predestinated us unto the adoption of children by Jesus Christ to himself, according to the good pleasure of his will'. In love the Father blessed us. In love he chose us in Christ. In love he beholds us holy and without blame before him. In love he predestinated us unto the adoption of children. In love he accepted and accepts us.

The God of Glory loves his people in Christ. He loves us because of Christ. He loves us as he loves Christ because we are one with Christ!

Our Saviour's purpose in all his work, and that for which he prayed as our great High Priest in John 17, is that we might be one in him and with him (v. 21). He declares that the glory he has as our Mediator he has given to us, that we may be one even as he and the Father are one (v. 22). All this great bounteous grace is to this end, 'That they may be made perfect in one; and that the world may know that thou hast loved them as thou hast loved me ... for thou lovedst me before the foundation of the world' (vv. 23, 24).

Divine predestination

In verse 5 the Apostle continues giving us reasons to bless, praise, honour, extol and adore our heavenly Father. Here the reason he gives is his great, gracious, eternal work of love called 'predestination'. This is the Bible doctrine of predestination. I give it to you in the very language of Holy Scripture. 'In love', God our Father, 'predestinated us unto the adoption of children by Jesus Christ to himself, according to the good pleasure of his will, To the praise of the glory of his grace, wherein he hath made us accepted in the beloved ... In whom also we have obtained an inheritance, being predestinated according to the purpose of him who worketh all things after the counsel of his own will: That we should be to the praise of his glory, who first trusted in Christ' (Ephesians 1:4, 5, 6, 11, 12).

Our Father adopted us and named us as his children in eternal election before the world was made (1 John 3:1). Because we were adopted in eternity, he sent the Spirit of his Son into our hearts in regeneration, giving us the nature of his Son (Galatians 4:6, 7; 1 John 3:2). He will soon bring us unto himself as his children in the final phase of our adoption (Romans 8:15-21; 1 John 3:1, 2). Then, we 'shall be delivered from the bondage of corruption into the glorious liberty of the children of God' (Romans 8:21).

To himself

Our God and Father has 'predestinated us unto the adoption of children in Jesus Christ to himself' – to himself. Those are weighty, precious words – to himself. Not merely to happiness, to blessings in time or to blessings in eternity, not to all the creation of God with all that the whole world can supply but 'to himself'. What wondrous grace is contained in these words. Our God and heavenly Father, the God and Father of our Lord Jesus Christ, has 'predestinated us unto the adoption of children by Jesus Christ unto himself, according to the good pleasure of his will'.

His good pleasure

All this, he has done, Paul tells us at the end of verse 5, 'according to the good pleasure of his will'. We were not blessed according to our will but 'according to the good pleasure of his will'. We were not chosen according to our will but 'according to the good pleasure of his will'. We were not adopted according to our will but 'according to the good pleasure of his will'. We were not predestinated according to our will but 'according to the good pleasure of his will'. We were not accepted according to our will but 'according to the good pleasure of his will'.

Our Saviour's delights were with us from everlasting and it was our Father's good pleasure from everlasting to save us! Well might we pray continually, 'Do good in thy good pleasure unto Zion: build thou the walls of Jerusalem' (Psalm 51:18). In all things God performs his good pleasure and my heart says, 'Let him do his pleasure'.

Glorious grace

The Lord our God ought to be ceaselessly blessed by us because he has eternally blessed us in election, in predestination and in adoption. We read in verse 6 that he has done all this, 'to the praise of the glory of his grace'. The purpose of God in the salvation of poor, doomed, damned, hell-bent, hell-deserving sinners is that we should be, 'to the praise of the glory of his grace'.

There are other Divine attributes manifested in the salvation of sinners by Christ. The wisdom of God devised the plan of redemption. The power of God accomplishes the work of regeneration. The immutability of God is the security of our souls. In fact, all the attributes of the Triune God are gloriously displayed in the salvation of sinners. However, grace is the fountain head of salvation. Grace is conspicuous throughout the whole work.

Grace is to be seen in our election. 'There is a remnant according to the election of grace.' Grace is evident in our redemption. We have been 'justified freely by his grace, through the redemption that is in Christ Jesus'. Grace is the basis of our calling. God, 'hath saved us and called us with an holy calling, not according to our works, but according to his own purpose and grace, which was given us in Christ Jesus before the world began'. Certainly, all who are born of God know we are justified, pardoned, adopted, accepted and blessed of God according to the riches of his grace toward us in Christ Jesus.

There is a golden thread of grace running through the whole of the believer's history from his election before all worlds to his admission into eternal glory in heaven. All along the way, 'grace reigns through righteousness unto eternal life'. There is no point in the history of a saved soul upon which man can put his finger and say, 'I did that. This part of my salvation was my own work. I have this by my own merit.' Every blessing we receive from God, in time or eternity, comes to us through the channel of free and sovereign grace in Christ.

Boasting excluded, pride I abase,
I'm only a sinner, saved by grace.

Boasting is excluded because all human merit is excluded. In the vocabulary of God's church 'merit' is an unknown word. It is banished from our speech forever. Our only shoutings over the foundation stone and the top stone are, 'Grace, grace unto it!'

The salvation of our souls is the glory of his grace! Grace quickens the dead, enlightens the blind and makes the dumb shout and sing for joy. Grace pardons the guilty. Grace justifies the ungodly. Grace brings prisoners out of their prison-house and sets the captive free. Grace communicates Divine holiness to unholy sinners. Grace raises the poor out of the dust, the beggar out of the dunghill and sets them among princes, even the princes of God's people. Grace gives immortal dignity to the most degraded. Grace strengthens the weak, confirms the feeble, upholds the faint. Grace preserves the tempted, revives the languishing and restores the fallen. Grace brings poor vile worms into communion with God the Father, God the Son, and God the Holy Ghost. Grace brings countless millions of once poor, wretched sinners to ineffable glory and makes them more glorious than the holy angels. All this is, 'to the praise of the glory of his grace'. Not only to the praise of his grace but, 'to the praise of the glory of his grace'.

It is as if Paul is telling us that God's glory is made more glorious in the manifestation of the riches of his grace in Christ. To crown the whole, all these unspeakable gifts of God the Father are the result of his own everlasting love and his own free, sovereign grace given us in Christ before the foundation of the world!

In its planning, in its purchase, in its performance, in its preservation and in its perfection our salvation is 'to the praise of the glory of his grace'. Therefore, we bless God forever, saying, 'Not unto us, O LORD, not unto us, but unto thy name give glory, for thy mercy, and for thy truth's sake' (Psalm 115:1).

Accepted

'Wherein he hath made us accepted in the Beloved.' In his great, boundless, infinite, free, eternal grace the God and Father of our Lord Jesus Christ, our heavenly Father, 'hath made us accepted in the Beloved'. What a climax this is to the Father's eternal works of grace! First, chosen in Christ. Second, predestinated to glory in Christ. Third, accepted in Christ as eternally one with him and everlastingly united to him! Considered one with him forever! What unspeakable blessedness those words convey! 'He hath made us accepted in the Beloved.'

Remember, Paul has not yet mentioned the gracious works of God the Son or God the Holy Spirit. He has not yet spoken of our redemption by Christ or our being called by the Spirit. Our acceptance is here spoken of as something done before redemption was needed.

We were accepted as a holy people in Christ before we became unholy by Adam's transgression. We were accepted as justified from sin before sin was committed. Being accepted in Christ we were made the sons of God before we were made the sons of Adam. We were accepted as a redeemed people in Christ before redemption became necessary.

When God the Holy Spirit declares that all who come to trust Christ in time were 'accepted in' Christ before the world was made, this is what he is telling us: we are eternally one with Christ. We are in him as the members are in the body, united to him as the head is united to the body, eternally and everlastingly inseparable from Christ! God our Father always sees us in Christ, only in Christ. The God of glory, our heavenly Father, embraces us and looks upon us in Christ with immutable, eternal complacency, with delight and satisfaction!

No fact is more constantly spoken of in the New Testament and none is more comforting, than the fact of our union with Christ. The Church of God is so really united to her Head that she is positively one with him. We are the bride and Christ is the Bridegroom. We are the branches, and he the Vine. We are the body, and he the glorious Head. Every individual believer is thus united to Christ and one with him. As Levi was in the loins of Abraham when Melchizedek met him so was every believer chosen in Christ and blessed with all spiritual blessings in heavenly places in him before the worlds were made. We have been spared, protected, converted, justified and accepted solely and entirely by virtue of our eternal union with Christ.

The soul can never obtain peace until, as Ruth, she finds rest in the house of her Kinsman, who becomes her Husband, Jesus the Lord. Joseph Irons said,

> I am as sure as I am of my own existence that wherever God the Holy Spirit awakens the poor sinner by his mighty grace, and imparts spiritual life in his heart, nothing will ever satisfy that poor sinner but a believing assurance of eternal union with Christ. Unless the soul obtains a sweet and satisfactory consciousness of it in the exercise of a living faith, it will never 'enter into rest' this side eternity.

Nothing this side of heaven can be more blessed than the confidence of our oneness with Christ. Spurgeon said, 'To know and feel that our interests are mutual, our bonds indissoluble and our lives united, is indeed to dip our morsel in the golden dish of heaven'.

We are eternally and unalterably one with Christ, justified in his glorious righteousness, holy in his spotless holiness, perfect in his perfection and lovely in his loveliness! 'In whom we have redemption through his blood, the forgiveness of sins, according to the riches of his grace' (Ephesians 1:7). That is grace. Free grace! It is the grace of the God and Father of our Lord Jesus Christ. It is eternal grace!

Chapter 5

Measuring Mercy

Having predestinated us unto the adoption of children by Jesus Christ to himself, according to the good pleasure of his will.

(Ephesians 1:5)

How we rejoice in the fact that God's covenant mercies are sure and everlasting mercies. 'His mercies are new every morning' and 'his mercy endureth forever'. The mercy of God is in Christ. John Gill wrote, 'Mercy is displayed only in and through Christ. God out of Christ is a consuming fire.' It is only in Christ that God proclaims his name to be 'gracious and merciful'. Christ is the Mercy-seat in whom sinners obtain mercy. If we would be saved we must, like the publican, cast ourselves upon the mercy of God in Christ (Luke 18:13). Edmund Jones wrote,

I'll go to Jesus though my sin
Hath like a mountain rose;
I know His courts I'll enter in
Whatever may oppose.

Prostrate I'll lie before His throne
And there my guilt confess;
I'll tell Him I'm a wretch undone
Without His sovereign grace.

I can but perish if I go;
I am resolved to try,
For if I stay away I know
I must forever die.

But if I die with mercy sought,
When I the King have tried,
This were to die (delightful thought!)
As sinner never died!

How can I describe the mercy of God in Christ? 'Thy mercy is great unto the heavens' (Psalm 57:10). God's mercy transcends our loftiest thoughts. 'For as the heaven is high above the earth, so great is his mercy toward them that fear him' (Psalm 103:11). God's mercy to sinners in Christ is infinite, beyond measure and utterly indescribable. The Bible tells us that it is great mercy, rich mercy, abundant mercy, plenteous mercy and that there is a multitude of mercies from God for sinners in Christ Jesus.

My experience

I cannot begin to describe the mercy of God but I can tell you something of the mercy I have found in Christ. This is what I have experienced. God's preventing, prevenient mercy (Psalm 59:10) preserved me unto the appointed time of love and brought me to the place where he saved me by his grace. His forbearing mercy (Romans 2:4) made him longsuffering with me in my rebellion and brought me to repentance. The Lord's pardoning mercy (Isaiah 55:6-8) has put away my sins by the blood of Christ. His comforting mercy (2 Corinthians 1:3, 4) sustains my soul in hope as he enables me to remember and trust his promises, his providence, his presence and his propitiation. This is my soul's comfort, 'Thy mercies are new every morning'.

I cannot measure the mercy of God and you cannot. 'Thy mercy is great above the heavens' (Psalm 108:4). 'The earth, O LORD, is full of thy mercy' (Psalm 119:64). No, we cannot measure God's mercy but God can and does.

'According to'

In the first chapter of Ephesians God the Holy Spirit inspired the Apostle Paul to use the words 'according' and 'according to' six times to measure his great mercy toward us in Christ; in predestination, in adoption, in redemption, in providence and in effectual calling (Ephesians 1:3-20). The word 'according' is the word God uses to measure his mercy to us. The word 'according' means 'in agreement with', 'in harmony with', 'guided by', and 'measured by'.

The Spirit of God uses this word 'according' in the Book of God to teach us that every blessing we receive from the hand of God's mercy is measured to us by the eternal, unalterable purpose and will of God in Christ our Saviour.

Everything God does for poor sinners in time is measured, regulated and guided by the sovereign purpose and will of God in eternity. The heaven he prepares for us, the salvation he bestows upon us, the providence he brings to pass for us, everything God does for his chosen is measured out and accomplished by the purpose of his grace and the will of his love.

Cause of rejoicing

Here is a cause for unceasing joy in our souls. 'Rejoice in the Lord alway: and again I say, Rejoice! Let your moderation be known unto all men. The Lord is at hand.' That the thrice holy God should save any of us is a wonder of his sovereign mercy. That he should make such great and glorious provisions for our souls' everlasting welfare is a cause for unceasing joy and praise. That he should save sinners like us at such a great price (the price of his own dear Son's precious blood) should inspire in our souls the greatest possible humility, gratitude and devotion.

All spiritual blessings

First, we are told that every spiritual blessing of grace, every heavenly mercy is bestowed upon needy sinners according to, by the measure of, God's sovereign election. 'Blessed *be* the God and Father of our Lord Jesus Christ, who hath blessed us with all spiritual blessings in heavenly *places* in Christ: According as he hath chosen us in him before the foundation of the world, that we should be holy and without blame before him in love' (Ephesians 1:3, 4).

God's choice and election of his people is not the result of something we do, but the cause of everything he does for us in Christ. It was the fact of his election by God unto salvation and eternal life in Christ that sustained David's heart in the trials and troubles of life and rejoiced his soul as he lay upon his deathbed. Indeed, this is a doctrine full of joy and comfort to every child of God. 'Blessed is the man whom thou choosest, and causest to approach unto thee, that he may dwell in thy courts: we shall be satisfied with the goodness of thy house, even of thy holy temple' (Psalm 65:4). 'Although my house be not so with God; yet he hath made with me an everlasting covenant, ordered in all things, and sure: for this is all my salvation, and all my desire, although he make it not to grow' (2 Samuel 23:5).

Predestination and adoption

Second, we are told that predestination and adoption are mercies measured to us 'according to the good pleasure of his will' (Ephesians 1:5).

What does that mean? It means no unexpected children are ever brought into God's family! When children are unexpected, parents are unprepared. But when a couple has been married a while they plan and prepare themselves to bring a child into the world. When the young couple gets the good news they start preparing their home for a baby; nursery, crib, clothes, etc.. Everything is done beforehand. Even the baby's name is selected with care.

It is so with all who are born into the family of God in time. Preparations were made for us by our heavenly Father before the world was made. Sometimes you and I are surprised by the conversion of a person. We may be surprised, but God is not. Our heavenly Father wrote his name in the Lamb's Book of Life before the world began! He was chosen in Christ in eternity. The Lord God, the Almighty, our good and gracious heavenly Father, predestined everything that comes to pass in time just for that poor sinner he intends to save.

Redemption and forgiveness

Third, God the Holy Spirit tells us our redemption by the precious blood of Christ and the forgiveness of our sins by his blood is measured to us 'according to the riches of his grace'. 'In whom we have redemption through his blood, the forgiveness of sins, according to the riches of his grace' (Ephesians 1:7).

Redemption is 'through his blood'. All who are redeemed by the precious blood of Christ, all for whom the Son of God obtained eternal redemption, have 'the forgiveness of sins'. The measure of these companion mercies; redemption and forgiveness, is 'the riches of his grace'. Grace planned it. Grace provided it. Grace performed it. Grace applies it. Grace will complete it in the resurrection. Grace will have the praise of it.

Effectual calling and faith

Fourth, our effectual calling by God the Holy Spirit and the gift of faith in Christ, by which chosen, redeemed sinners experience God's saving grace, are mercies measured to us by the power of God and the will of God (Ephesians 1:19; Romans 8:28; 2 Timothy 1:9). God ordained that we should be called. God ordained the time of our call. 'The time of love.' God ordained the means by which we must be called in gospel preaching and God performed the call.

There is a purpose in God's call and the call is on purpose. We are 'called according to his purpose'. None is called accidentally. God meant to call us. He called us for the purpose of making us like his dear Son, the Lord Jesus and in calling us made us 'partakers of the divine nature'. By irresistible grace and omnipotent mercy the Lord God has made us new creatures in Christ, men and women with a new nature, 'created in righteousness and true holiness'.

Regeneration and conversion

Fifth, in Titus chapter 3, we see regeneration and conversion, this new creation work of grace, performed in God's elect according to the measure of infinite mercy. 'After that the kindness and love of God our Saviour toward man appeared, Not by works of righteousness which we have done, but according to his mercy he saved us, by the washing of regeneration, and renewing of the Holy Ghost; Which he shed on us abundantly through Jesus Christ our Saviour; That being justified by his grace, we should be made heirs according to the hope of eternal life' (Titus 3:4-7).

What kind of love chose us to salvation in Christ? Free love! What kind of grace contrived the scheme of salvation? Eternal grace! Why does God show mercy to such sinful creatures of abject misery as we are? Because of 'his great love wherewith he loved us', God 'who is rich in mercy' saved us by his grace! (Ephesians 2:4-10)

Strength for the day

Sixth, the Lord God in great mercy gives us strength for every day, for every trial, for every trouble, for every burden as it is needed by the measure of his own glorious power. 'Strengthened with all might, according to his glorious power, unto all patience and longsuffering with joyfulness' (Colossians 1:11). 'And he said unto me, My grace is sufficient for thee: for my strength is made perfect in weakness. Most gladly therefore will I rather glory in my infirmities, that the power of Christ may rest upon me' (2 Corinthians 12:9).

Here God's elect are assured of his grace in Christ, and of the absolute sufficiency of it always and in all things. One of the names of our great God is El-Shaddai, which means God All Sufficient.

It is sufficient grace because it is effectual grace. Today there is much talk about grace, but those who talk about it talk about a grace that lacks efficacy. That is not the grace of our God. God's grace is effectual grace. It is always sufficient because it is always effectual. Let us ever remember that God's grace in Christ is sufficient for us for everything and at all times. Sufficient to accomplish all his saving purpose, sufficient to pardon, justify, regenerate, sanctify and preserve us. It is sufficient in every time of need; sufficient in health and sufficient in sickness, sufficient in joy and sufficient in sorrow, sufficient in life and sufficient in death, sufficient in judgment. It is sufficient to present us faultless before the presence of his glory forever.

The strength we have as believers to walk worthy of the Lord unto all pleasing, the strength we have to be fruitful in every good work, increasing in the knowledge of God, is according to his power. We have no more strength in ourselves to trust Christ and serve him than we do to save ourselves. He says, 'Without me ye can do nothing'. Child of God, hear what God your Saviour says to you, 'My grace is sufficient for thee'. We are made strong by his grace in the experience of our weakness, made 'strong in the grace that is in Christ Jesus' (2 Timothy 2:1).

Supply for the way

God's mercy is measured to us by the love of God, by the will and purpose of God, by the grace of God and by the glorious power of God. In Philippians 4:19 we have one more great boon of mercy and its measure. Our supply for the way is measured to us day by day according to the riches of the glory of God in Christ Jesus. 'But my God shall supply all your need according to his riches in glory by Christ Jesus.'

Our daily supplies, all our temporal and eternal needs, all our physical and spiritual needs, are met and supplied to us 'according to his riches in glory by Christ Jesus'. What a statement! What a promise! God's coffers are infinite and God's coffers are full! His riches are untold. No famine, no great depression, no panic, no disease, no discomfort, no drought, no pestilence can diminish his supply!

All these boons of mercy are ours by faith in Christ. Thank God, these boons of mercy are not measured to us by the measure of our faith. They are measured to us by Christ, the Object of our faith. All God's blessings are in Christ. We were not present when he deposited them in him. That was done before the world began, so the blessings do not depend on us. Trust Christ. In all things, look away from yourself to Christ. Trust him. Depend on him. Believe him. 'As ye have therefore received Christ Jesus the Lord, so walk ye in him.'

Chapter 6

'Accepted In The Beloved'

To the praise of the glory of his grace, wherein he hath made us accepted in the beloved.

(Ephesians 1:6)

One of the most delightful, assuring, comforting, glorious things revealed in the whole Book of God is found in Ephesians chapter one. This great chapter is all about Christ our Saviour and the grace that is ours by him and in him.

'Grace', what a great word that is! Phillip Doddridge wrote, 'Grace! 'Tis a charming sound, harmonious to the ear'. To those who have tasted the bitterness of their sin and come to know and feel their depravity, grace is indeed a charming sound, harmonious to the ear. Every saved sinner, every heaven-born soul adores, extols and delights in grace. God's grace is his glory and God's grace is our joy.

> Blessed *be* the God and Father of our Lord Jesus Christ, who hath blessed us with all spiritual blessings in heavenly *places* in Christ: According as he hath chosen us in him before the foundation of the world, that we should be holy and without blame before him in love: Having predestinated us unto the adoption of children by Jesus Christ to himself, according to the good pleasure of his will, To the praise of the glory of his grace, wherein he hath made us accepted in the beloved (Ephesians 1:3-6).

Here, Paul, writing by divine inspiration, tells us that God almighty has from all eternity, chosen, predestinated, adopted and blessed us in Christ, 'to the praise of the glory of his grace, wherein he hath made us accepted in the beloved'.

With those words God the Holy Spirit reveals and declares to us one of the most comforting and delightful truths of Holy Scripture, that is, there is an everlasting, indissoluble, immutable union between the Lord Jesus Christ and his people.

Our acceptance in Christ is spoken of as something accomplished by the Lord God himself from eternity. It is not something accomplished by us in time. Because it is something done by God and done by God from eternity, it cannot in any way be dependent upon us. 'I know that, whatsoever God doeth, it shall be forever: nothing can be put to it, nor any thing taken from it: and God doeth *it,* that *men* should fear before him' (Ecclesiastes 3:14).

Let men hoot and holler all they want to about man's part in salvation, man's will, man's work and man's contribution but our text declares, 'He' God the Father, 'hath made', from all eternity, before the foundation of the world, 'us', all God's elect, 'accepted', highly favoured, honoured, pleasing and delightful to God himself, 'in the Beloved', the Lord Jesus Christ, our Saviour. John Kent wrote,

'Twixt Jesus and the chosen race
Subsists a bond of sovereign grace,
That hell, with its infernal train,
Shall ne'er dissolve nor rend in vain

Hail! Sacred union, firm and strong,
How great the grace, how sweet the song,
That worms of earth should ever be
One with incarnate Deity!

One in the tomb, one when He rose,
One when He triumphed o'er His foes,
One when in heaven He took His seat,
While seraphs sang all hell's defeat.

This sacred tie forbids our fears,
For all He is or has is ours;
With Christ, our Head, we stand or fall,
Our Life, our Surety, and our All!

A beloved person

Our great Saviour, the Lord Jesus Christ, the Son of God, is revealed here as, 'The Beloved'. I cannot imagine a title or name more appropriate for our Redeemer. This sweet, golden name is the one name that suits our Saviour in all his relationships with the Triune God, the angels of heaven and his people in heaven and upon the earth.

The Lord Jesus Christ is the Beloved of the Father's heart (Matthew 3:17; 17:5). None of us can imagine how dear and beloved the Son of God is to the Father. Who can enter into the relationships of the three divine Persons in the eternal Trinity? We cannot imagine the kind of love the Father has for his Son but we have abundant evidence of it and many illustrations of it in the Scriptures.

God the Son was one with the Father and beloved by him as our Surety in the counsels of grace in eternity (Proverbs 8:22-31).

In the covenant of grace all the blessings of grace were bestowed upon chosen sinners 'in the Beloved'; only 'in the Beloved' (Ephesians 1:3; 2 Timothy 1:9, 10).

When the Lord God stooped to create all things out of nothing, the Father called to the Son and said, 'Let us make man in our image, after our likeness' (Genesis 1:26). 'And without him was not anything made that was made' (John 1:3).

Everything that God the Father has done and decreed to be done has been done to glorify the Son, 'that in all things he might have the preeminence' (Colossians 1:18). God the Son lived upon the earth as a man, died as our Substitute and lives again as our exalted Prophet, Priest and King in heaven that he might glorify the Father. He is the Father's Beloved!

The Lord Jesus Christ is the Beloved of the blessed Holy Spirit. It is the office work and good pleasure of God the Holy Ghost, in all his gracious operations and influences, to glorify the Lord Jesus Christ.

> Howbeit when he, the Spirit of truth, is come, he will guide you into all truth: for he shall not speak of himself; but whatsoever he shall hear, *that* shall he speak: and he will shew you things to come. He shall glorify me: for he shall receive of mine, and shall shew *it* unto you (John 16:13, 14).

The Holy Spirit never draws attention to himself. He has come to glorify Christ. When he is present, when he is working; Christ is preached, Christ is worshipped and Christ is exalted.

The Lord Jesus is the Beloved of all the heavenly angels. I am not stretching the Scriptures when I assert that the heavenly angels, those heavenly spirits who wait constantly before his throne, look upon the Lord Jesus Christ as the Beloved. It is before his throne that they bow. It is his praise they sing. It is his will they wait to perform (Isaiah 6:1-3).

Without question, the Lord Jesus Christ is the Beloved of all his people. Saved sinners everywhere, in heaven above and scattered throughout all the earth, look upon the Son of God as their Beloved (Song of Solomon 1:14, 16; 2:3, 8-10, 16, 17; 5:2, 4, 9-16; 6:2, 3; 7:10; Isaiah 5:1).

Never was the term 'beloved' so full of meaning, so well deserved, and yet so incapable of expressing all that is meant by it as when it is applied to the Lord Jesus Christ. He is our Beloved. 'We love him, because he first loved us' (1 John 4:19). We do not love him as we should. We do not love him as we would. We do not love him as we soon shall. But we do truly love him! How our hearts rejoice to look up to heaven upon the Son of God and call him, 'Beloved'. The love of God is shed abroad in our hearts by the Holy Ghost. His love for us has kindled in our hearts a flame of undying love for him that neither life nor death can quench. The Lord Jesus Christ is the Beloved of our souls because he is our Saviour (1 Corinthians 16:22; 1 Peter 2:7). Blessed is that person who can, with a heart of gratitude, faith and love lift his eyes to heaven and say, 'Christ is my Beloved. I am my Beloved's and my Beloved is mine.' Do you know this beloved Saviour? Do you know the Son of God? Is Jesus Christ your Beloved? If he is, I want you to see, know and rejoice in the next thing revealed in our text.

An everlasting union

Our everlasting union with Christ is the source and spring of all the blessings and benefits of grace that we enjoy in this world and hope to enjoy in the world to come.

In this first chapter of Ephesians, the Holy Spirit very specifically states that everything is in Christ. In the first fourteen verses of this chapter the words 'in Christ', or their equivalent are used fourteen times. The Spirit of God means for us to understand that all the blessings and benefits of God's covenant grace are ours only by virtue of our union with Christ.

Our everlasting union with the Son of God is the basis of our safety and security, too. God's elect are as safe and secure as Christ himself, for we are 'accepted in the beloved'. No doctrine is sound that does not recognise the everlasting union of God's elect with Christ. When a sinner believes on the Lord Jesus Christ he begins to enjoy a personal, manifest union with Christ. That is a blessed theme. But our union with Christ began long before we believed on him. Our faith in Christ is not the cause of our union with him, but the manifestation of it. 'Who hath saved us, and called *us* with an holy calling, not according to our works, but according to his own purpose and grace, which was given us in Christ Jesus before the world began, But is now made manifest by the appearing of our Saviour Jesus Christ, who hath abolished death, and hath brought life and immortality to light through the gospel' (2 Timothy 1:9, 10).

Fivefold union

The subject of Ephesians 1:6 is not our manifest union with Christ in time, but our everlasting union with him from eternity. Our everlasting union with Christ is a fivefold union. When Paul writes that we are 'in the beloved', he means we who now believe, all who have believed and all who shall believe are in Christ from everlasting in these five ways.

1. An election union

Our everlasting union with Christ is an election union. We were chosen in him before the foundation of the world. This election union is the basis of all God's gracious operations towards and in his people (Ephesians 1:4-6).

Salvation must begin with someone's choice. Religion says it begins with your choice, man's choice. The Bible, however, declares it begins with God's choice. God's choice of sinners unto salvation is what the Bible calls 'the election of grace' (Romans 11:5). Election is the basis and first part of God's salvation. Without election no one would be saved. Though election is personal and distinguishing, we were not chosen separately and distinctly as individuals, alone and apart. We were chosen in Christ. There is no election of grace apart from Christ. There is no union with Christ apart from the election of grace. Christ was chosen to be the Redeemer (Isaiah 42:1-4). We were chosen to be the redeemed (2 Thessalonians 2:13, 14). Isaac Watts wrote,

> Christ be my first Elect, He said,
> Then chose our souls in Christ our Head.

Here is the blessedness of the doctrine of election. It guarantees our eternal security. Our election and our Saviour's election stand or fall together. The Lamb's Book of Life, which begins with the inscription of his name, is the same register that holds our names. Until the pen of hell can scratch out his name, it cannot scratch out our names!

2. A legal, suretyship union

Our everlasting union with Christ is a legal, suretyship union. As the surety and the debtor represented by him are one before the law, so the Lord Jesus Christ and his people are one before God in a legal sense. He became our Surety in the covenant of grace before the worlds were made or ever the earth was. 'By so much was Jesus made a surety of a better testament' (Hebrews 7:22).

As the Surety of the covenant Christ drew near to the Father in the name of his elect, made himself our Substitute and laid himself under obligation to God to pay our debts. He would satisfy all the demands of God's law, justice and righteousness for us. He would procure, on the grounds of strict justice, all the blessings of grace and glory for us. John Gill wrote, 'Christ and his people being one, in a law sense, their sins become his, and his righteousness becomes theirs'.

When Christ became our Surety before God, he became totally responsible to God for us, to pay our debts, fulfil our obligations and bring us to glory (John 10:15, 16). When Christ became our Surety God ceased to look for satisfaction from us. The Lord God, the Triune Jehovah, trusted Christ as our Surety from eternity (Ephesians 1:12). When Christ became our Surety our salvation was finished insofar as the Lord our God is concerned (Romans 8:28-30; 2 Timothy 1:9; Revelation 13:8). When Christ became our Surety our eternal salvation in time and eternal security became a matter of absolute certainty. We had our being in Christ and with Christ from eternity. Until he ceases to live we cannot cease to live!

The Lord Jesus Christ, our Covenant Surety, is our Legal Head and Federal Representative before God. As Adam was the federal head of all men, so Christ is the Federal Head of all the elect (Romans 5:12-19; 1 Corinthians 15:21, 22).

Everything that Adam did in the Garden he did, not as a private individual but as the federal representative of all the human race. All his acts were representative acts. Had Adam been obedient to God all the descendants of that original man would have been partakers of all the benefits of his obedience to God. But Adam was not obedient. He sinned. He fell. He died. We all sinned, fell, and died in him.

In exactly the same way, the Lord Jesus Christ is the Federal Head and Representative of God's elect. He was our Federal Head from eternity. He is our Federal Head now. He shall be our Federal Head forever.

Christ was our Federal Head and Representative in the covenant of grace before the world began. He was given for a covenant to the people. He is the Mediator,

Messenger and Surety of that covenant. It was made with him, not as a single or private Person, but as the Head and Representative of God's elect who were given to him as a people to save. What he promised in the covenant, he promised for us. What he received in the covenant, he received for us. Thus, we were blessed in him and saved in him before the world was made (Ephesians 1:3, 4; 2 Timothy 1:9).

When the Lord Jesus Christ obeyed the law of God and made it honourable, we were in him, obeying the law and making it honourable. When Christ suffered and died under the wrath of God, we suffered and died in him; 'Crucified with Christ'. C. H. Spurgeon wrote, 'Justice looks upon the chosen as though they themselves had suffered all that Christ suffered, as though they had drunk the wormwood and the gall and had descended into the lowest depths'.

When Christ was buried in the earth we were buried with him. When the Son of God arose from the dead we arose with him, triumphant and victorious. When he ascended into heaven and took his place at the right hand of the Majesty on High we ascended with him and sat down with him in his Father's throne, as possessors of heaven and all its glory with him, our Federal Head and Representative.

We see not yet all things put under the feet of man, but we see it as a matter of certainty that all things shall be put in subjection to him in the new creation, for 'we see Jesus' seated upon yonder glorious throne, from henceforth expecting until his enemies shall be made his footstool (Psalm 8:1-9; Hebrews 2:9).

3. A mystical union

Our everlasting union with Christ is a mystical union. I do not know a better way to express this aspect of our union with our Saviour than by using the word 'mystical'. We are one with him in the sense that we are members of his body, not in a physical way, but in a spiritual sense (Ephesians 5:30; Hebrews 2:11-14).

I cannot begin to explain this mystery. The fact is I do not understand all that I know about it. But this I do know, God's elect have a greater union with Christ than the members of our physical bodies have with our heads. We are one with Christ; as the head is one with the body, as the Father and the Son are one (John 17:21), in his glory as the God-man (John 17:22), as the objects of the Father's love (John 17:23, 24).

4. A willing marriage union

Once chosen sinners are born of God, once we are given life and faith in him, once we are manifestly in Christ, our everlasting union with him is a willing, marriage union. The Son of God chose us and espoused us to himself from eternity. Now, he has won our hearts! Conquered by his love, we love him!

5. A vital union

Our everlasting union with Christ is a vital union. It is vital both to him and to us. Our union with the Lord Jesus Christ is so essential and vital that without it we could never be saved and Christ could never be complete as our Mediator and Head. 'I am the vine, ye *are* the branches: He that abideth in me, and I in him, the same bringeth forth much fruit: for without me ye can do nothing. If a man abide not in me, he is cast forth as a branch, and is withered; and men gather them, and cast *them* into the fire, and they are burned' (John 15:5, 6). '(The church) is his body, the fulness of him that filleth all in all' (Ephesians 1:23).

A glorious position

The Holy Spirit tells us that we have been made 'accepted in the beloved'. The word translated 'accepted' in our text is a much stronger word than our English word 'accepted'. This word means, 'highly favoured, laudable, praiseworthy'. Now we are not and never could be 'accepted' before and by the holy Lord God, except in Christ the Beloved. But in him, in the Beloved, every believer, every sinner chosen, redeemed and called by grace, is so completely and totally accepted of God that even in the eyes of the holy, omniscient Lord God, we are highly favoured, laudable, and praiseworthy! Let me show you three things.

First, our acceptance with God is thorough, complete, total and absolute. To be 'accepted in the beloved' is to be justified from all things, freed from all sin, the objects of divine complacency and delight and worthy of our heavenly inheritance (Colossians 1:12).

Second, our acceptance with God is only 'in the Beloved'. God the Father is well pleased with his Son; and he is well pleased with us in his Son. 'In whom' not with whom, 'I am well pleased' (Matthew 17:5).

Third, our acceptance with God in Christ is everlasting and therefore immutable. Bless God, our acceptance does not depend upon us. It did not begin with us. It is not maintained by us. It cannot be altered by us. Though we fell in our father Adam, yet were we 'accepted in the Beloved'. Though we came forth from our mother's wombs speaking lies we were still 'accepted in the Beloved'. Though we spent our days, from our youth up, in wanton rebellion against God and in league with hell, we were still 'accepted in the Beloved'. Though after the Lord God has saved us by his wondrous grace we sin and fall a thousand times a day, as we all do, yet it stands in the Scripture that we are 'accepted in the Beloved'. What a glorious position this is. You and I who believe are 'accepted in the Beloved' (Romans 4:8; Psalm 89:19-37).

Unchangeable His will,
Though dark may be my frame;
His loving heart is still
Eternally the same:
My soul through many changes goes,
His love no variation knows.

Our text reveals a beloved Person, the Lord Jesus Christ, an everlasting union, 'in the beloved', a glorious position, 'accepted in the beloved'. There is something else, too.

A divine operation

Look at the text one more time. 'He hath made us accepted in the Beloved.' Grace is stamped upon the whole thing. From beginning to end, the work of our acceptance is God's operation. Our text is saying, 'Salvation is of the LORD'. Our being in Christ and acceptance in Christ must be the work of God alone because no one else existed when it was done. It is a work finished from eternity! God the Father put us in the Beloved by his sovereign decree because of his everlasting love for us. God the Son made us acceptable and accepted. God the Holy Spirit made our acceptance manifest to us (2 Timothy 1:10), by divine regeneration and by giving us faith in Christ.

If this day you believe on the Lord Jesus Christ, the Lord God has made you 'accepted in the Beloved'. Your faith in Christ is the gift of his grace, the fruit of being 'accepted in the Beloved'. Your faith in him is the evidence of your being 'accepted in the Beloved'. Your faith in Christ is the assurance of your being 'accepted in the Beloved'. He who has begun his good work of grace in us, making us 'accepted in the Beloved', will complete his work and make us perfect in and with the Beloved (John 13:1; Philippians 1:6). Let us give all praise, honour, and glory to our great God alone.

Chapter 7

'Redemption Through His Blood'

In whom we have redemption through his blood, the forgiveness of sins, according to the riches of his grace.

(Ephesians 1:7)

'Redemption through his blood'. What a glorious subject this is! Nothing is more needful and nothing is more delightful than 'redemption through his blood'.

In verses 3-6 the Holy Spirit has, by the pen of his servant the Apostle Paul, shown us the gracious works performed for us by God the Father before the world was made, works by which he saved us from everlasting. Here, he begins to declare the works of God the Son, which were accomplished in time. In Hebrews 4:3, the Spirit of God tells us that, 'the works were finished from the foundation of the world'. But here he speaks of redemption as a work performed and accomplished in time. That is not a contradiction. That which was done by the purpose and decree of God in eternity is and must be executed and accomplished by the power of God in time. Both the Father's eternal work and the accomplishments of the Son in time are 'according to the riches of his grace'.

Redemption presupposes a very grave situation. It presupposes captivity, bondage and slavery. Were we not a fallen, captive, enslaved race there would be no need for redemption. But God's elect, like all other people, 'were by nature the children of wrath, even as others'. We were born in captivity to sin (Psalm 58:3), in bondage to Satan and under the curse of the law (John 3:36).

Redemption is the complete deliverance of chosen sinners from that captivity, bondage and curse into the glorious liberty of the sons of God by the purchase of his blood and the power of his grace.

Redemption is the theme of the Bible. It is promised, prophesied, portrayed and proclaimed throughout the pages of Inspiration. Everything in the Old Testament pointed to it. Everything in the New Testament explains and declares it. Everything in heaven has reference to it.

Redemption is the dominant theme of my thoughts in prayer, meditation and worship. Redemption is the dominant theme of my praise and thanksgiving. Redemption is the dominant theme of my conversations with men. Redemption is the dominant theme of my preaching.

If I did not preach 'redemption through his blood', I would not preach at all. I mean if I did not preach redemption through his blood every time I stand to preach, I would not pretend to be God's preacher. 'For I determined not to know any thing among you, save Jesus Christ, and him crucified' (1 Corinthians 2:2).

'Redemption through his blood' is the one thing you must have. Without redemption you must perish. Someone must suffer for your sins. Someone must pay for your crimes, either you or a Substitute. But someone must pay.

Redemption has been accomplished, purchased, and obtained for chosen sinners through the precious blood of the Lord Jesus Christ and all who trust him have it.

'In whom'

First, the Purchaser of redemption is the Lord Jesus Christ, the Son of God. Notice those first words in verse 7, 'In whom'. All the blessings of God's free grace for time and eternity are in Christ, 'In whom we have redemption through his blood'. Christ is the Author of our redemption. He was called and appointed to be our Redeemer in eternity in the covenant of grace, and freely agreed to it as our Substitute (Psalm 40). In the fulness of time he was sent to accomplish the redemption of a chosen multitude. 'But when the fulness of the time was come, God sent forth his Son, made of a woman, made under the law, To redeem them that were under the law, that we might receive the adoption of sons. And because ye are sons, God hath sent forth the Spirit of his Son into your hearts, crying, Abba, Father' (Galatians 4:4-6).

Jesus Christ, as our near Kinsman, had the right and the ability to redeem us. 'By his own blood he entered in once into the holy place, having obtained eternal redemption for us' (Hebrews 9:12). Redemption is His. He did it! He obtained it! He owns it! It resides in him. He is made redemption to us (1 Corinthians 1:30).

We will never appreciate the greatness of redemption, until we appreciate the greatness of our Redeemer. What a vast, immense work that must be that required the God of Glory to become a man! How immense that work must be that could be accomplished by nothing less than the sacrifice of God's darling Son. 'For thy Maker is thine husband; the Lord of hosts is his name; and thy Redeemer the Holy One of Israel; The God of the whole earth shall he be called' (Isaiah 54:5).

'We'

Second, the objects of redemption are God's elect, 'we' who are actually redeemed! Paul says, 'In whom we have redemption through his blood'. Everywhere the Bible speaks about redemption it speaks of it as an effectual work of Christ accomplished for a specific people (Revelation 5:9; Isaiah 53:10-12; Galatians 3:13, 14).

Who then are the 'we' in this text? Who are those people redeemed by the blood of Christ? We are not left to guess and speculate about this. The chapter tells us exactly who the 'we' are who have 'redemption through his blood'.

All who were blessed in verse 3. All who were chosen in Christ before the foundation of the world in verse 4. All who were 'predestinated unto the adoption of children' in verse 5. All who are 'accepted in the beloved' in verse 6. All who are forgiven of all sin in verse 7. All who have obtained the inheritance of grace in verse 11. All who have faith in Christ in verse 13. All who are sealed in grace by the Spirit of God and have the earnest of the inheritance in verse 14.

Universal redemption is universal nonsense! We preach an effectual Saviour who has obtained – and in whom we have – an effectual redemption.

'We have'

Third, Paul shows us the fact of redemption. 'In whom we have redemption through his blood.' This vast work of redemption is spoken of as a thing possessed. We have redemption. Yes, our Lord Jesus declared it to be finished when he died as our Substitute (John 19:30). Yes, he is the Lamb slain from the foundation of the world (Revelation 13:8). Yes, the work was 'finished from the foundation of the world' (Hebrews 4:3). Yet, it was accomplished in time and it is something God's elect come to possess in time.

Redemption is a work of God with vast, infinite dimensions. It reaches through all time and through all eternity. It is as vital in the experience of it as it is in the accomplishment of it. Though we were chosen in Christ, predestinated to the adoption of children in Christ and accepted in Christ from eternity, yet, having forfeited all right to these blessings by the sin and fall of our father Adam and our whole nature being thereby degraded and ruined; were it not for redemption through his blood we must have remained in the captivity of sin, under the heavy penalty of the law's curse and unfit to enjoy the privileges of adoption forever. What unspeakable blessings are included in that word 'redemption'.

Redemption is the present, everlasting possession of every believer. It is not something we hope to have. It is something we have right now. Being redeemed, I am right now and forever, freed from sin (1 John 3:5; Romans 6:18), freed from Satan (Romans 6), freed from the law (Romans 7:1-4; 8:1; 10:4) and a possessor of everlasting life!

'His blood'

The fourth thing revealed in our text is the price of our redemption, 'His blood'. 'In whom we have redemption through his blood.'

His blood represents his life sacrificed for us. 'The life of the flesh is in the blood.' His blood is a man's blood. Man sinned. Man must suffer. His blood is God's blood (Acts 20:28). His blood is enough. 'Payment God cannot twice demand, first at my bleeding Surety's hand, and then again at mine.' His blood is covenant blood (Hebrews 13:20). His blood is eternal blood (Revelation 13:8; 1 Peter 1:18-20). His blood is sprinkled blood (Hebrews 9:12-14). His blood is assuring blood (Hebrews 10:19-22). The price of our redemption was his blood. 'Ye are bought with a price.'

'The forgiveness of sins'

Fifth, the result of redemption is 'the forgiveness of sins'. Wherever there is redemption through his blood there is the forgiveness of sins. You cannot have one without the other.

Forgiveness was purchased for us by the blood of Christ. Forgiveness is given to us upon the merit of his blood. Forgiveness is ours in exactly the same sense that it is Christ's. He was released from the load and from the charge of sin when he had fully paid the debt of sin and so are we (1 Peter 4:1; 1 John 4:17). God has forgiven us of all past sins. He has forgiven us of all present sins. He has forgiven us of all future sins. He has removed them from us. 'As far as the east is from the west, *so* far hath he removed our transgressions from us' (Psalm 103:12). He casts them into the depths of the sea. He blotted them out. 'I, *even* I, *am* he that blotteth out thy transgressions for mine own sake, and will not remember thy sins' (Isaiah

43:25). He will not impute them to us (Romans 4:8). 'Blessed *is* the man to whom the Lord will not impute sin' (Romans 4:8). He has purged them away. He will not remember them against us forever. He will never deal with us any the less graciously because of our sins.

Robert Hawker wrote, 'So infinitely extensive in its efficacy is redemption from sin in all its consequences, that it reacheth through all time, and through all eternity. And so infinitely great in its power, that it "cleanseth us from all sin" (1 John 1:7)'.

'The riches of his grace'

Sixth, the cause of redemption is 'the riches of his grace'. 'In whom we have redemption through his blood, the forgiveness of sins, according to the riches of his grace. Grace planned it. Grace provided it. Grace performed it. Grace applies it. Grace will complete it. Grace will have the praise of it.

In the light of this great and blessed gift, 'redemption through his blood', I cannot avoid saying to you who have this great gift, 'Ye are not your own, for ye are bought with a price: therefore glorify God in your body, and in your spirit, which are God's'. Since God chose you, redeemed and saved you, you belong to him. It is true all people belong to God as creatures belong to their Creator, as property to its owner, as subjects to their ruler. All things were made by God and for God and all are ruled by God's sovereign will. This is God's right as the Sovereign of all his creatures (Romans 9:15-26). Yet, we who believe belong to God as a child belongs to its father, a wife to her husband, a willing bond slave to his master. Ours is an intimate, loving, family relationship with the eternal God.

We belong to God by the sovereign purpose of his grace. In eternity God said, 'I will be their God, and they shall be my people'. Were it not for God's electing grace no one would ever be saved. Indeed, were it not for God's election and determination to save some the world would never have been created. We belong to God because he chose us as his own (2 Thessalonians 2:13, 14).

We are the Lord's by the special purchase of his Son. Paul said, 'Ye are bought with a price'. It is not expected that the ungodly and unbelieving should seek the honour of Christ. They were not redeemed by him. But it is most reasonable that we should willingly give ourselves to the service of our Saviour's glory. He bought us out from under the curse of the law (Galatians 3:13).

We belong to our God by the saving power and grace of his Holy Spirit (Ephesians 2:1-5; Psalm 110:3). We were lost, helpless, depraved and spiritually dead. But the Spirit of God came to us and called us to life. He created faith in our hearts, and brought us to Christ by his sovereign, irresistible power and grace. He made us willing, voluntary bond slaves of the Lord Jesus Christ. We belong to God by the solemn profession of our faith. Following our Lord in baptism we have publicly declared to all the world our faith in and allegiance to the Lord Jesus Christ (Romans 6:4-6). Baptism is the believer's obedient, public confession of faith. It identifies us as those who belong to God. Since we belong to God it is only reasonable we should glorify God in our bodies and in our spirits, which are God's.

If Christ has redeemed you, you belong to him. By your own profession of faith, you have willingly, voluntarily given yourself up to the claims of Christ. Because you belong to Christ, you have nothing to fear and everything to give you comfort. You are a child of God, an heir of God, a joint-heir with Jesus Christ (1 John 3:1; Romans 8:17). You are not your own provider. It is a father's responsibility to provide for his children and our heavenly Father provides for his own (Matthew 6:31-34). You are not your own guide. It is the responsibility of the shepherd to guide his sheep and the Lord who is our Shepherd guides us through this world (Psalms 23:1-6; 37:23, 24). You are not your own protector. It is the king's duty to protect his people, the husband's to protect his wife and Christ, who is our Husband and King, protects his own with sovereign power (Isaiah 43:1-5).

Because we have willingly given ourselves to Christ as voluntary bond slaves we are to live under his dominion willingly and completely (Luke 14:25-33). Being the bond slaves of Christ we must not follow our own will, serve our own interests, or lend our service to another. A bond slave has no property, no rights and no time of his own. He should have no will of his own. He has voluntarily resigned himself and all that he has to his Master. 'Ye are not your own.'

Because we belong to God, we have no legitimate concern in this world but to glorify him. Our heart's only desire should be, 'Father, glorify thy name' (John 12:28). We have no right to serve any cause in this world, except the glory of God our Saviour. Everything we are, everything we own, everything we control, every relationship of our lives must be made subject to the glory of God. Our flesh rebels against complete subservience to God. We can never give the kind of allegiance to God that we desire in this world. Yet, we strive after commitment to Christ, the complete consecration of our beings to the glory of our God. May God the Holy Spirit give us grace to pursue total commitment to Christ, 'In whom we have redemption through his blood, the forgiveness of sins, according to the riches of his grace'.

Chapter 8

Grace Abounding

In whom we have redemption through his blood, the forgiveness of sins, according to the riches of his grace; Wherein he hath abounded toward us in all wisdom and prudence; Having made known unto us the mystery of his will, according to his good pleasure which he hath purposed in himself: That in the dispensation of the fulness of times he might gather together in one all things in Christ, both which are in heaven, and which are on earth; even in him: In whom also we have obtained an inheritance, being predestinated according to the purpose of him who worketh all things after the counsel of his own will: That we should be to the praise of his glory, who first trusted in Christ.

(Ephesians 1:7-12)

The more I taste and experience God's grace the more overwhelmed I am by it, the more I realise how little I know of it the more I feel utterly incapable of describing it. When I talk about the grace of our God I almost always speak of it as 'free grace', 'sovereign grace', 'rich grace', 'amazing grace', 'matchless grace', 'eternal grace', 'immutable grace', 'everlasting grace', 'effectual grace', 'wonderful grace' or 'abundant grace'. Yet, even if we use all those adjectives together, speaking of 'God's wondrous, sovereign, eternal, everlasting, amazing, matchless, rich, free, effectual, wonderful and abundant grace in Christ', we would not be speaking in hyperbole. We would still fail to adequately state even the little we know of the grace of our God. The fact is, our experience of grace defies human language to define it, declare it or even describe it.

Ephesians 1

The first chapter of Ephesians is all about the abounding grace of the Triune God toward poor, needy sinners in Christ. In verses 3-6, the Apostle set before us the mercy, grace and love of God the Father in what he did for us and gave to us in Christ before the world was made. In verse 7, he shows the mercy, grace and love of God the Son in redemption accomplished for us by the shedding of his blood at Calvary. In verses 7-12, writing by inspiration of the Holy Spirit, Paul shows the mercy, love and grace of God the Holy Spirit in the abounding revelation of grace.

One subject

Our translators give us the six verses in Ephesians 1:7-12 as one sentence. Every phrase in this long sentence sets before us different aspects of one subject. That subject is the revelation of God's grace to us. Paul is describing both the work of God the Son, our Lord Jesus Christ in the accomplishment of redemption and the work of God the Holy Spirit in the application of redemption to chosen sinners in regeneration and conversion. In verse 7, we are told redemption is ours in Christ, 'In whom we have redemption through his blood, the forgiveness of sins, according to the riches of his grace'. In verses 8 and 9, we read, 'Wherein he hath abounded toward us in all wisdom and prudence; Having made known unto us the mystery of his will, according to his good pleasure which he hath purposed in himself'. The first word in verse 8, 'Wherein', connects the work of God the Holy Spirit in us with the work of God the Son for us at Calvary and the work of God the Father in eternity. It declares all are according to the riches of God's grace in Christ. Paul is telling us exactly the same thing he states in 1 Timothy 1:14. 'And the grace of our Lord was exceeding abundant with faith and love which is in Christ Jesus.'

Wisdom revealed in redemption

Without question, the Spirit of God is here declaring that God's grace is revealed, and, 'he hath abounded toward us in all wisdom and prudence', in the redemption of our souls by Christ. 'Wisdom' refers to God's infinite knowledge. In Ephesians 3:10, Paul is talking about this same grace revealed in the gospel, and calls it 'the manifold wisdom of God'. In 1 Corinthians 1:21-23, he calls the gospel the wisdom of God and the power of God by which we are saved. It was the wisdom of God that found a ransom for our souls in his own dear Son. The gospel of Christ is the revelation of wisdom that is so infinitely higher than the wisdom of this world that the carnally wise call it foolishness.

'Prudence' refers to the great, infinitely great, skill by which our God accomplished his wise and good purpose in sacrificing his darling Son for us at Calvary. God sending his Son into the world to suffer in our stead, and to satisfy his law and justice for us was not only an act of special, boundless grace and peculiar favour, it was also the demonstration of his infinite wisdom. 'He hath abounded toward us in all wisdom'. God's grace is gloriously displayed in all its riches, wisdom and prudence in the redemption of our souls by Christ. The gospel by which redemption is preached is, 'the manifold wisdom of God'. When it is revealed to us by his Spirit the gospel makes us 'wise unto salvation', revealing the holy Lord God to be both just and Justifier, 'a just God and a Saviour'.

What wisdom is seen in the work of redemption and in appointing such a Mediator as Christ to reconcile man to God! What wisdom is revealed in our God choosing to secure and set forth his highest honour, glory and praise in redeeming lost sinners by the sacrifice of his Son, 'for the praise of his glory'. What infinite prudence and skill in God's overruling all the affairs of providence to accomplish the work. Adam's fall, Tamar and Judah, Lot's incest, David and Bathsheba, Herod's decree, Caesar's order, Judas' betrayal, the crucifixion, the Roman method of execution all worked to accomplish God's will.

The gospel proclaims the salvation of lost sinners by a Substitute, a crucified Redeemer. It was a mystery hidden from the world. Hidden so fully that the world could never have discovered it. Hidden in God, in his heart and mind, in his purpose and decree, until Christ came. Hidden still from lost sinners until Christ comes by his grace and reveals it. We preach 'the wisdom of God in a mystery, even the hidden wisdom … which none of the princes of this world knew', or could know.

'In whom the God of this world hath blinded the minds of them which believe not, lest the light of the glorious gospel of Christ, who is the image of God, should shine unto them. For we preach not ourselves, but Christ Jesus the Lord; and ourselves your servants for Jesus' sake. For God, who commanded the light to shine out of darkness, hath shined in our hearts, to *give* the light of the knowledge of the glory of God in the face of Jesus Christ' (2 Corinthians 4:4-6).

Wisdom revealed by grace

Not only is the wisdom and prudence of God revealed in our redemption by Christ, 'according to the riches of his grace', 'he hath' in the revelation of grace, by the power and grace of his Holy Spirit in the conversion of our souls, 'abounded toward us in all wisdom and prudence; having made known unto us the mystery of his will, according to his good pleasure which he hath purposed in himself' (vv. 8, 9).

We are like all men by nature, foolish and unwise. In regeneration, effectual calling and conversion God the Holy Spirit has caused us to know wisdom in the hidden part. God has given us, 'the Spirit of wisdom and revelation in the knowledge of' Christ (Ephesians 1:17). He has given us the mind of Christ, spiritual light, knowledge and understanding, by which we are now able to discern and know all things spiritual (1 Corinthians 2:1-16; 1 John 2:20). These two verses in Ephesians 1:8, 9 comprehend the whole work of God the Holy Spirit in us, from regeneration until grace is finished in glory. 'Wherein he hath abounded toward us in all wisdom and prudence; Having made known unto us the mystery of his will, according to his good pleasure which he hath purposed in himself.'

How we ought to admire and adore the matchless grace of God the Father who chose us, adopted us and accepted us in Christ before the world was made! How we ought to admire and adore the wondrous grace of God the Son who redeemed us with his precious blood at Calvary and obtained for us the forgiveness of all sin! How we ought to admire and adore the matchless grace of God the Holy Ghost who has revealed Christ in us to the saving of our souls! Truly, he is the Almighty 'Zaph-nath-paaneah', as Pharaoh called Joseph, the Revealer of hidden things (Genesis 41:45). So essential is the work of God the Holy Spirit that none can be saved without it. The Spirit's work of grace in us is just as vital, just as necessary, as the work of the Father in eternity and the work of the Son at Calvary. It is by the Spirit of God alone that chosen, redeemed sinners are brought into the experience and enjoyment of the blessings of grace given to us in Christ before the world began and purchased for us by the blood of Christ at Calvary. His it is to take of the things of Christ and reveal them to the soul. His it is to convince of sin, of righteousness, and of judgment (John 16:8). All the knowledge of Christ, faith in Christ and acquaintance with Christ that we possess is ours only by the gracious operations of the Holy Spirit. Until God the Spirit quickened and regenerated us we were dead in trespasses and sins and children of wrath, even as others (Ephesians 2:1-5).

Robert Hawker wrote, 'All the actions of the newborn child of God, leadings to the throne, access to the throne, and acceptation at the throne in Christ are the immediate work of God the Holy Ghost. Hence Paul prays for the Church, that the Lord, (that is, the Spirit) might lead their hearts into the love of God and into the patient waiting for Christ (2 Thessalonians 3:5).'

The mystery of his will

By the revelation of his grace, abounding toward us in all wisdom and prudence, in all the wisdom and skill of his infinite Being, God the Holy Ghost has 'made known unto us the mystery of his will, according to his good pleasure which he hath purposed in himself' (v. 9). He set it all out before us in Christ and revealed to us how our names were written in heaven before the world began. He has brought immortality and life to light by the gospel, causing us by the gospel to hear the good news of our salvation in Christ (Ephesians 1:13, 14; 2 Timothy 1:9, 10).

Grace was ours, salvation was ours, acceptance was ours, forgiveness was ours before we even knew we needed it, ours in Christ from eternity! We knew nothing about it until God the Holy Ghost, 'abounded toward us in all (the) wisdom and prudence' of his grace, revealing Christ and giving us faith in him.

It is this work of God the Holy Spirit that causes us to know our interest in our Saviour. That is what is meant by him making known to us the mystery of his will. When we behold the vast pile of sin reaching up to heaven, our hearts break within us. Ezra puts it, 'When I heard this thing, I rent my garment and my mantle, and plucked off the hair of my head and of my beard, and sat down astonied' (Ezra 9:3). At the same time, by the mighty operation of grace, he causes us to see the blood of Christ washing all our sins away, so, 'the iniquity of Israel shall be sought for, and there shall be none; and the sins of Judah, and they shall not be found' (Jeremiah 50:20). This is grace indeed. It abounds like the ocean, burying in its bosom the high and horrible mountains of my sin. God's grace is the vast, infinite sea into which he has cast my sins! Christ's blood is the vast, infinite sea that rises above all the high water-marks of sin and the aboundings of sin (Micah 7:18, 19; Romans 5:20, 21). That was his purpose, which he purposed in himself before the world was. The purpose he has revealed by his abounding grace!

A great gathering

In verse 10, we read about the gathering of all things together in Christ at God's appointed time, 'according to his good pleasure which he hath purposed in himself'. Here God the Holy Spirit opens to us the very heart of God in all his designs of grace toward his elect. Here he shows us that which has occupied the mind of the Triune Jehovah from everlasting. It is the eternal purpose and heart determination of the Triune God to glorify our Lord Jesus Christ.

All things were decreed for him. All things centre in him. All things are ruled by him. All things shall give praise to him. The dispensation of all events and the fulness of times are all moving in one direction, to this one point of termination. Like countless rays of light converging to one centre, all things are soon to meet 'in him'. It is repeated for wonder and for emphasis, 'even in him'. Here the Spirit of God is telling us that the ultimate manifestation of the glory of Christ in saving our souls (which is the only visible revelation there ever has been or can be of the glory of the Triune God) is the only reason why God created the universe (Romans 11:33-36; Colossians 1:18-20). How dear to God the God-man, our Mediator, the Lord Jesus Christ, is. How dear he ought to be to us. Try to imagine what the gathering together of all things in Christ shall be in that day. What glory he shall have when he comes to be glorified in all his saints and to be admired in all them that believe (2 Thessalonians 1:10).

An inheritance obtained

Now, read verse 11. 'In whom also we have obtained an inheritance, being predestinated according to the purpose of him who worketh all things after the counsel of his own will'. Here are four glorious facts. 1. We were predestinated to the eternal inheritance of heaven with Christ. 2. Our great God, in all the affairs of time, works all things together to accomplish that great purpose of his grace, to bring his elect into the possession of their predestined inheritance (Romans 8:28-30). 3. This inheritance, whatever it is, is altogether in Christ. The inheritance is by him, from him, with him and in him. Christ is our inheritance and 4. We have already obtained it (John 17:5, 20; Ephesians 2:6; Hebrews 12:22-24).

Why?

Why? Why has our great and glorious God been so gracious to us? Why is his grace so continually abounding and super-abounding toward us? Why did he save us? Why did he love us, choose us, adopt us, accept us, redeem us and forgive us all our sins in Christ? Why has he made known to us the indescribable wisdom and prudence of his grace? He did it all, 'That we should be to the praise of his glory, who first trusted in Christ' (v. 12). It shall be the everlasting glory of the Triune God to be known as God our Saviour! 'That in the ages to come he might show the exceeding riches of his grace in *his* kindness toward us through Christ Jesus' (Ephesians 2:7). 'To whom God would make known what *is* the riches of the glory of this mystery among the Gentiles; which is Christ in you, the hope of glory' (Colossians 1:27).

Chapter 9

Wisdom And Prudence

Wherein he hath abounded toward us in all wisdom and prudence; Having made known unto us the mystery of his will, according to his good pleasure which he hath purposed in himself.

(Ephesians 1:8, 9)

Our text tells us that the sovereign work of God in redemption and grace is the exercise of infinite wisdom and prudence, infinite knowledge and insight, infinite brilliance and skill. God's grace abounds toward us 'in all wisdom and prudence'.

'The mystery of his will', is what God the Holy Spirit has made known to us in the revelation and experience of grace, giving us faith in Christ. He has revealed our eternal election and redemption by Christ, 'which he hath purposed in himself'. 'The mystery of his will' is all that Paul has declared in verses 3-7.

Our God not only saves his elect in the only way we could be saved, but in the very best way. As is always the case, God's way is the best way. Let me show you the obvious wisdom and prudence of his grace. I said 'show'. I did not say 'explain'. Explain it, I cannot. In fact, I can only show you the little that is obvious. We shall spend eternity diving into the depths of divine 'wisdom and prudence' and soaring in the heights of God's infinite, boundless grace toward us in Christ.

Secrets revealed

Our Lord Jesus says in John 15:15, 'I have called you friends; for all things that I have heard of my Father I have made known unto you'. God's everlasting love for us, his eternal purpose of grace toward us, even the redemption of our souls by Christ are secret things, known only to God, until they are revealed to us and in us by the Holy Spirit's gift of faith in Christ. 'Faith is the substance of things hoped for, the evidence of things not seen' (Hebrews 11:1). When faith is given, the mystery is revealed (2 Corinthians 4:6; Ephesians 1:13, 14; 2 Timothy 1:9, 10).

Conversion

That is what happens in conversion. We have a beautiful picture of it in the opening verses of the Bible. 'In the beginning God created the heaven and the earth. And the earth was without form, and void; and darkness *was* upon the face of the deep. And the Spirit of God moved upon the face of the waters. And God said, Let there be light: and there was light' (Genesis 1:1-3). Paul told the Thessalonian saints that he knew their election because God had given them faith in Christ by the power and grace of God the Holy Ghost (1 Thessalonians 1:4, 5); and we know our own election by our God given faith in Christ.

The wisdom of grace

Only the all-wise God could devise and execute the sovereign purpose of his grace toward us. Behold the great wisdom of God in grace and worship him. I see the manifold wisdom of God in his choice of his Son to be our Redeemer, in his determination to accomplish redemption by substitution, in the glorious incarnation of Christ, in the life of Christ in this world, in the sacrificial, sin-atoning death of Christ and in the glorious exaltation of Christ.

1. The choice of his Son

God's choice of his Son to be our Redeemer displays his infinite wisdom. I do not pretend to understand the deep, hidden mysteries of the covenant of grace, the oaths and agreements of the Triune Godhead. I know God does not need to plan, devise, or work out anything in his great mind. He knows everything. I know a covenant was made (Jeremiah 31:31-34), that God the Father made proposals to his Son for the accomplishment of our redemption (Psalm 2:8; John 10:16-18), which our Saviour voluntarily accepted (Isaiah 50:5-7). I know these transactions of grace between God the Father and God the Son were sworn to by the Triune Jehovah, and secured the salvation of an elect multitude before the world was made (Hebrews 6:17-19; 8:10-12). In the covenant of grace, as it is revealed to us in the Scriptures, God the Father proposed the conditions upon which redemption would be accomplished. God the Son pledged himself to satisfy all the demands and conditions required by the holy law, character and will of God. God the Holy Spirit promised to effectually apply all the blessings of grace, earned by Christ's obedience, to the elect.

These are things that took place before the world began when no one and nothing existed but the eternal God (Ephesians 1:3-6; 3:11; 2 Timothy 1:9). In those great, eternal counsels of grace, God set his heart upon his dear Son, and chose him to be the Person who would perform the great work of redemption.

Christ is the Redeemer of God's own choosing. Therefore, he is called God's elect (Isaiah 42:1). When God set his eye upon his Son, choosing him to save his elect, he said with regard to all his elect, 'Deliver him from going down to the pit: I have found a ransom (an atonement)' (Job 33:24). 'I have laid help upon one that is mighty; I have exalted one chosen out of the people' (Psalm 89:19).

The wisdom of God in choosing Christ to be our Redeemer is evident in many ways. We rejoice in the love, mercy and grace of God but it was the wisdom of God which found a way for a holy God to embrace fallen, sinful men and women in love, mercy and grace. How we ought to admire the wisdom of God in providing such a Redeemer!

Christ is in every way a fit and proper Person to be our Redeemer. He who undertakes to redeem sinners, satisfy justice, make reconciliation for transgressors, and atone for sin must be a divine Person. None but God could be equal to the great work of redemption. He must be One who is infinitely holy. None could take away the infinite evil of sin but One who is infinitely pure. None can make satisfaction, except him who is of infinite worth and merit.

He must be a Person of infinite ability. The work of redemption is a great and mighty work, requiring both wisdom and power belonging only to God. He must be a Person infinitely dear to God. In order for God to place infinite value upon the Redeemer's work the Redeemer himself must be infinitely dear to God, the Beloved One of his heart, the Apple of his eye, the Darling of his affections (John 3:16; Romans 5:8; 1 John 4:9, 10).

Our Redeemer must also be a person who has an absolute right to redeem. He must be one who is free of all personal obligation and responsibility. If he is a servant or a subject he has no right to redeem. He cannot merit anything. A servant has nothing of his own, no price to offer and no merit before his master. Though Christ freely became Jehovah's Servant to do his will in redeeming us, he is not in any way God's subject. He is God's equal for Christ is God and has the right to redeem.

The Redeemer had to be a person of infinite love and grace! No one else would undertake a work so costly for a creature so worthless as man. Behold, how he loved us! Once more, the one chosen to be our Redeemer must be a person of infinite truth and faithfulness. He must be immutably true and unalterably faithful. Else he could not be trusted to carry on the great work to the horrible, ignominious death of the cross. God the Father found in his Son a fit person to be our Redeemer and trusted the whole affair of redemption to him (Ephesians 1:12, 13).

This is great wisdom. God found a Redeemer for sinners in the Person of his dear Son! But there is more. The only fit person to be our Redeemer is the Lord Jesus Christ, the Son of God. Not only was there no other way for a holy God to save fallen man but by the redemption that is in Christ, there is no other person who could be our Redeemer but Christ. The whole work must be on his shoulders alone! No man could make atonement, because all are guilty. No angel could redeem, because all are finite. God the Father could not redeem us, because in the divine economy he is the One whose justice must be satisfied. God the Spirit could not redeem us because he is the One by whom the blessings of redemption are conveyed to us, pleading the merits of the Redeemer.

Who but God, infinitely wise, could have thought to make Christ our Redeemer? Had God asked the angels or the sons of Adam none could ever have found the Redeemer we must have. But, thank God, he found a Ransom and the Ransom he found is his own dear Son, the Lord Jesus Christ.

2. Wisdom in substitution

God's wisdom is revealed in his determination to accomplish redemption by substitution. Having chosen Christ to be our Redeemer, the Lord God contrived the way in which he would accomplish redemption. The way he devised, indeed, the only way in which he could accomplish redemption is by substitution. The Son of God was made to be, and voluntarily became, our Representative, Surety and Substitute for the accomplishment of redemption (Romans 3:24-26; Hebrews 7:22). Before the world began God's own dear Son became our Substitute. He stood in our place. God determined that his Son, the Lord Jesus Christ, must have the sins of his people made his, must take our guilt upon himself, must suffer the utter extremity of the law's penalty to the full satisfaction of justice.

Not only did God determine to make Christ our Substitute, he looked upon him from eternity as the Substitute slain for the salvation of his people and looked upon us as sinners redeemed by the precious blood of his dear Son (Romans 8:29, 30). Wondrous grace! 'The works were finished from the foundation of the world.'

3. Wisdom in the incarnation

The incarnation of Christ wonderfully reveals the manifold wisdom of God (Isaiah 7:14; 9:6; 2 Corinthians 8:9; Philippians 2:5-8). No mind but the infinite mind of the infinite God could conceive and accomplish such a thing as this. The great, eternal, incomprehensible God assumed our nature and came into this world. 'The Word was made flesh and dwelt among us.' God the Son became the Son of Man! God became one of us! He who is the eternal Jehovah became Jehovah's Servant. The infinite, omnipotent God became a finite, feeble man! He who is the eternal Spirit was born of a woman. The immortal God became flesh and blood! God who is independent, self-sufficient and all-sufficient, stood in need of food, clothing and shelter. God who owns all things became a man who owned nothing. He who upholds all things by the word of his power lived upon the charity of men. God who knows all things had, as a man, to learn how to walk, talk, read and write. He who wrote the law and gave it to Moses in the Mount became subject to the law, and performed obedience to the law as a Man. The holy Son of God came under the obligation and sentence of the law as a guilty sinner when he was made sin for us. He who is life was made to die. God who is infinitely, immutably, unchangeably happy was made to suffer sorrow, pain, torment and death. He who is the object of God's perfect love became the object of God's unmitigated wrath. The great sovereign of heaven and earth became a worm (Psalm 22:6). The eternal God died as our Substitute! No man can even grasp the reality of the incarnation, much less understand it. But God, in infinite wisdom, purposed it before the world was and brought it to pass for the accomplishment of our redemption (Galatians 4:4-6).

4. Wisdom in Christ's life

The life of our Lord Jesus in this world reveals the manifold wisdom of God. If this gospel were the invention of men the Saviour would have been born in a palace, raised in royalty, trained with dignity, surrounded by riches and presented with all the pageantry of one of the devil's popes. But this thing is not of man. This is God's work! When God's Son came into the world to redeem man he was born in a stable, raised in poverty and lived in obscurity. When he came to announce his Messiahship and the inauguration of his kingdom he rode into Jerusalem upon an ass's colt. He died as a common malefactor. He was buried in a borrowed tomb. But what is the purpose, meaning and significance of Christ's earthly life?

In order to be our Saviour, the Lord Jesus lived in this world in perfect submission and faith toward God as a man (Hebrews 2:10, 11, 17, 18). He endured all the trials, temptations and sorrows of manhood in this world so he might be touched with the feeling of our infirmities. He knows all the emotions of manhood. The only difference between him and us is that he knew no sin. He is holy, harmless, undefiled and separate from sinners. He lived in this world. He lived by faith in God. He lived in submission to our Father's will.

Our Saviour lived a life of representative obedience to God (Romans 5:19). He worked out and brought in a perfect righteousness for us. Under more severe temptations and conflicts than any of us can ever know our Mediator was perfectly obedient. He fulfilled and obeyed the ceremonial law. He fulfilled and obeyed the moral law. He even submitted to the civil laws of human governments.

5. Wisdom in the cross

The sacrificial, sin-atoning death of the Lord Jesus Christ is a display of the manifold wisdom of God (Galatians 1:3-5).

This is the means, the only possible means, by which the great and holy God could redeem, justify and save guilty sinners. Nothing but divine wisdom could have devised such a plan. When it was announced in heaven, the angels must have been filled with astonishment. Nothing in all the world is more wonderful.

Christ, who is God blessed forever, infinitely and essentially happy, endured the greatest sorrow, suffering and agony of the universe. The supreme Lord and Judge of the world was arrested, tried and condemned by vile men. He who is the living God, the Fountain of life was put to death. The Creator of the world was crucified by his own creatures. The God of glory was beaten, spit upon and mocked by brutal men. He who is infinite good died by indescribable cruelty. The King of heaven was buried in the earth. Yet, this ignominious death was the means of Christ's greatest honour. By his death he both glorified God and saved his people.

Be sure you understand what happened at Calvary. Be sure you know the meaning of Christ's death. The Lord Jesus died by his own voluntary will (John 10:17, 18). He died as the Substitute for his people (John 10:11, 15; 2 Corinthians 5:21; Galatians 3:13), under the penalty of sin for the satisfaction of divine justice (Isaiah 53:9, 10). He effectually accomplished redemption when he died (Hebrews 9:12). Justice was satisfied. Sin was put away. Salvation was purchased. The blood of Christ left nothing to chance. When he cried, 'It is finished' all the hosts of God's elect were forever redeemed, justified and sanctified!

6. Wisdom in the exaltation

Sixth, the wisdom of God is evident in the glorious exaltation of Christ. 'Wherefore God also hath highly exalted him, and given him a name which is above every name: That at the name of Jesus every knee should bow, of *things* in heaven, and *things* in earth, and *things* under the earth; And *that* every tongue should confess that Jesus Christ *is* Lord, to the glory of God the Father' (Philippians 2:9-11).

Divine wisdom saw it was needful and expedient that he who died for us upon the cross should be raised from the dead and seated at the right hand of the majesty on high as the Supreme Governor of the universe. The exaltation of Christ assures us of the salvation of God's elect (John 17:2), comforts us with the knowledge of his good providence (Romans 8:28, 32), gives us assurance of perpetual pardon and acceptance at the throne of God (1 John 2:1, 2), promises exaltation and glory to every believer (Revelation 3:21) and is the pledge of his final triumph.

This great Redeemer and the great redemption he has accomplished is the wisdom of God. He is the power of God unto salvation to every believer. By means of this great scheme of redemption and grace, God achieved the highest ambition of his own great heart. He gave Christ all preeminence (Colossians 1:18).

The prudence of grace

A wise father takes care of his family with both immediate and future provision. The wiser the father and the greater his abilities the more certain and secure the provisions are. Our heavenly Father has, in infinite wisdom, provided all things for us and with infinite prudence, skill and insight he accomplishes his designs.

I see the grace of God abounding toward us in prudence in the sacrifice of his darling Son for the accomplishment of our redemption. 'We speak the wisdom of God in a mystery, even the hidden wisdom, which God ordained before the world unto our glory' (1 Corinthians 2:7).

I see great prudence in the means God has ordained for the salvation of his elect. God has chosen to save sinners by the foolishness of preaching (Romans 10:17; 1 Peter 1:23-25). The message he employs, the glorious gospel of Christ, is the revelation of infinite wisdom. The men he employs to preach that message are themselves a constant display of infinite prudence. 'For ye see your calling, brethren, how that not many wise men after the flesh, not many mighty, not many noble, *are called*: But God hath chosen the foolish things of the world to confound the wise; and God hath chosen the weak things of the world to confound the things which are mighty; And base things of the world, and things which are despised, hath God chosen, *yea,* and things which are not, to bring to nought things that are: That no flesh should glory in his presence' (1 Corinthians 1:26-29).

I see great prudence in the way God's grace abounds to his chosen in the experience of it (John 16:8-11; Psalm 107). He slays that he may make alive. He wounds that he may heal. He strips that he may clothe. He empties that he may fill. He imprisons that he may set the prisoner free. He abases that he may exalt. He condemns that he may pardon.

The warfare

I see great prudence in the means our God has chosen to employ to preserve his saints in grace and the means he has chosen to secure our perseverance. He has fixed it so we are in constant need of his grace, in constant need of his Son, in constant need of his forgiveness, in constant need of his mercy. He has given us and repeatedly supplies us with grace and faith by which we are sweetly inclined and bound to seek him (2 Corinthians 12:7-10; Hebrews 4:16; 1 John 1:9; 2:1, 2).

How often I sleep, though my heart wakes. How often when my Saviour comes, I refuse him. Yet, he puts his hand into my heart, dropping the sweet-smelling myrrh of his grace into my wretched soul and graciously causes me to awake, arise, and seek him, until at last, I find him. Then, he brings me into his banqueting house and spreads his banner of love over me. He causes me to know more fully with every experience of his affection that many waters cannot quench his love, neither can the floods of my sin drown it! 'Wherein he hath abounded toward us in all wisdom and prudence; having made known unto us the mystery of his will, according to his good pleasure which he hath purposed in himself.'

'O the depth of the riches both of the wisdom and knowledge of God! how unsearchable *are* his judgments, and his ways past finding out! For who hath known the mind of the Lord? or who hath been his counsellor? Or who hath first given to him, and it shall be recompensed unto him again? For of him, and through him, and to him, *are* all things: to whom *be* glory for ever. Amen' (Romans 11:33-36).

Chapter 10

The Mystery Of His Will

Having made known unto us the mystery of his will, according to his good pleasure which he hath purposed in himself: That in the dispensation of the fulness of times he might gather together in one all things in Christ, both which are in heaven, and which are on earth; *even* in him.

(Ephesians 1:9, 10)

'Canst thou by searching find out God? Canst thou find out the Almighty unto perfection?' Never! The wisdom and power of God are made known to all men in creation and to some extent even his goodness. However, that revelation of God is not enough to satisfy a soul convinced that God is holy, to quieten a conscience convicted of sin and to soothe a heart bowed down with a load of guilt. A guilty sinner wants to know, 'How can I be just with God? How can his justice be satisfied, his wrath appeased, his anger propitiated? How may I know he is my God, my Father? How may I be assured he loves me, has pardoned me of all my sin and accepts me?'

Could you comprehend all God's great works of creation, were you able at once to enter 'into the treasures of the snow', comprehend 'by what way is the light parted' and the wind scattered, were you able to 'bind the sweet influences of Pleiades' and 'loose the bands of Orion', give strength to a horse, teach the hawk to fly and command the eagle to soar on high, even if you could draw out leviathan with a hook and play with him like a bird, still the question that must be answered before you can live in this world in peace is this: 'How then can man be justified with God? Or how can he be clean that is born of a woman?'

'Canst thou by searching find out God? canst thou find out the Almighty unto perfection?' Never! Even the knowledge of God that you might gain by reading his law is, at best, vague and shadowy. True, the holiness of God is set forth in its precepts, the justice of God in its threatenings, but the law can never be more or less than the Spirit declares it to be: 'the ministration of death and condemnation' (2 Corinthians 3:7-9). The law says you must be justified but can never justify you or show you how to be justified. It breathes not a sound of mercy to a poor sinner. It speaks of death but not of life; of condemnation but not of salvation. It asserts authority and reflects the holiness and wrath of God, but not one beam of hope does it throw on the gloomy path of a terrified soul rushing to eternity!

'Canst thou by searching find out God? canst thou find out the Almighty unto perfection?' – Never! But, blessed be his name, God can be known, known by sinful men and known with satisfaction, peace and joy. In fact, he is thus known by many to whom he has 'made known … the mystery of his will, according to his good pleasure which he hath purposed in himself'.

In Ephesians 1:9, 10, the Apostle Paul confirms this. May God open our eyes, to behold wondrous things out of his Word. May we see the wonders of the mystery of his will revealed in the gospel and know in our hearts the wonders of redemption and grace in Christ. 'In whom we have redemption through his blood, the forgiveness of sins, according to the riches of his grace; Wherein he hath abounded toward us in all wisdom and prudence' (Ephesians 1:7, 8).

The mystery

What is the mystery of his will? Whatever it is, it is being revealed to us. It is something God the Holy Ghost has made known and is making known by the revelation of Christ in us. It is spiritually discerned and understood by the gift of his grace. 'Having made known unto us the mystery of his will, according to his good pleasure which he hath purposed in himself' (Ephesians 1:9).

The mystery revealed is something that at one time was secret, or hidden, but now is revealed in Christ. The term 'mystery' refers to God's secret purpose, once hidden, but now revealed. Paul is talking about what we did not know and could not know until it was revealed to us and in us, something now known and understood by all who are born of God and taught of him. Paul is telling us that the gospel of our salvation is the unveiling a divine secret. It is like the reading of a will (Hebrews 9:14-28). The 'mystery' is a secret, into which we must be initiated. In this sense the gospel is a mystery. In fact, though the Word of God is written in simple language, everything written in the Book of God is a mystery that lies beyond the reach of human understanding. If you and I understand anything God has revealed in his Word, it must be revealed in our hearts by his Spirit in the experience of grace. This word 'mystery' is found 22 times in the New Testament. It is always related to the unveiling of God's redemptive purpose in Christ.

The gospel

In Romans 16, the mystery of his will is identified as the gospel of Christ revealed by preaching. 'Now to him that is of power to stablish you according to my gospel, and the preaching of Jesus Christ, according to the revelation of the mystery, which was kept secret since the world began, But now is made manifest, and by the scriptures of the prophets, according to the commandment of the everlasting God, made known to all nations for the obedience of faith' (Romans 16:25, 26).

Heavenly glory

In 1 Corinthians 2:1-11, the Holy Ghost tells us the gospel of Christ, the mystery of his will, reveals what God has prepared for those who are his elect.

'And I, brethren, when I came to you, came not with excellency of speech or of wisdom, declaring unto you the testimony of God. For I determined not to know any thing among you, save Jesus Christ, and him crucified. And I was with you in weakness, and in fear, and in much trembling. And my speech and my preaching *was* not with enticing words of man's wisdom, but in demonstration of the Spirit and of power: That your faith should not stand in the wisdom of men, but in the power of God. Howbeit we speak wisdom among them that are perfect: yet not the wisdom of this world, nor of the princes of this world, that come to nought: But we speak the wisdom of God in a mystery, *even* the hidden *wisdom,* which God ordained before the world unto our glory: Which none of the princes of this world knew: for had they known *it,* they would not have crucified the Lord of glory. But as it is written, Eye hath not seen, nor ear heard, neither have entered into the heart of man, the things which God hath prepared for them that love him. But God hath revealed *them* unto us by his Spirit: for the Spirit searcheth all things, yea, the deep things of God. For what man knoweth the things of a man, save the spirit of man which is in him? even so the things of God knoweth no man, but the Spirit of God.'

The church

Ephesians 3 declares that the mystery of Christ refers to the fact that Jew and Gentile are one in Christ, that all who trust the Son of God are one in him and one with him, 'heirs of God, and joint-heirs with Christ'.

'For this cause I Paul, the prisoner of Jesus Christ for you Gentiles, If ye have heard of the dispensation of the grace of God which is given me to you-ward: How that by revelation he made known unto me the mystery; (as I wrote afore in few words, Whereby, when ye read, ye may understand my knowledge in the mystery of Christ) Which in other ages was not made known unto the sons of men, as it is now revealed unto his holy apostles and prophets by the Spirit; That the Gentiles should be fellowheirs, and of the same body, and partakers of his promise in Christ by the gospel: Whereof I was made a minister, according to the gift of the grace of God given unto me by the effectual working of his power. Unto me, who am less than the least of all saints, is this grace given, that I should preach among the Gentiles the unsearchable riches of Christ; And to make all *men* see what *is* the fellowship of the mystery, which from the beginning of the world hath been hid in God, who created all things by Jesus Christ: To the intent that now unto the principalities and powers in heavenly *places* might be known by the church the manifold wisdom of God' (Ephesians 3:1-10).

Although Israel was typically God's covenant people in the Old Testament, it was never God's purpose to save only Jews. That physical nation was made the beneficiary of God's goodness that the blessing of grace might be bestowed upon all God's elect scattered among the nations of the world. God plainly told Abraham that his blessing upon him was that in him all the families of the earth would be blessed (Genesis 12:1-3). The Apostle Paul tells us the blessing of Abraham is the gift of God's Spirit in the new birth, the gift of God's grace flowing to chosen sinners in the fountain of Christ's precious, sin-atoning blood (Galatians 3:13, 14).

Physical Israel was typical of another nation; a chosen, holy nation and royal priesthood called 'the Israel of God' (Galatians 6:16; 1 Peter 2:7-9). This is the Church of God. This holy, spiritual nation is God's elect whom he scattered in his wrath but gathers by his grace out of every nation, kindred, tribe and tongue.

In Ephesians 5, we see that this mystery of the gospel which is now revealed to us is the assurance of God's eternal purpose of grace concerning his church. It is the revelation of what God Almighty has done and will do for us in Christ. 'Husbands, love your wives, even as Christ also loved the church, and gave himself for it; That he might sanctify and cleanse it with the washing of water by the word, That he might present it to himself a glorious church, not having spot, or wrinkle, or any such thing; but that it should be holy and without blemish. So ought men to love their wives as their own bodies. He that loveth his wife loveth himself. For no man ever yet hated his own flesh; but nourisheth and cherisheth it, even as the Lord the church: For we are members of his body, of his flesh, and of his bones. For this cause shall a man leave his father and mother, and shall be joined unto his wife, and they two shall be one flesh. This is a great mystery: but I speak concerning Christ and the church' (Ephesians 5:25-32).

My prayer

I pray for you and for myself, as Paul did for the Ephesian saints, that God may grant eyes to see the wonders of his grace and love in the redemption of our souls by Christ Jesus, that we 'might be filled with all the fulness of God' (Ephesians1:17-19; 3:14-19).

All these things revealed in Holy Scripture and proclaimed in the gospel are mysteries hidden from men 'in whom the God of this world hath blinded the minds of them which believe not'. Until God the Holy Spirit reveals them in the sweet experience of grace, no matter how clearly they are preached, explained and illustrated, they will remain a mystery. But to the heaven born soul, to the sinner called and taught of God, as Christ is known by the gift of faith, 'the mystery of his will' is revealed (John 6:45, 47; 1 Corinthians 2:1-7, 12-15; Galatians 1:15, 16).

God's purpose of grace

The mystery spoken of in verse 9, which God the Holy Spirit makes known in the revelation of grace, is God's eternal purpose of grace in Christ. The gospel reveals the mystery of God and of Christ. The doctrine of the gospel sets before us 'the mysteries of the kingdom of God' (Matthew 13:11; Luke 8:10). The mystery of his will revealed to God's elect in the experience of grace, that mystery apprehended by faith, specifically makes known: First, our eternal union with Christ our Covenant Head, with our election and acceptance in him before the world was made (Ephesians 1:3-6; Romans 8:28-30). Second, redemption by Christ, our incarnate God (Ephesians 1:7-9; 1 Timothy 3:15, 16). Third, our effectual call by God the Holy Ghost assuring us of eternal glory with Christ (Ephesians 1:13, 14). Fourth, the mystery of the new creation (2 Corinthians 5:17; Colossians 1:26-29).

All of this great work of grace is 'according to his good pleasure, which he hath purposed in himself'. The Lord God has chosen to whom he will make known the wondrous mystery of his grace, when he will make it known and the means by which he will make it known in the preaching of the gospel!

The fulness of times

'That in the dispensation of the fulness of times he might gather together in one all things in Christ, both which are in heaven, and which are on earth; even in him'

(Ephesians 1:10). What is 'the dispensation of the fulness of times?' The word 'dispensation' does not refer to dispensationalism. It means 'the administration', 'the economy' or 'the stewardship' of the fulness of times. 'The dispensation of the fulness of times' is the accomplishment of God's eternal purpose in time, the execution of that which God purposed in eternity. Here, it specifically refers to the final, full accomplishment of redemption and grace by Christ. There is a time appointed called, 'the times of restitution of all things, which God hath spoken by the mouth of all his holy prophets since the world began' (Acts 3:21). In that great day, our Lord Jesus Christ will at last redeem, or deliver, God's creation from the curse and all the evil consequences of sin (Romans 8:18-23; 2 Peter 3:11-13).

As a result of our Saviour's redemption work this world will be purged of all sin and restored to its pristine beauty. Not so much as a blade of grass will be allowed to bear the curse brought upon it by sin. When all things are created new, righteousness shall again flourish in the earth! The slime of the serpent's trail will not be found in God's creation.

The gathering together

But what is the gathering together of all things in Christ? 'That in the dispensation of the fulness of times he might gather together in one all things in Christ, both which are in heaven, and which are on earth; even in him'.

The words 'gather together', literally mean 'gather together again'. Here the Spirit of God assures us all things will be reunited in Christ, all things in heaven and all things in earth. Primarily, he is talking about the gathering of all God's elect but he includes the whole of God's creation. There is a similar statement in Colossians 1. There Paul is also speaking of this great mystery God has made known to us by the gospel. He assures us of the ultimate glory of Christ our Redeemer in all things. 'For it pleased *the Father* that in him should all fulness dwell; And, having made peace through the blood of his cross, by him to reconcile all things unto himself; by him, *I say,* whether *they be* things in earth, or things in heaven' (Colossians 1:19, 20).

When our Lord Jesus Christ comes in his glory and makes all things new, there will be a gathering together of all things in heaven and earth, a reconciliation of all things 'in him, even in him', to the glory of God. What a day it will be! No wonder John closes the Book of God with this prayer, 'Even so, Come, Lord Jesus'.

Chapter 11

The Great Gathering

That in the dispensation of the fulness of times he might gather together in one all things in Christ, both which are in heaven, and which are on earth; *even* in him.
(Ephesians 1:10)

I cannot think of a single statement or verse in the Book of God that declares a more vast, all-encompassing subject than Ephesians 1:10, 'That in the dispensation of the fulness of times he might gather together in one all things in Christ, both which are in heaven, and which are on earth; *even* in him'.

This text opens to us the very heart of God and declares that the whole of his intention, design and purpose in eternal predestination is to glorify his dear Son, our Lord Jesus Christ, in all things. Here God the Holy Ghost shows us how, from all eternity, the mind of Jehovah has been occupied with this solitary grand concern: the glorification of his Son in all things. All things were decreed for him. All things centre in him. The dispensation of all events and the fulness of times are pursuing this one point of termination, the glory of Christ.

Notice the emphasis given by the Spirit of God, 'even in him'. With that added emphasis the Lord God, our heavenly Father, seems to say, 'Now listen children. This is very important. You need to know and remember it. In the dispensation of the fulness of times I will gather together in one all things in Christ, both which are in heaven, and which are on earth; even in him.' We have a similar statement in Colossians 1:20, 'And, having made peace through the blood of his cross, by him to reconcile all things unto himself; by him, *I say*, whether *they be* things in earth, or things in heaven'. The object and purpose of God in all his works of creation, providence, judgment and grace is stated fully and clearly in Ephesians 1:10.

I have no hope of entering into the depths of this vast declaration of God's eternal purpose of grace in Christ. I have studied it with increasing awe, reverence and gratitude for nigh fifty years. The more I study it the more I realise I have not yet begun to enter into the wonders of grace here set before us. All I can do is give you a brief sketch of what I see of our God's infinite wisdom and prudence along the shorelines of this great ocean of grace. Everything God has done, is doing and will do hereafter is moving toward the accomplishment of this one great end. 'That in the dispensation of the fulness of times he might gather together in one all things in Christ, both which are in heaven, and which are on earth; even in him'.

The dispensation

First, Paul speaks of a period of time that he describes as 'the dispensation of the fulness of times'. What period of time is this talking about? What is meant by 'the dispensation of the fulness of times?' As in all things, we must seek the answers to those questions in the Book of God alone.

It refers to the management of a household or the management, oversight and administration of another person's property or business. In Ephesians 3:2, the Apostle Paul speaks of the ministry God had given him as a 'dispensation of the grace of God'. That is what it is to be called into the ministry. It is to be given a 'dispensation of the grace of God', a stewardship of grace in the house of God.

Here, the word 'dispensation' refers to the universal dominion of our Lord Jesus Christ, by which he executes the will of God in time (John 17:2; Romans 14:9). As Paul states it in Ephesians 1:20-22, the Lord God gave his Son the reins of universal monarchy 'when he raised him from the dead, and set him at his own right hand in the heavenly places, Far above all principality, and power, and might, and dominion, and every name that is named, not only in this world, but also in that which is to come: And hath put all things under his feet, and gave him to be the head over all things to the church'. All power in heaven and in earth belongs to the God-man, our Mediator, the Lord Jesus Christ, that he might execute his eternal purpose in the salvation of his people to the everlasting 'praise of the glory of his grace'. That is the meaning of the word 'dispensation' in our text.

The fulness of times

But what is meant by 'the dispensation of the fulness of times'? Again, look into the Word of God for the answer. Our text tells us God's eternal purpose of grace is to be accomplished in the fulness of times by the gathering together of all things in heaven and on earth in Christ. The other place in which we find a similar statement is in Galatians 4:4-6. 'But when the fulness of the time was come, God sent forth his Son, made of a woman, made under the law, To redeem them that were under the law, that we might receive the adoption of sons. And because ye are sons, God hath sent forth the Spirit of his Son into your hearts, crying, Abba, Father'.

The 'fulness of times' obviously began with the first advent of our Lord Jesus Christ, his incarnation. Yet, Ephesians 1:10 tells us it is something not yet fulfilled. So the fulness of times refers to the whole gospel age. It began with our Saviour's first advent and will continue until his glorious second advent, culminating in the fulfilment of God's everlasting covenant and the full salvation of all his elect in Christ. This is what Paul speaks of in Romans 11:25-29: 'For I would not, brethren, that ye should be ignorant of this mystery, lest ye should be wise in your own conceits; that blindness in part is happened to Israel, until the fulness of the Gentiles be come in. And so all Israel shall be saved: as it is written, There shall come out of Sion the Deliverer, and shall turn away ungodliness from Jacob: For this *is* my covenant unto them, when I shall take away their sins. As concerning the gospel, *they are* enemies for your sakes: but as touching the election, *they are* beloved for the fathers' sakes. For the gifts and calling of God *are* without repentance.'

The contemplation of Christ's dominion, executing all the will and purpose of God in providence, and that culminating in the complete salvation of God's elect, and the final gathering together of all things in Christ, was glorious in Paul's eyes. It ought to be glorious in ours, too (Romans 11:33-36).

A reuniting

The word translated 'gather together' suggests many things. It might be better translated 'gather together again', 'reunite' or 'restore'. There was a time when all things were one. In the original creation, the angels of God were one, but they were divided by sin. Adam was one with the angels but sin divided men from the angels of God. All creation was one with Christ the Creator until sin entered. How horrible and sad, how far reaching the consequences of sin are in God's creation!

Sin has separated man from God and separates men from men. We were created as one, then sin entered. Since the day sin entered man has been divided. We are divided by race, by face and by place! The more we try to unite the human race, the more we are divided!

After the fall of Adam, our parents were expelled from the Garden of Eden and fallen man was scattered as one race over the face of the earth. After the flood mankind was divided into three races, and scattered through the earth. Since that day, the divisions and scatterings have constantly multiplied. No culture, no society, no civilization has ever stopped or even slowed the division.

The word translated 'gather together' also conveys the idea of 'recapitulation', or 'summarisation'. It suggests a mathematical sum, the total of things added together. Taken in this sense, it refers to the final summing up of all things in Christ: All the blessings and promises of the covenant, all the types, shadows and sacrifices of the law, all the prophecies and promises of the Old Testament, all the revelation of God in Holy Scripture, all the hosts of God's elect. Christ is the sum total of all.

Again, those words, 'gather together in one', might be translated 'reduce to one'. In a word, when all is said and done that must be said and done, 'Christ is All, in all'. Everything will at last be reduced to this that he might have the pre-eminence, that he might be the Firstborn among many brethren. What is grace, but Christ? What is redemption, but Christ? What is salvation, but Christ (1 Corinthians 1:30)? What is heaven, but Christ? What is the Church, but Christ? What is the glory of God, but Christ? What is the will of God, but Christ? What is God, but Christ (Colossians 2:9, 10)!

Scattered to gather

I have no doubt that the primary thing intended by Paul's declaration in Ephesians 1:10 is the gathering together of all God's elect in Christ. The fact is, our God, according to the abounding wisdom and prudence of his grace has scattered his elect across the face of all the earth in judgment that he might in his great mercy gather them all together in one in Christ, for the everlasting praise and glory of his own great name. We see this fact stated so commonly throughout the Scriptures that it is astounding it is so commonly overlooked (Deuteronomy 30:3; Jeremiah 31:10; Ezekiel 11:17; 20:34, 41; John 11:49-52).

In redemption, by the sacrifice and blood atonement of his dear Son, the Lord Jesus Christ, the Lord God gathered together all his elect in one in Christ. God was in Christ reconciling the world of his elect unto himself, not imputing our trespasses unto us, but imputing all our sin to his darling Son who was made sin for us, that we might be made the righteousness of God in him (2 Corinthians 5:17-21).

In the redemption of our souls at Calvary, all God's elect were brought together before his holy law and justice in one Head, the Lord Jesus. All the sins of God's elect were gathered together in him when he who knew no sin was made sin for us, all were made to meet on him, punished in him to the full satisfaction of justice, and put away by him, 'in whom we have redemption through his blood, the forgiveness of sins, according to the riches of his grace'.

In regeneration and effectual calling, by the omnipotent grace and almighty mercy of God, the Holy Spirit gathers God's elect one by one into his garner by the preaching of the gospel (Matthew 13:24-30; Mark 13:27; Luke 3:17). The gospel we preach is the fan by which the Son of God purges his threshing floor, separating the chaff from the wheat, the precious from the vile and gathers his wheat into his store. Gathered out of every nation, kindred, tribe and tongue, gathered from all the divided peoples of the earth, in Christ we are made one (Colossians 3:10, 11).

Then, when our blessed Saviour comes again in his glory he will gather all his elect together in resurrection glory. Paul calls this 'our gathering together unto him' (2 Thessalonians 2:1). He describes the majesty of it in 1 Thessalonians 4:13-18. 'But I would not have you to be ignorant, brethren, concerning them which are asleep, that ye sorrow not, even as others which have no hope. For if we believe that Jesus died and rose again, even so them also which sleep in Jesus will God bring with him. For this we say unto you by the word of the Lord, that we which are alive *and* remain unto the coming of the Lord shall not prevent them which are asleep. For the Lord himself shall descend from heaven with a shout, with the voice of the archangel, and with the trump of God: and the dead in Christ shall rise first: Then we which are alive *and* remain shall be caught up together with them in the clouds, to meet the Lord in the air: and so shall we ever be with the Lord. Wherefore comfort one another with these words'.

'Our gathering together unto him'. What a blessed prospect! Let those five words echo through our souls. 'Our gathering together unto him'. What a gathering that will be! No wonder Paul calls this 'the blessed hope' of every believing heart.

This gathering will take place at the end of the world, in the day when Christ returns to earth the second time, when 'the fulness of times' is finished. Our Saviour went away in the clouds of heaven and in the clouds of heaven, he will return. Visibly, in the body, he will return. The very first thing Christ will do will be to 'gather together' his people. 'And he shall send his angels with a great sound of a trumpet, and they shall gather together his elect from the four winds, from one end of heaven to the other' (Matthew 24:31).

The sleeping saints will be raised first. Then the living saints will be changed, 'in a moment', 'in the twinkling of an eye'! It is written, 'The dead in Christ shall rise first: Then we which are alive and remain shall be caught up together with them in the clouds, to meet the Lord in the air: and so shall we ever be with the Lord' (1 Thessalonians 4:16, 17).

When every member of Christ is found, and not one is left behind, when soul and body, those old companions, are once more reunited, that will be a great 'gathering'. All gathered together in one, in Christ, even in him. Adam and Eve, Abel and Noah, Abraham and Lot, Isaac and Isaiah, Rahab and Ruth, Tamar and Bathsheba, Paul and Barnabas, Peter and John, David and Don!

Children of God, we have no reason to fear in the day of gathering, however fearful the signs that may accompany it. Before the final destruction of all things begins, we will be hidden in the secret place of the Most High.

What miracles of grace will be revealed in that day! We will see some in heaven whom we never expected would have been saved at all. The confusion of tongues will finally be reversed and done away. The assembled multitude will cry with one heart and in one language, 'See what God has done!'

We shall be gathered by Christ, gathered unto Christ, gathered in Christ and gathered with Christ. All the family will be gathered. We will all be of one mind in all things. We will all be presented faultless before the presence of his glory, with exceeding joy. We will never part! All sorrow will be gone forever.

Then, when all the saints are gathered to glory and all the wicked forever cast into hell, our Lord Jesus Christ will make all things new and we will see all things reconciled to God in that glorious day called the 'restitution of all things'. 'What a day, glorious day that will be.'

Chapter 12

Predestinating Love

Blessed *be* the God and Father of our Lord Jesus Christ, who hath blessed us with all spiritual blessings in heavenly *places* in Christ: According as he hath chosen us in him before the foundation of the world, that we should be holy and without blame before him in love: Having predestinated us unto the adoption of children by Jesus Christ to himself, according to the good pleasure of his will, To the praise of the glory of his grace, wherein he hath made us accepted in the beloved. In whom we have redemption through his blood, the forgiveness of sins, according to the riches of his grace; Wherein he hath abounded toward us in all wisdom and prudence; Having made known unto us the mystery of his will, according to his good pleasure which he hath purposed in himself: That in the dispensation of the fulness of times he might gather together in one all things in Christ, both which are in heaven, and which are on earth; *even* in him: In whom also we have obtained an inheritance, being predestinated according to the purpose of him who worketh all things after the counsel of his own will: That we should be to the praise of his glory, who first trusted in Christ.

(Ephesians 1:3-12)

God almighty, the one true and living God, the God of the Bible, is a God of purpose; sovereign, eternal, unalterable purpose. All that comes to pass in time is brought to pass by the hand of our God, 'According to the eternal purpose which he purposed in Christ Jesus our Lord' (Ephesians 3:11). This eternal purpose of God is what the Bible calls 'predestination'. Charles Buck said, 'Predestination is the decree of God whereby he hath for his own glory fore-ordained whatever comes to pass'.

In Ephesians 1:5, God the Holy Ghost tells us that all who are made the children of God in time were in love 'predestinated ... unto the adoption of children by Jesus Christ to himself, according to the good pleasure of his will'. In verse 11, he tells us that we who believe on the Son of God have obtained an inheritance in Christ, 'being predestinated according to the purpose of him who worketh all things after the counsel of his own will'.

Bible Doctrine

There is absolutely no question about the fact that the Word of God teaches the doctrine of predestination. It is taught throughout the Scriptures and clearly stated in numerous passages of Inspiration (Exodus 4:21; Proverbs 16:4; Daniel 4:35; Matthew 11:26; 25:34; John 6:37; 17:2-24; Acts 2:23; 4:28; 13:48; Romans 8:29, 30; 9:11; Ephesians 1:3, 6, 11; 3:11; 2 Thessalonians 2:13; 2 Timothy 1:9, 10; 1 Peter 1:1, 2; Revelation 13:8; 17:8).

The basis of our faith is the Word of God and the Word of God alone. We do not believe the doctrine of predestination because it is a logical and reasonable part of a theological system, though it is both logical and reasonable. We do not believe this doctrine, or any other doctrine for that matter, simply because it has been upheld and maintained by true believers throughout the ages of Christianity, though it cannot be denied that the Church of God has always taught God's sovereign predestination. Yet, neither logic nor history is the basis of our faith. The basis of our faith is the Word of God alone. We believe this doctrine, rejoice in it and preach it from the housetops because it is plainly taught in Holy Scripture.

There is no question about the fact that predestination is a Bible doctrine. It is taught throughout the Bible. The only question that needs to be answered is this: What does the Bible teach about predestination?

This is one doctrine that is often deliberately misrepresented by those who oppose it but also ignorantly misrepresented by those who try to defend it. I once heard Bro. Henry Mahan say, 'It is hard to say whether this doctrine has suffered more in the camp of its enemies or in the camp of its friends'. That is the reason it is important to carefully search the Scriptures to see what the Bible does and does not teach about Divine Predestination.

Misrepresentations

There are four things commonly taught by men about predestination which the Word of God does not teach.

The Bible does not teach that impersonal, stoic thinking that says, 'Whatever will be will be'. That is nothing but philosophical fatalism. It attempts to remove from man all responsibility for his actions and for his condition in life. We do not believe man is the master of his own destiny but we do believe every man is responsible for his own soul and every man's destiny is his own responsibility.

The Word of God does not teach the religious fatalism which says, 'The elect will be saved no matter what'. We do believe the Bible doctrine of election. It is impossible to believe the Bible and not believe in election. However, the Word of God never suggests, or even allows the possibility, that 'the elect will be saved no matter what'. The Scriptures plainly declare that no one will ever be saved who does not hear the gospel (Romans 10:17), believe on the Lord Jesus Christ (Mark 16:15, 16), acknowledge and confess his sin (1 John 1:9), repent and bow to Christ (Luke 13:5) and persevere in the faith (Matthew 10:22). God has predestinated the use of specific means for the accomplishment of his purposes and the use of those means is as necessary and as certain as the end itself.

The Word of God nowhere teaches or implies that God has arbitrarily predestinated some to go to heaven and some to go to hell. The all-wise God never does anything arbitrarily. He has a wise and good purpose for everything he does and everything he purposed from eternity. Without question, the everlasting condemnation of the reprobate was as much a part of God's decree as the salvation of the elect.

The Bible speaks as plainly about 'the vessels of wrath fitted to destruction', as it does about 'the vessels of mercy, which he had afore prepared unto glory' (Romans 9:21-24). However, we must never fail to recognise that God's predestination, while securing the salvation of the elect by God's hand alone, leaves the responsibility for every sinner's damnation upon his own shoulders. The elect, the vessels of mercy, are prepared for glory by God's free grace in Christ; whereas the reprobate, the vessels of wrath, are fitted to destruction by their own sin and wilful unbelief. Salvation is always set before us in the Bible as being God's work, and God's work alone. Damnation is always set before us in the Bible as being man's fault and man's work alone.

Divine predestination is not based upon God's foreknowledge. Predestination is not God's foreknowledge of what would come to pass, but his purpose and determination of what must come to pass. It is not the result of what God knew man would do. Rather, predestination is what he determined he would do. The fact is, nothing could be absolutely foreknown that was not absolutely predetermined.

That which is foreknown must have been foreordained. God knew the end of all things from the beginning because he had predestinated the end from the beginning.

The scriptures do teach

Having said all this, let us see what the Scriptures do teach about this glorious doctrine of predestination. Essentially the doctrine of divine predestination is this: before the world began, God sovereignly predestinated all his elect to be conformed to the image of his dear Son, the Lord Jesus Christ. This he accomplishes in time by his sovereign, irresistible, immutable grace.

Eternal predestination is God's sovereign work. Carefully observe the language of Scripture. 'He also did predestinate.' 'He' is the original cause of all things. 'He' is the source of salvation. Everything springs from him. It is written, 'All things are of God' (2 Corinthians 5:18). 'For of him, and through him, and to him, are all things: to whom be glory for ever' (Romans 11:36).

Predestination is God's eternal purpose of grace toward his elect. It is God's determination to save his elect. It is his settled determination concerning the everlasting destiny of chosen sinners before the world began. The object of predestination is the salvation of the elect and divine predestination is absolutely free and unconditional. This work of God was finished before the world began. Predestination is an immutable, unalterable work of God's free grace in Christ. God's predestination is his gracious purpose to save specific sinners, his purpose of grace founded upon and arising from his everlasting love.

Salvation is accomplished by the irresistible power of God's grace, according to the sovereign purpose of God in his eternal decree, through the merits of Christ's blood and righteousness as the sinner's Substitute. It is not my will that saves me, but God's will. It is not my will that brings me to Christ, but God's will.

Salvation is accomplished by God's purpose. No one ever gets saved by chance or accident. Salvation is God's work! It is God's deliberate work. It is a work which the Lord God almighty purposed to accomplish from eternity. The means, or method, by which he would accomplish this glorious work was devised and resolved upon from eternity in the eternal covenant of grace and counsel of peace.

Hail sovereign love that first began
The scheme to rescue fallen man;
Hail matchless, free, eternal grace,
That gave my soul a hiding place!

This is God's plan. In eternal mercy he determined to save a people for the glory of his own great name by the substitutionary sacrifice of his dear Son. The death of Christ at Calvary was no accident or after-thought with God. Our Lord Jesus Christ went to the cross to accomplish our salvation by death as our Substitute according to his Father's own determinate counsel (Luke 22:22; Acts 2:23; 4:28).

It was God almighty who determined the time, place and circumstances of Christ's birth. It was God alone who determined the time and instrument of his Son's betrayal. It was God the Father who determined the time, place and circumstances of his Son's execution at the hands of wicked men. It was God who determined what the results of his Son's sacrificial death upon the cross would be. The Father resolved from eternity to save chosen sinners by the sin-atoning death of his own darling Son (Isaiah 53:10, 11). All of this the Lord God resolved upon and predestinated for his own glory in the salvation of his elect. He chose to save sinners by the sacrifice of Christ, through the power of his grace, without any aid or assistance from them and for the glory of his own great name (Psalm 106:8).

O the love that drew salvation's plan,
O the grace that brought it down to man,
O the mighty gulf that God did span,
At Calvary!

For the elect

Whatever predestination brings to pass and accomplishes is for God's elect. Read your Bible again. Predestination concerns God's chosen people. It secures their salvation, their preservation and their glory. Predestination is much, much more than an abstract theory of theological speculation. Predestination is one of the most practical, blessed and glorious doctrines revealed in Holy Scripture.

Predestination does not keep anyone out of heaven. People often look upon predestination as a frightful monster which stands at the gate of heaven and arbitrarily shuts multitudes out, saying, 'No, you cannot come in. You cannot be saved no matter how much you want to be because you were not chosen and predestinated to salvation.' Nothing could be further from the truth!

Any sinner who is lost at last and goes to hell will do so as the result of deliberate action on his part. If you go to hell, it will be your own fault. If you refuse to walk in the light God has given you, that is your fault. When you are cast into hell you will acknowledge the justice of God in casting you into hell.

Reprobation is always presented to us in the Book of God as a judicial act. Judgment is an act of justice. It is something God does in justice in response to man's sin. God sends blindness because men and women choose not to see. He sends hardness of heart to those who harden their hearts against him. He sends men to hell because they will not bow to his Son. Men and women can argue with that fact until they experience it in hell but that is what God declares. If you go to hell, it will be no one's fault but your own! 'O Jerusalem, Jerusalem, *thou* that killest the prophets, and stonest them which are sent unto thee, how often would I have gathered thy children together, even as a hen gathereth her chickens under *her* wings, and ye would not! Behold, your house is left unto you desolate' (Matthew 23:37, 38). 'And with all deceivableness of unrighteousness in them that perish; because they received not the love of the truth, that they might be saved. And for this cause God shall send them strong delusion, that they should believe a lie' (2 Thessalonians 2:10, 11).

Do you understand what I am telling you? If you go to hell, it will be your own fault alone. You will have no one to blame but yourself. But if anyone is saved, it will be God's work alone; the result of deliberate effort on God's part. We will have no one to thank and praise for it but God. God's salvation began in eternal predestination. Without predestination we would all be damned. Predestination is the guarantee of salvation for God's elect! God Almighty predestinated all things for the everlasting salvation of his elect and the glory of his name. In other words, all that comes to pass in time was purposed by God in eternity, purposed for our souls' everlasting good and God's everlasting praise (Romans 8:28-30).

That is Paul's doctrine in this glorious first chapter of Ephesians.

The object

The object of our God in predestination is that we should be conformed to the image of his own dear Son. The one thing God is determined to accomplish in us by his purpose, providence, power and grace is forming the exact likeness of his elect to the Lord Jesus Christ. God predestinated us to be conformed to the image of his Son! 'And we know that all things work together for good to them that love God, to them who are the called according to *his* purpose. For whom he did foreknow, he also did predestinate *to be* conformed to the image of his Son, that he might be the firstborn among many brethren.'

By the sin and fall of our father Adam we all became sinners. We lost God's image in which we were created, we forfeited life, communion, fellowship and acceptance with him forever. But God's purpose was not overthrown when Adam sinned. It was executed exactly according to his sovereign will and wisdom. 'For since by man *came* death, by man *came* also the resurrection of the dead. For as in Adam all die, even so in Christ shall all be made alive' (1 Corinthians 15:21, 22).

God Almighty was determined from the beginning to glorify himself in his creation by rescuing a multitude which no man can number from Adam's fall and restoring them to his image, perfectly and forever, through another representative man, the God-man, Christ Jesus. God looked upon his Son from eternity with such joy and delight that he said, 'I will have an innumerable multitude of sons and daughters just like him'. When predestination has done its work, every chosen sinner will be exactly conformed to the image of God's dear Son, 'holy and without blame' before God himself!

We are conformed to Christ in his nature, he is begotten of God and so are we. We are conformed to Christ in his relationship, he is the Son of God and we are the sons and daughters of the Almighty (1 John 3:1). We must be conformed to Christ in his experience. Like Christ, we must learn obedience through the things we suffer; like him, we must endure abuse from men; like our Master, we must suffer the attacks of Satan; like Christ, we must struggle against temptation and sin. We must be conformed to Christ in his character. Like him, we must be consecrated to God; like him, we must live by God's Word; like him, we must seek our Father's will; like him, we must be loving, kind and tender toward one another. We must at last be conformed to the image of Christ in his glory. This is salvation; perfect, complete, finished salvation, to be with Christ and be like Christ forever!

This salvation, from start to finish, is accomplished by God, according to his own sovereign purpose of grace in predestination. God predestinated from eternity who will be saved. God predestinated from eternity the means by which he would save us. God predestinated from eternity the time of our salvation. God predestinated from eternity all the events and circumstances necessary for and leading to our salvation. God predestinated from eternity the place where he would save his chosen. God predestinated from eternity our place in glory. God predestinated from eternity everything required to bring us safely home.

For Christ's sake

The ultimate end of our great God in predestination, as in all other things, is the exaltation and glory of our Lord Jesus Christ. God has determined to glorify himself in glorifying his glorious Son. He has predestinated us unto the adoption of sons that Jesus Christ his eternal, only-begotten Son, might be the firstborn among many brethren. He has caused us to obtain the full inheritance of grace and glory in Christ, 'that we should be to the praise of his glory, who first trusted in Christ' (Romans 11:33-36; Colossians 1:16-18).

Predestination gives Christ the pre-eminence. Christ is the centre of God's decrees. He is the Head of a new, elect race. He is the centre and glory of heaven. Predestination gives Christ pleasure. His delights were with the sons of men before time began. Now he has a race of men in whom and with whom he delights! He loves them and they all love him. This was the joy set before him, for which he endured the cross, despising the shame. This is the reward of his labour. Predestination gives Christ praise. God has arranged everything so that the population of heaven will owe everything to Christ, so that everyone in glory-land will chant Immanuel's praise alone and Immanuel's praise forever!

This is the glorious doctrine of predestination in which we rejoice. It is a most profitable doctrine. Thank God for his predestinating love! It destroys every basis of human pride. It exalts the glory of Christ and the grace of God. It gives us a purpose in evangelism. It gives us a sure hope before God (2 Samuel 23:5). It puts us at peace with God's providence. It opens the doors of heaven to sinners and guarantees that some shall enter therein. It shuts us up to God! It brings everlasting praise to the Lord Jesus Christ, our Saviour, causing ransomed sinners to glory in him forever (Revelation 5:7-14).

Chapter 13

Predestination And Providence

In whom also we have obtained an inheritance, being predestinated according to the purpose of him who worketh all things after the counsel of his own will.

(Ephesians 1:11)

Predestination and providence are inseparable twins of grace set before us in Ephesians 1:11. Divine providence is the daily, constant and sovereign rule of our God over all things for the accomplishment of his eternal purpose of grace in predestination, working 'all things together after the counsel of his own will'. Predestination is the sovereign, eternal, immutable, unalterable purpose of God almighty by which he has ordained and ordered, according to his own will and good pleasure, all things which come to pass in time.

Divine providence is the accomplishment of God's sovereign will and purpose. Providence is God doing in time what he purposed in eternity. Predestination is God's purpose. Providence is God's execution of his purpose.

Be sure you understand the doctrine of Holy Scripture with regard to the providence of God. Nothing in the universe happens by luck, chance, fortune or accident. Everything that comes to pass in time was purposed by our God in eternity and is brought to pass by his wise and good providence. Nothing comes to pass in time that God did not purpose in eternity, in sovereign predestination. Nothing comes to pass in time except that which God sovereignly brings to pass in his providence.

That which God predestinated in eternity and brings to pass in his providence is for the good of his elect and the glory of his name. Let us see if that is truth or heresy. What does the Word of God say? 'Let God be true, and every man a liar.'

'Surely the wrath of man shall praise thee: the remainder of wrath shalt thou restrain' (Psalm 76:10).

'The LORD hath made all *things* for himself: yea, even the wicked for the day of evil' (Proverbs 16:4).

'A man's heart deviseth his way: but the LORD directeth his steps' (Proverbs 16:9).

'The lot is cast into the lap; but the whole disposing thereof *is* of the LORD' (Proverbs 16:33).

'The king's heart *is* in the hand of the LORD, *as* the rivers of water: he turneth it whithersoever he will' (Proverbs 21:1).

'Remember the former things of old: for I *am* God, and *there is* none else; *I am* God, and *there is* none like me, Declaring the end from the beginning, and from ancient times *the things* that are not *yet* done, saying, My counsel shall stand, and I will do all my pleasure: Calling a ravenous bird from the east, the man that executeth my counsel from a far country: yea, I have spoken *it,* I will also bring it to pass; I have purposed *it,* I will also do it' (Isaiah 46:9-11).

'And at the end of the days I Nebuchadnezzar lifted up mine eyes unto heaven, and mine understanding returned unto me, and I blessed the most High, and I praised and honoured him that liveth forever, whose dominion *is* an everlasting dominion, and his kingdom *is* from generation to generation: And all the inhabitants of the earth *are* reputed as nothing: and he doeth according to his will in the army of heaven, and *among* the inhabitants of the earth: and none can stay his hand, or say unto him, What doest thou?' (Daniel 4:34, 35)

'Now I Nebuchadnezzar praise and extol and honour the King of heaven, all whose works *are* truth, and his ways judgment: and those that walk in pride he is able to abase' (Daniel 4:37).

The very best commentary I have ever read on Ephesians 1:11 is Romans 8:28, 'And we know that all things work together for good to them that love God, to them who are the called according to *his* purpose'. If we learn what is taught in these twenty-five words about God's providence we will rejoice in God our Saviour.

A delightful persuasion

First, the inspired writer speaks of a delightful persuasion. 'We know ... ' The word *'know'* in this sentence refers to a knowledge beyond speculation, theory, doctrine or even sound judgment. It is the knowledge of a confident, assured persuasion based upon fact and experience. It is my prayer that God will graciously and thoroughly convince us of these things as he did the Apostle Paul. 'We' – all true believers – 'know'. But how do we know? What is the basis of this knowledge?

We know these things by the revelation of God's Word (Psalms 84:11; 91:1-16; Proverbs 12:21; Hosea 2:18).

We know these things, and walk in the comfort of God's providence because of the inner witness and anointing of God the Holy Ghost who teaches us all things, by whom we have the mind of Christ (1 Corinthians 2:16; 1 John 2:20).

We know the wisdom and goodness of God's adorable providence because we have experienced it. Bro. Rolfe Barnard used to say, 'We only believe what we experience'. Are you persuaded of what Paul teaches us here? If you are, you have a persuasion that will keep your soul in peace. Indeed, this is the only persuasion that will keep your soul in peace, 'When sorrows like sea billows roll'.

A divine providence

Second, the Holy Spirit reveals a divine providence by which all things are ordered, ruled and disposed of in time. 'We know that all things work together for good.'

Providence is God's government of the universe. This is a subject of deepest importance. If we have a proper view of God's providence we will see the hand of God and the heart of God in everything, in all the experiences of our lives. Let us never talk like the unbelieving Philistines who said, 'It was a chance that happened to us' (1 Samuel 6:9). Believers talk like Job who said, 'Naked came I out of my mother's womb, and naked shall I return thither: the LORD gave, and the LORD hath taken away; blessed be the name of the LORD' (Job 1:21). Like Eli, who said, 'And Samuel told him every whit, and hid nothing from him. And he said, It *is* the LORD: let him do what seemeth him good' (1 Samuel 3:18). Like David, who said, 'And David said to Abishai, and to all his servants, Behold, my son, which came forth of my bowels, seeketh my life: how much more now *may this* Benjamite *do it?* let him alone, and let him curse; for the LORD hath bidden him. It may be that the LORD will look on mine affliction, and that the LORD will requite me good for his cursing this day' (2 Samuel 16:11, 12).

God is never idle. He is the one Person who is always on the job. He never needs to rest, recuperate or regroup! God almighty, our God and heavenly Father, is always at work governing the world.

You may sometimes think, 'God is not doing a very good job of running this world'. I have often heard fools say, 'If God was running everything, then this or that would not happen'. You might, in your imaginary great depth of wisdom, propose a lot of changes. Could not the Almighty easily put an end to sickness, poverty, war, sin, crime, disease, famine, earthquakes and death? Indeed, he could. But God almighty will not be dictated to by us! Who are we to dare set ourselves up as instructors to the all-wise God? He 'worketh all things after the counsel of his own will'.

Four things

Let me remind you of four things about God's providence.

God's providence is mysterious. 'O the depth of the riches both of the wisdom and knowledge of God! how unsearchable *are* his judgments, and his ways past finding out! For who hath known the mind of the Lord? or who hath been his counsellor? Or who hath first given to him, and it shall be recompensed unto him again? For of him, and through him, and to him, *are* all things: to whom *be* glory forever. Amen' (Romans 11:33-36).

His judgments are a great deep. His ways are past finding out. God always has his way. His ways are not our ways. His way is always right and best.

God's providence is minute. 'But the very hairs of your head are all numbered' (Matthew 10:30).

Divine providence is all inclusive! God rules everything, great and small, everywhere and always! 'The LORD hath prepared his throne in the heavens; his kingdom ruleth over all.'

God is in control of all inanimate matter; the creation, the Red Sea, the Jordan river, the crowd that followed Korah, the fiery furnace, the whirlwind, the shadow to go backward. Our God is in total control of all irrational creatures; the flies, frogs and locusts in Egypt, the whale that swallowed Jonah, the cock that crew for Peter.

Our God and heavenly Father controls, absolutely and totally, all rational creatures, too. He controls all men and women everywhere, good and bad, in the good they do and in the evil they perform. All angels, all demons and Satan himself are under the total control of our God (Psalm 76:10; Isaiah 14:24-27).

We have no trouble believing God controls good things and good people but those are not things that bother me. It is the bad stuff that disturbs me. I want to know who is in control of wickedness and evil. He is the One I will worship. Many have trouble with this. They do not understand that God truly is God, as fully in control of hell as of heaven, as totally in control of wickedness as of righteousness.

What about sin? What about the fall? C. D. Cole wrote, 'God allows sin because he is able to overrule it for his own glory. God is not the Author of sin; but he is the Controller and Director of sin. God is not the Causative Force, but the Directing Agent in the sins of men. Men are rebellious; but they have not pushed God off his throne. They are not out from under his control'.

William Plumer wrote, God our Saviour, 'Jesus Christ upholds, preserves, and governs the worlds which he has made! Thus all creatures, from the smallest insect which is seen by the microscope up to the archangel which worships before the eternal throne, all events, from the falling of a hair of the head to the destruction of nations by famine, pestilence and war, all rule and authority, from that of a petty official, to that of thrones and principalities in heaven, the material universe, from the least particle which floats in the sunbeam to the grandest system of worlds which roll in immensity, all hang dependent on his powerful providence! And if one link in the chain of that dependence were broken they would all rush headlong to destruction! Jesus always has governed this world and he shall ever hold the sceptre over it, until his last foe shall be vanquished and his last hidden one made victorious'.

God's providence is mysterious, minute and all-inclusive. But be sure you get this fourth thing. God's providence is good! 'All things work together for good to them that love God, to them who are the called according to his purpose'. No event in history is isolated from any other event. 'All things work together.' Not necessarily immediate good, not necessarily temporal good but spiritual good, eternal good, collective good.

Actually, that which is truly good for me is very often the exact opposite of that which is presently good. It is good for me to know Christ and be found in him. If God has to cripple me or cripple my child to get my attention and then turn my eyes and my heart to Christ, that is good! It is good to fellowship with God and walk humbly before him; to be a blessing to others, to be weaned from this world, to continue in the faith, to die in the faith and to rise in glory and be like Christ! Whatever God sees fit to use to accomplish these things for us and in us is good!

Someone has said: Too much joy would intoxicate me, too much misery would drive me into despair, too much sorrow would crush me, too much suffering would break my spirit, too much pleasure would ruin me, too much defeat would discourage me, too much success would puff me up, too much failure would keep me from doing anything, too much criticism would harden me, too much praise would exalt me.

God knows exactly what we need. His providence is wisely designed and sovereignly sent for our good! Let him send and do what he will.

A designated people

Third, Paul speaks of a designated people, 'We know that all things work together for good to them that love God, to them who are the called … ' This promise of God is not for and is not given to everyone. It is a special promise made to a special people. It is God's promise 'to them that love God, to them who are the called'.

A declared purpose

Fourth, here is a declared purpose according to which God almighty rules, governs and disposes of all things. 'We know that all things work together for good to them that love God, to them who are the called according to his purpose.'

Whenever you read or quote or even think of Romans 8:28, be sure you do not leave out those last four words. You will never understand anything in this Book; you will never understand anything God does; you will never understand the mystery and wonder of Divine Providence, until you understand that God does everything 'according to his purpose'.

When I read those last four words of Romans 8:28, the first thing that comes to my mind, the first thing I want to know is, 'What is his purpose?'

You may think it is impossible for us to know the purpose of God. In a sense that is true. It is written, 'The secret things belong unto the LORD our God' (Deuteronomy 29:29). We must never attempt to pry into the future. What God has purposed for us is God's business. Our business is to trust him.

However, the very next line of that text reads, 'The secret things belong unto the LORD our God: but those things which are revealed belong unto us and to our children for ever'. The reason why these things are revealed is, according to Deuteronomy 29:29, 'that we may do all the words of this law'. That is to say, that we may learn to trust the Lord our God.

God's goal for his elect is absolute, full, eternal glorification in Christ and with Christ. Nothing less will satisfy his purpose or honour his name.

Chapter 14

'Who First Trusted In Christ'

That we should be to the praise of his glory, who first trusted in Christ.
(Ephesians 1:12)

After faithfully preaching the gospel of God's free and sovereign grace in Christ for nearly 50 years, on the last day of his life in this world, on 6 April, 1827, Robert Hawker quoted Ephesians 1, verses 3-12 of Holy Scripture to some friends and briefly explained their meaning. When he got to verse 12, 'That we should be to the praise of his glory who first trusted in Christ,' the old pastor paused and asked, 'Who first trusted in Christ?' Then he made this answer: 'It was God the Father who first trusted in Christ'.

Who?

The word translated 'who' in verse 12 is a plural pronoun. That fact has led many good commentators to object to Hawker's interpretation of the words, suggesting instead that Paul must have had in mind Old Testament believers, the early Jewish believers or the apostles themselves.

But Hawker's interpretation is, in my opinion, the only interpretation that fits Paul's language, though it is true that the masculine article translated by the English pronoun 'who' must refer to more than one person. It is written in the plural because it refers to the entire Godhead: Father, Son and Holy Spirit.

You see, all three Persons in the Holy Trinity trusted the Lord Jesus Christ, our Mediator and Surety, with all the purpose and glory of the Triune God as it is set forth in this passage. In this paragraph God the Father is spoken of as the Covenant Spokesman for the Holy Trinity. We are saved to the praise of the glory of the Triune God, Father, Son and Holy Ghost, not just to the praise of the glory of the Father. Christ is spoken of as the Covenant Spokesman for his elect, as our Surety.

This interpretation is even more obvious when we realise the word translated 'trusted in' is a perfect participle implying an action completed in the past, once and for all, not needing to be repeated. It is a word used nowhere else in the Bible. When the Scriptures speak of our faith in Christ another word is used. The words here, 'trusted in', could be more accurately translated 'fore-hoped in', or 'hoped in beforehand', or 'hoped in advance'. So when the question is asked, 'Who first trusted in Christ?' the answer Paul gives in this text is, 'The Triune God, for whose glory and by whose grace we are saved in Christ'.

Nothing else will fit the context in which our text is found. Paul is talking about the inheritance we have obtained in Christ already, from eternity, according to God's sovereign, blessed, eternal purpose of grace in Christ our Surety. He is explaining to us the mystery of God's will revealed in Christ in Ephesians 1:7-12.

In the first fourteen verses of Ephesians, the Apostle Paul tells us three times that the purpose of the Triune God in our salvation is that we should be to the praise of his glory. One reason given why we should desire his glory is given in these words, 'That we should be to the praise of his glory, who first trusted in Christ'.

The covenant

Our heavenly Father entered into a covenant with his Son on our behalf before the world began for the saving of our souls. In Hebrews 13:20, it is called 'the everlasting covenant'. Frequently it is called the 'new covenant'. This covenant was made in eternity between the Triune God; God the Father, God the Son and God the Holy Ghost and Christ our Mediator and Surety, but it was made for us. Insofar as the benefits and blessings of it to us are concerned it is an unconditional covenant. The Lord God said, 'I will love them freely. I will be their God; and they shall be my people'.

This everlasting covenant of grace is a sure covenant, a covenant which infallibly secured and guaranteed to God's elect all the blessings of salvation and eternal life in Christ (2 Samuel 23:5; Jeremiah 31:3, 31-34; 32:38-40).

The only condition to the covenant and the blessings of grace and salvation promised in it was the obedience of the Son of God as our Surety unto death. 'Now the God of peace, that brought again from the dead our Lord Jesus, that great shepherd of the sheep, through the blood of the everlasting covenant, Make you perfect in every good work to do his will, working in you that which is wellpleasing in his sight, through Jesus Christ; to whom *be* glory for ever and ever. Amen' (Hebrews 13:20). There never was a danger of that condition not being met by the Son of God! There was never the slightest possibility of failure on his part. He was willing to obey. He was able to obey. He did obey his Father's will even unto death, even unto the shedding of his blood, 'the blood of the everlasting covenant'.

The Father's trust

Having found a ransom for our souls in the Person of his own Son, our heavenly Father gave his chosen into the hands of his Son, as sheep into the hands of a shepherd, and trusted him with the salvation of our souls and the glory of his own great name. In the covenant of grace, before the world began, when the Son of God volunteered to become our Surety, God the Father trusted his elect and all his purposes of grace toward his elect, into the hands of his dear Son. God the Father trusted Christ as our Surety, Shepherd and Saviour long before we did (John 6:37-39).

Thus it is that the Lord Jesus Christ spoke of all his sheep as being his sheep, which he must bring into the fold, long before many of his sheep were born. He spoke of the 'all' as his present possession, though he declared plainly that they were not yet in his fold. 'And other sheep I have, which are not of this fold: them also I must bring, and they shall hear my voice; and there shall be one fold, *and* one shepherd' (John 10:16).

In the everlasting covenant of grace God the Father trusted his Son, our all glorious Christ, with the salvation of his elect and thus with the glory of his name from everlasting. When our Saviour had finished his great work of redemption, whereby he secured the salvation of all the chosen, he asked and the Father gave to him as the just reward of his obedience, the glory he had with him before the world began. 'These words spake Jesus, and lifted up his eyes to heaven, and said, Father, the hour is come; glorify thy Son, that thy Son also may glorify thee: As thou hast given him power over all flesh, that he should give eternal life to as many as thou hast given him. And this is life eternal, that they might know thee the only true God, and Jesus Christ, whom thou hast sent. I have glorified thee on the earth: I have finished the work which thou gavest me to do. And now, O Father, glorify thou me with thine own self with the glory which I had with thee before the world was' (John 17:1-5). Notice that the glory given him when he had finished his work is the glory he had with him, as our trusted Surety, before the world began.

Our trust

'In whom ye also trusted' (Ephesians 1:13). At the appointed time of mercy, grace and love, every chosen, redeemed sinner is born again and called by the irresistible power and grace of God the Holy Spirit to faith in Christ. This God-given faith is not the trust of some imaginary Jesus who tries to save but cannot do it without the consent of man. Oh, no! That Jesus is an idolatrous figment of man's depraved imagination! This God-given faith is faith in the same Christ the Father trusted from eternity, the almighty covenant Surety who cannot fail!

Trustworthy

If God the Father has trusted his glory to his dear Son as our Substitute and Saviour, and trusted the salvation of our souls to his hands, how we ought to trust him with our immortal souls and with all that concerns us. If the Father trusted him he is a trustworthy Saviour! Upon the basis of this covenant our heavenly Father accepted us and blessed us with all spiritual blessings in Christ from eternity (Romans 8:28-30; Ephesians 1:3-6).

Our Surety

How is the Lord Jesus Christ our Surety and what work does he perform on our behalf as our Surety? It is said one picture is worth a thousand words. In Genesis 42:36-38, Reuben volunteered to be a surety for Benjamin but Jacob would not allow it. Why? Because our Surety is he who came from the tribe of Judah, not from the tribe of Reuben. He is 'the Lion of the tribe of Judah'. When Judah volunteered to be surety for Benjamin, Jacob agreed to it. 'And Judah said unto Israel his father, Send the lad with me, and we will arise and go; that we may live, and not die, both we, and thou, *and* also our little ones. I will be surety for him; of my hand shalt thou require him: if I bring him not unto thee, and set him before thee, then let me bear the blame for ever' (Genesis 43:8, 9).

As Judah became surety for Benjamin, the Lord Jesus Christ became Surety for God's elect in the covenant of grace.

What is a surety?

A surety is one who approaches one person on the behalf of another person. He is a representative man who lays himself under obligation to another person for the one he represents. In this sense Christ is our Surety. He drew near to his Father on our behalf and laid himself under obligation to God for us. 'Then said I, Lo, I come:

in the volume of the book *it is* written of me, I delight to do thy will, O my God: yea, thy law *is* within my heart' (Psalm 40:7, 8).

A surety is one who strikes hands with another in solemn agreement. Suretyship is, to a man of honour, a voluntary bondage. 'My son, if thou be surety for thy friend, *if* thou hast stricken thy hand with a stranger, Thou art snared with the words of thy mouth, thou art taken with the words of thy mouth' (Proverbs 6:1, 2). When Christ became our Surety, he voluntarily placed himself in bondage to his Father until his service was performed. He snared himself with the words of his own mouth (Isaiah 50:5-7; John 10:16-18).

This is what the Lord Jesus Christ did as our Surety in the Covenant of Grace, before the world began. He drew near to the Father on the behalf of his elect; he promised to faithfully perform all that the Triune Jehovah required for the salvation of his people; he struck hands with the Father in solemn agreement.

God the Father trusted his elect people into the hands of his dear Son as our Surety and the matter of our salvation was then and there settled forever (Ephesians 1:12; 2 Timothy 1:9, 10).

How did Christ become our Surety?

With men a Surety is a guarantor, a co-signer who is jointly responsible with the principal debtor for the payment of a debt. Not so with Christ!

Our Lord Jesus Christ did not merely agree to meet our obligations to God's law if we, by some circumstance or condition, became incapable of meeting our obligations. Our blessed Saviour, as our Surety, took the whole of our obligation before the law of God upon himself.

With men a surety may be legally forced into suretyship. A father is legally responsible for the debts and legal liabilities of his minor children. But Christ voluntarily and cheerfully placed himself in servitude to God's law and subject to his will as the Surety of his own elect. From the instant he became Surety for his people he became Servant to his Father (Isaiah 42:1; 49:3; John 10:17, 18). The Lord Jesus Christ is an absolute Surety by voluntary consent.

When he became our Surety Christ took the whole of our debt upon himself. He became responsible for all our obligations. As soon as he was accepted as our Surety we were released from all of our debts and obligations to God's holy law.

As soon as God accepted his Son as our Surety he set us free. He ceased looking to us for satisfaction. He freed us from all bondage, all curse, all penalty and all obligation. He looked to his Son alone for satisfaction of our debts (Job 33:24).

When Christ became Surety for us our sins were made his. Our sins were made his and placed to his account. He became responsible for them. Christ was made to be sin for us when he hung upon the cursed tree. But they were made his and he became responsible and accountable for our sins when he became our Surety (Psalms 40:12; 69:5; Isaiah 53:6; 2 Corinthians 5:21).

When the Lord Jesus Christ became our Surety we were then and there redeemed, justified, pardoned, made righteous and accepted in the Beloved. God's forbearance, patience and long-suffering with this world is due to the suretyship engagements of Christ. God's eye has always been on the blood. It is the blood of Christ, our Surety, that held back the hand of God's judgment when Adam sinned. It is that same precious blood that holds back the judgment of God upon the earth today (2 Peter 3:9).

The Old Testament saints were pardoned, justified and forgiven upon the basis of Christ's obedience as our Surety, though he had not yet actually rendered that obedience. 'These all died in faith, not having received the promises, but having seen them afar off, and were persuaded of *them,* and embraced *them,* and confessed that they were strangers and pilgrims on the earth. For they that say such things declare plainly that they seek a country. And truly, if they had been mindful of that *country* from whence they came out, they might have had opportunity to have returned. But now they desire a better *country,* that is, an heavenly: wherefore God is not ashamed to be called their God: for he hath prepared for them a city' (Hebrews 11:13-16).

Those blessed saints of old had knowledge of and faith in Christ as their Surety (Job 19:25-27; Psalms 32:1-4; 119:122; Isaiah 38:14).

The Lord Jesus Christ became our Surety by his own voluntary will. He was accepted as our Surety in the Covenant of Grace before the world began. God, the Triune Jehovah, trusted him as the Mediator and Covenant Surety of his elect (Ephesians 1:12-14).

What did the Lord Jesus Christ agree to as our Surety?

When Christ became our Surety he made certain promises in the name of his covenant people which he is honour-bound to perform. These promises were voluntarily made, without any constraint or force, except the constraint of his own love and the force of his own grace. Now, having made those promises, he is bound to perform them, bound by his own honour, snared by the words of his own mouth. What are those promises? What did our great Surety agree to do? Basically, our eternal Surety agreed to do two things.

First, he agreed to meet and perfectly fulfil all our responsibilities to God. Standing as our Surety, in an absolute sense, Christ did not simply assume part of our responsibility in a given area. He became absolutely responsible for his people in all things. He agreed to render that perfect obedience to the law, 'establishing righteousness for us', which we were obliged to do. He agreed to work out a legal righteousness for his people. 'I have finished the work.' He agreed to satisfy the penalty of the law as our Substitute. By his perfect obedience, in life and in death, our great Surety magnified the law and made it honourable.

Second, Christ our Surety agreed to bring all his elect safe to glory (John 6:39, 40; 10:16). The Lord Jesus Christ became responsible to bring God's Benjamins safely home. 'If I bring them not unto thee, and set them before thee, then let me bear the blame forever'. It is because of his suretyship engagements for his elect that our Lord says, 'Them also I must bring'. What our Surety has sworn to do, he must do.

He reconciled us to God in his sin-atoning death. He entered into heaven as our Covenant-Head and claimed our eternal inheritance in our name as our Surety. He will, in the last day, present all of his elect faultless before the Father's glory with great joy. In that day, he will appear without sin. We will appear without sin. His Father will say again, 'Well done!'

'Behold my servant, whom I uphold; mine elect, *in whom* my soul delighteth; I have put my spirit upon him: he shall bring forth judgment to the Gentiles. He shall not cry, nor lift up, nor cause His voice to be heard in the street. A bruised reed shall he not break, and the smoking flax shall he not quench: he shall bring forth judgment unto truth. He shall not fail nor be discouraged, till he have set judgment in the earth: and the isles shall wait for His law' (Isaiah 42:1-4).

Be sure to grasp the teaching of Holy Scripture regarding the matter of our acceptance before God. Our acceptance is in Christ our Surety. Our acceptance is from everlasting to everlasting. Our acceptance is absolute and unconditional. Our acceptance means that God the Father, our heavenly Father, looks upon us in Christ as perfect in him, and has done so from eternity. He declares, 'It must be perfect to be accepted'. Being 'accepted in the beloved', our heavenly Father has blessed us with all spiritual blessings in Christ from eternity and has promised to bless us forever for Christ's sake (Ephesians 1:3; 2 Timothy 1:9). The Lord God commanded Aaron, his high priest, to bless his people symbolically because he had sworn from eternity, for Christ's sake, saying, 'I will bless them' (Numbers 6:27). Bless us he has, and bless us he shall, because our Surety is a faithful Surety, a Surety worthy of the everlasting trust of the Triune God.

Children of God, we are in the grip of God's grace and we have been from eternity. Therefore, he would not let us go and will not let us go.

Some years ago on a hot summer day in south Florida a little boy decided to go for a swim in the old swimming hole behind his house. In a hurry to dive into the cool water he ran out the back door leaving behind shoes, socks and shirt as he went. He raced into the water not realising that as he swam toward the middle of the lake an alligator was swimming toward the shore. His mother, in the house, was looking out the window. She saw the two as they got closer and closer together. In utter fear she ran toward the water yelling to her son as loudly as she could. Hearing her voice, the little boy became alarmed and made a U-turn to swim to his mother. It was too late. As he reached her the alligator reached him. From the dock, the mother grabbed her little boy by the arms just as the alligator snatched his legs. That began an incredible tug-of-war between the two. The alligator was stronger than the mother but the mother was much too passionate to let go. A farmer happened to drive by, he heard her screams and raced from his truck, gun in hand. He took aim and shot the alligator.

Remarkably, the little boy survived. His legs were extremely scarred by the vicious attack of the animal and on his arms were deep scratches where his mother's fingernails dug into his flesh in her effort to hang on to the son she loved. The newspaper reporter who interviewed the boy after the trauma, asked if he would show him his scars. The boy lifted his trouser-legs. Then, with obvious pride, he said to the reporter, 'But look at my arms; I have scars on my arms, too. I have them because my Mom wouldn't let go'.

You and I can identify with that little boy. We have scars, too. No, not from an alligator or anything quite so dramatic. We have the scars of a painful past. Some of those scars are unsightly and have caused us deep regret but some wounds are because God has refused to let go. In the midst of your struggle, he has been there holding on to you. You are in the grip of his grace. He did not and will not let you go.

Chapter 15

'Your Salvation'

That we should be to the praise of his glory, who first trusted in Christ. In whom ye also *trusted,* after that ye heard the word of truth, the gospel of your salvation: in whom also after that ye believed, ye were sealed with that holy Spirit of promise, Which is the earnest of our inheritance until the redemption of the purchased possession, unto the praise of his glory.

(Ephesians 1:12-14)

I rejoice in the many descriptions of salvation given by God himself in Holy Scripture. This is how the Word of God describes our salvation. The very first time the word 'salvation' is found in the Bible, it is called God's salvation (Genesis 49:18). The Book of Hebrews declares it is 'eternal salvation' (5:9). Jude speaks of the salvation of God's elect as their 'common salvation' (v. 3). It is a salvation enjoyed in common, equally and fully by all God's elect. In Hebrews 2:3, the Holy Spirit tells us our salvation in Christ is a 'great salvation'.

That is a good description of salvation, 'so great salvation'. It comes from the great God. It is for great sinners. It comes to us through the merits of the great Saviour. It flows to us from the great reservoir of God's great grace; the heart of God and the love of God! It secures for us a great inheritance in heaven. God's salvation is 'so great salvation' that no words can adequately describe it.

Isaiah 45:17, describes this thing we call salvation as an 'everlasting salvation'. Salvation is eternal both ways. It is from everlasting and to everlasting. If salvation is God's work it is an everlasting work. 'I know that, whatsoever God doeth, it shall be for ever: nothing can be put to it, nor any thing taken from it: and God doeth *it,* that *men* should fear before him' (Ecclesiastes 3:14).

Sinners saved by grace shall never perish. We are saved beyond the reach of condemnation or even danger. God's love is an everlasting love. God's election is everlasting election. God's grace is everlasting grace. Christ's redemption is an everlasting redemption. The Spirit's seal is an everlasting seal.

Yet no description of salvation can be found that is sweeter, more delightful, comforting or more satisfying to our souls than that which is found in Philippians 2:12. Here the Spirit of God declares to believing sinners that God's eternal, great, everlasting salvation is 'your own salvation'. 'Wherefore, my beloved, as ye have always obeyed, not as in my presence only, but now much more in my absence, work out your own salvation with fear and trembling'.

If you are saved, the salvation you have is 'your own salvation'. God devised it for you. Christ purchased it for you. The Holy Spirit brought it to you and wrought it in you. It is yours forever! If you trust the Lord Jesus Christ, all that is included in that word 'salvation' is your personal property and possession forever. It belongs to you by the gift of the grace of God. 'Work out your own salvation with fear and trembling.' That does not mean, 'Work that you might be saved'. It means, 'Work outwardly what God has worked inwardly'. Here is an assurance. 'For it is God which worketh in you both to will (to desire) and to do of his good pleasure.' If you are saved, the salvation God has wrought in you is 'your own salvation'. That great, glorious, eternal, everlasting, common salvation God has wrought in us is distinctly ours. In Ephesians 1:12-14, it is called 'your salvation'.

There are five things clearly taught in these three verses about your salvation and mine. Believer, child of God, your salvation is designed for divine praise, 'That we should be to the praise of his glory'. It is based upon a divine trust, 'That we should be to the praise of his glory, who first trusted in Christ'. It is obtained and enjoyed by a divine gift, 'In whom ye also trusted, after that ye heard the word of truth, the gospel of your salvation'. It is secured by a divine seal, 'In whom also after that ye believed, ye were sealed with that holy Spirit of promise'. It is assured by a divine pledge, 'Which is the earnest of our inheritance until the redemption of the purchased possession, unto the praise of his glory'.

Divine praise

First, the Spirit of God tells us our salvation in and by Christ is a salvation designed for divine praise. 'That we should be to the praise of his glory.' That salvation revealed in Holy Scripture always honours the Lord God. It is a salvation becoming the character of God. If your salvation does not honour God alone, your salvation is a delusion.

The purpose of God in all things is the glory of his own great name. It is why he has saved us (Psalm 106:8). It is the end of predestination, election, adoption, redemption and calling, 'That we should be to the praise of his glory'. Our salvation is first and foremost for 'the praise of his glory, who first trusted in Christ'.

Divine trust

Second, the salvation of our souls is a salvation based upon a divine trust. 'That we should be to the praise of his glory, who first trusted in Christ'. The Apostle Paul, writing by divine inspiration, tells us of a twofold trust in the Lord Jesus Christ. He tells us God the Father trusted Christ as the Mediator and all who are born of God trust him as the only Mediator between God and man.

The Holy Spirit informs us God the Father trusted his Son long before we came to trust him. In the covenant of grace, before the world began, when the Son of God volunteered to become our Surety, God the Father trusted his elect and all his purposes of grace toward his elect, into the hands of his Son. God the Father trusted Christ as our Surety, Shepherd and Saviour long before we did (John 6:37-39).

Thus it is that the Lord Jesus Christ spoke of all his sheep as being his sheep, which he must bring into the fold, long before many of his sheep were even born. He spoke of them all as his present possession though he declared plainly that they were not yet in his fold (John 10:16).

In the everlasting covenant of grace, God the Father trusted his Son with the salvation of his elect and thus with the glory of his name from everlasting. When our Saviour had finished his great work of redemption whereby he secured the salvation of all the chosen, he asked and the Father gave to him, the glory he had with him before the world began (John 17:1-4; Hebrews 1:1-3; 10:1-14).

'In whom ye also trusted.' At the appointed time of mercy and love, every chosen, redeemed sinner is born again and called by the irresistible power and grace of God the Holy Spirit to life and faith in Christ.

Divine gift

Third, if you are saved, your salvation is a salvation obtained and enjoyed by a divine gift. 'In whom ye also trusted, after that ye heard the word of truth, the gospel of your salvation.' Our trust in Christ, like all other blessings of grace, is the gift of God, the result of divine election and predestination and the operation of his grace in us (Ephesians 2:8, 9; Colossians 2:10-12).

Notice here that the object of all true, saving faith is a 'whom', not a what! 'In whom ye also trusted.' What is involved in this matter of trusting Christ?

Trust in Christ first demands a renunciation of self. There can be no trust in Christ until we cease to trust in ourselves. Christ is the last refuge of man. Our experience of grace verifies that fact, does it not? When we first began to be troubled in conscience and were made to tremble before God's holy law, we tried everything to obtain peace; reformation, repentance, religious duties and countless other things. We sought forgiveness of sin and rest in our souls by trying to save ourselves by the merit of something we could do. Thank God, he swept away every refuge of lies we made for ourselves! He made every staff upon which we leaned a spear to pierce our hands. He made our righteousnesses stink as filthy rags before him and sweetly forced us to flee to Christ alone for refuge, glorying only in him.

Faith in Christ, trusting in him alone as our Saviour is glorifying God. He who ordained our salvation, to the praise of his own glory, causes us to glorify him. By trusting in Christ we magnify and glorify each attribute of God in particular. To trust in Christ is to glorify the justice and truth of God, taking sides with God against ourselves. 'The soul that sinneth, it shall die.' 'It shall be perfect to be accepted.' 'Without holiness no man shall see the Lord.' 'The unrighteous shall not inherit the kingdom of God.'

Trusting in Christ glorifies the truth of God. 'He that believeth on the Son hath everlasting life.' 'Whosoever believeth in him shall receive remission of sins.' 'Whosoever believeth in him shall not be ashamed.' 'Whosoever believeth that Jesus is the Christ is born of God.' 'Whosoever shall call upon the name of the Lord shall be saved.' 'Believe on the Lord Jesus Christ, and thou shalt be saved.'

Trust in Christ glorifies the mercy, love and grace of God. It is by God's free love, his immaculate mercy and his omnipotent grace that miserable, hell-deserving sinners are rescued from misery, crowned with blessing and raised to joys everlasting. Faith in Christ puts heaven in our souls and gives all the glory to our great God for his glorious grace and salvation.

When God graciously causes stout-hearted rebels to bow before him, trusting Christ, he makes sinners saved by his grace his glory in the earth (Isaiah 46:12, 13). Our God says of his elect, 'They shall come up with acceptance on mine altar, and I will glorify the house of my glory' (Isaiah 60:7). Imagine that! The God of Glory calls us 'the house of my glory'. In his indescribable, condescending grace our great God stoops to be glorified in us. Trusting his darling Son, we glorify the Triune God. 'Whoso offereth praise glorifieth me: and to him that ordereth *his* conversation *aright* will I shew the salvation of God' (Psalm 50:23).

The sweet incense of trust, faith and gratitude ascends day and night from the altar of love in the believing heart to the glory of God. When Christ returns to earth it will be to be glorified in his saints. When the end comes and he delivers up the kingdom to God, even the Father, then shall the faithful lift up their voices, which shall never cease, and every note and sound shall be glory to God and to the Lamb. Thus we who trust in Christ are to the praise of His glory.

How did we, who were dead in trespasses and in sins, come to trust in the Lord Jesus Christ? Look at verse 13 again, 'In whom ye also trusted, after that ye heard the word of truth, the gospel of your salvation'. Here, and throughout the Word of God faith follows hearing. It never precedes hearing. Faith in Christ comes by hearing the Word of God (Romans 10:17; 1 Peter 1:23-25).

Divine seal

Fourth, ours is a salvation secured by a divine seal. 'In whom also, after that ye believed, ye were sealed with that holy Spirit of promise.' A better reading would be, 'Having believed, ye were sealed'. This is not talking about a second work of grace but about the result of God-given faith in Christ. The sealing work of the Spirit is mentioned after the experience of faith because our salvation is attested to and revealed only after we believe. Actually, we have a threefold seal from God.

The seal of the Father's foreknowledge. 'Nevertheless the foundation of God standeth sure, having this seal, The Lord knoweth them that are his. And, Let every one that nameth the name of Christ depart from iniquity' (2 Timothy 2:19).

The seal of the Son's love. 'Set me as a seal upon thine heart, as a seal upon thine arm: for love *is* strong as death; jealousy *is* cruel as the grave: the coals thereof *are* coals of fire, *which hath a* most vehement flame' (Song of Solomon 8:6). 'Saying, Hurt not the earth, neither the sea, nor the trees, till we have sealed the servants of our God in their foreheads' (Revelation 7:3).

The seal of the Spirit's work of grace. 'And grieve not the holy Spirit of God, whereby ye are sealed unto the day of redemption' (Ephesians 4:30). It is this seal of the Spirit that gives us the full assurance of faith by which we call God our Father and draw near unto him by the blood of Christ. It is this seal of the Spirit, the gift of faith, that assures the believing sinner of a saving interest in Christ. The seal identifies ownership and preserves the one sealed.

My wife was, for many years, a certified notary public. She was often asked to notarize deeds and documents. When she did she sealed them with her registered, legal seal. Why? That seal verified the legitimacy of the document or deed as a legally valid thing. It cannot be altered. Anyone holding the deed can point to the seal stamped upon it, without doubt or hesitation, as final evidence that the deed is sure and cannot be cancelled.

That is what Ephesians 1:13 declares. When the Spirit of God stamps his seal upon the heart the believer is assuredly certified that he is chosen, redeemed, called, and saved. Fear and doubt vanish. He can say, 'I am my Beloved's, and my Beloved is mine'. He realises that salvation is his in Christ. He confidently cries, 'Who shall lay any thing to the charge of God's elect? It is God that justifieth. Who is he that condemneth? It is Christ that died, yea rather, that is risen again, who is even at the right hand of God, who also maketh intercession for us. Who shall separate us from the love of Christ?' Nothing 'shall be able to separate us from the love of God, which is in Christ Jesus our Lord' (Romans 8:33-35, 39).

This assurance is the work and gift of God the Holy Spirit. Man cannot obtain it for himself. One man cannot give it to another. It is the result of God given faith in Christ. It is the deep impression which the Spirit alone can imprint. He who lives in the steady realisation that he is a child and heir of God, that he is dead to the world, and that he is raised high above the range of Satan's darts lives in peace. By this blessed seal of the Spirit, we know and are assured that we have 'passed from death unto life'.

Divine pledge

And fifth, God the Holy Spirit dwelling in us is the pledge of resurrection glory. 'The redemption of the purchased possession'. Ours is a salvation assured by a divine pledge. 'Which is the earnest of our inheritance until the redemption of the purchased possession, unto the praise of his glory' (v. 14).

The seal of the Spirit is that which gives us the assurance of salvation. The Spirit of God is the earnest of our inheritance, assuring us of it until the resurrection, here called the redemption of the purchased possession.

The seal of God the Holy Spirit in us sheds abroad in our hearts the love of God, assuring us that we are God's and that heavenly glory is ours in Christ. 'The Spirit itself beareth witness with our spirit, that we are the children of God: And if children, then heirs; heirs of God, and joint-heirs with Christ; if so be that we suffer with *him,* that we may be also glorified together' (Romans 8:16, 17).

With this great salvation, we have this great promise, 'Ye shall not be ashamed nor confounded world without end'.

Chapter 16

'The Redemption Of The Purchased Possession'

In whom ye also *trusted,* after that ye heard the word of truth, the gospel of your salvation: in whom also after that ye believed, ye were sealed with that holy Spirit of promise, Which is the earnest of our inheritance until the redemption of the purchased possession, unto the praise of his glory.

(Ephesians 1:13, 14)

God the Holy Spirit, having created faith in us, is the 'holy Spirit of promise' by which the believer is sealed in Christ, 'Which is the earnest of our inheritance until the redemption of the purchased possession, unto the praise of his glory'. All who are born of God are sealed by God the Holy Ghost, sealed unto the resurrection.

The sealing

First, the sealing of the Spirit spoken of in verse 13 is the blessed witness of the Spirit with our spirits that we are the children of God, by which he sheds abroad the love of God in our hearts, assuring us that salvation is ours in Christ. Giving us faith in Christ and 'good hope through grace', he tells us all grace is ours and glory too. In a word, by giving us his Spirit, as 'the Spirit of adoption, whereby we cry, Abba Father', our God puts his seal upon his own work and stamps it as genuine.

'He that hath received his testimony hath set to his seal that God is true' (John 3:33). Receiving the testimony God has given of Christ by faith, the believing sinner has proof in his own heart that Jesus Christ is the Son of God and that he is himself born of God. It is written, 'This is the record, that God hath given to us eternal life, and this life is in his Son. He that hath the Son hath life; and he that hath not the Son of God hath not life' (1 John 5:11, 12).

Spirit of promise

Second, all this work of grace in us is performed by the 'holy Spirit of promise', by God the Holy Spirit who was promised, who comes in fulfilment of the promise.

It is the Spirit of God who verifies and confirms in every believer the promise made by God, who cannot lie, to give eternal life to his elect before the world began (Titus 1:2). Paul is here referring to the many promises of the Spirit spoken by our Lord and written in the Scriptures (Jeremiah 50:4; Ezekiel 36:27; 37:14; 39:29; Joel 2:28; Galatians 3:13, 14). While he was yet on the earth the Lord Jesus assured his disciples that when he had gone to the Father, he would send them the Comforter, even the Spirit of truth, to abide with us forever (Luke 11:13; 24:49; John 14:16, 17, 26; 15:26; 16:7-15). After his resurrection he commanded the apostles to abide in Jerusalem until they had received 'the promise of the Father', referring to the gift of the Holy Spirit (Luke 24:49; Acts 1:4; 2:16-22, 33).

Paul seems to refer to the promise God made to Abraham when he said, 'In thee shall all nations be blessed' (Genesis 12:3; 28:14; Galatians 3:8). Abraham's Seed, by whom the blessing of the covenant comes to God's Israel is Christ (Galatians 3:17). The blessing of the covenant to which that promise refers is the 'holy Spirit of promise'. One of our Saviour's objects in redeeming us from the curse of the law was that we should receive the promise of the Spirit. The indwelling of God the Holy Spirit as the source of truth, holiness, consolation and eternal life is the great gift Christ secured for us by his death on the cross. 'Christ hath redeemed us from the curse of the law, being made a curse for us ... That the blessing of Abraham might come on the Gentiles through Jesus Christ; that we might receive the promise of the Spirit through faith' (Galatians 3:13, 14).

Let us ever give thanks for the 'holy Spirit of promise' and his mighty operations of grace in us. Without him we would still be dead in trespasses and sins; lost and blind, ignorant of the blood of atonement shed for us by our Lord Jesus Christ, without a ray of comfort, incapable of faith, hope or even of prayer, and incapable of worshipping and praising our God for his great salvation. Until God the Holy Spirit gives us life and faith in Christ, sealing us by his grace, we cannot know the love of God and cannot know our interest in Christ and his great salvation. But now, by the Spirit of God dwelling in us, we are not only convinced of our sin, we are convinced of Christ's righteousness and of our freedom from judgment and condemnation by the redemption he accomplished for us at Calvary. Now, since the Spirit of God has sealed us, giving us faith in Christ, we draw near to the thrice holy God by the blood of Christ in 'full assurance' of acceptance.

The earnest

Third, it is the 'holy Spirit of promise, which is the earnest of our inheritance'. He is the pledge or the earnest of our incorruptible, never fading inheritance in heaven. This bequest is our Father's gift. It belongs to the children of God. It comes to us by the death of Christ the Testator and is ours forever by him, with him, and in him.

The 'holy Spirit of promise' is called 'the earnest of our inheritance' or the pledge of it, because, being a part of it, he assures us we shall possess the whole. He certifies it is the right of all who trust Christ to possess the heavenly inheritance, and makes us 'meet to be partakers of the inheritance of the saints in light', by giving us a new, righteous nature, forming Christ in us, making us partakers of the divine nature (2 Corinthians 5:1; Colossians 1:2; 2 Peter 1:4; 1 John 3:9).

An 'earnest' is a part of the whole. If you purchase a house or a piece of property you are required to make a down-payment, earnest money, which is part of the price of the property. It is your binding pledge to pay the full price at a specified time. In this sense the blessed Spirit of promise has been given to us in saving grace as 'the earnest of our inheritance'. His gifts and grace, his teaching, influence and operations; his quickening, reviving, renewing, anointing, indwelling and sealing are pledges of the truth and reality of the inheritance of God's covenant children.

But the earnest is not only a pledge of the whole, it is part of the whole. The 'holy Spirit of promise', which we have received, is part of the inheritance awaiting us in glory. In the Levitical law the first fruits were not only a pledge of the whole harvest, but part of it. The down-payment or deposit on a piece of property is not only a pledge to pay the whole price of the property, it is part of the price. The 'holy Spirit of promise', 'the earnest of our inheritance', is part of the inheritance.

Let there be no confusion about the indwelling of the Holy Spirit as the earnest of our inheritance. The Spirit of God dwelling in us is the Spirit of Christ (John 14:16-18; Romans 8:9, 10). The earnest of the inheritance is Christ and the full inheritance is Christ. Here we have Christ in grace, 'Christ in you, the hope of glory'. Soon we shall have the full inheritance, Christ in glory. Christ is revealed in us here. There we shall see him face to face. Christ is with us here and the same blessed Christ, in all the fulness of his presence and love, will be ours in heaven.

Prepared for heaven

J. C. Philpot wrote, 'Heaven is a prepared place for a prepared people. Holy are its inhabitants, holy its employments, holy its enjoyments'. The Holy Spirit, therefore, in his sealing, sanctifying operations and in the communication of a holy, spiritual, and divine nature (2 Peter 1:4) is the earnest of this holy and heavenly inheritance, making us, as the Apostle says (Colossians 1:12) 'meet to be partakers of the inheritance of the saints in light'.

Fourth, and this is very important. The righteousness of Christ imputed to us in justification makes us worthy of the inheritance, while the righteousness of Christ imparted to us in regeneration makes us fit for the inheritance. Until Christ is formed in us and we are made partakers of the divine nature by regenerating grace, we are not made 'meet to be partakers of the inheritance of the saints in light'.

Until we know something of the teaching, work, and witness of the Holy Spirit here, and are made partakers of a new, holy, spiritual and heavenly nature, we have no pledge of our interest in the inheritance of the saints. A carnal, unsanctified, unholy, unrenewed heart is utterly incapable of knowing, entering into, longing after and loving an inheritance incorruptible, undefiled, 'that fadeth not away'.

In summary, while the solitary basis of our hope before God is the finished work of Christ, it is Christ in us who is our hope. The basis of our hope is the work of God for us, altogether outside our experience. But hope itself is the work of God in us, grace experienced in our souls, 'Christ in you, the hope of glory'. This is the fulfilling of the Word of God in us. 'Whereof I am made a minister, according to the dispensation of God which is given to me for you, to fulfil the Word of God; *Even* the mystery which hath been hid from ages and from generations, but now is made manifest to his saints: To whom God would make known what *is* the riches of the glory of this mystery among the Gentiles; which is Christ in you, the hope of glory' (Colossians 1:25-27).

Every holy desire, heavenly affection, gracious longing, spiritual enjoyment, and believing hope, is a pledge of an interest in the glorious inheritance of the saints in light. Love, joy and peace; a calm tranquillity and blessed acquiescence in the will of God, and every ravishing view of Christ, 'with open face beholding as in a glass the glory of the Lord, are changed into the same image from glory to glory, even as by the Spirit of the Lord' (2 Corinthians 3:18). These are those things by which God's chosen vessels of mercy are 'afore prepared unto glory' (Romans 9:23), pledges of our inheritance above and heaven begun on earth.

Every delight we have in Christ, every bowing of our hearts to him, every setting of our affection upon our all-glorious Redeemer, as 'the chiefest among ten thousand' and 'altogether lovely', everything that turns us to our Saviour, 'looking for the mercy of our Lord Jesus Christ unto eternal life', is a pledge of the inheritance by which we are prepared for that which awaits us in eternity.

The 'holy Spirit of promise, which is the earnest of our inheritance', makes heaven real to our souls. 'Christ in you, the hope of glory', is both the firstfruits of glory, assuring us of the full inheritance and the foretaste of glory. That means that heaven will not be a strange, new experience for us but the fulfilment of that which God has begun in us by his grace. The psalmist sang, 'The Lord will give grace and glory' (Psalm 84:11). Grace is glory begun and glory is grace finished. He who began the work will finish it (Philippians 1:6; 1 Thessalonians 5:23, 24). Heavenly glory will immeasurably and infinitely enlarge, expand, and amplify the gifts of grace that we enjoy here by the 'the Holy Spirit of promise, which is the earnest of our inheritance' but it will reveal and bestow nothing new. We will see our Saviour face to face and know him even as we are known, yet even now we enjoy 'seeing him who is invisible' and 'know the love of Christ, that passeth knowledge'.

There we will be pure, even as God is pure, and holy as he is holy; but even now we are 'partakers of the divine nature', which 'cannot sin', because it is 'born of God'. There our peace shall never be disturbed by doubt or fear and Satan shall assault no more; but even now the peace of God, which 'passeth all understanding' keeps our hearts and minds through Christ Jesus. There our joy shall be a vast ocean; but even now we 'rejoice with joy unspeakable and full of glory'. There we shall enter into 'an exceeding and eternal weight of glory', even the very glory which the Father gave to Christ before the foundation of the world; but even now, with the Holy Spirit of promise dwelling in us, we 'are come unto mount Sion, and unto the city of the living God, the heavenly Jerusalem, and to an innumerable company of angels, To the general assembly and church of the firstborn, which are written in heaven, and to God the Judge of all, and to the spirits of just men made perfect, And to Jesus the mediator of the new covenant, and to the blood of sprinkling, that speaketh better things than that of Abel' (Hebrews 12:22-24).

Resurrection redemption

Fifth, the Apostle Paul tells us that the inheritance to which we have been predestined is ours already. We have already obtained it by grace. The 'holy Spirit of promise' is the earnest, the firstfruits, the pledge, and the assurance that we shall one day possess it fully. He keeps us sealed in grace 'until the redemption of the purchased possession'. What do those words mean? Redemption is the complete deliverance of our souls and bodies from the fall of our father Adam and from all the consequences of sin, 'into the glorious liberty of the children of God' (Romans 8:21). It is deliverance from the curse of the law by the blood of Christ, deliverance from the death of sin in regeneration, and deliverance from all the consequences of sin in the resurrection, here called 'the redemption of the purchased possession'. The gift of faith in regeneration brings with it the seal of the Spirit, the assurance of our redemption by the blood of Christ, the assurance of salvation accomplished by our Substitute. And the Spirit of God dwelling in us, giving us eternal life in Christ, assures us we shall at last possess the resurrection that is ours in Christ.

There is a day appointed by our God when Christ will deliver his elect, his purchased possession, into the full glory of their inheritance. All whom he bought and purchased with the price of his precious, sin-atoning blood shall in the resurrection be delivered from corruption into incorruption, from mortality into immortality, from sorrow and sighing into joy unspeakable and full of glory, from trial and trouble into triumph, from sin, death and the grave into life and holiness.

Yes, resurrection glory will be ours because God the Father chose us in eternal love, God the Son redeemed us with his blood and God the Holy Ghost has sealed us and is the earnest of the glory awaiting us in eternity. We know that 'we are not of them who draw back unto perdition; but of them that believe to the saving of the soul' (Hebrews 10:39). Resurrection glory will be the end of redemption, 'the redemption of the purchased possession'. In the resurrection morning, when the dead in Christ shall be raised incorruptible then the redemption of the body will be complete. Then we will enter into our inheritance fully. Then we shall fully possess Christ as our inheritance and Christ will fully possess us as his inheritance. Unto that day the Holy Spirit seals us (Ephesians 4:30), assuring us of our interest in the inheritance as the earnest of it and securing to us the certain possession of it.

To his glory

Sixth, then mortality will be swallowed up in life 'unto the praise of his glory'. All shall be accomplished to the praise of the glory of God the Father, 'who first trusted in Christ', by whom we are chosen and predestinated; and to the praise of the glory of God the Son, by whom we are redeemed, in whom we have obtained the inheritance, and in whom we trust; and to the praise of the glory of God the Holy Ghost, by whom we are sealed, who is the earnest of our inheritance until that day.

'Then *cometh* the end, when he shall have delivered up the kingdom to God, even the Father; when he shall have put down all rule and all authority and power. For he must reign, till he hath put all enemies under his feet. The last enemy *that* shall be destroyed *is* death. For he hath put all things under his feet. But when he saith all things are put under *him, it is* manifest that he is excepted, which did put all things under him. And when all things shall be subdued unto him, then shall the Son also himself be subject unto him that put all things under him, that God may be all in all' (1 Corinthians 15:24-28).

Chapter 17

'Sealed'

In whom ye also *trusted,* after that ye heard the word of truth, the gospel of your salvation: in whom also after that ye believed, ye were sealed with that holy Spirit of promise, Which is the earnest of our inheritance until the redemption of the purchased possession, unto the praise of his glory.

(Ephesians 1:13, 14)

God the Holy Spirit, having created faith in us, is the 'holy Spirit of promise' by which the believer is sealed in Christ, 'Which is the earnest of our inheritance until the redemption of the purchased possession, unto the praise of his glory'.

I have gone through the Book of God several times marking those things we are told God has sealed. Every time, I have been both instructed and blessed in my soul. May God the Holy Spirit be pleased to open the Scriptures by his grace and reveal to us these things that are sealed in the fresh experience of his grace!

A sealed Saviour

First, the Lord Jesus declares that he, as the Son of Man who gives everlasting life to all who trust him, is a sealed Saviour. 'Labour not for the meat which perisheth, but for that meat which endureth unto everlasting life, which the Son of man shall give unto you: for him hath God the Father sealed' (John 6:27).

'For him hath God the Father sealed.' What does that mean? The word that is translated 'sealed' throughout the New Testament means 'stamped for security, preserved, or kept secret'. The sentence might be translated, 'Him hath the Father sealed, God'. If that is the case, John is telling us the same thing Peter announced on the Day of Pentecost. 'Ye men of Israel, hear these words; Jesus of Nazareth, a man approved of God among you by miracles and wonders and signs, which God did by him in the midst of you, as ye yourselves also know: Him, being delivered by the determinate counsel and foreknowledge of God, ye have taken, and by wicked hands have crucified and slain' (Acts 2:22, 23). God the Father has demonstrated beyond question that this Man is God.

This is one of those many, precious places in Holy Scripture in which we see in very few words a huge volume of sacred theology. Here, in just seven words, our Lord Jesus declares that all three persons of the Triune Godhead concur and co-operate in the great work of redemption by Christ Jesus. Robert Hawker says, 'There is a peculiar blessedness in these sweet portions, which at one view, represent the Holy Three in One, unitedly engaged in the sinner's redemption'.

Who could be the 'him' here spoken of, if not the Lord Jesus? Who other than God the Father could seal him? With whom was Christ sealed and anointed, except God the Holy Spirit? Who but God could give such a full, instructive and blessed testimony to the glorious foundation-truth of the whole Bible in just seven words? 'For him hath God the Father sealed'.

Let us ever behold, as the warrant of our faith, the divine authority of the Lord Jesus Christ, the Son of Man, our Mediator. He and he alone is infinitely suited for our poor soul's need, in every state and every circumstance. The validity of all his gracious acts as our Substitute is founded in this, 'For him hath God the Father sealed', marked and stamped from eternity by his choice, appointment and decree, as the Lamb slain, marked and stamped in time by his Spirit. It was the Spirit of Jehovah that was upon him when he was anointed 'to preach the gospel to the poor, ... to heal the broken hearted, to preach deliverance to the captives, and the recovering of sight to the blind, to set at liberty them that are bruised, to preach the acceptable year of the Lord'. This great Saviour, whom God the Father has sealed, is thus held forth and recommended by the great seal of heaven to every poor sinner who needs his salvation. Every act of his love, word of his lips, deed of his hands, work of his grace proclaims the Lord Jesus as him whom 'God the Father hath sealed'. Help us, O Lord God, by your blessed Spirit, to receive Christ the Saviour as the One sealed by God and to rest in nothing short of being sealed by your Spirit.

A sealed book

Second, in Revelation 5:1-7 we are told about a sealed book. This book is the book of God's eternal decrees. It represents God's purpose of grace in predestination, which includes all things. It is to this book that our great Surety referred when he said, 'Lo, I come: in the volume of the book it is written of me, I delight to do thy will, O my God' (Psalm 40:7, 8; Hebrews 10:5-10). William Hendriksen said of this book, 'It symbolizes God's purpose with respect to the entire universe throughout history, and concerning all creatures in all ages and unto all eternity'.

The Lord our God is a God of purpose; eternal, unalterable purpose (Isaiah 46:9-11). The object of God's purpose of grace in predestination is the effectual accomplishment of the everlasting salvation of his elect (Romans 8:28-30). All that comes to pass in time was purposed by God in eternity (Romans 11:36). In election, God chose a people whom he would save. In predestination, he sovereignly ordained all things that come to pass to secure the salvation of his chosen. In providence, he accomplishes in time what he purposed from eternity.

As John saw it, the book of God was closed, a mystery sealed with seven seals. These seven seals do not represent a fanciful 'seven dispensations' of time. The book with writing within and on the back and sealed with seven seals simply means that God's purpose is full, complete, perfect and unalterable. Nothing can be added to it, nothing taken from it. The seven seals also tell us that God's purpose of grace is unknown and unrevealed; a secret known only to God until Christ reveals it.

A sealed people

Third, in Revelation 7 we read of a sealed people. There is a vast multitude of people in this world called 'the elect', a people chosen in eternity and redeemed at Calvary who must be sealed by the Spirit of grace. When God saves a sinner, that sinner is sealed by the Holy Spirit, marked as God's own, secretly preserved and kept by God the Holy Spirit. This sealing of the Spirit is symbolised in the Old Testament rite of circumcision. The sealing of the Spirit is what the Bible calls the circumcision of the heart made without hands (Romans 2:29; Colossians 2:11, 12).

'And grieve not the holy Spirit of God, whereby ye are sealed unto the day of redemption' (Ephesians 4:30). We would be wise to make this verse the motto of our daily walk. Is God the Holy Spirit grieved when a child of God forgets the Lord Jesus and by indulgence in any sin loses sight of those sufferings which he endured because of sin? Yes, he is grieved, communion with God the Father is interrupted, and the agonies and bloody sweat of our dear Saviour forgotten when any ransomed soul lives a loose and careless life. Shall I grieve the Holy Spirit, my Divine Keeper, by the allowance of wickedness? God forbid! Would you grieve for me, O Lord, at such a sight? Can it be possible that a poor worm of the earth, such as I am, should excite such regard and attention? Such considerations should be enough to keep us from evil. Yet we run eagerly after the poisonous ooze of our own depraved hearts, except the Lord Jesus himself keep us from the evil by his blessed Holy Spirit!

Blessed Lord God, withdraw not your restraining influences; leave us not for a moment to ourselves! If you keep us, we shall be well kept. Blessed Son of God, 'Cast me not away from thy presence; and take not thy Holy Spirit from me'. Let me not grieve him by whom I am sealed unto the day of redemption.

God's Church in this world is a sealed fountain. 'A garden inclosed *is* my sister, *my* spouse; a spring shut up, a fountain sealed' (Song of Solomon 4:12). The Church of Christ is a garden flourishing with good works, works done for him, works which he has created in us. She is a garden planted by his grace and watered by his Spirit, so thoroughly and effectually watered that she has become herself a fragrant, fruitful fountain of gardens and living waters, with streams flowing out of her into all the world to refresh the earth. Our works, the works of God's Church performed for Christ, are never counted by us as being worthy of anything. We know that if we did all things perfectly we would only have done what we should have done. We constantly repent even of our best, noblest, most righteous works, because 'all our righteousnesses are filthy rags' before the holy Lord God. But he whom we love and serve looks upon our puny works as his pleasant fruits. They are rich, sweet fragrances, the smell of which delights his heart. They are works of faith and love. They are works produced by him and honoured by him. That which is done by faith in Christ, arising from a heart of love for him, is honoured and accepted by him. Let us ever rest in his love, walk in communion with him, and faithfully serve our Redeemer who loved us and gave himself for us.

A sealed vision

Fourth, in Isaiah 29 we learn that there are many in this world to whom the gospel of Christ and the Word of God is a sealed vision. 'Stay yourselves, and wonder; cry ye out, and cry: they are drunken, but not with wine; they stagger, but not with strong drink. For the LORD hath poured out upon you the spirit of deep sleep, and hath closed your eyes: the prophets and your rulers, the seers hath he covered. And the vision of all is become unto you as the words of a book that is sealed, which *men* deliver to one that is learned, saying, Read this, I pray thee: and he saith, I cannot; for it *is* sealed: And the book is delivered to him that is not learned, saying, Read this, I pray thee: and he saith, I am not learned' (Isaiah 29:9-12). The Book of God is a sealed vision (1 Corinthians 2:14) to every sinner left to himself.

A sealed vengeance

In Deuteronomy 32 we see a fifth thing that is sealed. Here, as in Isaiah 29, the word translated 'sealed' is, of course, a Hebrew word; and the meaning is slightly different. The word means 'closed up, ended, stopped'. In this chapter the Lord warns the ungodly who have no understanding and do not trust Christ and do not worship God, that the vengeance and wrath that he shall execute upon them is a sealed vengeance for the time appointed. Sinner, be warned; you will not escape the vengeance of God, except you take refuge in Christ (Deuteronomy 32:34, 35).

A sealed bag

All who are taught of God come to Christ and live by him. All who come to Christ find, in coming to him, that their sins are in a bag cast behind God's back into the depths of the sea of forgetfulness. So the sixth thing described in the Scriptures as a sealed thing is a sealed bag. 'My transgression is sealed up in a bag, and thou sewest up mine iniquity' (Job 14:17). In ancient times when men died at sea, their bodies were placed in a weighted bag, sewn together and sealed. Then they were dropped overboard into the sea. That is what God has done with our sins. They are cast 'into the depths of the sea'. When Christ died he put away all our sins. They were buried in the sea of God's infinite forgiveness, put away, never to be brought up again. God almighty will never charge us with sin, impute sin to us, remember our sins against us or treat us any the less graciously because of our sin. That is forgiveness! 'Blessed is the man to whom the Lord will not impute sin.'

When Job asks in Job 14:16, 'Dost thou not watch over my sin?' The obvious answer is, 'Yes'. If he finds any, we are forever damned; but that cannot be, because he has cast them away in a sealed bag. 'In those days, and in that time, saith the LORD, the iniquity of Israel shall be sought for, and *there shall be* none; and the sins of Judah, and they shall not be found: for I will pardon them whom I reserve' (Jeremiah 50:20).

A seal desired

Seventh, is a seal desired. 'Set me as a seal upon thine heart, as a seal upon thine arm: for love *is* strong as death; jealousy *is* cruel as the grave: the coals thereof *are* coals of fire, *which hath a* most vehement flame' (Song of Solomon 8:6).

This is a prayer which arises from the earnest hearts of God's believing children. Yet it is a prayer any sinner desiring mercy, grace and salvation might make at the throne of grace. 'Set me as a seal upon thine heart, as a seal upon thine arm'. The allusion is to the high priest in Israel. The prayer is twofold: we long to know we have an interest in the love of Christ's heart and we long to experience the power of his arm (Exodus 28:12, 29, 30, 36-38).

Believers know the meaning of this prayer by personal experience. It is the longing, the desire of a sinner seeking grace, to know that his name is engraved upon the Saviour's heart. In the language of the Psalmist, we say to the Lord Jesus, 'Say unto my soul, I am thy salvation'. I desire an interest in your love; but I want more. I want to know I have an interest in your love. Write my name in your heart, engrave it as a signet upon your heart so I may see it and know it. There are many whose names are written on our Lord's heart who do not yet know it. Christ has loved them from eternity. His heart has been set upon them from everlasting. But they have not yet seen the signet with their names written upon it. In all of his work our great High Priest bears the names that are upon his heart.

For them he makes intercession (John 17:9, 20; 1 John 2:1, 2). He bore their sins in his body upon the cursed tree (1 Peter 2:24; 3:18). He endured all the wrath and fury of divine judgment to the full satisfaction of justice for them (Isaiah 53:9-11). He made atonement for them, putting away their sins by the sacrifice of himself (Hebrews 9:26). He obtained eternal redemption for them by the merit of his blood (Hebrews 9:12). He pronounces the blessing of God upon them (Numbers 6:24-27; Ephesians 1:3-6).

We want to know by personal experience the power of our Saviour's arm. We want always to see and know that our Redeemer's heart and hand are eternally engaged for us, engaged to accomplish our everlasting salvation. This is our soul's desire. We want to know and be assured that the Lord Jesus Christ is our High Priest, our Advocate, our sin-atoning Mediator before God. If we can know that we have a place in his heart of love and that his arm is set to do us good, we want no more. All is well with our souls. His arm preserves us, protects us, provides for us. This is the prayer we make. What more could we desire than this? 'Set me as a seal upon thine heart, as a seal upon thine arm.'

Four pleas

Anytime we go to God in prayer, it is wise to not only make our request known to him, but also to offer a plea, an argument, a reason why he should grant the thing we ask. Be sure you understand this: the only grounds upon which we can appeal to God for mercy are to be found in God himself (see Psalm 51:1-5). Our hope, our basis of appeal with God must be found in him. Do you see how the spouse here urges her request? She says, 'Make me to know your love for me, because I know this concerning your love. It is as strong as death. It is as firm as the grave. It is as intense as fire. It is as unquenchable as eternity.' With these four pleas, we back up and press our suit for mercy.

Show me your love, for your love is strong as death. 'Love is strong as death.' The love of Christ is as irresistible as death and the love of Christ triumphed over death for us. As death refuses to give up its victims so the love of Christ refuses to give up its captives. Nothing shall ever cause the Son of God to cease loving his people, nothing will induce him to let them go.

Show me your love, for your love is as firm as the grave. 'Jealousy is cruel as the grave.' These words would be more accurately translated, 'Jealousy is as hard as hell'. Our Lord is jealous over his people. He will not allow those whom he loves to be taken from him. You will more likely see the gates of hell opened, the fires of hell quenched and the spirits of the damned set free, than see the Son of God lose one of those who are engraved upon his heart (Romans 8:28-39). Those whom God has chosen he will never refuse. Those Christ has redeemed he will never sell. Those he has justified he will never condemn. Those he has found he will never lose. Those he has loved he will never hate.

Show me your love, for your love is as intense as fire. 'The coals thereof are coals of fire, which hath a most vehement flame.' These words seem to allude to that fire which burned at the altar and never went out. The coals of fire were always kept burning in the typical Levitical dispensation. The flame was originally kindled by God. It was the work of the priests to feed it with sacred fuel. The love of Christ is like the coals of that altar which never went out. And more, the love of Christ for his own elect is vehement, blazing, intense and never diminishes. The only cause of his love for us is in himself. There is nothing to compare with his love. The love of Christ for his elect is free, sovereign, eternal, saving and immutable.

Show me your love, for your love is as unquenchable as eternity. 'Many waters cannot quench love, neither can the floods drown it' (Song of Solomon 8:7; Romans 8:37-39). No other love is really unquenchable but our Saviour's love is. His love is eternal and everlasting, immutable and unalterable. The love of Christ is infinitely beyond that of a father or a mother, a brother or a sister, a husband or a wife. The love of Christ passes knowledge. Nothing in heaven, earth or hell can extinguish or cool the love whose dimensions are boundless (Ephesians 3:14-19).

Our Redeemer's love is compared to fire that cannot be quenched. As such it is affirmed that 'waters', 'many waters' cannot quench it. Christ's love for us is something floods cannot drown (Psalms 69:15; 93:3). The waters of God's wrath could not quench the love of Christ for his people. 'Having loved his own which were in the world, he loved them unto the end.' It was our Saviour's matchless love for us that made him willing to endure all the horror of God's wrath in our stead.

The waters of shame and suffering sought to quench and drown it. They would have hindered its outflow and come between the Saviour and the cross. It leaped over all the barriers in its way. It refused to be extinguished or drowned. Its fire would not be quenched. Its life could not be drowned. The waters of death sought to quench it. Billows of death went over the great Lover of our souls. The grave tried to cool and quench his love but it proved stronger than death. Neither death nor the grave could alter or weaken his love for us. Love defied and defeated death.

Even the flood of our sins could not quench the love of Christ for us. The waters of our unworthiness could not quench nor drown the love of Christ for our souls. Love is usually attracted to that which is loveable. When something ugly, unlovely, unattractive comes, human love withdraws from its object. Not here. Our unfitness did not quench the love of Christ. It refused to be torn away.

The waters of our long rejection sought to quench it. Though the gospel showed us that personal unworthiness could not arrest the love of Christ, yet we continued to reject him and his love. We continued to hate him and despise his love. His love rose above our enmity. It rose above our unbelief and overcame our hardness. In spite of everything we are and have done his love was unquenched.

Though he saved us by his matchless grace, the waters of daily inconsistency still seek to quench his love, but blessed be his name, without success. Even after experiencing his adorable grace we are constantly spurning his love! What inconsistencies, coldness, unbelief, worldliness, hardness and ungodliness daily flow from us against the Saviour's love? Yet it survives all. It remains unquenched, unquenchable and unchanged! All these evils in us are like 'waters', 'many waters', like 'floods', torrents of sin, waves and billows of evil, all constantly labouring to quench and drown the love of Christ! They would annihilate any other love, any love less than his. But our Saviour's love is unchangeable and everlasting.

Chapter 18

Three Whats And A Who

The eyes of your understanding being enlightened; that ye may know what is the hope of his calling, and what the riches of the glory of his inheritance in the saints, And what *is* the exceeding greatness of his power to us-ward who believe, according to the working of his mighty power, Which he wrought in Christ, when he raised him from the dead, and set *him* at his own right hand in the heavenly *places*.

(Ephesians 1:18-20)

In this passage of Holy Scripture, the Apostle Paul told the saints at Ephesus his desire for them. These are the things he prayed that God would do for his saints. This is what Paul means by God giving us the Spirit of wisdom and revelation in the knowledge of Christ.

Opened eyes

'The eyes of your understanding being enlightened.' All depends on the seeing eye. A scene may be fair, light may be bright but if you are blind, all is in vain.

Zedekiah had his eyes put out by the king of Babylon. Then he was taken down to the imperial city but saw nothing of it. There were vast halls and palaces, hanging gardens and a city wall which was the wonder of the world. Babylon is called by the prophet 'the glory of kingdoms, the beauty of the Chaldees' excellency' (Isaiah 13:19). But the blinded monarch beheld nothing of all the grandeur of the Golden City. To him its beauty was no more than the beauty of a dungeon.

That is the way it is with us by nature. Spiritually, we are blind and see nothing. Fallen man has no knowledge or apprehension of spiritual things, no power to discern eternal good. Our foolish heart is darkened. The Lord must first enlighten the eyes of our understanding or else, however precious the truth and however clearly it may be stated, we shall never be able to comprehend it (John 3:5-8).

'The eyes of your understanding' are the eyes of your heart. The things of God are seen by the heart, not by carnal reason. There are a thousand things which God has revealed which we shall never understand and yet, we can know them by faith, by experience and by grace. Our Saviour says, 'Blessed are the pure in heart: for they shall see God'. The purifying of the heart is the enlightening of the spiritual eye. Strange as it may seem, the true eye of the renewed man is seated in the heart, not in the head. Holy affections enable us to see and even to understand divine things. I pray the eyes of our hearts may be enlightened that we may know the things of God. May God grant us that unction of the Holy Ghost and the mind of Christ to cause us to truly know all things (1 John 2:20-27).

Believers too

Paul's prayer here was offered for believers, for converted people, for those who had faith in Christ Jesus and love to all the saints. Yet he says he never ceased to pray that their eyes might be enlightened. There is good reason for this. He who sees most still needs to have his eyes enlightened to see more. How little we see of the glory of God! How little we see of our all-glorious Christ! May God give you, may God give me, opened eyes to see and know the Lord Jesus Christ!

'Finally, my brethren, rejoice in the Lord. To write the same things to you, to me indeed *is* not grievous, but for you *it is* safe. Beware of dogs, beware of evil workers, beware of the concision. For we are the circumcision, which worship God in the spirit, and rejoice in Christ Jesus, and have no confidence in the flesh. Though I might also have confidence in the flesh. If any other man thinketh that he hath whereof he might trust in the flesh, I more: Circumcised the eighth day, of the stock of Israel, *of* the tribe of Benjamin, an Hebrew of the Hebrews; as touching the law, a Pharisee; Concerning zeal, persecuting the church; touching the righteousness which is in the law, blameless. But what things were gain to me, those I counted loss for Christ. Yea doubtless, and I count all things *but* loss for the excellency of the knowledge of Christ Jesus my Lord: for whom I have suffered the loss of all things, and do count them *but* dung, that I may win Christ, And be found in him, not having mine own righteousness, which is of the law, but that which is through the faith of Christ, the righteousness which is of God by faith: That I may know him, and the power of his resurrection, and the fellowship of his sufferings, being made conformable unto his death; If by any means I might attain unto the resurrection of the dead' (Philippians 3:1-11).

Even those who stand on the top of Pisgah's lofty mount and are favoured to gaze upon the glories of Immanuel's land have not yet begun to perceive the things which God has prepared for them that love him. Yes, God the Spirit has revealed the glory of Immanuel's Land to us in his Word. We know the things revealed but we see little. 'But as it is written, Eye hath not seen, nor ear heard, neither have entered into the heart of man, the things which God hath prepared for them that love him. But God hath revealed *them* unto us by his Spirit: for the Spirit searcheth all things, yea, the deep things of God (1 Corinthians 2:9, 10).

If believers need to have their eyes enlightened, how much more must you who are without Christ. You are altogether blind. You were born blind and Satan takes care yet further to darken your mind. You are engulfed in great darkness, in the gloom of spiritual death. You meet with darkness in the daytime and grope in the noonday as in the night. May Christ Jesus touch you! May the Spirit bring his sacred ointment to make you see. It is not mine to give you eyes, but let me tell you what is to be seen, hoping that God will open your eyes and make you see!

The hope

Here is the first 'what' spoken of in our text. 'What is the hope of his calling?' If you would see the hope of his calling, you must be called of God; effectually, irresistibly called to life and faith in Christ by God the Holy Spirit. There is no seeing without calling. If God has called you to life and faith in Christ by his grace, there are some things you see (John 16:8-11). You see the exceeding sinfulness of sin, the insufficiency of your own righteousness, the beauty, glory, fulness, and suitability of Christ as Saviour, the excellency, truth and blessedness of the gospel.

But what is it that Paul desires for us to see? What does he mean when he speaks of 'the hope of his calling'? What is the hope of his calling? Perhaps he is referring to that which is our hope, Christ Jesus himself. I am sure he has Christ in mind when he speaks of 'the hope of his calling'. Christ crucified is the only basis of hope for poor sinners. Christ is our Hope. 'Christ in you', the new birth (2 Corinthians 5:17), is that which gives us hope. The earnest of the Spirit, making us partakers of the divine nature seals this blessed hope to our hearts.

Certainly, 'the hope of his calling' includes that blessed security of grace that gives us peace in the prospect of trials and temptations in life and in the death, judgment, and eternity we must soon face. The glorious second Advent of our Saviour is called 'the blessed hope'. 'The hope of his calling' is that good hope through grace, bestowed upon us with the gift of faith that enables us to live in the blessed anticipation of the glory awaiting us with Christ in heaven (Revelation 21:1-5; 22:1-7).

Rich inheritance

Here is the second 'what'. 'What the riches of the glory of his inheritance in the saints'. Oh, what riches await us in Christ. A crown of life! A crown of glory!

But this 'what' speaks not of the riches awaiting us. Paul says, I want you to know 'the riches of the glory of his inheritance in the saints'. What can that be? Shall God, the Triune Jehovah find riches for himself in us? Indeed, he will (Ephesians 2:7). 'He shall see of the travail of his soul, and shall be satisfied'.

'And you *hath he quickened,* who were dead in trespasses and sins; Wherein in time past ye walked according to the course of this world, according to the prince of the power of the air, the spirit that now worketh in the children of disobedience: Among whom also we all had our conversation in times past in the lusts of our flesh, fulfilling the desires of the flesh and of the mind; and were by nature the children of wrath, even as others. But God, who is rich in mercy, for his great love wherewith he loved us, Even when we were dead in sins, hath quickened us together with Christ, (by grace ye are saved;) And hath raised *us* up together, and made *us* sit together in heavenly *places* in Christ Jesus: That in the ages to come he might shew the exceeding riches of his grace in *his* kindness toward us through Christ Jesus. For by grace are ye saved through faith; and that not of yourselves: *it is* the gift of God: Not of works, lest any man should boast. For we are his workmanship, created in Christ Jesus unto good works, which God hath before ordained that we should walk in them (Ephesians 2:1-10).

His power

Now we have the third 'what'. 'What is the exceeding greatness of his power to usward who believe, according to the working of his mighty power, which he wrought in Christ when he raised him from the dead.' The power by which we believe, the power wrought in us and working in us, is the life-giving, life-sustaining, resurrection power of God (Psalms 65:4; 110:3; Revelation 20:6).

The 'Who'

Be sure you get this last thing. Do not get so caught up with the 'whats', that you miss the 'Who'. All this power, all this grace, this salvation, this life is 'in Christ'. The Lord Jesus Christ is our covenant Surety, our righteous Representative, our crucified Substitute, our ascended Saviour, our faithful Advocate, our exalted Lord!

Chapter 19

The Power Of Faith

Wherefore I also, after I heard of your faith in the Lord Jesus, and love unto all the saints, Cease not to give thanks for you, making mention of you in my prayers; That the God of our Lord Jesus Christ, the Father of glory, may give unto you the spirit of wisdom and revelation in the knowledge of him: The eyes of your understanding being enlightened; that ye may know what is the hope of his calling, and what the riches of the glory of his inheritance in the saints, And what *is* the exceeding greatness of his power to us-ward who believe, according to the working of his mighty power, Which he wrought in Christ, when he raised him from the dead, and set *him* at his own right hand in the heavenly *places*, Far above all principality, and power, and might, and dominion, and every name that is named, not only in this world, but also in that which is to come: And hath put all *things* under his feet, and gave him *to be* the head over all *things* to the church, Which is his body, the fulness of him that filleth all in all.

(Ephesians 1:15-23)

We hear much talk about faith. Everyone is encouraged to exercise faith. Preachers and religious leaders everywhere tell us that everyone has the power in himself to believe on Christ and be saved. We are assured that all men can, somehow or other, muster faith from within and cause themselves to be born-again. We are told that faith and the new birth are the result of man exercising his will. That all sounds very good to the ears of proud worms who like to think they control God, but it is completely contrary to Holy Scripture. What does the Word of God say?

The Bible says, 'All men have not faith'. It tells us, men and women receive Christ and are born-again 'not of blood, nor of the will of the flesh, nor of the will of man, but of God'. 'Not by might, nor by power, but by my Spirit, saith the Lord'. The Scriptures declare, consistently, 'So then, it is not of him that willeth, nor of him that runneth, but of God that showeth mercy'.

In short, the religion of the world, of whatever label, be it Conservative, Liberal, Fundamental, Papist, Protestant, Pentecostal, Baptist, Buddhist, Jewish, Islam, Hinduism, Voodooism is all freewill, works-based religion. The whole world is drunk on the wine of Babylon's fornication! The religion of the world, the religion of Babylon, the religion of antichrist exalts man and sets God in subjection to man's will. The Word of God, in contrast, debases man and exalts the power and grace of God. Modern fundamentalism makes salvation partly a work of man and partly a work of God, thereby robbing God of his glory. The gospel of Christ makes salvation altogether the work of God and gives all the glory for it to him alone.

If men do not have the power and ability to repent and believe the gospel for themselves, where does faith come from? That question naturally arises when we assert the helplessness of dead sinners. It deserves an answer. In the first chapter of this great epistle of Ephesians, the Apostle Paul, writing by divine inspiration, tells us that we believe 'according to the working of his mighty power'.

Omnipotent power

To believe on the Lord Jesus Christ with all our heart is one of the simplest things in the world. To trust Christ, to depend on his power and faithfulness is such a childlike act of trust that one sees no great difficulty in it. Yet to bring the human heart to exercise simple faith in the Saviour is a work of most astounding power. Before any man will come to Christ by faith he must be the subject of divine power. His pride must be brought down. His will must be broken. His passions must be subdued. Otherwise, he will never accept the mercy and grace of God in the person of his Son, Jesus Christ the Lord.

This is a work only God can perform. God the Holy Ghost is the Author and Giver of faith. It is not of ourselves. It is the gift of God. Twice our text uses the strongest possible language to show the almighty power of the Omnipotent God that is exercised in bringing a human soul to believe on the Lord Jesus Christ, and in bringing that believing soul to heaven at last. Notice carefully the first expression, 'The exceeding greatness of his power'. In our English translation these expressions seem almost redundant. But Paul's purpose is to use the most emphatic language so that his meaning could not be missed by any except those who are wilfully ignorant. The first expression, 'The exceeding greatness of his power', is a very amazing one. It might read, 'The super-excellent, sublime, overcoming or triumphing greatness of his power'. The second phrase, 'According to the working of his mighty power', is even more emphatic. It is a Hebrew manner of speech, forced to do the duty of the Greek tongue. It could be read, 'The effectual working of the might of his strength', or 'The energy of the force of his power'.

It seems that Paul was not content to say, 'You believe through the power of God', or 'through the greatness of that power', but 'through the exceeding greatness of his power'. He was not satisfied with declaring that the salvation of man is the result of God's power. He stretches language as far as possible and says, 'Salvation is the result of the efficacious activity of the power of God's might'.

No amount of straining can ever get rid of the grand doctrine which this text contains. The bringing of a soul to simple faith in Jesus Christ and the maintenance of that soul in the life of faith, displays an exercise of omnipotence such as God alone could put forth.

Faith's definition

Faith is an act of the heart giving credit to the testimony of the gospel. It is the desire, expectation and confidence of eternal salvation by the righteousness of Christ and his shed blood. Before any of us can have the knowledge of Christ, our eyes must be enlightened. Before any of us can grow in the grace and knowledge of Christ, we must continually be enlightened by God the Holy Ghost. 'The eyes of your understanding being enlightened'.

Saving faith has three parts. These three things are required if a man truly has faith in Christ. First, there must be a knowledge of Christ as he is revealed in the gospel. Second, there must be an agreement with the gospel message. Third, there must be an active, personal trust or confidence in the person and work of Jesus Christ.

Faith in Christ is a most precious gift of God's grace. It is the first and principle grace of the Holy Spirit. From faith comes all other graces. 'Without faith it is impossible to please God.' Faith is also a progressive grace. There is weak faith and strong faith. People grow in faith. All true faith is saving faith. All who truly believe in Christ alone for everlasting life have everlasting life. 'Whosoever believeth that Jesus is the Christ is born of God.' 'He that believeth on the Son of God hath everlasting life.'

Faith is a permanent grace. Once a person has been given faith in Christ, it cannot be lost. Faith is an active grace. We live by faith. Faith realises and confidently expects the hope of the promise of God. It is 'the substance of things hoped for, the evidence of things not seen'.

Divine power

Our text says that we 'believe according to the working of his mighty power'. Faith can only be produced by the power of God. (John 6:29; Matthew 16:16, 17; Romans 12:3; Ephesians 2:8; Colossians 2:12; Hebrews 12:2).

We should not be surprised to read in the Book of God that faith is God's work and not man's when we remember what the work of salvation really is. The salvation of a soul is a creation. 'Therefore if any man *be* in Christ, *he is* a new creature: old things are passed away; behold, all things are become new. And all things *are* of God, who hath reconciled us to himself by Jesus Christ, and hath given to us the ministry of reconciliation' (2 Corinthians 5:17, 18). Regeneration is not a reformation of principles, it is the creation of life. The new birth is not a decision for Christ, it is the creation of Christ in the soul. God alone can create.

Salvation is more than a creation. Salvation involves destruction. There must be a destruction. The old man must be destroyed. The stony heart has to be taken away. In the physical creation there was nothing to oppose God's work; but in the new creation there is much that fights against God that must be destroyed. Our wills oppose this creation. They must be bowed. Our sins oppose this creation. They must be overcome. Satan's power opposes this creation. It must be bound. As God alone can create, so God alone can destroy.

The work of salvation is a transformation (Romans 12:2). Those who have been given faith in Christ know how great this transformation is. The desire of your heart becomes the garden of the Lord. The stones of the brook become the children of Abraham. The Lord takes a man covered with spots and washes him whiter than snow. Christ takes one whose heart is sinful and cleanses him with his own precious blood, so that he becomes fair and lovely.

Can this be the work of any but God? God alone creates faith where there was once only unbelief. God alone turns the thief into an honest man. God alone turns the adulterous heart into virgin purity. God alone takes one who is drunk with wine and fills him with his Spirit.

Remember also that the conversion of a sinner is constantly compared to the quickening of the dead. The new birth is the resurrection of the dead, the first resurrection. 'And you hath he quickened, who were dead in trespasses and sins; Wherein in time past ye walked according to the course of this world, according to the prince of the power of the air, the spirit that now worketh in the children of disobedience: Among whom also we all had our conversation in times past in the lusts of our flesh, fulfilling the desires of the flesh and of the mind; and were by nature the children of wrath, even as others. But God, who is rich in mercy, for his great love wherewith he loved us, Even when we were dead in sins, hath quickened us together with Christ, (by grace ye are saved;) And hath raised us up together, and made us sit together in heavenly places in Christ Jesus: That in the ages to come he might shew the exceeding riches of his grace in his kindness toward us through Christ Jesus. For by grace are ye saved through faith; and that not of yourselves: it is the gift of God: Not of works, lest any man should boast. For we are his workmanship, created in Christ Jesus unto good works, which God hath before ordained that we should walk in them' (Ephesians 2:1-10).

We were dead sinners. We had been dead a long time. The Spirit of God comes in sovereign power and gives us life.

The analogy

In this text Paul gives us an analogy between faith in Christ and our Saviour's own resurrection from the dead.

The Lord Jesus Christ was really dead and so were we by nature. We lost the image of God. We lost the favour of God. We lost holiness. We became spiritually dead and were insensible of our death. Christ Jesus was among the dead in his tomb and we also were among the dead. 'Children of wrath even as others.'

When Christ was raised from the dead, God sent a heavenly messenger, clothed with power, to take away the stone from his tomb. Whenever God saves a sinner from his sins, he sends a messenger, clothed with the power of the Divine Word, to take away the stone. He takes away the stone of ignorance, of error, of pride, of self-righteousness and of despair.

The stone being removed, Christ our Saviour came forth from among the dead. He was raised to die no more. So it is with the heaven-born soul! We are raised by the power of God from among the dead. We are resurrected, brought to life, never to die again (Revelation 20:6).

Our resurrection from the dead is by Divine, sovereign power. 'As the Father raiseth the dead, and quickeneth whom he will, even so the Son quickeneth whom he will.' What shall we say of those who think that conversion is wrought by the free-will of man, who ascribe man's salvation to his own disposition or willingness of heart? When I see the dead in the cemetery walking by their own power, then I will expect ungodly sinners to turn to Christ by the power of their will! The resurrection of Christ came by irresistible power and so does ours. The resurrection of Christ was glorious and so is ours. The resurrection of Christ is everlasting, and so is ours. But there is more in our text than Christ's resurrection. He also ascended and was made to sit down at the right hand of God. So are we! 'Quickened together with Christ.' We have been raised above this world so that it no longer sees us! We are ascended to the very throne of God with Christ. This is the place of honour. This is the place of pleasure. This is the place of power. Children of God, here is our hope. All who have experienced this spiritual resurrection by Divine power shall also ascend to the very throne of God in the Resurrection Day!

'But I would not have you to be ignorant, brethren, concerning them which are asleep, that ye sorrow not, even as others which have no hope. For if we believe that Jesus died and rose again, even so them also which sleep in Jesus will God bring with him. For this we say unto you by the word of the Lord, that we which are alive *and* remain unto the coming of the Lord shall not prevent them which are asleep. For the Lord himself shall descend from heaven with a shout, with the voice of the archangel, and with the trump of God: and the dead in Christ shall rise first: Then we which are alive *and* remain shall be caught up together with them in the clouds, to meet the Lord in the air: and so shall we ever be with the Lord. Wherefore comfort one another with these words' (1 Thessalonians 4:13-18).

Chapter 20

Christ The King

Which he wrought in Christ, when he raised him from the dead, and set *him* at his own right hand in the heavenly *places*, Far above all principality, and power, and might, and dominion, and every name that is named, not only in this world, but also in that which is to come: And hath put all *things* under his feet, and gave him *to be* the head over all *things* to the church, Which is his body, the fulness of him that filleth all in all.

(Ephesians 1:20-23)

Jesus Christ is King over all the earth! That is the message of the New Testament and the message of our text, Ephesians 1:20-23. Our Redeemer has been exalted to the throne of everlasting dominion. We need to recognise this, rejoice in it and proclaim it. If we worship the Son of God, if we worship the Lord Jesus Christ, we must know him in his kingly office and worship him as the King.

The prophet Isaiah had a prophetic, pre-incarnation vision of the King. He said, 'I saw also the Lord sitting upon a throne, high and lifted up, and his train filled the temple'. He told us that when Christ came, he would enter into his kingdom through humiliation. Another prophet, Zechariah, said, 'Rejoice greatly, O daughter of Zion; shout, O daughter of Jerusalem: behold, thy King cometh unto thee; he is just, and having salvation; lowly, and riding upon an ass, and upon a colt the foal of an ass … He shall speak peace unto the heathen: and his dominion shall be from sea even to sea, and from the river even to the ends of the earth' (Zechariah 9:9, 10). Zechariah's prophecy was fulfilled on the eve of our Lord's crucifixion.

As Jesus rode into Jerusalem to enter his kingdom by the door of his cross, the multitude cried out saying, 'Blessed be the King that cometh in the name of the LORD: peace in heaven, and glory in the highest' (Luke 19:38).

Many of God's saints lose great blessings because they limit their thoughts about Christ to one aspect of his life and grace for them. Some focus their minds on the Saviour's birth in Bethlehem's manger. Others think only of his exemplary life of mercy. We frequently limit our thoughts to the Saviour's death at Calvary. Of course, I would encourage you to think upon these things and speak of them. These are all matters of vital importance. Deny any one of them and you deny the gospel. We can never think or speak too much about Christ. Nevertheless, our Redeemer's death at Golgotha was not the termination of his history. He arose from the grave and was exalted to a heavenly and eternal throne. It is the privilege of faith to follow the Lamb of God into the holiest of all and see him seated upon the throne of grace, as King of kings within the veil.

Within the veil

In the closing portion of Paul's prayer in Ephesians 1, we are reminded that the risen Redeemer has been given all power, authority and dominion. In these verses Paul breaks out into praise and adoration for the exaltation of Christ our King. Christ has been given the sceptre of the universe as the God-man Mediator. As the Head of the Church he has gone within the veil, 'Whither the forerunner is for us entered'.

How that ought to strengthen our faith and encourage our hearts! He is worthy of our fullest trust. There is no room for doubt or uncertainty. The Lord God values the obedience and death of Christ above all else. He accepts it for our perfect redemption and to prove it he has exalted our Redeemer to the throne of eternal glory as the reward of his obedience as our Redeemer. God the Father has given the supreme place of honour in heaven to the very one who bore our sins and died in our place. This he has done for us! God, the Triune Jehovah, raised Christ from the dead and exalted him to his own right hand to be an everlasting King and Priest for his Church.

The place of our King

Paul is here talking about the power of God by which we believe. The power 'which he wrought in Christ, when he raised him from the dead, and set him at his own right hand in the heavenly places'.

The Lord Jesus Christ was raised from the dead and exalted to a kingly throne by the power of God because he suffered and died for his people. The throne of our King is the reward of his humiliation and death.

The Lord Jesus Christ is himself equal with God. Christ our God greatly humbled himself and became a man. Though a man, a real man, he is yet God over all, blessed forever! If we are to be exalted to heaven, we must be humbled upon the earth.

As the God-man, our Mediator, our Lord Jesus Christ, suffered and died in obedience to his Father's will. As the reward for his suffering and death, God the Father raised him from the dead and set him upon the throne of everlasting dominion. Soon everyone in heaven, earth and hell will bow to Christ the King, confessing him as Lord over all.

The Lord Jesus Christ is sitting as a King in heaven. Paul's expression, 'set him as his own right hand', is not to be forced into a literal interpretation. It is a metaphor. The Scriptures plainly show us that Christ is not actually and permanently seated. In Acts 7 we read of 'the Son of man standing on the right hand of God' (Acts 7:56). He is the One 'who walketh in the midst of the seven golden candlesticks' (Revelation 2:1). 'In the midst of the elders, stood a Lamb' (Revelation 5:6). He stands to receive repenting sinners! He stands to intercede for his elect (Zechariah 3). He stands to receive dying saints (Acts 7). He stands to fulfil the purpose of God (Revelation 10)

When the Scripture speaks of Christ sitting in heaven, it must be interpreted as a figure of speech. It indicates at least four things.

Christ's being seated in heaven indicates that he is resting from a finished work (Hebrews 1:3). His sacrificial services and sufferings are ended. The Old Testament priests could never finish their work. Among the furnishings of the tabernacle there was no chair. However, Christ sat down, having finished his work (Hebrews 10:11, 12). Christ's being seated in heaven indicates that he has begun a new work. He has ended the work of his expiation for sin; and he has begun the administration of his kingdom (John 17:1-5). Christ's being seated in heaven indicates the supreme honour and dignity placed upon him (Romans 14:9; Revelation 5:9-14). Christ's being seated in heaven indicates a state of everlasting continuance. His humiliation was temporary and came to its end; his exaltation and dominion are eternal (Isaiah 16:5; Daniel 7:14).

The Lord Jesus Christ is seated at God's right hand. Again, this is to be understood figuratively. God does not have a body. He is Spirit. When he uses the terms relating to a body to describe himself he does so in a figurative sense. The right hand is the place of blessedness (Psalm 16:11). The right hand is the place of honour (Hebrews 1:13). The right hand is the place of power (Matthew 26:64).

The pre-eminence of our King

In verse 21 we see the pre-eminence of our king. 'Far above all principality, and power, and might, and dominion, and every name that is named, not only in this world, but also in that which is to come.'

God the Holy Ghost is here telling us about the God-man, our Saviour. As God, he already possessed the honour described here. But as our Mediator, the humanity of Christ is exalted. He rules as the Son of David above all creatures in dignity, glory and authority. Yonder, he sits as King, as David's Son and David's Lord upon the throne of David.

This is what the Apostle had reference to when he said, 'God was manifest in the flesh, justified in the spirit, seen of angels'. The angels now, for the first time, saw, gazed upon, and rejoiced in the vision of the Godhead in the glorified humanity of the Son. What the angels saw in the ascended, exalted Christ, the nations of the world have proclaimed to them through the preaching of the gospel, namely, the boundless mercy, grace and love of God and the surpassing glory of Christ.

Our exalted King is also our High Priest. 'Now of the things which we have spoken *this is* the sum: We have such an high priest, who is set on the right hand of the throne of the Majesty in the heavens; A minister of the sanctuary, and of the true tabernacle, which the Lord pitched, and not man (Hebrews 8:1, 2).

He is a priest upon the throne. He rules as a king, but he intercedes as a priest. He is our Melchizedek. He has neither father nor mother. He is King of righteousness. He is King of peace.

Christ our King is a universal Monarch. He is King over all angels. He is King over all devils. He is King over the world to come. He is the King over heaven, the King over earth and the King over hell! Before this King, all shall bow!

We may again draw comforting and encouraging inferences from this verse. Is Christ a king? Then we are kings in him. Is Christ a priest? Then we are priests in him. With such a King as Christ, the kingdom is surely safe. Has God given Christ pre-eminence? Then, children of God, give pre-eminence to Christ your King.

The power of our King

Read verse 22 and rejoice in the power of our king. 'And hath put all *things* under his feet, and gave him *to be* the head over all *things* to the church.'

The Lord Jesus Christ has all power and authority throughout all the universe as our King. God has exalted Christ to such dignity and dominion that everything is under his power and brought in subjection to him (Psalm 8:6; Hebrews 2:8, 9).

All creatures are under the rule of Christ our King. The Triune God has made Christ Lord (Acts 2:36). He is Lord of all (Acts 10:36). He is Lord over all (Romans 10:12). He is Lord both of the dead and the living (Romans 14:9). He rules in providence over all things. He governs the lives of all men. History is shaped by the hand of our King.

King Jesus rules for the benefit of his Church. Christ has been given absolute and universal rule so that he may give eternal life to his elect (John 17:2). It is by the power of Christ that the Church carries out her mission (Matthew 28:18, 19). Because Christ rules, his Church is safe. No weapon formed against her shall prosper. Our King orders the affairs of the universe for his Church. There is a mystical union between Christ and his Church. He is the Head, therefore he received honour. He is the Head, therefore he is Governor. He is the Head, therefore he is the Guide.

The pleasure of our King

Verse 23 declares the pleasure of our king. Though Christ is a universal King, his pleasure is in his people. 'Which is his body, the fulness of him that filleth all in all.'

We are his body, one with him, and one with all who are in him. As our Mediator, the Lord Jesus Christ must have all the members of his body, for the fulness of his body and his satisfaction. There cannot be a Redeemer without the redeemed. There cannot be a Shepherd without sheep. There cannot be a Head without a body. There cannot be a Bridegroom without a bride. 'For in him dwelleth all the fulness of the Godhead bodily. And ye are complete in him, which is the head of all principality and power' (Colossians 2:9, 10).

We have all fulness in Christ our King; the fulness of redemption, the fulness of pardon, the fulness of grace, the fulness of righteousness, the fulness of sanctification, the fulness of glory, the fulness of heaven, the fulness of eternity, the fulness of God. Philip Doddridge wrote,

> Hail to the Prince of life and peace,
> Who holds the keys of death and hell!
> The spacious world unseen is His,
> And sovereign power becomes Him well.

In shame and torment, once He died,
But now He lives forever more;
Bow down ye saints around His seat,
And, all ye angel bands, adore.

So live forever, glorious Lord,
To crush Thy foes, and guard Thy friends!
While all Thy chosen tribes rejoice
That Thy dominion never ends.

Worthy Thy hands to hold the keys,
Guided by wisdom and by love;
Worthy to rule o'er mortal life,
O'er worlds below and worlds above.

Forever reign, Victorious King!
Wide through the earth Thy name be known;
And call my longing soul to sing,
Sublimer anthems near Thy throne!

'Now unto the King eternal, immortal, invisible, the only wise God, *be* honour and glory for ever and ever. Amen' (1 Timothy 1:17).

Chapter 21

'It Is The Gift Of God'

And you *hath he quickened*, who were dead in trespasses and sins; Wherein in time past ye walked according to the course of this world, according to the prince of the power of the air, the spirit that now worketh in the children of disobedience: Among whom also we all had our conversation in times past in the lusts of our flesh, fulfilling the desires of the flesh and of the mind; and were by nature the children of wrath, even as others. But God, who is rich in mercy, for his great love wherewith he loved us, Even when we were dead in sins, hath quickened us together with Christ, (by grace ye are saved;) And hath raised *us* up together, and made *us* sit together in heavenly *places* in Christ Jesus: That in the ages to come he might shew the exceeding riches of his grace in *his* kindness toward us through Christ Jesus. For by grace are ye saved through faith; and that not of yourselves: *it is* the gift of God: Not of works, lest any man should boast. For we are his workmanship, created in Christ Jesus unto good works, which God hath before ordained that we should walk in them.

(Ephesians 2:1-10)

The apostle Paul realised that after his death many false teachers would spring up in the Church, who would pervert the gospel of Christ. That was Paul's fear; and that is my fear for you. The Apostle Paul wrote this epistle to the congregation at Ephesus, whom he dearly loved, hoping to establish their hearts in the doctrine of the gospel, lest they should be turned aside by the subtlety of Satan from 'the simplicity that is in Christ'.

The gospel which this great champion of the faith preached was plain and clear. He declared that all men are wicked, helpless, dead sinners and that salvation is altogether the gift of God's grace.

Another gospel

Needless to say, this is altogether a different gospel from that which is preached from the pulpits of the vast majority of churches today. That which is commonly preached in our day is not good news; it is, at best, good advice. The modern preacher pampers human pride. He speaks much about the power of man's will. He boasts of the natural goodness of man. He does not, out and out, deny grace, but the grace he preaches is weak and powerless without the help of man. We are advised of what we should do, but told little of what God has done for us. We are told that God offers men help, but they must first help themselves. The modern gospel gives promises that God will come to men, but first they must come to God. How this robs God of his glory in salvation!

We hear about a universal love but it is a love without any specific object or purpose. We hear about the gift of life but it is a gift without any definite benefactor, a gift that waits for you to unwrap it, open and take it. We hear about an atonement but it is an atonement that does not atone. It is an atonement that must yet be completed by the sinner's will. We hear about a substitute but it was a substitute for no one in particular. We hear about a redemption but it did not actually redeem. Much talk is made of a Saviour but he does not have power in himself to save. Consequently, when the preacher has finished his work, the poor sinner is left to help himself. Is this the gospel of the apostles? Not hardly!

Good news

Paul gives us a gospel that is truly the good news of heaven for poor sinners. He tells us that Jesus Christ, God's immaculate Son, has redeemed an innumerable company of men. By shedding his blood, Christ has washed away the sins of his people. He tells the hell-deserving sinner that God's justice has been satisfied by the death of his Son. Poor, helpless, depraved, bankrupt, dead sinners are told that there is a rich, powerful, holy and living Saviour, who is able to give life everlasting, who is able to save to the uttermost all who come to God by him. The gospel declares to the soul that is slain, being condemned by the law and despairing of life, that God can be just and yet justify the ungodly upon the merits of his Son alone. It tells men and women on the road to hell that God is calling out a people for his own name's sake.

Don't forget
Paul justifiably supposed we might soon become puffed up and forget the pit from which we were digged and the rock from which we were hewn. And, brethren, we are compelled to confess, 'We do, alas, forget too often'.

We very often forget the condition we were in when the Good Samaritan came to us. We are prone to forget what we are by nature. It seems we would always realise that we are what we are by the grace of God. But we do not. Therefore, Paul reminds us in these verses both of what we were, and what God's gracious hand has done for us.

In these verses God the Holy Ghost teaches us the exceeding sinfulness of sin, setting forth the miserable condition of man by nature and the super exceeding greatness of God's grace in salvation.

This is the gift of God. Now let us honour the grace of God in making such a gift to us. These verses are an inspired commentary on another statement from the pen of this same apostle. 'Where sin abounded grace did much more abound.'

Our sin
We are all sinners by nature. There are no exceptions. We see this clearly set before us in verses 1-3.

These three verses plainly and forcibly remind us this is the condition of all men by nature. Let us never forget this awful condition from which God has delivered us. 'I sink in deep mire, where there is no standing: I am come to deep waters, where the floods overflow me' (Psalm 69:2). 'For innumerable evils have compassed me about: mine iniquities have taken hold upon me, so that I am not able to look up; they are more than the hairs of mine head: therefore my heart faileth me' (Psalm 40:12).

This was David's confession. This was our Redeemer's confession. This is my confession! This was our condition when the Lord God found us by his grace, 'And you hath he quickened, who were dead in trespasses and sins' (Ephesians 2:1).

We all died in our father Adam and we were born in a state of spiritual death (Romans 5:12). We were dead, under the sentence of the law. We were dead, without the Spirit of life. We were dead, being separated from God. We were dead, without the image of God. We were dead, without holiness, without righteousness. We were dead, without any awareness of our condition. We were dead, without any ability to help ourselves. We were dead and thus repugnant and offensive to God, who alone is Life, who alone has life, and who alone gives life. We were dead, without hope!

Here is the course in which God's grace found us, 'Wherein in time past ye walked according to the course of this world, according to the prince of the power of the air, the spirit that now worketh in the children of disobedience' (Ephesians 2:2).

By nature, the sinner's will is governed by corrupt and hostile principles so that he goes on continually in a course of sin (John 3:19, 20; 5:40; Romans 8:7). We are bound by our corrupt nature. It takes no great argument to prove that something is radically wrong with mankind. Man is totally depraved. This does not mean that man is outwardly as evil and wicked as he might be. Men may be very virtuous in outward living. However, all men by nature are wicked and are governed by wicked principles. Sin is the nature of man.

The mind is defiled. 'God is not in all his thoughts' (Psalm 10:4). 'The carnal mind is enmity against God' (Romans 8:7). 'The natural man receiveth not the things of the Spirit of God' (1 Corinthians 2:14).

The heart is wicked. 'For out of the heart proceed evil thoughts, murders, adulteries, fornications, thefts, false witness, blasphemies' (Matthew 15:19). 'The heart is deceitful above all things, and desperately wicked' (Jeremiah 17:9).

The conscience is evil. 'Unto the pure all things are pure: but unto them that are defiled and unbelieving is nothing pure; but even their mind and conscience is defiled' (Titus 1:15).

Sinners live according to the course, the design and custom of this world. It is a dark course. It is a crooked course. It is a broad course. It is a hard course. It is a deceitful course. The course of this world promises pleasure and delight, but ends in pain and destruction.

Children of God, remember that you once lived like all other men, in the domain and under the dominion of Satan. 'Ye are of your father the devil, and the lusts of your father ye will do' (John 8:44).

The picture gets worse. Verse 3 describes our conversation, our way of life. When used in the Scriptures the term conversation means 'our company', 'our environment', 'our manner of life'. Here Paul reminds us of our manner of life as unbelievers. 'Among whom also we all had our conversation in times past in the lusts of our flesh, fulfilling the desires of the flesh and of the mind; and were by nature the children of wrath, even as others' (Ephesians 2:3). We were governed by the lusts of the flesh. We fulfilled the will of the flesh. We were children of wrath, abiding under the curse of the law. Wrathful, rebel children! Paul says this is true of all.

God's gift

The second thing Paul teaches us is that salvation is the gift of God (vv. 4-10). Here Paul uses the strongest language imaginable to show us that salvation is entirely the gift of God's grace. Here he shows us five distinct things about this gift and the goodness of God.

1. God's pleasure

'But God, who is rich in mercy, for his great love wherewith he loved us' (v. 4). Hear this and rejoice! It is God's pleasure to save sinners. 'He delighteth in mercy.' 'Fear not little flock; for it is your Father's good pleasure to give you the kingdom' (Luke 12:32).

In great mercy God interferes with the will and way of man (1 Timothy 1:13). God is rich in mercy. The love of God is active and always engaged for us (1 John 3:1). His love is eternal. His love is perfect. His love is particular. His love is sacrificial. His love is saving.

2. God's power

'Even when we were dead in sins, hath quickened us together with Christ, (by grace ye are saved;) And hath raised *us* up together, and made *us* sit together in heavenly *places* in Christ Jesus' (vv. 5, 6). Salvation is always the result of a direct exertion and effectual application of God's almighty power.

There is such a vital union of our souls with the Lord Jesus Christ that when God quickened him and raised him from the dead, we were quickened and raised in him. Salvation is a resurrection from the dead. Almighty God must give new life because sinners have none of their own. Only God's power can raise the dead (John 5:24, 25; Revelation 20:4-6). When this life came, we were dead. This life is the implantation of Christ in the heart. This is all of grace. By this spiritual resurrection, we are made the heirs of heaven.

Our spiritual resurrection is but the pledge of our bodily resurrection yet to come. If we are in Jesus Christ, it is certain that we shall be with Jesus Christ. He will never leave us.

3. God's purpose

'That in the ages to come he might shew the exceeding riches of his grace in *his* kindness toward us through Christ Jesus' (v. 7). It is God's purpose to glorify his grace and kindness in the saints throughout the ages in Jesus Christ.

4. God's praise

'For by grace are ye saved through faith; and that not of yourselves: *it is* the gift of God: Not of works, lest any man should boast' (vv. 8, 9). Once again Paul takes great care to ensure that God receives all praise for the salvation of sinners.

God must be praised because salvation is the work of his eternal grace (2 Timothy 1:9). We receive the blessings of salvation by simple childlike faith. But lest we should think that we can claim credit for our faith, Paul asserts that even faith is the gift of God (Matthew 16:17). There is no room for any man to boast in salvation (Romans 3:20, 27, 28; 4:2; 9:16; 11:6; 1 Corinthians 4:7).

5. God's performance

'For we are his workmanship, created in Christ Jesus unto good works, which God hath before ordained that we should walk in them' (v. 10). Salvation is not merely a gift which God offers to men, leaving it up to their will to receive or reject it. Salvation is a gift God effectually bestows upon and works in dead sinners, performing a miracle of grace.

All believers are the work of God's hands. We are new creatures in Christ Jesus. We are created to walk in righteousness. This is the purpose of election (Ephesians 1:4; 2 Thessalonians 2:13). This is the power of grace.

Children of God, remember the rock from whence you are hewn and the hole of the pit from whence you have been dug! Never forget, 'By the grace of God I am what I am'.

Chapter 22

Life From The Dead

And you *hath he quickened*, who were dead in trespasses and sins.
(Ephesians 2:1)

The Apostle Paul is here speaking of the church at Ephesus and, indeed, of all of those who were chosen in Christ Jesus, accepted in him, and redeemed by his blood. He says of all who are born-again, 'You hath he quickened, who were dead in trespasses and sins'.

Mysterious work

The new birth is a mysterious work of God's grace. Only those who have experienced it can understand it. In the things of God, knowledge can only be gained by personal experience. 'Except a man be born again he cannot see the kingdom of God.' If you would understand regeneration, you must be born-again. If you would understand faith, simple as it is, you must believe. If you would understand forgiveness, you must be forgiven. I repeat, the new birth is a mysterious thing, a work of God's omnipotent mercy for us and in us.

Not all the outward forms on earth,
Nor rites that God has given,
Nor will of man, nor blood, nor birth,
Can raise a soul to heaven.

The sovereign will of God alone
Creates us heirs of grace:
Born in the image of His Son,
A new, peculiar race.

The Spirit, like some heavenly wind,
Blows on the sons of flesh;
Creates anew, by grace divine,
And forms the man afresh.

Our quickened souls awake and rise
From the long sleep of death;
On heavenly things we fix our eyes,
And praise employs our breath.

Isaac Watts

Dead brought to life

God has quickened us who were dead in trespasses and sins, that is, spiritually dead. We were full of vigour towards everything that is contrary to the law and holiness of God. We walked according to the course of this world. But, as to everything spiritual, we were not only somewhat incapable, somewhat weakened, we were actually and absolutely dead. We had no sense with which to comprehend spiritual things. We had neither eye that could see, nor ear that could hear, nor a heart that could understand.

Dead but different

We were dead, all of us. Yet we were not all exactly like one another. Death may be universal over a certain number of bodies. Yet those bodies may look very different from each other. The dead that lie on the battlefield; torn, mutilated and corrupting in the sun, are a hideous sight. But your deceased loved one, lying in his coffin, is somewhat more acceptable to the eye. The corpse still looks like life. Yet your loved one is just as dead as the bodies lying in pieces on the battlefield. Corruption has not yet done its work. Tender care has guarded the body from what must surely come upon it. Yet there is death, sure, complete, total death in the one case as well as the other.

Equally, we have many who are lovely, moral and very admirable to look upon, like the rich young ruler the Saviour looked upon and loved. Yet they are still dead. We have others who are drunken, profane and unchaste. They are dead, too, but not more dead than others. Certainly, their deadness has left its terrible traces more plainly visible, but death is the same. Sin brings forth death and death brings corruption. Whether we were as corrupt as others is not so very important. The point is we were all dead. Though some were trained by godly parents, well instructed in the gospel and brought up under the sound of faithful and fervent gospel preaching, you were still dead, just as dead as the most profane blasphemer, just as dead as the harlot in the street, just as dead as the murderer on death row. We were all dead.

Resurrected

Ephesians 2:1 tells us that, though we were dead, Christ has come by his Spirit, and raised us out of the grave. This text brings us Easter tidings. It sings of resurrection. It sounds in our ears as the trumpet of new life. It introduces us into a new world of joy and gladness. We were dead, but we are made alive by Christ Jesus the Lord.

Understand this, the doctrine of Holy Scripture is that man by nature, since the fall, is dead. He is a corrupt, ruined thing. In a spiritual sense, utterly and entirely dead. If any shall come to spiritual life, it must be the quickening of God the Holy Ghost that brings 'life from the dead', given to us sovereignly through the good will and pleasure of God, not for any merits of our own, but entirely of his own abounding and infinite grace. In summary, every person born into this world is spiritually dead; and spiritual life can come only by the power and grace of God the Holy Spirit.

Our text tells us three things. May God seal them to our hearts forever, and cause us that have experienced 'life from the dead' to walk in the newness of life with joy and thanksgiving.

1. Were dead

First, you were dead! What a solemn sight is presented to us by a dead body! The thought is overwhelming! Soon this body must be a house of worms! These sockets that house my eyes, now so full of life, will soon become empty holes. This body, now full of life, will soon be still, stretched out in a coffin, laid in a grave and eaten of the most loathsome creatures!

Perhaps you can hardly realise the thought. Perhaps it is too hideous for you. But try, as well as you can, to get the idea of a dead corpse. When you have done this, please understand the meaning of our text, 'You were dead'. Just as the body that has been laid in the grave, you were dead. We all died in our father Adam. 'Wherefore, as by one man sin entered into the world, and death by sin; and so death passed upon all men, for that all have sinned' (Romans 5:12). 'For since by man *came* death, by man *came* also the resurrection of the dead. For as in Adam all die, even so in Christ shall all be made alive' (1 Corinthians 15:21, 22).

God created Adam in the perfection of mature manhood. Adam was the father and representative head of all the human race. God made a covenant with Adam which could have secured life for us all. Yet under the threat of divine judgment, Adam broke God's covenant, plunging himself and all the race into spiritual death. We are all dead under the sentence of the law (Romans 5:18-21).

Through the fall of our father Adam we became guilty of sin. Now death reigns over all men. We are born with a corrupt nature inclined toward every manner of evil. We sin daily, being bound by a sinful nature.

Because of sin, we are all born under the curse and condemnation of God's holy law. We were condemned to spiritual death. We are sentenced to physical death. We are subject to eternal death.

Three examples

Though we are all dead by nature, the manifestations of death are not the same in us all. During his earthly ministry, our Lord raised three people from the dead. I do not find that during his lifetime he raised more than three. Each of these resurrections were performed for the purpose of our instruction. Each of them teaches us some singular truth about spiritual resurrection. These resurrections were first the young maiden, Jairus' daughter (Luke 8), second was the widow's son (Luke 7), who was in his coffin at the city gate, and perhaps the most significant of all was Lazarus (John 11). Let me show you a singular thing about each.

Jairus' daughter

Jairus' daughter had just died. She was in her bed. She was dressed like the living. She still had some signs of life in her. Her cheeks were still red. She was not yet cold with death. Her body was not yet in the coffin. It is thus with many, especially our children. But remember, she was dead.

Many are around us who seem outwardly to be as much alive as anyone. They are very moral. They are accepted in society. Their consciences are not yet seared and cold with sin. They have not yet begun to decay. Yet, they are dead!

The widow's son

Next, is the case of the widow's son. His case is far different. He was in his coffin. No one now came very near him. His cheeks were hollow. His eyes were glazed. His body was cold; and, like the young maid, he was dead. Death was much more manifest in this young man. It is thus with many, many I fear of our own households. The corruption of sin has begun its work. Already their hearts are cold. They are no longer welcome company. You can see in their eyes the gaze of death. They are dead!

Lazarus

Then, there is the case of Lazarus. His was the worst case. He was already corrupt. He was sealed off from all society. Death had thoroughly done its work. Thus, too, it is with many around us! Death of sin has thoroughly corrupted them. They are altogether the outcasts of society. All have lost hope for them. But I want you to know that even Lazarus was raised by Christ. Though outwardly more corrupt, he was no more dead than the young maiden.

We are all dead; but what does it mean to be dead? When a man is dead, he has lost all sense. He cannot hear. He cannot feel. He cannot smell. He cannot touch. When a man is dead, he has lost all desire. When a man is dead, he has lost all power. When a man is dead, he has lost all fellowship with the living. When a man is dead, he begins to decay.

2. Made Alive

Such was our case. We were dead. But if we have been born again, we have been made alive! The new birth is nothing less than 'life from the dead'. It is a spiritual resurrection (John 5:21, 24, 25). There is a blessed and mystical union between Christ and his people. We were raised with Christ by representation. We were raised with him in regeneration. We shall be raised with him in the resurrection.

This spiritual resurrection is accomplished only by the power of Christ. Man has nothing whatever to do with his spiritual resurrection. It is the voice of Christ that gives dead sinners life. It was the voice of Christ that gave life to Jarius' daughter, the widow's son and Lazarus. His voice is sovereign. His voice is particular. His voice is powerful. He condescends to use unworthy preachers to proclaim his Word but only he can make it the voice of life. Happy I am that his voice can give life to the corrupting Lazarus as easily as it can to the fair maiden.

How do we know when this life comes? For this I can only speak what I have experienced. The first consciousness of new life brings pain (Romans 7:9-13).

Next, when a man is brought from death to life, he sees all things new. For the first time sin appears as sin. Christ appears glorious. Holiness appears wonderful. God appears gracious. The gospel appears majestic. When a man is born-again, he has many questions, he makes many blunders. He is introduced into a new world. He has new desires. He has new joys. He is likely to make many mistakes.

3. Now alive

Our text tells us you are alive. We were dead, but now we are alive! If we are alive, then let us live! Do not dwell among the dead. Live above this graveyard. Speak to God as a living child to a living Father. Do not be held by the grave clothes of the law. Feed upon the Bread of Life. Drink from the life-giving Fountain.

We are alive and we are one with Christ! We are alive, then let us love him who gave us life! We are alive, then let us rejoice! We are alive, then let us anticipate the future! Heaven awaits! Over us death has no power (Revelation 20:6).

We are alive. Let us now learn! Learn of Christ. Learn of his love, his kindness. Learn of his promises. Learn of his glory. Live for the glory of Christ, who alone gives and sustains life. Walk in love, seek him, trust him, and make him known.

More about Jesus I would know,
More of His grace, to others show,
More of His saving fulness see,
More of His love who died for me.

More about Jesus let me learn,
More of His holy will discern;
Spirit of God, my teacher be,
Showing the things of Christ to me.

More about Jesus in his Word,
Holding communion with my Lord,
Hearing His voice in every line,
Making each faithful saying mine.

More about Jesus on his throne,
Riches in glory all his own,
More of His kingdom's sure increase,
More of His coming – Prince of Peace.

Chapter 23

'His Grace'

But God, who is rich in mercy, for his great love wherewith he loved us, Even when we were dead in sins, hath quickened us together with Christ, (by grace ye are saved;) And hath raised *us* up together, and made *us* sit together in heavenly *places* in Christ Jesus: That in the ages to come he might shew the exceeding riches of his grace in *his* kindness toward us through Christ Jesus. For by grace are ye saved through faith; and that not of yourselves: *it is* the gift of God: Not of works, lest any man should boast.

(Ephesians 2:4-9)

Almost all professing Christians profess to believe that salvation is by grace. The Bible states the fact of salvation by grace alone so frequently and so clearly that you can hardly find any who claim to be Christians who openly deny it. The trouble is that the vast majority of men and women, and the vast majority of preachers, talk about grace in such a way that they frustrate the grace of God. The grace they talk about is not grace at all, but works and free-willism, presented in the name of grace!

It is therefore needful that we be constantly and clearly instructed in the doctrine of the grace of God. Ephesians 2:4-9 tells us about 'his grace', that grace that comes from God who sits upon, and sovereignly rules this universe from his lofty 'throne of grace'. This text tells us how God saves sinners by 'his grace'.

Important message

Three times the inspired Apostle tells us in this short passage that God has saved us by his grace. This message is important for four reasons. First, salvation by grace destroys all room for human boasting (1 Corinthians 4:7).

If your idea of salvation allows you to boast that the difference between you and other people is something you are, something you have done, something you decided, or something you willed, you do not yet know the gospel of the grace of God. You have not yet been taught of God. You do not yet know God. No man, no flesh, can glory before God! God's people know better than to boast even of their repentance and faith. We know that even these things are the gifts of God and the operations of his grace in us (Acts 5:31; 11:17; Romans 2:4; 1 Corinthians 3:5; Ephesians 1:19; 2:8; Philippians 1:29; Colossians 2:12).

Second, salvation by grace alone means that God gets all the praise, honour, and glory for it. God the Father gets all praise for planning it. God the Son gets all praise for purchasing it. God the Holy Ghost gets all praise for performing it (Ephesians 1:3-14). 'As it is written, he that glorieth, let him glory in the Lord.'

Here is a litmus test for all doctrine. If it makes you proud, if it causes you to look to yourself and say, with regard to any aspect of salvation, 'I did that', it is not the doctrine of the grace of God. If, on the other hand, it causes you to bow humbly before God and say, 'Not unto us, O Lord, not unto us, but unto thy name give glory', then you can be sure it is according to the doctrine of the grace of God.

Third, this message is important because any mixture of works with grace, any mixture of merit with mercy, any mixture of what you do with what God does is not only a terribly evil thing, but utterly damning to your soul. We are saved by grace alone, through faith alone, in Christ alone. Grace plus anything is not salvation but damnation. Faith plus anything is not salvation but damnation. Christ plus anything is not salvation but damnation (Romans 11:6; Galatians 5:2, 4).

Fourth, this message is important because very few professing Christians, very few preachers and consequently, very few people in this world know what grace is. Most imagine grace is a desire in the heart of God to save sinners and something God offers to men. Or they think grace is God giving men a chance to be saved and grace is something God gives them to use to work out their own salvation. Nothing could be further from the truth. The Bible never talks this way about grace.

Grace is both an attribute of God and the work and operation of God by which he saves sinners. Whenever you think about grace or talk about it, always remember that as it is described in the Bible, grace has four distinct characteristics. Remember, I am talking about 'his grace', God's grace. Any definition of grace that violates any of these four characteristics is in direct opposition to the Word of God. His Grace is eternal (2 Timothy 1:9, 10). His Grace is immutable (Malachi 3:6; Romans 11:29). His Grace is sovereign (Romans 9:11-24). His Grace is effectual (Ephesians 2:8, 9).

Wherever God bestows his grace, salvation is the result. Grace is not the offer of salvation or a chance to be saved. Grace is the accomplishment of salvation. Here are seven things the Word of God reveals about 'his grace'. The Bible shows us that God's grace is: covenant grace, prevenient grace, regenerating grace, justifying grace, sanctifying grace, sufficient grace and keeping grace.

Covenant grace

First, the grace of God, by which we are saved, is set forth in the Word of God as covenant grace (Ephesians 1:2-6; 2 Timothy 1:9, 10).

Salvation is the result of a covenant made between the three Persons of the Holy Trinity before the world began. In that blessed, firm and everlasting covenant of grace, four things happened. 1. People were chosen unto salvation (2 Thessalonians 2:13, 14). 2. A ransom was found for the redemption of the chosen (Job 33:24; Revelation 13:8). 3. A seal was pledged, 'Hurt not the earth, neither the sea, nor the trees, till we have sealed the servants of our God' (Revelation 7:3). 4. The salvation of God's elect was secured in divine predestination (Romans 8:28-30). Saving grace is covenant grace. You cannot understand what the Bible teaches about grace unless you begin in eternity, in the everlasting covenant.

Prevenient grace

Second, 'The grace of God that bringeth salvation' is prevenient grace. Preachers do not talk about this much anymore because preachers, for the most part, know nothing about the grace of God. However, a common theme of meditation and preaching in earlier times was God's prevenient grace. The word 'prevenient' means preceding. Prevenient grace is the secret operation of grace that precedes and prepares the way for God's saving grace. Prevenient grace is illustrated in many ways in the Word of God. Here are just three aspects of it.

1. Prevenient grace is formative grace. 'Before I formed thee in the belly I knew thee; and before thou camest forth out of the womb I sanctified thee, *and* I ordained thee a prophet unto the nations' (Jeremiah 1:5).

2. Prevenient grace is restraining grace. 'Hitherto shalt thou go and no further!' 'Abimelech had not come near her … God said unto him in a dream, Yea, I know that thou didst this in the integrity of thy heart; for I also withheld thee from sinning against me: therefore suffered I thee not to touch her' (Genesis 20:4, 6).

3. Prevenient grace is overruling grace. 'For perhaps he therefore departed for a season, that thou shouldest receive him for ever' (Philemon 15). 'For she did not know that I gave her corn, and wine, and oil, and multiplied her silver and gold,

which they prepared for Baal' (Hosea 2:8). 'Surely the wrath of man shall praise thee: the remainder of wrath shalt thou restrain' (Psalm 76:10).

How I rejoice and give thanks to God for his free covenant grace and for his secret prevenient grace. It is this prevenient grace that keeps and preserves his elect throughout their days of rebellion unto the day of their calling (Jude 1).

Regenerating grace

Third, the grace of God by which we are saved is regenerating grace. The new birth is a regeneration, a resurrection from the dead, a new creation. It takes something more than the choice and decision of your free-will to accomplish that! It takes the grace of God. Ephesians 2:1-10 describes God's regenerating grace.

Verses 1-3 show us the condition of man. 'And you hath he quickened, who were dead in trespasses and sins: Wherein in time past ye walked according to the course of this world, according to the prince of the power of the air, the spirit that now worketh in the children of disobedience: Among whom also we all had our conversation in times past in the lusts of our flesh, fulfilling the desires of the flesh and of the mind; and were by nature the children of wrath, even as others'.

Verses 4-6 talk about the call of God. 'But God, who is rich in mercy, for his great love wherewith he loved us, Even when we were dead in sins, hath quickened us together with Christ, (by grace ye are saved;) And hath raised *us* up together, and made *us* sit together in heavenly *places* in Christ Jesus:'

Verse 7 demonstrates the cause of mercy. 'That in the ages to come he might show the exceeding riches of his grace in *his* kindness toward us through Christ Jesus'.

Verses 8-10 display the character of grace. It always operates alone. It is always effectual. 'For by grace are ye saved through faith; and that not of yourselves: *it is* the gift of God: Not of works, lest any man should boast. For we are his workmanship, created in Christ Jesus unto good works, which God hath before ordained that we should walk in them.'

The grace of God does not offer eternal life. It produces it! The grace of God does not advise sinners to be born again. The grace of God is that by which sinners are born again.

Justifying grace

Fourth, the grace of God by which sinners are transformed, saved and made to be saints is justifying grace. 'Being justified freely by his grace through the redemption that is in Christ Jesus' (Romans 3:24).

I know justification was accomplished long before regeneration is experienced. We were justified in the purpose of God eternally (Romans 8:29), in the Lamb slain from the foundation of the world. We were justified by the purchase of blood at Calvary when our Saviour died for us and paid our debt.

However, in our experience of things, justification comes to us and is known by us after regeneration, after we are born of God, as the result of our faith in Christ's blood atonement (Romans 3:24-28).

All who trust the Lord Jesus Christ are justified freely by the grace of God, without the works of the law. That means three things: 1. We are completely forgiven of all sin by the blood of Christ in effectual redemption. 2. The righteousness of Christ is imputed to us in free justification. 3. We 'shall not come into condemnation'. We are 'accepted in the beloved'.

Thank God for that grace that freely justifies helpless, guilty sinners.

Sanctifying grace

Fifthly, God's grace is sanctifying grace. 'Know ye not that the unrighteous shall not inherit the kingdom of God? Be not deceived: neither fornicators, nor idolaters, nor adulterers, nor effeminate, nor abusers of themselves with mankind, Nor thieves, nor covetous, nor drunkards, nor revilers, nor extortioners, shall inherit the kingdom of God. And such were some of you: but ye are washed, but ye are sanctified, but ye are justified in the name of the Lord Jesus, and by the Spirit of our God' (1 Corinthians 6:9-11).

Many are sadly confused about sanctification. Many who really appear to believe that salvation is by grace alone, when they come to the subject of sanctification make it to be a work of God and man together! However, the language of the Bible clearly declares sanctification to be a work of grace alone. God's sanctifying grace is threefold: 1. We are sanctified by the decree of God from eternity (Jude 1), 2. We are sanctified by the blood of Christ in redemption (Hebrews 10:10), and 3. We are sanctified by God the Holy Ghost in regeneration (2 Thessalonians 2:13).

Like every other aspect of salvation, sanctification is by grace alone, in Christ alone. You will search the New Testament in vain to find a solitary reference to partial or progressive sanctification. Sanctification is never referred to as something we do for God. It is something God does for and in us.

However, though our sanctification in Christ is perfect and complete, not partial and progressive as many imagine, sanctification is a continuous thing that causes every believer to grow in grace and consecrate himself to Christ.

Sufficient grace

Sixth, God's grace is sufficient grace (2 Corinthians 12:7-10). There is an infinite, super-abounding, overflowing sufficiency in the grace of God to meet all the needs of all his people forever. No matter who you are, no matter what your needs may be, no matter what circumstances you are in, if you are a believer, if you trust the Lord Jesus Christ, the Lord God says to you, 'My grace is sufficient for thee'. I am here to tell you it is so.

His grace is sufficient to sustain you in your trials (Isaiah 43:1-5). His grace is sufficient to uphold you in temptation (1 Corinthians 10:13). His grace is sufficient to enable you to do his will. Someone said, 'The Spirit of God will never lead you where the grace of God will not keep you'. 'Faithful is he that calleth you, who also will do it.' His grace is sufficient to uphold, sustain, provide for and protect his servants and to make their labours effectual to the souls of men. 'Our sufficiency is of God.' His grace is sufficient especially for his fallen saints. 'But go your way, tell his disciples and Peter that he goeth before you into Galilee: there shall ye see him, as he said unto you' (Mark 16:7).

In your last hour, when you come to the swelling of the Jordan and are about to cross over to the other side, you will yet hear him say, 'My grace is sufficient for thee'.

Keeping grace

1 Peter 5:10 tells us one last fact about God's saving grace. It keeps us. It is keeping grace. 'But the God of all grace, who hath called us unto his eternal glory by Christ Jesus, after that ye have suffered a while, make you perfect, stablish, strengthen, settle *you.*'

If you are a believer, God's keeping grace is as sure to you now as his covenant grace was before ever you were born (Philippians 1:2-6). The grace of God is grace that cannot be altered, destroyed or taken away, not even by anything we may do.

The grace of God alone is that which distinguishes one sinner from another. 'For who maketh thee to differ *from another*? and what hast thou that thou didst not receive? now if thou didst receive *it*, why dost thou glory, as if thou hadst not received *it*?' (1 Corinthians 4:7).

'Let us therefore come boldly unto the throne of grace, that we may obtain mercy, and find grace to help in time of need' (Hebrews 4:16).

Chapter 24

'But God'

But God, who is rich in mercy, for his great love wherewith he loved us.
(Ephesians 2:4)

In Ephesians chapter 2, the Apostle Paul paints a dark, dark picture; a gloomy picture of our race. It is the same picture drawn by all the prophets and apostles used of God to write this Book. We are all sinners by nature, lost and ruined by the sin and fall of our father Adam.

Paul does not paint this picture any darker than it should be or any darker than it has been painted by those who preceded him. For example: Moses wrote in Genesis 6:5, 'God saw that the wickedness of man was great in the earth, and that every imagination of the thoughts of his heart was only evil continually'.

In chapter 15, verses 15 and 16, Job wrote, 'Behold, he putteth no trust in his saints; yea, the heavens are not clean in his sight. How much more abominable and filthy is man, which drinketh iniquity like water.'

David, in Psalm 14, verses 2 and 3, said, 'The Lord looked down from heaven upon the children of men, to see if there were any that did understand, and seek God'. He found that, 'They are all gone aside, they are altogether become filthy: there is none that doeth good, no not one'. David wrote again, 'Every man at his best state is altogether vanity' (Psalm 39:5).

In Isaiah 64:6, Isaiah said, 'We are as all as an unclean thing'. Prior to this he said; 'Woe is me! for I am undone; because I am a man of unclean lips, and I dwell in the midst of a people of unclean lips' (Isaiah 6:5). Here he says, 'We are all as an unclean thing, and all our righteousnesses (our goodness) are as filthy rags; and we do all fade as a leaf; and our iniquities like the wind, have taken us away'.

Dead

Paul takes up this picture and paints it himself. He says in Ephesians 2:1 that we were dead. 'You … who were dead in trespasses and sins.'

What are trespasses? Have you ever seen a sign on the side of a fence out in the woods or out on a farm somewhere that says, 'No Trespassing'? That means you are not to walk on that land. Trespassing is walking on forbidden property, on forbidden ground. That is what we are, trespassers. God said, 'Thou shalt not, thou shalt not, thou shalt not' and we did anyway. We are trespassing; we are dead in our trespasses and in our sins. 'By one man sin entered the world, and death by sin; and so death passed upon all men.' 'The wages of sin is death.'

Our sins killed us. Paul says that we are dead. Somebody might say, 'There's a little life in everybody'. No, not spiritually speaking. We are dead spiritually. We are not dead mentally or dead physically; but we are dead spiritually.

God said to Adam in the garden concerning the forbidden fruit, 'In the day that thou eatest thereof thou shalt surely die' (Genesis 2:17). He died and we died in him. That is what the Scripture says; and this is what Paul is saying here. 'You who were dead, dead in your trespasses and in your sins.'

Walked

'Ye walked.' That was our walk, our lives, and the bent of our wills. We walked according to the course of this world, just like all other rebels. 'All we like sheep have gone astray; we have turned every one to his own way.'

'Ye walked according to the course of this world.' We lived not according to God's Word, and not according to God's will, but according to the 'prince of the power of the air (Satan), the spirit that now worketh in the children of disobedience'.

We were will-worshippers; 'we all had our conversation (our behaviour, our manner of life) … in the lust of our flesh'. We did not care about our souls, only for our bodies. We were driven by greed, covetousness, materialism, passion and ambition. We had our behaviour in the desires and passions of our flesh.

Not only that, we were slaves to the lusts of our flesh and the desires of our mind. What we did not do, we thought. There are restraints on the flesh; there are all kinds of fences around about the flesh that prevent men from doing what they would do. There are no fences around the imagination. There is no restraint on the imagination. Nothing is safe and nothing is holy from the human mind and the human heart. We may not do something, but we think it. Others do it and we condemn them in self-righteous pride. We think it, then justify ourselves, as if we were righteous! But the fact is, we are all by nature slaves to the lusts of our flesh and the desires of our mind. That is where we were when God called us by his grace. It is what we are by nature.

God looks on the heart. He said, 'Ye are they which justify yourselves before men; but God knoweth your hearts'. 'That which is highly esteemed among men is an abomination in the sight of God.'

God haters

In Ephesians 2 Paul goes on to say, Ye 'were by nature the children of wrath'. Who's wrath? God's wrath. We were angry with God, and our consciences sensed God's anger with us. You might say, 'I'm not angry with God'. The Scripture says, 'The carnal mind is enmity against God'. All of us, by nature, are angry with God and are God haters!

Men do not hate their god, the gods of their imagination. Men do not hate their conception of God. Men hate the true and living God as he is revealed in his Word, and as He is revealed in the person and work of his Son, the Lord Jesus Christ. That hatred of God was demonstrated and is proved by the treatment that God's Son received when he came to this earth.

He was and is the perfect God and the perfect man. He lived on this earth in perfect righteousness, perfect goodness, perfect holiness. Men spit in his face and nailed him to a cross and said, 'We are not going to have you reign over us. We will let Caesar reign over us. We will let our Pharisees reign over us; but God is not going to reign over us.'

As others

We 'were by nature the children of wrath, even as others'. Who are these 'others'? They are as the angels that kept not their first estate, even as citizens of Noah's generation, before the flood, of whom God said, 'I will destroy man whom I have created'. They are even as the Sodomites, even as those who crucified Christ, for the Scripture says, there is no difference, 'for all have sinned, and come short of the glory of God'.

What a terrible picture! What a horrible revelation! What a hopeless situation! Dead, dead in trespasses and sin, walking in the bias of our will, the direction of our lives, the course of this world!

We are slaves, servants, bond-servants of the prince of the power of the air, having our conversation in the lust of our flesh, fulfilling the desires of our flesh and our mind, by nature under God's judgment, under God's wrath. The Scripture says, 'God is angry with the wicked every day' and 'He that believeth not the Son shall not see life; but the wrath of God abideth on him'. What a terrible situation!

'But God'

Is there no hope? Jeremiah said there's no hope as far as man is concerned. 'Can the Ethiopian change his skin, or the leopard his spots? Then may ye also do good, that are accustomed to do evil.'

Is there no hope? After hearing Christ's discourse with the rich young ruler, the disciples asked him, 'Who then can be saved?' If that's the condition of the best man we ever knew, 'Who then can be saved?' He said, 'With men it is impossible'. What God demands we cannot produce. What justice demands we cannot give. It is impossible! 'But with God all things are possible.'

There is good news. 'But God' is our hope. There is nothing we can do; but there is something God can do. 'But God, who is rich in mercy, for his great love wherewith he loved us, Even when we were dead in sins (even when we were in this condition), hath quickened us together with Christ, (by grace ye are saved:)' Not by works, by grace. Not by decision, by grace. He 'hath raised us up together, and made us sit together in heavenly places in Christ Jesus: That in the ages to come he might shew the exceeding riches of his grace in his kindness toward us through Christ Jesus'.

Why is it so much easier to think evil than to think well? Why is it so much easier to hate than to love? Why is it so much easier to hold a grudge than to forgive? It is because of the wretched condition we are in because we were born in Adam, shapen in iniquity, conceived in sin, brought forth into this world, enemies of God. 'But God.'

Men are dead in sin, guilty before the law, unable to please God, unwilling to bow to Christ. 'But God.' Only Christ can do something about it. If you look to a preacher you are hopeless. If you look to a creed you are helpless. 'But God.'

We were without hope, without help, without Christ, 'But God.' God purposed, God planned, God determined to do something about it and God did what he planned, purposed and determined.

God is going to have a people. We would not have God but God said, 'I will be their God; and they shall be my people'. We did not want God but he wanted us. God will have his will!

Sinner's hope

The remedy is not what we have done for God. It is what God has done for us. Here is the remedy for sinful man, 'But God'.

In Adam we were dead in trespasses and sin, hopeless and helpless. 'None eye pitied thee' in your blood, in your filth, in your corruption, in your depravity, in your deadness, in your grave of iniquity, unwilling and unable, and God came by (Ezekiel 16:6-14). He said, 'I saw you just like you were, and I loved you anyway'. 'But God commendeth his love toward us, in that, while we were yet sinners, Christ died for us'.

'Salvation is of the LORD'. He planned it. He purposed it. He purchased it. He executed it in the person of his Son. He brings it and applies it to the hearts of chosen, redeemed, needy sinners. He sustains it and perfects it by his grace. 'He which hath begun a good work in you will perform it until the day of Jesus Christ.' He will make all of his children like his Son, the Lord Jesus Christ.

Rich in mercy

'But God who is rich in mercy.' Our guilt is higher than the mountains and deeper than the sea. 'But God' is rich in mercy. Ask Mary Magdalene about the riches of his mercy; seven devils living in one woman but our Lord Jesus Christ was rich in mercy to her.

Ask Saul of Tarsus who was wrapped up in his religious hatred, in his religious tradition, in his religious pride. What an arrogant, haughty, proud religionist he was. He was a legalist and a moralist. He said he was blameless concerning the law. He persecuted our Lord's Church. He put God's saints in prison and had them put to death. He held the coats of those who stoned Stephen, the first Christian martyr. He stood there in smug, self-righteous indignation and watched him die. Ask him about the riches of God's mercy. He said, 'But I obtained mercy'.

Ask the woman at the well. She was married five times and was living with a man who was not her husband. She was the talk of the town. She was hiding, sneaking her way to the well at high noon. Ask her about the riches of his mercy.

Ask the thief on the cross. They took him outside the city wall and nailed him to a tree. Ask him about the riches of God's mercy. Ask him to whom Jesus said, 'Verily I say unto thee, To day shalt thou be with me in paradise'.

Christ Jesus 'is able (and willing) to save to the uttermost, them that come to God by him'. Your sins will never keep you out of heaven, but your righteousness will. He is the friend of sinners. He came to save sinners. He died for the ungodly. He delights to show mercy. He says, 'Though your sins be as scarlet, they shall be as white as snow; though they be red like crimson, they shall be as wool'. 'Come unto me, all ye that labour and are heavy laden, and I will give you rest.' 'Herein is love, not that we loved God, but that he loved us, and sent his Son to be a propitiation for our sins.'

Any grace we have is God's grace. Any love is God's love. Any fruit is God's fruit. 'Of him are you in Christ Jesus, who of God is made unto us wisdom, and righteousness, and sanctification, and redemption: that, according as it is written, He that glorieth, let him glory in the Lord.' There is nothing good in us, 'But God, who is rich in mercy, for his great love wherewith he loved us, Even when we were dead in sins, hath quickened us together with Christ.'

O gift of gifts, O grace of faith!
My God, how can it be,
That Thou, who hast discerning love,
Shouldst give that gift to me?

Oh, grace! Into unlikeliest hearts,
It is thy boast to come,
The glory of thy light to find,
In darkest spots a home.

Chapter 25

'The Exceeding Riches Of His Grace'

That in the ages to come he might shew the exceeding riches of his grace in *his* kindness toward us through Christ Jesus.

(Ephesians 2:7)

This verse of Scripture makes it plain that Paul fully expected the gospel of the grace of God to be preached in the ages to come. He knew that the gospel of grace must be preached in every part of the world.

No improvement

Paul was assured there could be no improvement made upon the gospel. This man was fully persuaded that the very same gospel Christ preached, the gospel that turned the world upside down in days of the early church, would be the gospel that God would use to gather his elect from the four corners of the earth in all future ages. I think Paul is also telling us that as this gospel has been the means of saving men throughout the ages, it will be the theme of our songs throughout the ages of eternity, too.

Eternity itself will not improve the gospel. When all the saints are gathered in heaven, they shall still talk and sing of the wonders of love revealed in Jesus Christ our Lord. As we walk the golden streets of the celestial city, we shall stand before the listening crowds of angels, principalities and powers, and think it our greatest joy to tell what the Lord has done for us by 'the exceeding riches of his grace'.

Unalterable

The gospel of God is unalterable. Paul did not anticipate the removal of this ancient landmark. He knew many false teachers and false religions would rise up to pervert the gospel. But he also knew God would preserve his truth throughout the ages.

The gospel of Christ has the same power today as it had at the dawn of the church. It is still the battering ram of the church against the gates of hell. God has shown it in the ages gone by and he will yet show in the ages to come, how the gospel of Christ and him crucified is 'the power of God, and the wisdom of God'. We dare not cease to proclaim the mercy of God as it is displayed in the sin-atoning death of his dear Son. We have an innumerable company of witnesses, from the church of the Old Testament, from the Apostles of the New and in all the years of this gospel age who are united in testifying to us that Jesus Christ is 'able also to save them to the uttermost that come unto God by him'.

These infallible assurances strengthen our confidence and inflame our hearts so that we are bold to say with the Apostle, 'As much as in me is, I am ready to preach the gospel … For I am not ashamed of the gospel of Christ: for it is the power of God unto salvation to everyone that believeth; to the Jew first, and also to the Greek.'

By faith

God has used this gospel to save multitudes of sinners. These multitudes of converts in the days of old stand as monuments to free and sovereign grace. They show us there is salvation for sinners because they possessed everlasting salvation.

The gospel declares salvation accomplished and tells us this salvation can be the portion of sinful men. It may be had upon the terms God has laid down; simply believing on the Lord Jesus Christ. The saints of old obtained it by faith in Christ and so may we. Doubt should be put out of the question. Every needy, trembling sinner should flee quickly to the refuge of mercy in Jesus Christ. Many have fled to him and found mercy. Surely, we can do the same. He has never rejected any. He will not reject us.

The God of all grace has saved to the uttermost all who have come unto God by him. Therefore sinful men ought eagerly to come to Christ at once and put their trust in the Lamb of God who alone is worthy to be trusted. Then will God's purpose in this text be accomplished, that in the ages to come it should be made known by all who have received his kindness, that there are riches, exceeding riches, super-abounding riches of grace for poor sinners in Christ Jesus. Here is a royal subject, 'The Exceeding Riches Of His Grace'.

All who have ever been converted stand as monuments to this truth: God's grace is rich, free and merciful in Jesus Christ for all who trust him.

God's purpose in grace

Paul has spent all of his efforts in these first two chapters of Ephesians showing us that salvation is altogether a marvellous work of God's free and sovereign grace in Christ. He has described the rich blessings of grace, the wonder of grace and the condescension of grace. He has shown us the power of grace in supplying us a spiritual resurrection. Now he will show us why he has spoken so much about God's grace. It is because God has determined 'in the ages to come' to show the exceeding riches of his grace by us.

The grace God has shown to his people is an encouragement to sinners. The salvation of these Ephesians stands as a remarkable example of God's grace. These people were steeped in idolatry. They were given to every imaginable vice. Yet God saved them and he still saves such sinners today.

The salvation of the earliest Christians is a pattern of God's grace to encourage sinners everywhere and in every age to trust him. God saved a cheating Publican like Zacchaeus. God saved a woman who was an adulteress. God saved a woman who was a harlot. God saved a wild Gadarene. God saved a man who was a condemned and dying criminal. God saved a proud, self-righteous Pharisee. God saved sinners in Nero's house. Surely, God will save such as I am if I will trust him.

Paul's own conversion was a pattern of God's grace to all future ages. 'Howbeit for this cause I obtained mercy, that in me first Jesus Christ might shew forth all longsuffering, for a pattern to them which should hereafter believe on him to life everlasting' (1 Timothy 1:16).

Paul was guilty of horrid crimes of self-righteousness but he obtained mercy. God saves all sinners just like he saved Paul. 'And he said, The God of our fathers hath chosen thee, that thou shouldest know his will, and see that Just One, and shouldest hear the voice of his mouth' (Acts 22:14). He was chosen. He was redeemed. Christ was revealed to him; and God's will was made known to him.

The grace that God has shown to his people sets forth his glory in salvation. This is the primary reason for all of God's gracious dealings with men. That we should be 'to the praise of the glory of his grace' (Ephesians 1:6). 'Nevertheless he saved them for his name's sake, that he might make his mighty power to be known' (Psalm 106:8). It is the glory of God to be gracious. God is to be praised for the work of his grace.

The grace of God that has been shown to his people should be the singular subject of the pulpit. The gospel of grace is to be preached fully. Man's ruined condition must be preached. God's free election must be proclaimed. Christ's perfect atonement must be sounded out. The gracious calling of God the Holy Ghost must be made known. The perfect preservation of God's people must be upheld. The gospel of Christ is the life and strength of the church.

The grace God has shown to his people will be the theme of eternal worship. 'And they sung a new song, saying, Thou art worthy to take the book, and to open the seals thereof: for thou wast slain, and hast redeemed us to God by thy blood out of every kindred, and tongue, and people, and nation; And hast made us unto our God kings and priests: and we shall reign on the earth' (Revelation 5:9, 10).

'After this I beheld, and, lo, a great multitude, which no man could number, of all nations, and kindreds, and people, and tongues, stood before the throne, and before the Lamb, clothed with white robes, and palms in their hands; And cried with a loud voice, saying, Salvation to our God which sitteth upon the throne, and unto the Lamb' (Revelation 7:9, 10).

'And after these things I heard a great voice of much people in heaven, saying, Alleluia; Salvation, and glory, and honour, and power, unto the Lord our God' (Revelation 19:1).

God's provision by grace

Ephesians 2:7 speaks of 'the exceeding riches of his grace'. Here our English language is poor compared to the Greek. In the Greek you can readily see how Paul stretches his mind to the utmost degree, searching for words suitable to describe the riches of God's grace. It is as though he said it is God's purpose to show the super-abounding, excessive, overflowing riches of his grace. I could heap up more adjectives but it is impossible to show the extent of Paul's meaning in the English tongue.

God's grace has bestowed upon us a rich treasure of mercy. 'Blessed be the God and Father of our Lord Jesus Christ, who hath blessed us with all spiritual blessings in heavenly places in Christ'. Here are just a few tokens of his grace:

God's grace is the source of election. His redemptive grace is seen in giving his Son for us. God's prevenient grace is manifest in his care for us before we were saved. His grace preserves us unto salvation (Jude 1) and his regenerating grace has been demonstrated to us in the effectual call of his Spirit.

God graciously received us as sons (1 John 3:1, 2). He spoke pardon and peace to our hearts. He instructs us in his Word. He guides us in his ways. He upholds us, restores us, and preserves us.

Does anyone ask, 'What has God done for us in grace?' We might better ask, 'What has he not done for us?'

The grace we have received at God's hand has been rich grace indeed! The riches of God's grace are without measure and without limit. God's grace excels above all observation. We have not yet begun to observe the wealth of divine grace. God's grace is rich beyond our understanding. God's grace is greater than our sins. 'Where sin abounded, grace did much more abound' (Romans 5:20).

Look at the mountains of our sins. Grace has removed them all. God's grace is rich above all measure. It is higher than our sins for it brings us to the throne of the Most High. It is deeper than our sins for it has reached to the depth of man's depravity and brought up jewels for heaven. It is wider than our sins for it has removed them as far as the east is from the west. As for the length of God's grace, it is from everlasting to everlasting.

There is a beginning to man's sin but there is no beginning to pardoning love! Before there was a sinner there was a Saviour. Before there was a crime there was a Redeemer. Before there was transgression there was mercy. Before there was an offended justice there was a satisfied Justifier. His grace is everlasting!

God's exceeding riches of grace have been fully manifested to us. His grace has been shown to us particularly. When we resisted his grace, he resolved to overcome our folly. Christ comes to us just as we are, in our alienation and in our enmity. He brings everything we need in his hands.

The more we learn how his grace works, the richer his grace appears. He loved us freely. He chose us unconditionally. He removed our sins by his blood. He sent his Word to heal our souls. He gave us life by his Spirit. He subdued our hearts by his power. Ever since our conversion the Lord has held on to us by his grace and never ceased to be kind. He loves us perfectly. He will never divorce his spouse.

God's place for grace

Perhaps the most blessed thing about the exceeding riches of God's grace is this. It is shown to us through Jesus Christ. The place of grace is Jesus Christ. We see his precious blood on every blessing grace bestows upon us.

> There's ne'er a gift his hand bestows,
> But cost his heart a groan.

All things come to us through Jesus Christ. He is the golden Channel of eternal love, the Window through which grace shines, the Door by which it enters. Look at the kindness of God toward us through Christ and never cease to praise him!

His kindness is demonstrated in all of his work for us. For us, he became a man. For us, he lived a life of suffering and obedience. He fulfilled all righteousness for us. For us, he died at Calvary. For us, he rose from the dead. For us, he intercedes in heaven.

Christ Jesus receives sinners in kindness. He deals with his sinning people in kindness. He provides for our every need in kindness. Oh, with what great kindness he intercedes for us in heaven! He waits for us in heaven in kindness.

'In ages to come', in heaven's endless glory, the Triune God will show to wondering worlds 'the exceeding riches of his grace, in his kindness toward us, through Christ Jesus'. Imagine that! May God seize our hearts with wonder at his rich grace.

Children of God, we shall never know, until we have reached eternal glory, our debt to the exceeding riches of his grace. Then we will stand before God to the amazement of all creatures.

When this passing world is done,
When has sunk yon glaring sun,
When we stand with Christ in glory,
Looking o'er life's finished story,
Then, Lord, shall I fully know—
Not till then—how much I owe.

'Now unto him that is able to keep you from falling, and to present *you* faultless before the presence of his glory with exceeding joy, To the only wise God our Saviour, *be* glory and majesty, dominion and power, both now and ever. Amen' (Jude 24, 25).

Chapter 26

'Saved Through Faith'

For by grace are ye saved through faith; and that not of yourselves: *it is* the gift of God.

(Ephesians 2:8)

Except you believe on the Lord Jesus Christ you cannot be saved. Faith in Christ is as essential to salvation as election, redemption and regeneration. Salvation is through faith.

'By grace are ye saved?' The grace of God is the fountain, the source, the cause of salvation. It is because God is gracious that sinful men are chosen, redeemed, forgiven, converted, justified, sanctified and saved. It is not because of anything in them, or anything that ever can be in them, that they are saved but because of the boundless love, goodness, pity, compassion, mercy and grace of God.

Look at the great source and cause of salvation. Here is a rich fountain. Look at the pure river of the water of life that flows from the throne of God and of the Lamb. What an abyss the grace of God is! Who can comprehend it? Like all the rest of the divine attributes, the grace of God is infinite. God is full of love, because 'God is love'. God is full of goodness because God is good. The very name 'God' is but a shortened form of the word 'good'. Unbounded love and goodness are the very essence of the Triune God. It is because 'his mercy endureth for ever', that men are not consumed. It is because 'his compassions fail not', that sinners are drawn to him and forgiven. It is because 'he delighteth in mercy', that sinners obtain mercy.

Get a firm hold on this statement, 'By grace are ye saved'. Otherwise you might fall into the error of supposing, as many do, that your faith is the source of eternal salvation. Faith is the work of God's grace in us. No man can say that Jesus is the Christ, but by the Holy Ghost. 'No man can come to me', says our Lord, 'except the Father which hath sent me draw him' (John 6:44). That faith by which we come to Christ is the result of the creative, effectual, drawing power of God's omnipotent grace. Grace is the first and last cause of our salvation. Faith, important as it is, is only a part of the machinery which grace employs. We are saved 'through faith', but it is 'by grace'. Let us sound forth those words with a clarion voice, 'By grace are ye saved'.

Faith is the channel or conduit of grace. I have frequently stood at a large dam and watched the water rush with great power through those huge pipes at its base. The rush of the water is frightening because of its power. At other times, I have gone and looked at the pipes when there was no water in them. Any child can perceive the power is not in the pipe. The pipes are but the channel through which the water flows. All the power is in that great lake on the other side of the dam. So it is with faith.

Grace is the great lake, the great reservoir, of salvation. Faith is only the pipe by which we receive salvation. Grace is the fountain of life. Faith is the channel by which divine mercy flows to the thirsty sons of men. Faith is not the fountain and source of salvation. It is only the channel through which salvation flows.

Faith is a precious gift of God's grace but we must never so highly exalt faith as to make it the cause of salvation. That is the grace of God alone. Never make a Saviour out of your faith. Do not think of faith as though it were the source of salvation. Life is found by looking unto Jesus, not by looking unto our faith. By faith all things become possible to us. Yet, the power is not in faith, but in the God upon whom faith relies.

The righteousness of faith is not the moral excellence of faith, but the righteousness of Jesus Christ, which faith appropriates. The peace we enjoy is not derived from our faith. It comes to us from him who is our Peace, the hem of whose garment faith touches.

The words of the Apostle show us the source of salvation, 'By grace are ye saved'. They also show us the channel of salvation, 'Saved through faith'.

Here is the doctrine of the text. Salvation is bestowed upon sinful men freely by God's rich grace and we receive this gift of life by faith in Jesus Christ.

Thus far in the Book of Ephesians we have looked at the many beauties and riches of God's grace, which is the source of our salvation. Though I have only skimmed the surface of that great reservoir, I think it is needful for us now to look at the channel.

Perhaps the simplest and clearest way for me to approach this subject is to try to answer some very basic questions about faith. Here are four questions I want to answer.

What is faith?

Today we hear much talk about faith. People are urged to believe. Men, women and children are urged to make a profession of faith. Men place bumper stickers on their cars saying, 'Keep the faith'. But what does all that mean? What is faith?

Perhaps it would be helpful, first of all, to show you what faith is not. Satan has substituted many kinds of faith for saving faith. Some people have what might be called a human faith. That is, what they believe is founded upon the authority and testimony of men. There are men who make a profession of religion intellectually, because they have a historical faith. They give mental assent to the historical truths revealed about Christ in the Scriptures (James 2:17). There is a faith produced in men as the result of witnessing miracles (John 2:23; 6:66). Others have only a temporary faith. They are the people who give assent to the truths of the gospel. They find them, for a time, both interesting and desirable. But, after a while, when the privileges and advantages of religion are crowded out by the cares of the world, they leave the profession of their faith (Luke 8:12-14).

What we call saving faith is something more than this. Saving faith is faith in the Lord Jesus Christ. It is wrought in the heart by God. God the Holy Spirit persuades us that Christ is the Messiah and gives us a desire and expectation of the promises of the gospel in him. Saving faith depends on the blood and righteousness of Christ for all blessings. It is obedience to his call.

Saving faith is made up of three things; knowledge, assent and trust. The knowledge of Christ is necessary for the exercise of faith (Romans 10:13-17). You cannot trust an unknown Saviour any more than you can come back from where you've never been! Knowledge of Christ comes through the preaching of the gospel. Man must be taught and convinced of sinfulness so he will know his need of Christ. Man must be taught and convinced of his impotence so he will feel his need of Christ. Man must be persuaded of the fulness and ability of Christ to save.

However, knowledge alone is not faith. There must also be an assent, or agreement, with the testimony of God concerning his Son (John 6:45). Being taught of God, we believe that Jesus is the Christ (Daniel 9:24). Along with knowledge and assent, there must be trust in Christ.

Saving faith is believing that Jesus is the Christ, that he is what he is said to be in the Word of God and that he has done all that the Book of God declared the Christ must do. It is trusting he will do what he promised to do and expecting this from him, we believe that Christ is God in human flesh and that he died and rose again to save sinners. We believe Christ will save all who come to him in faith and repentance. We expect everlasting glory at his appearance.

Saving faith is looking to Christ (Isaiah 45:22). Saving faith is coming to Christ (Matthew 11:28). Saving faith is fleeing to Christ (Hebrews 6:18). Saving faith is laying hold of Christ (Isaiah 27:5). Saving faith is clinging to Christ (Song of Solomon 3:4). Saving faith is leaning upon Christ (Song of Solomon 8:5). Saving faith is receiving Christ (John 1:12). We receive him as Christ our Prophet to teach us the will of God. We receive him as Christ our Priest to intercede for us before God. We receive him as Christ our King to rule over us as God.

Saving faith is feeding upon Christ, living upon the Bread of Life (John 6:54). Saving faith is not an experience of yesterday, but the present reality of the believer's life (Habakkuk 2:4; Romans 1:17; Galatians 3:11; Hebrews 10:38; 11:6).

Faith in Christ is one of the three abiding graces of the Holy Spirit. 'Now abideth faith, hope, and charity'. Faith is a most precious gift of God's grace. It may sometimes be weak faith, but true faith, weak or strong, once it is bestowed will never be taken from us. Faith renders to us the reality of God's promises and the experience of God's love.

Where does faith come from?

The answer to this question is given in the Book of God with utmost clarity. Faith is not the work of man. It is the work of God in man. Faith does not spring from man's imagined freewill, but from God's omnipotent, sovereign will and irresistible grace and power. Listen to the Scriptures. 'But as many as received him, to them gave he power to become the sons of God, even to them that believe on his name: which were born, not of blood, nor of the will of the flesh, nor of the will of man, but of God' (John 1:12, 13). 'This is the work of God, that ye believe on him whom he hath sent' (John 6:29). 'Ye are risen with him through the faith of the operation of God' (Colossians 2:12). Paul's prayer for the Thessalonians, and for us all, was 'That our God would count you worthy of this calling, and fulfil all the good pleasure of his goodness, and the work of faith with power' (2 Thessalonians 1:11).

God the Father must draw you to Christ or you have no faith and will not come (John 6:44, 45). God the Son is the Author and Finisher of our faith. God the Holy

Spirit produces faith in chosen, redeemed sinners by the Word (John 6:65). Saving faith is a revelation of Jesus Christ in the heart causing men to trust him. 'It is the gift of God.'

God has chosen to save sinners through faith, that the whole work might appear to be of his grace, for faith gives all the glory to God alone. 'Therefore *it is* of faith, that *it might be* by grace; to the end the promise might be sure to all the seed; not to that only which is of the law, but to that also which is of the faith of Abraham; who is the father of us all' (Romans 4:16).

How can I get faith?

This is a great question to many. They say they want to believe but cannot. A great deal of nonsense is spoken and written on this subject. I want to be very practical in my answer to this question. How can I get faith? What must I do in order to believe? You must do nothing. You must look for nothing. You must simply believe!

Think much upon the Lord Jesus Christ. Seek the Lord. Seek him in his Word. Seek him by prayer! Seek him in the preaching of the gospel! Yes, you must seek the Lord, but you will never seek him until you are sought of him. Yes, you must believe, but only God can give you faith in Christ. Yes, you must turn to Christ, but only God can turn you.

I sought the Lord, and afterward I knew
He moved my soul to seek Him, seeking me.
It was not I that found, O Saviour true;
No, I was found of Thee.

Thou didst reach forth Thy hand and mine enfold;
I walked and sank not on the storm-vexed sea.
'Twas not so much that I on Thee took hold,
As Thou, dear Lord, on me.

I find, I walk, I love, but oh, the whole
Of love is but my answer, Lord, to Thee!
For Thou wert long beforehand with my soul;
Always Thou lovedst me!

What is the result of faith?

The result of faith is salvation; eternal, free, everlasting salvation by the grace of God. 'By grace are ye saved through faith.' Faith receives justification. Faith receives adoption. Faith receives redemption. Faith receives peace. Faith receives sanctification. Faith performs nothing but receives everything.

'Believe on the Lord Jesus Christ, and thou shalt be saved.' The result of faith is salvation (Romans 10:1-13).

Chapter 27

'We Are His Workmanship' – God's Masterpieces

For we are his workmanship, created in Christ Jesus unto good works, which God hath before ordained that we should walk in them.

(Ephesians 2:10)

Paul has been arguing throughout the first nine verses of this chapter that salvation is altogether the work of God's free grace and not the result of human works. 'Not of works lest any man should boast ... for we are his workmanship'. In this tenth verse he proves that human merit has nothing whatever to do with our salvation.

Paul's argument

Our text begins with the word 'for' and that indicates an argument. It is as though Paul had said, 'Here is a conclusive proof that salvation cannot be the result of our good works, because all of our good works are the result of God's grace'. All who are saved by the grace of God are the workmanship of God. With each of us, this argument holds strength, for we know it not only by revelation but by experience as well. With this we fully agree. 'By grace are ye saved through faith; and that not of yourselves: it is the gift of God; not of works lest any man should boast; for we are his workmanship'.

God's creation

The word 'workmanship' is 'masterpieces'. God's elect are God's masterpieces, his best work, his highest work, his signature work. We are so completely the workmanship of Jehovah that we are also called his creation. We were 'created in

Christ Jesus'. Surely none would be so foolish as to claim to be his own creator! Such a supposition would be absurd upon the very face of it. It would be a misuse of language to speak of anything creating itself. Whatever, therefore, we are in Christ Jesus is the result of God's work upon us and in us; and it cannot be the cause of that work.

God's purpose

Our text gives yet another argument. Our good works, be they what they may, are the subjects of God's eternal decree. 'Which God hath before ordained that we should walk in them.' It is certainly true that we purpose for ourselves a life and walk of good works. We choose and determine in our heart to walk in them. But long before we resolved to walk the path of holiness, God's purpose for us was settled.

Here is Paul's argument. If good works are ordained by God as well as the salvation of which they are the result, then the whole matter must be the result of sovereign, predestinating, effectual grace and there is no place left to impute salvation to human works. The tree is not the result of its fruit, for the fruit is created with the tree; it is the one purpose for which the tree was made. Good works are not the cause of salvation but the result of it; good works are a part of God's purpose in saving men.

Paul's doctrine

There are some who make good works to be meritorious and the cause of salvation. In this they greatly err, perverting the gospel of Christ. But there is another great error in the opposite direction which is employed by Satan to destroy the souls of men. This is the error of the 'carnal Christian' doctrine. Many suppose that since good works are not meritorious they are not necessary. We are told that a man may be a true believer and yet live in ungodliness. He may choose to walk in good works that he may obtain greater reward in heaven. If he does not choose to do so, he will still be saved, only with the loss of reward.

In our text Paul firmly denies that good works are meritorious. He also insists good works are necessary. Salvation is altogether a matter of divine grace; therefore good works cannot cause it, yet good works are the fruit of the work of grace and are therefore necessary.

There are three things clearly taught in our text in the development of this subject.

The believer's origin

First, 'We are his workmanship, created in Christ Jesus'. Here we have the singular origin of all believers. All Christians are the workmanship of God, whether Jews or Gentiles. We owe our being to the work of God alone whether we are among the strongest believers, like Paul, or among the weakest, as we may be. As many as are truly saved and brought into union with Christ, every member of the family of God, are the workmanship of God.

The origin of our being, not only as men but even as Christians, is God alone. No man ever became a Christian by chance. Spiritual life is not the reform and moral development of our old nature. When our nature matures to its fullest years, it only becomes more vile. Even after we are born-again that old man within us is as evil as ever.

It is an utter impossibility to suppose that spiritual life could arise from our dead nature. Death may produce corruption but it will never produce life. Developed manhood is but developed sin. The Bible knows nothing of evolution but it does speak of degeneration, decay and depravity. 'When lust hath conceived, it bringeth forth sin: and sin, when it is finished, bringeth forth death' (James 1:15).

Darkness never produces light, filth never produces purity, hell never brings forth heaven, depravity never produces grace. If we are believers, if we are saved, if we are Christians, we are God's workmanship.

We are his workmanship from the very beginning. God marks the stone he will have while it is yet in the quarry. God cuts the stone from its mountain. He hews it, squares it, polishes it, refines it and makes it his own jewel. We might use David's language, 'Thine eyes did see my substance, yet being unperfect; and in thy book all my members were written, which in continuance were fashioned, when as yet there was none of them' (Psalm 139:16). God chose us. The Lord first taught us our need. Jehovah first gave us holy fears and holy desires. He gave us spiritual life. He called us to himself. God himself spoke the peace of pardon and forgiveness to our heart.

We are his workmanship now. There is nothing in us that is perfect, except Christ, that new man created in us in righteousness and true holiness. We are his workmanship. He has not yet finished this masterpiece; but he is working on it even now. He chips off the rough places and sands down the coarse edges; he refines the work according to his own will, like the potter does the clay. He strengthens our faith by trials. He increases our patience by afflictions. He draws forth our love by his providence. He teaches us to pray by showing us our need. He subdues our sin by chastisement.

Furthermore, we will be God's workmanship to the very last. 'Being confident of this very thing, that he which hath begun a good work in you will perform it until the day of Jesus Christ' (Philippians 1:6). Rest assured, my brethren, that God will complete his work in you! He will not allow any other hand to put even one finishing touch to his masterpiece, not even your own.

All of this is very comforting to remember. It should stir up our hearts to magnify the Lord. Dwell upon his skill, think on his wisdom and magnify his name. Remember his power and magnify his name. Remember his loving patience and magnify his name.

Our text also shows us the peculiar manner of God's work in us. 'We are his workmanship, created in Christ Jesus'. Our new life is the creation of God in Christ Jesus. Just as God created the heavens and the earth out of nothing just so in the spiritual creation God created us out of nothing. We were without form and void, but the Spirit of God moved upon us. We were darkness but God gave us light. We were dead but he gave us life.

In the first creation God made all things by his Word. 'The worlds were framed by the Word of God'. Likewise, our spiritual creation was effected by the Word of God. 'So then faith cometh by hearing, and hearing by the word of God' (Romans 10:17). 'Of his own will begat he us with the word of truth, that we should be a kind of firstfruits of his creatures' (James 1:18). 'Being born again, not of corruptible seed, but of incorruptible, by the word of God, which liveth and abideth for ever' (1 Peter 1:23). God's Son came and spoke life into our hearts (Hebrews 4:12). God sent his servant to preach the gospel and implanted in us faith in his Son. In the work of creation the Lord is alone and unaided.

Our text tells us this new creation is in Christ Jesus. We were first created in Adam and our father Adam plunged us into spiritual death. We are created anew in Christ Jesus, the second Adam, and he gives us eternal life. We were in Christ from everlasting. We are created anew in Christ by his own power.

Here is hope for poor sinners. Salvation is not a matter of works. It is a divine creation, and no one is beyond the creative power of God.

The blessed object

Second, look at the blessed object of God's new creation. What is the purpose or object of our creation? Our text spells it out plainly, 'We are his workmanship, created in Christ Jesus unto good works, which God hath before ordained that we should walk in them'. We were not created because of good works, but unto good works!

When Adam was created, God made him for his own glory. This was and is the chief end of man. How was Adam to glorify God? The Lord put Adam in the garden 'to dress it and keep it'.

When God creates his elect anew in Christ Jesus, it is to the end that we may glorify him by good works. We are placed in the garden of the Lord and it is ours to dress and keep it. To you the great Father says, 'Son, go work today in my vineyard.' Now what are those good works which we are to perform? We are to perform works of love. Our works are regulated by love to God. Our works are to be works of love to man.

We are to perform works of faith. Faith is to characterise and motivate our actions in our homes, workplaces, churches, travel and interactions with those around us. A good work is a work of faith, done for Christ, motivated by love and gratitude (Mark 14:3-9). 'Whatsoever ye do in word or deed, do all in the name of the Lord Jesus' (Colossians 3:17).

How can we perform these works of love and faith? We must be enabled by Christ's presence and follow Christ's example. Our Lord Jesus Christ gave us a plain example of the work of love in John 13 when he washed the disciples' feet. He was tender and kind. He was longsuffering and patient. He was forgiving. He sought the good of others at great self-sacrifice. Whatever Christ did he did in faith, with an eye to his Father's glory and upon his Father's promise. We must do so, too. 'Whatsoever is not of faith is sin' (Romans 14:23).

Our text says we are to walk in good works. God has ordained this to be the habit of our lives, not just an occasional gesture.

The beneficial ordination

Third, we have the beneficial ordination. 'Which God hath before ordained that ye should walk in them.' God has not only decreed our salvation, he has also ordained that his people be a holy people, zealous of good works. Godliness is the purpose of divine predestination, it is the design of Christ's redemptive sacrifice (Titus 2:11-14).

If God has ordained that you be a new creature he has also ordained that you live as a new creature; prayerful, godly, sanctified and upright. Godliness does not consist in outward things. 'For the kingdom of God is not meat and drink; but righteousness, and peace, and joy in the Holy Ghost. For he that in these things serveth Christ is acceptable to God, and approved of men. Let us therefore follow after the things which make for peace, and things wherewith one may edify another' (Romans 14:17-19). The fruit of the Spirit is love, joy and peace toward

God. It is longsuffering, gentleness and goodness toward man. It is faith, meekness, and temperance in our own hearts.

God has personally prepared every Christian for good works. If the Lord God makes a bird to fly it is the best flying machine possible. If God makes a worm to turn the soil, nothing can better it. When God makes a Christian he equips him with the presence and power of Christ to walk in good works. God has not only prepared you for his work, he has also prepared the work for you. God prepares the man for the hour and the hour for the man.

Children of God, labour today in the Master's vineyard, for 'the night cometh, when no man can work' (John 9:4). Soon, very soon, our day of work will end. Then we shall shine forth as 'his workmanship' and as God's masterpieces.

Chapter 28

'Good Works'

For we are his workmanship, created in Christ Jesus unto good works, which God hath before ordained that we should walk in them.

(Ephesians 2:10)

We know that faith works by love and that all who are in Christ Jesus are admonished to be 'careful to maintain good works'. James tells us that true, saving faith in the Lord Jesus Christ is faith that is demonstrated and shown by good works. Here, in Ephesians 2:10, God the Holy Spirit tells us that all who are born of God are 'His workmanship, created in Christ Jesus unto good works, which God hath before ordained that we should walk in them'. If God has ordained that all who are new creatures in Christ walk in good works, then all who are new creatures in Christ Jesus shall and do walk in good works.

Know three things

1. Salvation is by grace alone. God's grace in Christ is free, sovereign, unconditional, eternal and unchangeable. Grace planned our salvation and provided us with a Redeemer who purchased our pardon with his blood. Christ produced life in us by his Spirit, preserves us in life and faith and will present us faultless before the presence of God's glory in eternity. 'By grace ye are saved.' Grace cannot be resisted and cannot be frustrated. It is always effectual. God's grace is not, in any way, determined by or dependent upon the will, works and worth of the sinner. Grace is free!

2. Good works have nothing whatever to do with the accomplishment, preservation or consummation of our salvation in Christ. Neither our election nor our redemption, neither our calling nor our sanctification, neither our preservation, nor our glorification are determined by our works. The moment you make room for works you push grace out. If you attempt to win, enlarge or maintain God's favour by your works you 'are fallen from grace', you have departed from the gospel of the grace of God and 'Christ shall profit you nothing'. Any mixture of works with grace is not salvation, but damnation.

3. All who are saved by grace walk in good works. Though we are sinners still, though sin is mixed with and mars everything we think and do so that our best works of righteousness are filthy rags, nevertheless, believers are men and women of good works. They carefully strive to maintain such works on earth that glorify God our Saviour. Believers are motivated by gratitude and love to do so, because we are saved by grace.

But what are those good works? Does the Word of God tell us? Churches and religion of every kind and brand – Papist and Baptist, Buddhist and Methodist, Jewish and Mohammedan, Presbyterian and Pentecostal – have long lists of things they try to compel people to do or not do. They call the doing, or not doing, of them 'good works' or even 'works of righteousness'. 'Touch not, taste not, handle not.'

Many people think they are doing good works for God by living austere lives of strict separation from the world. They strictly obey certain, self-imposed rules, or the rules of religious customs and traditions and think they are maintaining good works. Most people think that outward deeds of morality, outward obedience to the law of God, or outward performance of religious duties are good works. Religious people imagine, vainly, that good works are measured by the clothes they wear, what they eat or drink, or refuse to eat or drink. They think it has to do with whether or not they attend movies, sports activities and watch television. Such works impress men but they are not what the Bible calls 'good works'. I know they are not what God is talking about when he speaks of good works in the Word of God. I know that because good works are works of faith. Only people who trust Christ can perform the 'good works' spoken of in our text. All who trust Christ perform those 'good works'. You do not have to be a believer not to smoke, drink, cuss and chew, and not to run with those who do!

So, I ask again, 'What are those good works?' Does the Word of God tell us? Can we open the Book of God and find in this Book certain, specific things, examples of 'good works' that every believer performs and walks in? Can we find such 'good works' only a believer can perform and walk in? Indeed we can. I have searched this Book and have found in it five things, five 'good works' in which believers walk; five things only a believer can do.

Repentance

First, every heaven born soul, every saved sinner, everyone who trusts the Lord Jesus Christ lives in repentance. I have repented. I am repenting. I shall continue to repent. I repent of my sin; what I am. I repent of my sins; the evil I do. I repent of my righteousness.

Repentance is to a believer a state of being. Repentance causes us to come to Christ, confess our sins and seek his grace continually. None but a believer will repent and all true believers do repent.

'Blessed is he whose transgression is forgiven, whose sin is covered. Blessed is the man unto whom the LORD imputeth not iniquity, and in whose spirit there is no guile. When I kept silence, my bones waxed old through my roaring all the day long. For day and night thy hand was heavy upon me: my moisture is turned into the drought of summer. Selah. I acknowledged my sin unto thee, and mine iniquity have I not hid. I said, I will confess my transgressions unto the LORD; and thou forgavest the iniquity of my sin. Selah. For this shall every one that is godly pray unto thee in a time when thou mayest be found: surely in the floods of great waters they shall not come nigh unto him. Thou art my hiding place; thou shalt preserve me from trouble; thou shalt compass me about with songs of deliverance. Selah' (Psalm 32:1-7).

'Have mercy upon me, O God, according to thy lovingkindness: according unto the multitude of thy tender mercies blot out my transgressions. Wash me throughly from mine iniquity, and cleanse me from my sin. For I acknowledge my transgressions: and my sin is ever before me. Against thee, thee only, have I sinned, and done this evil in thy sight: that thou mightest be justified when thou speakest, and be clear when thou judgest. Behold, I was shapen in iniquity; and in sin did my mother conceive me. Behold, thou desirest truth in the inward parts: and in the hidden part thou shalt make me to know wisdom. Purge me with hyssop, and I shall be clean: wash me, and I shall be whiter than snow. Make me to hear joy and gladness; that the bones which thou hast broken may rejoice. Hide thy face from my sins, and blot out all mine iniquities. Create in me a clean heart, O God; and renew a right spirit within me. Cast me not away from thy presence; and take not thy Holy Spirit from me. Restore unto me the joy of thy salvation; and uphold me with thy free spirit. Then will I teach transgressors thy ways; and sinners shall be converted unto thee. Deliver me from bloodguiltiness, O God, thou God of my salvation: and my tongue shall sing aloud of thy righteousness. O Lord, open thou my lips; and my mouth shall shew forth thy praise. For thou desirest not sacrifice; else would I give it: thou delightest not in burnt offering. The sacrifices of God are a broken spirit: a broken and a contrite heart, O God, thou wilt not despise' (Psalm 51:1-17).

'If we confess our sins, he is faithful and just to forgive us our sins, and to cleanse us from all unrighteousness' (1 John 1:9).

Love

Second, every believer walks in love; real love not a sham pretence. Every believer has genuine love for God and his people, not just a showy talk of love. Saving faith is 'faith which worketh by love'. Believers love the Lord Jesus Christ (1 Corinthians 16:22; 1 John 4:19). Believers love God, love his Word, love his law and love his ways. It is easy to say, 'I love the Lord' and sing, 'O how I love Jesus', but the only way love for Christ can be seen is in love for his people. All believers love one another (1 John 3:16-19).

This brotherly love is manifest by very specific deeds. Love provides for its object. Love protects. Love covers weaknesses, flaws and sins. 'Hatred stirreth up strifes: but love covereth all sins' (Proverbs 10:12). Love forgives, forbears and excuses. 'And be ye kind one to another, tenderhearted, forgiving one another, even as God for Christ's sake hath forgiven you. Be ye therefore followers of God, as dear children; And walk in love, as Christ also hath loved us, and hath given himself for us an offering and a sacrifice to God for a sweetsmelling savour' (Ephesians 4:32-5:2).

Submission

Third, faith in Christ teaches the believer to practise submission. Faith is submission to Christ as my Lord, the continual submission of myself to him. Faith in Christ is walking in the Spirit. Walking in the Spirit is walking in submission to God, my Saviour. This submission to Christ as my Lord shows itself in a very practical way. I submit my will to his will. I submit myself to his Word; his doctrine and ordinances.

This submission to Christ as my Lord shows itself in a very practical way. Believing children submit to their parents. Believing wives submit to their husbands. Believing men submit to God-ordained authority. Believers submit to God's servants (Hebrews 13:7, 17). Submission for believers is a way of life.

Perseverance

Fourth, believers, that is, people who trust Christ alone as their Lord and Saviour, persevere to the end. All believers do and only believers do. 'He that endureth to the end shall be saved' (Matthew 10:22). 'The righteous also shall hold on his way, and he that hath clean hands shall be stronger and stronger' (Job 17:9). 'They went out from us, but they were not of us; for if they had been of us, they would no doubt have continued with us: but they went out, that they might be made manifest that they were not all of us' (1 John 2:19). 'Now the just shall live by faith: but if any man draw back, my soul shall have no pleasure in him. But we are not of them who draw back unto perdition; but of them that believe to the saving of the soul' (Hebrews 10:38, 39).

What are the good works which all true believers perform and walk in all the days of their lives? Repentance, love, submission, perseverance and worship.

Worship

Fifth, all believers, all who are born of God and are taught of God worship him in Spirit and in truth. 'For we are the circumcision, which worship God in the spirit, and rejoice in Christ Jesus, and have no confidence in the flesh' (Philippians 3:3). 'But the hour cometh, and now is, when the true worshippers shall worship the Father in spirit and in truth: for the Father seeketh such to worship him. God is a Spirit: and they that worship him must worship him in spirit and in truth' (John 4:23, 24). All who are born of God, all believers, live before God in repentance. They walk in love. They submit to God and to one another. They persevere in the faith and continue in the grace of God. They worship God.

One example

In Mark 14 we have an example of all five of these things in something our Saviour calls 'a good work'.

'After two days was the feast of the passover, and of unleavened bread: and the chief priests and the scribes sought how they might take him by craft, and put him to death. But they said, Not on the feast day, lest there be an uproar of the people. And being in Bethany in the house of Simon the leper, as he sat at meat, there came a woman having an alabaster box of ointment of spikenard very precious; and she brake the box, and poured it on his head. And there were some that had indignation within themselves, and said, Why was this waste of the ointment made? For it might have been sold for more than three hundred pence, and have been given to the poor. And they murmured against her. And Jesus said, Let her alone; why trouble ye her? She hath wrought a good work on me. For ye have the poor with you always, and whensoever ye will ye may do them good: but me ye have not always. She hath done what she could: she is come aforehand to anoint my body to the burying. Verily I say unto you, Wheresoever this gospel shall be preached throughout the whole world, this also that she hath done shall be spoken of for a memorial of her' (Mark 14:1-9).

Our Lord said, 'She hath done a good work'. How marvellous and great is this praise coming from the lips of the Son of God! We read of no other work done by a human being on this earth called by the Son of God 'a good work'. It was a work of faith, a work of gratitude, a work of love, a work for Christ alone, and a work she could do. 'She hath done what she could.'

Chapter 29

Grace Alone

And you hath he quickened, who were dead in trespasses and sins; Wherein in time past ye walked according to the course of this world, according to the prince of the power of the air, the spirit that now worketh in the children of disobedience: Among whom also we all had our conversation in times past in the lusts of our flesh, fulfilling the desires of the flesh and of the mind; and were by nature the children of wrath, even as others. But God, who is rich in mercy, for his great love wherewith he loved us, Even when we were dead in sins, hath quickened us together with Christ, (by grace ye are saved;) … For by grace are ye saved through faith; and that not of yourselves: it is the gift of God: Not of works, lest any man should boast … Now therefore ye are no more strangers and foreigners, but fellowcitizens with the saints, and of the household of God; And are built upon the foundation of the apostles and prophets, Jesus Christ himself being the chief corner stone; In whom all the building fitly framed together groweth unto an holy temple in the Lord: In whom ye also are builded together for an habitation of God through the Spirit.

(Ephesians 2:1-22)

Grace, what a wonderful word! The Greek word for grace is beautifully meaningful. It refers to that indescribable something that causes one to love someone; that which causes one person to be attracted to another. It is very near the word love. In some instances the Greeks would use the word grace to refer to a burst of generosity that would bestow a lavish gift, unmerited, without the thought of reward or return of kindness. The Apostles took this word, beautiful as it was, and made it even more so. They exalted it to heavenly use. They used the word grace to describe the love and mercy of God in Jesus Christ for his people.

Grace originally referred to a gift. Then it referred to the forgiveness of a debt. If a man could not pay his debt and the lender freely forgave the debtor it would be out of grace. Finally, grace came to refer to the mercy of God in forgiving us and saving us. This is the way God saves sinners. 'Noah found grace in the eyes of the LORD.' 'By grace ye are saved.' All of us were perishing like the falling leaves of autumn; but God in his goodness and mercy saved us. He did it by grace alone.

Because God is gracious, sinners are welcome at the throne of grace. Because God is abounding in infinite love, he forgives us. His mercy endures forever. Therefore we are not destroyed. It is because of God's marvellous and majestic grace that we are saved. Grace is in God. Paul insisted that salvation is altogether a matter of grace throughout his writings. Above all other truths, he wanted this truth to grasp our hearts. He stated it twice in this chapter. He stated it both positively and negatively. 'By grace are ye saved through faith; and that not of yourselves: it is the gift of God: not of works, lest any man should boast.' Salvation is something God has done for us by grace alone. It is delivered to us as a gift of love and mercy.

> Grace! 'Tis a charming sound,
> Harmonious to mine ear,
> Heaven with the echo shall resound,
> And all the earth shall hear.

Criminal doctrine

Children of God, understand this. The criminal doctrine, the damning heresy against which the church of God must contend in all ages, especially in this day of antichrist darkness, is salvation by works. The great opponent to the truth as it is in Jesus Christ is the pride of the human heart that convinces man that he can, at least in part, be his own Saviour. This error is the mother of all heresies. It is the universal doctrine of Babylon. It is through this falsehood that the pure stream of truth has been polluted. It is my firm conviction that 'grace alone' must be our relentless message to this generation. 'By grace ye are saved.' Departure from this message is the root of all religious error, the cause of all heresy.

In all times, when this doctrine has been obscured, the church has either become heretical or Laodicean. She has either held some dangerous and damnable heresy, or she has held the gospel of God with such feeble hands that she has lost her power and her enemies have prevailed over her, like the Philistines over Israel. The mightiest men of all ages in the history of Christ's church, those who have done the most good for God's kingdom and the world at large, have been those who made 'grace alone' their message.

In Augustine's day, there had been a grievous falling away from the simplicity of the gospel. God raised up this man to preach the glorious truth of salvation by grace to his generation. If men had heard his voice, the great heresy of Rome would have been stayed, at least for a while. Popery would have been an impossibility. Later, when Romanism had become very strong, the Lord raised up Martin Luther who taught this great central truth of Christianity, that sinners are justified by faith rather than by works. After Luther came another distinguished teacher of the doctrine of grace, John Calvin. Calvin was even more clearly instructed in the gospel of grace than Luther. He pushed the grand doctrine of the gospel to its proper consequences.

Calvin preached this great staple doctrine, the message of Ephesians, the message of Scripture, 'By grace ye are saved'. It is common in these days to call preachers who dwell mainly on this doctrine, 'Calvinists'. We accept that title gladly. It indicates that our message is the message of grace. We assert again and again that the truth Calvin preached was the thunderous message of Augustine, before him. More importantly, this is the message Paul preached and the message our Lord Jesus preached. The gospel of God is the gospel of 'grace alone'.

We desire to preach the truth, the whole truth, and nothing but the truth. Therefore, we proclaim salvation by grace alone. 'By grace ye are saved.' In doing so we keep the best of company. John Knox preached this message throughout Scotland. In England God had his voices of truth as well. There was the mighty Dr John Gill, Benjamin Keach, John Rippon, John Bunyan, Philip Doddridge, Augustus Toplady and Charles Spurgeon. In America, who can deny that God wrought wonders in his kingdom as Jonathan Edwards and George Whitfield carried the message of grace into our open fields?

But we are not the followers of mere men. We hold dearly those doctrines revealed in Scripture that these men, and many others, have boldly proclaimed. 'Grace alone' was the grand message of the church in days of old when it declared, 'By grace ye are saved', and it is to this truth the church must return if we are to stem the tide of heresy and shake the earth again. God give us men who will not be ashamed to declare to all men; rich and poor, black and white, learned and unlearned, 'By grace ye are saved'.

Salvation is altogether a work of God's grace. That is the doctrine of this Book, the doctrine of this epistle, the doctrine of this chapter. 'Grace alone' is the message of the gospel.

Grace alone

I intend to drive this nail until my hammer is worn out. Like Jephthah of old, I have lifted my hand to God and I cannot go back. Salvation is by grace alone! 'Salvation is of the LORD.' From start to finish salvation is by the grace of God alone. There is no part of salvation which is, even in the slightest degree, dependent upon or determined by, the will of man or the works of the flesh.

Election is the free eternal choice of God's sovereign grace to save some of Adam's race without any consideration of personal merit, potential merit, or pre-known merit (Romans 9:11-13; 2 Thessalonians 2:13, 14).

Redemption is the particular, effectual ransom of God's elect out from under the curse of the law by the death of Christ (Isaiah 53:8; Galatians 3:13; Hebrews 9:12). Man does nothing to make redemption complete or effectual.

Justification is God making sinners the very righteousness of God in Christ, without works (Romans 4:3-5). We are made 'the righteousness of God' without doing anything righteous, just as Christ was 'made sin for us' without ever committing sin (2 Corinthians 5:21; Romans 5:19).

Regeneration is the spiritual resurrection of dead sinners to life in Christ (John 5:25; Revelation 20:6). The dead sinner does nothing to make himself live! Repentance, faith and conversion are the results of the new birth, not its cause.

Sanctification is holiness imparted to the child of God in regeneration. The holy seed implanted, the holy nature created in us bears fruit unto God, not by the energy of the flesh, but by the power of the Spirit (1 John 3:9, 10).

Perseverance is the believer's continuation in grace. It is necessary but it is not our work. It is the work of Christ who gives us eternal life, holds us in his hand and will not let us go (John 10:27-29).

Heaven is the reward of righteousness, bestowed upon those who merit eternal glory by being 'in Christ'. It is given to men and women, in all its blessed fulness, not by anything we do, have done or can do, but by the blood and righteousness of Christ freely bestowed upon us in saving grace (Colossians 1:12).

To make any part of salvation dependent on works is to deny the grace of God altogether and trample underfoot the precious blood of Christ (Galatians 5:1-4).

Why?

Why is God gracious to us? Our text teaches us God is gracious to sinners. But what is the cause of his grace? Certainly, the cause is not to be found in us (Isaiah 1:2-6).

The very mention of the word grace destroys all supposed human merit. There was no beauty in us. There was no goodness in us. There was no wisdom in us. There was no power in us. There was no inclination to anything good in us.

It is obvious to everyone who reads his Bible that fallen man has nothing in him or about him to attract God's mercy and grace. Therefore, the cause of his grace must be something outside of us.

God is gracious to us because he loves us (Ephesians 2:4; Jeremiah 31:3). God loved us eternally (Ephesians 1:4). God loved us particularly (Romans 9:13). God loved us perfectly. God loved us freely. God loved us graciously. He gave us his Son because he loved us (1 John 4:9, 10; John 3:16). He adopted us as his sons because he loved us (1 John 3:1). He gave us his grace because he loved us (2 Timothy 1:9). He gave us himself because he loved us (1 John 3:16). He is gracious to us simply because he delights to show us grace (Romans 9:11-18).

Message of grace

What does the gospel of grace proclaim? What is the message of grace? You will observe that Paul addresses certain people to whom he says, 'Ye are saved'. He does not say, 'Ye shall be saved,' or 'Ye hope to be saved'. He speaks to them as people already saved. Now, there are no people upon the face of the earth to whom it can be said, 'Ye are saved', unless it can also be said of them, 'Ye are saved by grace'. I see two things in this.

First, the Apostle speaks of a present salvation. The gospel of grace proclaims a present salvation to all who trust Christ. He speaks not of people who would be saved when they died, or who hoped to be saved in some future state. Paul addresses those who are saved, who had salvation in their possession. It does not honour Christ for his people always to doubt their salvation. A present salvation cannot consistently be preached by those who hold to a system of salvation by works. No works-monger can claim a present salvation. The Arminian claims he is saved but he does not know whether he will be saved tomorrow or not. A present salvation can be proclaimed only by a gospel which proclaims, 'By grace are ye saved'.

The gospel of grace proclaims that salvation in all its fulness, all its riches, all its length and breadth, depth and height, is a present reality to be enjoyed now.

God's law is now silenced. My sins are now pardoned. I am now justified. I am now God's son. Augustus Toplady understood this when he wrote,

> The terrors of the law, and of God,
> With me can have nothing to do;
> My Saviour's obedience and blood
> Hide all my transgressions from view.
>
> My name from the palms of His hands
> Eternity will not erase;
> Impressed on His heart it remains
> In marks of indelible grace.
>
> Yes, I to the end shall endure,
> As sure as the earnest is given;
> More happy, but not more secure,
> The glorified spirits in heaven.

Second, the gospel of grace proclaims a perfect salvation (Hebrews 7:25). We teach that the moment a man believes in Christ, he is completely and perfectly saved. He is not put into a salvable state. He is not half saved. He is not in danger of being lost. He is saved and saved perfectly. I truly believe that though the saints in heaven have received the ultimate crown of salvation, they are not more perfectly saved than the poorest sinner on earth who believes in Christ. 'Giving thanks unto the Father, which hath made us meet to be partakers of the inheritance of the saints in light' (Colossians 1:12). 'For in him dwelleth all the fulness of the Godhead bodily. And ye are complete in him, which is the head of all principality and power' (Colossians 2:9, 10).

Our salvation was completely accomplished when our triumphant Saviour cried, 'It is finished'. He finished a perfect obedience to God for us. He endured the penalty of the law for us. He washed away our sins. He reconciled God to us.

When a man receives Christ as Saviour, God gives him a perfect salvation. The good news of heaven is not 'Christ can save'. It is 'Christ has saved'. We are accepted in the Beloved. We are righteous. We are secure (John 4:14; 10:28-30). We are complete in Christ.

Only the gospel of grace can proclaim salvation as a present reality. The legalist cannot make this claim. The ritualist cannot make this claim. The Roman Catholic cannot make this claim. The Arminian cannot make this claim.

But the gospel of grace enables the child of God to claim with confidence, 'I know whom I have believed, and am persuaded that he is able to keep that which I have committed unto him against that day'.

Still, there is more. The gospel of God, the gospel of the grace of God, proclaims an eternal salvation. The salvation proclaimed by the preaching of grace alone is salvation finished from the foundation of the world (Romans 8:28-30; Ephesians 1:2-6; 2 Timothy 1:9, 10; Hebrews 4:3).

The meaning of grace

What does grace mean as it is used in the Scriptures? Lewis Sperry Chafer said, 'When used in the Bible to set forth the grace of God in the salvation of sinners, the word 'grace' discloses not only the boundless goodness of God and his kindness toward man, but reaches far beyond and indicates the supreme motive which actuated God in the creation, preservation, and consummation of the universe ... It is nothing less than the unlimited love of God expressing itself in measureless grace'.

Grace is the good favour of God. There is nothing in us that could ever merit God's esteem or give him such delight as to lead him to bestow upon us the blessings of eternal salvation. If we ask why any individuals are rescued from the ruins of the fall and enabled to believe in Christ, the only answer is, 'Even so, Father: for so it seemed good in thy sight' (Matthew 11:26). We were not saved because of our talents. We were not saved because of our wealth. We were not saved because of our good character. We were not saved because of the excellence of our disposition. There is much in us to repel God, but nothing to attract him.

Grace is the marvellous operation of God. It was God who gave us our first holy desire. It was God who made us willing to hear the gospel. It was God who gave us faith. It was God who gave us repentance. It was God who gave us life. I will go yet further and say that if God brought us within one foot of the gates of heaven and left it for us to enter in, we would all surely perish.

Someone may say, 'Is it not man's duty to repent and believe the gospel'. I reply, 'Yes, indeed it is'. But I am not talking about man's duty, I'm talking about his ability. If the poor beggar owes the local grocery store a thousand dollars, it is his duty to pay, but he doesn't have the ability. It is our duty to repent and believe, but we have no power. But here is the glory of God's grace. He gives us repentance and faith. Grace is the sovereign prerogative of God. He says, 'I ... will be gracious to whom I will be gracious'. Grace alone preserves us to life everlasting. Grace alone gives us eternal glory.

Inferences

What inferences may be drawn from the doctrine of grace? If we are saved by grace we should be humble. If we are saved by grace we should have great compassion on those who are not saved.

John Newton wrote, 'A Calvinist who gets angry with the ungodly is inconsistent with his profession. He knows that no man can receive this doctrine except by the grace of God; so, if God has not given these men the grace to receive this doctrine, rather pray for them than get angry with them, and ask that they may receive the truth in which your soul delights.'

If we are saved by grace, then nothing should bring us discomfort. Are you afflicted? You are saved by grace. Are you poor? You are saved by grace. Are you neglected and despised? You are saved by grace. Are you sick? You are saved by grace.

If we are saved by grace, we should be utterly devoted to him who saved us by his grace. The headstone of God's spiritual temple shall be brought forth with shoutings, crying, 'Grace, grace unto it'. Let us now begin the heavenly shout. 'Grace, grace unto it!' 'Grace, grace unto it!' John Newton, again, wrote,

Amazing grace! How sweet the sound
That saved a wretch like me!
I once was lost, but now I'm found –
Was blind, but now I see.

When we've been there ten thousand years,
Bright shining as the sun,
We've no less days to sing God's praise,
Than when we first begun!

Chapter 30

'One Body'

Wherefore remember, that ye being in time past Gentiles in the flesh, who are called Uncircumcision by that which is called the Circumcision in the flesh made by hands; That at that time ye were without Christ, being aliens from the commonwealth of Israel, and strangers from the covenants of promise, having no hope, and without God in the world: But now in Christ Jesus ye who sometimes were far off are made nigh by the blood of Christ. For he is our peace, who hath made both one, and hath broken down the middle wall of partition between us; Having abolished in his flesh the enmity, even the law of commandments contained in ordinances; for to make in himself of twain one new man, so making peace; And that he might reconcile both unto God in one body by the cross, having slain the enmity thereby: And came and preached peace to you which were afar off, and to them that were nigh. For through him we both have access by one Spirit unto the Father. Now therefore ye are no more strangers and foreigners, but fellowcitizens with the saints, and of the household of God; And are built upon the foundation of the apostles and prophets, Jesus Christ himself being the chief corner stone; In whom all the building fitly framed together groweth unto an holy temple in the Lord: In whom ye also are builded together for an habitation of God through the Spirit.

(Ephesians 2:11-22)

All of God's elect are one with Christ; eternally one, mystically one and vitally one. In Christ all God's elect are one in Christ, 'One body'.

God's church, His family on earth,
Though by the world unknown,
Are people of a heavenly birth,
And in our Saviour one.

Our Father is the God above,
The Sovereign on His throne.
And Christ, our Brother-King, in love,
He claims us as His own!

Indwelt by God the Spirit we
Are one in faith and love,
And one with Christ eternally,
Our home – Heaven above!

Oh, let us keep the unity,
The blessed bond of peace,
A loving, caring family, —
All sinners saved by grace!

Christ's delight

Our Lord Jesus Christ delights to see his people walking together as one spiritual body. One reason for his death at Calvary was that he might reconcile all his elect to one another in one body. He came to this earth as the Good Shepherd in order to gather his sheep into one fold. His desire for his church was very plainly expressed in his high priestly prayer for her, just before his death. 'Neither pray I for these alone, but for them also which shall believe on me through their word; that they all may be one … I in them, and thou in me, that they may be made perfect in one'.

Oh, how it must grieve the Spirit of God, how it must grieve the Son of God to behold the church splits, denominational divisions, strife and carnal schisms that are prevalent in his church today.

I wish we could truly learn, in a practical way, by the grace of God, that all true believers are 'one body in Christ'. We are all members of one church universal. We are all of the same royal family. We have one elder Brother. We have one heavenly Father. We are all redeemed by one sacrifice. We all have one Head. We live by one Spirit and in one Spirit. We are all members of one spiritual body. We have one hope. We have one name. We have one inheritance.

It is my soul's desire to promote the spiritual unity of God's church and kingdom. Any who know me know I have no intention of denying my baptism, nor my Baptist heritage. Certainly, I must and am determined to continue to uphold the great doctrines of the gospel commonly known as Calvinism. I must denounce as heresy any rival doctrine. Yet, I am bound under God, and by the love of Christ, to regard and treat as brethren all who confess Jesus Christ alone as their Saviour and Lord, trusting the Son of God as their only hope for heaven. I must let nothing divide me from any of my brethren.

Church universal and local

This must be our attitude universally but it must also be our attitude in the local assembly. We all are members one of another. We all profess the same faith. We all have been baptised with the same baptism. Let all who long to walk in obedience to Christ and honour him walk in love with one another! So long as anyone professes faith in Christ he is to be embraced as my brother and shown the same love Christ has shown me.

We can do nothing about the attitude and conduct of others. We are not responsible for another person's actions and attitude. But we are responsible for our own. The commandment of Christ is that you 'love your enemies'. Do good to those that abuse you. 'Pray for them that despitefully use you.' When you do, you will find peace in your soul and you will lead others in the way of peace. If that is how we are to treat our enemies, how much more our brothers and sisters in Christ.

One body

Our text teaches us that all of God's people, whether Jew or Gentile, male or female, black or while, rich or poor, learned or unlearned, are 'one body in Christ'.

> The church's one Foundation
> Is Jesus Christ our Lord;
> She is His new creation,
> By water and the Word;
> From heaven He came and sought her,
> To be His holy bride;
> With His own blood He bought her,
> And for her life He died.

Elect from every nation,
Yet one o'er all the earth,
Her charter of salvation,
One Lord, one faith, one birth;
One holy name she blesses,
Partakes one holy food,
And to one hope she presses,
With every grace endued.

Though with a scornful wonder,
Men see her sore oppressed,
By schisms rent asunder,
By heresies distressed,
Yet, saints their watch are keeping,
Their cry goes up, 'How long?'
And soon the night of weeping,
Shall be the morn of song.

Mid toil and tribulation,
And tumult of her wars,
She waits the consummation
Of peace forever more;
'Til with the vision glorious
Her longing eyes are blest,
And the great church victorious
Shall be the church at rest.

Yet she on earth hath union,
With God the Three in One,
And mystic sweet communion,
With those whose rest is won.
O happy ones and holy!
Lord, give us grace that we,
Like them the meek and lowly,
On high may dwell with Thee.

All true believers are 'one body in Christ', through the blood of his cross. It is our duty and privilege to live and serve him as one.

The church of Jesus Christ is not a building made of wood and stone. It is not a denomination. It is all of God's elect; redeemed by the blood of Christ and called by God the Holy Spirit.

I see three things in this portion of Holy Scripture.

Our sorrowful past

First, because all division in Christ's kingdom is caused by pride, Paul begins by once again stripping us of all grounds for human pride. He would have us to remember what we were in times past. Nothing helps us to overcome our pride and nothing inspires sympathy like the remembrance of our past. What a sad, sorrowful past it is we are here called to remember.

We were members of a divided race (v. 11). 'Wherefore remember, that ye being in time past Gentiles in the flesh, who are called Uncircumcision by that which is called the Circumcision in the flesh made by hands.' Since the tower of Babel, all the human race has been divided and at war. Division is the curse of the earth. Unity is the mark of the new creation.

Our divisions are manifest in many ways, but the root and essence of them all is pride. The Jew despises the Gentile. The rich despise the poor. The white despise the black. The black despise the white. The learned despise the unlearned. The unlearned despise the learned.

We were desperately and hopelessly ruined (v. 12). 'That at that time ye were without Christ, being aliens from the commonwealth of Israel, and strangers from the covenants of promise, having no hope, and without God in the world'. God created a perfect race in our father Adam and blessed him with all things needful. But, through sin, the human race was ruined. Notice how Paul describes our ruin and poverty by nature.

1. We were without Christ. This does not mean that before conversion Christ had never been gracious to us (Ephesians 1:3, 4). Yet, though loved of God and redeemed by the blood of Christ, though blessed of God and accepted in the Beloved from everlasting, before God saved us, we were without Christ. What does that mean? What does it mean to be without Christ? We were without righteousness. We were without forgiveness. We were without peace. We were without favour. We were without strength. We were dead in trespasses and sins.

2. We were aliens from the commonwealth of Israel. This cannot mean that we had no part in the Jewish race; for even after conversion we are not made Jews in

a physical sense. Paul means we had no part with the people of God, 'The Israel of God'. We were opposed to God's people. We had no inheritance with God's people. We had none of the privileges of God's people.

3. We were strangers to the covenants of promise. Here Paul has reference to the covenant of grace. He speaks of it in the plural because it was reaffirmed from patriarch to patriarch, and from generation to generation. We were strangers to the blessings and promises of God's covenant.

4. We were without hope. In Adam we lost all hope. We were without the hope of life and filled with fear and despair, filled with a sense of dread; dreading death, dreading judgment, dreading eternity.

5. We were without God in the world. Paul does not say that we were abandoned by God for God had not cast off his elect. Paul's meaning is we were among the mass of fallen, sin-laden, lost, doomed and damned mankind. Being of that race, we were Godless. We had no knowledge of God. We had no desire for God. Everything in us was opposed to God.

But now, in Christ Jesus, we are divinely reconciled (v. 13). 'But now in Christ Jesus ye who sometimes were far off are made nigh by the blood of Christ'. Now we are in Christ, by a living experience of faith. Now we who were far off from God and the blessings of God are brought near to him. Now we are drawn nigh and reconciled to God by the blood of our Lord Jesus Christ.

Our Saviour's performance

Second, in the next verses Paul describes how we were made nigh by the blood of Christ. He calls for us to remember our past, to remember what the Lord Jesus Christ has done for us.

Christ is our peace. He is our peace with God. He has reconciled us to God. Christ is the peace of our own hearts. He gives us peace by giving us faith in himself. He speaks peace to our hearts. He gives us a peaceful confidence in God's goodness. He gives us a peaceful rest in God's promises. He gives us peace with God's providence.

Our Lord Jesus Christ gives us peace one with another. He has made all true believers one in himself. He has made us one body through the cross. 'For he is our peace, who hath made both one, and hath broken down the middle wall of partition between us; Having abolished in his flesh the enmity, even the law of commandments contained in ordinances; for to make in himself of twain one new man, so making peace; And that he might reconcile both unto God in one body by the cross, having slain the enmity thereby' (vv. 14-16).

He has broken down the wall that separated us. This refers to the ceremonies of the law which divide the Jew and Gentile. In the new creation of grace, Christ has destroyed all walls of separation; walls of religious prejudice, walls of racial prejudice, walls of social prejudice, walls of political prejudice.

The Lord Jesus Christ has broken down the wall that separated us from God by his death at Calvary, 'having abolished in his flesh the enmity, even the law of commandments'. He has broken down the wall of divine justice against us. He has broken down the wall of our sins.

All who are redeemed by the blood of Christ are one in him. Christ has made us one body through the gospel. 'And came and preached peace to you which were afar off, and to them that were nigh' (v. 17).

When our Lord Jesus Christ died at Calvary, he accomplished our peace with God. In him we were fully justified. In him we were perfectly reconciled.

Now, by the preaching of the gospel, he comes to us, both Jew and Gentile, and proclaims peace by his blood. He does this through his word. He does this by the Spirit in our hearts.

Christ has made us one body by the mighty operations of his grace in the new birth. 'For through him we both have access by one Spirit unto the Father' (v. 18). In due time he sends the Spirit of adoption into our hearts. We all have the same Spirit. All who are born of God live by the Spirit, live in the Spirit and have the Spirit of God living in them. We all come to God in the same way. By faith in Christ. We all have liberty as sons in Christ.

Then, in verses 19-22 the Holy Spirit shows us some of …

Our satisfying privileges

Third, behold the great, soul-satisfying privileges of grace that are ours as one body in Christ. We are Christ's new creation. We are his church, his kingdom, his spiritual Israel, his heavenly Jerusalem. All grace is ours through his cross. Here Paul shows us the blessed results of us being 'one body in Christ'.

We have a satisfying fellowship. 'Now therefore ye are no more strangers and foreigners, but fellowcitizens with the saints, and of the household of God' (v. 19). We are one with all of God's people. Christ is ours. We are made partakers of the divine covenant. All the promises of God in Christ Jesus are to us yea and amen. We have a blessed and sure hope. We have God and all that is his! God's love is mine. God's grace is mine. God's power is mine. God's wisdom is mine. God's holiness is mine. God's justice is mine. God's world is mine.

We have a sure Foundation (v. 20). 'And are built upon the foundation of the apostles and prophets, Jesus Christ himself being the chief corner stone.' Our Foundation is the doctrine of the apostles and prophets, and their doctrine is the doctrine of the gospel; ruin by the Fall, redemption by the blood, regeneration by the Holy Ghost.

We have the same Foundation as the apostles and prophets. The Foundation of the prophets was Christ alone. The Foundation of the apostles was Christ alone. The Foundation of the church is Christ alone (Isaiah 28:16). Christ is the Foundation upon which we are built. Christ is the Foundation that joins the walls of his church. Christ is the chief, or pre-eminent, Cornerstone of his church. Christ is the tried Foundation. Christ is the sure Foundation.

We have a spiritual formation, being fitly framed together. ' In whom all the building fitly framed together groweth unto an holy temple in the Lord' (v. 21). God the Holy Spirit graciously forms and fits every member of Christ's church in its proper place.

We are God's holy temple. The temple is not yet complete. But John gave us a picture of the church and temple of God when it will be finished. It will be a city four square and fully inhabited, 24 seats and 24 elders around the throne, 144,000 saints. In the midst of it is the glory of God and of the Lamb!

We have a splendorous future (v. 22). 'In whom ye also are builded together for an habitation of God through the Spirit.' What can be more blessed than to dwell in God's house, with God's people, 'an habitation of God through the Spirit'?

God's church shall be made perfect in one. We are the habitation of God. Soon, we shall be complete in the Lord. All division will be ended. All strife will be over. Christ will be all.

Children of God, we are one body in Christ. Let us then labour for the unity of God's church and labour together, keeping 'the unity of the Spirit in the bond of peace'.

Chapter 31

Ruin, Reconciliation, Restoration

But now in Christ Jesus ye who sometimes were far off are made nigh by the blood of Christ.

(Ephesians 2:13)

The subject of this text should be precious to every child of God. It speaks of the wondrous grace and condescending love of our heavenly Father. The God of glory, who was justly offended by our sin and rebellion against him, has taken his chosen into a union with himself through the blood of Jesus Christ his Son.

This text is a gate of pearl leading into the excellent glory and everlasting grace of God. Happy is the man, happy is the woman who has entered into blessed union with God through this gate. It turns upon two diamond hinges: 'In Christ Jesus' and 'By the blood of Christ'.

The wonderful privilege that our text speaks of is that we 'are made nigh'. The delightful blessing, however, is ours only 'in Christ Jesus' and 'by the blood of Christ'.

Here is a sea of love, an ocean of boundless peace and a rich fountain of free grace. May God the Holy Ghost, whose words we have before us, open our hearts and refresh our spirits with the sweet consolation of this text. We, who were once separated and far off from God by sin, are now 'made nigh' in Christ Jesus by the sacrifice of his blood. Paul here presents to us three stages of our history:

Ruin

Ephesians 2:13 speaks first of our ruin by the sin and fall of or father Adam. 'Ye who sometimes were far off.' Each of us were by nature far off from God and ruined by sin. We were ruined by a fall; but God did not originally create man in a sinful condition. When Adam was created and placed in the Garden, he had a blessed nearness to God. Adam was created in the very image of God. He was the only being in creation made in the likeness of God. He was given intellect, emotion, and will and thus he was like God. He had a body like that which God had ordained and prepared for his Son when he would come into the world. He was a representative man, like Christ. Adam walked and conversed with God in the Garden. Adam enjoyed the provision of God's hand. Adam enjoyed dominion over God's creatures.

But Adam sinned against God, plunging himself and all his race into a state of separation and alienation from God. Adam was our representative before God, so that we acted in him, and were charged with all his deeds. We were made sinners, made guilty of sin (Romans 5:19). We were judged guilty and condemned (Romans 5:18). We died spiritually (Romans 5:12).

What does this spiritual death involve? We lost God's image. We lost God's favour. We lost all righteousness. We lost our moral freedom. We died spiritually. Man was made body, soul and spirit. When we sinned in Adam, the spirit in man died and man has been, since the fall, body and soul, without spirit. In the new birth we receive the spirit of life and are made whole again; body, soul and spirit (1 Thessalonians 5:23).

Not only were we ruined by the fall of our Father Adam, we were also ruined by birth (Psalms 51:5; 58:3). By birth, fallen man is far off from God. We were without Christ. To be without Christ is to be without life, without righteousness, without pardon, without peace, without light and without understanding.

We were aliens from the commonwealth of Israel. We had no fellowship with God's people and did not share the blessings of God's people. We were strangers to the covenant of promise, without hope, godless and ruined in this world.

There are many who oppose the doctrine of original sin because they do not like being charged with Adam's transgression. But we all have sin enough of our own, for we were also ruined by choice. We sin like all other men. We sinned as children. We sinned as adults. We even sin as believers.

Reconciliation

Second, the Apostle shows us the way of our reconciliation. We are now reconciled to God 'in Christ Jesus' and 'by his blood'.

Children of God, we are made near unto God because we are in Christ Jesus. We have a covenant union with Christ.

We are in our Saviour's heart from eternity. In his heart, the Lord Jesus Christ cherished thoughts of love for his people before the world began. 'I have loved thee with an everlasting love: therefore with loving kindness have I drawn thee' (Jeremiah 31:3). 'As the Father hath loved me, so have I loved you' (John 15:9).

We were all chosen at one time and our names were written in the Book of Life, beneath the name of Christ our great head before the world was made (Revelation 13:8). 'In thy book all my members were written, which in continuance were fashioned, when as yet there were none of them' (Psalm 139:16).

The same register that records Christ's eternal Sonship records our sonship. Destroy his Sonship and yours must perish. But as long as he stands as the Son of God, so must all the elect sons stand.

The name Jesus Christ heads the list in that blessed Book of Life; and until the pen of hell can run through that name, it cannot run through any other.

The Book of Life contains a list of all who shall inherit the celestial city. We are in that book which is sealed with seven seals of perfection and completion, which none but the Lion of the Tribe of Judah has prevailed to open.

We are in Christ's hand as our Surety and Protector. We are in Christ's loins, so that we are in a mystical way one with him.

But I must go a step further. Our text speaks of a real, vital and present union with Christ. All who are in Jesus Christ in the eternal and everlasting Covenant of Grace shall, in due time, be in him by a living union. I know I am in waters over my head. I have no hope of understanding, let alone explaining this union but this I know, we are in his very Person! We are wedded to him. This is a mystical and mysterious union, but it is, nevertheless, real and true. Christ and I are one!

'Twixt Jesus and the chosen race
Subsists a bond of sovereign grace,
That hell, with its infernal train,
Shall never dissolve, nor rend in twain!

Hail sacred union, firm and strong,
How great the grace, how sweet the song,
That worms of earth should ever be,
One with incarnate Deity!

In the moment of regeneration the soul is made alive in union with Christ. This is a living, vital union. Do you have this union? Without it all that I have been talking about is only speculative theory. We are in Christ, like the branch is in the vine. We are in Christ, like the babe is in the womb. We are in Christ, like the brain is in the head, like the heart is in the body!

Are you in Christ Jesus? Does Christ live in you? Is Christ your dependence? Do you believe on the Son of God? Do you bear fruit from Christ? Do you love Christ? Is his presence heaven and his absence hell to your soul? Are you wedded to him by faith and love? Do you feed upon the Lord Jesus Christ?

Happy is that soul who can say by faith, 'Blessed be God! I am one with Christ! I was in his heart, his book, his hands, his loins from eternity. I know that I was, for I am now in him by living union. I know that I am in him because he is in me. And I know that he is in me because I trust him.' Such a soul is happy, satisfied, and secure.

We are made near to God through the blood of Christ. The blood of Christ is the symbol of the covenant and the blood of Christ is the symbol of divine vengeance. The blood of Christ is the satisfaction of the law. The blood of Christ is the putting away of sin. By the blood of his cross the Lord Jesus made peace for us and reconciled us to God (Colossians 1:20-22). We receive that reconciliation by faith in him (Romans 5:1-11) but it was made by Christ at Calvary.

'Therefore if any man be in Christ, he is a new creature: old things are passed away; behold, all things are become new. And all things are of God, who hath reconciled us to himself by Jesus Christ, and hath given to us the ministry of reconciliation; To wit, that God was in Christ, reconciling the world unto himself, not imputing their trespasses unto them; and hath committed unto us the word of reconciliation. Now then we are ambassadors for Christ, as though God did beseech you by us: we pray you in Christ's stead, be ye reconciled to God. For he hath made him to be sin for us, who knew no sin; that we might be made the righteousness of God in him' (2 Corinthians 5:17-21).

Our text tells us that we are nigh to God now! When we stand before God in heaven, we shall not be more near to God than we are now!

Restoration

Third, the Apostle shows us our restoration. 'But now in Christ Jesus ye who sometimes were far off are made nigh by the blood of Christ.' In Christ we are restored to God's image. We are near to God, and restored to God's favour. We are now made righteous. We are now sanctified and made holy. We are near to God. What can that mean? We have Christ. We are members of God's kingdom. We are partakers of the Covenant of Promise and have a sure Hope. We have God himself.

'And the very God of peace sanctify you wholly; and I pray God your whole spirit and soul and body be preserved blameless unto the coming of our Lord Jesus Christ. Faithful is he that calleth you, who also will do it.' Here in 1 Thessalonians 5:23 is the only place in the Word of God where these three words describing the whole man in Christ are used together.

Paul here tells us that the nature of the believer is compounded of spirit, soul and body. The spirit is the immortal part of our being, which by our fall in Adam is dead in trespasses and sins, but by the Holy Ghost, in every child of God, is quickened to a new and spiritual life. Now, being part of Christ it can die no more. It is holy and without blame in Christ forever. The Psalmist speaks of the soul when he tells us that when the breath of man leaves him, he returns to his earth and his thoughts perish (Psalm 146:4). The body, of course, is the mere mass of flesh and bones, this earthly tabernacle that must soon be dissolved.

The spirit, before the new birth, like all the mass of Adam's race, is dead in trespasses and sins. When a sinner is born again by the grace and power of God the Holy Ghost, when we are made partakers of the divine nature by that sovereign act of omnipotent mercy, God gives his elect all things that pertain to life and godliness; and we are made 'partakers of the divine nature' (2 Peter 1:3, 4).

This is what all of that means. Christ makes sinners whole again. He completely restores his lost ones. The new-born babe in Christ is born perfect in all his parts. In respect to the spiritual life imparted to the heaven born soul, he is as holy as it ever can be in heaven, perfectly holy (Hebrews 12:14; 1 John 3:9). That new man created in us by the grace of God is 'created in righteousness and true holiness' (Ephesians 4:24). That new man is 'Christ in you, the hope of glory' (Colossians 1:27). 'Grow it will in grace', wrote Robert Hawker, 'as a new-born child grows in nature. But like a child in nature, it will have no other nature, but the same forever in which it is new-born.'

We are born again, 'not of corruptible seed, but of incorruptible, by the word of God, which liveth and abideth forever' (Peter 1:23). The thinking faculty, our soul, and the body which is only flesh and bones, are not renewed until the resurrection. We groan, anxiously awaiting that blessed day (Romans 7:24; 8:23).

Let us draw near to God continually; by prayer, by praise, through his word, and by feeding upon Christ. Let us live near our God in sweet communion. Let us trust him, love him and seek to know him. If we are now made nigh by the blood of Christ, now in such blessed nearness to God, let us live unto God, let us live for heaven and not for this world! Horatius Bonar wrote,

A mind at perfect peace with God:
Oh, what a word is this!
A sinner reconciled through blood:
This, this indeed is peace.

By nature and by practice far,
How very far from God!
Yet now by grace brought nigh to Him
Through faith in Jesus' blood.

So nigh, so very nigh to God,
I cannot nearer be;
For in the person of His Son,
I am as near as He.

So dear, so very dear to God,
More dear I cannot be;
The love wherewith He loves the Son,
Such is His love to me!

Why should I ever anxious be
Since such a God is mine?
He watches o'er me night and day,
And tells me, 'Mine is thine'.

Chapter 32

'He Is Our Peace'

For he is our peace, who hath made both one, and hath broken down the middle wall of partition *between us.*

(Ephesians 2:14)

'He is our peace.' Those four one syllable words speak volumes, assuring us of that peace God gives his people by Christ Jesus as the result of his redemptive accomplishments as our Mediator. It is clear from this second chapter of Ephesians that God the Holy Ghost intends for us to understand that Jesus Christ is our peace in a threefold sense: he is our peace with God first, then, he is our peace in our own consciences, finally, Christ is our peace with one another.

1. Peace with God

Christ is our peace with God. 'Now in Christ Jesus ye who sometimes were far off are made nigh by the blood of Christ' (Ephesians 2:13). 'And all things are of God, who hath reconciled us to himself by Jesus Christ' (2 Corinthians 5:18).

This peace with God is by the blood-work of our Saviour, the Lord Jesus Christ. More than anything else, the Bible speaks of the blood of Christ obtaining for his elect all the great benefits and blessings that are ours in him. We have been purchased by his blood (Acts 20:28). We have propitiation by his blood (Romans 3:25). We have been justified by his blood (Romans 5:9). We have redemption through his blood (Ephesians 1:7). Our consciences are cleansed by his blood (Hebrews 9:14). We are sanctified through his blood (Hebrews 13:12). Our election is through the sprinkling of his blood (1 Peter 1:2). We are ransomed by his blood (1 Peter 1:18, 19). We have been set free from sin by his blood (Revelation 1:5). We who were afar off have been brought nigh by his blood (Ephesians 2:13). We have peace through his blood (Colossians 1:20).

The precious blood of Christ is central to all we are and all we have as the children of God. His blood was the ransom price of our souls, the price of our redemption and the expiation of our sin. Think much of the blood! Thank God for the blood, the precious, sin-atoning blood of our Lord Jesus Christ. By the shedding of his blood 'he is our peace'. Without the shedding of his blood, there is no remission. Without the shedding of his blood, there is no peace.

The Lord Jesus Christ has torn down the wall that separated his people from God. Now, through his death and resurrection, there is 'peace on earth and good will toward men'. When sin is put away, God has no reason for warfare against us. Christ has put away our sins by the sacrifice of himself; and, therefore, peace is established between God and our souls.

2. Peace in our consciences

God is at peace with us through the blood of Jesus Christ long before he subdues our wills and brings us to enjoy his peace by faith. But thanks be unto God, Jesus Christ does come into our hearts with regenerating power and gives peace to the hearts and consciences of his people. C. H. Spurgeon rightly observed, 'Peace with God is the treaty; peace in the conscience is the publication of it'.

Peace with God is the fountain, peace in the conscience the stream that flows from it. Peace was made in the court of divine justice in heaven when Christ's blood made an atonement for our sins and peace is declared in the heart when he sends forth his Spirit into our hearts crying, 'Abba Father'.

3. Peace with each other

Then, having sealed our peace with God and subdued our hearts in peace toward God, the Lord Jesus Christ binds us to one another with the bonds of love and peace. He brings us into his kingdom of righteousness and peace.

All of this Jesus Christ is. 'He is our peace.' Not only a friend to peace but peace itself. As he is our righteousness, our life and our sanctification, he is our peace. Not only has he brought in everlasting righteousness, he is himself our righteousness. He has not only made and proclaimed peace, he is our peace. Jesus Christ is the peace of all who trust him.

Christ our peace

How is Christ our peace? We have Christ as our peace entirely as a gracious act of almighty God. He has given us his Son as our peace in the covenant of grace and peace. When God made man there was a bond of perfect love and unity between them. God was at peace with man and man was at peace with God. They had sweet fellowship and communion with one another, walking together in the garden. But when Adam sinned, immediately a quarrel began between God and man. Eating the forbidden fruit broke the peace and ever since that day, there has been a quarrel between the creature and the Creator.

It is a mutual quarrel. God is angry with man. 'God judgeth the righteous, and God is angry with the wicked every day. If he turn not, he will whet his sword; he hath bent his bow, and made it ready. He hath also prepared for him the instruments of death; he ordaineth his arrows against the persecutors' (Psalm 7:11-13).

I know that God's elect are eternally accepted in Christ, eternally righteous, holy and sanctified in Christ, eternally justified and eternally reconciled by the blood of the Lamb slain from the foundation of the world; but none know it until they are reconciled to God in the sweet experience of his grace. All are sinners. All have broken God's law. All have earned God's wrath.

All men by nature are opposed to God. We are opposed to his holiness, his sovereignty and his will. We are opposed to his Word and we are opposed to his salvation. Every part of our being is, by nature, enmity against God. 'The carnal mind is enmity against God: for it is not subject to the law of God, neither indeed can be' (Romans 8:7).

Fallen man is God's enemy; hating God, opposed to God, fighting God relentlessly, because fallen man's understanding is darkened. His will is hardened. His heart is wicked. 'For from within, out of the heart of men, proceed evil thoughts, adulteries, fornications, murders, thefts, covetousness, wickedness, deceit, lasciviousness, an evil eye, blasphemy, pride, foolishness: All these evil things come from within, and defile the man' (Mark 7:21-23).

This quarrel between God and man is a growing quarrel. It increases day by day as we pursue our lusts, rebellion and practise sin against him. On God's part this quarrel is righteous. He has every reason to be angry and offended with us. Our sins are debts. We are indebted to God and we have nothing with which to pay off our debts. Our sins are trespasses against God's law and we cannot repair it. We have broken every commandment many times. We have robbed God of his glory and despised his Son.

Our sin is treason against the crown rights and dignity of the King of heaven. Did you ever wonder why it is our Saviour said that when he sends his Spirit in grace the very first thing he does is convince the heaven-born sinner of sin 'because they believe not on me'? The essence of all sin is the despising of Christ, the Son of God, the King of heaven. We despise his righteousness, his sacrifice, his salvation and his dominion and authority as Lord.

Christ the Mediator

Unless this quarrel is taken up by someone who can settle it, it will be an everlasting quarrel. When there are feuds between men they may last a lifetime but death puts an end to them. Not this quarrel. Death brings the sinner to an endless state of misery and torment where he will eternally wax worse and worse in his hatred of God, cursing and blaspheming his name. God will eternally go on hating and punishing him.

In reference to this quarrel between God and men, Jesus Christ is our peace. He stepped forward in the covenant of peace and volunteered to undertake our cause, to take up the quarrel and settle it. He is the Mediator. He is the Daysman. He steps between the two quarrelling parties and brings us together. To do this, he must deal first with one and then with the other.

God has graciously condescended to settle this quarrel through his Son, the Man Christ Jesus, the one Mediator between God and men. Peace is the gift of God. 'The LORD will give strength unto his people; the LORD will bless his people with peace' (Psalm 29:11). Peace comes only through Jesus Christ. 'Peace I leave with you, my peace I give unto you: not as the world giveth, give I unto you. Let not your heart be troubled, neither let it be afraid' (John 14:27). 'These things I have spoken unto you, that in me ye might have peace. In the world ye shall have tribulation: but be of good cheer; I have overcome the world' (John 16:33). This peace which Christ gives guards our hearts. 'And the peace of God, which passeth all understanding, shall keep your hearts and minds through Christ Jesus' (Philippians 4:7).

But how do we have peace? Christ our Mediator has dealt with God. God had to be satisfied before peace could come. The wall of partition which separated us from God had to be removed. The law of accusation had to be satisfied (Galatians 3:13; 4:4, 5). Our sins had to be put away.

Nothing but blood would satisfy God's justice (Hebrews 9:22). Nothing but the violent death of God's own Son, could satisfy the demands of his holiness. It must be the blood of the Son of God that its merit may be of infinite value. It must be the blood of the Son of Man that the very nature that sinned would be punished. Jesus Christ must die a violent death so that God's anger with sin might be demonstrated. Our Lord Jesus Christ came into this world to satisfy the holiness, righteousness, justice and truth of the Triune Jehovah (Psalm 40:6-8) and Jehovah has been satisfied.

Having made satisfaction for us with the Father, the Saviour now deals with man. God has reconciled his chosen to himself by the obedience and death of his Son. The Bible never speaks of God being reconciled to his people, only of us being reconciled to God. Now his people must be won and reconciled to him.

Christ sends forth his Spirit through the preaching of the gospel and persuades you to be God's friend. By the saving power of his grace, God the Holy Ghost wins you to Christ (Psalm 65:4). He shows Christ's beauty to you. He opens your blinded eyes with the light of the gospel. He breaks your hard heart with conviction. He humbles your stubborn will with repentance. He causes you to gladly receive the Saviour (Psalm 110:3). He gives you a new heart; and, before you know it, you have fallen in love with the Saviour.

Having made peace between God and man, the Lord Jesus Christ is also our peace with one another. There will never be peace between the seed of the woman and the seed of the serpent. But in Christ Jesus, all of his people are one and are at peace with one another (Colossians 3:11). We have a common Saviour. Christ has put away all carnal distinctions. He gives his people love for one another.

Peace by faith

How do sinners obtain this peace and enjoy it? The gospel which we preach is the gospel of peace (Luke 1:76-79).

The only way sinners can obtain peace is by faith in the Lord Jesus Christ. Trust him who is our peace, and peace is yours. You cannot have it any other way. No priest can give you peace. No ritual can give you peace. No sacrifices can give you peace. No works of your own can give you peace. No amount of earthly possessions can give you peace.

When the Spirit of God comes to our hearts in regeneration he sovereignly proclaims peace by the gift of faith in Christ. 'Therefore being justified, by faith we have peace with God through our Lord Jesus Christ' (Romans 5:1). There is peace in Jesus Christ for all who want it. It is to be had by faith, by faith in the Son of God, by reconciliation to God in and by his dear Son (Matthew 11:28-30).

As peace is obtained by faith so we walk with God in peace only by faith in Christ. 'Rejoice in the Lord alway: and again I say, Rejoice. Let your moderation be known unto all men. The Lord is at hand. Be careful for nothing; but in everything by prayer and supplication with thanksgiving let your requests be made known unto God. And the peace of God, which passeth all understanding, shall keep your hearts and minds through Christ Jesus' (Philippians 4:4-7).

What then?

If Christ is our peace, what then? What follows? I can tell you this: if Christ is my peace then he has reconciled me to God and to all that is his; his person, his purpose, his salvation and his providence.

If Christ is my peace and Christ is your peace then we are at peace with one another. 'For he is our peace, who hath made both one, and hath broken down the middle wall of partition between us.'

Sinner, lay down your enmity, raise the white flag of surrender in your soul to King Jesus and take him for your peace or God will be your enemy forever.

Children of God, learn to enjoy Christ as your peace. 'Thou wilt keep him in perfect peace, whose mind is stayed on thee: because he trusteth in thee' (Isaiah 26:3). 'Trust in the LORD with all thine heart; and lean not unto thine own understanding. In all thy ways acknowledge him, and he shall direct thy paths' (Proverbs 3:5, 6).

When temptations assail us, Christ is our peace. When darkness surrounds us, Christ is our peace. When enemies oppose us, Christ is our peace. When tribulation is upon us, Christ is our peace.

Chapter 33

'Jesus Christ Himself'

Now therefore ye are no more strangers and foreigners, but fellowcitizens with the saints, and of the household of God; And are built upon the foundation of the apostles and prophets, Jesus Christ himself being the chief corner *stone*

(Ephesians 2:19, 20)

'Jesus Christ himself.' What an ocean there is in those words. In which direction shall we turn our thoughts? There may not be a richer, fuller text in all the volume of Holy Scripture than that which we have before us in these three words found in Ephesians 2:20. 'Jesus Christ himself.' Here is a treasure chest full of jewels. Here is a banqueting table spread for our souls upon which to feed forever. May it please God the Holy Spirit, our Divine Comforter and Teacher, to reveal 'Jesus Christ himself' to our hearts and give us grace to trust, love and worship him. O Lord God, give us 'Jesus Christ himself' and we have all and abound. We desire nothing but our Immanuel.

Christ not doctrine

'Jesus Christ himself' should always be the prominent thought of our minds and the meditation of our hearts. Our theology ought to be 'Jesus Christ himself'. He must be the Centre and Head of all. In him are hid all the treasures of wisdom and knowledge. Too many, I fear, are altogether consumed with doctrine. They may indeed be precisely orthodox, and they should be, but they are harsh, bitter and divisive in their orthodoxy. Let us love every word that fell from the lips of our dear Lord and his apostles. Let us contend earnestly for the faith once delivered to the saints. But it is essential for us to hold all doctrine in connection with 'Jesus Christ himself'. Truth isolated from Jesus Christ is hard, cold and lifeless.

Christ not experience

There are others who delight in what they call experimental preaching, preaching which sets forth the inner life experiences of the believer, both in the rage of his depravity and the triumph of grace. In its proper proportion, this is good. But 'Jesus Christ himself' should be proclaimed, not our frames and feelings, doubts and fears, struggles and victories. We study ourselves in vain. The more you see your own heart, the more you will be filled with despondency and despair. 'Looking unto Jesus' is far better, indescribably better for your soul than looking unto yourself. Self-examination is needful but our faith is not in ourselves. It is in Christ alone. Our faith is not in our righteousness, but his righteousness. Our faith is not in our faith, but his faithfulness.

Christ not law

Then there are others who place all importance upon the commandments of God. Their supreme happiness is when they hear someone preaching legal precepts. But the design and purpose of the law is to point us to Christ. The law is not our God, Christ is! We are not under the law, but under grace. Moses was a prophet to point us to our Saviour, but Moses is not our Saviour. Christ is our Saviour! Moses was a prophet to point us to our Lord, but Moses is not our Lord. Christ is our Lord!

'Jesus Christ himself' is the precept we must follow. He is the Way. 'Jesus Christ himself' is the doctrine we believe and preach. He is the Truth. 'Jesus Christ himself' is the experience we must have. He is the Life. He is all my salvation; all my desire. Let us never insult our Lord by despising his doctrine. Do not neglect the precepts of Christ in the gospel so transgressing the authority of Christ.

Our salvation

I begin by emphasising that 'Jesus Christ himself' is the salvation of sinful men. When our Lord Jesus Christ was conceived in the womb of the virgin Mary, the angel of the Lord appeared to Joseph and said, 'She shall bring forth a son, and thou shalt call his name JESUS; for he shall save his people from their sins'. When Mary and Joseph brought their newborn baby boy to Jerusalem to present him to the Lord, according to the law of Moses, Simeon took the child into his arms, and said, 'Lord, now lettest thou thy servant depart in peace, according to thy word: for mine eyes have seen thy salvation'. Learn this: salvation is not in any system of doctrine; it is not in any church; it is not in any experience; it is not in any human work. Salvation is in a Person, 'Jesus Christ himself', the God-man.

I am a saved sinner, saved by the grace of God because he 'loved me, and gave himself for me'. He gave his crown, his throne and his joys in heaven for us, but that was not all. He gave himself; he gave his life on earth. He renounced all the comforts of life and bore all its woes. He gave his body and his blood, but the sum of it is this: he gave himself for me (2 Corinthians 8:9; Galatians 2:20).

Listen to the words of the Apostle. 'Christ also loved the church, and gave himself for it.' 'Who his own self bare our sins in his own body on the tree.' There was no limit to the suffering and grief of our Lord Jesus Christ for us. Though Job suffered indescribably great things in his time of trial, the Lord God put a limit to his suffering. When the Lord God sent his Son to suffer for sinners, no reserve was made. He gave himself. 'He saved others; himself he cannot save', because he himself was the very essence of his sacrifice.

It is because he is who he is that the Lord Jesus was able to redeem us. It was the dignity of his blessed person that gave merit and efficacy to his work of redemption. Jesus Christ is God, able to bear all the wrath and fury and infinite justice of an angry God, and satisfy its every claim. Jesus Christ is man, like ourselves, able to suffer the just penalty of our sins. When we think of our redemption, let us always remember 'Jesus Christ himself' is the essence of it.

It is for this reason that 'Jesus Christ himself' must be the only object of our faith. The Triune God always directs sinners to look to Jesus Christ himself; our Divine Mediator, our Covenant Surety, our Sin-atoning Substitute, to Jesus Christ himself for salvation. 'Look unto me, and be ye saved, all the ends of the earth: for I am God, and there is none else' (Isaiah 45:22). 'Come unto me, all ye that labour and are heavy laden, and I will give you rest' (Matthew 11:28). He does not say look to my life, look to my death, look to my cross, come to my ordinances or come to my servants. His command is, 'Look unto me'. 'Come unto me'. Here is our way of life, 'Looking unto Jesus the author and finisher of our faith'.

It is a very simple thing to trust in Christ alone. We make faith in Christ complicated by our carnal reason and complex creeds. Faith in Christ is not at all complicated. I might be puzzled with many things about the atonement but I can believe in Jesus Christ himself. I might be staggered by the many mysteries of theology but I can trust in Christ. He who loved me, lived for me, bled for me, gave himself for me, I cannot distrust. 'Lord, I believe; help thou mine unbelief.'

Our gospel

Second, I want to show you that 'Jesus Christ himself' is our gospel. He is the substance of the gospel of God. Christianity is a mass of miracles and a body of wonders. But the miracle of our religion is Christ. The wonder of wonders is he whose name is 'Wonderful'. There is nothing so wonderful about the gospel as 'Jesus Christ himself'. The gospel is the good news of heaven, and Christ is the embodiment of that good news. The gospel is the wisdom of God, and Christ is Wisdom. The gospel is a word from God, and Christ is the eternal Word. The gospel is the revelation of God, and God is revealed to men only in the Person and work of 'Jesus Christ himself'.

We need no other proof of the gospel; Jesus Christ is God's final word to men (Hebrews 1:1-3). He is God manifest in human flesh. His character is so perfect even his enemies could find no fault in him. 'Jesus Christ himself' is not only the proof of the gospel, he is the marrow and essence of the gospel we believe and preach. When Paul preached the gospel, he preached Christ in all the fulness of his redemptive glory (Acts 20:27; 1 Corinthians 2:2). If you want to know what Christ taught, study 'Jesus Christ himself'. He is the incarnation of the truth which is revealed by him and in him. He lived what he taught. Hear his voice. He says, 'Come and see'. Study his wounds and you will learn his philosophy. 'That I may know him, and the power of his resurrection', is the highest degree of education. He is the end of the law and the essence of the gospel. When we have preached the whole counsel of God to the full, we may close by saying, 'Now of the things which we have spoken, this is the sum: We have an high priest, who is set on the right hand of the throne of the Majesty in the heavens' (Hebrews 8:1).

'Jesus Christ himself' is the power of the gospel. The power by which the gospel spreads through the earth is not the eloquence of the preacher, nor the precision of our logic, nor the programs of our churches, but 'Jesus Christ himself'. 'The pleasure of the LORD shall prosper in his hand.' It is in heaven that he rules all things for the advance of his truth and the progress of his kingdom. His hand directs the wheel of providence. By his power, the church militant becomes the church triumphant. If a sinner is converted, it is by the power of 'Jesus Christ himself'. If peace rules in our hearts, it is because Christ manifests himself to us. If we walk in the newness of life, it is by the power of Christ who dwells in us.

Christ is the gospel, so let us study him and study to know him. While he was here upon the earth, he taught his disciples; the object of his teaching was that they might know him (Philippians 3:10). They did not learn fast but it was clear what his object was. 'Have I been so long time with you, and yet hast thou not known me, Philip?' When he was risen, he walked with the disciples on the road to Emmaus, and 'beginning at Moses and all the prophets, he expounded unto them in all the Scriptures the things concerning himself'. Whatever else we may be ignorant of, it is essential that we know 'Jesus Christ himself'.

We must know his character, nature, mind, spirit, will, work and power. It is the work of God the Holy Spirit to show us the things of Christ. 'He shall glorify me: for he shall receive of mine, and shall shew it unto you' (John 16:14). The purpose and end of the Bible is that we might know 'Jesus Christ himself'. No subject so moves the heart, so arouses the conscience, so stirs the soul, so satisfies the desires and so calms the fears of men as 'Jesus Christ himself'. God forbid that I should ever cease from preaching 'Jesus Christ himself'. There is no fear of exhausting this theme. His word is still true, 'I, if I be lifted up from the earth, will draw all men unto me'.

Our love

Third, Christ is the object of our love. For all of God's people, this is both our testimony and desire, 'We love him, because he first loved us' (1 John 4:19). We have intense affection for his blessed person and sincere gratitude for his salvation. We love the Lord Jesus Christ, our Saviour, because he is the embodiment of everything true, lovely and good (Philippians 4:8).

O Spirit of God, cause me to love my Christ superlatively! 'Lovest thou me more than these?' To love him above any other. To love him more than any occupation. To love him rather than this world. To love him, and not myself!

If we love the Lord Jesus Christ, our love for him must be a God-given, divinely created and divinely sustained love. It has one singular object. It is a settled love. It causes us to desire his glory. True love desires the blessedness of its object above all else. Because we love 'Jesus Christ himself', we delight in love for his people. Through him we have a union of brotherly love for all his people. Since we love him we delight to serve him, with all that we have, in any place, in any capacity.

Our joy

Fourth, Jesus Christ is himself the source of all our joy. How our hearts ought to bubble over with joy when we realise what blessedness we have in our dear Saviour, the Lord Jesus Christ! I may lose my health, but 'Jesus Christ himself' is mine. I may lose my family, but Christ is mine. I may be filled with pain and sorrow, but 'Jesus Christ himself' is mine. I may be weak, I may be sinful, but 'Jesus Christ himself' is mine. He is holy and he is my Holiness.

Can we not rejoice in all things knowing the presence of 'Jesus Christ himself?' In prosperity rejoice, not in your prosperity, but in 'Jesus Christ himself'. In bounty rejoice in 'Jesus Christ himself'. In leanness rejoice in 'Jesus Christ himself'. In temptation rejoice in 'Jesus Christ himself'. In bereavement rejoice in 'Jesus Christ himself'. In life rejoice in 'Jesus Christ himself'. In death rejoice in 'Jesus Christ himself'. 'Rejoice in the Lord always: and again I say, Rejoice. Let your moderation be known unto all men. The Lord is at hand' (Philippians 4:4, 5).

Our rule

Fifth, 'Jesus Christ himself' is our rule of life, the model after which we seek to mould our lives. Christ is the law by which we live (John 13:12-17; 1 Peter 2:20, 21). Copy the character of the Son of God and you will not err. Let us 'follow the Lamb whithersoever he goeth'. 'And grieve not the holy Spirit of God, whereby ye are sealed unto the day of redemption. Let all bitterness, and wrath, and anger, and clamour, and evil speaking, be put away from you, with all malice: And be ye kind one to another, tenderhearted, forgiving one another, even as God for Christ's sake hath forgiven you. Be ye therefore followers of God, as dear children; And walk in love, as Christ also hath loved us, and hath given himself for us an offering and a sacrifice to God for a sweetsmelling savour' (Ephesians 4:30-5:2).

Our heaven

Sixth, 'Jesus Christ himself' is heaven to our souls. I do not pretend to understand all of Ezekiel's vision, Daniel's prophecy or John's record of the Revelation. I do not know all that heaven shall be, but this I know is heaven to my soul – 'The name of the city from that day shall be, the LORD is there' (Ezekiel 48:35).

With Christ himself in heaven, we will not be plagued with any of our present infirmities. With Christ there shall be no corruption, no fading, no separation, no devil, no curse, no sin, no strife, no division, no darkness, no confusion, no sorrow, no regrets, no sickness, no bereavement, no death.

With 'Jesus Christ himself' in heaven, we shall have all we desire in perfection. We shall have complete knowledge with Christ. We shall have complete holiness. We shall have perfect rest. We shall have perfect satisfaction. We shall have perfect communion with all the saints. 'Jesus Christ himself' is all my hope, expectation, and desire in heaven. Christ is heaven. Heaven is Christ to my soul.

Chapter 34

'The Household Of God'

Now therefore ye are no more strangers and foreigners, but fellowcitizens with the saints, and of the household of God; And are built upon the foundation of the apostles and prophets, Jesus Christ himself being the chief corner *stone*; In whom all the building fitly framed together groweth unto an holy temple in the Lord: In whom ye also are builded together for an habitation of God through the Spirit.
(Ephesians 2:19-22)

The church of God is 'the household of God', the family of God, 'the household of faith'.

Visible dwelling place

In the Mosaic Age of the Old Testament, God had a visible dwelling place among men. The Shekinah was seen between the wings of the cherubs which overshadowed the mercy-seat. In the tabernacle, while Israel journeyed in the wilderness, and in the temple after they were established in the land of promise, there was a visible manifestation of Jehovah in the place dedicated to him.

But everything in the Old Testament was typical of something higher and nobler to be revealed in Christ. The Jewish form of worship was only a picture or a shadow of which the gospel is the substance. It is a sad fact that fallen men and women like to retain those old, weak and beggarly elements of the law. We should never do so. We should never substitute the shadow for the substance! Those carnal ordinances of worship employed under the law were given to point us to that which is real, heavenly and spiritual in the gospel. It is disgraceful to hear men and women speak as they do with regard to 'holy places' and 'holy buildings'. When I was a boy, I heard sermons which would make men and women think that brick, mortar and wood could be made holy. Is there in this gospel age any such thing as a 'holy place'? Is there any spot where God dwells particularly? Of course not! It is ridiculous for men to speak of 'the holy land', 'the sacred desk', or 'the sanctuary'.

Listen to the words of our Lord. 'Believe me, the hour cometh, when ye shall neither in this mountain, nor yet at Jerusalem, worship the Father ... But the hour cometh, and now is, when the true worshippers shall worship the Father in spirit and in truth: for the Father seeketh such to worship him' (John 4:21, 23). Remember again the words of the apostle at Athens. 'God that made the world and all things therein, seeing that he is Lord of heaven and earth, dwelleth not in temples made with hands' (Acts 17:24).

Carnal 'holy things'

When men talk of 'holy things' and 'holy places', they seem to be ignorant of all things spiritual. Can holiness dwell in brick and mortar? Can there be such a thing as a sanctified steeple? Can it possibly be that there is such a thing as a holy window or a godly door? I am amazed when I think of how addled men's brains must be when they impute holiness to buildings! If these popish superstitions were true, the sparrows that build their nests in church steeples would be holy! Yet, because these superstitions are so appealing to our carnal minds this is an extravagance of error into which we are all very inclined to run.

Somehow, when we enter our places of worship, we think we have entered into a holy place. Men speak of church buildings in terribly idolatrous ways. Some dare not to eat in the church building for fear of divine wrath falling upon them. Many never touch the utensils of the Lord's Table, fearing they might contaminate them!

Let us drive away, once and for all, the idea that holiness is connected with anything physical. Let us put away such superstitions with regard to places and things. You may depend upon it, one place is as consecrated as another if God will meet with us there. Wherever we meet with true hearts to worship God, that place becomes, for the time being, our Bethel. It is for us 'the house of God'.

'The house of God'

What mother or father has not been perplexed by the question of their young child, 'Daddy (Mummy), where does God live?' Our text tells us that God has a habitation, a house, a place of residence. I'm interested in that. Aren't you?

There is such a thing as the house of God but it is not an inanimate physical structure. The household of God is a living, spiritual temple. 'In whom', that is, in Christ, 'ye also are builded together for an habitation of God through the Spirit'. The house of God is built with the living stones of converted men and women. The church of God which Christ purchased with his own blood is where God dwells.

Let me make one clear remark with regard to our places of worship. Though they have no sanctity in themselves, yet, by their association, they are places of great blessedness to us. Any place where God meets with me is precious to my heart. Frequently, the Lord God reveals himself to us in this place of worship and for that reason, we hold it dear. Wherever we meet with God is sacred, holy ground, not in the place itself, but in the fact God has met us in that place. Where we hold fellowship with God, where God makes bare his holy arm; be it in a barn, an open field, a church building, that place is consecrated to us by Jehovah's presence.

Yet, it is not so consecrated as to cause us any superstitious awe. It is blessed because we remember the tokens of God's presence that fall on us there; the sweet hours of fellowship we enjoy in that place with the Triune God and his people.

One household

First, the apostle shows us that all true believers are members of the household of God. 'Now therefore ye are no more strangers and foreigners, but fellowcitizens with the saints, and of the household of God'.

I shall begin by answering a question about which there is much confusion in our day. What is the church of God? There are many groups which claim to be the church of God. The Papists tell us the true church is the Roman Catholic church. The Campbellites do not hesitate to affirm they are the only true church. They call themselves, 'The Church of Christ'. The Russellites are quick to inform us that the 'Jehovah Witnesses' are the church. The Mormons are equally determined to convince men that, 'The Church of Jesus Christ of the Latter-Day Saints' is the true church. Regrettably, some Baptists have assumed the attitude of Rome. They say only the Baptist Church is the true church, and only certain Baptists at that. Each of these make the fatal mistake of thinking the trueness of the church is seen in things that are physical, not spiritual. Their foundation is in history, not in a Person.

The church of Jesus Christ is not a denomination! The church is not a physical building. The church of God consists of those whose names are written in the book of God's eternal election, the men and women who were purchased by the blood of Christ, and called and regenerated by the Holy Spirit (Acts 20:28; Ephesians 5:25-27; Hebrews 12:22-24).

Under the Old Testament economy, all Gentiles were strangers to the household of God, and all men by nature are strangers to this spiritual household. We were all dead in sin. We all walked in the course of this world. We were all under the dominion of Satan. We all were in bondage to our own hearts' lusts. We were all children of wrath, cursed and condemned by the law of God.

In the flesh, by nature, we were all alienated from God. Without God! Without Christ! Aliens from the people of God. Strangers to the promises of God. Without hope and in the world.

But watch this. The Apostle delightfully turns our attention away from what we once were, what we know full-well we are by nature, to what we now are in Christ by the grace of God, telling us that we are members of 'the household of God'.

The Lord Jesus Christ has torn down the wall that separated us from God. He has removed the mountain of our sins by his precious, sin-atoning blood. He has broken down the law that was against us by his sacrifice. He has removed the wall of our unbelief by his grace.

The Lord Jesus Christ has removed the wall that separated us from one another. 'Brethren' is a pleasant sound! We are indeed 'brethren' in Christ, with Christ, through Christ, 'brethren' one with another. Jew and Gentile are one in Christ. Male and female are one in Christ. Black and white are one in Christ. Rich and poor are one in Christ. We become one with God's family, only by faith in Christ.

In our text Paul uses a very endearing term to describe God's church. We are called 'the household of God'. What can that sweet term mean? As the household of God, we are the place of his rest. As the household of God, we are the place of his delight. A man's house is the place where he reveals himself. There he sits his children on his lap, hugs them and takes them to his heart. There he reveals the depths of his love. There he opens his heart. There he reveals his secrets and makes known his plans.

As the household of God, we are the centre of all that he does, the singular object of all his work and all his care (Romans 8:28). If we are 'the household of God', will not our God defend, protect and preserve us? O my Soul, cast all your care upon him who cares for you!

What trouble we make for ourselves in this world of darkness and woe. All the cities, states and nations of this world are just a mist, a vanishing vapour. All of them together are less than the small dust of the balance, less than a drop in a bucket, less than nothing, less than vanity. For these things we fret, fight, war and die. Here is a holy nation, a city whose Builder and Maker is God, 'The New Jerusalem', 'The Heavenly Jerusalem', 'The Israel of God', 'The Church of the

Living God'. Ours is an eternal inheritance in a city with gates of pearl, streets of gold, walls of jasper, and everlasting bliss. The church of God is 'The Household of God'. Ours is the citizenship of heaven.

In 'the household of God' we live in sweet communion and fellowship with the Father, and with his Son Jesus Christ. We are not strangers to, but live constantly upon, the love of God; the Person, glory and grace of Christ, and the renewing influences of God the Holy Ghost. Robert Hawker said, 'Oh! The felicity, even now, of an heir of heaven! Oh! The glory that soon shall be revealed!'

Christ the Foundation

Second, we are taught that the church is built upon Jesus Christ as its only foundation. 'And are built upon the foundation of the apostles and prophets, Jesus Christ himself being the chief corner stone; In whom all the building fitly framed together groweth unto an holy temple in the Lord' (Ephesians 2:20, 21).

Our foundation is not the apostles and prophets, but the doctrine of the apostles and prophets, and their doctrine is the doctrine of the gospel. 'Jesus Christ himself.' The apostles and prophets join together to show us the truth of the gospel: ruin by the fall, redemption by the blood, regeneration by the Holy Ghost.

We are all built upon the same foundation that the apostles and prophets were built upon. The foundation of the prophets was Christ. The foundation of the apostles was Christ. The foundation of the church in every age is Christ alone (Psalm 118:22; Isaiah 28:16; Matthew 21:42; 1 Corinthians 3:11; 1 Peter 2:6). We do not build ourselves on the foundation. We are built upon the foundation. Faithful men build upon Christ the foundation by the preaching of the gospel; build not with wood, hay, and stubble, but with the gold, silver and precious stones of the gospel.

Christ is the only foundation upon which our hopes are built. He is the foundation of our faith. He is the foundation of our righteousness. He is the foundation of our comfort. He is the foundation of our glorious hope. Christ is the foundation-stone that supports his church. Christ is the foundation-pattern upon which his church is built. Christ is the corner-stone that joins the walls of the church together. Christ is the chief, or pre-eminent corner-stone of his church. Christ is a tried foundation. Christ is a sure foundation.

'The household of God', the church of God, is here described as a building of the Lord. We are built upon Christ by God himself. God drew the plans for this building in eternity. God chose every stone for his building. Jesus Christ purchased and purified the stones which God had chosen. The Holy Spirit goes to the quarry and cuts out the stones. He breaks them out of the rock-bed of fallen humanity with the law. He forms them into the proper shape by the gospel. He places them into the building by omnipotent grace. There is never the sound of a saw or hammer (man's work) in the building of God. 'And the house, when it was in building, was built of stone made ready before it was brought thither: so that there was neither hammer nor axe nor any tool of iron heard in the house, while it was in building' (1 Kings 6:7). As Christ is the only foundation of 'the household of God', Christ is the only door by which we can enter into the house.

The church, 'the household of God', is also described in our text as God's holy temple, 'an holy temple in the Lord' (v. 21). The pavement of this temple is the pure gold of divine love. The bulwarks of this temple are 'Salvation is of the LORD'. The beauty of this temple is God himself, the Triune Jehovah; Father, Son and Holy Ghost, revealed, seen and known in the crucified God-man, Christ Jesus. The strength of this temple is the right hand of the Almighty.

Saints of God, look what God has made us to be by his mercy, love and grace. Rejoice and sing. We are built by the power of God, built upon the foundation, Christ our God, built as the temple of God.

God's dwelling

Third, the apostle shows us that the church is the place of God's dwelling. 'In whom ye also are builded together for an habitation of God through the Spirit' (Ephesians 2:22).

When chosen, redeemed sinners are brought into saving union with Jesus Christ, we come into a blessed union with his people. 'We are built together.' This is what we profess in our baptism. 'For as the body is one, and hath many members, and all the members of that one body, being many, are one body: so also is Christ. For by one Spirit are we all baptised into one body, whether we be Jews or Gentiles, whether we be bond or free; and have been all made to drink into one Spirit' (1 Corinthians 12:12, 13).

All who are saved by the grace of God are one body in Christ. Each local assembly is one body in the Lord. Let us do everything we can to promote and protect the unity of God's family and the health of Christ's body. There should be no division in the body of Christ. We all have our proper place to fill in Christ's body. We should tenderly sympathise with our brothers' needs and help wherever help is needed. We should esteem one another highly in love for Christ's sake, each esteeming the other better than himself. We should walk in love for one another, as members of the same family, the same body, forgiving one another and forbearing one another in love for Christ's sake.

Each congregation of believers is built together for 'an habitation of God through the Spirit'. This speaks of life and vitality. Too many churches are houses, but not habitations. Formality is not necessarily worship. We need God's presence. Where the Holy Spirit is absent, his presence is faked! 'For where two or three are gathered together in my name, there am I in the midst of them' (Matthew 18:20).

I do not doubt Paul had in his mind's eye the great wonder of the world at Ephesus, the temple the Ephesians built to their dunghill idol, Diana. If so, Paul used that image to turn the minds of those saints at Ephesus to the indescribably greater beauty and glory of God's church and temple in this world, 'the household of God'. But Ephesians 2:22 reaches beyond any local church, reaches beyond God's church on the earth, and speaks of the future glory of 'the household of God'. We are builded together that we may be the everlasting 'habitation of God through the Spirit', the very tabernacle (dwelling place) of God with men (Revelation 21:1-22:5). This household of God will be in every way perfect and complete. There will be no vacant places in her walls, no empty seats at her table. There will be no flaws in the church triumphant. I think I can see the heavenly multitude. Can you? Can you see Mary? Manasseh? David? Rahab? The Dying Thief? John Kent wrote,

Hail, sacred day that shall declare
The jewels of the Son of God;
Designed to deck His crown, they were
Chosen of old and bought with blood.

To make salvation free and full,
Mary adorns Christ's diadem;
Her crimson stains are white as wool;
She shines a bright, distinguished gem.

Manasseh, too, through sovereign grace
Was not in Satan's den to lie;
But in this crown to fill a place,
And raise the Saviour's triumph high.

There David shines without a stain;
Uriah's blood shall ne'er be known,
For like a millstone in the sea
Are all his black transgressions thrown!

Rahab, the harlot, that fair stone,
Sank not in Tophet's endless flame;
When Jesus conquered for His own,
His coronet contained her name.

The dying thief, behold him too,
This matchless diadem adorn;
A pearl of no inferior hue,
Though from the gloomy gibbet torn.

No wanting gem, no absent stone,
Shall e'er be seen when Christ appears,
Each in his place, about His crown,
Shall beam and shine to endless years.

God's household will soon be made perfectly one (John 17:23). We will be the eternal habitation and glory of God. Just imagine that.

Children of God, let us each do whatever we can to maintain the sweet unity of the Spirit, the bond of peace in Christ, as his church, as 'the household of God'.

Oh, may God give us grace to live in expectation of the fulness of our Father's house, rejoicing in the security that is ours as 'the household of God'.

Chapter 35

'For This Cause'

For this cause I Paul, the prisoner of Jesus Christ for you Gentiles, If ye have heard of the dispensation of the grace of God which is given me to you-ward: How that by revelation he made known unto me the mystery; (as I wrote afore in few words, Whereby, when ye read, ye may understand my knowledge in the mystery of Christ) which in other ages was not made known unto the sons of men, as it is now revealed unto his holy apostles and prophets by the Spirit; That the Gentiles should be fellowheirs, and of the same body, and partakers of his promise in Christ by the gospel: Whereof I was made a minister according to the gift of the grace of God given unto me by the effectual working of his power. Unto me, who am less than the least of all saints, is this grace given, that I should preach among the Gentiles the unsearchable riches of Christ; And to make all men see what is the fellowship of the mystery, which from the beginning of the world hath been hid in God, who created all things by Jesus Christ: To the intent that now unto the principalities and powers in heavenly places might be known by the church the manifold wisdom of God, According to the eternal purpose which he purposed in Christ our Lord: In whom we have boldness and access with confidence by the faith of him.

(Ephesians 3:1-12)

Every man who is engaged in work has a cause for which he labours. Some causes are noble and worthy of commendation. Others are selfish and worthy of censure. There are many who give themselves to the worthy cause of philanthropy. They sacrifice time, talents and money to relieve the sufferings, poverty and misery of the human race. There are men and women who are dedicated to the cause of freedom, seeking to maintain the freedom and liberty we enjoy. Men live and die for a cause; otherwise, their lives are without purpose and meaning.

We too have a cause. Ours is the cause of Christ, the cause of the gospel. Sadly, very few in the pulpit or the pew realise this. Preachers commonly make the defence of some particular creed their cause. They study and labour and reason with men to win them to their creed. In our day, the church of Jesus Christ is often divided simply because the man who occupies the pulpit spends his labours defending some pet doctrine. Countless preachers make the mistake of engaging in politics or social issues – abortion, temperance, or whatever, and their passion becomes the cause for which they live. As the man in the pulpit takes up a mistaken cause, so do those who hear him. To many, the purpose for which the church exists is vague and undefined. It does not really matter what the cause becomes, the point is, God's people are led to substitute something other than the gospel as their cause.

The Apostle Paul announces his subject as he opens this third chapter of Ephesians, 'For this cause'. There was one purpose, one cause, which inspired the zeal of this old man. He shows us throughout his epistles that the church of Jesus Christ has only one purpose, one cause for her being. What is that cause?

There is only one cause worthy of all our efforts as God's people in this world. The church of our Lord Jesus Christ is to be engaged always in the work of making known the marvellous grace and wisdom of God revealed in the gospel.

I have said it before, and I say it again, the church of Jesus Christ is here for the spread of the gospel. The church is not a community centre. It is not a social club. It is not an organisation for entertainment. If the church fulfils its responsibility to any community and to our generation, it will be a preaching centre, a sounding board for the gospel.

Paul's example

The Apostle Paul was a wise and loving servant of God. As we observe in this chapter, it was very much the practice of this man to mingle prayer with his instruction. He made intercession to God for these saints, knowing that all his teaching would be vain and useless unless God made it effectual. This is an example every preacher should follow, praying earnestly that God the Holy Ghost may attend our labours, making them effectual and crowning them with success.

In Ephesians 3:1-12, Paul instructs the saints of God about their purpose for being upon the earth, God's purpose for the existence of his people in this world, and particularly God's purpose for setting a gospel church in any community. He tells them what his commission from God was in this matter.

As the servant of Christ, I have but one cause. The church of Christ has but one cause. Our cause is Christ. Our cause is the gospel. We have no other.

'For this cause I Paul, the prisoner of Jesus Christ for you Gentiles, If ye have heard of the dispensation of the grace of God which is given me to you-ward' (vv. 1, 2). Here are three lessons from Paul's words.

Hardship and reproach

First, Paul shows us that for Christ's sake, 'for this cause', the cause of the gospel, he endured relentless hardship and reproach. He here gives us an account of himself as the apostle of Jesus Christ. He shows us some of the trials and difficulties he endured for the gospel's sake. It is obvious that Paul's language is more easily adapted to the preacher than to anyone else. But remember he wrote these words to the Ephesian church, so they would understand and appreciate the purpose and responsibility of the ministry.

The Apostle Paul suffered greatly for having preached the gospel doctrine he set forth so clearly in chapters 1, 2. Everywhere he went, he preached salvation by free grace in Christ, our omnipotent, effectual Saviour. He dared to preach the gospel to the Gentiles. He declared that believers are free from the law and that the sabbath days and ceremonies of the law are meaningless. In breaking with all Jewish tradition, Paul asserted that Jew and Gentile were one in Jesus Christ.

The gospel was committed to Paul for the sake of God's elect among the Gentiles. It was particularly committed to him for the sake of God's elect at Ephesus, for the Church at Ephesus. God does not put any man into the work of the gospel for his own benefit, or as something to be used for his benefit. Men who are called, gifted and sent of God into the blessed work of the ministry are called, gifted and sent to a specific people, a sphere of service in the cause of Christ.

Paul tells us he suffered 'for you Gentiles'. Here is the grace of God; a Jew going to prison for his love to Gentiles (Acts 21:27-33). He was a prisoner 'for this cause'. Faithful servants of Christ must declare his truth, however disagreeable it may be to some, or regardless of the cost. Paul was the prisoner of Jesus Christ, not of Caesar, but of Christ, and he knew it. Christ's servants, if they become prisoners, are his prisoners, and Christ does not despise his prisoners. Paul did not suffer as a criminal. He suffered as a preacher. What an example Paul sets before us! He said, 'But none of these things move me, neither count I my life dear unto myself, so that I might finish my course with joy, and the ministry, which I have received of the Lord Jesus, to testify the gospel of the grace of God' (Acts 20:24). When the believers at Caesarea tried to persuade him not to go to Jerusalem, he replied, 'What mean ye to weep and to break mine heart? for I am ready not to be bound only, but also to die at Jerusalem for the name of the Lord Jesus' (Acts 21:13).

Like Paul, we may be called to suffer for Christ and the gospel, but the things we may be called to suffer are really nothing. We may suffer the loss of reputation. We may suffer the loss of worldly goods. But when we are called upon to suffer in this world, let us think nothing of it. Rather rejoice in that which Christ gives us, and follow Paul's example in suffering (Philippians 1:29; 2:16, 17; 1 Peter 2:20-24). It is a fact that none of us have ever really had to suffer very much. Usually that which we suffer from others, we bring on ourselves. But there is a cause for which all of God's people must be willing to suffer, and that is 'for this cause', the gospel of Jesus Christ. If we suffer for Christ's sake, then Christ will own us, care for us and protect us. The fact is, all God's people are required to suffer for Christ's sake. There are no exceptions. 'Yea, and all that will live godly in Christ Jesus shall suffer persecution' (2 Timothy 3:12). 'Ye shall be hated of all men for my name's sake: but he that endureth to the end shall be saved' (Matthew 10:22). If we are made to suffer for the gospel, the cause for which we suffer is a noble one.

The important thing for us is that we be willing to suffer for the cause of the gospel. If I'm willing to suffer for Christ, I'm willing to live for him. If I'm willing to suffer for the cause of Christ, I'm willing to give for the support of his cause. If I'm willing to suffer for the cause of Christ, I'm willing to work for his cause and I'm willing to go anywhere to preach the gospel.

Divine revelation

Second, for the cause of the gospel, we are enlightened by divine revelation (vv. 3-7). Paul informs us that he had been taught the gospel by revelation, and God had appointed him to the ministry, gifting and qualifying him for its work. The gospel is a mystery revealed (vv. 3-6). The mystery of the gospel is spoken of in many ways in Scripture. It is called the mystery of godliness, the mystery of faith and the mystery of Christ. The doctrine of the gospel is spoken of as the mysteries of the kingdom of heaven. The doctrine of the gospel is a mystery that can only be received by faith when it is revealed by God the Holy Ghost. The doctrine of the Trinity, the doctrine of Christ's person, the saint's union with Christ, and the resurrection of the dead are mysteries revealed.

The blessed gospel doctrine of salvation by Christ is a deep mystery revealed in a few words: predestination, election, redemption, regeneration, salvation in Christ alone, by grace alone, through faith alone. This mystery is received by faith.

The mystery of the gospel, of which Paul has given us the summary in a few words, was, in other ages, hid from the sons of men (v. 5). Under the Old Testament economy, it was hidden from the sons of men in types and shadows and prophecies.

It was revealed in part to some men (Adam, Abraham, David, Isaiah), but not so clearly and as extensively as it now is. Even now, the gospel is the mystery of Christ hidden from men by nature (2 Corinthians 4:3, 4).

The mystery of the gospel is made known by revelation, only by divine revelation. Paul does not here suggest that he received a revelation that no one else had received. Indeed, he declares that this was a revelation made known to all the apostles and prophets of our Lord. The mystery of the gospel is revealed in Sacred Scripture. 'Search the scriptures; for in them ye think ye have eternal life.' The mystery of the gospel is revealed in Jesus Christ (Hebrews 1:1-3). It is revealed in the hearts of men 'by the effectual working of his power'.

The mystery of which Paul here speaks is the mystery of the kingdom of heaven. It is the union of all believers in Christ Jesus (v. 6). Jew and Gentile have an equal inheritance in Christ, and all who are in Christ are one. The only medium by which men are born into this blessed kingdom is the gospel (1 Peter 1:23-25).

Paul very pointedly reminds us that God alone is the source and authority of any true gospel ministry (v. 7). Many false teachers made charges against Paul's authority as an apostle and mocked him because of his imprisonment. But Paul's confidence was this; he was God's servant. As the gospel is of divine origin, so the ministry of the gospel is of God. Paul was made a minister. He did not make himself, neither did any man make him a minister. God made him a minister (Galatians 1:1). John Gill wrote, 'He is a true minister of the gospel who is called of God to the work of the ministry, and is qualified by him with grace and gifts for it; and who faithfully discharges it according to the ability God has given'.

You can be sure of this; if God calls a man to the work of the ministry, he graciously gifts him for the work. Paul was not called because of his natural gifts or his great education. He was gifted of God for the work of the ministry. This is the gift of understanding and explaining the Scriptures. The work of the gospel is accomplished 'by the effectual working of his power'. It is the power of God that makes a preacher. It is the power of God that makes his message effectual.

Our responsibility

Third, for the cause of the gospel, we are trusted with great responsibility (vv. 8-12). The greatest privilege and heaviest burden, the highest honour and the most demanding responsibility upon the earth is laid upon the shoulders of the man who is called to the work of the gospel, the man who is called of God to preach the gospel. He must preach all the counsel of God, constantly and faithfully preaching the gospel of Christ in the exposition of Holy Scripture. He is responsible to preach to eternity bound sinners with immortal souls. 'Who is sufficient for these things?' Blessed be God, our sufficiency is not of ourselves, but of God!

Every God-called man knows he is a sinful man, unworthy of the office. 'We have this treasure in earthen vessels.' He is commonly more tempted of Satan than anyone else. He sees the enormity of his own iniquity, transgression and sin. At the same time, he sees the greatness of God's mercy, grace and love in Christ and the greatness of Christ's sacrifice (Isaiah 53:1-12; 2 Corinthians 5:20, 21).

The subject of every faithful man's preaching, the theme of every God-honouring pulpit is 'the unsearchable riches of Christ'. Our all-glorious Christ, the God-man our Saviour, is full of riches. He is rich in power and in glory. He is rich in holiness, righteousness and truth. Christ our Mediator is rich in forgiveness, grace, love and wisdom. The riches of Christ for his people are unsearchable. We shall be telling them to one another throughout the endless ages of eternity! Here is the great, unutterable delight of the gospel ministry, we proclaim to men, who are in the poverty of sin, 'the unsearchable riches of Christ'.

It is the great privilege and responsibility of God's servants to make known the mystery of Christ (vv. 9-11). We must proclaim the gospel to all men with simplicity so they may see the riches of Christ. We must be reminded constantly that the gospel is all about Christ, that the Word of God is all about Christ, and that all things centre in Jesus Christ. In verse 10, the Holy Spirit tells us a remarkable thing. The angels of heaven attend the ministry of the word to learn from the church the manifold wisdom of God. 'Unto whom it was revealed, that not unto themselves, but unto us they did minister the things, which are now reported unto you by them that have preached the gospel unto you with the Holy Ghost sent down from heaven; which things the angels desire to look into' (1 Peter 1:12). That which the angels desire to learn from us is not Jesus Christ, the perfection of wisdom, for they are before him day and night, but they desire to learn the wisdom of God in the gospel as it is known and experienced by saved sinners like you and me. They desire to learn of election, redemption, justification, pardon and preservation.

The gospel we preach is the eternal gospel of God, 'according to the eternal purpose which he purposed in Christ Jesus our Lord' (v. 11). 'In whom we have boldness and access with confidence by the faith of him' (v. 12). The confidence and joy of God's people are in Christ Jesus. In him we have boldness of access to the Father, and are confident of his everlasting love and our acceptance in him. We are confident of righteousness brought in, redemption accomplished, and sins put away. We are confident of his promises, and his faithfulness, and the hope of heaven's glory.

Chapter 36

God's Preachers – Their Authority, Their Attitude, Their Ambition

Wherefore I was made a minister, according to the gift of the grace of God given unto me by the effectual working of his power. Unto me, who am less than the least of all saints, is this grace given, that I should preach among the Gentiles the unsearchable riches of Christ; And to make all men see what is the fellowship of the mystery, which from the beginning of the world hath been hid in God, who created all things by Jesus Christ.

(Ephesians 3:7-9)

God the Holy Spirit intends for the churches of Christ to have a proper appreciation and high esteem for God's preachers, those men who are ascension gifts of Christ to his church. He would have you to know as much as you can know about the men themselves and their labour for your souls, that you may 'esteem them very highly in love for their work's sake. And be at peace among yourselves' (1 Thessalonians 5:13). Churches who love and highly esteem their pastors are at peace. Labouring together for the cause of Christ, they just overlook things that might otherwise make it impossible for them to get along. As soldiers in battle, they have one far more important than themselves that unites them, namely, Christ. They have a cause more important than themselves, the gospel. They have a nation more important than themselves, the Israel of God. Churches who despise God's gift to them, churches who despise their pastors are never peaceable households.

God's preachers, their authority, their attitude and their ambition is the subject in Ephesians 3:7-9. There is no greater work in the church or in the world than that of preaching the gospel. It is an awesome thing to stand before men as God's spokesman. I prepare every sermon with great fear and trembling before God. Each time I stand in the pulpit I stand in the name of God to proclaim the gospel of God to immortal souls who must soon meet God in judgment. That is my greatest fear and my greatest delight, my heaviest burden and my greatest joy. Oh, what a blessing! Oh, what a joy! Oh, what a responsibility! To declare the unsearchable riches of God's grace in Jesus Christ to eternity bound sinners.

The love of Christ my soul constrains
To seek the wandering souls of men;
With cries, and pleas, and tears to save,
To snatch them from the fiery grave.

My life, my blood, I here present,
If for my God they may be spent.
Fulfil Your sovereign purpose, Lord!
Your will be done, Your name adored!

Give me Your strength, O God of grace
To run and finish well my race!
Your faithful servant I would be:
Your grace, Your constant grace I need!

The work of the ministry is great. It requires all of a man, and more. It is too great for a man. 'Who is sufficient for these things?' I want you to be aware of the great magnitude of this work. Pray for your pastor, holding up his hands for the work, realising that your pastor is but a man; a weak, sinful man. Pray that the Lord will raise up labourers and thrust them out into his vineyard.

Church history

The history of God's church is written around the men who have occupied her pulpits. When the pulpit has been strong, the church has been strong. When the pulpit is dry, dead and weak, the church is dry, dead and weak. The greatest blessing God can give to a town or community is a preacher, a man who boldly and plainly declares the gospel of his free and sovereign grace in Christ Jesus, a man who dares to preach the Book as it is, who dares to stand up on his feet and confront rebel sinners with the claims of Christ the King! The greatest curse that can come upon a land is for God to silence his messengers. When John Bunyan was shut up in Bedford prison, it was not God's judgment upon Bunyan; it was God's judgment upon England. The greatest famine a people can know is a famine of gospel preaching. '*Behold, the days come, saith the Lord GOD, that I will send a famine in the land, not a famine of bread, nor a thirst for water, but of hearing the words of the LORD: And they shall wander from sea to sea, and from the north even to the east, they shall run to and fro to seek the word of the LORD, and shall not find it*' (Amos 8:11, 12).

I hear from people all the time who live in huge, rich cities and others who live in small, out of the way places, who live in the midst of such famine. There are church buildings everywhere, but no place to worship God, no place to hear the gospel, no place to hear from God. The church can prosper and grow without her fine buildings, her beautiful music, her organised Sunday Schools, and her many programs. But if a church does not have a man to proclaim the gospel of God under the anointing of God, she has nothing.

In the verses before us, Paul gives the description he was inspired by God the Holy Ghost to give us. Here we are not looking merely at a famous character in history. When we look for a pattern for the ministry, a pattern for preachers and preaching, let us not look at Calvin, or Luther, or Gill, or Spurgeon. Look rather at Christ and his apostles. Paul writes to us as God's apostle. What he records was given by the inspiration of God the Holy Spirit for our learning. Every true gospel preacher is made to be God's preacher by the gift and power of God for the glory of Christ and the salvation of sinners. In Ephesians 3:7-9, we have three things that characterise every man called, gifted and sent of God as a gospel preacher.

Their authority

'Whereof I was made a minister, according to the gift of the grace of God given unto me by the effectual working of his power' (v. 7). First, God's preachers are men under God's authority. If there is anything that this generation needs to learn about preachers, it is this: God alone makes a preacher, and God's preachers are men under divine authority. They are not hired. They are not fired. They are not controlled by men or circumstances.

Gospel preachers are made by God. Paul was made a preacher of the gospel, a preacher of the mystery of Christ (Ephesians 1:3-2:22), a minister of the dispensation of the grace of God by God. No man can make himself a preacher. No Bible college or seminary can make a preacher. No single man or group of men can make a preacher. Men are made preachers by the gift of the grace of God. There was nothing in Paul by nature that qualified him for the work of the ministry, and nothing that disqualified him. There is nothing in a man's past life that qualifies him to be a preacher, and nothing that forbids him from the work.

Gospel preachers are the servants of God. Being God's servants they are men under God's authority. They are not June-bugs on a string. They delight to serve God. They are men under commission from heaven. As God's servants, gospel preachers serve the interests of Christ's kingdom for the glory of Christ and the salvation of sinners. As the servants of God, God's preachers; God called pastors, rule Christ's church (Hebrews 13:7, 17).

A pastor must rule the house of God but he must do so with patience and gentleness (1 Timothy 1:12-16; 2 Timothy 2:24-26). He must rule the house of God firmly and boldly, just as a husband is required by God to rule his house (1 Timothy 3:4, 5). He must rule by the Word of God.

The Apostle Paul was gifted by God for the work of the gospel. So, too, is every true gospel preacher. A very great part of the call to the ministry is the gifts for the ministry. John Gill wrote, 'He is a true minister of the gospel who is called of God to the work of the ministry, and is qualified by him with grace and gifts for it, and who faithfully discharges it according to the ability God has given'.

God gives his servants a desire for the ministry. He gives them not only a desire to preach, but a desire to serve the souls of men. 'If a man desire the office of a bishop, he desireth a good work' (1 Timothy 3:1). God gives his servants understanding in the Scriptures. He gives his servants ability to explain and communicate the things of God. God gives his servants the ability to lead men.

The Apostle Paul was not only gifted for the ministry, he was qualified to be God's servant by the power and will of God. As Paul was a sinner saved by the grace and power of God, so every man called and sent of God to preach the gospel first knows the power and grace of God in the overwhelming experience of his saving grace in Christ. Before a man can preach to others, he must be himself a child of God; he must himself be born of God. In all things, this man Paul is held before us in the Book of God as an example of what a preacher ought to be. He was filled with the Holy Ghost, bold and fearless before men. He was a man addicted to the study of the Scriptures and fervent in prayer. He was a man of constant labour. He was a self-sacrificing man; full of love, full of faith and full of hope. He was a man whose heart was set upon Christ and eternity.

If a man is God's servant, he is aware of the fact that he is a man commissioned from heaven, under God's authority, doing God's work. God's servants are not sent to be social workers. They are not sent to be counsellors. They are not sent to be ambulance chasers. They are not sent to be politicians. The servant of God is the messenger of Christ. 'As my Father hath sent me, even so send I you' (John 20:21). God determines his place of service. God gives him the message for the hour. And to God he gives account. Here is Paul's testimony of his authority as a preacher. This is the testimony of every God-called man. 'I was made a minister, according to the gift of the grace of God given unto me by the effectual working of his power'.

Their attitude

'Unto me, who am less than the least of all saints, is this grace given, that I should preach among the Gentiles the unsearchable riches of Christ' (v. 8). Second, we have the example that Paul gives to all preachers concerning their attitude toward the blessed work of the ministry. As God's preacher, Paul had a great attitude regarding the work to which the Lord God had called him. I am fully persuaded that, in a great measure, the success or failure of a man's ministry will depend on his attitude toward the work. This eighth verse shows us four things about Paul's attitude. It is no marvel to me that God used this man so greatly.

1. God's preachers, like Paul, think very little of themselves. 'Unto me, who am less than the least of all saints, is this grace given.' This was Paul's own, truthful estimation of himself. He was not guilty of a false modesty. When he looked at himself, he saw less than the least of all saints. He had stubbornly refused to trust Christ, wishing himself accursed from Christ, until he had wasted most of his life. He had been a blasphemer and persecutor; and though God had forgiven him of his sin, he could never forgive himself. He was keenly aware of his gifts and keenly aware of God's super-abundant grace. The longer he walked in the company of Christ, the lower his opinion of himself became.

Someone pointed out Paul's development: as a young believer, he said, 'I am less than the least of all the apostles'. Later on, he said, 'I am less than the least of all saints'. Just before he died, he said, 'I am the chief of sinners'. Oh, Spirit of God, give me greater and greater revelations of Christ, that I may have a lower and lower opinion of myself. 'He must increase, but I must decrease' (John 3:30).

2. Like Paul, God's preachers think very highly of God's saints. Paul had a low opinion of himself and a high opinion of his brothers and sisters in Christ, a very high opinion of the family of God. Those two things always go together, a low opinion of self and a high esteem of others.

He was not unrealistic. He saw many weaknesses in the saints and he boldly rebuked them. Yet he saw that all who were God's saints were in Christ, and in that, he saw perfection. The church of Jesus Christ, with all her spots and wrinkles, is the fairest society upon the earth. She is lovely in the eyes of Christ, and it ought to be in our own eyes as well. Paul thought very lovingly of his congregation. He counted it a great grace that he was permitted to preach among the Gentiles.

Peter had a much more respectable audience. He was the apostle of the circumcision. He preached among the aristocratic Hebrews. James was pastor of that huge, big city church, First Baptist Church of Jerusalem. Paul was sent to preach to Gentile dogs. Oh, how he rejoiced to preach the gospel to the ignorant masses of the Gentiles and bring the outcasts home to the Lord Jesus! Read the first chapter of Romans and you will see how debauched and depraved the Gentiles had become. But Paul was sent to labour among them and he preferred them to any other audience. I love to see preachers fall in love with the place of their calling.

Spurgeon said, 'I never knew a man succeed among a people unless he preferred them to all others as the objects of his care. When ministers despise their congregations, their congregations are very likely to despise them; and then usefulness is out of the question. When a man thinks himself above his work, the probability is that he is in the clouds altogether, or stands in the way of some practical worker of a more commonplace kind, who would do the work he is despising.'

Paul dearly loved the Jews, his kinsmen according to the flesh, but the Gentiles were his flock. It is wonderful to watch God wed a man to his congregation and wed his congregation to him.

3. God's preachers, like Paul, think very highly of their work. 'Unto me, who am less than the least of all saints, is this grace given, that I should preach.' This man looked upon the work and labour of the ministry as a great gift from God, an honour bestowed, a favour granted. The greatest title he ever took to himself was 'Paul, a servant of Jesus Christ' (Romans 1:1). He threw up his hands in grateful amazement that so great an honour could be bestowed upon him.

This man, this preacher, had a very clear understanding of the work God had called him to do. 'That I should preach.' He was called to be a preacher. He kept to his work and he preached everywhere. This is the work of the ministry in every age and in every place. God's servants are preachers. Nothing else; just preachers.

Paul realised the seriousness, the weight and the magnitude of his work. He keenly felt his weakness before it. Yet he calls the work of the ministry a grace. It was a grace given to him to enrich his own soul.

4. Here is the crowning attitude of Paul toward his ministry. This man had the highest possible thoughts of his subject. 'That I should preach among the Gentiles the unsearchable riches of Christ.'

The unsearchable riches of Christ were his one and only theme. All he had to say was contained in that one word – Christ. All he aimed at was to glorify him. He did not feel restricted by this one subject. He realised that in Christ there were riches unsearchable (1 Corinthians 1:23, 24; 2:1-5). He preached to men the unsearchable riches of Christ. He preached his glorious person, his covenant engagements, his wondrous incarnation, his sin-atoning death, his mighty resurrection, his heavenly intercession, his sovereign rule, his second coming and his purchased inheritance.

Here then is Paul's attitude toward the ministry. 'Unto me, who am less than the least of all saints, is this grace given, that I should preach among the Gentiles the unsearchable riches of Christ.'

Gospel preaching is not defending points of doctrine, but declaring the boundless mercy and grace of God to poor, needy sinners in Christ. I think hell must roar with laughter when preachers stand in the pulpit and try to untie theological knots no one is aware of, and argue debates no one cares about.

Until I find a message more glorious than Christ crucified, more needful than free grace, more delightful than infinite mercy, more comforting than absolute forgiveness, more assuring than perfect righteousness, more compelling than redeeming blood, more hopeful than heavenly glory and more joyful than the infinite, immutable love of God in Christ, I am determined to preach nothing else, but Jesus Christ and Him crucified. 'God forbid that I should glory, save in the cross of our Lord Jesus Christ, by whom the world is crucified unto me, and I unto the world'. Christmas Evans said, 'The flame of Calvary's love is intense, and should cause a glow in the pulpit'.

Every man who is sent of God to preach is sent of God to preach Christ crucified, always, in all places, in all his fulness (1 Corinthians 1:17-2:5). Christ crucified is 'all the counsel of God' (Acts 20:27). He is the singular subject of Holy Scripture. He is the sum and essence of all true doctrine. He is the life of all gospel ordinances. He is the secret ingredient of all true worship. He is the mercy-seat in whom God meets with men. He is the motive of all godliness, obedience, service and devotion. He is the reward of heavenly glory.

Jesus Christ is our God. Jesus Christ is our Saviour. Jesus Christ is salvation. He is the Way to heaven, and he is Heaven. He is the Revealer of truth, and he is Truth. He is the Giver of life, and he is Life. 'Christ is all.'

When we talk about Divine sovereignty, we are declaring that Jesus Christ is Lord. When we proclaim God's glorious work of predestination, we are showing how that sinners have been predestinated to be conformed to the image of Christ. God's election is God's choice of some to everlasting salvation in Christ, and for Christ's sake.

Total depravity, a thoroughly biblical doctrine, is God's revelation of our need of Christ. Limited atonement is the biblical assurance of effectual redemption and grace by Christ; the declaration that all for whom Christ died shall be saved. Irresistible grace, or effectual calling, is the almighty, irresistible revelation of Christ in the soul by God the Holy Ghost, which causes the chosen to come to him. Regeneration is the implanting of Christ in us. Justification is the righteousness of Christ made yours by God's free grace. Faith is trusting Christ. Sanctification is Christ being formed in us, begun in regeneration and consummated in glorification. Perseverance is Christ holding our hearts by grace and keeping us in life and faith.

Baptism is the believer's public confession of faith in Christ. Being symbolically buried in the watery grave and raised with him, we confess our faith in his finished work of redemption as our Substitute. The Lord's Supper is our blessed remembrance of Christ. Eternal life is knowing Christ. Heaven is being with Christ and like Christ, perfectly and forever.

Preaching is telling people about Christ. Anything else is not preaching. Call it what you may; it is not preaching!

Their ambition

'And to make all *men* see what *is* the fellowship of the mystery, which from the beginning of the world hath been hid in God, who created all things by Jesus Christ' (v. 9). Paul, thirdly, declares the great ambition of God's preachers. They all have the same great and glorious ambition. That one glorious, all absorbing ambition is to make Christ known to all men and to glorify him in the eyes of all men.

'How beautiful upon the mountains are the feet of him that bringeth good tidings, that publisheth peace; that bringeth good tidings of good, that publisheth salvation; that saith unto Zion, Thy God reigneth' (Isaiah 52:7).

Chapter 37

'The Unsearchable Riches of Christ'

Unto me, who am less than the least of all saints, is this grace given, that I should preach among the Gentiles the unsearchable riches of Christ.

(Ephesians 3:8)

The Apostle Paul considered it his greatest privilege to be the servant of the Most High. To be allowed of God to preach the gospel was to him a cause of joy and thanksgiving. He did not look upon his calling as drudgery. He went about his work with intense delight.

Delightful labour

I have no hesitancy in asserting that every man called, gifted and sent of God as his messenger, every man allowed of God to preach the gospel, experiences the same delight. The burden is heavy. The work is demanding. It consumes the whole of a man. The labour is intense. Yet, I cannot imagine a greater joy than the blessed work of preaching the gospel of Jesus Christ. I have the high honour and great privilege of proclaiming to poor, lost, ruined, doomed, damned, hell-bent rebels the mercy, love and grace of God in Christ Jesus!

Were I sent of God with nothing but a stern message of judgment, with no terms of peace from the throne of grace, declaring that every rebel must be forever damned; I could not do the work without a weeping, heavy, broken heart. Were I nothing but a messenger of doom, there could be no joy in my work, only sorrow. But, blessed be God, that is not the case! Everywhere I go, I am sent of God with the white flag of peace to proclaim free and full pardon by the precious blood of Christ to the very people who shed his blood! Every man sent of God to preach is sent of God to preach the gospel, to proclaim the message of hope; the glad tidings of salvation by grace through faith in the Lord Jesus Christ.

Angelic preachers

Only once, were the angels of heaven sent as preachers of the gospel. How did they go about their work? What was their message? – 'Glory to God in the highest, and on earth peace, good will toward men.' They were not sent to preach hell-fire and damnation. They were sent to preach heavenly grace and salvation! The glad tidings of great joy were set to music and announced with holy joy and celestial song, 'Glory to God in the highest, and on earth peace, good will toward men'.

Office magnified

The gospel of Christ is a message of life, peace, pardon and eternal bliss. It should fill the hearts of both those who preach it and those who hear it with joy unspeakable. Faithful men, like the Apostle Paul, always make it their business to magnify their office as preachers of the everlasting gospel. I admonish every man, whose soul is fired with the love of Christ, aspire to this work. Covet this best gift. May the Holy Ghost call many to the work and thrust them into the gospel vineyard! The harvest is great. The labourers are few.

Humbled preacher

Paul magnified his office. He was honoured by and thankful for the work the Lord God trusted to his hands. His labour and his usefulness exceeded that of his peers (2 Corinthians 11:23). But his usefulness did not bloat him with pride. It broke him and humbled him. Abundance of grace is the best remedy for pride. Those who are empty, especially those who have nothing to do, usually have a very high opinion of their abilities. Those who are called and used of God mourn their sin, their weakness, their inability and their failure. If you would like to feel how utterly insignificant and powerless you are, if you would know your nothingness, give this a try: try preaching 'the unsearchable riches of Christ' to eternity bound sinners for the glory of God.

Our message

I know and freely acknowledge my weakness and inability as a preacher and a pastor. I know little about being a preacher and even less about being a pastor. But there is one thing about which I have no perplexity and no question. I am never at a loss about what I should preach. Ephesians 3:8 tells us what every preacher is to preach every time he preaches. He is to preach 'the unsearchable riches of Christ'.

It is the high and holy calling of every gospel preacher to relentlessly proclaim to poor sinners 'the unsearchable riches of Christ'. It is every preacher's responsibility to preach 'Jesus Christ, and him crucified'. I do not know what God will do for our generation. But this I know, if God blesses anything to the souls of men for their eternal good, it will be preaching Christ and him crucified.

The Lord Jesus Christ is full of riches indescribable; more, he is full of riches beyond imagination for all who are united to him by living faith. I see three things in Ephesians 3:8: a glorious person, a generous portion, a gracious purpose

A glorious person

First, the gospel of God is the revelation and declaration of a glorious person; and that person is our Saviour, the Lord Jesus Christ. It is the great joy of the gospel preacher to declare unto men 'the unsearchable riches of Christ'. The glories of Christ, whom once he persecuted, were Paul's one and only theme. All he had to say was contained in the fulness of that one word, 'Christ'. All he aimed at was the glory of Christ. This noble apostle did not labour for ceremonies, nor creeds, nor orthodoxies, nor denominations, nor philosophies, nor parties. He did not make any effort to exalt any man or the church as a whole. His soul's desire was to exalt Christ. He looked upon the glories of Christ's person as being full of riches unspeakable. He had deep insight into the truth which he preached. It was his delight to find within the person, offices and work of Christ rich veins of truth he could never exhaust.

The Lord Jesus Christ is glorious in his essential Person. Perhaps there is no text of Scripture which more distinctly sets forth the Person of our blessed Redeemer than 1 Timothy 3:16, 'And without controversy great is the mystery of godliness: God was manifested in the flesh, justified in the Spirit, seen of angels, preached unto the Gentiles, believed on in the world, received up into glory'.

Everywhere in the Scriptures, the Lord Jesus Christ is spoken of and worshipped as God (Isaiah 7:14; 9:6; Acts 20:28; Romans 9:5; 1 John 3:16). I do not pretend to understand the mystery of the sacred Trinity; but, with all of our hearts, we believe in and worship God in the Trinity of his Sacred Persons: Father, Son, and Holy Ghost (1 John 5:7). Jesus Christ is God, the second Person of the Holy Trinity, in every way one with and equal to God the Father and God the Holy Spirit. Others may make him merely a great man or an angelic creation, but we worship him who is himself God, and no other. We behold in the blessed Saviour deity itself, 'For in him dwelleth all the fulness of the Godhead bodily'.

Christ is the creator, without whom was not anything made that was made. Christ is the preserver of all things, by whom all things consist. Christ possesses all the attributes of divinity. He is eternal, immutable, omnipotent, omniscient, omnipresence, just, faithful, holy. He is truth, goodness, grace, mercy and love.

Here upon the earth, in our humanity, Christ's Godhead was evident in him. The winds knew him and were silent at his command. The waves obeyed him. The angels worshipped him and ministered to him. Devils feared him, obeyed him and fled from him. Diseases were healed by his touch and his word, for both were omnipotent. The dead lived at his command, for his voice was the voice of the Almighty. He was God, even while to mortal eye he was only the carpenter's son.

Jesus Christ is the revelation of God (John 1:1-3, 14-18; 1 John 1:1-3). Either Jesus Christ is himself God, or he is an imposter and deceiver of men's souls; and all who worship him are guilty of idolatry. Away with such arguments. God has spoken and Christ is God! He was worshipped as God in the Old Testament. He was worshipped as God in his earthly ministry. He is worshipped as God today.

This great God, our Saviour, became a man that he might be the Saviour of men. Jesus Christ our Lord is all God and all man. Just as truly as Christ is the eternal God, he is man. He was conceived of the Holy Ghost in the womb of the blessed virgin with a real human body and soul. See his marvellous condescension (2 Corinthians 8:9; Philippians 2:5-7). The Lamb of God descends in the fulness of time to Bethlehem's manger; there he lies, a babe wrapped in swaddling clothes.

He grew in stature and wisdom as a man. He was tempted as a man. He has experienced the secrets of our nature: Pain, sorrow, hunger, thirst, even death when he was made sin for us. See him as he makes his pilgrimage from Bethlehem to Calvary, working out a perfect righteousness for his people.

Look again at him, if you have eyes to see, as he is stretched upon the cursed tree between heaven and earth. See there the venom and hatred of men. See there the wrath and justice of God. See there the grace and mercy of the Saviour. Hear his word of forgiveness, 'Father forgive them'. Hear his word of promise, 'Today thou shalt be with me in paradise'. Hear his cry of anguish, 'My God! My God! Why hast thou forsaken me?' Hear his word of suffering, 'I thirst'. Hear his word of victory, 'It is finished'. Hear his word of contentment, 'Father, into thy hands I commend my spirit'.

Look again! See his shed blood. In that crimson fountain, our sins are washed away! Behold the Saviour on the third day, early in the morning, as he rises from the tomb, conqueror of death and the grave. Redemption is finished. The law is fulfilled. Salvation is accomplished. Look upon our Saviour's glorious person. See him if you can. The King ascends to heaven; he sits gloriously upon his throne. He rules all things. He represents and intercedes for us. He preserves and waits for us.

He who sits in heaven is there by divine right. He is there as a sympathising High Priest, having earned the right by his obedience unto death as the man Christ Jesus. Today, he has put aside his garments of servitude, and laid aside the towel wherewith he washed his disciple's feet. All power is his in heaven and earth. He is crowned with universal glory as God (Colossians 2:9, 10; Revelation 4 and 5).

The Lord Jesus Christ is glorious in his eternal promises. 'All the promises of God in him are yea, and in him Amen.' In old eternity our blessed Redeemer entered into covenant agreement with the Father for our redemption. He volunteered to be our Mediator. He struck hands with the Father as the Surety of our redemption, and promised to suffer in our place. He promises to save all who come to God by him and bring them to the Father's house. He promises to keep all his sheep. He said, 'They shall never perish'. He promises to provide all our needs, love us unto the end, and never to leave us.

It is this glorious Person we delight to preach. Yes, preach all the doctrine of the gospel, but don't preach them apart from the Person of Christ. I fear that many make the mistake of preaching doctrine instead of preaching Christ. Certainly the doctrine is to be preached but the doctrine is a robe worn by the Saviour, and never apart from him. Christ himself is the sum of all true doctrine. Justification is by Christ the Justifier. Sanctification is by Christ the Sanctifier. Glorification is by Christ the Glorifier. In preaching, let Christ have no rival!

A generous portion

Second, to preach 'the unsearchable riches of Christ' is to set before you a very generous portion for your soul. The prophet Jeremiah comforted his soul with this blessed statement, 'The Lord is my portion, saith my soul; therefore will I hope in him'. If we can claim Christ as our portion, we shall desire nothing else; for those who have him have all. Is this not Paul's meaning when he says that he was sent to preach 'the unsearchable riches of Christ'? We preach a great Saviour to great sinners. His name is 'Mighty to Save'.

Look into the unsearchable riches of Christ; the portion of his people. The Lord Jesus Christ has unsearchable riches of love to sinners. He so loved the souls of men that the only word used to describe it is 'so'. We see the love of Christ in the way he deals with sinners. How his love radiates in his reception of them! He carried the gospel to the Samaritan adulteress. He freely forgave the woman who had been an harlot. He graciously sought Zacchaeus. He spoke tenderly to the woman taken in adultery. We ourselves were condemned, but he died in our place. There is no love to compare with his love.

Christ has riches of pardon for those who, trusting him, confess their sin. He has such unsearchable riches of pardon that no amount of guilt can possibly transcend the efficacy of his precious blood. He will never charge a man with sin who is washed in his blood. He so cleanses us from sin that he neither sees nor remembers sin in us. So thorough is his pardon that he never treats us any the less kindly because of our sin.

Christ Jesus has unsearchable riches of peace to comfort troubled hearts. He made peace for us with God, and proclaims peace in our own hearts. He gives us comfort and peace in all our circumstances. 'He is our peace!' Do you weep for your sin? Christ has a handkerchief to wipe away your tears. Are you sad because you are bereaved? Christ is a loving companion. Are you downcast because a friend has betrayed you? Christ is 'a friend that sticketh closer than a brother'.

Christ has riches of wisdom to guide and direct our lives. He has unsearchable riches of joy for those who walk with him. The company of Christ is joyful company indeed. He has unsearchable riches of contentment too. The man who can say, 'I have enough', is the richest man in the world. And my friend, if you have Christ, you have enough.

Christ has unsearchable riches of provision for his house. He provides your every need from the abundant storehouse of creation and from the overflowing, super-abundant storehouse of his grace! The Lord Jesus has unsearchable riches of grace for all who come to him. He has grace to save, justice to make you righteous, holiness to sanctify, mercy to preserve and power to make you perfect. The riches of Christ are unsearchable and we shall be learning more of their depth and height, length and breadth forever. They shall be best known in eternity.

A gracious purpose

Third, as we proclaim to sinners 'the unsearchable riches of Christ', the gospel we preach displays a gracious purpose. But it would be of little comfort to just hear that Christ is rich. Here is the blessedness of his unsearchable riches. He intends to bestow his riches upon sinners. 'For ye know the grace of our Lord Jesus Christ, that, though he was rich, yet for your sakes he became poor, that ye through his poverty might be rich' (2 Corinthians 8:9). What mercy! What grace! What a Saviour!

Chapter 38

Angelic Lessons

To the intent that now unto the principalities and powers in heavenly places might be known by the church the manifold wisdom of God.

(Ephesians 3:10)

The Apostle Paul, writing by Divine inspiration, tells us that 'the principalities and powers in heavenly places', the angels of God, attend the worship of God's saints and listen intently to the faithful preaching of the gospel. They listen that they might learn, by the lips of a saved sinner, the wonders of 'the manifold wisdom of God' in redeeming his elect by the precious blood of his Son, the Lord Jesus Christ.

Elder-born creatures

Remember that compared with us, the angels are the elder-born creatures of God. They have been with our Triune Jehovah since before this material universe was created by him. These angels kept their first estate when Satan led one-third of the heavenly hosts in rebellion against their Creator. They have never displeased him, sinned against him, or refused his will and pleasure.

Yet we are never told that the angels learned the manifold wisdom of God by any means other than this. The wonders of redemption are 'things the angels desire to look into' (1 Peter 1:12). Therefore, they gather with God's saints in public worship, listen to our songs and prayers and praises, and attentively hear the preaching of the gospel that they might learn from us 'the manifold wisdom of God' displayed in our redemption by Christ. I find that astonishing. Don't you?

Observing creation

These holy angels were with God when he made the heavens and the earth. 'In the beginning' when God said, 'Let there be light: and there was light', when the first ray of light blazed through the heavens like a living finger to touch the earth and awaken its beauty, the angels were there. 'The morning stars sang together, and all the sons of God shouted for joy.' Yet, though they were with the great Creator during the seven days of creation, though they saw the cattle after their kind, and the fowls of the air after their kind, and the fish of the sea, and all the plants, we do not learn that, in all of this, there was made known unto the holy angels, 'the manifold wisdom of God'. Even when man, the Creator's last great creature, walked through Eden with his fair bride by his side, when they stood up to praise their Creator, though they were 'fearfully and wonderfully made', though in the minds and bodies of our first parents, Adam and Eve, there was a display of wisdom unrivalled in the creation, still 'the manifold wisdom of God' was unknown to the angels of God.

Lift your eyes to the worlds above. When the stars were kindled like glowing flames by him who is Light, still to these celestial creatures 'the manifold wisdom of God' was a secret mystery hidden. Even in all the dispensations of divine providence, apart from the church, 'the manifold wisdom of God' has been hidden from these heavenly creatures. They look upon Christ, our Glory-man Mediator, who has accomplished eternal redemption for us. They, seeing him sitting yonder upon his throne with undimmed eye, veil their faces at his footstool, and cry, 'Holy, Holy, Holy', Lord God of Sabaoth. Yet, standing as they do nearest to the eternal throne, they do not learn, 'the manifold wisdom of God', except as they come to church with saved sinners, like Sunday School children to learn their lesson.

By the church

Only by the church do the angels of God learn, 'the manifold wisdom of God'. Here the Apostle Paul shows us that the angelic hosts are instructed in Divine wisdom as they behold God's work for and in his church. There is more of God's wisdom displayed in the church than in all of creation. More of God's wisdom is revealed in the church, which he purchased with his own blood, than even heaven with all its splendours could otherwise reveal. More of the wisdom of God is displayed in the saving of our souls than in building the arches of the skies.

There is an ingenious toy called the kaleidoscope. Each time you turn it, you see some new form of beauty, so it is with the church of Christ. Look at her from any angle and you will behold the beauty of divine wisdom displayed in her. The word 'manifold' is used as if to compare salvation, Christ's redemption and God's free grace, to a precious treasure wrapped up in many folds. First this, then the next, then the next must be unfolded; as you unwrap fold after fold, you find something precious each time. 'The manifold wisdom of God' is displayed in his eternal counsel and conduct forming and perfecting his church. This wisdom is the study of angels and should be the study of saints as well.

God's purpose

'The manifold wisdom of God' is made known to the angels by God's purpose for the church. I have no doubt that the great object the angels desire to look into is God's purpose and plan to save the church by Christ. To those holy, heavenly creatures this is something before which they bow with admiration and wonder.

If the Triune God had taken counsel with all the creatures of heaven and earth, and it had been the responsibility of that council to devise a plan whereby God might be just and yet the justifier of the ungodly, they would have failed. I am sure that it is a great question with the angels, as it is with men, 'How then can man be justified with God? or how can he be clean that is born of a woman? Behold, even to the moon, and it shineth not; yea the stars are not pure in his sight. How much less man, that is a worm? and the son of man, which is a worm?' (Job 25:4-6).

Without doubt, the celestial spirits consider with delight the fact that in God's way of saving his church, all the divine attributes are clearly displayed. Above all of God's creatures, the angels know that God is just. They saw Lucifer when God cast him out of his habitation because of sin, falling like lightning. God is just. But that fact is nowhere displayed as it is upon Calvary where his Son hangs and bleeds, 'the just for the unjust, that he might bring us to God'.

The angels see in our salvation the great wonder of justice and peace reconciled. They see God as sternly as if there were no mercy in him, smiting his Son for the sins of his people with all the fulness of his wrath. They see him as merciful as if he were not just, embracing his people as though they had not sinned, loving us with a love that could not have been greater had we never transgressed. The angels behold with wonder that God so hates sin that he slew his only begotten Son, when he was made sin for us. Yet, 'God so loved the world, that he gave his only begotten Son, that whosoever believeth in him should not perish, but have everlasting life'.

All the infinite attributes of God shine out at once in all their combined glory and splendour around the cross. This is the wonder of men and angels. In the cross we see God's anger and his love. We see his power and his tenderness. We see his greatness and his goodness. We see his immutability and his wisdom.

But further, when the angels see that by this great scheme of grace, all the ruin that sin brought upon mankind is removed, they wonder at the wisdom of God. Our Lord Jesus said, 'I restored that which I took not away'. Did we lose Eden in Adam? The Lord Jesus Christ has given us a better Paradise. Did we lose the dignity of our manhood by the fall? Christ has raised us to a higher dignity. In him the angels are subject to us. Did we lose our spotless purity by sin? In Christ we are justified, righteous and sanctified through his blood. Did we lose our communion with God? In Christ 'we have access by faith into this grace wherein we stand'. Did we lose heaven in Adam? In Christ we have an eternal inheritance in heaven.

God in infinite wisdom made this mischief of sin to destroy itself. The dragon is pierced with his own sting. Goliath is slain with his own sword. Death is slain by the death of a man. Sin is put away by the great sin-offering, 'who his own self bare our sins in his own body on the tree'. Sin was slain by sin when Christ was made sin for us! 'For as in Adam all die, so in Christ shall all be made alive.'

Moreover, by this great plan and purpose of grace and salvation by the atonement of Christ, God is more glorified than he would have been if there had been no fall. In this the angels behold 'the manifold wisdom of God'. God could have made a race that would not have sinned; but he did not. He ordained that his chosen go astray for a season, because he would have us attached to him by bonds of love, grace and gratitude. Suppose for a moment we had not fallen. We could never have sung of redeeming grace and dying love. We could never have been made one with Christ and love him as we now love him. We could never have known God as we now know him. Thus, in God's purpose and plan for the church, the angels behold 'the manifold wisdom of God'.

God's purchase

'The manifold wisdom of God' is also made known to the angels by God's purchase of the church. The Lord Jesus did not purchase his church out of the hands of Satan. Satan had us in his power; but we were never his property. God our Saviour purchased us out from under the bondage, curse and condemnation of his own holy law. The church is a treasure hidden in a field and the pearl of great price.

'The manifold wisdom of God' is displayed to the angels in the great fact that Christ was made the Covenant Head and Representative of his church that he might purchase it with his own blood. It is God's eternal purpose to redeem his church by the substitutionary sacrifice of his Son. We are one with Christ in his heart from all eternity. We were one with him while he was upon the earth, one with him at Calvary, one with him in the resurrection, and one with him upon the eternal throne.

God's power

Look again, and see 'the manifold wisdom of God' made known to the angels by God's power in the church. The conversion of every child of God is a display of infinite power and wisdom. It is the greatest miracle that can ever be imagined. Are we not living proof of this? Remember, brothers and sisters, what you were and what you still are by nature. 'Now the works of the flesh are manifest, which are these; Adultery, fornication, uncleanness, lasciviousness, idolatry, witchcraft, hatred, variance, emulations, wrath, strife, seditions, heresies, envyings, murders, drunkenness, revellings, and such like: of the which I tell you before, as I have also told you in time past, that they which do such things shall not inherit the kingdom of God (Galatians 5:19-21). Always remember where you were, what you were, and what you are by nature; and ever hold in precious, thankful memory what God has done for you in Christ by his grace.

'Know ye not that the unrighteous shall not inherit the kingdom of God? Be not deceived: neither fornicators, nor idolaters, nor adulterers, nor effeminate, nor abusers of themselves with mankind, Nor thieves, nor covetous, nor drunkards, nor revilers, nor extortioners, shall inherit the kingdom of God. And such were some of you: but ye are washed, but ye are sanctified, but ye are justified in the name of the Lord Jesus, and by the Spirit of our God' (1 Corinthians 6:9-11).

'But of him are ye in Christ Jesus, who of God is made unto us wisdom, and righteousness, and sanctification, and redemption; That, according as it is written, He that glorieth, let him glory in the Lord' (1 Corinthians 1:30, 31).

The angels behold the manifold wisdom of God by the church in the work of God the Holy Ghost in the calling of sinners to Christ by the gospel. He convicts you by the law. He breaks your heart by the gospel. He heals you by the ministry of peace. He brings you to Christ. The wisdom of God is seen in conforming sinners to the image of Christ in sanctification, not by works, but by grace.

God's preservation

'The manifold wisdom of God' is made known unto the angels by God's preservation of the church. The angels have seen God's wisdom in preserving the church through every dispensation of time and providence. At first, the church was indeed small. God called only a man or a family here and there; Adam and Eve, Abel, Enoch, Noah, Abraham. Then God called twelve tribes, then a nation. He preserved his church in Egypt and in the wilderness. He revealed more of his wisdom little by little under the types and shadows of the Mosaic dispensation, until, finally, the Sun of Righteousness arose with healing under his wings.

The angels have seen God's wisdom in preserving the church through all of her persecutions and heresies by which Satan has sought to destroy her. No harm has been done. The earth always opens to help the woman, even when it appears that the world is devouring her! God's church has prevailed, is prevailing, shall prevail, and always prevails.

The angels have beheld God's manifold wisdom in preserving his church in all the trials and experiences of her members. In wisdom he has kept us from temptation when we were weak. In wisdom he has given us strength. In wisdom he brings us in the valley that we may learn to call upon him. In wisdom he brings us to the mountain tops that we may rejoice in him. In wisdom he strips us of all earthly comfort that we may learn to trust in him, saying, 'Though he slay me, yet will I trust in him'. In wisdom he takes our most darling relations that we may learn to love him. It is the wisdom of God that works all things together for our good; and it is the faithfulness of God that preserves us in all our trials (Malachi 3:6).

God's perfection

Finally, observe that 'the manifold wisdom of God' is made known to the angels by God's perfection of the church. When the last of God's people shall be brought in, and the angels shall wander through the heavenly streets and talk with the redeemed, they will know by the church 'the manifold wisdom of God'.

God, our God, the Triune Jehovah, will have a people out of every kindred, nation, tribe, tongue, culture, rank and class of society. They shall all be one. My brethren, we shall sit down in the kingdom with Abraham, Isaac and Jacob. In that day all things shall be reconciled to God. In that day the saints shall enjoy the perfection of glory, and God alone shall receive all praise and honour (Ephesians 5:25-27).

See how much interest the angels have in the gospel. Let us make it our lifelong study. We walk in the company of angels. They serve us, they protect us, they care for us, but they desire to learn from us. Imagine the joy of the heavenly host, created and sent forth by the Triune God to be ministering spirits to his elect, when our Lord Jesus Christ presents us in his own perfection before his Father's throne!

Chapter 39

A Family Prayer (My Prayer For You)

Wherefore I desire that ye faint not at my tribulations for you, which is your glory. For this cause I bow my knees unto the Father of our Lord Jesus Christ, Of whom the whole family in heaven and earth is named, That he would grant you, according to the riches of his glory, to be strengthened with might by his Spirit in the inner man; That Christ may dwell in your hearts by faith; that ye, being rooted and grounded in love, May be able to comprehend with all saints what *is* the breadth, and length, and depth, and height; And to know the love of Christ, which passeth knowledge, that ye might be filled with all the fulness of God. Now unto him that is able to do exceeding abundantly above all that we ask or think, according to the power that worketh in us, Unto him *be* glory in the church by Christ Jesus throughout all ages, world without end. Amen.

(Ephesians 3:13-21)

The Apostle Paul was deeply affected by a heart-felt closeness and union which he had with all the saints in Jesus Christ, God's elect, his family. He lived, preached, and suffered for the sake of his family, the church. The prayer contained in this third chapter of Ephesians is an example of the love of faithful pastors for God's people. I take the Apostle's words for my own. Paul's prayer for his family, the church, is my prayer for you. May God be pleased to grant it for Christ's sake.

In the previous verses, Paul had described to the church his attitude toward the ministry. To this man, preaching the gospel was not an irksome task that he was required to perform. It was his great joy to preach among the Gentiles the unsearchable riches of Christ. He counted it a gift of God's grace. Therefore, he was content to preach Christ, even when it meant he must endure many hardships, many even from those for whom he laboured.

Paul was now a prisoner at Rome, imprisoned for preaching the gospel, by the very people to whom he preached, yet his concern was not for himself or for his physical welfare. It was for the spiritual welfare of God's saints. He wrote to the Church at Ephesus with the heart of a pastor, the kind of pastor God promises to give his people (Jeremiah 3:15). Listen to his words of concern.

'Wherefore I desire that ye faint not at my tribulations for you, which is your glory' (v. 13). This servant of God endured many hardships. He was reproached as an evil-doer. He was stoned, beaten and imprisoned. Eventually, he was slain. All of these things he endured gladly. It is true that by the exercise of human wisdom and expedience he could have avoided them. Why then did he endure these things? He did it for the elect's sake, for Christ's body's sake, for the church. He endured all this for the redeemed of the Lord, for you and for me. It was for the sake of preaching the gospel among the Gentiles and confirming their faith in the gospel, that Paul suffered. He was concerned these Ephesian saints might be ashamed of him, the prisoner of Christ. Therefore, he made this prayer for his family, the church of God, that it might grow and be strengthened in the love of Christ.

The picture

There could hardly be a more impressive picture than the Apostle on his knees in a Roman prison interceding for his beloved brethren. Next to the view of our Lord praying in Gethsemane is the picture of the Apostle Paul on his knees in Rome. Here, in supplication and prayer, the stocks and chains fall from him, and he is free. His spirit soars. Paul thus triumphantly writes in jail before he is executed. In the second letter to his son in the ministry, Timothy, he speaks of his imprisonment; then he says, 'But the word of God is not bound'. God's Word could never be imprisoned. The Word of God is free so the spirit of God's servant is free, though his body is in bonds. What a marvellous example he sets before us. May God give us such hearts, so that our care is not for ourselves, but for others.

> Lord, help me to live from day to day,
> In such a self-forgetful way
> That through the day and when I pray,
> My life may be for others.

Help me in everything I do
To ever be faithful and true
And know that if I would serve You
I must be serving others.

Let self be crucified and slain,
Buried, and never rise again!
In union with Your darling Son,
Use me, my God, for others.

If we who preach the gospel could learn this lesson, God might be pleased to use us. We must learn not to seek a name for ourselves, but the everlasting good of the people we serve. We labour not for fame and fortune, but for the glory of Christ and the good of immortal souls. How happy would the church of God be if we could each learn to live for others, if each esteemed the other better than himself, if we spent our lives for one another! In all things, let us seek to spend ourselves and be spent of God for the benefit of his people. How he has blessed me, if he makes me a blessing to you!

The purpose

'For this cause I bow my knees unto the Father of our Lord Jesus Christ, Of whom the whole family in heaven and earth is named' (vv. 14, 15). I fear that too often we rush into the presence of God in an irreverent manner. We sometimes pray because it is expected. We go through the motions of prayer without any real purpose in mind. When our prayers lack purpose they are only vain repetitions and an offence to God. We need to order our words before God as he directs us by his Spirit.

Paul here declares a clear and distinct purpose in prayer, 'For this cause'. When you and I go to God in prayer, we should do so with a definite cause or purpose. Paul had a specific cause for which he sought the Lord. He was seeking God's strength for his brethren to prevent them from fainting or falling. Nothing is more desirable to a minister than that his hearers would persevere in the way of faith and righteousness; that nothing would turn them away from Christ; that God would graciously keep them and preserve them for Christ's sake.

Only the Lord God can keep you. Only God can keep me. This is God's work. The perseverance and preservation of the saints is a gift of God's grace. He has promised to do it. 'And I give unto them eternal life; and they shall never perish, neither shall any man pluck them out of my hand' (John 10:28). 'Being confident of this very thing, that he which hath begun a good work in you will perform it until the day of Jesus Christ' (Philippians 1:6).

Still, we must never forget that God will be sought for his promises. His word is, 'Ask of me … and I will give it thee'. Paul was praying that God would make theses saints see the wondrous mystery of their fellowship in Christ. The church of God is one family, one family as a local church, one family with all God's saints on earth, one family with all God's saints in heaven.

Paul's prayer and heart's desire to God is the same that mine is for you, that you might be made partakers of all the promises of God by the gospel. The promise of life eternal, the promises of the Covenant, the promises of comfort and consolation, peace and joy, and the promises of strength and confident faith. Oh, how I pray that the Lord God will bless my labours for your souls to that end!

I am sometimes asked, 'How should we pray?' Here is Paul's answer, 'For this cause I bow my knees'. When we pray, it must always be on bended knees. I am not talking about physical posture. When we draw near to God in prayer, we should do so with reverence in our hearts. It is proper to express that reverence in any suitable means. Do not imagine any particular physical posture is necessary but be careful you do not employ any action or form in public that attracts attention to yourself. When Paul said, 'I bow my knees', he was expressing not the posture of his body but of his heart, a posture of faith, reverence, humility and submission.

'For this cause, I bow my knees unto the God and Father of our Lord Jesus Christ.' There is no true prayer except the prayer of faith to the Triune God (1 John 5:7). We pray to the God of Revelation and the God of Revelation is 'the Father of our Lord Jesus Christ'. He is the living and true God. He is the God of the sacred Trinity. He is the God revealed in Christ. He is God, our Father.

The petitions

'That he would grant you, according to the riches of his glory, to be strengthened with might by his Spirit in the inner man; That Christ may dwell in your hearts by faith; that ye, being rooted and grounded in love, May be able to comprehend with all saints what is the breadth, and length, and depth, and height; And to know the love of Christ, which passeth knowledge, that ye might be filled with all the fulness of God' (vv. 16-19). Inasmuch as Paul had a specific cause for which to pray, he had some specific things he desired God to do for his people. When we pray, we too should ask God to do definite things.

Here Paul asked that God would give four things to his brethren. These things I desire for each of you. Spiritual blessings are the best blessings. These are the things we should most earnestly seek, both for ourselves and for each other.

Paul prayed that we might have spiritual strength. 'That he would grant you, according to the riches of his glory, to be strengthened with might by his Spirit in the inner man' (v. 16). Spiritual strength comes to us according to the glorious riches of God. Strength is granted to us by his grace. We need strength to do the work of God, to resist temptation, to endure affliction and to live for the glory of God.

It is the presence of God the Holy Spirit with us that gives us strength. Strength from the Holy Spirit in the inner man is the best strength a man can possess. Let us seek this strength. Seek it for yourself, for your brethren, for your pastor.

How does the Holy Spirit strengthen our hearts? He leads us to trust in the fulness of Christ's strength. We are made strong only when we are made weak (2 Corinthians 12:1-10). When you think you are strong, you are very, very weak. The weaker we are, the stronger we are. God the Holy Spirit always makes us strong only by making us weak and thereby graciously teaches us to trust in the fulness of Christ and find strength in him (2 Samuel 22:33; Psalms 22:19; 28:7; 59:17; 118:14; Isaiah 12:2).

Paul prayed that we might be confirmed in Christ's love. 'That Christ may dwell in your hearts by faith; that ye, being rooted and grounded in love' (v. 17). Christ himself is the inhabitant of every believer's heart. He dwells there as a King in his palace. He dwells there as a Master in his home. He dwells there as a Friend with us.

Christ dwells in our hearts by faith. Faith opens the door to admit him. Faith receives him, retains him, submits to him and delights in his presence. Christ dwells in our hearts permanently. Christ comes into the hearts of his people sovereignly; he brings his welcome with him and he never departs.

What we need and desire is to be confirmed in his love. Without question, we need to have our love to him confirmed. However, that is not the way to settle things. That is not the way to settle soul trouble. We need assurance in our hearts that we are the objects of Christ's love, that perfect love which casts out all fear.

Paul prayed that we might be enabled of God to comprehend the boundless nature of Christ's love, that we, 'May be able to comprehend with all saints what is the breadth, and length, and depth, and height' (v. 18). I try in everything I write and preach to convey the wonders of our Saviour's love. I want to know and want you to know as much of Christ's love as mortals upon the earth are allowed to know about it. Knowing it we will admire it for the dimensions of Christ's love are boundless.

The love of Christ is as great as God himself. Who can know it to perfection? 'It is as high as heaven; what canst thou do? deeper than hell; what canst thou know? The measure thereof is longer than the earth, and broader than the sea' (Job 11:8, 9).

Yet, we have been made to comprehend that his love is without boundary. In its breadth it reaches to all nations, ages and conditions of men. In its length it is from everlasting to everlasting. In its depth it reaches to the lowest of sinners to retrieve and save them.

Study the love of Christ! Dwell much upon it. It will fill your heart with amazement, and it will satisfy your soul. This is my prayer for you, 'And to know the love of Christ, which passeth knowledge, that ye might be filled with all the fulness of God' (v. 19).

The praise

When we bow to God in prayer, we should have a definite cause, we should seek specific blessings and we should be careful to offer praise to him for his goodness. Let us praise him, our great and glorious Triune Jehovah, for his Person and for his power. 'Now unto him that is able to do exceeding abundantly above all that we ask or think, according to the power that worketh in us' (v. 20). There is an inexhaustible fulness in our God. His wisdom, power, grace and mercy extend beyond anything that we can ask or even think. Open your mouth ever so wide, and he is able still to fill it, and more. We have proof of God's all sufficiency in the Scriptures, in the history of God's saints, and in our own experience.

Let us ascribe praise to God in the church. 'Unto him be glory in the church by Christ Jesus throughout all ages, world without end. Amen' (v. 21). The church is the place where God's glory is revealed. He alone must be honoured in the church. He will preserve his church throughout all ages for his own glory. God is glorified in the church by Christ alone. He accepts our praise through Christ and that which gives him glory is the work of Christ.

Chapter 40

'For This Cause I Bow My Knees'

For this cause I bow my knees unto the Father of our Lord Jesus Christ, Of whom the whole family in heaven and earth is named, That he would grant you, according to the riches of his glory, to be strengthened with might by his Spirit in the inner man; That Christ may dwell in your hearts by faith; that ye, being rooted and grounded in love, May be able to comprehend with all saints what *is* the breadth, and length, and depth, and height; And to know the love of Christ, which passeth knowledge, that ye might be filled with all the fulness of God.

(Ephesians 3:14-19)

The Apostle Paul was not content to travail in birth for souls and to become a spiritual father to them. After sinners were saved by the grace of God, being born into Christ's Kingdom, he exercised the responsibilities of a nursing father to them. He cared tenderly for those souls to whom God had blessed his ministry. He desired to see them grow in the grace and knowledge of our Lord Jesus Christ. He laboured to feed their souls that their faith might mature and strengthen. He was parent, nurse and teacher. In fact, he became all things, as far as lay within his power, to his spiritual children.

Inspired by God the Holy Spirit, the Apostle knew it is needful for God's saints on this earth, struggling with their corruption, sin and unbelief, to know themselves to be the objects of God's everlasting, immutable and free love in Christ.

I bow

'For this cause I bow my knees unto the Father of our Lord Jesus Christ'. God's servant bowed his knees unto the God and Father of our Lord Jesus Christ, as the

Father of the whole family of Christ, in heaven and in earth. God the Father is, in every sense of the word, the God and Father of our Lord Jesus Christ. It is he who gave the Church to Christ before the foundation of the world (John 17:6; Ephesians 1:4). Happy and blessed are those who are taught and given grace by God the Holy Ghost to bow the knee before him! Oh, Spirit of God, bow the knee of my heart before him, who is the God and Father of our Lord Jesus Christ! Oh, that I may know thee, the only true God, and Jesus Christ whom thou hath sent!

Trinitarians

The Word of God constantly speaks of our great God in the Trinity (Tri-unity) of his Sacred Persons. The doctrine of the Trinity is never argued for, explained or defended in Holy Scripture. It is simply stated as a matter of fact; known, believed, and rejoiced in by all who know God.

If you never read anything Paul wrote except the epistle to the Ephesians, you would have to be convinced that the man who penned this epistle was a Trinitarian. Throughout this book, the inspired Apostle speaks of the Persons (plural) of the (one) Triune Godhead, and the operations of each for our salvation. In the very first chapter, he shows us how we were chosen by God the Father, redeemed by God the Son, and called by God the Holy Spirit.

Our hearts should be overwhelmed when we are made to realise each Person of the eternal Godhead has a personal interest in our immortal souls. We are loved by God; Father, Son and Holy Ghost. We are saved by God; Father, Son and Holy Ghost. Our eternal destiny will have its fulness in God; Father, Son, and Holy Ghost. We are Trinitarians. We worship one God in the Trinity of his Sacred Persons, the Triune Jehovah. Always hold it as a truth precious to your heart that each Person of the sacred Trinity loves you, provides for you and is one with you.

Look at vv.16-19. Here are three things we need, three things we should seek from our God constantly. The strength of the Holy Spirit (v. 16). The presence of Christ (vv. 17-19a). The fulness of God (v. 19b).

The strength of the Spirit

First, we need the strength of God the Holy Spirit. 'That he would grant you, according to the riches of his glory, to be strengthened with might by his Spirit in the inner man' (v. 16). We are weak creatures. 'Without me, ye can do nothing.' Without Christ, we cannot see or enter the Kingdom of God. We cannot pray, believe him, or understand his Word. Without Christ we cannot know the way, walk in the way, or help others along the way. 'Without me, ye can do nothing.'

That is what the Lord Jesus declares. It is what our experience teaches us. Yet, we all tend to think and act as though we are completely self-sufficient. We need spiritual strength, the strength of God the Holy Spirit. Such a prayer as Paul's is an admission of our need. Blessed is that man who is made to know his weakness, that he may seek to 'be strengthened with might by his Spirit in the inner man'.

The source of all that we need and desire from God is 'the riches of his glory'. We desire nothing but what comes to us 'according to his riches in glory'. God is glorious in all his attributes. His power is infinite. His love immeasurable. His mercy is boundless. His grace is indescribable. His wisdom is vast beyond imagination. His holiness is unapproachable. His justice is incomparable. His truth is matchless. His faithfulness is relentless. These are the riches of his glory. All of God's holy Being is a storehouse of riches to us. It is not his power to the exclusion of his mercy, nor his mercy to the exclusion of his power, nor his justice to the exclusion of his grace, nor his grace to the exclusion of his justice. Everything in God renders him glorious; that is the object of our adoration and hope.

What does all of that mean? God has joined his own glory to the good of his people! The Apostle Paul prayed that God would deal with his people according to the abundance of his grace and power, which constitutes his glory and makes him the source of all good. His glorious riches comprehend everything in his holy Being, all that makes him glorious.

We are prone to every evil. We have no strength of our own. We must have God's strength to perform our daily labours, to oppose the lusts of our flesh, to resist Satan's fiery darts, to endure affliction and to persevere in faith. To have this strengthening 'with might by his Spirit in the inner man', God must make us weak and keep us weak before him. That is what we learn from Paul's experience in 2 Corinthians 12. It is the work of the Holy Ghost to strengthen us, to make us weak that he might strengthen us. He strengthens us by leading us to the fulness of grace and strength in Christ. He strengthens us by shedding the love of God abroad in our hearts. He strengthens us by causing us to know our weakness and sweetly forcing us to look to Christ. 'When I am weak, then am I strong' (2 Corinthians 12:10). 'Though our outward man perish, yet the inward man is renewed day by day' (2 Corinthians 4:16).

The presence of Christ

Second, while we make our pilgrimage through this world, we need the presence of Christ (vv. 17-19a). God has determined that in all things Christ will have the pre-eminence. So it is with the believer. If we have Christ, we have all. Paul knew that so he prays, 'That Christ may dwell in your hearts by faith'.

The promise of his presence is that which our Lord uses throughout the Book of God to comfort the hearts of his people. All who are born of God are 'partakers of the divine nature'. Christ is formed in us, a new man 'created in righteousness and true holiness'. Saved sinners are people in whom Christ dwells. We are partakers of Christ by the Holy Spirit and partakers of the Holy Spirit by the presence of Christ in us. Where Christ is, there the Holy Spirit is. Where the Holy Spirit is, there Christ is.

Our Lord promised he would come to us and abide with us. 'I will not leave you comfortless; I will come to you. Yet a little while, and the world seeth me no more; but ye see me: because I live, ye shall live also … If a man love me, he will keep my words: and my Father will love him, and we will come unto him, and make our abode with him' (John 14:18, 19, 23). God the Father has placed all the fulness of grace in Christ; and those who have Christ want for nothing.

The place of Christ's presence is our hearts. What we want is for Christ to dwell in our hearts. It is not enough to have him in my thoughts. I must have him in my heart. It is not enough to have him on my lips. I must have him in my heart. Christ in the heart is the life of the soul (Romans 8:9, 10; Galatians 2:20). Christ dwells in the hearts of his people. He does not merely make an occasional visit to spend a few minutes, or a few hours, or a few days. The Lord Jesus Christ is the constant tenant of a saved sinner's inmost being.

He dwells in his chosen like a king in his palace. He dwells in his elect like a man in his home. He dwells in us perpetually because we are one with him. Where he once takes up his residence, he never totally and finally departs. He may hide his face; but he never forsakes. He may appear to have forsaken us, sweetly forcing us to seek him; but he never abandons the purchase of his blood; the love of his heart, the bride of his choice. The Lord Jesus Christ dwells in the hearts of saved sinners by faith. He never resides where he is not wanted. He must be a welcome guest, or he will not be a guest at all. He comes in uninvited, unwanted and unexpected. But when he comes, he brings his welcome with him and, creating faith in us, causing us to gladly receive him, embrace him, and commune with him.

Christ does not and cannot dwell in the heart of the unregenerate. Christ cannot dwell in the heart of any the Father has not given to him. In every heart where Christ dwells, the Lord God has given testimony, that the precious soul is a child of God, given by the Father, redeemed by the Son, and regenerated by the Holy Ghost.

And where Christ dwells in the heart by faith, there all other blessings follow (Ephesians 1:3-7). Rooted in Christ, we are one with Christ. Grounded in love, we feel all the sweet influences of love. Though the love of Christ is unsearchable and past finding out, yet we can, in some measure, comprehend that it reaches from everlasting to everlasting. Though its dimensions are infinite and it is a love 'which passeth knowledge', we know it to be a special, peculiar, free and gracious love, that runs through all time and to all eternity to his people.

When Christ dwells in the heart by faith, he assures us of his love. 'That ye being rooted and grounded in love.' Paul uses a metaphor that speaks of firmness 'rooted and grounded'. How blessed it is to be 'rooted and grounded' in the love of Christ! Rooted in it, like the great oak whose roots sink deep into the ground and wrap around a firm rock. Grounded like a skyscraper, built on a firm foundation.

I want you to know all that is knowable about the love of Christ. That ye 'may be able to comprehend with all saints what is the breadth, and length, and depth, and height'. Yet, when we have learned all that is knowable, the love of Christ is beyond our highest imagination. There is nothing in the salvation of your soul that is not built upon and flowing from the love of Christ.

To know the love of Christ is acquaintance with the greatest wisdom. John Calvin wrote, 'Almost all men are infected with the disease of desiring useless knowledge. Therefore, this admonition is very useful. What is necessary for us to know, and what the Lord desires us to contemplate, above and below, on the right hand and on the left, before and behind. The love of Christ is held out to us to meditate on day and night and to be wholly immersed in. He who holds to this alone, has enough. Beyond it there is nothing solid, nothing useful, nothing, in short, that is right or sound. Go abroad in heaven and earth and sea, you will never go beyond this without overstepping the lawful bounds of wisdom.'

The breadth of Christ's love is such that it extends to all ranks and races of men. The breadth of the Saviour's love encompasses the whole body of God's elect. We have the best understanding of the breadth of Christ's love when we realise that it reaches to our own lost and guilty souls. I never realised that the love of God was such a broad river until I found that it reached even to me! You can measure the breadth of the Saviour's love when you can measure the sins it covers. The breadth of Christ's love is displayed in his marvellous providence.

There is nothing that concerns the welfare of his people that is not important to our King. The hairs of our heads are all numbered. In all out afflictions he is afflicted. Can you begin to estimate all that the Redeemer has brought to your soul? When you can, then you can measure the breadth of his love.

What of the length of Christ's love. This love is without beginning and without a cause. It is without interruption. This is love without change and without end. Make this a life's study, 'To know the love of Christ'. Covet this. It is the best gift.

Plunge into the depths of the love of God. What an infinite ocean it is! For his love to us he became one of us and bore our sorrows. He was made sin for us! He was made a curse for us, forsaken of God for us! He suffered our death, endured our hell and stooped down to the very depths of human depravity to save us!

Sinner, you cannot have gone too deep for Christ's love to reach you! Fallen saint, you cannot have sinned too fully for Christ's love to forgive you!

Oh, that you might know the height of my Saviour's love! His love adopted us as children, gave us an inheritance in heaven, and is bringing us safe to glory. 'Behold, what manner of love the Father hath bestowed upon us, that we should be called the sons of God: therefore the world knoweth us not, because it knew him not. Beloved, now are we the sons of God, and it doth not yet appear what we shall be: but we know that, when he shall appear, we shall be like him; for we shall see him as he is. And every man that hath this hope in him purifieth himself, even as he is pure' (1 John 3:1-3).

The fulness of God

Third, I want to be, and I want you to be 'filled with all the fulness of God' (v. 19). What an expression! 'Filled with all the fulness of God.' We would not dare to use it if it were not given by inspiration. I will say very little about it because I know very little about it. Its meaning is beyond me. What can this mean, to be 'filled with all the fulness of God'?

To be filled with the fulness of God is to be filled up with God. Filled with a sense of his love. Filled with the salvation of his Son. Filled with his Spirit (Galatians 5:25; Ephesians 5:18). Filled with his grace. To be filled with the fulness of God is to have our souls so full of God that there is neither room, nor desire, for anything else.

I can perhaps illustrate the text better than I can explain it. If you were to go to the ocean and fill a bottle with water, seal it firmly, and then cast it into the ocean, the ocean would be in the bottle, and the bottle would be in the ocean. So it is with our souls. We have God in us, but we are in him. We are swallowed up in God's love, and we are to be full of God's love. May God grant that it will be so to each of us, for Christ's sake.

Chapter 41

The Family Of God

Of whom the whole family in heaven and earth is named.

(Ephesians 3:15)

This third chapter of Ephesians is built upon one word. If we understand Paul's usage of that one word, we will have a key to unlock the door of understanding for the entire epistle. That key word is 'family'. Paul's doctrine throughout this book is concerning the family of God.

Family

What is more precious to a man than his family? We all understand the meaning of the word 'family'. A family is a group of people living in one house, under the rule and government of a single head – the father. A family consists of men and women and their children; boys and girls, the descendants of common parents. We love our family. Family gatherings are natural, and right, and good. They are one of the very few pleasant things that have survived the fall of our race. Next to the grace of God, I know of no principle which unites people so much in this sinful world as family ties. Blood is a powerful bond. I have often seen people that will stand up for their family relations, simply because they are family. They refuse to hear a word against their kinsman, even when they have no sympathy for their tastes and ways. Anything which helps to keep the family feeling healthy ought to be commended. It is a wise thing when it can be done for the whole family.

Yet, family gatherings are sometimes sorrowful things. It would be strange, indeed, in such a world as this if they were not. There are few family circles that do not show gaps and vacant places as the years pass. Changes and death make havoc of our families. All other delights cannot entirely suppress those sad thoughts that rise up in us about faces we no longer see and voices we no longer hear. When our children grow up and begin to leave home, to go off to college or to pursue their careers, there is a sadness that mom and dad cannot avoid. We know that the time will soon come when the whole family will seldom be together again.

You who have enjoyed the privilege of being raised in loving, happy, godly families ought to cherish your families. Cherish every fond memory! Cultivate strong family ties of love and joy. But, at their very best, all earthly families must soon be broken.

Another family

But there is a great family of which I hope you will all be members. It is a family despised by many and not even known by some. But this is a family of more importance than any family on earth. It is the family of which our text speaks. It is the family of God. Here is a family which is everlasting. Not one member of this family shall ever perish! What privileges belong to this family; election, predestination, adoption, redemption, forgiveness, acceptance and providence. Oh, what riches belong to this family; the riches of God's covenant, the riches of his everlasting love, the riches of his grace, the riches of his goodness and of his glory.

All God's elect in heaven and in earth make up one holy family. I pray that each of you may be members of this family. Our family gatherings on earth must have an end someday. This is a family that will never have an end, a family in which there is no death, the family of God.

One family

The family of God is one. What is this family that the Bible calls 'the whole family in heaven and earth'? Of whom does it consist? In what respects are the people of God in heaven and earth one family? What do the Scriptures say?

The family of God consists of all true believers. God does not have one family of Old Testament saints and another family of New Testament saints. Nor does he have one family in heaven and another on earth. God's family is one in Christ. All real believers are in the family of God; all who have the Spirit, all who trust in Christ, every saint of every age, people, nation and tongue make up, 'the whole family' of God 'in heaven and earth'. The family of God includes all the household of faith. It is the same as the election of grace. Every man, woman and child who has ever been born again and trusted Christ as Saviour since the beginning of time is a member of this family.

Membership in this family does not depend on any earthly privilege (John 1:11-13). To be a member of this family you must be born-again (John 3:5-8). Christ alone can make you a living member of his family. It is his creation (2 Corinthians 5:17). Christ brings into his church daily such as should be saved (Acts 2:47).

The oneness of this family is set before us in the Book of God in many ways. Those the Lord loves in heaven and earth are one, because their names are written in one family register (Revelation 13:8; 17:8). That mystical roll which eye has not seen contains all the names of God's children. Look by faith upon that book and know that those names are all inscribed permanently there. The saints of God are one, because we have one family covenant, 'ordered in all things, and sure', a covenant made with us in Christ, our Head and Representative.

My God, the covenant of thy love,
Abides forever sure;
And in its matchless grace, I feel
My happiness secure.

We are one with all the human race in our father Adam, for in Adam we fell. We realise we are one in Adam, we are one family by the common sweat of the brow, the common tendency to sin, the common sorrows and troubles of Adam's fallen family. We realise it by the common certainty of death all men must face.

But, blessed be God, there is a another Adam, the last Adam, our Lord Jesus Christ, in whom all the elect are one family! It is with him that the family covenant stands as an everlasting covenant and a sure covenant. He has, from eternity, secured to all the chosen family all the blessings of the covenant.

Read the Book of God and see what Christ achieved for all his family. His death accomplished our redemption. His obedience brought our righteousness. His resurrection is the pledge of our life. His eternal honour is the guarantee of our eternal honour. His holiness is our holiness. His sanctification is our sanctification. His acceptance in heaven is our acceptance, and his glory is ours.

In Christ we have a nearer, surer and truer oneness with the saints in heaven than we do with the ungodly on earth. We are one in covenant headship with the spirits of just men made perfect, but not with the ungodly. We are fellow citizens with the glorified spirits above while upon earth we are strangers and foreigners.

How blessed it is to remember that the saints in heaven and earth have the covenant promises secured to them by the same seal. The sacrifice of the bleeding Lamb is the ground of acceptance for the saints above and for the saints below (Hebrews 12:24). God the Holy Spirit is the Seal of the family, by that circumcision made without hands in the new birth (Ephesians 1:13, 14).

We are one with the saints in heaven because we are all born of the same Father. God is Father to his whole family in heaven and earth. He loves us all, forgives us all, protects us all, and hears us all. All who are members of this family, whether in heaven or earth, have been born-again by the same Holy Spirit. We are all children of God by faith in Jesus Christ. We are all born of one Spirit. We are all sons and daughters of the Lord Almighty. We have all received the same Spirit of adoption, whereby we cry, 'Abba, Father'.

The nature of all regenerate people is the same whether in heaven or earth, for in all it is the living incorruptible seed which abides forever, that 'new man, which after God is created in righteousness and true holiness'. The saints above are called the sons of God, and so are we. They delight in holiness, so do we. They are the church of the firstborn, so are we. They love Christ, so do we. They are immortal, and so are we. Those saints above have shaken off the dust of earth and put on beautiful garments, but they are the same as we are in nature. On earth we are very near to being with them. So slight is the change that it takes place in the twinkling of an eye, we read 'to be absent from the body is to be present with the Lord'.

We are one with the saints in heaven, because we are all partakers of the same divine love. The love of God toward his children is not affected by their position. He loves those on earth just as he does those in heaven. He loves us all perfectly in his Son. Our gracious Father loves his people with a love surpassing thought, so that he gives himself to each one as an everlasting portion. What more can he do for the saints in heaven?

We are all one, because we are all heirs of the same promises, whether in heaven or on earth. As a sinner trusting Christ, as one who believes on the Son of God, I am assured by God that heaven in all its fulness is as much mine as it is Paul's or Peter's. They are there to enjoy it and I am waiting to obtain it; but I hold the same title deed as they do. As an heir of God and joint-heir with Christ, my heritage is as large and as broad as theirs. Their only right to heaven is the grace of God in Christ Jesus, his blood and his righteousness; and that is mine, too. Child of God, do not think that the Lord has set apart some very choice and special blessings for a few of his people. All things are yours. 'If children, then heirs.'

One more thing in this regard, the saints of heaven are one with us because they are members of the same body, and they cannot be complete without us (Hebrews 11:40). May the grace of God teach us that all true believers are our brethren. I warn you, unless you are a member of this family by the new birth, you must perish forever.

Inseparable family

The family of God is inseparable. Our text tells us of 'the whole family in heaven and earth', not of two families, nor of a divided family, but of one complete family. We feel pain and sorrow at the death of our loved ones but we are comforted in our sorrow because we are assured that death does not destroy God's family. Nothing can separate the members of God's family from one another.

Death does not separate the household of God. The separation caused by death is only an apparent separation. The family is still one. Death cannot separate us from our Elder Brother, the Lord Jesus Christ (John 17:24). Death cannot really separate us from one another. Were not the tribes of Reuben, Gad and Manasseh one with the rest of Israel, though separated by a broad river? So it is with God's Israel. The whole family in heaven and earth is one, though the swelling Jordan rolls between us.

We meet with the saints of God of every age in worship when we come to God through Christ. It is impossible to restrict our communion with the people of God by the boundaries of time and place. We are one in all the earth and one in heaven. We realise part of the family is in an Upper Room, but we are one family. We feed in different pastures but we are one flock. Sorrow does not separate the whole family in heaven and earth. Those in heaven are soldiers who have fought and won their rest. We are still in the battlefield but we are one army. Not even sin separates the family of the redeemed. The saints in heaven have been washed in the same fountain as those on earth. They wear the same garments as we do. They are justified by the same atonement.

Let me say also that the inseparable oneness of the family of God is presently displayed. The service of those who have departed blends with ours. They being dead yet speak. Are not the works of the apostles yet effectual? Today we are reaping the benefits of mighty and faithful soldiers of the cross who have gone before. The work of the faithful will abide many years after they have gone to glory. One sows, another waters, but God gives the increase. The saints upon the earth continue to reap the benefits of those who have gone ahead of us to heaven by their prayers. The prayers they offered before they died are often answered years after they have gone to heaven. Many a mother has died without an answer to her prayer, but it shall be answered. Many a pastor has died without seeing the prayer of his heart accomplished; but God hears the cry of the righteous.

Towering over all this, our oneness is presently displayed in the fact that Christ is the common joy of all the saints in heaven and earth. He is the object of our worship, the subject of our songs, the delight of our souls, the love of our hearts. We embrace him and he embraces us. He leads us and comforts us.

Family gathering

As the children of God, we anticipate a great gathering of the whole family. The prospects of our earthly families are uncertain. It is a great mercy that we do not know what a day may bring forth. We must all experience sorrowful separations. Many a fine boy will follow the prodigal's path. Many a fair daughter will follow the bent of her own will. Disease, pain, sin and death will break the happy family circle. To say the least, many families have gathered as a whole for the last time.

But, oh, how I thank God there is one family whose prospects are different! The future prospects of the family of God are not uncertain. They are all good. They are all happy. They are all sure! All the members of God's elect family shall be brought home (John 6:37, 38; 10:16, 28-30). The members of God's family shall have glorified bodies one day. All the members of God's family shall be gathered in one company at the last day (Ephesians 1:10). We shall be one in mind and judgment. We shall be one in perfect holiness. We shall be one in everlasting reward. We shall be one in the perfection of Christ's beauty.

Are you a member of the family of God? Children of God, love your family, promote your family, protect your family, speak well of your family. Family of God, take comfort. Comfort your hearts in sorrow. Comfort your souls in trouble. Others have run the race before you, and won. So shall you. Trust Christ, and all that belongs to and pertains to the whole family of God is yours. Seek in all things to honour our family name, the name of Christ, our God and Saviour.

Chapter 42

'The Love Of Christ'

And to know the love of Christ, which passeth knowledge, that ye might be filled with all the fulness of God.

(Ephesians 3:19)

In this passage the Apostle Paul tells us how he prayed for God's people and what he sought for them at the throne of grace. Remember who God's people are as they are described in this epistle. They are described as his chosen people, his predestined people, his redeemed people, his forgiven people, his blessed people, his accepted people and his regenerated people.

One distinguishing mark of God's people is they know the love of Christ. There are no exceptions. All those who have passed from death to life, whatever they may be ignorant of, they know the love of Christ. Without exception, those who are not saved, whatever else they may know, know nothing of the Saviour's love.

An ungodly man may know something about the love of Christ. He may realise the fact of it. He may see the theory of it. He may even be able to talk like a believer, expressing joy because of it. But to know the love itself, to taste its sweets, to realise personally, experimentally and practically the love of Christ shed abroad in our hearts by the Holy Ghost, is the privilege of the child of God, and the child of God alone. Into this experience the stranger cannot enter. This is the garden of the Lord, so well protected by walls and hedges that no wild boar of the woods can enter. This is the pasture for the Good Shepherd's sheep where he feeds them, refreshes them, and causes them to lie down in peace. Only the redeemed of the Lord can walk here.

Self-examination

Here is a question of self-examination. Do I know the love of Christ? Do I know its power? Is it shed abroad in my heart? Do I know that the Son of God loved me and gave himself for me? Is my heart quickened and warmed and attracted to him by the recognition of the fact that Christ has loved me, chosen me, redeemed me and set me as a seal upon his heart?

Every child of God knows the love of Christ; but God's children do not all know that love in the same measure. In the family of God there are babes, young men, strong men and even a few fathers. As we grow in the grace and knowledge of our Lord Jesus Christ, we grow in the knowledge of the love of Christ. The more I am made to know my unloveliness, the more I know his love. The more I know my weakness, the more I know the strength of my Saviour's love. The more I know my sin, the more I know the love of him who bare my sin in his own body on the tree. The more I know my unfaithfulness, the more I know the fulness and faithfulness of his love. The more I know my want of love, the more I know the fulness of his love. 'Many waters cannot quench love, neither can the floods drown it: if a man would give all the substance of his house for love, it would utterly be contemned' (Song of Solomon 8:7).

May God the Holy Ghost take us into the inner chamber with our dear Saviour and cause us drink of the spiced wine. May he be pleased to bring us into his heavenly banqueting house and set over us his banner of love! Come, my brother, come, my sister, to Pisgah's lofty heights and see all the length and breadth and depth and height of the love of Christ that passes knowledge!

The love of Christ might be compared to Jacob's ladder, reaching from heaven to earth. By it, God is brought down to man and man is brought up to God. Some of us are standing on the lower rounds or rungs. There are others who have ascended a bit higher. There are some who perhaps at this hour have just reached the top of the ladder, almost ready to step into the arms of Christ, who awaits them. There they shall rest in his love. With the eternal songs of heaven, they shall rejoice forever and ever. Here are some of the ways by which we may know the love of Christ. Yet we must never suppose that we know his love as we ought; for when we have come at last to heaven itself, the love of Christ is still such that it surpasses all knowledge. May God the Holy Spirit give us grace to know the love of Christ.

Doctrinally

If we would know the love of Christ, we must know what the Word of God teaches about it. If we would know what God teaches us in his Word about the love of

Christ, we must study the Word of God. We ought to study the Scriptures with care, attention and regularity, always depending upon the grace of God the Holy Spirit to teach us. We are admonished to search the Scriptures, for they speak of Christ. The servant of God is required to give himself constantly to the study of God's Word so he may feed the people of God. A pastor's work is done in his study, labouring in the Word of God. Every believer should seek to be thoroughly established in the faith once delivered to the saints. C. H. Spurgeon said, 'Depend upon it, doctrinal ignorance will always make churches weak; but where saints are fed upon the finest of the wheat, and are made to suck honey out of the rock, and to eat the manna and fatness of the gospel, they will, all other things being equal, become the strongest and most valiant believers on the face of the earth'.

This generation of lost religionists needs to be told there are certain things taught in the Word of God. The Bible is our Doctrine Book. The Bible is our Creed. The Bible is our Confession of Faith. We ought to be and want to be as charitable as possible to all men, yet we must believe and preach what God has written in his Word. The Bible alone is true. Anything that contradicts it is a lie.

The Word of God teaches us very precious truths about the love of Christ. 'And walk in love, as Christ also hath loved us, and hath given himself for us an offering and a sacrifice to God for a sweetsmelling savour'. 'Husbands, love your wives, even as Christ also loved the church, and gave himself for it' (Ephesians 5:2, 25).

Christ loved the church and gave himself for it for this specific reason: 'That he might sanctify and cleanse it with the washing of water by the word, That he might present it to himself a glorious church, not having spot, or wrinkle, or any such thing; but that it should be holy and without blemish (Ephesians 5:26, 27).

It is a sweet and blessed thing to know that Christ's love is without beginning. When as yet the world had not been made; when the sun, moon and stars slept in the mind of God, when there had never been heard the songs of the angels, when God dwelt alone in the delight of his own holy Being, then he loved us.

Our hearts leap for joy when we are made to see that God's Word teaches there are no changes in Christ's love. 'Having loved his own which were in the world, he loved them unto the end.' The Scriptures give us many demonstrations of Christ's love. He chose us to be his bride because he loved us. His delights were with us before the world was because he loved us. He became our Surety and Representative because he loved us. He took upon himself our nature because he loved us. He laid down his life in our place because he loved us. He intercedes for us in heaven, setting us as a seal upon his heart, because he loved us. He is coming to receive us into his house because he loved us.

Sadly, there is a tendency in some to make doctrinal knowledge everything. To my great sorrow, I have seen the doctrines of grace turned into a huge stone to be rolled at the mouth of the tomb of a dead Christ. I have seen what men call sound doctrine made into a seal to seal the dead Christ, lest by any means the power of his grace should come out to the salvation of sinners. Doctrine is the throne upon which Christ sits and when the throne is vacant, it has no attraction for us. It is the King, not the throne that we worship. The doctrines of the gospel are but the tongs of the altar. Christ is the Sacrifice of sweet-smelling savour. Doctrines are the garments of our Beloved. They all smell of myrrh, cassia and aloes. Yet it is not the garments we love, but the person of our Lord.

Learn the doctrine. Learn it well. But if your knowledge of the love of Christ is only what is taught in the catechism, you know nothing of his love. Let our doctrinal knowledge be precise, but let it be only the beginning.

Gratefully

All who have experienced the love of Christ know it gratefully. Do you not hold in grateful memory the hour when Christ first came into your heart? Some of us can remember the place and the hour that Christ met us. Oh! That day of days, that first day of spiritual life! Other days have lost their freshness to us, but not that day. That was the day of our marriage to our faithful and loving Husband. That was the day when first our souls were allowed to feast at the Father's table. That was a day when heaven came to earth and filled our souls.

Just at the time we had come to the end of ourselves, God the Holy Ghost came to us in saving power and shed abroad in our hearts the love of Christ to our souls! We had walked in the prodigal's way. We were burdened with the awesome load of sin. We felt we soon would be turned into hell. Well does my soul recall the bitterness of those days. My eyes would not close in sleep for fear. But then the Saviour revealed himself to my heart. Oh, child of God, do you not remember that happy day? The blessed Saviour spoke to your soul as you gazed with broken-hearted wonder upon him. He said, 'I died that you may live'. He said, 'Come weary one and rest'. He said, 'Come naked one and be clothed'. He said, 'Come sinful one and be cleansed'. Do you not well remember the joy that flooded your soul when you first trusted him and he spoke peace to your heart? You had heard of him before. Now you have him and you have learned of him (John 6:45).

We know his love and we are grateful for it. With the revelation of his love our dear Saviour reveals himself to us. He reveals himself to us in a way that the world cannot know. He teaches us his secrets. He opens his heart to us. Day after day, he comes to us. Night after night, he tucks us into bed. He is ever with us, and all that he has is ours. He speaks to us by the way. He comforts us in sickness. He goes with us in sorrow. He blesses us in affliction. He makes our hearts to burn within us when we think of him. Yes, we do know something of his love, for gratitude has been our teacher.

We are so grateful to Christ our Saviour that we have grown in love to him since the day we met him. Sometimes Satan tries to rob us of the joy of our Lord, insinuating that since we do not have the same feelings we had when first we knew him our knowledge of his love is not real. You know that the devil is liar from the beginning. Is Christ such a one that the more you know him the less you love him? Perish the thought! My heart rejoices to tell you I have found that my Lord and Master improves with acquaintance. The more I know of Christ, the more I want to know. I think I speak for all of God's people when I say that the more we experience of his lovingkindness, the more intensely we love him.

When we were first converted our hearts were full of fire and glitter. Why, we could hardly contain ourselves. But then our love was a very shallow thing. Now, perhaps, there is not so much flame, but there is an intense heat. Still waters run deep. When you first light a fire the kindling burns with great flame. Then the kindling goes out, but it leaves the coals red hot with an intense warmth.

Grateful souls, saved by the grace of God, receive every token of mercy as a letter from their absent friend, whom having not seen we love, because he loved me and gave himself for me. Having been much loved and so much forgiven, we love him much in response.

Practically

God's people know Christ's love practically. If you are going to make a soldier, you can never do it at West Point. The place to make a soldier is on the battlefield beside a veteran. If a young man wants to become a farmer, it will never be enough for him to read books on agriculture. The books are fine and good in their place. But farming is learned by going out into the fields with the farmer. The more we walk with Christ among men, imitating him, walking in his steps, the more we know his love in this practical sense (Ephesians 4:30-5:2).

Our Lord Jesus tenderly cared for the needs of men. He was compassionate kind and good. He entered into the sorrows of others, sympathising with them. He served his friends humbly and gladly, washing their feet. The love of Christ is patient, longsuffering and forgiving. His love is self-sacrificing and he is anxious to restore the fallen.

We learn Christ's love by obeying his commands. We live by his rule. 'And this is his commandment, That we should believe on the name of his Son Jesus Christ, and love one another, as he gave us commandment' (1 John 3:23). 'For this is the love of God, that we keep his commandments: and his commandments are not grievous' (1 John 5:3). If we would know the love of Christ, we must seek his will in all things and obey it.

His love is shed abroad in our hearts by the Holy Ghost in such a way that, as we come to know the love of Christ that passes knowledge, we begin to feel for the souls of men as he felt. That is what it is to know the love of Christ practically.

Meditation

One of the most effectual ways of knowing the love of Christ is meditation. If you would know Christ and his love, meditate on him and his love. Spend time embracing him, just holding him in your heart's arms, meditating on his sin-atoning sacrifice; the five wounds in his body, the bloody sweat, the cross, the passion. Think much about the God-man; the cross, the nails, the vinegar, the spear, the agonising cries. If you would know Christ's love, meditate upon him.

You men take time to embrace your wives. Take time to show them your love. You women take time to lovingly embrace your husbands. If you don't, you need to learn to do so. Children of God, take time to embrace your Saviour and to be embraced by him. Take Mary's place at his feet to hear what he has to say. Take John's place at his bosom to feel the beat of his heart. Go on further and cry, 'Let him kiss me with the kisses of his mouth: for thy love is better than wine'.

Let your lips of prayer meet his lips of blessing. Let your lips of thanksgiving meet his lips of benediction. There are heights and depths of Christ's love to be found by meditation that I cannot put into words. Oh, for grace to swoon at the feet of our Beloved! 'He brought me to the banqueting house, and his banner over me was love. Stay me with flagons, comfort me with apples: for I am sick of love. His left hand is under my head, and his right hand doth embrace me'.

Meditate upon his work, his sufferings, his triumphs, and his glorious Person. We shall never want for a subject of meditation if we know Christ's love.

Chapter 43

'O Come, Let Us Adore Him'

Now unto him that is able to do exceeding abundantly above all that we ask or think, according to the power that worketh in us, Unto him be glory in the church by Christ Jesus throughout all ages, world without end. Amen.

(Ephesians 3:20, 21)

Public worship

In the third chapter of Ephesians, writing by inspiration of God the Holy Ghost, the Apostle Paul gives us all that is needed for our public worship; preaching, prayer, and praise. As we open this chapter we have a sermon. Paul gives us a very warm declaration of the unveiling of the gospel mystery that the Gentiles are made partakers of the promise in Christ. It also contains a prayer. Verse 14 begins with these words, 'For this cause I bow my knees'. Then, Paul tells us of the marvellous blessings he sought from God on behalf of the church. In verses 20, 21, the chapter concludes with a hymn, a hymn of adoration and praise.

The doxology

Ephesians 3:20, 21 is an inspired doxology, an inspired hymn of praise to our God. This doxology grows out of and crowns the Apostle's message in the preceding chapters of this magnificent epistle. It should excite us to praise. When God has done such great good for us, we ought to freely pour out praise to his glorious name. We can, and should, do so with hope and expectation that even more good is sure to follow.

Gospel revealed

Reading this chapter, we find the Apostle speaking of the blessed revelation of the gospel in this gospel age. In the fifth verse, he says that it is now made known unto the sons of men. It was revealed under the Old Testament types and shadows, but not as it is now. Now, in this gospel age, it is fully and clearly revealed to his holy apostles and prophets by the Holy Ghost in the Holy Scriptures. Today, we live in the clear light of God's glorious revelation in the gospel. This gives us great reason for thanksgiving and praise.

In the eighth verse, Paul speaks of the relation of the gospel to himself. 'Unto me, who am less than the least of all saints, is this grace given.' Whatever the gospel may do for other men, it is of the greatest importance that we experience its power in us. We must personally be aware of our interest in Christ. Can you speak for yourself and say, 'Unto me … is this grace given'?

In the tenth verse, Paul speaks of the gospel in its relation to the angels. 'To the intent that now unto the principalities and powers in heavenly places might be known by the church the manifold wisdom of God.' The gospel even has its relation to the angels. They have always had something to do with it. They desire to look into it. They are ministering spirits sent forth to minister to those who shall be saved by the gospel. It is written of our Lord that he was 'seen of angels'. The angels of God rejoice over the conversion of sinners by the gospel and join with the redeemed in heaven to sing praises to the Lamb.

Next in verse sixteen, Paul speaks of the relation of the gospel to those who hear it. He prays that God would grant to those who hear the message of redemption and grace in Christ Jesus, 'according to his riches of glory, to be strengthened with might by his Spirit in the inner man'.

Having spoken of the relation of the gospel to men and angels the Apostle turns, in our text, with a full heart to speak of its relation to God himself. 'Now unto him that is able to do exceeding abundantly above all that we ask or think, according to the power that worketh in us, Unto him be glory in the church by Christ Jesus throughout all ages, world without end. Amen.'

Adoration

Our text speaks not of preaching or of prayer, but of praise. It really speaks of adoration. I hardly know how to describe adoration. It goes beyond praise. Praise is primarily something done with our lips. Adoration is an act of the heart. It is supreme worship, absolute worship. It is the act of giving all honour to God from the heart; reverence, esteem, praise, thanksgiving and love. The word 'adoration' is a compound word. It means 'kiss the hand'. O Spirit of God, let us, with our hearts, kiss the hand of our great God; Father, Son and Holy Ghost!

Adoration is the fulness, the height and depth, length and breadth of praise. It is the eloquent silence of the soul that is too full for language. In this spirit, I want us to approach this text. I pray that God will enable us to turn our eyes off of every other object and fix them fully on him.

Let us remember what the gospel does for us, so we may adore God for it. Let us fix our hearts upon the Lord God himself and adore him for himself and for his great ability to bless, to enrich, and to sanctify above all that we can ask or think. The greatness of God's ability should encourage our faith, strengthen our hope and humble us in adoration. Here are three things concerning God's ability to do us good which I trust will encourage your faith and confidence in him; the abundance of God's power, the appreciation of God's power, the adoration of God's power

The abundance of God's power

First, we are greatly encouraged to trust our God for all spiritual good by the abundance of his power. 'Now unto him that is able to do exceeding abundantly above all that we ask or think.' The primary subject of our text is set before us immediately. It is the ability of God. Oh, how I adore the ability of our God! It is God's great ability that gives confidence to the faith and hope of his people. What does Paul teach us about God's ability?

He tells us that we have not yet reached the bounds of God's infinite ability! He declares that God's ability is above all that we ask. That's some statement! We have asked great things of God. Have we not? I well remember how difficult my first prayers were. I felt myself so sinful and knew I did not deserve anything from God, but hell. Yet, I dared to ask the greatest of all gifts. I prayed, 'Forgive me, Father. I have sinned.' I was well enough convinced that he had freely forgiven others. But my sins were so vile I almost felt it was vain for me to seek forgiveness for myself. Yet I asked God for that great blessing.

Since then, I have asked many great things of God. I have pleaded with God to cleanse my polluted soul. I have begged him to heal my backsliding heart. I have prayed for the Almighty to deliver me from temptation. I turn to him for daily need. I ask him to guide me in the way I should go. How I have pleaded with him to hold my heart! These are great things to ask; but God, my God, has done them all.

Sometimes our prayers are limited by our sense of need. We do not really know what we need. The Scriptures tell us, 'The Spirit also helpeth our infirmities: for we know not what we should pray for as we ought'. How our hearts deceive us, so we do not know what we need! When we think we are strong, we are weak. When we think we are most righteous, we are most sinful. When we think we are spiritual, we are carnal. When we think we are full, we are empty. When we think we are well, we are sick. But, blessed be God! His ability to bless us is not limited to our sense of need. We ask for bread and water, but his fatlings and oxen are killed.

Our prayers are often greatly limited by our desires. Then sometimes when we do want great things, our faith is small and our prayers are limited by the smallness of our faith. Our Lord Jesus said to the blind men healed by his touch, 'According to your faith be it unto you' (Matthew 9:29). We bring little cups to the infinite, full, overflowing well and take home only a little water.

No man ever yet believed God as he ought to be believed. When we come to him for great blessings we do not really pray for them as we do not really believe him, and our prayers fail. But God is not limited by the weakness of our faith. 'If we believe not, yet he abideth faithful: he cannot deny himself' (2 Timothy 2:13).

Paul does not stop here. He goes on to tell us God's ability to bless us is also above all that we think. Our thoughts, even at their best, are not his thoughts, neither are our ways his ways. As high as the heavens are above the earth, so high are his thoughts above our thoughts and his ways above our ways. God can do more than we have ever thought. We who are God's people often think of what he will do for us in heaven. Oh, blessed thoughts they are. I tell you that God can and will do more than has ever entered into your heart! 'As it is written, Eye hath not seen, nor ear heard, neither have entered into the heart of man, the things which God hath prepared for them that love him' (1 Corinthians 2:9). Will he take away all sorrow? Yes, and more. Will he wipe away all tears? Yes, and more. Will he remove all pain? Yes, and more. Will he remove sin? Yes, and more. Will he give perfection? Yes, and more. Will he give perfect love, peace, rest, delight, joy, knowledge, holiness and life? Yes, and more. Will he give Christ? Yes, yes, he will give Christ. But we have not yet come to the limit of his ability. He will give us more in Christ than we have ever imagined.

I am trying to convince you, and myself, that God's ability to bless us is so abundant that it exceeds measure. It is without limit! Pile blessing upon blessing for a millennium, you shall not reach the bounds of his ability. Put together the minds and hearts of all the apostles and prophets, and all the saints of all ages, still God's ability to do us good goes beyond our combined thoughts.

Let us use God's ability continually, for it can never be diminished. Our prayers should never be restrained and limited. We cannot ask too much of God. There can be no presumption upon God's ability. 'Let us therefore come boldly unto the throne of grace, that we may obtain mercy, and find grace to help in time of need' (Hebrews 4:16). He bids us come to him without fear. He tells us to come to him for grace. He calls for us to come to him for help.

The appreciation of God's power

Second, though God's power is altogether beyond our ability to ask or think, Paul gives us a hint that we know something about it. He suggests that all who know him have in them, in their own hearts' experience of his great grace, an appreciation of his power. God's great, infinite ability is 'according to the power that worketh in us'. We cannot begin to comprehend the fulness of God's ability, but in our own experience, we perceive something of its exceeding abundance, above all that we ask or think. Each of us who are born-again, who have been made new creatures in Christ, are constrained to confess it is true to our experience that God has already done for us more than we have either asked or thought.

God chose us to be his own before we ever thought of him. God's Son became our Redeemer and died in our place at Calvary when we had never thought of him. Regeneration, that resurrection of the spiritually dead, came to us when we asked not for it. 'I was found of them that sought me not.' Faith came to us as God's gift, though we had no ability to trust our Saviour.

We have asked for many blessed graces and found God able to do exceeding abundantly above all that we ask or think. He is able to forgive our sin by his Son, able to deliver from temptation, to comfort in sorrow, to revive the backsliding heart, to give joy in affliction and heal the sick. He is able to keep that which we have committed unto him and give triumph in death. We have sometimes asked great things of God, but even in giving us these things, he has done exceeding abundantly above all that we ask or think. We asked for forgiveness; he gave us his Son! We asked for cleansing; he made us his sons. We asked for pardon; he made us righteous. We asked for salvation; he made us one with him. We asked for life; he gave us his Spirit! We asked him to save us from hell; he gave us heaven.

We all returned like the prodigal, desiring only to be made as one of the Father's hired servants. But what has our God done? He gave us the ring of love, the robe of righteousness, and the fatted calf of provision.

The adoration of God's power

Third, our text sets before us the adoration of God's power which ought to possess our very souls. 'Unto him be glory in the church by Christ Jesus throughout all ages, world without end. Amen.'

No longer in darkness I'm walking,
For the Light is now shining on me,
And now unto others I'm telling
How He saved a poor sinner like me.

And when life's journey is over,
And I the dear Saviour shall see,
I'll praise Him forever and ever,
For saving a poor sinner like me.

'Come, let us adore him.' Let us adore him with our lips, our heart and our life. Let us adore him with our house and in his house. Let us adore him with our faith.

I call upon you, my brother, my sister, adore him. Adore the Almighty! Let him have glory in the church by our perpetual praise. When he receives glory from the church, then his glory will be in the church. His glory is his presence. His glory is his beauty. His glory is his power. His glory is his goodness. His glory is his salvation.

God's glory is revealed in the church by Jesus Christ. Then, let Christ be exalted in our hymns, our prayers, in our preaching and in our thoughts. God will receive praise from us only through the mediation of Christ. Here is the unity of the Godhead. The Father's glory is in his Son. The Son's glory is in his Father. The Spirit's glory is the revelation of God in Christ.

Let God, our God, the Triune Jehovah; Father, Son and Holy Ghost, alone be adored 'throughout all ages, world without end'. Let him be adored throughout all the ages of our lives. Let him be adored throughout all the ages of the church. Let him be adored throughout the endless ages of eternity!

Praise God from whom all blessings flow,
Praise Him all creatures here below,
Praise Him above ye heavenly host,
Praise Father, Son, and Holy Ghost.

Chapter 44

A Exhortation To Unity And Peace

I therefore, the prisoner of the Lord, beseech you that ye walk worthy of the vocation wherewith ye are called, With all lowliness and meekness, with longsuffering, forbearing one another in love; Endeavouring to keep the unity of the Spirit in the bond of peace. *There is* one body, and one Spirit, even as ye are called in one hope of your calling; One Lord, one faith, one baptism, One God and Father of all, who *is* above all, and through all, and in you all. But unto every one of us is given grace according to the measure of the gift of Christ.

(Ephesians 4:1-7)

The Psalmist David wrote, 'Behold, how good and how pleasant it is for brethren to dwell together in unity' (Psalm 133:1). He admonishes us to 'pray for the peace of Jerusalem' (God's church and kingdom), saying, 'they shall prosper that love thee' (Psalm 122:6). In David's opinion, nothing was more needful, nothing more desirable for us, and nothing more to be sought and promoted by us, than the unity and peace of God's saints in this world.

The Apostle Paul was of the same opinion. While he was a prisoner at Rome, awaiting execution, he wrote this epistle to the Church at Ephesus. After giving us instruction in the gospel of God's free and sovereign grace in Christ, he admonishes us to walk worthy of our high and holy calling as the children of God. The matter of first importance he mentions is the unity and peace of God's Church in this world.

Our great Saviour prayed for the unity of his Church throughout the ages. 'That they all may be one; as thou, Father, art in me, and I in thee, that they also may be one in us: that the world may believe that thou hast sent me' (John 17:21).

What could be of more importance? What could be more beneficial? What could be more blessed? The hymn writer Joseph Swain wrote,

How sweet, how heavenly is the sight,
When those that love the Lord,
In one another's peace delight,
And so fulfil His Word.

When each can feel his brother's sigh,
And with him bear a part,
When sorrow flows from eye to eye,
And joy from heart to heart.

When free from envy, scorn, and pride,
Our wishes all above,
Each can his brother's failing hide,
And show a brother's love.

When love, in one delightful stream,
Through every bosom flows,
And union sweet, and dear esteem,
In every action glows.

The challenge

Here is Paul's exhortation, 'I therefore, the prisoner of the Lord, beseech you that ye walk worthy of the vocation wherewith you are called' (v. 1). In this opening verse Paul urges us to walk in a manner that is worthy of our high and holy calling as the sons of God.

Notice who it is that presents us with this challenge. 'I the prisoner of the Lord.' Paul was a prisoner at Rome but he looked upon himself as the prisoner of the Lord. He was not ashamed of his sufferings, they were the result not of evil, but of good. He was aware that even the evil which he suffered at the hands of men came from the hand of his God. He was convinced that the gospel of Christ and the souls of men were worth the suffering he presently endured for them (Acts 20:24; 2 Corinthians 4:1-18).

Faithful men, faithful servants of Christ, are faithful to the souls of men and faithful in preaching the gospel, no matter how disagreeable they are to some, and no matter what the cost may be to themselves. Gospel preachers must be instant in season and out of season.

Though Paul was in prison at Rome, he knew he belonged to Christ. There are times when God's servants become prisoners; but they are his prisoners, and he tenderly cares for them. Our Lord never thinks less of us because of the reproaches men heap upon us, or the evil they do to us. Let us faithfully adhere to Christ, for he will never forsake us.

Paul was a prisoner at Rome, but his concern was not for his own well-being, but for the Church of Christ. He fulfilled his own exhortation. 'Look not every man on his own things, but every man also on the things of others' (Philippians 2:4).

Paul has given us a good foundation for this challenge. 'I therefore, beseech you.' 'Therefore', also, refers to all that Paul had taught up to this point. It is as if he were saying, 'Since God has done so much for you in Christ, I call upon you to walk as he would have you to walk'.

Here is the challenge, 'Walk worthy of the vocation wherewith ye are called'. We are called the sons of God; therefore we should walk like the Son of God. We are called Christians, therefore let us walk in the way of Christ. We are called the heirs of heaven, let us then walk not as other men walk. We are called believers, therefore let us walk not as unbelievers. This exhortation is frequently given to us in the Word of God (Colossians 1:10; 1 Thessalonians 2:12; 1 Peter 1:15).

Our calling

Our calling is to a life of faith and love. When the gospel is preached, the servant of God calls men to this holy vocation. But here the Apostle speaks particularly of that internal and irresistible call of the Spirit that brings chosen, redeemed sinners into the kingdom of God.

It is a call out of darkness into light. It is a call out of bondage into liberty. We were called out of death into life. We were called out of the kingdom of darkness into the kingdom of God's dear Son. We were called out of the wicked men of this world into fellowship with the children of light. This is a high, holy and heavenly calling without repentance. Once it is given, it is never rescinded. To walk worthy of this calling is to walk with Christ, 'the prize of the high calling of God', ever before our eyes. 'I press toward the mark, for the prize of the high calling of God in Christ Jesus.' To walk worthy of our calling is to walk onward, persevering unto the end. Bow your back into the wind and press on.

Are we called by the Holy Spirit? Then let us walk worthy of our calling. To walk worthy of it is to walk in light as children of light. It is to walk in the liberty wherewith Christ has made us free. It is to walk in faith, leaning upon the staff of his promise. It is to walk in the ways of Christ, emulating his love, patience, temperance, longsuffering and gentle forbearance.

The conduct

This is the exhortation. This is the challenge. 'Walk worthy of the vocation wherewith ye are called.' How are we to behave ourselves as we meet with this challenge? If we are called as God's children into the fellowship of his Son, we want to walk as he would have us to walk. Therefore, secondly Paul shows us the conduct which is agreeable to this calling and promotes unity. 'With all lowliness and meekness, with longsuffering, forbearing one another in love; Endeavouring to keep the unity of the Spirit in the bond of peace' (vv. 2, 3).

We do not walk worthy of our calling unless we are faithful friends to God's saints. Nothing is pressed upon us more earnestly or more frequently in the Scriptures than brotherly love. Love is the law of Christ's kingdom. It is the lesson of his school. It is the garment of his people. In these two verses Paul gives us some things which are demonstrated in the life of one who is governed by the love of Christ. These are things that promote and secure unity and peace among God's people. If we would walk worthy of our calling, we must walk 'with all lowliness and meekness, with longsuffering, forbearing one another in love; endeavouring to keep the unity of the Spirit in the bond of peace'.

There are many precious promises to men and women of this character. 'The meek shall eat and be satisfied' (Psalm 22:26). 'The LORD lifteth up the meek' (Psalm 147:6). 'The LORD taketh pleasure in his people: he will beautify the meek with his salvation' (Psalm 149:4). 'The meek also shall increase their joy in the LORD' (Isaiah 29:19). 'Blessed are the meek: for they shall inherit the earth' (Matthew 5:5). 'Whosoever exalteth himself shall be abased; and he that shall humble himself shall be exalted' (Matthew 23:12).

Who are these meek ones? What is the meekness spoken of in Holy Scripture? Moses is an example of it. He was a truly meek man. The meekness that possessed him made Moses comfortable, confident and courageous as he walked with God. He knew who and what he was; a sinner, but a sinner chosen, redeemed, called and saved by the grace of God. He knew whose he was, God's! He knew what God would have him do, and he would not be turned aside from doing it.

Such meekness is essential to every man called and sent of God to preach the gospel; essential to success in the ministry. 'And the servant of the Lord must not strive; but be gentle unto all men, apt to teach, patient, in meekness instructing those that oppose themselves; if peradventure God will give them repentance to the acknowledging of the truth' (2 Timothy 2:24, 25).

If you are to profit by the preaching of the gospel, you must hear the Word with meekness. No one profits by the preaching of the gospel, no one profits by the faithful exposition of Holy Scripture, except those who meekly bow to the revelation of God. 'Wherefore lay apart all filthiness and superfluity of naughtiness, and receive with meekness the engrafted word, which is able to save your souls' (James 1:21).

Meekness is a Christ-like spirit. Paul urged his exhortation upon the Corinthians by 'the meekness and gentleness of Christ'. Our Lord said, 'Take my yoke upon you, and learn of me; for I am meek and lowly in heart' (Matthew 11:29). How did our Lord show his meekness? 'He was oppressed, and he was afflicted, yet he opened not his mouth: he is brought as a lamb to the slaughter, and as a sheep before her shearers is dumb, so he openeth not his mouth' (Isaiah 53:7). 'When he was reviled, he reviled not again; when he suffered, he threatened not; but committed himself to him that judgeth righteously' (1 Peter 2:23). That is it! Meekness is, in its essence, the committing of myself to him that judgeth righteously.

Such meekness is a very precious thing in the sight of God. 'The ornament of a meek and quiet spirit, which is in the sight of God of great price' (1 Peter 3:4). Meekness and lowliness of mind is rare and seldom seen because it is contrary to human nature. Meekness and lowliness of mind is that sweet disposition of grace that causes saved sinners to disown themselves and give up their lives to God. Lowliness of mind is that humility which causes men to have low thoughts of themselves and high esteem for others. Meekness is that excellent disposition of the soul which makes us unwilling to provoke others and prevents us from being easily provoked by others. These things are opposed to pride, envy, jealousy, anger, wrath and malice. Peevishness is ours by nature. Meekness is given to us only by the grace of Christ.

If we would keep the unity of the Spirit in the bond of peace, we must be longsuffering with one another. Longsuffering is patiently bearing the reproaches, injuries and infirmities of others, for Christ's sake (Galatians 6:1-3). The Lord our God has been longsuffering to us; and we ought to be longsuffering with one another.

Perhaps one of our greatest needs is loving forbearance. Love covers a multitude of sins. If we love someone we will try to hide their faults. The love of Christ experienced in the soul makes saved sinners forbearing with one another. That person who is truly and most fully aware of the depravity of his own heart, his own propensity to every evil, and his own liability to fall into any sin, being loved of God and forgiven of all, is least likely to judge the faults of others, and most likely to forgive their offences. Without these things, there can be no unity and peace.

Earnestly endeavour

As I have said, these things are contrary to our nature, therefore, we must labour, we must earnestly endeavour, to keep the unity of the Spirit. Yes, this is a unity of heart, affection and purpose produced in God's people by the gracious indwelling of God the Holy Spirit. Yet, it is a gift of grace we must endeavour to keep. Pride destroys it. 'Only by pride cometh contention.' Loving humility preserves it. By the Holy Spirit we are united to one another in Christ, so that all of God's people are one. We should earnestly endeavour to keep this spirit of oneness. Let us resolve to let nothing divorce our hearts, but let us pray for one another and care for one another.

Bond of peace

Look at the last line of verse 3. 'Endeavouring to keep the unity of the Spirit in the bond of peace.' The bond of unity is peace. Peace is that cord which binds us together and gives us strength. If you take many small sticks, useless in themselves and useless by themselves, and bind them together with a strong rope, bound together, those small, useless sticks become strong and useful.

Peace makes us one; but bickering, strife, quarrelling, and discord divide us. Let us then be careful to seek peaceable things, and to stir one another up to peace, to keep 'the bond of peace'. Govern your thoughts for peace. Govern your tongue for peace. Govern your life for peace.

This is what it is to be filled with the Spirit. 'And be not drunk with wine, wherein is excess; but be filled with the Spirit; Speaking to yourselves in psalms and hymns and spiritual songs, singing and making melody in your heart to the Lord; Giving thanks always for all things unto God and the Father in the name of our Lord Jesus Christ; Submitting yourselves one to another in the fear of God' (Ephesians 5:18-21).

This is what it is to follow Christ. 'If there be therefore any consolation in Christ, if any comfort of love, if any fellowship of the Spirit, if any bowels and mercies, Fulfil ye my joy, that ye be likeminded, having the same love, being of one accord, of one mind. Let nothing be done through strife or vainglory; but in lowliness of mind let each esteem other better than themselves. Look not every man on his own things, but every man also on the things of others. Let this mind be in you, which was also in Christ Jesus' (Philippians 2:1-5).

This is what it is to live for God. 'But the fruit of the Spirit is love, joy, peace, longsuffering, gentleness, goodness, faith, meekness, temperance: against such there is no law. And they that are Christ's have crucified the flesh with the affections and lusts. If we live in the Spirit, let us also walk in the Spirit' (Galatians 5:22-25).

The constraint

All of these things are good and noble. But they will soon be forgotten unless you have an effectual motive that will cause you to strive after them. Therefore, the third thing Paul sets before us is the constraint for unity and peace. 'Endeavouring to keep the unity of the Spirit in the bond of peace. There is one body, and one Spirit, even as ye are called in one hope of your calling; One Lord, one faith, one baptism, one God and Father of all, who is above all, and through all, and in you all' (vv. 3-6).

The Church of God is one body, one with Christ and one in Christ. It is composed of saints of all generations, both Old Testament and New Testament saints; saints of every nation, kindred, tongue, tribe and age; saints in heaven and saints on earth. All true believers are one body in Christ. Therefore we should not bite and devour one another. We should not despise one another (1 Corinthians 12:15-20). We should love, nourish, and cherish one another.

We have been made partakers of one Spirit, the Holy Spirit of God. Therefore we should be one. He has convinced us of sin, righteousness and judgment. He is the Spirit of adoption who helps us to go to our Father in prayer and comforts us. Let us be one, for he is grieved when we are divided.

We should be one, because we are all called in one hope. Christ is our hope. We all hope for the same thing in heaven, Christ and all his glory. There are no degrees in the inheritance for which we hope. We shall all possess it fully. We are all loved with the same love, redeemed by the same blood, called by the same Spirit, accepted by the same righteousness and saved by the same grace. We shall all wear the same crown.

We should all be one, because we all have one Lord. The Lord Jesus Christ by right of creation is Lord of all. By right of redemption he is Lord over his Church. Let us then live as one! He is the Head and we are all his members.

There is but one faith and all who have come to God by faith in Christ are one. That one faith is the faith of the gospel. Christ died for our sins, was buried, and rose again, according to the Scriptures. This is a God given faith. This faith unites us to Christ and all who are his. Do we live by the same faith? Then let us be one.

The Church of God is one, because we are all baptised with one baptism. We were all baptised, immersed into an entirely new life in God the Holy Spirit (1 Corinthians 12:12, 13). Baptism confesses one death and one resurrection. It is performed upon one people – believers. It is done in one way, by immersion in a watery grave. It is done in one name – the name of God the Father, the Son, and the Holy Ghost. Are we all baptised with the same baptism? Then shall we not be one?

Children of God, we are one because there is one God. There are not many gods, but one God. 'I am the LORD, and there is none else, there is no God beside me' (Isaiah 45:5). He is above all in his supreme excellency. He is through all, working through us all in his marvellous providence and grace. 'For it is God which worketh in you both to will and to do of his good pleasure' (Philippians 2:13). And, blessed be his name, God is in us all. He is in us to save us, to sanctify us, protect us, strengthen us, unite us and to preserve us.

To every one

Paul gives us one more motive, one more sweet constraint of grace, by which he urges and inspires us by the Spirit of God to unceasingly strive, labour and earnestly endeavour to 'keep the unity of the Spirit in the bond of peace'. You have it in verse 7. 'But unto every one of us is given grace according to the measure of the gift of Christ.'

To every one of us who are saved by God's rich, free grace in Christ Jesus, 'is given grace according to the measure of the gift of Christ'. All the grace of God's salvation. The grace of life and faith in Christ. Grace to serve our God and Saviour with his body, the Church.

Children of God, we are one. Then let us be one for Christ's sake. Blessed Father, Son and Holy Spirit, hasten the day when we shall be made perfect in one, even as you are one.

Chapter 45

The Fulfilling Of All Things

But unto every one of us is given grace according to the measure of the gift of Christ. Wherefore he saith, When he ascended up on high, he led captivity captive, and gave gifts unto men. (Now that he ascended, what is it but that he also descended first into the lower parts of the earth? He that descended is the same also that ascended up far above all heavens, that he might fill all things.) And he gave some, apostles; and some, prophets; and some, evangelists; and some, pastors and teachers; For the perfecting of the saints, for the work of the ministry, for the edifying of the body of Christ: Till we all come in the unity of the faith, and of the knowledge of the Son of God, unto a perfect man, unto the measure of the stature of the fulness of Christ: That we henceforth be no more children, tossed to and fro, and carried about with every wind of doctrine, by the sleight of men, and cunning craftiness, whereby they lie in wait to deceive; But speaking the truth in love, may grow up into him in all things, which is the head, even Christ: From whom the whole body fitly joined together and compacted by that which every joint supplieth, according to the effectual working in the measure of every part, maketh increase of the body unto the edifying of itself in love.

(Ephesians 4:7-16)

The King is gone. Our blessed Lord and Saviour has been taken from our midst. From the Mount of Olives, where in agonising conflict his garments were dyed in blood, he has mounted in triumph to his throne in heaven. Having obtained eternal redemption for us, our sin-atoning Substitute entered into the holy place of the

Triune God and sat down upon his throne. After having shown himself for forty days among his beloved disciples, giving them abundant proof that he was really risen from the dead, and comforting them with his wise instructions, he was taken up. Slowly rising before their astonished eyes, he gave them his blessing as he disappeared into the heavens. Like Jacob, whose departing act was to bestow blessings upon his twelve sons and their descendants, our Lord poured out his blessing upon his Church as he ascended up into glory.

But now he is gone! His voice of wisdom is silent before us. His place at the table is empty. His voice is heard no more by mortal ears. It would have been very easy to have found reasons why he should not go. Had it been a matter of choice to us, we certainly would have begged him to stay, unless God had given us grace to say, 'Not as we will, but as you will'. The natural desire of our souls would have pleaded, 'Abide with us'.

What a comfort it would have been to those disciples to have their Teacher present with them. It would have been a great consolation to that persecuted band to see their Leader visibly at their head. Difficulties would disappear, problems would be solved, perplexities removed, trials made easy and temptations averted, if only he would not go. Let Christ himself, their own dear Shepherd, be near, and the sheep would be peaceful and secure. Had he been there they could have gone to him in every affliction, like those of whom it is written, they 'gathered themselves together unto Jesus, and told him all things'.

Yes, to the unbelieving minds of his weak children, it seemed most expedient for Christ to stay. How sad, how perplexed, how troubled his disciples were after his death as they buried him in the heart of the earth. How excited they were when they learned he was risen from the dead. How confused they must have been as they watched him ascend up into heaven, departing from them. A great multitude of chosen sinners must yet be converted. With the eloquence of his gracious words and the arguments of his loving miracles, surely the multitudes could be easily won. If he put forth his power, the battle would soon be over. His voice could awaken the dead. The personal presence of Christ is worth more than thousands of prophets and apostles. That's the way flesh thinks. We suppose that if Christ were visibly present among us, the progress of the Church would be like that of a triumphant army passing through the world.

That is the way flesh and blood reasons. But our thoughts are not his thoughts, neither are our ways his ways. All our thoughts in this matter must be silenced by our God's own declaration. He says, 'It is expedient for you that I go away'. He might have told us that his majestic presence was expected by the saints in heaven to fulfil their happiness. He might have said it was proper for him to return to the reward of his home after such a long exile. He might have added it was proper that he should return to his Father and to the angels of light. But our tenderhearted Lord knew the fears of his disciples. He knew that those fears arose from their personal interests. Therefore, he comforted them by letting them know it was for their good he was going away. 'It is expedient for you that I go away.'

He has gone, and though our weak minds cannot comprehend it, it is better for us that he is now seated in heaven than to have his physical, bodily presence with us here. Oh, we would delight to have him here! There are thousands of places upon this earth where women would delight to kiss his feet, and men would rejoice to unloose the laces of his shoes. But he has gone away to the mountains of myrrh and the hills of frankincense. He no longer sits at our tables. No longer does he walk our streets. He is now leading his heavenly flock by the fountains of living water, and feeding them in the garden of God.

But we who are his sheep below should never imagine that we have lost anything by the ascension of our great Shepherd. No! We are the gainers of it. The Master himself says, 'It is expedient for you that I go away'. Our Lord Jesus has gone into heaven for the benefit of his redeemed. He has gone to glory for the good of his chosen. Let us bow in quiet submission before his throne, asking God the Holy Ghost to teach us some profitable things from the ascension of our Saviour.

Here, the Holy Spirit tells us the ascension of our Lord Jesus into heaven is the fulfilling of all things. Having fulfilled all things, 'by his own blood he entered in once into the holy place, having obtained eternal redemption for us', and sat down as King on his throne. Now, our Mediator, Substitute and great High Priest rules all things from his throne of grace in heaven for the perfecting of his Church.

The ascended Christ

In this text we are assured of this fact: Our Lord Jesus Christ has now ascended into heaven (vv. 8-10). 'Wherefore he saith, When he ascended up on high, he led captivity captive, and gave gifts unto men. (Now that he ascended, what is it but that he also descended first into the lower parts of the earth? He that descended is the same also that ascended up far above all heavens, that he might fill all things.)'

David's prophecy

Here the Apostle Paul expounds to us the meaning of David's words in Psalm 68:18. There David made a plain prophesy of the ascension of our Lord Jesus Christ long before he came into the world. This Psalm is a prophetic declaration of

Christ's resurrection, ascension and glory as our Substitute. 'Thou hast ascended on high, thou hast led captivity captive: thou hast received gifts for men; yea, for the rebellious also, that the LORD God might dwell among them. Blessed be the Lord, who daily loadeth us with benefits, even the God of our salvation. Selah. He that is our God is the God of salvation; and unto GOD the Lord belong the issues from death' (Psalm 68:18-20).

Verse 18, says, 'Thou hast ascended on high'. Having accomplished all that he came here to accomplish, having redeemed his elect from all sin and having brought in everlasting righteousness for us, when he had made an end of sin, having obtained eternal redemption for us, the Lord Jesus took his seat in glory by the merit of his own blood as our Mediator.

'Thou hast led captivity captive.' We do not have to guess what this means. The Apostle Paul tells us that our all-glorious Christ, 'Blotting out the handwriting of ordinances that was against us, which was contrary to us, and took it out of the way, nailing it to his cross; And having spoiled principalities and powers, he made a show of them openly, triumphing over them in it' (Colossians 2:14, 15). The Son of God took every enemy of our souls into captivity. That includes Satan (Revelation 20:1-3).

Next, we read, 'Thou hast received gifts for men; yea, for the rebellious also, that the LORD God might dwell among them'. The ascended Christ, who entered into heaven as a Forerunner for us, received gifts for us? What gifts? All the gifts of grace, righteousness and salvation for men, even for us rebels who 'were by nature the children of wrath, even as others', that God the Holy Spirit might come down here and dwell in our hearts in grace (John 16:7-11), and that the Holy Lord God might dwell among us forever in the world to come. As the result of this, he daily loads us with the benefits of grace.

Psalm 68:19, says, 'Blessed be the Lord, who daily loadeth us with benefits, even the God of our salvation. Selah.' Just think about that! He daily loads us with mercy and grace, forgiveness and righteousness, a refuge for our souls and peace, and access to God and Divine promises.

Verse 20 continues, 'He that is our God is the God of salvation; and unto GOD the Lord belong the issues from death.' He who is our God, he alone and none but he, this holy Lord God, Jesus Christ our almighty, effectual Saviour, he is the God of salvation. To him and to him alone belong the issues from his death. That is to say, all the fruits, benefits and blessings issuing from his death as our Substitute are his to give.

Place and state

Our blessed Saviour, the Lord Jesus Christ, ascended into glory. When Paul says that 'he ascended up on high', he speaks both of the place to which he ascended in his human nature, the highest heaven, and particularly that state to which he was advanced, for then he was highly exalted in the eternal glory.

Our blessed Redeemer, having risen from the dead, is gone into heaven where he sits at the right hand of the Majesty on high. What does this mean?

Victorious King

First, it means that Jesus Christ is a victorious King. God has crowned him with glory and honour above his fellows. Heaven is his throne, and earth is his footstool. He shall reign with incontestable sovereignty until all of his enemies are put under his feet (Philippians 2:9-11).

As Christ ascended up to heaven, he led captivity captive. The allusion here is to the public triumphal parade of a Roman commander who led his captives, bound in chains, through the streets to make an open show of them. Our Lord triumphed at the cross, but his triumph was not complete until he both rose from the dead and ascended on high, having the keys of death and hell at his side. I say it again, the Lord Jesus Christ led into captivity all those who once held us captive.

The world, wherein we were once bound, is under the domain of Christ. The curse of the law by which we were condemned has been forever consumed in Christ. The sin which once enslaved us is forever drowned in the sea of Calvary's blood! Satan, who once took us captive at his will, is himself in the captivity of our Christ, bound in the chain of our great King's omnipotence. 'God is gone up with a shout, the LORD with the sound of a trumpet' (Psalm 47:5). 'And having spoiled principalities and powers, he made a shew of them openly, triumphing over them in it' (Colossians 2:15). Death, which once had the power over all flesh, is defeated. Christ arose crying, 'O death, where is thy sting? O grave, where is thy victory?'

Gates open

Second, the ascension of our Lord Jesus Christ is the opening of the gates of heaven for poor sinners. We are told he 'gave gifts unto men'. Having received power over all flesh, our Lord now gives the gifts of heaven to the sons of men (John 17:2). He received gifts as the God-man Mediator. And he gives the gift of life unto men.

David mentions a sweet and blessed fact that Paul was not inspired to mention in our text. In Psalm 68 the Holy Ghost inspired David to tell us that our Lord Jesus 'received gifts for men; yea, for the rebellious also'. Here is the greatness of his grace. Our glorious King persuades his enemies to lay down their arms and be at peace with him.

Justice satisfied

Third, the ascension of Christ is a declaration of Jehovah's satisfaction with our Saviour. The Triune God has accepted his righteousness for us. The Triune Jehovah has accepted his atonement for us. The Lord our God has accepted his Christ for us, and accepted us in him. The ascension of Christ means he is beyond the reach of the enemy, and we are too. We are more than conquerors through him! The ascension and glory of our Lord Jesus Christ is the guarantee of the salvation and glory of all who trust him.

First descended

There was something that was necessary to make the ascension of Christ possible. He first had to descend (vv. 9, 10). '(Now that he ascended, what is it but that he also descended first into the lower parts of the earth? He that descended is the same also that ascended up far above all heavens, that he might fill all things.)'

It is evident David was aware of the fact that before the Messiah could ascend on high, he must first undergo deep humiliation, for his ascension is a proof of his humiliation. Here is another of the many proofs of our Lord's deity. He who is God the Son was the Son of Man long before he became a man, long before his humiliation. 'And no man hath ascended up to heaven, but he that came down from heaven, even the Son of man which is in heaven. And as Moses lifted up the serpent in the wilderness, even so must the Son of man be lifted up: That whosoever believeth in him should not perish, but have eternal life. For God so loved the world, that he gave his only begotten Son, that whosoever believeth in him should not perish, but have everlasting life' (John 3:13-16).

The Son of God, the Lord of Glory, descended into the lower parts of the earth in the incarnation. 'My substance was not hid from thee, when I was made in secret, and curiously wrought in the lowest parts of the earth' (Psalm 139:15). He humbled himself and became obedient unto death, even the death of the cross, and was buried in the earth. Our Lord Jesus humbled himself first, then he was exalted. First he descended, then he ascended. The same must be true of us. 'He that humbleth himself shall be exalted.'

The ascension of Christ, I say again, is the fulfilling of all things. He filled all the types and shadows of the Old Testament. He filled all the prophecies of Scripture. He fills all his offices; Prophet, Priest and King, for us. He fills his

Church with his power. He fills his people with his presence. He fills the world with his goodness. He fills heaven with his glory, having obtained eternal redemption for us.

The benefits

The ascension of Christ is indescribably beneficial to God's elect (vv. 7, 11-16). In verse 7 we are told every believer receives the fulness of grace from the ascended Christ. All our souls need is given to us by 'the measure of the gift of Christ'. He gives us pardon, righteousness, peace, joy and sanctification. He gives us his Spirit.

Another benefit that we have received by the ascension of Christ is the blessed ministry of the gospel by pastors according to God's own heart, who feed his Church with knowledge and understanding (vv. 11, 12). 'And he gave some, apostles; and some, prophets; and some, evangelists; and some, pastors and teachers; For the perfecting of the saints, for the work of the ministry, for the edifying of the body of Christ.'

He gave us the Apostles. Though they were chosen before his ascension, he gave them special power and authority afterwards. These apostles were given to teach us infallibly the doctrine of the gospel.

He gave us the Prophets. These were not the prophets of the Old Testament, but men like Agabus, who are Divinely gifted to understand the hand of God in providence, making proper and powerful application of the Scriptures. They are men who, like the sons of Issachar, are men who have understanding of the times and know what Israel ought to do (1 Chronicles 12:32).

He gave us the evangelists. These are itinerate preachers, missionaries, who go from one place to the other establishing gospel churches.

He gave us pastors who teach us the gospel (Jeremiah 3:15). God promised in the days of the Messiah that he would give pastors after his heart, who would feed the people with knowledge and understanding. The work of God's servants is here described in three ways (v. 12): He is to labour at perfecting, or unifying the saints. He is to labour in the ministry, dispensing the truths of the gospel. He is to labour for the edification of the Church. The pastor must labour for the salvation of God's elect and labour for the growth God's saints in the faith and knowledge of Christ.

The ascension of Christ, and his rule in heaven is for the purpose of completing his purpose and will for his Church (vv. 13-16). 'Till we all come in the unity of the faith, and of the knowledge of the Son of God, unto a perfect man, unto the measure of the stature of the fulness of Christ: That we henceforth be no more children, tossed to and fro, and carried about with every wind of doctrine, by the sleight of men, and cunning craftiness, whereby they lie in wait to deceive; But speaking the truth in love, may grow up into him in all things, which is the head, even Christ: From whom the whole body fitly joined together and compacted by that which every joint supplieth, according to the effectual working in the measure of every part, maketh increase of the body unto the edifying of itself in love.'

The Lord Jesus Christ will continue to work through the ministry of the gospel, until his Church is brought to perfection (v. 13). One great reason for Christ's gift of pastors to his Church is that the saints may be established in the faith, that his Church may be built up and grow up in mutual, family love. For that purpose he intercedes for us in heaven.

Let every pastor take great care to guard the walls of Zion from those deceitful, crafty heretics who would destroy God's Church (v. 14). Let every gospel preacher faithfully speak the truth in love (v. 15). Love for Christ. Love for your souls. Love for God's glory. Christ alone unites us in the Spirit, gives the bond of peace, and fitly joins us together by the effectual working of his power within us (v. 16).

I urge you to cherish the Church of God, the House of the living God, where Christ meets with and ministers to his elect by his Spirit through the preaching of the gospel. The great purpose for which God has established a standing ministry in his Church is the perfecting of the saints, for establishing the whole mystical body of Christ, in Christ, their glorious Head. When the Lord graciously gathers his people together, there he is, in the midst of them. Then, everything is made blessed and refreshing. There is life and prosperity, vitality and joy, where Christ walks in the midst of his Churches. The body is edified when the good will of him that dwelt in the bush dwells in the assembly of his saints. That good will flows from his heart into the hearts of his people and the fragrance and savour of Christ's name is as ointment poured forth.

'Having therefore, brethren, boldness to enter into the holiest by the blood of Jesus, By a new and living way, which he hath consecrated for us, through the veil, that is to say, his flesh; And having an high priest over the house of God; Let us draw near with a true heart in full assurance of faith, having our hearts sprinkled from an evil conscience, and our bodies washed with pure water. Let us hold fast the profession of our faith without wavering; (for he is faithful that promised;) And let us consider one another to provoke unto love and to good works: Not forsaking the assembling of ourselves together, as the manner of some is; but exhorting one another: and so much the more, as ye see the day approaching' (Hebrews 10:19-25).

Chapter 46

Christ Our Head

But speaking the truth in love, may grow up into him in all things, which is the head, even Christ.

(Ephesians 4:15)

The Apostle Paul is anxious to promote true Christian unity. To him there seemed no surer way to secure the unity of God's saints than to convince us that all true believers are members of one mystical body of which Jesus Christ is the head.

Christ the Head

It is by the preaching of the gospel that God saves sinners (Romans 10:17). In our text, in verse 15, Paul tells us it is by the regularly established ministry of the Word, by the preaching of the gospel in the house of God, that saved sinners 'grow up into him in all things, which is the head, even Christ'. This matter of Christ being the head of the church is of great importance. It is so important that Paul, writing by Divine inspiration, made it a dominant theme of two of his epistles. It is mentioned in three of the six chapters of Ephesians. In Ephesians 1:22, we are told God 'hath put all things under his feet, and gave him to be head over all things to the church'. Here in 4:15, we read Christ is the head of his body, the church. Then in 5:23 it says, 'Christ is the head of the church: and he is the saviour of the body'.

Colossians

The headship of Christ is a dominant theme also in the book of Colossians. In Colossians 1:18 we read, 'He is the head of the body, the church'. There the Spirit of God shows us that the headship of Christ is to be held in the highest esteem by us because it is placed side-by-side with the loftiest honours of our Lord Jesus. In the same breath, the Son of God is called 'the image of the invisible God, the firstborn of every creature', that is the Creator of all existence, and 'the head of the body, thc church'. Colossians 2:19 declares that Christ is 'the Head, from which all the body by joints and bands having nourishment ministered, and knit together, increaseth with the increase of God'.

Christ is the head of all things; he is the head of his body, the church. For any mere mortal to assume this title is equal to the blasphemy of a mere man assuming the mediatorial office of our Saviour. The Lord Jesus Christ is the only head of his body, the church, and all true believers are members of him.

The church

What is the church of which Christ is the head? The word 'church' means assembly. The church of Jesus Christ is an assembly of believers. It is the entire company of God's chosen, redeemed and called people. It is the whole community of the true followers of the Lord Jesus Christ. It is the assembly of those whose names are written in heaven (Hebrews 12:23). That entire body of people for whom the Lord Jesus Christ died at Calvary is the church of which he is the head.

Part of that church is in heaven, triumphant, part on earth, militant but these differences in place make no difference as to real unity. There is but one church in heaven and in earth. Neither does time cause any separation of this mystical body of Christ. The church is always one. The church of the Old Testament and the church of the New is one. The church of the apostles and the church of the Reformers is one. The church of the first century and the church of today is one. Of this one and only church the Lord Jesus Christ is the one and only head.

Blessed is that company of redeemed sinners who can call the Son of God, the God-man Mediator, their head. I pray that God the Holy Ghost will join you to Christ by faith this very hour if you are not now united to him. For those of us who are by faith joined to, and one with, Christ our head, I pray that God will graciously enable us to live as his body, as the members of Jesus Christ himself.

What is meant by our Lord's headship of the church? When the Scriptures tell us Christ is our head, what does it mean?

Competent head

The Lord Jesus Christ is the competent head of the church. As the head of his church he demonstrates many characteristics that show him to be just such a head as his body requires.

Christ is our sovereign and supreme head. The head is pre-eminent in the body. It is placed by nature as the uppermost member and all the rest are below it. The Lord Jesus Christ was exalted as head of all things to the church, 'that in all things he might have the preeminence'.

The Triune God made Christ pre-eminent over all his creation as a man. 'Thou art fairer than the children of men: grace is poured into thy lips: therefore God hath blessed thee for ever' (Psalm 45:2). 'My beloved is white and ruddy, the chiefest among ten thousand' (Song of Solomon 5:10).

As God has made Christ the head of all things in creation, each of us should make Christ alone the head of all things in our own hearts and lives. Let him be the head of your loves. Make him the head of your hopes. Make him the head of your desires. Let him be the head of your delights.

Christ is our suitable head. As his body, the church, has a human nature so does our head. It was necessary for our Saviour to assume that nature if he would redeem his elect. 'Forasmuch then as the children are partakers of flesh and blood, he also himself likewise took part of the same; that through death he might destroy him that had the power of death, that is the devil; And deliver them who through fear of death were all their lifetime subject to bondage. For verily he took not on him the nature of angels; but he took on him the seed of Abraham' (Hebrews 2:14-16).

We should never cease to marvel that the Son of God would stoop so low to ransom rebel worms. 'What is man, that thou art mindful of him? and the son of man, that thou visitest him? For thou hast made him a little lower than the angels, and hast crowned him with glory and honour' (Psalm 8:4, 5).

Christ is our supplying head. He nourishes and cherishes his body, supplying it with all that is needed. He supplies us with grace. He supplies us with daily needs upon the earth. He supplies us with wisdom and knowledge, making known to us the secrets of his heart. He supplies us with guidance and direction. 'I will instruct thee and teach thee in the way which thou shalt go: I will guide thee with mine eye' (Psalm 32:8). He who supplies us with grace will supply us with glory too.

Christ is our sympathising head. Oh, how our souls ought to be comforted to know that our head is touched with the feeling of our infirmities. He knows our temptations and helps us in them (Hebrews 2:17, 18; 4:15, 16).

He feels our afflictions and he will arise for our rescue. 'In all their afflictions he was afflicted, and the angel of his presence saved them: in his love and in his pity he redeemed them; and he bare them, and carried them all the days of old' (Isaiah 63:9).

Complete Head

Christ is also the complete head of the church. The Lord Jesus Christ is our head, because he is our representative. The head is the representative of the body. When we count the number of people in a place, we say we are counting heads, because the head stands for the body. It has always been God's pleasure to deal with men collectively as a body by means of representation. His great covenant transactions are with men in a body, not as individuals (Romans 5:12-21).

We fell in our father Adam, because he was the head of the race. Now Christ is the head of God's spiritual creation. He is our representative to God in the Covenant of Grace. We were chosen in him, redeemed in him, called in him, accepted in him, and we live in him. He said, 'Because I live, ye shall live also'.

Christ is also our head in a mystical, vital sense, as is explained in Ephesians 4:16. 'From whom the whole body fitly joined together and compacted by that which every joint supplieth, according to the effectual working in the measure of every part, maketh increase of the body unto the edifying of itself in love.'

The head is indispensable to the life of the body; even so, Christ is indispensable to the life of his people. He is our vital head. 'In him was life, and the life was the light of men.' Separation from Christ is spiritual death. Union to him is spiritual life. The life of every member of Christ's church is dependent upon the life of our head. From the Lord Jesus Christ alone every living child of God continually derives his life. 'For ye are dead, and your life is hid with Christ in God.'

The head is not only the source of life. It is also the seat of government. Man walks, speaks, eats and sleeps according to the direction of that mysterious something that is found in his head. Thus, Christ our head is the supreme governor of his body.

The head is also the glory of the body. The chief beauty of manhood is in the head. The remnant of the Divine image is best seen in man's head. The face of a man is his distinguishing glory. He holds his head erect toward the heavens. His face is not turned toward the earth like a beast. Beauty chooses her favoured seat in the features of the face. There you see the signs of majesty and tenderness, wisdom and love, courage and compassion. In this sense, too, Jesus Christ is our head. He is all the beauty of his church. She is properly called the fairest among women, because her head excels above all else in beauty. His beauty is our beauty (Ezekiel 16:14).

Yes, blessed be his name, our great Christ is our complete head; and we are complete in him (Colossians 2:9, 10).

Conjugal Head

Another figure that is used in the Scriptures to describe Christ as the head of the church is the conjugal, or marital head. As Eve was taken from the side of Adam, the church was taken from the side of Christ. He is espoused to us, and we are espoused to him as a chaste virgin. We are both anxiously awaiting the day of our marriage. As the husband is the head of the wife, so Christ is the head of the church (Ephesians 5:25-32).

Implications

What does this headship of Christ over his church imply? This is certain; since Christ is the only head of his body, the church, he alone can determine her doctrine. Our doctrine is not to be derived from the reason of man. Our doctrine is not founded upon the opinion of the church fathers. Our doctrine is not formulated by the councils of men. Nothing is to be received as a doctrine of Christ's church which is not plainly written in the Book of God.

Since Christ is our head, only he can lay down the laws of his church. The church has no power to make laws for herself. We do not have the right to form laws upon the opinions and traditions of men. Nor have we any right to make laws regulating the lives of others, either believers or unbelievers. The law of Christ's church is plainly set forth in the Book of God. We would do well to live by it. It is the law of faith. It is the law of love. It is the law of liberty. Whatever contradicts this, we must resist!

If Christ is our head, then his sole authority in all things must be rigorously maintained. I insist upon this because churches are so very apt to seek guidance from some other authority. Many today are guided by what they think will be the results of their activity. Many churches regulate their doctrine and their activity according to the whims of the times in which we live. Other churches have a sacred reverence for tradition.

Our hearts are assured of this fact, since Christ is the head of his church, then all things concerning her welfare are safe. Our head is safe so we are safe. Our triumph is sure. Our inheritance is secure. Christ's glory is certain.

The foundation

What is the foundation of Christ's headship of the church? Beyond all dispute Christ is head of the church by the decree of God. 'Thou art my Son; this day have I begotten thee. Ask of me, and I shall give thee the heathen for thine inheritance, and the uttermost parts of the earth for thy possession' (Psalm 2:7, 8).

Christ's headship rests upon the supremacy of his nature and the efficacy of his work (Philippians 2:8-11). He is God over all and blessed forever, the perfect Man, Firstborn among many brethren. He must be head, God decreed it and he earned it.

The Lord Jesus Christ is head of his church by the universal acclamation of all the members of his body (Revelation 5:9, 10). The saints in heaven and earth proclaim him Lord, and Head, and King.

Let him be crowned with majesty,
Who bowed His head to death:
And be His honours sounded high,
By all things that have breath!

Let us then reject any head, but Christ. We have no pope but Christ. We have no ruler but Christ. We have no authority but Christ. We have no law but Christ.

Our responsibility

What is our responsibility as members of Christ our head? We have a responsibility with regard to ourselves. We must make sure that we are united to Christ, not by a dead profession of religion, but by the living union of faith.

Is Christ our head? Let us be subject to him in all things. Submit to his Word, to his doctrine and his will; his worship, his ordinances and his providence. With the Lord as our head, how happy, content and satisfied we ought to be. Satisfied with his love and his righteousness. Satisfied with his ways and with his purposes!

We have a responsibility to our brothers and sisters in Christ, as members of Christ. Let us show them charity, brotherly kindness, gentleness and love in all things. Be careful not to hurt or offend those for whom Christ died, in word or in deed. Learn to be content with your place in the body of Christ, and serve the Lord with singleness of heart. Highly esteem one another for Christ's sake. Be compassionate toward all your brethren. Suffer with them in their afflictions and sorrows. Rejoice with them in their joys. Be ready to help your brethren in any way possible. Are they fallen? Lift them up. Are they hungry? Feed them. Are they tempted? Pray for them. Are they weary? Support them. Are they broken-hearted? Comfort them. Are they discouraged? Cheer them. Are they fearful? Assure them.

My brother, my sister, is Christ our head? Then all is safe and secure. Our head is safe in heaven and he must have his body (Ephesians 1:23). Jesus reigns. All is well.

Chapter 47

Living For Christ

This I say therefore, and testify in the Lord, that ye henceforth walk not as other Gentiles walk, in the vanity of their mind, Having the understanding darkened, being alienated from the life of God through the ignorance that is in them, because of the blindness of their heart: Who being past feeling have given themselves over unto lasciviousness, to work all uncleanness with greediness. But ye have not so learned Christ; If so be that ye have heard him, and have been taught by him, as the truth is in Jesus … And be ye kind one to another, tenderhearted, forgiving one another, even as God for Christ's sake hath forgiven you.

(Ephesians 4:17-32)

We are admonished in the Scriptures to do all things for the glory of God. And we want to do so. It is our joy as believers to seek the honour and glory of God our Saviour. We want to know God's will in all things. We seek to obey God's Word in the totality of our lives. In all things we want to be led by his Spirit, to the honour of our Lord Jesus Christ, and to adorn the doctrine of God our Saviour, living soberly, righteously and godly in this present evil world.

If you trust the Lord Jesus Christ, if you know him, if God has saved you by his grace, if you are washed in the precious blood of Christ, if you are born of God, if God the Holy Ghost has given you faith in Christ, I am sure of this, nothing is more important to you than living for him. You know you are not your own. You have been bought with the price of Christ's precious blood and you want to live for him.

Paul's purpose

When Paul wrote to his son in the faith, Timothy, he was very anxious that the young preacher should know how to conduct himself as Christ's servant. He said, 'These things write I unto thee ... that thou mayest know how thou oughtest to behave thyself in the house of God, which is the church of the living God, the pillar and ground of the truth' (1 Timothy 3:14, 15). Paul's concern for Timothy was very much the same as that which he expresses for the saints at Ephesus in our text.

Remember Paul's purpose in this chapter. He is trying to secure the unity of the saints. He has urged us to walk worthy of the vocation wherewith we are called. In the first part of the chapter, Paul carefully showed us that all true believers are indeed one in Christ. We are members of that one glorious body, the church, of which Jesus Christ is the exalted head.

The purpose for which the gospel ministry was established is the edification of the church so that all the members of Christ may grow up in him in the unity of faith and love. This is the prayer of our Lord Jesus himself, 'That they may be made perfect in one' (John 17:23). This was the great desire of Paul's heart. He knew that carnal divisions in Christ's kingdom were dishonouring to Christ our head, grieving the Holy Spirit of peace and dishonouring to our heavenly Father.

Exhortation continues

In verses 17-32, the Apostle continues with the same exhortation, 'That ye walk worthy of the vocation wherewith ye are called'. He has shown us the foundation for our unity. We are one with Christ and one in Christ. 'There is one body, and one Spirit, even as ye are called in one hope of your calling; One Lord, one faith, one baptism, One God and Father of all, who is above all, and through all, and in you all' (Ephesians 4:4-6).

We are one with Christ and one in Christ. That is the foundation upon which Paul tells us we must build. In verses 17-32, he teaches us how to build upon that foundation. In these verses, Paul is calling upon each of us to conduct ourselves in a manner which will promote unity. Here the divinely inspired apostle tells you and me how to live for Christ in this world. He carefully tells us what we should avoid and what we should practise if we would live for Christ, live for the glory of God, and live for the benefit of God's people in this world. This is how we promote the unity of the body of Christ.

There are four things in this passage by which Paul shows us how to live for Christ our Saviour. We must not live like other men (vv. 17-19). We must always remember who we are and whose we are (vv. 20-24). We must follow the example of Christ (vv. 25-29). We must seek the glory of God (vv. 30-32).

Walk not

First, if we would live for Christ, if we would 'keep the unity of the Spirit in the bond of peace', we must not live like other men. 'This I say therefore, and testify in the Lord, that ye henceforth walk not as other Gentiles walk, in the vanity of their mind, Having the understanding darkened, being alienated from the life of God through the ignorance that is in them, because of the blindness of their heart: Who being past feeling have given themselves over unto lasciviousness, to work all uncleanness with greediness' (Ephesians 4:17-19).

Throughout this world there is the prevalence of strife, division and chaos among men. It seems impossible for two men to be together for long without division. This was God's judgment at Babel. He sent confusion to our fallen race and it continues to this day. The reason for the terrible confusion of men is the depravity and sinful pride of man's heart. If we have been born-again, if we would honour God in our lives and be useful to one another, we cannot live like the men and women of this world.

'This I say, therefore, and testify in the Lord, that ye henceforth walk not as other Gentiles walk.' The word 'therefore' connects this exhortation to all that has gone before. It is as though Paul were saying, 'Because of your high calling and your responsibility to edify the body of Christ, you should no longer conduct yourselves as mere worldlings'. Paul speaks as God's messenger, with the authority of the Lord. His testimony is in the interest of Christ's cause.

We are no longer like other Gentiles, therefore we must not walk like them. Though we are Gentiles physically, by nature, we are now made fellow citizens with the saints. We are new creatures in Christ. We are the Israel of God. Let us live as those who are princes with God. Let us lay aside our former manner of life and not imitate the unregenerate people among whom we live.

Those who go on in their trespasses and sins, against every warning of God in the law, in providence and in the gospel, have their consciences seared as with a red-hot iron (v. 19). They are 'past feeling'. How sad and what a curse! They have no conscience to prick their hearts. God judicially takes from them all feeling that should turn them to him. They have no feeling of their sinfulness. They have no sense of their misery and danger. When men's consciences are seared, there are no bounds to their sin. They are entirely given over to the evil of their own hearts.

Whose we are

Second, if we would live for Christ, we must always remember who we are and whose we are. 'Ye are not your own. For ye are bought with a price: therefore glorify God in your body, and in your spirit, which are God's' (1 Corinthians 6:19, 20). That is what Paul tells us in verses 20-24, 'But ye have not so learned Christ; If so be that ye have heard him, and have been taught by him, as the truth is in Jesus: That ye put off concerning the former conversation the old man, which is corrupt according to the deceitful lusts; And be renewed in the spirit of your mind; And that ye put on the new man, which after God is created in righteousness and true holiness.'

We should not live like others because we are not the same as others. We have been taught of God and made new creatures in Christ. 'But ye have not so learned Christ.' That which makes the believer different from other men is that he has been taught by Christ himself. 'If so be that ye have heard him, and have been taught by him, as the truth is in Jesus.'

We have heard the voice of Christ speaking to us by the gospel. We have been taught by Christ himself, who dwells in our hearts as a Prophet to teach us the things of God. All who hear Christ and are taught of him learn by him. We have learned who he is; God over all and blessed forever, the Saviour of sinners. We have learned what Christ has done, he died as the sinner's Substitute. He intercedes for us in heaven. He forgives all our sin and gives us acceptance with God. He loves us, teaches and protects us. We have learned his truth. The truth of God resides in Christ, who is Truth! Apart from Christ there is no truth.

Since God has graciously revealed himself to us in Christ while others are left in their sins we should live as new men. We should live as new men because we are new. The old man within us is unchanged, as evil as ever. Having put off that old man, we must continually put him off, 'That ye put off concerning the former conversation the old man, which is corrupt according to the deceitful lusts' (v. 22). Paul uses the illustration of changing a garment. The sinner who is washed in the blood of Jesus Christ hates the very garments that are stained with sin.

The old man is our own sinful nature. He is not dead, but dying. He is not buried, but crucified. The old nature is still with us. The old man is never sanctified. He only gets more wicked with age. We must always be aware of his presence, but refuse to allow him dominion. The lusts of this old man within us are still corrupt and deceitful. They promise pleasure and profit, but give pain and poverty. They promise liberty but bring bondage. They promise satisfaction, but end in destruction. Sometimes the lusts of the old man assumes a religious face, filling men with pride and conceit, who think themselves to be something, when they are nothing.

The way to avoid the deceitful lusts of the old man is to have your mind constantly renewed in Christ Jesus. 'And be renewed in the spirit of your mind; And that ye put on the new man, which after God is created in righteousness and true holiness' (vv. 23, 24).

God's work

This putting off the old man and putting on the new is God's work, altogether God's work. He made us new creatures, giving us a new nature, a new heart, a new will and a new mind. He put Christ in us, making us 'partakers of the divine nature'. Who but God the Holy Ghost, who formed Christ in Mary's womb, could create him in us, 'the new man, which after God is created in righteousness and true holiness'? John Gill puts it thus, 'He only who renews the face of the earth year by year, can renew us daily in the spirit of our minds'.

Christ is the new man Paul is talking about (Jeremiah 31:22), 'Christ in you, the hope of glory' (Colossians 1:27). His righteousness is a garment pure and spotless which must be put on by the hand of faith. As long as we live in this world we must constantly look to Christ, trust Christ, and put on Christ with the hand of faith, putting off the old man, saying no to the deceitful lusts of the flesh. As we do, as we are enabled of God to put off the old man and put on Christ, we are renewed by his Spirit in the inner man.

Here God the Holy Ghost teaches us that the righteousness of God's elect is not the ceremonial righteousness of the law, but the real righteousness of Christ. Our holiness is not the pretend holiness of the Pharisees, but a genuine holiness of heart. Christ is our Righteousness in justification. Christ is our Holiness in sanctification. What a great motive our Divine Comforter here gives us to live for Christ!

Christ's example

Third, if we would walk worthy of our holy vocation and promote the unity of the Spirit in the bond of peace, if we would live for Christ, we must follow the example of Christ. 'Wherefore putting away lying, speak every man truth with his neighbour: for we are members one of another. Be ye angry, and sin not: let not the sun go down upon your wrath: Neither give place to the devil. Let him that stole steal no more: but rather let him labour, working with his hands the thing which is good, that he may have to give to him that needeth. Let no corrupt communication proceed out of your mouth, but that which is good to the use of edifying, that it may minister grace unto the hearers' (vv. 25-29).

The godliness Paul speaks of in these verses has nothing to do with meat and drink. It is not determined by the length of your hair, the observance of days, sabbath keeping, or any carnal, material thing. It has to do with following the example Christ has given us and being conformed to his image. Here Paul tells us some things by which we should adorn the doctrine of God our Saviour, as we seek to live for him. We must learn to live for the benefit of others, for the service of our brothers and sisters in Christ, as our Lord did (John 13:1-15). The most difficult part of that is learning to use our tongues for the good of our brethren.

God's glory

Fourth, if we desire to promote the unity of the saints and walk worthy of the vocation wherewith we are called, if we would live for Christ and for the glory of God in this world, we must seek the glory of God in all things. 'And grieve not the holy Spirit of God, whereby ye are sealed unto the day of redemption. Let all bitterness, and wrath, and anger, and clamour, and evil speaking, be put away from you, with all malice: And be ye kind one to another, tenderhearted, forgiving one another, even as God for Christ's sake hath forgiven you ' (vv. 30-32).

'Grieve not the holy Spirit of God.' God the Holy Spirit is grieved by us when we are at odds and mistreat one another. He has called us by his power. He has sealed us as the heirs of heaven. In spite of everything evil in us and every ungodly thing done by us, he has sealed us and keeps us until the day of redemption.

Spirit of God, give me grace to avoid those things that grieve you, those things so natural to my flesh and dishonouring to my God, by which others are injured. Bitterness is the disposition of a person with a razor-sharp tongue. Anger is fury, a strong sense of rage. Wrath is settled indignation against someone. Clamour is the malice of a person stirring up strife and discord. It is another word for brawling. Evil-speaking is slander, gossip and criticism. Malice is the spirit of hatred and revenge, delighting to inflict pain on someone.

Would you live for Christ? Would I? I will tell you how to do so. In all things, treat one another like God has treated and treats us, for Christ's sake. 'And be ye kind one to another, tenderhearted, forgiving one another, even as God for Christ's sake hath forgiven you.' 'Put on therefore, as the elect of God, holy and beloved, bowels of mercies, kindness, humbleness of mind, meekness, longsuffering; Forbearing one another, and forgiving one another, if any man have a quarrel against any: even as Christ forgave you, so also do ye' (Colossians 3:12, 13).

Chapter 48

In The School Of Christ

But ye have not so learned Christ; If so be that ye have heard him, and have been taught by him, as the truth is in Jesus.

(Ephesians 4:20, 21)

Our Lord Jesus says to all who come to him, to all who trust him, 'Learn of me' (Matthew 11:28-30). If we are God's children we are students at school. We are in the school of grace, in the school of Christ, and our lesson is the Lord Jesus Christ himself. May God graciously enable us to keep to our lesson so that we may ever learn Christ. One thing that separates the children of light from the children of darkness is this, we have learned Christ. We have heard him. We have heard the Shepherd's voice. We have been taught and are being taught by him; we have learned. We are in the school of Christ, learning to live for him, and to live for God.

This distinction should be manifest in every aspect of our lives. We are in the school of Christ. Paul has been writing concerning other Gentiles and the evil lives that they live. Now he tells us that as believers we ought not to walk as unconverted men ordinarily do. If we are indeed the children of God, if we are in the school of Christ, there is a manifest difference between us and the men of the world.

Marked distinction

There always has been and always will be a marked distinction between the woman's seed and the serpent's seed; between the righteous and the wicked, between those who follow Christ and those who follow the lusts of their flesh, the children of God and the children of the devil. The distinction is one made and maintained by God alone (1 Corinthians 4:7). It is God who puts a difference between Israel and Egypt. There is an everlasting distinction between nature and grace, between God's elect and the reprobate of this world. That distinction is made and maintained by God's sovereign and eternal election (2 Thessalonians 2:13, 14); God's eternal purpose of grace in predestination (Ephesians 1:3-6); Christ's particular and effectual redemption (Isaiah 53:4-10; Galatians 3:13, 14; Ephesians 1:7); the irresistible grace and effectual call of God the Holy Ghost (John 3:3-8; 6:63; Ephesians 2:1-10) and by God's gracious preservation of our souls in grace and faith (Philippians 1:6; 1 Peter 1:5).

That marked distinction is a distinction that is to be maintained by us as long as we live in this world. We are either dead in trespasses and sins or we are quickened by divine grace. We ought always to strive to live as those who are born of God and taught of God. As a believer, as a child of God, there are some things I know I just ought to do. I have learned these things, and am learning them in the school of Christ, being 'taught by him, as the truth is in Jesus'. I try to do specific things, and try to avoid others, because I want to honour God my Saviour. When I fail to do so, I am embarrassed. The fact is, there are some 'things that accompany salvation'. If you are God's child, there is something in you which is not to be found in the best of worldlings, something which is not discovered in the most admirable of carnal men. There is a higher something in your character which marks you as belonging to another family of men. You are in Christ, a new creature in him. The fact that Christ lives in you separates you from the rest of mankind.

Something learned

The great cause of this distinction is something we have learned. We have been taught of God. We have been made disciples in the school of Christ, 'But ye have not so learned Christ'. It is something which we have learned that makes us different from other people. Sitting at the Master's feet, and being taught of him, we learn of him. Being taught of him, we are distinguished from the mass of Adam's fallen race. God the Holy Spirit is our Teacher. He takes us to school. The Bible is our textbook. Christ is our lesson. The Holy Spirit has taught us something already. He is teaching us more now. He will continue to teach us more and more, until we shall know even as we are known.

Christ our Lesson

Christ Jesus the Lord is the lesson we must learn. Christ is the one lesson of Divine Revelation. Learn him and you learn all. If you do not learn him, then you learn nothing. Christ is the only lesson which will eternally profit your soul. This lesson is absolutely necessary. Hear his words …

'These words spake Jesus, and lifted up his eyes to heaven, and said, Father, the hour is come; glorify thy Son, that thy Son also may glorify thee: As thou hast given him power over all flesh, that he should give eternal life to as many as thou hast given him. And this is life eternal, that they might know thee the only true God, and Jesus Christ, whom thou hast sent' (John 17:1-3).

Do not misread Paul's words. He does not say, 'Ye have not so learned of Christ', but, 'Ye have not so learned Christ'. That is a very unusual expression. It is not usual to learn a person. But Paul says, 'Ye have not so learned Christ'.

The Apostle does not mean that God's people merely learn the doctrine of Christ. Many know what Christ taught who have not learned Christ. They have read their Bibles. Perhaps they even study the Scriptures. They know doctrine but they have not learned Christ. It is proper for us to learn about Christ, and value every word he has spoken. Still, that is not the lesson. We must learn Christ himself.

Our text is not about learning the precepts of Christ. You may learn all that Christ commands and still not learn him. You may learn all there is to know about believer's baptism and the Lord's Supper, yet miss Christ. You may read with great care our Lord's Sermon on the Mount, his many parables and discourses, and carefully mark his every precept, and still not learn him. Learning Christ is much more than merely learning about Christ. You may know much about Christ; whose Son he is, what he has done, what he is doing, where he is, what he is yet going to do, even how he will do it. You may know enough to be a teacher of others. You might be thought of as a theologian and yet, for all that, not learn Christ.

I know a great deal about many very famous people. I read their biographies. I know about their habits. I am even aware of some of their family secrets. But I cannot say I know them. So it is for many concerning Christ. They know all about him but they have not learned him. Beware of being satisfied with knowing about Christ yet not knowing him, not learning him. I am very much afraid for many who seem to always be increasing in knowledge but not in grace. Nothing is more dangerous to the soul of a man than a barren familiarity with sacred things.

Paul's meaning

What does it mean for a man to learn Christ? We must learn to know him. To know him is eternal life. This is the knowledge for which Paul gladly suffered the loss of all things. This is the one thing he desired. This is that better part, that one good thing, which Mary chose. 'That I might know him.'

I must know Christ personally. I must have intimate, personal acquaintance with Christ as a real Saviour. To learn Christ is to know his heart, voice, ways. 'Create in me a clean heart, O God; and renew a right spirit within me. Cast me not away from thy presence; and take not thy holy spirit from me. Restore unto me the joy of thy salvation; uphold me with thy free spirit. Then will I teach transgressors thy ways; and sinners shall be converted unto thee' (Psalm 51:10-13).

This is the very essence of all true religion. It is personal living with a personal Saviour, trusting a personal Redeemer, crying out to a personal Intercessor and personally receiving answers from one who loves us and reveals himself to us as he does not to the world. Spurgeon said, 'To many people, Christ is only a name to bow at, not a person to embrace'. We must know Christ's nature. We must know who he is. We know that Jesus Christ is God. This is more than a mere doctrinal understanding or theoretical opinion. We know that Jesus of Nazareth is God, because 'his eternal power and Godhead' have been proven in us. He has given us the Spirit of adoption, crying, 'Abba, Father'. Like Thomas, what we have experienced compels us to cry out, 'My Lord and my God'. I never cared much about reading arguments to prove the deity of Christ. I would as soon read a book which sought to prove the existence of my wife. Christ is my God! This is something that I know for myself. I have tried it and proved it and felt its power.

Only the most self-willed and deliberately blind fool would think of denying our Lord's humanity. But we know his humanity by our personal acquaintance with him. He has felt for us as none but a brother born for adversity could feel. He has watched over our griefs as only the 'man of sorrows' could. He has spoken to our hearts such words of cheer as only a tender companion is able; and he succours his tempted ones as only one can who has been tested, tempted and tried in himself.

To us, this is not a matter of doctrine alone. It does not need to be proved. We have seen him for ourselves. We have spoken with him personally (1 John 1:1-3). We not only believe his Word but our own hearts have tested and proved beyond all question that he is Immanuel, God with us. We have tasted that the Lord is gracious and good.

Another part of the lesson which we must learn is to know Christ in all the offices he bears for us. In our first Sunday School lessons we learned that the Lord Jesus Christ is Prophet, Priest and King. But now, we know it. I know Christ is my Prophet, for he has taken away my ignorance and shown me the things of God. Daily, he teaches me the will of God and guides me into the ways of God.

I know Christ is Priest with God for me. He has fulfilled all righteousness by his perfect obedience to the law and has satisfied God's justice for all my sins by his death. He washed my polluted soul in his blood; and now he intercedes for me in the presence of God. I know that Christ is my King because he has made me willing in the day of his power to bow myself to his gracious rule. My sinful lusts are stubborn and strong but he subdues my heart by his grace.

Do you understand what I am saying? There is many 'a master in Israel', like Nicodemus, who does not know these things. It is one thing to fluently talk about theology, quite another thing to know Christ. Doctors of Theology may know many things, yet never learn Christ. Those who know Christ have been taught of God.

We have not learned Christ until we know the sweet influences of his person. Learning Christ, we see what charms there are in him and we feel the power he has over our hearts in all circumstances. Did you ever feel the power of Christ break your heart? Have you learned his power to heal a broken heart? Has your heart ever become cold and indifferent, only to experience the joy of his grace that warms and revives? Have you known what it is to rest your weary soul on him? Does he renew your strength? Have you sat with him in heavenly places?

May God help us to learn Christ in this personal way, and the power of his presence in us. He will be to us, the Foundation upon which we are built, the Food upon which we live, the Water by which we are refreshed, the Righteousness with which we are clothed, the Hope by which we are satisfied, the Head to whom we are members, the Refuge to which we flee, the Crown for which we labour, the Holiness without which we cannot see the Lord.

We must learn to believe Christ. To learn Christ is to have faith in him. 'Every man therefore that hath heard, and hath learned of the Father, cometh unto me' (John 6:45). To believe Christ is to come to him, expectantly, like a sick man comes to the doctor, like a hungry man comes to food, like a thirsty man to the well.

We must learn to love Christ. Can we speak like Peter to our Lord, and say, 'Lord, thou knowest all things; thou knowest that I love thee'? Christ himself is so lovely that all who know him love him. 'Thou art fairer than the children of men' (Psalm 45:2). 'My beloved is white and ruddy, the chiefest among ten thousand … yea, he is altogether lovely' (Song of Solomon 5:10, 16). He has been so loving to my soul that I cannot refuse to love him. He loved me and gave himself for me. His is a love that passes all knowledge. None can resist it who have learned it!

We must learn to obey Christ. Let us walk not as other men but walk as we have Christ for an example (John 13:15). All who have learned Christ have learned his character, so that they obey his example. Although it is never perfect, it is our most intense desire to be conformed to the image of Christ. This is true godliness.

Not so learned

'Ye have not so learned Christ.' There are some people who vainly imagine they have learned Christ, who yet remain the same as they were before. Their lives are motivated by the same principles of lust and greed. Their hearts are fixed upon this world. They live as they did before. They still trust in themselves, that they are righteous. That simply cannot be. Those who have learned Christ are new creatures.

How we learned

The Spirit of God tells us how we have learned Christ. 'If so be that ye have heard him, and have been taught by him, as the truth is in Jesus' (v. 21).

We have learned Christ because we have heard him. Our faith finds its foundation in the Word of God alone. This is the Word of Christ, 'My sheep hear my voice'. We hear his voice by his Word, by the gospel. It is not enough to hear your pastor; you must hear Christ. It is not enough to be emotionally stirred; you must hear Christ. It is not enough to join the church; you must hear Christ. It is not enough to pray; you must hear Christ.

Christ speaks to us personally in the Scriptures. 'Search the Scriptures; for in them ye think ye have eternal life.' These are they that testify of Christ. The Holy Scriptures are able to make you wise unto salvation. The Word of God becomes the living Word of the living Saviour to our souls when the Lord Jesus Christ sends his Spirit to reveal himself by his Word (1 Corinthians 2:11, 14).

We can only learn Christ by Christ himself, for the truth is in him. Pilate ask, 'What is truth?' Many today ask the same question. I tell you Christ is the truth. He is the embodiment of truth. All truth is in him. He is the truth that sets men free, for he is the truth of God. Study Christ, for to learn him is to learn truth.

Study everything in its connection with Christ. Doctrine without Christ is only an empty tomb. Commandments without Christ are only impossible precepts. Experience without Christ is only fanaticism. No matter what good we have done, unless we have learned Christ, we shall be damned. Multitudes are damned eternally for not learning Christ.

Learn Christ. He will sweeten your spirit. He will arouse your affections. He will subdue your passions. Prize this lesson above all else. 'That I may know him, and the power of his resurrection, and the fellowship of his sufferings, being made conformable unto his death' (Philippians 3:10).

Chapter 49

The Body Of Christ, 'Members One Of Another'

Wherefore putting away lying, speak every man truth with his neighbour: for we are members one of another.

(Ephesians 4:25)

In the fourth chapter of the book of Ephesians, God the Holy Spirit inspired the Apostle Paul to give us very needful, specific instructions about our privileges and responsibilities as 'members one of another' in the body of Christ. God's saints are each given grace to fill their place in the body of Christ, grace to function in their place for the good of the whole body and the glory of God.

Many members

Several times in this fourth chapter, Paul refers to the body of Christ, not his physical body, but his spiritual body, the church of God. He tells us in verse 25 that 'we are members one of another'. Christ is the head and believers are the body; and as we are the body of Christ, we are members one of another.

'There is one body' (v. 4). Each member of Christ's body is 'fitly joined together' (v. 16) to Christ the head, and to every other member of the body by God the Holy Ghost. The Apostle tells us throughout his epistles that there is one body. Though there are many local churches, there is only one true, elect, redeemed church of the firstborn, whose names are written in heaven. There are many congregations, but only one body. There are many clans, but only one family. Christ is the head of that family and that body (Mark 3:31-35).

All who are truly united to Christ by faith are one body in Christ, one church of the living God; Jew and Gentile, rich and poor, learned and unlearned, black and white, male and female, in heaven and on earth. I do not saying that all religionists, all professors of religion and all church members are members of this body. I am saying that all true believers are one body in Christ.

Chosen

The members of this body were all chosen in Christ by God the Father before the foundation of the world. 'Ye have not chosen me, but I have chosen you, and ordained you, that ye should go and bring forth fruit, and that your fruit should remain: that whatsoever ye shall ask of the Father in my name, he may give it you' (John 15:16). 'Blessed be the God and Father of our Lord Jesus Christ, who hath blessed us with all spiritual blessings in heavenly places in Christ: According as he hath chosen us in him before the foundation of the world, that we should be holy and without blame before him in love: Having predestinated us unto the adoption of children by Jesus Christ to himself, according to the good pleasure of his will, To the praise of the glory of his grace, wherein he hath made us accepted in the beloved' (Ephesians 1:3-6). 'But we are bound to give thanks alway to God for you, brethren beloved of the Lord, because God hath from the beginning chosen you to salvation through sanctification of the Spirit and belief of the truth: Whereunto he called you by our gospel, to the obtaining of the glory of our Lord Jesus Christ' (2 Thessalonians 2:13, 14).

God's church, the church of our Lord Jesus Christ, is his elect, chosen church.

Redeemed

Members of this body were all redeemed by Christ in his substitutionary sacrifice at Calvary (Isaiah 53:4-12; 1 Corinthians 1:30; Colossians 2:9, 10: Hebrews 10:12-17). Not all men and women are elect, and not all are redeemed; but every member of Christ's body, the church, was purchased by the precious blood of God's dear Son at Calvary. When you think about redemption you should always think of these five words: special, sovereign, substitution, satisfaction, success.

Born again

The members of this body, the church of the living God, are all alive, quickened, born again, called, awakened and regenerated by the Holy Spirit through the preaching of the gospel of Jesus Christ. 'And you hath he quickened, who were dead in trespasses and sins' (Ephesians 2:1). 'Forasmuch as ye know that ye were not redeemed with corruptible things, as silver and gold, from your vain conversation received by tradition from your fathers; But with the precious blood of Christ, as of a lamb without blemish and without spot' (1 Peter 1:18, 19).

Believers

All the members of this body, the church of God, are believers. They all believe on the Lord Jesus Christ as he is revealed in the Scriptures. We love and trust him as our Prophet to teach us, our Priest to save us and as our King to rule over us.

There is no debate in God's family, no argument among God's children about who Christ is, what he has done, where he is now or what he is doing. All God's children confess he is Lord. His blood is effectual. His power is omnipotent. If he has all power, nobody else has any. His intercession prevails. 'He shall not fail.'

New creatures

The members of this body, all of them, are new creatures in Christ. 'Therefore if any man be in Christ, he is a new creature: old things are passed away; behold, all things are become new' (2 Corinthians 5:17).

Every member of Christ's body, the church, is a new creature. The old man in us is not a new creature. Flesh is not a new creature. Adam is not a new creature. The old man, flesh, is not a member of Christ's body, but that 'new man created in righteousness and true holiness', that which 'is born of God', 'Christ in you, the hope of glory', is this new creature of grace. As new creatures, we love God's Word, long for his will, and walk after his Spirit. Consider the following passage.

'Simon Peter, a servant and an apostle of Jesus Christ, to them that have obtained like precious faith with us through the righteousness of God and our Saviour Jesus Christ: Grace and peace be multiplied unto you through the knowledge of God, and of Jesus our Lord, According as his divine power hath given unto us all things that pertain unto life and godliness, through the knowledge of him that hath called us to glory and virtue: Whereby are given unto us exceeding great and precious promises: that by these ye might be partakers of the divine nature, having escaped corruption that is in the world through lust' (2 Peter 1:1-4).

The first four verses of this chapter are one sentence, all dealing with one thing. Peter declares the wonder of the new birth, the glorious work of regeneration. The first word of verse 4 (whereby) refers us back to the call of God the Holy Spirit. It is by the call of God the Holy Spirit that God bestows these great and precious promises of his grace, making us everlasting partakers of the divine nature.

Persevere

The members of this body will continue in the faith. True faith never quits. God's people persevere in faith. All believers keep on believing because they cannot do otherwise. We persevere in faith because our God perseveres in grace!

We 'are kept by the power of God through faith unto salvation ready to be revealed in the last time' (1 Peter 1:5). 'All that the Father giveth me shall come to me; and him that cometh to me I will in no wise cast out … And this is the Father's will which hath sent me, that of all which he hath given me I should lose nothing, but should raise it up again at the last day' (John 6:37, 39).

'My sheep hear my voice, and I know them, and they follow me: And I give unto them eternal life; and they shall never perish, neither shall any man pluck them out of my hand' (John 10:27, 28).

United

The members of God's church, the members of this body, are united. They are one body and members of one another (1 Corinthians 12:12-27; Ephesians 4:16, 25).

Members of the body love, care for and take care of, one another. 'With all lowliness and meekness, with longsuffering, forbearing one another in love' (Ephesians 4:2). 'Owe no man anything, but to love one another' (Romans 13:8). Love is a principle of the heart. It cannot be produced by law, created by argument, or developed by resolution. It is the work of God's grace in the heart (1 John 4:7, 8). It is the fruit of the Spirit and the companion of faith.

Love is the royal law of Christ our king (1 John 3:23). Love is not only the commandment of Christ, it is the evidence of his grace and presence (John 13:34, 35). Love is exemplified for us by Christ. How did Christ love us? He loved us in spite of our sins and failures and in spite of the fact we did not love him. He loves us with a love that never died. He loved us enough to die for us (Romans 5:6-8). And his love is longsuffering, patient, kind and forgiving.

Members of the same body are one, united to and unified with one another, always working together as one (Ephesians 4:3). This is not an outward show of unity. It is a real unity of heart, purpose, spirit and desire. God is glorified where the perfections of his nature and attributes are recognised, where the work of his hands is praised, where his dear Son is honoured, where his mercy and grace in Christ are believed and received, and where his people walk in love. Members of the same body do everything they can to make other members as comfortable, attractive, acceptable and commendable as possible (Ephesians 4:32).

Chapter 50

'Grieve Not The Holy Spirit'

And grieve not the holy Spirit of God, whereby ye are sealed unto the day of redemption.

(Ephesians 4:30)

Here is a text of Scripture by which our lives should be motivated and ruled every hour of every day. Oh, for grace to wear it upon my heart everywhere I go, just as I wear my wedding ring on my finger every day and everywhere I go, as a constant reminder of the one who put it there almost 47 years ago.

'Grieve not the Holy Spirit.' Those five words should be engraved upon the heart of every man, woman and child who bears the name of Christ. Paul has admonished us to 'walk worthy of the vocation wherewith we are called' in Christ Jesus. He has shown us how we should endeavour 'to keep the unity of the Spirit in the bond of peace'. Now he comes to enforce his exhortation with arguments drawn from the love and grace of God that we have experienced as believers.

His argument is this. You should be careful to live in such a way that your lives promote Christian unity, because everything that hinders the unity of the Spirit and breaks the bond of peace among God's children is grieving to 'the Holy Spirit of God, whereby ye are sealed unto the day of redemption'.

The fact that the Holy Spirit can be grieved is a very clear proof of this distinct personality. It would be a very difficult thing for us to imagine that a mere influence, or a mere spiritual emanation could be grieved. We can only grieve a person. Inasmuch, then, as the Holy Spirit may be grieved, we see he is a distinct personality of the sacred Trinity. Let us never rob him of the glory and honour which is his due. Ever worship and reverence him as God.

Our text also reveals the close connection between the Holy Spirit and the believer. If he is grieved by our shortcomings and sins, then certainly he must have a very tender and affectionate interest in us. C. H. Spurgeon said, 'He is not a God who reigns in solitary isolation, divided by a great gulf, but he, the blessed Spirit, comes into such near contact with us, takes such minute observations, feels such tender regards, that he can be grieved by our faults and follies'.

The word 'grieve' is a painful one but there is honey in the rock. It is a delightful thought that he who rules heaven and earth, is the Creator of all things and the infinite, ever-blessed God, condescends to enter into such a tender relationship with his people that he can be grieved by our actions. What a marvel this is! God the Holy Ghost is grieved with the faults, failings and foulness of our poor souls!

There is something very touching in this admonition, 'Grieve not the Holy Spirit of God'. It does not say, 'Do not make him angry'. A more tender term is used, 'Grieve him not'. Some men are so hard and cruel that it causes them no pain to make another person angry. Indeed, many of us are hardly touched when we know that another person is angry with us. But where is the heart so hard that it is not moved when we know we are the source of another's grief?

Grief is a mix of anger and love. It is anger, but all the gall is removed. Love sweetens the anger and turns the edge of it, not against the person, but against the offence. A loving father sees the offence of a son and is grieved. There is anger in him, but his anger is against his son's sin. There is a deep love that neutralizes his anger, and he is grieved. Instead of wishing the child ill as punishment for sin, he looks on the sin as the ill. He grieves to know his child has injured himself by sin.

Perhaps you would care little that you made someone angry without cause. But to grieve another would cause you great distress of heart. When you have grieved a dear companion, or a loving parent, or a good friend, you cannot rest until you have done your best to take away the grief. When we see anger in one another, we immediately begin to feel hostility. Anger begets anger. Grief begets brokenness.

We have all experienced this. When you were a small child, and you did something wrong, if your mother or father punished you in anger, you became hostile and pouty. But if you felt that they were deeply hurt and grieved, your heart was broken; you sought to remove their grief by your own repentance. You see, grief produces pity and pity is a very near kinsman to love. We love those we have caused to grieve. Do you see what a sweet expression this is? 'Grieve not the Holy Spirit of God'.

The blessed Spirit of God can be grieved only by sinners who are loved of God; and that fact ought to make us anxious never to grieve him.

The Person

Who is this blessed Person we are urged not to grieve? 'Grieve not the Holy Spirit of God'. This is an outstanding fact. The Holy Spirit, the third Person of the Triune Godhead, may be grieved by us. That loving, tender Spirit, who has taken it upon himself to quicken us from our death in sin, and to be the Sanctifier of our souls by that new life implanted in us, may be grieved.

He is our Divine Instructor, Illuminator and Comforter. He takes the things of Christ and shows them to us. He dwells in us. He guides us by his power and presence. Yet by us, he is grieved. He is life to our souls, dew to our graces, light to our minds and comfort to our hearts. Yet he may be grieved by us. The heavenly Dove of peace may be disturbed. The Celestial Fire can be quenched. The Divine Wind is resisted. The blessed Paraclete is far too often treated with despite. So the admonition comes with force, 'Grieve not the Holy Spirit of God'.

I will not try to prove that the Holy Spirit of God is one of the Persons of the sacred Trinity. To the child of God that is an evident truth. 'There are three that bear record in heaven, the Father, the Word, and the Holy Ghost; and these three are one' (1 John 5:7). The wilfully ignorant unbeliever can never be convinced of such truth by all the logical arguments of the most learned orator. This is a truth given to men only by Divine revelation. We know that the Holy Spirit is more than a mere influence, power, or emanation of God. He is himself the blessed God, equal in eternity, dignity, power and glory with the Father and the Son.

Human language

We know that the language of our text speaks of God the Holy Spirit in human terms. God the Spirit does not know passion and suffering as we do. But he is described in human language so that we can know his attitude toward us and toward our sin. We must never lose the comforting assurance that the Holy Spirit takes the same deep interest in us as loving parents take in a dear but wayward child. This is a marvel of his free-grace. This loving grief of the Holy Spirit may be traced to his holy character and perfect attributes. Sin everywhere must be displeasing to the Spirit of holiness; but sin in his own people is grievous to him. He would not be the Spirit of Truth if he could approve of that which is false in us. He would not be perfectly pure if he could approve of that which is impure in his people. We could not believe him to be holy if he did not grieve over our unholiness.

It is the very nature of his Holy Being to be vexed with sin. Everything which falls short of his own nature must be grievous to him. He helps our infirmities; but he grieves over our sin. Robert Hawker wrote, 'If Lot was vexed with the filthy conversation of the wicked from day to day, what must be the feeling of God the Holy Ghost, at the daily view of indwelling corruption, and out-breaking sin, in his redeemed ones?'

This grief of the Holy Spirit is an indication of his love for us. He grieves over our sins, because he knows what pain we bring upon ourselves by sin, and how much communion and joy we lose by our disobedience. Like a loving parent, he would keep us from this. He knows the backslider's way and the sorrow it brings.

His grief is like that of a mother for her wrong-doing prodigal. She is not grieved for the pain he has caused her. She is grieved because she knows the pain that the prodigal's way will bring upon her son. 'Thine own wickedness shall correct thee, and thy backslidings shall reprove thee' (Jeremiah 2:19).

The Holy Spirit is grieved by the sins of his people for Christ's sake. The Holy Spirit knows the value of the Saviour's blood, the cost of our redemption. He grieves when he sees sin in us which is traitorous to the Saviour's love. He grieves when we forget our solemn obligations to our Master. He grieves over us when we undervalue and dishonour our blessed Redeemer by our sin, indifference and unbelief, when we fail to cherish and glorify the One he was sent to glorify in us.

It seems evident from this fourth chapter of Ephesians that the Holy Spirit of God is grieved for the church's sake. He knows how useful we might be if we would live up to our privileges. How he is grieved by lazy, indolent preachers. The divine Comforter is grieved when God's servants become slack and fail to comfort God's people by the gospel (Isaiah 40:1, 2).

We are watchmen; but how little do we truly watch over the souls committed to our trust? We are messengers of God to perishing souls; but how little do we seek God's message for the hour? We are sent to sow the good seed of the gospel, but too often we take up time of our hearers with silly talk. The Holy Spirit came to the earth to testify of Christ. He is grieved when the churches do not hear that testimony of the gospel of the glory of Christ sounded from their pulpits.

God the Holy Spirit is grieved with preachers who ought to labour in the Word and doctrine of Christ for the good of men's souls, who waste their time on trifles! The cause of his grief is both in the pulpit and in the pew.

The reason

We are admonished not to grieve the Holy Spirit; but why should we be so careful not to grieve him? Paul gives us the answer plainly. Here is the reason Paul gives why we should not grieve the blessed Holy Spirit of God. By him 'ye are sealed unto the day of redemption'. Those words imply much.

His love

They imply the Holy Spirit's great love for us. We who are the children of God are the objects of his love. If we are truly persuaded that another person loves us, we are furnished with a powerful motive not to grieve him. Behold, therefore, the love of the blessed Spirit for you and do not grieve him. The Holy Spirit's love for us was very early. The Spirit of God is one of those high contracting parties in the Covenant of Grace. The Father loved us. He chose us to be his own. Christ loved us. He assumed the responsibility of redeeming us by the sacrifice of himself. The Holy Spirit loved us. He took upon himself the task of giving us eternal life by virtue of Christ's blood and righteousness. All that may be said of the love of the Father and the Son is equally true of the love of the Spirit. His love for us is without beginning. It is eternal. He loves us infinitely and perfectly. The love of the Spirit for us, as that of the Father and the Son, is free, electing love that cannot change.

There are many acts of love that the Holy Spirit has performed for us. We were placed in Christ in eternal election by the Holy Spirit. 'God hath from the beginning chosen you to salvation through the sanctification of the Spirit and belief of the truth' (2 Thessalonians 2:13). Before we were converted, in the days of our youth, the Holy Spirit often rebuked our tender consciences. It was the Spirit of God who graciously brought us under the influence of the gospel. Now you have discovered the mystery of God's love, do you not marvel at the mighty prevenient grace the Holy Spirit exercised toward you long before you knew him?

Hear the Word of the Lord, 'Jude the servant of Jesus Christ, and brother of James, to them that are sanctified by God the Father, preserved in Jesus Christ, and called' (Jude 1). Frequently, he kept you from a course of vice by which you would have destroyed yourself. Many of us are worshipping God, rather than in prison, only because he powerfully hedged up our way of rebellion. We blasphemed the name of God, despised the grace of Christ, and stubbornly resisted the sweet wooing of the Spirit himself; but his love was never repelled. 'Many waters cannot quench love, neither can the floods drown it' (Song of Solomon 8:7).

Do you see how the Holy Spirit overruled your obstinate rebellion for your good? Wonder of wonders! God the Holy Spirit, out of his pure love for us, has brought us safely to the time and place of our calling. Child of God, does not your heart leap within you to remember that blessed hour when first the Holy Spirit led you to Calvary and revealed Christ as your Substitute? He sheds abroad the love of God in our hearts by the revelation of Christ in us (Romans 5:6-11). He gives us faith in Christ, as the Spirit of adoption (Galatians 4:4, 5).

Here is another marvel of his love. He comes to our souls and teaches us the things of Christ for our comfort. The consolation of the Holy Spirit is a display of his great love. He heals your broken heart. He keeps you in the hour of temptation and revives your weary spirit. He strengthens your faith and graciously helps you in prayer. 'Likewise, the Spirit also helpeth our infirmities: for we know not what we should pray for as we ought; but the Spirit himself maketh intercession for us with groanings which cannot be uttered. And he that searcheth the hearts knoweth what is the mind of the Spirit, because he maketh intercession for the saints according to the will of God' (Romans 8:26, 27).

Here is one more token of the Holy Spirit's love I dare not fail to mention. God the Holy Spirit dwells in us! He is our constant, intimate companion! He is the faithful friend of fickle, frail, faltering, falling, sinful folk like you and me!

His sealing

Let me never grieve one who loves me so! But there is another reason which should strongly restrain us from grieving the Holy Spirit. By him we are 'sealed unto the day of redemption'. The Holy Spirit is the seal of the New Covenant. 'If a man love me, he will keep my words: and my Father will love him, and we will come unto him, and make our abode with him (John 14:23). 'Behold, the tabernacle of God is with men, and he will dwell with them, and they shall be his people, and God himself shall be with them, and be their God' (Revelation 21:3).

This sealing of the Holy Spirit has a fourfold purpose. First, it is a seal of attestation. Hereby we are confirmed as the sons of God. 'Circumcision made without hands!' Second, it is a seal of appropriation. When God sends forth the Spirit of his Son into our hearts, 'crying, Abba, Father', he lays claim to his purchased possession. Third, it is a seal of assurance. If we have the Spirit of God dwelling in us, we are assured that the promise of eternal glory is ours. Fourth, it is a seal of preservation. The presence of the Holy Spirit in us is that which preserves us safe and secure 'unto the day of redemption'.

Day of redemption

All who are born again by the Spirit of God are sealed by him unto the day of redemption. What is this 'day of redemption?'

The day of death for believers is the day of redemption. In the hour of death, God's elect are delivered from the encumbrance of the body. In that day, we shall be delivered from the body of sin and death and from all sorrows and afflictions. We shall be delivered from the reproaches and persecutions of men, the temptations of Satan, sin and shame. We shall be delivered from our doubts, fears and unbelief. What a day of redemption the day of the resurrection will be for Christ's redeemed! Our bodies will be redeemed from mortality, corruption, weakness and dishonour. This body will be refined and spiritualised, so as not to stand in need of natural sustenance. We will be perfectly suited for the everlasting glory that awaits.

Our Lord Jesus tells us the day of redemption is the Day of Judgment in Luke 21:28. It is that day when Christ shall appear in glory, and all his saints with him. At that great day, he will put us; body, soul and spirit, into the possession of everlasting blessedness. We shall have perfect communion with Christ, perfect commitment to Christ, and perfect conformity to Christ!

The grieving

How is the Holy Spirit grieved? I am now speaking of those who are truly born-again, those who love the Lord Jesus Christ. The holiness, justice and wrath of our God is incensed against the wicked. But with us, he is grieved. The Spirit of God is in your heart and it is very easy to grieve him. Sin is as easy as it is wicked and the Holy Spirit is grieved by our sin.

The Holy Spirit is grieved when we put his work in the place of Christ's. Many today exalt the work of the Holy Spirit and diminish the honour and glory of Christ, whom the Holy Spirit was sent to magnify. The Spirit of Christ always gives Christ the pre-eminence. The way to honour the divine Spirit is to honour Christ. Do not seek after the tongues of angels; seek a tongue to speak of Christ's glory. Do not seek the gifts of miracles; seek the miracle of Christ's righteousness. Do not seek fanciful dreams and visions; seek a vision of the glory of God in Jesus Christ.

God the Holy Ghost is the holy, pure, unspotted Spirit of God; and he is grieved with sin. He is grieved with our carnal lusts, covetousness and our corrupt communication. He is grieved with our callousness toward one another. The Holy Spirit is the Spirit of Peace. He is grieved by anything that brings discord and division to the church of Christ. All bitterness, wrath, anger, quarrelling and malice are contrary to him. Gossip, slander and evil words drive him from us. He is grieved by our coldness and indifference to our Saviour. He is grieved whenever a child of God forgets the Lord Jesus, and loses sight of those pains he endured for sin? Yes, God the Holy Ghost is grieved, communion with God the Father is interrupted, and the agonies and bloody sweat of the Lord Jesus are forgotten when sin is indulged.

The Holy Spirit is grieved by the ingratitude that keeps God's people from prayer and from worshipping God (Song of Solomon 5:1-8; Revelation 3:20). Only a thankless heart can neglect the sacred volume of Scripture which the Holy Spirit has given us. Only contempt for Christ keeps us from the assembly of his saints (Matthew 18:20). The Holy Spirit is greatly grieved by our unbelief. Nothing could be more grievous to the Spirit of Truth than to question his truthfulness. How dare we ever doubt God?

Perhaps that which grieves the Spirit of God more often and more cruelly than anything else is our pride. We are such proud creatures that we even become proud of God's mercies to us. Some of us are so full of this venom of the serpent that when God is pleased to slightly use us, our heads get so elated we are sure soon to fall. I assure you God will abase all those who exalt themselves. He knows how to unhorse the proud Pharisee. Let us boast only in the Lord. 'My soul shall make her boast in the LORD, the humble shall hear thereof and be glad.' 'He that glorieth, let him glory in the LORD.'

The consequence

What is the result of grieving the Holy Spirit of God? I know grieving of the Holy Spirit will never end in the destruction of God's children. No heir of heaven can perish, neither will the Holy Spirit be taken from him. But, if we are God's children, he will not allow us to persist in grieving him (Isaiah 54:7-10; Jeremiah 2:19).

What misery we bring upon ourselves when we grieve the loving, heavenly Dove! How God must love us. Would the infinite God grieve for me? Can it be possible that a poor worm of the earth, such as I am, should excite such regard and attention from the Almighty? The very thought of it should have constant power over us.

Shall I grieve the Holy Spirit of God? Shall I quench those sweet influences which first quickened me? Shall we recompense the kindness which called us from death to life and formed Christ in us by grieving him? Had he left us alone, we would to this day be dead in trespasses and sins!

Except the Lord keep us, we shall not be kept from any evil. But, oh, our gracious God, if you keep us, we are well kept. Holy Spirit of God ever lead us to our all-precious, all-glorious, all-merciful Christ. Ever sprinkle our hearts with his precious blood. Keep us always in Gethsemane, always at Calvary, always at the Throne of Grace.

We cannot mortify the deeds of the body and live unto God but you can mortify the deeds of the body in us. You can make us live unto God. Do it, for Christ's sake. Amen.

Chapter 51

'For Christ's Sake'

And be ye kind one to another, tenderhearted, forgiving one another, even as God for Christ's sake hath forgiven you.

(Ephesians 4:32)

This text speaks plainly and tenderly of the love of God to his people and the love for one another that God gives to his people. The sense of this verse is given in similar words by this same Apostle in the book of Colossians. 'Put on therefore, as the elect of God, holy and beloved, bowels of mercies, kindness, humbleness of mind, meekness, longsuffering; forbearing one another, and forgiving one another, if any man have a quarrel against any: even as Christ forgave you, so also do ye. And above all these things put on charity, which is the bond of perfectness' (Colossians 3:12-14).

As you know, the chapter and verse divisions of our English Bible were added by translators to assist us in finding passages with more ease. However, they sometimes occur in places that break up the thoughts of the writer. This is the case here. When we read this latter part of the fourth chapter of Ephesians, we should include the first two verses of chapter five, for Paul's thought continues through those verses.

'And grieve not the holy Spirit of God, whereby ye are sealed unto the day of redemption. Let all bitterness, and wrath, and anger, and clamour, and evil speaking, be put away from you, with all malice: And be ye kind one to another, tenderhearted, forgiving one another, even as God for Christ's sake hath forgiven you. Be ye therefore followers of God, as dear children; and walk in love, as Christ also hath loved us, and hath given himself for us an offering and a sacrifice to God for a sweetsmelling savour' (Ephesians 4:30-5:2).

The imagery here is beautiful. It pictures the golden altar of incense with its perfume, its ascending sweetsmelling odour, coming up to God. Here we see that our Redeemer, the Lord Jesus Christ, is a sweetsmelling, acceptable offering to God, both as the ground of our forgiveness and as the example of our conduct.

The blessed purity of our holy faith is obvious, not only in its precepts, but in the character of the God it reveals. There is not an excellency which we can imagine that is not seen shining brightly in the Person of our Lord Jesus Christ. There is no line of conduct in which we should excel as believers that does not point us to Christ Jesus, our Lord and Master, as the example of it.

Mercy's motive

We are urged to constantly exercise the tender spirit of forgiveness, not by pointing us to the law of Moses, nor by showing us the virtues of such a spirit, but by pointing us to God our Father, who 'for Christ's sake' has forgiven us.

What nobler motive can we require for loving and forgiving one another? What manner of people ought we to be who have such a high example of mercy? As we run the race that is set before us, we must be 'looking unto Jesus the author and finisher of our faith'. Christ is both the object of our hope and the example of our obedience. May the God of all grace grant grace to follow him.

Our text urges us to love one another and forgive one another continually. Paul sets before us the example of God himself. God's forgiving love is so fascinating that we could dwell upon it for many hours, and it would still be as fresh as the morning dew. As we meditate upon God's forgiving love, may we gather grace by which to follow his example, forgiving one another even to seventy times seven.

The only motive that has caused God to forgive us of our sins is the loving sacrifice of his dear Son; and we should follow his example, forgiving one another 'for Christ's sake'.

All gifts of grace

Our text teaches us that all the gifts of God's mercy, love and grace, every good thing the Lord our God bestows upon us, comes to us for Christ's sake.

This is a lesson with which we should all be familiar. It is a lesson we all must learn. We use these words very often, 'for Christ's sake'. We talk about doing a certain thing and refusing to do another, 'for Christ's sake'. Do not misunderstand me. This should be our motive in all things. But I dare say, few of us have ever stopped to consider the force and meaning of those three words, 'for Christ's sake'. It is certain that I lack both the understanding and the ability to give you the fulness of their meaning. This much is clear, every good thing that God bestows upon the sons of men, especially the forgiveness of their sins, is done 'for Christ's sake'. That is the plain assertion of our text.

Forgiveness

It is the glory of God's grace to forgive our sin, but he only forgives sin 'for Christ's sake'. 'In whom we have redemption through his blood, the forgiveness of sins, according to the riches of his grace' (Ephesians 1:7).

God forgives sin for the sake of the atonement the Lord Jesus Christ has accomplished at Calvary. Here is a marvel of God's grace! The just Lawgiver, the glorious King, our great God, readily passes over our offences because of the expiation for sin which Christ offered as our Redeemer. Without the suffering and death of Christ, God could never forgive sin. 'Without shedding of blood is no remission.'

If we could but realise what sin is, we would readily perceive that it can only be forgiven 'for Christ's sake'. Sin is an affront to God's holy character; therefore, it must be destroyed. Sin is the breach of God's holy law; therefore, it must be punished. Sin is an attack upon God's government of the universe; therefore, it must be condemned. Sin is man's attempt to assassinate the Almighty!

John Bunyan said, 'Sin is the dare of God's justice, the rape of His mercy, the jeer of His patience, the slight of His power, and the contempt of His love'. If God could allow sin to go unpunished, it would be the worst calamity that could ever befall the universe, for it would be a license for all creatures to rebel. This is probably the best argument for those who advocate capital punishment. I am neither defending nor opposing that. I will leave it in the hands of Caesar. But it serves to illustrate my point. Sometimes, in the affairs of state, the lawgiver must execute death upon the murderer in mercy toward society. Otherwise, life would be in jeopardy and everything would be insecure. Therefore, it becomes mercy to write out the sentence of death upon the criminal as a deterrent to murder. This is the case with God in reference to sin and sinners. It is his very love as well as his holiness and justice which compels the severity of his judgment. For the honour of God and the good of his creation, sin cannot be blotted out until a suitable atonement is made.

Justice satisfied

But here is God's great mercy, love and grace. He has supplied his own Son to make that sacrifice demanded by his justice. God, 'for Christ's sake', forgives sin, because his holiness and justice have been fully satisfied. Until we see the Son of God dying in the sinner's place, it is impossible for us to conceive that sin might be forgiven. But Christ's death shows us how God can be both just and the justifier of the ungodly. That is the message of the incarnation (Hebrews 10:1-22).

Our sorrow cannot wipe the slate clean. Our repentance cannot answer for the sins of the past. We could never make any sacrifice that would satisfy Divine justice, neither in this world, nor the world to come. But come with me to Calvary, see there the bleeding Lamb of God and you will easily see that God may be just and yet justify the ungodly. Behold Christ Jesus, 'Whom God hath set forth to be a propitiation through faith in his blood, to declare his righteousness for the remission of sins that are past, through the forbearance of God; To declare, I say, at this time his righteousness: that he might be just, and the justifier of him which believeth in Jesus' (Romans 3:25, 26).

Our Representative

God has forgiven us because of the representative character of our Lord Jesus Christ. It must never be forgotten that we originally fell and became sinners by a representative. Our father Adam stood before God as our representative in the Garden of Eden. We should never object to this arrangement because that is also the hope of our race.

The angels fell individually, one by one; and they are irretrievably lost forever. There is no hope of restoration for them. But since we fell in Adam, our representative, there remained for us the possibility of rising in another Adam. Therefore, in the fulness of time, God sent forth is Son, Christ Jesus, made of a woman, made under the law as the last Adam. Standing as our Representative, he undertook in the covenant of grace to remove our sins and to fulfil the conditions of our forgiveness.

According to the law, in as much as man had sinned, a man must die; therefore, Christ assumed our nature. Man must perfectly obey the law, so Christ rendered a perfect obedience. Man must suffer the penalty of Divine wrath, so Christ died. As our Representative, having borne the penalty of the law he fulfilled for us, Christ Jesus is justified before God. And he ever lives before God as our Representative, so that we are justified in him (Romans 5:12-19).

His love for Christ

I will go a little further and say that God forgives our sins for the sake of his love for Christ. It is always the joy of God to express his love for his Son. We cannot begin to understand the wondrous mystery of the sacred and eternal love between the Father and the Son. Throughout all the ages, yea, before the ages began, they have enjoyed loving fellowship with one another. They have always been one in their designs. They have never differed upon any purpose. Indeed, they cannot differ, for they are one. When our Lord says, 'Father … glorify thy Son', he is so united to the Father that he says, 'that thy Son also may glorify thee'. God forgives sin because he loves his Son. Blessed be God, there is no sin that he will not forgive 'for Christ's sake'.

Once more, our great and ever-gracious God forgives sin for the sake of glorifying Christ. Christ took the shame of our sins that he might glorify the Father. Now his Father delights to magnify him by forgiving sin on his account.

Sinner, here is the ground upon which you may pray with hope, 'Lord, I am a vile sinner. There is nothing in me but sin. I have nothing to offer you. But would it not be for the glory of Christ to forgive such a sinner as I am?' 'For thy name's sake, O LORD, pardon mine iniquity; for it is great' (Psalm 25:11).

Prayers accepted

Not only has God forgiven our sins, but he hears our prayers 'for Christ's sake'. What can God refuse when it is sought for the sake of his Son? Let this be the constant guide of our prayers, 'for Christ's sake'.

God accepts our labours and our sacrifices only 'for Christ's sake'. We 'offer up spiritual sacrifices, acceptable to God by Jesus Christ' (1 Peter 2:5). Ever bear in mind that our noblest labours and most costly sacrifices are not acceptable to God, except by Christ. Do your service 'for Christ's sake', and God will accept it. Come to worship 'for Christ's sake', and God will be worshipped by you. Offer your prayers to God 'for Christ's sake', and your prayers will be heard. Offer your songs of praise 'for Christ's sake', and your songs will be embraced by the Lord God. Give your money 'for Christ's sake', and God will accept it.

Every blessing

Remember this, every blessing and promise of God in the covenant is yours 'for Christ's sake', and be thankful. Are you loved of God? It is 'for Christ's sake'. Are you God's elect? It is 'for Christ's sake'. Are you redeemed? It is 'for Christ's sake'. Are you accepted? It is 'for Christ's sake'. Are you the sons of God? It is 'for Christ's sake'. Are you instructed? It is 'for Christ's sake'. Are you sealed with God's Spirit? It is 'for Christ's sake'. Are you saved? It is 'for Christ's sake'.

Let this truth humble our hearts and make us thankful, giving all praise, honour, and glory to Christ. 'For who maketh thee to differ from another? and what hast thou that thou didst not receive? now if thou didst receive it, why dost thou glory, as if thou hadst not received it?' (1 Corinthians 4:7).

Forgiveness done

Notice the words of our text, 'God for Christ's sake hath forgiven you'. Here Paul speaks with confidence and finality of a great blessing God has given to every believing soul for the sake of his Son. 'God for Christ's sake hath forgiven you'.

These words show us the certainty of our forgiveness. The forgiveness of sin is not something to be hoped for when we come before the judgment seat. It is not the prize for which we run. It is a blessing conferred upon us which we receive when we come to the Lord Jesus Christ by faith.

We receive the declaration of pardon in our hearts the moment we believe. The pardon of sin is not a matter of hope, but a matter of fact.

> The vilest offender who truly believes,
> That moment from Jesus a pardon receives.

If Christ took your load, then your load cannot remain on your back. If Christ paid your debts, then they do not stand in God's book against you. God has so completely forgiven our sin 'for Christ's sake' that it shall never be mentioned against us forever!

Continual forgiveness

God's forgiveness of our sin is continuous. 'If we confess our sins, he is faithful and just to forgive us our sins, and to cleanse us from all unrighteousness' (1 John 1:9). 'If we walk in the light, as he is in the light, we have fellowship one with another, and the blood of Jesus Christ his Son cleanseth us from all sin' (1 John 1:7). Once pardon is given, sin continues to be forgiven. When we are in doubt, unsure of our pardon, it is still sure and true. He who believes on the Son of God is not condemned, even if his own heart condemns him. 'For if our heart condemn us, God is greater than our heart, and knoweth all things. Beloved, if our heart condemn us not, then have we confidence toward God' (1 John 3:20, 21).

Free forgiveness

This forgiveness of sin is absolutely free and unconditional on our part. God has forgiven us, 'for Christ's sake' alone. It was not because of our faith, or our repentance, for even these are given to us, 'for Christ's sake'. Purely of his own love he delights to show mercy to us, 'for Christ's sake'.

Full forgiveness

Mark this and rejoice: God has forgiven us fully! The whole, horrible list of our sin was destroyed at once. All our transgressions were swept away. All were carried away with that crimson flood, so fully removed that not one trace of them is found.

> Because the sinless Saviour died,
> My sinful soul is counted free;
> For God, the Just, is satisfied
> To look on Him and pardon me!

My sins against a holy God and his law are forgiven. My sins against his gospel are forgiven. My sins against my body are forgiven, and my sins against my neighbours are forgiven.

Oh, my soul, this thought is too great for me! The sins of my body and my mind, as numerous as the sands of the sea, as great as the sea itself, are all removed from me as far as the east is from the west. All my evil was rolled into one great mass, laid on my Surety, and made his. Having borne it in my stead, Christ has made an end of sin forever! O blessed Redeemer! O blessed forgiveness! Our dear Saviour, the Lord Jesus Christ took the handwriting that was against us and nailed it to the cross to show to the entire universe that its power to condemn us has ceased.

Do you want assurance? Look to the risen Redeemer. There, at the right hand of the Majesty on High, is your assurance. He says concerning the demands of the law, 'Paid in full'.

Eternal forgiveness

This forgiveness which God has given us, 'for Christ's sake' is an eternal forgiveness. Our God will never rake up our past offences and require them at our hand. It is an irreversible forgiveness. Though we sin a thousand times a day, as we all do, he will never look upon us without pronouncing us clean through the blood of Christ. We will not be dealt with any less graciously because of our sin.

One another

The next lesson that the Holy Spirit gives us in this text is most practical. 'For Christ's sake' we should freely forgive one another. Each of us requires the forgiveness of another. We have a great deal to forgive in other people, but there is always a great deal more to be forgiven in ourselves by our brethren. For me to forgive my brother is a very small thing in comparison with God forgiving me. Here is the inspiration, the motive for forgiveness that we cannot resist. If we are truly God's children, we should forgive one another, 'for Christ's sake'. Forgiveness is Christ-like and honours Christ.

Our forgiveness of one another must be even as God, 'for Christ's sake', has forgiven us. We should forgive our brethren even before they repent and seek forgiveness and without them asking for it, simply, 'for Christ's sake'.

Will you not forgive, 'for Christ's sake', regardless of the offence? Listen to the words of Christ himself. 'If ye forgive men their trespasses, your heavenly Father will also forgive you: But if ye forgive not men their trespasses, neither will your Father forgive your trespasses' (Matthew 6:14, 15). Yet this forgiveness is not something done by force or compulsion, it is done willingly, 'for Christ's sake'.

This spirit of forgiveness will make your own life and your life in Christ's family sweet. Let us not follow the example of Ham who uncovered his father's nakedness. But be like Shem and Japheth who covered their father's shame. Do not publish your brother's faults, but cover them with love and forgiveness.

Saints of God, let this be the motive for all you do. Do it, 'For Christ's sake'. Children of God, make this subject the theme of your meditations and praises, 'God for Christ's sake hath forgiven you'.

Bold shall I stand in that great day,
For who ought to my charge shall lay!
Through Jesus' blood absolved I am,
From sins tremendous curse and shame!

Chapter 52

Five Gracious Exhortations

And be ye kind one to another, tenderhearted, forgiving one another, even as God for Christ's sake hath forgiven you. Be ye therefore followers of God, as dear children; And walk in love, as Christ also hath loved us, and hath given himself for us an offering and a sacrifice to God for a sweetsmelling savour.

(Ephesians 4:32-5:2)

Were you to ask me to give you a single passage by which to regulate and govern your life for the glory of God, I would read to you this passage. If you should ask me for a portion of Scripture that would teach you how to live peaceably with yourself and others in your home, in the world and in the church, I would tell you to read Ephesians 4:32-5:2.

In this passage of Scripture, the Apostle Paul adopts the strongest, most persuasive, most reasonable and most gracious arguments imaginable to urge us to be kind, tenderhearted, gracious, forbearing, forgiving and loving in all our relations and connections with one another. Believers ought always to be a blessing to one another, never a hindrance and never an offence. It does matter how we live in this world. Someone is watching you whose life may be greatly affected by what you do, for better or for worse.

Do you want to be a blessing to other people? Do you want to help others? Do you want to minister to others? Do you want to build up others? Rather than hurting, hindering, offending and tearing down; rather than driving people away from Christ, the gospel and the worship of God, would you like to be a magnet to draw them in? Are you interested in the glory of God, the church of Christ and the souls of men? If you are, here are 'Five Gracious Exhortations'. I pray that God the Holy Spirit will graciously enable us to obey them.

Kind

First, 'Be ye kind one to another'. I love that word, 'kind'. I love to be around kind people. I want to be kind. The word 'kind' means good, thoughtful, courteous, amiable. To be kind toward one another is to entertain gracious thoughts toward each other, look pleasantly upon each other, speak favourably to and about one another and mutually serve one another for good.

Kindness is exactly the opposite of everything mentioned in Ephesians 4:31. 'Let all bitterness, and wrath, and anger, and clamour, and evil speaking, be put away from you, with all malice.'

'Bitterness' is oppression, hardness and ill-will. 'Wrath' is the heat of emotion that follows bitterness. 'Anger' is the intent to hurt. 'Clamour' is an out-breaking of anger and wrath into tumult, strife and division. 'Evil speaking' is reproach and slander, arising from a bitter, resentful heart. 'Malice' is an intent to hurt or even destroy, the vengeful emotions of an envious, jealous, bitter heart.

These vile works of the flesh are natural to us all, natural to fallen men and women. We are all petty and vindictive by nature. Nevertheless, these abominable, wicked things ought never to characterise saved sinners. They are what our fallen nature is, but we must never indulge them. We ought to be kind to one another.

Henry Clay once said, 'I'd rather be right than be president'. Well, I would rather be kind than be right. Kindness is always right! Someone once said, 'Be kind. Remember that everyone you meet is fighting a hard battle'. John Blanchard wrote, 'Kindness is a language that the deaf can hear and the blind can see'.

Kindness is the honey that takes the edge off another person's bitterness. Kind words are music in a world of trouble and the surest end to strife. 'A soft answer turneth away wrath: but grievous words stir up anger' (Proverbs 15:1). If we would be both peaceful and useful, let us 'be kind one to another'.

Tenderhearted

Second, be ye 'tenderhearted'. God, give me a tender heart. The word means sympathetic, compassionate, full of pity. The only other time this word is used in the Bible is in 2 Chronicles 13:7. There we read that Rehoboam, the son of Solomon, 'was young and tenderhearted'. Therefore, he could not fight against his enemies. I know we must fight the good fight of faith, contend for the truth, and defend the honour of God. But may we never be contentious, hard and unmerciful.

I repeat, this is my prayer. God, give me a tender heart, a heart sensitive to the direction of your Spirit and obedient to your will, a heart sensitive to the glory of Christ and to the needs and feelings of others, especially my brethren.

Forgiving

Third, 'Be ye kind one to another, tenderhearted, forgiving one another, even as God for Christ's sake hath forgiven you'. The secret to peace and happiness in any association with other human beings is forgiveness. You cannot live long with anyone in peace and harmony until you learn to forgive. And we, of all people in the world, ought to be a forgiving people. Saved sinners, forgiven transgressors, pardoned offenders have great reason to be gracious and forgiving.

By the grace of God, through the blood and righteousness of the Lord Jesus Christ, by the free grace and abundant mercy of God, I have been forgiven of all my sins. I ought to quickly forgive any evil done to me. I have been pardoned all my transgressions. I should pardon any transgression another may commit against me. I have been cleansed of all my iniquities. I dare not refuse to forgive the indescribably lesser iniquities committed by others. Grace bestowed makes people gracious. Mercy tasted makes people merciful. Love felt makes people loving. Forgiveness experienced makes people forgiving (Matthew 6:5-15; Luke 11:1-4).

You and I who trust Christ have been forgiven by God of all sin. We have been forgiven for Christ's sake through the merits of his blood! Forgiven fully and forgiven freely! Let us therefore forgive one another. No man or woman has ever done anything to or against me that can even begin to compare with what I have done to and against my God, both before he saved me and since. If God in heaven has forgiven me, I surely ought to forgive you of anything (Romans 5:1-8).

We never so touch the ocean of God's love as when we forgive and love our enemies. We should all have a large cemetery in which we bury the faults and offences of others. We are to forgive one another just like God for Christ's sake has forgiven us. We should forgive freely and fully from our heart, before forgiveness is sought, for Christ's sake. We should forgive and forget.

Followers

Fourth, 'Be ye therefore followers of God as dear children'. The word 'followers' here is imitators. Paul is urging us to follow the example of God himself in all things by imitating him. We are to follow his will, follow his Spirit, follow his Word and follow his example. Particularly, we are to follow God in acts of mercy, kindness and forgiveness.

We are to be followers of God 'as', or because we are his 'dear children'. You and I, believing on the Lord Jesus Christ, are the sons and daughters of the Almighty by adopting grace and covenant mercy; by regenerating power and by faith in Christ.

Love

Fifth, 'And walk in love'. We are to love God. That is the first great commandment; but love for God does not exist except in the hearts of heaven-born spirits who love one another (1 John 4:19-5:1). In our text, Paul is urging us to walk in love one toward another. Love is more than sentiment. It is service. It is more than passion. It is commitment. To love someone is to live for them. Love is the constant, self-abasing, self-sacrificing commitment of myself to the welfare of the people I love.

Love is the law by which Christ governs his kingdom. 'The love of Christ constraineth us'. Love is the fruit of saving faith. 'The fruit of the Spirit is love.' Love is easily defined and quickly perceived (1 Corinthians 13:4-8). Love is giving, not taking. Love is serving, not being served. Love is forgiving, not retaliating. Love is overlooking faults, not exposing them. Love is covering sin, not digging it up. Love is forbearing, not getting even. Love is helping, not hurting.

'Though I speak with the tongues of men and of angels, and have not charity, I am become as sounding brass, or a tinkling cymbal. And though I have the gift of prophecy, and understand all mysteries, and all knowledge; and though I have all faith, so that I could remove mountains, and have not charity, I am nothing. And though I bestow all my goods to feed the poor, and though I give my body to be burned, and have not charity, it profiteth me nothing. Charity suffereth long, and is kind; charity envieth not; charity vaunteth not itself, is not puffed up, Doth not behave itself unseemly, seeketh not her own, is not easily provoked, thinketh no evil; Rejoiceth not in iniquity, but rejoiceth in the truth; Beareth all things, believeth all things, hopeth all things, endureth all things. Charity never faileth: but whether there be prophecies, they shall fail; whether there be tongues, they shall cease; whether there be knowledge, it shall vanish away. For we know in part, and we prophesy in part. But when that which is perfect is come, then that which is in part shall be done away. When I was a child, I spake as a child, I understood as a child, I thought as a child: but when I became a man, I put away childish things. For now we see through a glass, darkly; but then face to face: now I know in part; but then shall I know even as also I am known. And now abideth faith, hope, charity, these three; but the greatest of these is charity' (1 Corinthians 13:1-13).

Here is the example of love by which we are to pattern our lives. We are to 'walk in love, as Christ also hath loved us, and hath given himself for us for a sweetsmelling savour to God'. Christ loved us with a free, unconditional, everlasting distinguishing love. Even so, we are to love one another freely.

Chapter 53

Live For God

Be ye therefore followers of God, as dear children; And walk in love, as Christ also hath loved us, and hath given himself for us an offering and a sacrifice to God for a sweetsmelling savour … For we are members of his body, of his flesh, and of his bones. For this cause shall a man leave his father and mother, and shall be joined unto his wife, and they two shall be one flesh. This is a great mystery: but I speak concerning Christ and the church. Nevertheless let every one of you in particular so love his wife even as himself; and the wife see that she reverence her husband.

(Ephesians 5:1-33)

It has been my heart's desire and unceasing prayer every day for the past 50 years that the Lord God would give me grace to live for him. I want to live for God.

I am more and more convinced that Christianity, true Christianity; true faith in Christ, is nothing less than the utter consecration of myself to God my Saviour, the devotion of my life to the will, honour and glory of the Lord Jesus Christ. That is exactly what our Lord Jesus teaches us (Matthew 16:25; Mark 8:35, 36; Luke 9:24; 14:25-33; 17:33; John 12:25). In the fifth chapter of Ephesians, God the Holy Ghost tells us what it means to 'Live For God'.

God's dear children

We are inspired to live for God by the fact that we are God's own dear children. Nothing can be more inspiring to devotion and consecration towards God than the fact that the God of heaven has made me – me of all people – his own dear child. Therefore, the Spirit of God says to you and me; sinners saved by the grace of God, washed in the blood of Christ, born again by God the Holy Spirit, 'Be ye therefore followers of God, as dear children; And walk in love, as Christ also hath loved us, and hath given himself for us an offering and a sacrifice to God for a sweetsmelling savour' (vv. 1, 2).

Let us imitate God our Father in all things, forgiving one another for Christ's sake. Forbearing one another's faults and weaknesses for Christ's sake. Walking in love, one toward another, for Christ's sake, loving one another 'as Christ also hath loved us, and hath given himself for us an offering and a sacrifice to God for a sweetsmelling savour'. What motive can induce such behaviour? What can inspire such love? God has made us his own 'dear children' by election (Galatians 4:4-6), by redemption (Ephesians 1:3-6), by regeneration (1 John 3:1, 2).

Denying ungodliness

If we would live for God, we are told by God the Holy Ghost that we must do so 'denying ungodliness and worldly lusts, we should live soberly, righteously, and godly, in this present world' (Titus 2:12). Paul does not leave us to guess what that ungodliness is that we must avoid. In Ephesians 5:3-13, he tells us exactly what that ungodliness is that we must deny.

'But fornication, and all uncleanness, or covetousness, let it not be once named among you, as becometh saints; Neither filthiness, nor foolish talking, nor jesting, which are not convenient: but rather giving of thanks' (vv. 3, 4).

Oh God, my God, teach me to live in a constant state of giving thanks to you for all your abundant grace in Christ Jesus! Thankful hearts are obedient hearts.

'For this ye know, that no whoremonger, nor unclean person, nor covetous man, who is an idolater, hath any inheritance in the kingdom of Christ and of God. Let no man deceive you with vain words: for because of these things cometh the wrath of God upon the children of disobedience. Be not ye therefore partakers with them. For ye were sometimes darkness, but now are ye light in the Lord: walk as children of light' (vv. 5-8).

We know what we are by nature. We know that this is where we were and what we were when God saved us by his grace. But, blessed be his name, we are washed, we are sanctified, we are now justified by the Spirit of our God and by the precious blood of our Lord Jesus Christ! So, let us live for him (1 Corinthians 6:9-20).

'(For the fruit of the Spirit is in all goodness and righteousness and truth;) Proving what is acceptable unto the Lord. And have no fellowship with the unfruitful works of darkness, but rather reprove them. For it is a shame even to speak of those things which are done of them in secret. But all things that are reproved are made manifest by the light ...' (vv. 9-13).

Awakening required

If we would live for God, we have learned, by long experience, that awakening, constant awakening, is required. 'Wherefore he saith, Awake thou that sleepest, and arise from the dead, and Christ shall give thee light' (v. 14).

We are alive. Yes, bless God, we are alive, made alive in Christ! Christ is our life, and we live in Him. We have been raised from the dead by the Spirit of God in the new birth. If you trust Christ, that is true of you. If I trust Christ, it is true of me. Faith in Christ is the evidence. But, like Sarah's womb, there is a deadness in us, a deadness we feel. We feel ourselves as good as dead and utterly impotent. There is a deadness, a lifelessness about us, while we live in this body of flesh, that puts us in constant need of awakening, reviving and enlivening.

Here we are called upon to awaken ourselves. It is our responsibility. But every heaven-born soul knows we can no more awaken ourselves now than we could awaken ourselves in the beginning. We must be awakened that we may awake and rise from the dead (Song of Solomon 4:16-5:9). 'Quicken us, and we will call upon thy name' (Psalm 80:18).

It is distressing to know what poor, sinful creatures we are. But nothing short of this painful, humbling knowledge of ourselves will break us and convince our proud hearts that it is Christ alone who is our strength and salvation. This spiritual poverty and leanness of soul is a blessed thing, designed by our ever-gracious, all-wise God to endear Christ the more to our hearts (Romans 7:14-25). Our Saviour has promised that all who mourn for him shall be comforted (Matthew 5:4).

Understanding God's will

If we would live for God, we must know God's will. So, in Ephesians 5:15-21, we are given instruction by God himself, by which to understand what his will is.

'See then that ye walk circumspectly, not as fools, but as wise, Redeeming the time, because the days are evil. Wherefore be ye not unwise, but understanding what the will of the Lord is. And be not drunk with wine, wherein is excess; but be filled with the Spirit; Speaking to yourselves in psalms and hymns and spiritual songs, singing and making melody in your heart to the Lord; Giving thanks always for all things unto God and the Father in the name of our Lord Jesus Christ; Submitting yourselves one to another in the fear of God.'

Redeeming the time, buying up the opportunity God has given us while we pass through this world, let us walk circumspectly, doing that which is right (v. 15). Let us be filled with the Spirit, live under the control of God the Holy Ghost, ruled by his Word (v. 18), speaking to ourselves in the psalms, hymns, and spiritual songs recorded in Holy Scripture, singing and making melody in our hearts unto the Lord (v. 19). Praise is always good for the soul. 'Giving thanks always for all things unto God and the Father in the name of our Lord Jesus Christ' (v. 20). Thanksgiving always makes life easier and makes our Lord's yoke lighter. 'Submitting yourselves one to another in the fear of God' (v. 21). We will not greatly err in any relationship if we simply submit ourselves to one another, fearing God.

Married to Christ

If we would live for God, let us live in the constant awareness of this blessed fact: we are married to Christ. Christ is married to us and we are married to the Lord Jesus Christ. What could be more inspiring and compelling? What could more effectually cause us to consecrate our lives to him than the constant remembrance of this sweet fact?

'Wives, submit yourselves unto your own husbands, as unto the Lord. For the husband is the head of the wife, even as Christ is the head of the church: and he is the saviour of the body. Therefore as the church is subject unto Christ, so let the wives be to their own husbands in every thing. Husbands, love your wives, even as Christ also loved the church, and gave himself for it; That he might sanctify and cleanse it with the washing of water by the word, That he might present it to himself a glorious church, not having spot, or wrinkle, or any such thing; but that it should be holy and without blemish. So ought men to love their wives as their own bodies. He that loveth his wife loveth himself. For no man ever yet hated his own flesh; but nourisheth and cherisheth it, even as the Lord the church: For we are members of his body, of his flesh, and of his bones. For this cause shall a man leave his father and mother, and shall be joined unto his wife, and they two shall be one flesh. This is a great mystery: but I speak concerning Christ and the church. Nevertheless let every one of you in particular so love his wife even as himself; and the wife see that she reverence her husband' (vv. 22-33).

This blessed, blessed union of Christ and his church was beautifully portrayed in the Garden before the fall when God created Eve out of Adam's side, presented her to him, and married them.

Christ is the Head of the church. He is the Saviour of his body. Christ loved the church and gave himself for his church. We have our life from him, by his death. And we have our life in union with him, being married to him. His purpose from everlasting has been that he might sanctify his church, make us holy and at last present his church to himself 'a glorious church, not having spot, or wrinkle, or any such thing; but that it should be holy and without blemish'.

Chapter 54

Imitating God

Be ye therefore followers of God, as dear children.

(Ephesians 5:1)

The Amplified Version translates Paul's words in Ephesians 5:1, 'Therefore be imitators of God [copy him and follow his example], as well-beloved children [imitate their father]'. Paul here urges us to be 'imitators of God'. That is how we ought to live in this world, as 'imitators of God'.

We live in a day that prizes originality. Men are forever striving to be original. One of the greatest ways to express disdain for a man in our day is to say, 'He never had an original thought in his life'. We are all horribly proud creatures! Pride is never so proud as when it enters the realm of religion. One of those things I constantly urge young preachers not to do is strive for originality. The proud longing for originality is one reason why the old, old gospel of the grace of God is seldom heard from the pulpit. It would be a good thing for the church of Christ if her preachers learned that the only thing original about them is original sin.

The same is true of us all. Our text calls us to the noble duty of being 'imitators of God'. May God the Holy Ghost fire your soul and mine with a desire to be like the Most High.

Give and forgive

The apostle urges us to give and forgive. If we are imitators of God let us give, for he is always giving. Give, for if he did not continually give, our lives would cease. Give, for he gives to all men liberally and upbraids not. Give, for every good and perfect gift comes from above. Let us be imitators of God, the constant and generous Giver, who spared not his own Son, but delivered him up for us all. 'Thanks be unto God for his unspeakable gift.'

Then comes that which is a much harder task, but that which is the joy and delight of God's saints. If we are God's children, let us forgive, for the Lord our God graciously forgives. 'God for Christ's sake hath forgiven you.' He has blotted out our transgressions. He has cast our sins into the depth of the sea. He has removed our iniquities from us as far as the east is from the west. God has buried our offences in the tomb of forgetfulness. Therefore, let us freely forgive the offences of others, that when we bow our knees we can pray without hypocrisy, 'Forgive us our debts. as we forgive our debtors'.

May these two things be prominent features of your life and mine as God's dear children; giving and forgiving. Giving to the needy and forgiving the guilty. Giving to the cause of Christ and the furtherance of the gospel. Giving to our missionaries and preachers. Forgiving those who offend us.

Doing these things, we walk in love as Christ also has loved us. Christ has given himself for us, and through his precious blood God has faithfully and justly forgiven us of all sin. Oh Spirit of God, give me grace to blend giving and forgiving into one God-like life, imitating my God!

The command

Consider the command itself, 'Be ye therefore followers (imitators) of God'. To many this command has little meaning. Many have weak, unscriptural and irreverent ideas about God. Since they think little of God, they think it is an easy thing to imitate him and presume they do so fairly well. But for those who know God, this is a tremendously weighty thing to consider. We have seen the glory, majesty, holiness and supremacy of God. How can sinners imitate the Almighty?

Very practical

What we have before us in Ephesians 5:1 could not be more practical. There is nothing mystical, sentimental or speculative about it. This is an eminently practical exhortation. It points to continued action of the best kind: 'Be ye imitators of God'.

Paul does not tell us simply to go and meditate upon God, but he tells us to imitate him. Meditation is a good, pleasant and profitable thing for our souls. It will instruct you, strengthen you, comfort you, inspire your heart and make your soul stedfast. By all means, meditate upon God. Meditate upon him as God the Father, God the Son, and God the Holy Ghost. Meditate on his salvation, his providence, and his goodness.

But do not stop at meditation. We must go on to the imitation of God himself. It is good to make Mary's excellent choice, sitting at the Saviour's feet and hearing his word but now we must arise and follow his steps. How I thank God for his serving Marthas at church! Thank God for those who work hard to give generously, mow the grass, shovel the snow, maintain the flowers and clean the building, and for those who visit the sick and entertain guests.

The apostle does not say to us, 'Be ye admirers of God', but 'be ye therefore imitators of God'. We do admire God; of course, we do. The pure in heart see God, and are filled with reverent admiration. With the seraphim, every renewed soul cries, 'Holy, Holy, Holy is the LORD of hosts'. 'Who is like unto thee, O LORD, … glorious in holiness, fearful in praises, doing wonders?' But we must not be satisfied with admiring God. We show our admiration of him by carefully imitating him. The imitation of God is the highest and most sincere way of admiring him.

This exhortation does not even stop at adoration of God. Adoration arises from meditation and admiration. It is one of the highest forms of worship. We serve God greatly when we adore him. Our whole lives should be marked by adoration. Not only on Sundays, at certain set hours, in the assembly, in our closets but always and in all things let us adore God. Thus, adoration becomes a practical imitation of him. Our adoration is proved to be sincere by imitation.

True worship of God involves imitating him in meditation, admiration and adoration. We must study to be like him. We want a resemblance between God and us otherwise, our knowledge of him is but a cold form, our faith is but a dead profession and our praise is but an empty compliment. How can we say we love God if we do not desire to be like him?

As dear children

Truly, the command here given is most practical. But Paul's exhortation treats us as we are. It treats us as children. 'Be ye imitators of God, as dear children.' Being God's dear children, we are to simply copy the example of God as he is revealed in our dear Saviour, the Lord Jesus Christ. The Spirit of God does not here require us to strike out like men and be original. He simply requires us to copy Christ. Like a child in school copies his letters, the children of God are to copy his Son. We must follow him by faith, trusting in his grace. You cannot follow God until you are born of God (John 3:3-8). Faith in Christ is where you must begin.

You cannot imitate God if you do not know him. We must be possessors of the knowledge of the Lord, that only comes by the Holy Ghost. Until Christ is revealed in us, we cannot imitate him.

Then, being God's own dear children, we must be careful not to invent a pretended holiness or godliness of our own. We copy the holiness and godliness of our Saviour. The Pharisees added many things to the commandments of God, just as religious people do today. But the children of the kingdom simply follow the Master. The kingdom of heaven is not in meats, and drinks, and carnal things, but in righteousness, and peace and joy in the Holy Ghost.

Not legalism

'Be ye imitators of God, as dear children.' This is not a matter of legal obedience, but a matter of grace. Believers are not driven to godliness by the whip of the law. We are called to be imitators of God as his dear children, as children who delight in the law of God after the inward man. 'Be ye imitators of God, as dear children.' The children of grace imitate God because of the sweet bonds of the gospel from a willing heart. You do not have to force your children to imitate you. They do it naturally, even in their games. Nothing could make us more useful to one another than obedience to this exhortation, 'Be ye imitators of God'. As we imitate God our Saviour, we benefit one another. As we imitate God, we honour the gospel. As we imitate our God, we serve his church and kingdom well.

The argument

Carefully weigh the argument Paul uses to secure our obedience. The precept is, 'Be ye imitators of God'. The argument is this, 'as dear children'. This is the greatest privilege and highest title that a mere mortal can have.

We are the children of God! We are God's children by eternal adoption in Christ and divine predestination. We are his children by sovereign regeneration and by faith in Jesus Christ. We are his children now; 'Beloved, now are we the sons of God'. In as much as we are now the children of God, by almighty power and grace, it is only reasonable that we should be imitators of God.

Not only are we the children of God; but we are his 'dear children'. We are children beloved of God. Is not this a mighty and tender argument, irresistible to your soul? 'Behold, what manner of love the Father hath bestowed upon us, that we should be called the sons of God.'

The encouragements

Perhaps some of you are thinking that while this is a great subject, it is too great for me. How am I to imitate God? I want us to think of the encouragements we have to obey this precept. God has made great provisions for us that we may be like him. I will only hint at a few in order to encourage our hearts to seek more and more of his likeness.

God has graciously made us his children. I speak to believers. You are the sons and daughters of God. If we are to be imitators of God, we must first be his children. By the new birth, we are renewed in the divine image.

God has given us his divine nature. 'According as his divine power has given to us all things that pertain to life and godliness, through the knowledge of him that hath called us to glory and virtue: whereby are given unto us exceeding great and precious promises: that by these ye might be partakers of the divine nature, having escaped the corruption that is in the world through lust' (2 Peter 1:3, 4).

If we are truly born again as God's children, he has implanted a new nature, a new man, a new heart within us. The old nature, the old man, and the old heart are still there, but God has placed within us his Seed, even Christ the Lord. 'Christ in you, the hope of glory.' 'Therefore if any man be in Christ, he is a new creature: old things are passed away; behold, all things are become new. And all things are of God, who hath reconciled us to himself by Jesus Christ, and hath given to us the ministry of reconciliation; To wit, that God was in Christ, reconciling the world unto himself, not imputing their trespasses unto them; and hath committed unto us the word of reconciliation. Now then we are ambassadors for Christ, as though God did beseech you by us: we pray you in Christ's stead, be ye reconciled to God. For he hath made him to be sin for us, who knew no sin; that we might be made the righteousness of God in him' (2 Corinthians 5:17-21).

God has given us his Holy Spirit. 'Likewise the Spirit also helpeth our infirmities' (Romans 8:26). We are weak, but he strengthens us. We are ignorant, but he teaches us. We fall, but he lifts us up! We are languishing, but he revives us. We are nothing, but his grace is sufficient. He has promised, 'My grace is sufficient for thee'.

The Lord God has graciously given us the example of Christ as a pattern for our lives. 'For I have given you an example, that ye should do as I have done to you' (John 13:15). Christ is the embodiment of the eternal God. He is the express image of his person, the brightness of his glory. In Christ we see God. If we would be like God we must follow Christ's example (Philippians 3:10).

God graciously gives us personal communion with himself. If we would be like God, we must fellowship with him. We must walk with him. We must live with him. Nearness to God gives likeness to God. The more you see God, the more God will be seen in you.

God has given us his Word. 'Thy Word is a lamp unto my feet, and a light unto my path' (Psalm 119:105). If you would know God's will, go to the Holy Bible, his Word. There he reveals his will and his way. Search it out, and follow it. In the pages of Holy Scripture, we have the counsel of infinite wisdom.

Our obedience

God give us grace to obey this precept, 'Be ye therefore imitators of God, as dear children'. The Holy Spirit dwells in us to make us like Christ in all things, to be like him is to be like the Most High. Being like Christ is the fruit of the Spirit. The works of the flesh are many. But the fruit of the Spirt is one (Galatians 5:22, 23).

The fruit of the Spirit is a Christlikeness toward God himself. The fruit of the Spirit is the treatment of other men as Christ himself treated them. Be longsuffering with the faults of others. Treat one another with gentleness, kindness, tenderness. Show goodness and mercy to one another, even as God shows goodness and mercy to you. 'Be ye therefore merciful, as your Father also is merciful' (Luke 6:36).

The fruit of the Spirit is living by faith in God, loving one another, and submitting to God our Father in all meekness. Exercise self-control and restraint in all things by the power of the Spirit who dwells in you.

And never forget that the imitation of God is 'the fruit of the Spirit'. It is not by the power of the flesh that we are conformed to the image of Christ, but by the power of the Spirit. Let us boast nothing of ourselves, but give all glory to his grace.

If God requires us to be imitators of him by forgiving men of their wrongs for Christ's sake, then God must be ready to forgive sinners for Christ's sake. If God requires us to be imitators of him by being truthful and honest with them, then God will surely keep his Word to us. From all that is written here, I must conclude that God is a dear Father to all believers. He treats us with kindness, tenderness and patience. He loves us dearly. He will never turn his love away from us.

Let this be your fervent prayer, your inmost desire, 'O God, my Father, give me the grace of Christ, the power of your Spirit and such faith in you, that I may imitate you as a beloved child'.

Is this your desire? Do you long to be like Christ your God? Then you shall be satisfied. You shall awake in his likeness. 'We know that when he shall appear, we shall be like him, for we shall see him as he is.' We will be like him, full of love. We will be like him, free from sin. We will be like him, robed with glory.

Chapter 55

'Walk In Love'

And walk in love, as Christ also hath loved us, and hath given himself for us an offering and a sacrifice to God for a sweetsmelling savour.

(Ephesians 5:2)

Our Lord gave us his great commandment, that we should love one another. For this he earnestly made supplication while he was upon the earth. Today he intercedes for the saints in heaven that they may be made perfect in one. The church of Christ is one in thought, in purpose, in desire and in faith. The joy of that blessed unity is our oneness of heart, a oneness created by the love of God 'shed abroad in our hearts by the Holy Ghost which is given unto us' (Romans 5:5). Being one with Christ, we are one in Christ. We enjoy the love of God flowing from heart to heart.

An exhortation

In Ephesians 3, we find the Apostle Paul praying that we might know this love. In chapter 4, he gave us instructions about how this love is to be practised. Now in chapter 5, the Apostle moves from prayer and instruction to exhortation. In our text, Paul commands us to practise the love of Christ.

It is good for us to pray for more love but the way to nurture and cultivate love is to 'walk in love'. The more we practise love, the more loving we become. You will notice in this chapter that Paul sets before us several very practical duties that the people of God must perform. In them all, there is one dominant motive, one pre-eminent foundation, and that is love.

Love is the sum of the law. By it, the law is fulfilled. Love is the rule of Christ's kingdom. It is the principle governing the hearts of God's elect. In the new birth, the seed of love is planted in the heart, and that seed brings forth the fruit of love in the lives of God's children.

Love is essential

Love is not something that is an optional extra. This is not an add-on grace. This is not something you choose. Love is essential. Without love, there is no Christianity, no life, no salvation. If you have not love, you are not of God, for God is love. 'He that loveth not knoweth not God.' Are we the people of God? If so, we both should and must 'walk in love', and we do.

Two directions

This love runs in two directions. We love God and we love one another. Here we have Paul's second direction for a life of godliness. 'Walk in love, as Christ also hath loved us.' In verse one he exhorts us to imitate God. Here we are exhorted to imitate Christ, God's Son. The exhortation is, 'Walk in love'. The motive by which it is enforced is the example of Christ's love. Since it is by the love of Christ that we are reconciled to God, we should imitate his love. In this, as in all things, Christ himself is our pattern and example. We are to love one another as Christ loved us. Listen to the Scriptures. 'Hereby perceive we the love of God, because he hath laid down his life for us: and we ought to lay down our lives for the brethren' (1 John 3:16). 'Love one another; as I have loved you' (John 13:34). 'This is my commandment, That ye love one another, as I have loved you' (John 15:12).

Children of God, is not this an irresistible motive, constraining our hearts to love one another? Can we sin against such matchless love as is given us in Christ Jesus? Do we despise that love that caused him to bleed and die in our stead? God forbid! Let us walk in love.

Heaven's hope

We live in the hope and expectation of heaven. And what is heaven? It is a world of love. 'Charity (love) never faileth ... And now abideth faith, hope, charity (love), these three; but the greatest of these is love' (1 Corinthians 13:8, 13). Love is that gift of grace that shall endure through all eternity. In heaven, we will forever walk in love toward God and one another. When the saints of God walk in love, they enjoy a little of heaven upon the earth. May God the Holy Ghost enable us to do more than pray for love. Let us walk in love as Christ has loved us.

That which the Holy Spirit here teaches us is unmistakable. The Lord Jesus Christ showed us such great love in giving himself as a sacrifice to God for us, that all true believers are bound to walk in love.

Love's example

Here is the example of love in the text, 'Christ also hath loved us, and hath given himself for us an offering and a sacrifice to God for a sweetsmelling savour'.

We must never fall into the error of looking upon the death of Christ as nothing more than a moral example of dedication and love. His death was much more, infinitely more than that. The death of Christ was a substitutionary atonement for sin. It was the satisfactory payment for our transgressions. It was the death of death. It was the reconciliation of God and man. It was the end of sin. It was the accomplishment of righteousness. Yet at the same time, we must remember that it was a noble example. 'Christ also suffered for us, leaving us an example, that ye should follow his steps' (1 Peter 2:21). In Ephesians 5:2, Paul shows us the death of Christ as an example of love that should be imitated by the people of God.

Love revealed

The Lord Jesus Christ loved us. We may search the Scriptures, search the world, search out heaven itself, but we will never find any other principle that motivated the Son of God to die in the place of sinners than this, 'Christ also hath loved us'.

It is true that Christ came into the world to suffer and die in obedience to his Father's will. Yet our Lord was not forced into obedience. He was Jehovah's willing Servant (Exodus 21:1-6). He undertook the work of our redemption by a voluntary agreement to his heavenly Father's will. 'Therefore doth my Father love me, because I lay down my life, that I might take it again. No man taketh it from me, but I lay it down of myself. I have power to lay it down, and I have power to take it again. This commandment have I received of my Father' (John 10:17, 18). In the covenant of everlasting grace, Christ agreed to all the stipulations of the covenant for our redemption because he loved his Father and loved us.

It was our blessed Saviour's great love for us that constrained him to become our Surety, our Substitute and our Redeemer. He 'loved me, and gave himself for me' (Galatians 2:20). 'Unto him that loved us, and washed us from our sins in his own blood' (Revelations 1:5).

It was not anything in us that constrained the Son of God to die in our stead. He agreed to be our Redeemer before ever the earth was. Before there was a sinner, Christ was our Redeemer. Before God's law had been broken, Christ was our pardon. Before we transgressed God's law, Christ was our Righteousness. Certainly, there were no foreseen merits in us that caused Christ to become our Surety. As he looked upon the future ages of mankind, he saw nothing but sin, rebellion, hatred of God and foolishness of heart.

Out of the abundant freeness of his grace Christ Jesus loved us, and became our Substitute. He loved us freely, fully and perfectly from all eternity. From eternity, he declared, 'My delights were with the sons of men' (Proverbs 8:31). Because of his great love for us he 'gave himself for us'. O blessed gift! O blessed Giver! 'Thanks be unto God for his unspeakable gift' (2 Corinthians 9:15).

The gift

Behold the gift; 'Himself'. Christ gave himself as our Representative in the Covenant, and as our Kinsman in the incarnation. He gave himself as the Man of Sorrows throughout his earthly life. He gave himself as our Priest in Gethsemane, and as our Substitute at Calvary. He gave us his throne, his glory, his majesty, his power, his riches and his dignity, but he gave more. He gave himself. He 'through the eternal Spirit offered himself without spot to God' (Hebrews 9:14). 'Who loved me, and gave himself for me' (Galatians 2:20). 'Christ also loved the church, and gave himself for it' (Ephesians 5:25). 'Who his own self bear our sins in his own body on the tree' (1 Peter 2:24). He gave all his divinity, his humanity, his holiness, his righteousness, and his being.

Here is the blessed wonder of grace, 'Christ also hath loved us, and hath given himself for us'. Sinners that we are, vile as we are, wretched as we are, he gave himself for us. It was for our pardon, our salvation, our eternal life that Christ died.

Justice vindicated

The substitutionary death of Christ in our stead demonstrates the justice and holiness of God. God hates sin. He will by no means clear the guilty. Sin must be punished. The only way that it can be removed is in the manner that God has prescribed, through the death of Christ. 'Whom God hath set forth to be a propitiation through faith in his blood, to declare his righteousness for the remission of sins' (Romans 3:25).

Christ gave himself for us to vindicate the honour of God's holy law. God's authority was violated by man's rebellion. His law was broken. If God did not execute the penalty of the law upon fallen man, his justice would fall to the ground. God could not remove the curse until the law was satisfied. 'But when the fulness of time was come, God sent forth his Son, made of a woman, made under the law, to redeem them that were under the law' (Galatians 4:4, 5). 'Christ hath redeemed us from the curse of the law, being made a curse for us: for it is written, Cursed is everyone that hangeth on a tree' (Galatians 3:13).

Indescribable love

Christ secured our eternal happiness and peace at a dear price. 'Greater love hath no man than this, that a man lay down his life for his friends' (John 15:13). 'Herein is love, not that we loved God, but that he loved us, and sent his Son to be the propitiation for our sins' (1 John 4:10). By the substitutionary death of Christ, we have the greatest possible revelation of divine love.

Sinner, read the Book of God and tremble. God has put a mark upon sin. If he spared not his own Son when he was made sin for us, you may be assured he will not spare you in the Day of Judgment, unless your sins are removed by the blood of Christ. Children of God, read this and rejoice. 'He gave himself for us', to satisfy the demands of God's law, justice and wrath. We are accepted in him, never to die.

Sacrifice to God

Look at the manner in which the death of Christ is described. It was 'an offering and a sacrifice to God'. The death of Christ was an offering of peace to secure our reconciliation to God. And it was a sacrifice of blood to atone for our sins. The law of God required both a burnt peace offering (Leviticus 4:26-35) and an offering of blood (Leviticus 16) to make atonement for the transgressor. This should remind us of several things.

We should be reminded of the misery we were in. We have broken God's law. We have offended God's holiness. We have rebelled against God's government. Therefore, Christ reconciled us to the offended God. He appeased God's just wrath and he took away our sin. Behold the love and mercy of God to us. 'God so loved the world, that he gave his only begotten Son, that whosoever believeth in him should not perish, but have everlasting life' (John 3:16).

Let us never forget that the only means of redemption is by the sin-offering and propitiatory sacrifice of Jesus Christ. 'Without shedding of blood is no remission' (Hebrews 9:22). 'For he hath made him to be sin for us, who knew no sin: that we might be made the righteousness of God in him' (2 Corinthians 5:21).

Before sin can be removed, there must be a sacrifice such as God will accept as a full satisfaction for sin. That sacrifice is none other than Jesus Christ. With that sacrifice found, nothing else is needed. He says of Christ, 'I have found a ransom'.

Sweetsmelling Savour

One last thing that I would have you to observe about this great example of love is that the Holy Lord God is altogether satisfied with the sacrifice of Christ for us. His sacrifice is 'for a sweetsmelling savour to God'. Here the Scripture speaks of God after the manner of men. Men are delighted with sweet aromas. Therefore, to show us the satisfaction that God has in the death of Christ, it is presented as a sweetsmelling savour, a sweetsmelling aroma, a sweetsmelling odour.

God is satisfied with the person offered, his own Son. He is satisfied with the obedience he offered, the sufferings he endured and the price he paid, 'His own blood'. God showed his satisfaction by the resurrection and exaltation of Christ.

Love's walk

Using the great love of Christ for us, which brought him to die in the place of sinners, Paul teaches us to follow his example. Since Christ loved us in such great measure, those who are redeemed by his blood should walk in love. This does not signify an act or two occasionally performed, but the constant tenor of our lives should be the exercise of love. We are taught to walk in love to our God and Saviour, the Lord Jesus Christ. 'We love him, because he first loved us.' If God has so loved us that he gave his only begotten Son to have us, and Christ so loved us that he died in our place, surely, we ought to walk in love to him.

It is impossible for us to truly love men if that love does not flow from love to God. Listen to the words of the Apostle John, 'By this we know that we love the children of God, when we love God, and keep his commandments' (1 John 5:2). There is no genuine love upon earth, except that which has God as its primary object. The first impression of the love of Christ upon our hearts produces in us a love to God. This is the foundation and motive of everything in the life of the believer. 'For the love of Christ constraineth us; because we thus judge, that if one died for all, then were all dead: And that he died for all, that they which live should not henceforth live to themselves, but unto him that died for them, and rose again' (2 Corinthians 5:14, 15).

Christ Jesus died for us, not only to secure our salvation, but also to win our hearts to himself. When we are made 'partakers of the divine nature', we are made partakers of the love of God, causing heaven born souls to have a fervent love to God, that directs all our actions to his glory, and gives us a desire to honour him in all things.

What, then, is it to walk in love toward God? To walk in love is to do all things because of love to Christ. Let all acts of worship and devotion, deeds of service to Christ and the deeds of life be done with love.

Whatever you do, let it be done because of love and gratitude, which is the life, soul and heart of godliness. Pray, seeking your desires because of love for Christ. Obey God's Word from a heart desiring to honour him whom we love. If we do not walk in love toward God, everything we do is nothing but a show of religion, a mere form of godliness!

Love never weighs cost. If we love Christ we will lay all things at his feet. We will suffer all things for him, endure all things for him and give up all things for him.

> Were the whole realm of nature mine,
> That were a present far too small;
> Love so amazing, so divine,
> Demands my soul, my life, my all.

For his glory, we will give our time and our possessions. For his glory, we will give up our dearest companions. For his glory, we will give ourselves; our strength, our will, our pleasures, our lives.

But there is more involved in this admonition to walk in love than loving God. You and I are to walk in love toward our fellowmen. Our Saviour teaches us both by example and precept to love all men. We should walk in love toward our brethren and toward our enemies. Deal with them in kindness, tenderness and compassion, doing them good and not evil. The love of Christ in us must overrule all the prejudices that divide the hearts of men. To walk in love is to walk sympathetically, patiently and forgiving toward men. It is to walk seeking to do them good.

Love's constraint

Love to God and our fellowmen is the rule and law by which God's kingdom is governed. 'The love of Christ constraineth us.' If I am not ruled by love, I am not the subject of the King of love. If I do not have a heart of love, I am not a child of God, who is love. If I am born-again by God's Spirit, redeemed by the blood of his dear Son and chosen by his grace, I am constrained to walk in love.

The love of Christ is shed abroad in our hearts, as a motive and principle constraining us to love. We are constrained to love our enemies because he loved us when we were yet his enemies. We are constrained to love our brethren because they are redeemed with the same precious blood. We are constrained to love Christ because he has loved us and given himself for us.

The love of Christ is a pattern and example constraining us to imitate his love. We are constrained by its freeness to love even those who give no love in return. We are constrained by his humiliation and sacrifice to so love him that we give all to him; and do all because we love him.

'Above all these things put on charity (love), which is the bond of perfectness.' May God give us grace both to know and to walk in the love of Christ.

How condescending and how kind
Was God's eternal Son!
Our misery reached His heavenly mind,
And pity brought Him down.

This was compassion like a God,
That when the Saviour knew,
The price of pardon was His blood,
His pity ne'er withdrew.

When justice by our sins provoked,
Drew forth its dreadful sword,
He gave His soul up to the stroke,
Without a murmuring word!

Chapter 56

'Children Of Light'

But fornication, and all uncleanness, or covetousness, let it not be once named among you, as becometh saints; Neither filthiness, nor foolish talking, nor jesting, which are not convenient: but rather giving of thanks. For this ye know, that no whoremonger, nor unclean person, nor covetous man, who is an idolater, hath any inheritance in the kingdom of Christ and of God. Let no man deceive you with vain words: for because of these things cometh the wrath of God upon the children of disobedience. Be not ye therefore partakers with them. For ye were sometimes darkness, but now are ye light in the Lord: walk as children of light: (For the fruit of the Spirit is in all goodness and righteousness and truth;) Proving what is acceptable unto the Lord. And have no fellowship with the unfruitful works of darkness, but rather reprove them. For it is a shame even to speak of those things which are done of them in secret. But all things that are reproved are made manifest by the light: for whatsoever doth make manifest is light. Wherefore he saith, Awake thou that sleepest, and arise from the dead, and Christ shall give thee light.

(Ephesians 5:3-14)

In Ephesians 5 verses 1 and 2, the Apostle urges us to 'walk in love'. In verses 3-14, he shows us that imitating God, walking in love, living in this world 'as God's dear children', involves the totality of our lives. To imitate God is to live for God. To walk in love is to live for God. In this passage the Apostle Paul urges us to 'walk as children of light'.

Sun of righteousness

The prophet Malachi gave us a very peculiar name by which Christ Jesus is revealed. The prophet tells us that the Messiah, in whom his faith was fixed, would be revealed in this manner: 'The Sun of righteousness (shall) arise with healing in his wings'. It was in this character that our Lord was revealed. John said, 'In him was life; and the life was the light of men. And the light shineth in darkness; and the darkness comprehended it not' (John 1:4, 5). Today, our Lord still stands forth in heaven as 'the Sun of Righteousness'. He says, 'I am the light of the world'.

As the sun is hidden from view in the darkness of night, and there is only a reflection of the sun's light seen in the moon, even so, the church of Christ is the reflection of the great Sun of Righteousness in this dark world. Christ, the Sun, is in heaven, hidden from view to this world of darkness. But he has not left himself without a witness in the world. His church reflects the light of his life, his glory, and his grace to men who grope about as drunken men in the darkness of sin. Listen to the Master's own words. 'I am the light of the world: he that followeth me shall not walk in darkness, but shall have the light of life' (John 8:12). To those who have been born again by his Spirit and follow him, our Lord says, 'Ye are the light of the world. A city that is set on an hill cannot be hid' (Matthew 5:14).

A great danger

You see, there is a great danger of our light not being seen in this dark world. There is the great danger of our light being hidden under a bushel. Our Lord knew that this danger existed, so he admonished us in these words, 'Let your light so shine before men, that they might see your good works, and glorify your Father which is in heaven' (Matthew 5:16). The Apostle Paul saw the danger of God's people being affected by the darkness of sin all around them; and he warned them to avoid the ways of darkness. 'That ye may be blameless and harmless, the sons of God, without rebuke, in the midst of a crooked and perverse nation, among whom ye shine as lights in the world; holding forth the word of life' (Philippians 2:15, 16). If we are the children of light, our lives should be such a reflection of the great light of the Sun of Righteousness, that, as his very being was a reproof to men's evil deeds, men are also reproved by our conversation in this world.

Are we children of light, loved and chosen of God, redeemed, purchased, and bought by the precious blood of the Lord Jesus Christ, born again and called, sanctified and sealed by God the Holy Ghost? Are we children of light? If so, let us walk in the light. If not, I pray that God will cause the Sun of Righteousness to shine the light of his glory into our hearts that we may be healed of all darkness (1

John 1:5-7). If we have been translated from the kingdom of darkness into the kingdom of God's dear Son by almighty grace, it is our honour and responsibility to walk as children of light. In verses 3-14, Paul continues his exhortation to walk in love. If we walk in love to God and to our fellowmen, we must walk in the light of Christ. This portion of Holy Scripture teaches us three things I want you to see.

Avoid darkness

First, as children of light, we must avoid the ways of darkness (vv. 3-7). These verses contain a caution against all manner of uncleanness. To enforce his warning, the Apostle shows us the remedy for these evils and gives strong arguments to dissuade their practise.

In chapter four, we were admonished to be imitators of Christ by exercising self-sacrifice. Here, we are urged to avoid self-indulgence. The love of Christ constrains us to avoid vices that are unbecoming to the saints of God. Paul does not mince words in his denunciation of evil. Some things are inconsistent with godliness; it is our responsibility and our honour to avoid them. 'But fornication, and all uncleanness, or covetousness, let it not be once named among you, as becometh saints; Neither filthiness, nor foolish talking, nor jesting, which are not convenient: but rather giving of thanks' (vv. 3, 4).

The vices Paul gives here is only a sample of those which are condemned in the Scriptures. These things are natural to men. They are common among unregenerate men. But they are sins that should never be named among God's elect. As we shall see, Christ alone provides the example, motive and power to overcome them.

Paul begins by denouncing every form of sexual perversion. Fornication is specifically the unlawful sexual behaviour of two single people, but it seems to include illicit relationships of every description. Fornication is contrary to the law of God. It is a work of the flesh. Yet it was common in Paul's day. Many pagan religions promote such behaviour. In our day, fornication has become a matter of indifference to many, even in the church of Christ.

All uncleanness goes beyond fornication to include adultery, incest, sodomy, and every unnatural lust. Paul is talking about impurity, not only of deeds, but also words, thoughts, intents of the heart, desires and filthy passions. All of them are denounced. The phrase 'all uncleanness' covers a wide range!

Covetousness here goes beyond a desire for gain. Covetousness usually has reference to an inordinate desire for worldly gain. Here it seems to be in reference to a beastly, inordinate and selfish lust. It is self-assertion, regardless of the injury done to others. 'Thou shalt not covet thy neighbour's wife' (Exodus 20:17).

If we are the children of God, if we are Christ's, such behaviour is unbecoming to us. Such vices ought never to be committed, much less should they be common among us. We are God's saints, his holy ones. Such things should never be named among us. We were set apart by God in eternal election for himself. Our sins have been pardoned by the blood of Christ. We are sanctified by the power and presence of God the Holy Spirit, being made 'partakers of the divine nature'. We have separated ourselves unto God in believer's baptism. How can we that are washed, justified and sanctified live any longer to the lusts of our flesh?

Not only must we avoid sexual perversions, but as children of God, we bridle our tongues. My tongue, perhaps the most influential member of my body, should be employed for the edification of the body of Christ. It should speak the truth in love. I should make it my conscious duty not to injure my brother with my tongue.

Filthiness and foolish talking

Men and women in this world are constantly overflowing with filth. Their gestures, their actions, their language is designed to excite lust; but the children of God ought not to speak in such a manner. As men and women whose hearts are fixed upon eternity, our speech should not be foolish talking; vain, idle, empty words.

Jesting

Jesting is that wicked sense of humour people employ at the expense of hurting others. It is what we call 'cutting a man down'.

Many twist this text to mean that God's people should never use humorous speech. It was not intended to teach that. I think Elijah was being somewhat humorous when he said to the prophets of Baal, 'Cry aloud: for he is a god; either he is talking, or he is pursuing, or he is in a journey, or peradventure he sleepeth, and must be awaked' (1 Kings 18:27). Paul simply means that God's people should avoid all filthy and harmful talk. This manner of speech is not convenient. It is unbecoming of the holy calling to which we have been called.

What is the remedy for these vices? How are they to be avoided? Paul answers the question by saying 'but rather giving of thanks'.

William Hendriksen said, 'When mind and heart are centred on 'all things bright and beautiful' which God grants to us and still has in store for us, the interest in squalid indecency will vanish'.

It is edifying to ourselves and to one another, and it is honouring to God, for us to use our tongues for praise and thanksgiving, rather than for filthy, foolish and hurtful language. Let clarion praise replace clever phrases.

In order to enforce these prohibitions, the apostle uses the strongest possible arguments to prevent us from living like other men. 'For this ye know, that no whoremonger, nor unclean person, nor covetous man, who is an idolater, hath any inheritance in the kingdom of Christ and of God. Let no man deceive you with vain words: for because of these things cometh the wrath of God upon the children of disobedience. Be not ye therefore partakers with them' (vv. 5-7).

Paul uses the strong language of these two verses to stress this point. Immorality and salvation are opposites. Indecency and godliness are contrary. They cannot go together. Children of God do not follow the example of the wicked. No one who lives in ungodliness has any inheritance in the kingdom of heaven.

Paul adds a word of explanation to the words 'covetous man'. He says such a man is an idolater. He is an idolater because his god is his own belly. He never has his fill of sin. He lives for sensuality and worships the same material things as the heathen. Paul is not telling us that men and women who have fallen into those vices cannot be saved, but if they persist in their sin and do not repent, seeking pardon by the blood of Christ, their sins will shut them out of heaven.

Heaven is here spoken of as the kingdom of God and of Christ. It is the kingdom of Christ as God. It is his kingdom by right of his divine Being. It is his kingdom by right as Mediator between God and man, by right of his Mediatorial obedience.

There is no way of coming into the kingdom of life, but by Christ. It is in his hands. His righteousness alone gives us title to it. Christ preserves us unto his heavenly kingdom and will put us in possession of it. With the loving heart of a true pastor, Paul warns these Ephesians of the certainty of God's wrath upon sin. 'Let no man deceive you with vain words: for because of these things cometh the wrath of God upon the children of disobedience' (v. 6).

No one who continues to practise pagan vices, either from force of old habit and the course of least resistance, or because he has adopted some pretended excuse, no one shall escape the wrath of God (Revelation 21:27; 22:15).

Do not be deceived about sin. In the words of Matthew Henry, 'Those who flatter themselves and others with hopes of impunity in sin do but put a cheat upon themselves and others'. God must punish sin! His wrath is now coming on the children of disobedience because of sin.

Children of God, you and I are to live above these things. We must not be partakers with wicked men. As a father pleads with his children, whom he dearly loves, so this prisoner of Jesus Christ, who was facing certain death, pleads earnestly with those who are called by the name of Christ, 'Be not ye therefore partakers with them' (v. 7).

These things are displeasing to God our Father. They dishonour God's holy name. They are contrary to the purpose of Christ's death to purify us unto himself. Though we well deserved God's wrath, yet he has not appointed us to wrath, but has forgiven us by the shed blood of Christ. If you partake of their evil way of life, you must also partake of their judgment, because, after all, you are one of them.

Children of light

Second, if we have been renewed by the grace of God, we must walk as the children of light. 'For ye were sometimes darkness, but now are ye light in the Lord: walk as children of light: (For the fruit of the Spirit is in all goodness and righteousness and truth;) Proving what is acceptable unto the Lord. And have no fellowship with the unfruitful works of darkness, but rather reprove them. For it is a shame even to speak of those things which are done of them in secret. But all things that are reproved are made manifest by the light: for whatsoever doth make manifest is light' (vv. 8-13).

The ungodly are always found among God's saints. In every local church where God's saints are found, there are some who are believers in name only. The ungodly among God's saints are warned with the threat of divine judgment. But Paul now turns to speak to those who have been truly born again. He woos us to obedience from a far stronger motive. It is as though he were saying, 'The warning I have given was given to awaken those who are secure in sin; but now for you who are truly God's people, consider the love, grace and mercy of God in Christ, and let this secure your obedience'. Child of God, think of your high and holy calling. Be done forever with the works of darkness. Let us 'walk in the light, as he is in the light'. Remember that once you were darkness. 'For ye were sometimes darkness, but now are ye light in the Lord: walk as children of light' (v. 8).

Once we were like all other men, dwelling in darkness. Not only were we in the dark, but we were darkness. We were exceedingly blind, ignorant and depraved, not knowing the things of God. For years, our hearts were blinded by the darkness of sin (Isaiah 9:2). But now we are the children of light. God has 'delivered us from the power of darkness, and hath translated us into the kingdom of his dear Son' (Colossians 1:13). The eyes of our understanding have been enlightened.

Now we see the exceeding sinfulness of sin. We have been made to see the insufficiency of our own righteousness before God. We see the true way of life, salvation and purity by Christ. We have some light into the mysteries of the gospel. We have been given a glimpse of the invisible glories and realities of heaven. All of this we have because the light of the glory of Christ shines in our hearts.

Since God has done so much for us, we cannot resist his claims upon us. We will 'walk as children of light'. We do fall into darkness, but we walk in the light. The knowledge of God and his will is the standard of our lives. His righteousness and holiness rule our thoughts, our attitudes, our words and our actions. The Word of God is our rule. The Son of God is our example. The Spirit of God is our guide, and the glory of God is our aim.

As our translation from darkness to light came by divine power alone, even so, the light in which we now walk is only the fruit of the Spirit. '(For the fruit of the Spirit is in all goodness and righteousness and truth;)' (v. 9).

Light is never the product of human labour. It is the fruit of the Spirit. John Gill put it like this, 'The allusion is to fruit of trees. The believer is a tree of righteousness. Christ is his root. The Spirit is the sap which supports and nourishes; and good works, under the influence of his grace, are the fruit.'

Children of light bear the fruit of goodness, not malice. Goodness is sympathy, forgiveness and forbearance. God the Holy Ghost produces righteousness in the children of light. Righteousness is right behaviour, the joy of doing what is right before God. It is the fruit of the new man created in us in righteousness and true holiness. Holiness of character, created in the new birth, results in right conduct.

The Spirit of truth in us causes the children of light to walk in truth. Truth is integrity and reliability. It is opposed to dishonesty and hypocrisy. God's children, according to God's own Word, are 'children that will not lie' (Isaiah 63:8). You may think, 'That is not me', and you are right, if you look at yourself in Adam. We went astray from the womb speaking lies; and our hearts are altogether deceitful.

What, then, are we to understand by these words, 'Children that will not lie'? We are not to look at these children as they appear in union with Adam, or when left to themselves, but as they stand in blessed union with him who is 'the Truth', and as they are guided by the Spirit of truth into communion with the God of truth.

'Children that will not lie', bow before God and confess what sinners they are, owning the sovereignty of his grace that plucked them as brands from the burning, the efficacy of his blood that has put away their sin and the perfection of his righteousness that makes them 'meet to be partakers of the inheritance of the saints in light'. That is exactly what the Holy Spirit declares in 1 John 1:7-10. Every heaven born soul walks in the light and will not lie before God.

Not only must we dread and avoid that which God hates, we must walk in the way God approves. 'Proving (showing) what is acceptable unto the Lord' (v. 10).

The only righteousness God will accept is the righteousness of Christ, so we must walk before him in that righteousness by faith, constantly relying upon God in all things with our eyes fixed on Christ. For Christ's sake, God accepts our works of love and faith in him. We must walk in obedience to God our Saviour and we must walk in love one to another. Living by faith in Christ and love to one another, the light in us reproves the unfruitful works of darkness.

'And have no fellowship with the unfruitful works of darkness, but rather reprove them. For it is a shame even to speak of those things which are done of them in secret. But all things that are reproved are made manifest by the light: for whatsoever doth make manifest is light' (vv. 11-13).

As children of light we should have no fellowship with darkness. This does not mean we are to have nothing to do with wicked men, or we should not associate with them. It simply means we must not share in their evil deeds or give any approval to their deeds. If we avoid the ways of darkness, our lives will be a reproof of sin. You do not have to go around telling people what they do is wrong. It is far better to walk in the light than to talk about light.

Time to awake

Third, it is now time to awake from the sleep of darkness and to walk in the light! 'Wherefore he saith, Awake thou that sleepest, and arise from the dead, and Christ shall give thee light' (v. 14).

Sinner, this is God's word to you! 'Arise, shine; for thy light is come, and the glory of the LORD is risen upon thee. For, behold, the darkness shall cover the earth, and gross darkness the people: but the LORD shall arise upon thee, and his glory shall be seen upon thee' (Isaiah 60:1, 2). Some of you are yet in darkness. I warn you of God's wrath and bid you to awake. No darkness shall ever enter the city of light. In the Day of Judgment, your sins will be seen in his light. Awake now!

Will you sleep in death, while the light of life is so near at hand? Can you sleep while danger is imminent? Death and sin have stupefied you. It is time now to awake. The light of Christ's gospel shines upon you. Will you still continue to sleep? Awake, for the Sun of Righteousness has risen with healing in his wings. Soon the night of judgment will come.

My brother, my sister, this is the word of God to you, too, 'Arise, shine, for thy light is come; and the glory of the LORD is risen upon thee'. Awake, for time is short. Awake, for Christ is near. Awake, for men are perishing. Arise from among the dead, for we are risen with Christ. Awake, arise, Christ will give you light.

Are we the children of light? Then, let us walk in the light, adorning the doctrine of God our Saviour in all things.

Chapter 57

'Awake, Thou That Sleepest'

Wherefore he saith, Awake thou that sleepest, and arise from the dead, and Christ shall give thee light.

(Ephesians 5:14)

'Awake thou that sleepest.' That is the call of God to you and me, the call of God the Holy Ghost to his people, the call of God the Father to his chosen, the call of God the Son to his redeemed, the call of the Lord Jesus Christ to his bride, his beloved, his church. 'Awake thou that sleepest.'

The promise given at the end of this verse makes it clear that this is the call of God to his elect. The call is, 'Awake thou that sleepest'. The promise is, 'Christ shall give the light'. What a blessed word from our God this is to such poor, needy souls as we are.

'Wherefore', because Christ the Light, the Sun of Righteousness, who alone is Life and who alone gives light; because the Sun of Righteousness is risen with healing in his wings, because the light of the Sun of Righteousness is both efficacious and accessible, God the Holy Ghost says to you and me, 'Awake thou that sleepest'.

'He saith.' But where does our Lord say that? Paul is not here giving a direct quotation from the Old Testament. We do not find a text like this recorded anywhere in the Old Testament Scriptures. But remember, Paul wrote by inspiration. Frequently, he quoted not the very words of Scripture, but the infallible spirit of the Scriptures. In our text, it may be Paul is giving us the sense or the meaning of what was written in the prophecy of Isaiah. Accordingly, there are several passages similar to our text in that prophecy.

'The people that walked in darkness have seen a great light: they that dwell in the land of the shadow of death, upon them hath the light shined.' This passage refers to Christ, the Messiah, who came to enlighten the world by his gospel. We see its fulfilment in Matthew 4:16, 'The people which sat in darkness saw great light; and to them which sat in the region and shadow of death light is sprung up'.

'Thy dead men shall live, together with my dead body shall they arise. Awake and sing, ye that dwell in dust: for thy dew is as the dew of herbs, and the earth shall cast out the dead' (Isaiah 26:19). This, too, was fulfilled for us, and in us, by Christ. 'But God, who is rich in mercy, for his great love wherewith he loved us, Even when we were dead in sins, hath quickened us together with Christ, (by grace ye are saved;) And hath raised us up together, and made us sit together in heavenly places in Christ Jesus' (Ephesians 2:4-6).

But that which comes nearest to the words of our text is found in Isaiah 60:1, 'Arise, shine; for thy light is come, and the glory of the LORD is risen upon thee'. Isaiah 60 gives us a prophecy of the blessed state of the church in this gospel age. We are exhorted to rouse ourselves up, to be mindful of the grace of God, holding forth the light of the gospel of the glory of Christ, proclaiming Christ everywhere for the salvation of his elect.

The Spirit of God is warning us not to fall into the habits of the children of darkness. He is urging us to come out of all darkness and walk as children of light. May God the Holy Spirit, whose Word this is, cause us to hear our Saviour's voice. It comes to us with a command and a promise. 'Awake thou that sleepest, and arise from the dead, and Christ shall give thee light.'

Robert Hawker said, 'In whatever sense we consider the call, either to awaken in the first act of regeneration, or to rouse from a sleepy, drowsy frame, in the after stages of life, the call is most blessed. For Christ, in both instances, and in every other, is the sole life, and light of his people.'

Our first call

What child of God can read our text and not be overwhelmed with remembrance of that first regenerating, life giving call of God the Holy Ghost, by which we were brought out of darkness into light, out of death into life; that call by which the Light of Life shined into our hearts by the power of God?

God's elect, though given by the Father to the Son before all worlds, are spiritually dead until God the Spirit, by his omnipotent grace and power calls them from darkness to light. They are as completely dead in trespasses and sins as all the rest of Adam's fallen race. Before God called us to life and faith in Christ, we had no knowledge of our everlasting union with Christ and all the blessings of grace given to us in and with Christ from everlasting. Until we were called to life, we had no interest in these blessings and no capability of enjoying them. We were 'dead in trespasses and sins'. But when we were called, all this was brought to light in our souls (2 Corinthians 4:6; 2 Timothy 1:9, 10).

Only after the Sun of Righteousness arises upon us and in us with healing in his wings, only after we have been called from death to life do we see. It is then that the heaven-born soul is first awakened to see his sin and guilt before God. This causes him to mourn. He sees the remission of sins accomplished by Christ, which causes him to repent and turn to God in reconciliation. He sees there is righteousness and complete justification by Christ. Seeing justice satisfied by Christ causes him to have 'a good hope through grace'.

What can be more wonderful? What can be more delightful than the sweet experience of God's grace by the call of God the Spirit? Having escaped the shipwreck of fallen humanity, standing safe on the shore with Christ, by God's sovereign grace, we look back and behold the great gulf over which God has brought us, the abyss from which he has delivered us, and see the multitudes stranded where we were, sinking to rise no more, lost forever! We are constrained to lift our hearts to the God of all grace and cry, 'Lord, how is it that you have manifested yourself to us, and not to the world?' (John 14:22). Oh, my God, let me never get over the wonder of your grace (1 Corinthians 6:9-11, 19, 20).

After calls

Ephesians 5:14 certainly has reference to those after calls, the many, countless after calls of grace that come to our souls when we fall into that death-like sleep of lethargy and indifference toward our dear Saviour that so often seizes us. As in the beginning, none but God can awaken us, and blessed be his name, he does!

It is a great mercy of our Redeemer that he comes frequently to awaken us. You have been sleeping, but now your heart is waking and you long for Christ's presence. Be careful not to spurn his love and grace. Awaken to him, rise to him, open your heart to him, and he will give you the light of his presence.

Sad condition

Here is a sad and sorrowful condition into which believers are prone to fall. It is described as sleep and death. 'Awake thou that sleepest, and arise from the dead.'

If we are honest with ourselves, we all have abundant reason to confess with the hymn writer …

> Prone to wonder, Lord I feel it,
> Prone to leave the God I love:
> Here's my heart, O take and seal it,
> Seal it for Thy courts above.

Surely, every renewed soul will confess that we often feel exactly like the bride in the Song of Solomon. We are often sleeping, but there is within us a spirit inclining us to awaken as well. 'I sleep, but my heart waketh.' We read in the parable that both the wise virgins and the foolish all slept at midnight. Yes, even the wise, the children of light, often sleep.

The sweet doctrine of the gospel, the Persons of the Godhead, heaven and hell, sin and holiness, death and eternity do not always have a powerful influence on our hearts and lives. Faith may be lulled to sleep in the darkness of this world, so that God's people become more and more subject to the desires of the flesh.

What is this evil of which Paul speaks? A condition of unconscious lifelessness and carelessness is what it is. He who sleeps takes all for granted in religion. Thoughts of whether or not he is a believer never arouse his soul. He has no question about that. He believes he is. He thinks he is and that is enough for him. He is secure. He also becomes indifferent about the souls of other men. Those who are in this dull and lifeless condition seem to be altogether unmoved by all the appeals and constraints of the gospel.

This slumbering spirit spreads itself over everything else. The sleeping saint does not enjoy the Word of God. If he reads it, the text is meaningless. If he hears it, he thinks the preacher does not preach as he once did. All the joy of life is gone out of him. The hymns that used to arouse his spirits are only words now. He prays only as a formal exercise. His closet is full of cobwebs. His own heart has not been inspected in many a day. How often churches go about their work heartlessly, because they are fast asleep! There are some who get into such a lifeless state they are forever looking for evidence of life. Sleeping souls get unhappy and difficult.

Let me say just a word or two concerning the cause of this horrid death sleep. We are inclined to it by nature. Naturally, we are very much alive to everything carnal, and dead to everything spiritual (Matthew 26:41).

Men will go fast asleep if they are overtaken with the laziness of neglect. Neglect prayer, neglect reading the Scriptures, neglect the preaching of the Word, neglect the fellowship of the saints, and you will soon be fast asleep.

Frequently, the warm sun of prosperity sends many to sleep. When God blesses us with the goodness of his providence, we become like men who have eaten a large meal. We fall fast asleep. Once George Whitfield had a young friend who inherited a large estate. His prayer for the young man was very wise. He prayed that God would give his friend grace to persevere under such a great trial.

Nothing more quickly puts people to sleep than the intoxication of spiritual pride. We become proud of our church, proud of our doctrine, proud of our condition, proud of our knowledge, proud of our accomplishments, proud of our usefulness, and we fall fast asleep.

Christ's call

The Lord Jesus Christ lovingly calls us to awake and arise. 'Wherefore he saith, Awake thou that sleepest, and arise from the dead.' May the love of Christ awaken us. May our slumbering hearts feel his stirring us to life.

Christ lovingly seeks the company of believers. It is true, Christ seeks unconverted souls. He seeks lost sheep. But he also seeks wandering sheep. He is not done with the believer when he has converted him. After conversion, it is his joy to hold fellowship with his people (Song of Solomon 4:16; 5:2-16).

The Lord Jesus often knocks at the heart's door of his people. 'Behold, I stand at the door and knock: if any man hear my voice, and open the door, I will come in to him, and will sup with him, and he with me' (Revelation 3:20). You would think our hearts would always be open to him but they are not. He stands and knocks. He delights to be in our hearts. It is not his pleasure that we should sit alone.

This voice of Christ is not only the voice of loving patience, it is also the voice of wisdom. The Saviour knows that we are losing much by our sleeping. The thief is robbing us while we sleep. The sower of bad seed is planting his tares while we sleep in the night watch. In loving wisdom, he says, 'Awake!'

Nothing but the voice of our Beloved can awaken this poor heart. 'My beloved put in his hand by the hole of the door, and my bowels were moved for him' (Song of Solomon 5:4). O child of God, is your heart now moved for him? Then, awake and open to him.

He speaks to us in the gospel and in providence. Christ has been saying, 'Awake, awake, awake', to some of us hundreds of times. You were sick a few months ago. That was the voice of Christ saying, 'Awake'. Recently you suffered a loss in business. It was the voice of Christ shaking you from your slumber. A dear loved one was taken from your home. It was Christ saying, 'Awake'. The other day you read a text that came crushing to your soul. It was the voice of Christ saying, 'Awake'. A sermon came home to your heart last week. You knew the preacher was talking to you. That was the voice of Christ saying, 'Awake'.

Shall the ever-blessed Christ stand always at the door with its rusty hinges? Shall he always say, 'Open to me'? Shall he always be shut out? Will you never open the door and say, 'I have missed you! Come in now and sup with me, that I may sup with you'?

This is a voice that comes to us personally. He does not say, 'Awake all of you'. He says, 'Awake thou'. This call places the responsibility upon our shoulders. If we sleep, it is because we choose to do so. Listen to the words of our Lord. 'This is the condemnation, that light is come into the world, and men loved darkness rather than light, because their deeds were evil' (John 3:19). I fear that some of you are not just sleeping. You are altogether dead in trespasses and sins. May God send to you his life-giving voice, that you may awake and live.

Gracious promise

Here is a gracious promise held out to those who obey the Master's call. 'And Christ shall give thee light.' Those who awake and arise to Christ shall have the light of Christ. He will give us light to instruct us in the Scriptures, to guide us in his way, to know his will and to rejoice our hearts.

In Revelation 3:20, it is promised that those who arise and open to Christ shall enjoy his blessed presence. He promises to come in and sup with those who open to him. His presence will be food to our souls and will give us power to overcome. And we will enjoy his presence throughout all of eternity.

A Question

Why should you and I be awakened and arise to Christ? I could give many answers to that question, but I will limit myself to just a few. Let us awake, for the time is short and men are perishing. O think of that word 'eternity'. Think of the souls of men. Think of the coming judgment. Think of the terrors of hell (1 Corinthians 15:34).

Children of heaven, 'Now it is high time to awake out of sleep: for now is our salvation nearer than when we believed' (Romans 13:11). Can we sleep when heaven is at hand? The Sun of Righteousness is risen with healing in his wings, so let us awake and arise and be healed.

Chapter 58

'Redeeming The Time'

See then that ye walk circumspectly, not as fools, but as wise, Redeeming the time, because the days are evil.

(Ephesians 5:15, 16)

Throughout this chapter of Ephesians, the Apostle Paul is giving us direction and instruction for walking as children of light, as we make our pilgrimage through this world. He states his case both positively and negatively. Paul plainly tells us that there are some things the children of light should not do; and there are certain things we must carefully adhere to. 'For ye were sometimes darkness, but now are ye light in the Lord: walk as children of light.'

As children of light, we are to prove what the will of the Lord is in our daily conversation. Also, we are to 'have no fellowship with the unfruitful works of darkness'. Because we are constantly in danger of foolishly sleeping away the hours of the day, Paul exhorts us to diligence, saying, 'Awake thou that sleepest, and arise from the dead, and Christ shall give thee light'. Then in verses 15 and 16, he tells us how to walk in the light, 'See then that ye walk circumspectly, not as fools, but as wise, Redeeming the time, because the days are evil'.

If we would 'walk circumspectly, not as fools', we must redeem the time the Lord God gives us in this world. What a solemn word we have before us in our text. What a needful exhortation this is, 'Redeeming the time, because the days are evil'.

Our text does not simply say, 'redeeming time'. That would have been a very wise statement. Time is a precious thing. But notice carefully what Paul says, 'Redeeming the time'. He uses the definite article 'the', calling our attention specifically to 'the time' God has given us, 'the time' of our life. It is the space of our opportunity that we must redeem.

The text could be read like this: 'Buying up the opportunity'. As believers, we should not wait for opportunity to fall into our laps. We must buy the opportunity. What does this mean?

A price

In buying anything a price must be paid. We part with one thing to obtain another. Merchants will not refuse to pay any price for such goods as they think will be profitable to them. So, the Spirit of God here tells us to not refuse to part with any temporary convenience to buy 'the time' our God gives us in the days of our lives. Time is such a precious commodity, so useful for the eternal glory of Christ and the souls of men, that we should spend any ease, carnal pleasure, or worldly convenience that we may buy it.

That which is purchased belongs to the buyer. Therefore, buy time to make it your own for spiritual advantage. Our translation uses the word 'redeeming'. It speaks of the recovery of a loss, the redeeming of that which has been lost, or pawned. Paul is obviously referring to our former misuse of time when we were children of darkness. In the days of our unregeneracy, before God saved us, we lost so much of our time to Satan, to the world and to vanity. Let us now employ every means to redeem it.

Again, this word 'time' properly signifies the opportunity or season. We must not let the opportunity, the season, slip away. 'As we have therefore opportunity, let us do good unto all men' (Galatians 6:10).

The reason

Why should we be concerned about 'redeeming the time'? Paul tells us, 'because the days are evil'. This may refer to the whole course of a person's life. 'Jacob said unto Pharaoh, The days of the years of my pilgrimage are an hundred and thirty years: few and evil have the days of the years of my life been' (Genesis 47:9). Our days in this world are few in themselves, but especially so in comparison with eternity. They are evil in regard to sin and misery. In heaven, they are neither few nor evil. Here, it is a mercy that they are few because they are evil. We can all say with the Saviour, 'Sufficient unto the day is the evil thereof' (Matthew 6:34).

The days in which Paul lived and served Christ were days of great wickedness, persecution and evil. His message to us is this; because there is great danger, see that you buy up every opportunity to serve and honour our God and Saviour, to serve the interests of his gospel, his church and his kingdom; to serve his people and do them good for the glory of Christ.

Time is one of the most valuable and precious things in the world. Once lost, it can never be regained. It is wise to do God's work in God's time. We all soon grow old and die. We must seize the opportunity before us and redeem the time we have.

Listen to the words of our Lord Jesus, 'I must work the works of him that sent me, while it is day: the night cometh, when no man can work' (John 9:4). This is our time of our opportunity. Let us use it for Christ.

We frequently complain, 'These are bad times'. The worse the times, the more diligent we should be. Instead of complaining of evil times, let us labour to reclaim the time and make it better. Let us by 'redeeming the time', live for eternity. The period of time that has been allotted us, wherein we may serve the Lord our God, his cause and his people, is brief, very brief. Therefore, let us redeem the time.

What are we to redeem?

What does the Spirit of God tell us to redeem? The answer is plainly given in our text, 'Redeeming the time'. Here the Apostle tells us we are to carefully take advantage of the time we have and employ every opportunity for the glory of God. Each of us have the space of the days of this life to do good for our immortal souls. The days of a man's life are but a preparation for eternity. How foolish it is to waste the only opportunity you have for the great work and business of your soul.

You young boys and girls, young men and women, 'Remember now thy Creator in the days of thy youth, while the evil days come not, nor the years draw nigh, when thou shalt say, I have no pleasure in them' (Ecclesiastes 12:1). You parents ought to frequently press upon your children the claims of Christ, the brevity of life and the reality of eternity. The sooner a child is converted the better. A small twig is more easily bent than a strong tree. The earlier a child is converted, the greater is his opportunity for serving God. You cannot begin too soon in your journey to heaven.

Some of you have already lost the time of your youth. Some of you are lost, without Christ. Up to this point, the days of your life have been wastefully spent in sin. Your days upon this earth are passing away and the wrath of God abides on you. Repent, trust Christ, be converted now and redeem the time. You must now redeem the time because there is little time left. Turn to Christ this hour, buy up the days that remain. God says, 'Seek ye the LORD while he may be found, call ye upon him while he is near' (Isaiah 55:6). It is a dangerous and foolish thing to let conviction die, as Felix stifled the pricks of his conscience. No iron is so hard as that which has been often heated and often cooled; none are so hardened in sin as those who have lost the advantage of conviction.

But Paul is here speaking to believers. Children of God, we must not serve God now and then, but our whole time should be spent for God and redeemed for his glory. May God grant 'that we being delivered out of the hand of our enemies might serve him without fear, in holiness and righteousness before him, all the days of our life' (Luke 1:74, 75). God's glory must be the ultimate end of all our actions. Our worship, our work, in our homes, even our recreation should be to the honour of our God (Galatians 2:20). We should be sensitive to the times when God speaks to us. Buy up the opportunity of receiving good from him. When he draws, let us run after him. When he knocks, let us open to him. When the waters are stirred, we should step in for cure. We should also buy up every opportunity to receive good from men. When God gives us the company of godly and wise men, we should seek to profit by it. How foolish some are who absent themselves from the preaching of the gospel, losing the opportunity when God might speak to them.

Far too often we miss opportunity of serving God by simply refusing to redeem the time. When God speaks to us, our response should be, 'When thou saidst, Seek ye my face; my heart said unto thee, Thy face, LORD, will I seek' (Psalm 27:8). When God gives us opportunity to speak or to do something for the good of another, we must buy it up. The Apostle Paul went from place to place, as God moved upon his heart, doing the will of God. God's work must be done by God's man, in God's place, in God's time.

Why should we redeem the time?

Writing to the Corinthians, Paul said, 'This I say, brethren, the time is short: it remaineth, that both they that have wives be as though they had none; And they that weep, as though they wept not; and they that rejoice, as though they rejoiced not; and they that buy, as though they possessed not; And they that use this world, as not abusing it: for the fashion of this world passeth away. But I would have you without carefulness' (1 Corinthians 7:29-32).

As believers, you and I need to be constantly reminded that the time we have in this world is very short. Hear the words of inspiration, and ask God to burn them in your heart. It is but a short journey from the cradle to the grave (Job 7:6; 9:25,

26; Psalm 90:10; Isaiah 40:7; James 4:14). The time for service is short. We cannot afford to lose our time in senseless talk, idle gossip and domestic scandals. We cannot afford to lose our time debating fine points of religious controversy or the trivialities that entertain other men. Let us be admonished to singleness of purpose.

Those who preach the gospel ought, above all other people, to redeem the time for the single purpose of uplifting the name of Christ to this perishing generation of eternity-bound souls! Spend out the days of your life for the glory of Christ. Seek opportunities of serving Christ's kingdom. Souls are perishing around you. Seek to do them good and win them to Christ. The time for suffering is short. 'Be patient therefore, brethren, unto the coming of the Lord. Behold, the husbandman waiteth for the precious fruit of the earth, and hath long patience for it, until he receiveth the early and latter rain. Be ye also patient; stablish your hearts; for the coming of the Lord draweth nigh' (James 5:7, 8).

How can we redeem the time?

Paul tells us to redeem the time, to buy up the opportunity, to ransom the season. But how can this be done? Here are two brief words of direction.

First, if we would redeem the time, we must live in the constant realisation of the brevity of life. 'So teach us to number our days, that we may apply our hearts unto wisdom' (Psalm 90:12). All of that time which is not spent for Christ is lost time. Our time is not ours to dispose of as we will. A believer is one who has given up himself entirely to God, and that includes our time. Paul said, 'For me to live is Christ'. He was saying my life is Christ's.

We have no time that cannot be serviceable to God, our Saviour. Morning, afternoon, evening and night, we should ask ourselves, 'What can I do for Christ?' We have a great deal of work to do, and a short time to do it. Let us spend our time in matters of most concern. When you go to bed at night, put this searching question to your heart, 'What have I done today? The day is gone. What has been done for the glory of God and the souls of men?'

Second, since time is so short and so precious, if we would redeem the time, we must live in a manner that is detached from all things in this world. Let us be as much detached from the dearest objects of this world as we may prudently be. 'It remaineth, that both they that have wives be as though they had none.' Though marriage is honourable in all, and the bed undefiled, a married believer must be in some respects as though he were not married. This is true of all earthly relations. We must learn to lean upon Christ alone and be willing to part with our dearest companion, and still cling to Christ.

Samuel Rutherford gave this advice. 'Build your nest upon no tree here: for you see, God hath sold the forest to death, and every tree whereon we would rest is ready to be cut down, to the end that we may flee and mount up, and build upon the Rock, and dwell in the holes of the Rock.' We must be detached from the sorrows of this world. 'They that weep, as though they wept not.' This world is a vale of tears. There are always some that weep. No sooner is the tear dried up on one cheek than it trickles down the other. But we live in the expectation of a world that knows no sorrow (2 Corinthians 4:15-5:1). And we must be detached from the joys of this world. 'They that rejoice, as though they rejoiced not.' It is right for us to use this world and to enjoy it. But we pursue Christ, not happiness or even joy.

We must be detached from the possessions of this world. 'They that buy as though they possessed not.' Whatever we may possess, we possess only as stewards. Use what God has given you for the glory of God; and be ready at a moment's notice to part with all you have for a greater inheritance. It is proper to use this world, but we dare not abuse it. Use all things, but use them in moderation. The Lord is at hand. The time is short!

'The fashion of this world passeth away.' We are living in a world that is passing away, where everything is temporal. Anyone who does not realise this is wilfully ignorant. Everything and everyone around us is decaying and dying. Beauty is decaying, strength is fading, riches are soon to vanish. This entire world and everything in it, as we now see it, will soon be gone. There is a promised world that is rapidly approaching. 'Nevertheless we, according to his promise, look for a new heavens and a new earth, wherein dwelleth righteousness. Wherefore, beloved, seeing that ye look for such things, be diligent that ye may be found of him in peace, without spot, and blameless' (2 Peter 3:13, 14).

When the Lord Jesus Christ has brought the last scene to the theatre of this world, and folded it up as a garment, he will create a new heavens and new earth. That new earth shall be real. It shall be full of righteousness. The new earth and all who inhabit it shall be eternal. We should live in the expectation of this new creation, of which Christ is the glory. Count nothing dearer now than you will count it in eternity. 'Set your affection on things above, not on things on the earth' (Colossians 3:2).

Let all who love the name of Christ be, 'Redeeming the time, because the days are evil'. Seek the honour of God. Seek the good of his kingdom. Seek the good of perishing souls. Seek his will and do it. Keep your heart in love to Christ and in anticipation of heaven.

Chapter 59

'Walk In The Light'

See then that ye walk circumspectly, not as fools, but as wise, Redeeming the time, because the days are evil. Wherefore be ye not unwise, but understanding what the will of the Lord is. And be not drunk with wine, wherein is excess; but be filled with the Spirit; Speaking to yourselves in psalms and hymns and spiritual songs, singing and making melody in your heart to the Lord; Giving thanks always for all things unto God and the Father in the name of our Lord Jesus Christ; Submitting yourselves one to another in the fear of God.

(Ephesians 5:15-21)

In the fifth chapter of Ephesians, we are directed to behave as the children of God in this world. Paul gives us the example of God and Christ to follow, admonishing us to exemplify the love of God in our daily lives. Then he shows us the foolishness of the ways of darkness, warning us to avoid them and 'walk as children of light'. Because we are always inclined to slumber and sleep in this world of darkness, God the Holy Ghost gives us an earnest exhortation in verse fourteen to awake. 'Wherefore he saith, Awake thou that sleepest, and arise from the dead, and Christ shall give thee light.'

Now, in verses 15-21, he says, 'Walk in the light'. He says, 'You know what you ought to do, now see to it!'

Not only must we awaken to the light, we must conscientiously 'walk in the light'. We have similar exhortations throughout the New Testament. 'Therefore we are buried with him by baptism into death: that like as Christ was raised up from the dead by the glory of the Father, even so we also should walk in newness of life' (Romans 6:4). 'This I say then, Walk in the Spirit, and ye shall not fulfil the lusts of the flesh' (Galatians 5:16). 'If we walk in the light, as he is in the light, we have fellowship one with another, and the blood of Jesus Christ his Son cleanseth us from all sin' (1 John 1:7) 'He that saith he abideth in him ought himself also so to walk, even as he walked' (1 John 2:6).

Are we the children of God? Are we redeemed by the blood of Christ? Do we abide in him who is the Light? Has Christ Jesus graciously awakened us to his light and life? If so, then we ought to walk on this earth as he walked. Let us 'walk in the light'. The way to overcome the power of darkness is to 'walk in the light'.

Our responsibility

The Holy Spirit here places the responsibility squarely on our shoulders. True, he must awaken us, and he must graciously uphold us, or we cannot meet that responsibility. Nonetheless, he tells us to awake and arise, and Christ shall give us light. His exhortation in this text is, 'Walk in the light'.

Read the book of Acts. When the church was filled with the Holy Spirit, they were filled with the graces of the Spirit. They walked in love toward God and man. They walked in obedient faith. They walked in submission to the will of God. They went everywhere preaching the gospel. The zeal with which their souls were fired was a zeal to glorify God and do good to the souls of men. They wanted to honour God's name, serve his kingdom and do his will. They were filled with the Spirit.

Do we want to honour God? Do we want to live for God? Then let us 'walk in the light'. Paul tells us three things we must do that we may 'walk in the light'.

Be wise

First, Paul tells us we must walk in wisdom. If we would live for God, we must be wise. 'See then that ye walk circumspectly, not as fools, but as wise, Redeeming the time, because the days are evil. Wherefore be ye not unwise, but understanding what the will of the Lord is' (vv. 15-17).

Our Lord taught us to be as 'wise as serpents and as harmless as doves'. Light implies understanding and wisdom. So, Paul here shows us that those who walk in light are wise. This is not worldly wisdom. We are prohibited from being wise in our own conceits. But spiritually, we should be wise. Paul gives us three areas in which men are usually foolish. He tells us in these three things to be wise.

If we would be wise, we must set our hearts upon the highest goals and walk straight toward them (v. 15). The unwise, those who have no insight in the things of God and eternity, are not aiming at the highest goal. Therefore, they do not care much about the way they walk. Like fools, they choose poverty over riches, sin over righteousness and darkness over light. But wise men have their hearts set upon God, Christ, eternity, life and salvation. They govern their lives accordingly.

Let us walk as wise not as fools. Make it your business to live by faith, trusting Christ, his finished work, his grace and his providence. Make God's Word the rule of your life, and Christ the example and pattern of your life. Seek the grace and guidance of God the Holy Ghost in all things, and walk in all things as becomes the gospel of Christ. 'Adorn the doctrine of God.'

Walk in wisdom toward men. In as much as possible, live without offence. Live as strangers in this world, as those who are looking for a better country. Live in such a way as will promote the glory of God and the good of men. To walk circumspectly is to walk accurately, exactly and in the right way, being taught of God with wisdom that is from above.

Wise men also make careful and diligent use of their time, 'Redeeming the time' (v. 16). People who waste time are great fools. Time is one of the most valuable and precious things in the world. It is neither stopped nor prolonged. Make wise use of your time for your own soul and for the everlasting good of others. Press as much labour for God into each day as you can.

If we would be wise, we must discern the will of the Lord, 'Understanding what the will of the Lord is' (v. 17). No one likes to be thought of as foolish; but those who do not set their hearts upon eternity, redeem the time before them, and seek to discern what the will of the Lord is, are great fools. Believers are the children of wisdom. We should not live like fools.

There is the secret will of God which is unknown to men. This is his purpose and decree. It is unknown to men until facts make it clear. When it is made known, we should delightfully submit to it. But our text, obviously, speaks of the revealed will of God. It is our responsibility not only to discern God's will, but also to obey it. God's will is revealed in his Word, by the illumination and direction of the Holy Spirit, and by his providence. Let us seek the will of our God and walk in it. 'Thy will be done', should be our prayer. These three things we should seek: the honour of God's name, 'Our Father, which art in heaven, hallowed by thy name'. The good of his kingdom, 'Thy kingdom come'. The doing of his will, 'Thy will be done'.

Be filled

Second, if we would walk in the light, we must walk under the influence of God the Holy Spirit, 'And be not drunk with wine, wherein is excess; but be filled with the Spirit' (v. 18). First, Paul says, 'Be wise'. Then, he says, 'Be filled'. Both are gifts of God and both are matters of personal responsibility.

One outstanding manifestation of foolishness is drunkenness. The man who is under the influence and control of strong drink is a great fool. But it is a great mark of wisdom for a man to be under the influence and control of the Spirit of God.

What is prohibited here? 'Be not drunk with wine.' There is nothing wrong with the exhilaration of heart and mind. In fact, that is encouraged in Scripture. Believers should not be always mournful, downcast and despondent. We have great reason to shout for joy. We should live in the fulness of joy unspeakable and full of glory. But it is wrong to seek excitement from the excessive use of wine.

It is the abuse of wine or strong drink that is here forbidden, not its use. The Scriptures do not teach the necessity of total abstinence, but of moderation. There was a great danger in the early church that some might be overcome by the immoderate consumption of wine, and there is still such a danger. Therefore, we have strong warnings against that abuse.

The pastor must be above reproach, not one who lingers by his wine (1 Timothy 3:3; Titus 1:7). Deacons similarly must be dignified, not addicted to much wine (1 Timothy 3:8). The aged women should also be reverent in their conduct, not enslaved to much wine (Titus 2:3). Wine and strong drink is a mocker. It is the devil's poor substitute for the unspeakable joy which God provides. It will not relieve the pressures and worries of life. It will not lift you up. It only brings men, who are given to it, down to the level of brute beasts. Drunkenness is an evil that seldom walks alone. It commonly brings men under the control of every evil lust. So, Paul says, 'Don't get drunk on wine'.

But there is a positive exhilaration that is godly and good. Instead of being controlled by the spirits of the bottle, live under the control of God the Holy Spirit. What does it mean to be filled with the Spirit? Being filled with the Spirit is not some trance-like, passive state, such as modern-day charismatics and Pentecostals speak of. Being filled with the Spirit is being under the influence, control and rule of the Spirit of God. We ought to be under the dominion and influence of his Spirit, just as the trees are under the influence of the wind. Just as a drunk is controlled by his wine, we should be controlled by the Holy Spirit (Acts 2:4, 13). A man filled with the Holy Spirit is filled with the graces of the Spirit. People are filled with the Spirit when the love of God is shed abroad in their hearts by the Holy Spirit. This is the best wine. To be filled with the Spirit is to be full of joy and peace.

Believers have the Holy Spirit given to them in all his fulness at the new birth. He is given as our Comforter, Guide, Teacher and our Seal. To be full of him is simply to be full of his influence, comforted by his presence, guided by his power, instructed by his wisdom, and assured by his love. What can be more blessed?

This is what Paul is teaching us. Getting drunk on wine leads to nothing better than debauchery. It will not give you any worthwhile pleasure, usable knowledge, or lasting contentment. It can never help you, but only hurt you. On the other hand, being filled with the Spirit will enrich you with precious treasures of lasting joy, deep insight and inner satisfaction. By this means, being filled with the Spirit, we will understand what the will of the Lord is; because the Holy Spirit is given as the Spirit of wisdom and understanding.

Be Thankful

Third, if we would walk in the light, we must walk in a way that honours God and benefits our brethren. 'Speaking to yourselves in psalms and hymns and spiritual songs, singing and making melody in your heart to the Lord; Giving thanks always for all things unto God and the Father in the name of our Lord Jesus Christ; Submitting yourselves one to another in the fear of God' (Ephesians 5:19-21).

As we are filled with the Spirit, we are enlightened and joyful and give jubilant expression to our knowledge of the will of God. To be filled with the Spirit is to do the will of God. The person who does God's will is a Spirit-filled believer.

What is the will of the Lord? Paul tells us plainly what the will of the Lord is for every saved sinner, all the time. It is the will of God that Spirit-filled believers edify themselves and one another in songs of praise to God (v. 19). What are we to sing? The psalms, hymns of praise and songs of grace. Our singing should not be the sentimental songs that stir natural emotions, but songs of God's grace, his power and his glory.

How are we to sing? 'Making melody in your heart.' We should sing with our voices, but the melody should be the melody of the heart unto the Lord. As we worship God in song, we should do so from a heart of deep love, affection and adoration towards God.

Why should we sing? We should sing to ourselves, to the Lord and to one another (Colossians 3:16). Our songs should be full of truth and instruct one another in the gospel. Our songs should admonish one another, comforting the sorrowful, uplifting the despondent, encouraging the fearful, assuring the doubtful.

It is the will of God that Spirit-filled souls, believing people, saved sinners, always give thanks unto him. 'Giving thanks always for all things unto God and the Father in the name of our Lord Jesus Christ' (v. 20). Thanksgiving is the grateful acknowledgment of God's greatness and glory and of his goodness and grace. It is our happy response to God's free favour. When we are giving thanks, worries tend to disappear, complaints vanish, courage is increased, peace is felt and

God is glorified. So, let us give thanks. The person who gives thanks to God recognises three things: first, the good that he enjoys abounds toward him from God's gracious hand. Second, he is totally unworthy of them. Third, the blessings of God are great and numerous.

When should we give thanks? 'Always.' We should give thanks after we have received the blessings of God. We should give thanks while we are experiencing God's blessings, we should even give thanks before the blessings are received. Jehoshaphat led the people into battle against Ammon and Moab, singing, 'Praise the LORD; for his mercy endureth for ever' (2 Chronicles 20:21).

For what are we to give thanks? Paul says, 'For all things'. Even as Paul wrote this exhortation, he was a prisoner at Rome, and for his bonds he gave thanks. Are we persuaded 'that all things work together for good to them that love God'? Then we should give thanks for 'all things'.

We should give thanks for everything that is withheld, as well as all we receive. We should give thanks for every temporal provision. We should especially give thanks for every spiritual blessing given to us in Christ; election, adoption, redemption, justification, calling and preservation. In Christ, all things are ours: things past, things present and things to come.

How must we give thanks? The answer is, 'in the name of our Lord Jesus Christ'. It is Christ who earned everything for us. God will accept our thanksgiving and praise only by him.

To whom must we give thanks? To 'God and the Father'. We give thanks to God, the Triune Jehovah, and our Father, the source of all good.

Paul concludes this exhortation by showing us that it is the will of God for us to be submissive to one another. The rule for the loving unity of God's family is that each member of the family prefer the good of others to his own good. It is only in this way that we can serve one another's good.

Again and again, our Lord taught his disciples that each one should be willing to be the least. We all should be willing to wash one another's feet. If we love our brethren, we will prefer their honour to our own (Romans 12:10; Philippians 2:3). Humility breeds peace for the edifying of the body of Christ. Pride breeds division. All division between brethren is caused, maintained and promoted by stupid, senseless, shameful, sinful pride (1 Peter 5:5). The apostle has shown us in these verses what it is to walk in the light. It is walking in wisdom, in the Spirit and in humility. Let us be wise, be filled and be thankful.

Chapter 60

'Understanding What The Will Of The Lord Is'

Wherefore be ye not unwise, but understanding what the will of the Lord is.
(Ephesians 5:17)

Were it possible to gather all the desires, ambitions, aspirations, goals and prayers of all God's saints in heaven and on earth into one expression, it would be this: 'Thy will be done'. Every believer delights to do the will of God! We see that fact in the lives and prayers of God's saints throughout the Book of God.

'I delight to do thy will, O my God: yea, thy law *is* within my heart' (Psalm 40:8). We know those words find their ultimate fulfilment in Christ, because the Holy Ghost tells us so in Hebrews 10:7-9. How we rejoice to know that Christ, our Substitute, delighted to fulfil the will of God for us! By obedience to God in our stead, the Lord Jesus obtained eternal redemption for us. His obedience to God is our righteousness. His blood is our atonement for sin. We are complete in Christ; we are accepted in him, because he delighted to do the will of God as our Substitute.

Yet the words of Psalm 40:8 were also David's words. They express the desire, ambition and driving force of every believer's heart. All who are born of God bear this mark of grace in the likeness of Christ. Believers, in their souls, delight to do the will of God. Our joy and happiness is not merely in receiving good from God, but in being of service to God. We desire to obey and serve our heavenly Father and do his will cheerfully at all times. God's will is our joy and delight.

More than that, we delight to see God's will done in and by others, too. Our heart's desire and most earnest prayer is, 'Our Father which art in heaven, Hallowed be thy name. Thy kingdom come. Thy will be done in earth, as it is in heaven' (Matthew 6:9, 10). God the Holy Ghost has taught every believer in the world to pray with Christ, 'Thy will be done'.

When the believing heart cries, 'I delight to do thy will, O my God'. The sense is: My heavenly Father, my God, in my heart of hearts, from the depths of my inmost soul, I delight to fulfil your will of purpose, to satisfy your will of pleasure, and to obey your will of precept'. We know that our heavenly Father, the God of the Bible, is a God 'who worketh all things after the counsel of his own will' (Ephesians 1:11). All who know him delight to do his will in all things.

God's precepts

As we read Holy Scripture, it is obvious God's will is set before us in three ways: his precepts, his pleasure and his purpose. It is the duty and responsibility of all men, women and children to obey the will of God revealed in his precepts.

God's precept is that which he requires and commands of his creatures. A wise and loving Father demands obedience from his children. God's pleasure is that in which he delights and that of which he approves. I delight in any child's willing obedience to his parents. God's purpose is what he is determined to accomplish.

These three things never contradict each other. They are never at odds. They are always in perfect harmony. They are, together, the will of God. Let us look at them one at a time, beginning with God's will of precept. This is his revealed will, that which he requires of men; that which he commands us to do.

When a person expresses his will to those under his authority, his revealed will is to them a law, a command, a precept, which they are responsible to obey. That which God has revealed to be his will and pleasure is to us a precept; a law and command which we are responsible to obey. God's will of command, or precept, made known to us, is our rule of duty (Ecclesiastes 12:13).

The moral requirements of God's law are revealed to all men by the light of nature, creation (Romans 1:18-20) and conscience (Romans 2:12-15). All men by nature, even the heathen and barbaric of ancient cultures, know that God is and that he requires of man that he love God supremely and love his neighbour as himself.

God revealed his will on Mt. Sinai in the Ten Commandments (Exodus 20:1-17; Romans 13:8, 9; Ephesians 6:2). The decalogue, commonly referred to as the moral law, reveals what God requires of all men in their relations to God and to one another. Though in Christ we are free from the yoke of the law's rule and its curse, these requirements are never altered.

The ceremonial law given to the nation of Israel was God's revealed will concerning worship in the Old Testament. It began when God commanded Israel to observe the passover (Exodus 12), and ended when Christ our Passover was sacrificed for us, when the handwriting of the ordinances was nailed to the cross (1 Corinthians 5:7; Colossians 2:14).

Since Christ has come and fulfilled all the requirements and types of the moral and ceremonial law, the revealed will of God to all men is set forth in the gospel of Christ. 'And this is his commandment, That we should believe on the name of his Son Jesus Christ, and love one another, as he gave us commandment' (1 John 3:23).

Because no man is capable of fulfilling the righteousness of God revealed in the law, Christ fulfilled the law in the place of sinful men. Now we fulfil the righteousness of the law by faith in him (Romans 3:31; 8:2-4). This is what God requires and commands of all men: 'Believe on the Lord Jesus Christ (1 John 3:23). Faith in Christ is the revealed will of God. This is God's precept. All men are responsible to obey it (John 3:36). In this sense, our renewed hearts say, 'I delight to do thy will, O my God'. 'Lord, I believe; help thou mine unbelief.'

God's pleasure

It is the desire of every believer to obey the will of God's holy pleasure in all things. A loving child wants to do more than merely avoid his father's disapproval. He seeks to know and do that which is his father's pleasure. A loving wife wants more than to do just what her husband requires. She wants to please her husband in all things. Similarly, the believer wants something indescribably greater than to avoid the wrath of God. He wants to do the will of God. He wants to do that which gives pleasure, satisfaction and delight to his heavenly Father. I know we cannot add to God's infinite pleasure. But we earnestly seek to do what pleases him.

There are some things revealed in the Bible that please God and those things that please God are all in Christ and only in Christ. The only way sinners can please God is by faith in his dear Son, the Lord Jesus Christ (Hebrews 11:5, 6).

'Wherewith shall I come before the LORD, and bow myself before the high God? shall I come before him with burnt offerings, with calves of a year old? Will the LORD be pleased with thousands of rams, or with ten thousands of rivers of oil? shall I give my firstborn for my transgression, the fruit of my body for the sin of my soul? He hath showed thee, O man, what is good; and what doth the LORD require of thee, but to do justly, and to love mercy, and to walk humbly with thy God?' (Micah 6:6-8).

Sadly, almost every commentator I have read on Micah 6:8 and every sermon I have been able to find on it interpret the text to mean, God requires men and women, in every department of life, to behave justly, honestly and uprightly, to be merciful and charitable to others and to live in humiliation before God. They tell us that this is the sum and substance of true religion and true godliness.

'But ye have not so learned Christ' (Ephesians 4:20). How I thank God that I have not so learned Christ! Notice what the text says. There is not a word in this verse about how we are to live before men, or what we are to do to and with men. God requires us to 'do justly, and to love mercy, and to walk humbly with thy God'.

'Do justly'

What is this requirement that we 'do justly' with God? This is not talking about treating men justly, though we should try to do that at all times. We should pay our bills, live honestly and treat people right. But God's prophet is talking about doing justly with God! How can I do justly with God? To 'do justly' is to confess that in ourselves, by reason of sin, we justly deserve his wrath and indignation, having broken all his righteous law. To do justly is to confess our sin. To do justly is to take sides with God against ourselves (Psalms 32:5; 51:4, 5; 1 John 1:9). To 'do justly' is to exercise that repentance toward God that only God himself gives, that only God himself can produce in a sinner by his grace.

'Love mercy'

Who does not love mercy? Everyone I know loves mercy, especially when he needs it. But anyone who has not been blinded to the Word of God by his own love of works religion must surely realise Micah is not telling us that salvation is to be had by loving mercy! Let us love to show mercy and exercise mercy, but you are a fool if you imagine you can win God's favour by being merciful. In Luke 1:72, we see that the mercy we must love is our Lord Jesus Christ himself, and God's salvation by him. Zacharias speaking of John the Baptist and his ministry as the forerunner of Christ, our Redeemer, said he came 'to perform the mercy promised'. That's the mercy we love. Christ Jesus the Lord himself, and the salvation he performed.

'Walk humbly'

Next we are told we must walk humbly with God. 'He hath shewed thee, O man, what is good; and what doth the LORD require of thee, but to do justly, and to love mercy, and to walk humbly with thy God?' To 'walk humbly with thy God' is to walk before God in the conscious awareness of my sin, trusting Christ alone as my Saviour, as being taught by God the Holy Ghost for the everlasting comfort of my soul (John 16:7-11; 1 Corinthians 1:30, 31; Philippians 3:3; Colossians 2:6).

As we please God by trusting his Son, there are some things revealed in the Scriptures that are displeasing and grievous to our Lord (Ephesians 4:17-5:1). 'The thing that David had done displeased the LORD' (2 Samuel 11:27).

I am fully aware of the fact that the only way sinful men and women can please God is by faith in Christ. 'By faith Enoch was translated that he should not see death; and was not found, because God had translated him: for before his translation he had this testimony, that he pleased God. But without faith it is impossible to please him: for he that cometh to God must believe that he is, and that he is a rewarder of them that diligently seek him' (Hebrews 11:5, 6). God is pleased with his Son. He is pleased with us in his Son (Matthew 17:5; Ephesians 1:6). He is pleased with our feeble efforts to please him for his Son's sake.

God's Purpose

We are assured in the Book of God that all things obey the secret will of God's eternal purpose. 'The secret things belong unto the LORD our God: but those things which are revealed belong unto us and to our children for ever, that we may do all the words of this law' (Deuteronomy 29:29).

Moses is not suggesting we can know nothing about divine predestination, or that God does not intend for us to study the subject. The only thing Moses is telling us is this, we do not know what God has predestined and what must come to pass. However, we do know what God requires of us and that is our duty. The Lord our God has purposed, decreed, and predestinated all things that have ever come to pass and all that ever shall come to pass (Psalms 115:3; 135:6; Isaiah 46:10; Daniel 4:35; Acts 2:23; 4:27, 28; 13:48; Romans 8:28-30; 9:15-18; Ephesians 1:11).

In this sense everything that is, has been, or shall be is the will of God. God is absolutely sovereign in directing the affairs of the universe. His will of purpose includes all things, evil as well as good, sin as well as salvation, error as well as truth. God's will of purpose is always perfectly accomplished (Romans 11:33-36).

C. D. Cole stated the matter like this. God's 'will includes whatsoever comes to pass. Hence, everything that comes to pass is providential and not accidental so far as God is concerned. He "worketh all things after the counsel of his own will" (Ephesians 1:11)'. He goes on to explain, 'The will of God includes the wicked actions of sinful men, but does not take away their blameworthiness. We may not see how this can be, but the Scriptures declare it and we should believe it. The Scriptures were not written to confirm our reasoning, but rather to correct it. On the day of Pentecost Peter said, concerning Jesus, "Him being delivered by the determinate counsel (will) and foreknowledge of God, ye have taken, and by wicked hands have crucified and slain" (Acts 2:23). And on a later occasion he said that Herod and Pilate, the Gentiles and the people of Israel were gathered together "For to do whatsoever thy hand and thy counsel (will) determined (Gk. predestinated) to be done" (Acts 4:27, 28). We may not be able to see how God can will or determine a sin without becoming the author of sin, but the fact remains that the greatest of all sins, the slaying of the Son of God, was divinely ordained.'

Because men are ever bent upon perverting the things of God, I must give a word of caution regarding the will of God. The sovereignty of God's purpose does not destroy man's responsibility, or even his will. Man's sin has put his will in bondage to sin, not God's purpose. God's purpose does not make God the author of sin. God is not the author of sin but he is the author of the good which he accomplishes by sin. When God says concerning all things, 'I will do all my pleasure', we rejoice to bow before him and say, 'Thy will be done'.

Two questions

Is it possible for a believer to miss or be out of the will of God? Yes, insofar as God's revealed will; his precept and his pleasure is concerned, a believer can miss, can disobey and can be out of the will of God. However, let it be understood and clear; no one, and no action performed by anyone, is ever out of the will of God's purpose. 'He worketh all things after the counsel of his own will.' Elimelech was out of God's will of precept and pleasure in going down to Obed-Edom; but this was overruled by God to accomplish his will of purpose and predestination for the salvation of his elect. David's actions in the matter of Uriah the Hittite, we are told, 'displeased the LORD'. Yet, God's will of purpose was accomplished thereby.

God's purpose is always accomplished, even when we are disobedient to his revealed will. That does not lessen our responsibility to any degree; but it does give us reason to adore and worship our God, whose purpose is ever wise and good.

How can I know the will of God? I almost said, 'How can I know the will of God for my life?' But that question is too big. How can I know the will of God for my life today? Let me answer that question with three statements. No one can determine what God's will for you is, except you. 'I conferred not with flesh and blood.' God reveals his will in three ways, by his Word, by his Spirit, and by his providence. God will reveal his will to all who seek his will in faith. 'Trust in the LORD with all thine heart; and lean not unto thine own understanding. In all thy ways acknowledge him, and he shall direct thy paths' (Proverbs 3:5, 6). Let this be our prayer. 'Thy will be done.' Let this be our determination. 'I delight to do thy will, O God.' Let this be our attitude. 'It is the Lord, let him do what he will.'

Chapter 61

'Be Filled With The Spirit'

And be not drunk with wine, wherein is excess; but be filled with the Spirit.
(Ephesians 5:18)

Amid all the happy-clappy, hand-waving tomfoolery of this modern, charismatic age of Pentecostal sorcery, someone needs to speak and speak clearly about the person and work of God the Holy Spirit. I repeat, with emphatic dogmatism, that the Apostolic Age is over, the Apostolic gifts of that age are no more and that no one today has the gifts of healing, of speaking in tongues or of prophecy.

But that does not mean that the work of God the Holy Spirit has ceased. It has not. This is distinctly the age of the Spirit (John 16:7-11; Acts 2). God the Holy Spirit is our divine Comforter and Teacher. God the Holy Spirit gives chosen, redeemed sinners life and faith in Christ. God the Holy Spirit is he who sheds abroad the love of God in our hearts and seals to us all the blessings and blessedness of God's covenant grace in Christ.

Yet, some questions need to be answered: Do I have the Holy Spirit? Do all believers have the Holy Spirit? What does it mean to be filled with the Holy Spirit?

Ephesians 5

I shall answer those questions for you from the Word of God. In the fourth and fifth chapters of the Book of Ephesians, the Apostle Paul, writing by divine inspiration, gives us very clear and very specific instructions about how we are to live in this world for the glory of God. He spent the first three chapters of this book telling us how God saved us by his free and sovereign grace in Christ.

God the Holy Ghost ever points us to Christ, glorifies Christ and speaks of Christ. He inspires faith, devotion and praise for our great Saviour, the Lord Jesus Christ. Religion talks about you, your goodness and your works. The Bible talks about God, his goodness and his work. Religion turns attention on you, your feelings, your experience, your sacrifice. The gospel of Christ focuses our attention upon Christ, his sacrifice, his accomplishments and his glory. Religion talks about being in the Spirit, feeling the Spirit and knowing the Spirit. God the Holy Spirit always talks about Christ, being in Christ, trusting Christ and knowing Christ.

Strange doctrine

The Jews accused Paul of setting forth strange doctrine, because he asserted that 'Christ is the end of the law'. They accused him of promoting licentiousness. The Gentiles also thought he preached strange doctrine because he taught God's saints to live soberly, righteously and godly in this present, evil world. They accused him of teaching asceticism, 'touch not, taste not, handle not'.

It is difficult for us to understand just how strange Paul's doctrine must have appeared to men and women living in Ephesus 2000 years ago. When those Ephesian converts first read the things Paul wrote in this chapter, they must have thought, at least initially, 'This doctrine is absurd. No one thinks like this.' In that day, particularly in the Gentile world, society was so degenerate by reason of prolonged idolatry that drunkenness, theft, lying, fornication, adultery, even sodomy, were common and acceptable. Debauchery was the norm of society.

Fornication was common practice. Theft a way of life. Lying a universal custom. It was only blameworthy if you were clumsy enough to be caught in a lie. Drunkenness was an ordinary condition of life. Even the great political and military leaders of those dark days were known for their drunkenness. At their public feasts they made a sport of gluttony and drunkenness. This was a problem that had to be dealt with at Corinth (1 Corinthians 11).

In many of the idolatrous religions, from which these Ephesians and other Gentiles had been converted, drunkenness and fornication were part of the religious rituals they practiced. It is difficult for us to realise the impact of Paul's exhortation, 'And be not drunk with wine, wherein is excess; but be filled with the Spirit'.

Christ's claims

The Apostle Paul, by inspiration of God the Holy Ghost, set before these Gentile converts, and us, the claims of Christ over our lives. He would not alter the gospel of God or compromise the claims of our Saviour, regardless of the circumstances.

Today, there is a return to the practices of those dark times. Fornication, adultery, lying, fraud, drunkenness and sodomy are becoming more and more common and more and more accepted with every passing day. The evil is even worse in our day because it is against the full light of the gospel. It is still true, men love darkness rather than light. There is a common tendency to bring the standard of the gospel down to men. The church has joined the world and the world has joined the church! Craving success in the eyes of men, preachers everywhere run to compromise the truth of God. They give people what they want to get a crowd.

Be warned, my brethren, it is our responsibility to set before men the pure Word of God, with which we are entrusted, without alteration. We dare not set up principles of outward piety, like the Pharisees, but we dare not compromise the principles God himself has established in his Word. We have been translated from darkness into light by the power of God. We are the sons of God. We should live as such. 'This I say therefore, and testify in the Lord, that ye henceforth walk not as other Gentiles walk, in the vanity of their mind, Having the understanding darkened, being alienated from the life of God through the ignorance that in is them, because of the blindness of their heart: Who being past feeling have given themselves over unto lasciviousness, to work all uncleanness with greediness. But ye have not so learned Christ' (Ephesians 4:17-20).

How are the people of God to avoid being engulfed in the ways of this world in which we live? How are we to resist the constant pressures of this evil world? Paul says, 'Be not drunk with wine, wherein is excess; but be filled with the Spirit'.

Joel's prophecy

The Prophet Joel told us that in the last day, the great day of the Lord, the Spirit of God would fall, not just upon a mighty leader here and there, as was the case in the Old Testament, but that the Holy Spirit would be poured out upon all flesh, Gentiles and Jews, with miraculous power (Joel 2:28-32). In days of old, the Spirit of God was mightily given to a Samson, a David or an Isaiah. Now, in this gospel day, all who call upon the name of the Lord; men, women, children have the Spirit of God. In those days, the work of the Holy Spirit was limited to the nation of Israel; now he is poured out upon all flesh.

Joel's prophecy had its accomplishment in the book of Acts. On the Day of Pentecost, Peter said, 'This is that which was spoken by the prophet Joel' (Acts 2:16). As a result of the death, resurrection and ascension of Christ, the Holy Spirit has been given to his church and kingdom. When a person is born-again, the Spirit of God is given to him. We are in Christ, and Christ is in us. We are in the Spirit, and the Spirit is in us. He indwells every believer. He is to our hearts the seal of heaven. He guides us by his gracious influence, preserves us, teaches us, sanctifies us, and comforts us. All of this is God's gracious work. But we have a responsibility toward him as well. Paul has told us we must be careful not to quench his operations in us. He said, 'Grieve not the Holy Spirit of God, whereby ye are sealed unto the day of redemption'. Now he shows us how we are to avoid grieving him. 'Be not drunk with wine, wherein is excess; but be ye filled with the Spirit.'

This is what Paul teaches us in this verse: As God's elect in this world, you and I must avoid drunkenness and be filled with the Holy Spirit.

A great evil

'Be not drunk with wine.' Paul has been talking about the unwise. A characteristic of those who are unwise is drunkenness. Those who are unwise are people who are unthinking, without understanding, senseless. Paul says to you and me, 'Be ye not unwise, but understanding what the will of the Lord is'. Christ is the Lord. Here Paul makes our Saviour's very godhead a very practical thing, entering into our everyday lives. He is God. His will is our law. Upon this basis, the Apostle says, 'And be not drunk with wine, wherein is excess'.

Nowhere in the Word of God do we find any prohibition of the lawful use of God's creation. 'There is nothing unclean of itself' (Romans 14:14). Let us use all things wisely, for the glory of God. What other people eat and drink is not our business. When churches draw up covenants forbidding the use of anything God has not forbidden they add the traditions of men to the commandments of God.

That which is here prohibited by the Spirit of God is drunkenness. 'Be not drunk with wine, wherein is excess.' Drunkenness (with wine, bourbon, weed or heroin) is a destructive course of life. Drunkenness is the crutch of a weakling, the spine of a coward, the excuse of a sluggard. It is a great evil.

A great gift

The great gift and blessing of God to his people in this world is the gift of the Holy Spirit. God the Holy Spirit is the ascension gift of Christ the King to his church and kingdom (Galatians 3:13, 14; 4:4-6).

True joy comes from being filled with the Spirit. If you would be full of joy, be full of the Holy Spirit. The divine Comforter causes us to forget the sharpness of our trials and to rejoice in God's purpose, goodness, and grace. When you have a severe trial, take a deep drink of the fountain of living water and be filled with the Holy Spirit. In sickness, you can rejoice; in poverty, you can sing; in bereavement, you can give thanks. Child of God, when you are sad the Holy Spirit will make you see what a great Saviour Christ is. He will fill you with the love of God and refresh your heart with the knowledge of redemption. He will make Christ your joy.

The filling

'Be not drunk with wine, wherein is excess; but be filled with the Spirit.' What is Paul talking about here? What is this filling of the Spirit? Paul is not talking about some ecstatic, unexplainable, emotional experience or fit of religion, such as the Pentecostals promote. This is an imperative command of Scripture. 'Be filled with the Spirit.' Scripture makes it plain what that command involves. You and I who are God's people are to be filled with the Spirit continually. This is not something only certain believers enjoy. Paul is saying, 'Be filled, all of you, with the Spirit'. May God give us grace to obey this command.

Drunkenness makes men forget their relationships and responsibilities, but the Holy Spirit causes us to remember them. Spirit-filled wives are submissive. Spirit-filled husbands are loving. Spirit-filled parents nurture their children in the Lord. Spirit-filled employers are good, thoughtful and generous. Spirit-filled workers are faithful, honest and hard-working. Being filled with the Holy Spirit is being continually under his influence, continually controlled by the Spirit of God. All true believers have the Spirit of God dwelling in them. 'God hath sent forth the Spirit of his Son into our hearts, crying, Abba, Father' (Galatians 4:6). 'If any man have not the Spirit of Christ, he is none of his' (Romans 8:9).

To be filled with the Holy Spirit is to believe God, to trust Christ. Paul is telling us, as God's children in this world, to live continually looking to Christ. This is the same thing as that for which he prayed in chapter 3. 'That Christ may dwell in your hearts by faith; that ye, being rooted and grounded in love, May be able to comprehend with all saints what is the breadth, and length, and depth, and height; And to know the love of Christ, which passeth knowledge, that ye might be filled with all the fulness of God' (vv. 17-19).

When we are commanded to 'put on Christ' and 'put on the new man', we are commanded to trust Christ, to be 'filled with the Spirit'. Wine can never fill; but the Spirit of God fills his people until they can say, 'My cup runneth over'. The Holy Spirit gives blessed rest, a quiet, unutterable peace. The Holy Spirit is our Teacher and we follow his teaching. What does he teach us? He teaches us of God's holiness, of our sin, and the gospel of the glory of Christ and his power to save.

The Holy Spirit is our Guide. He guides us to Christ and into all truth. We are to follow his lead as he guides us in the will of God.

The Holy Spirit is our Comforter. He comforts us by assuring us of God's love and our adoption. He comforts us by assuring us of our redemption in Christ. He comforts us with the assurance of our resurrection and eternal glory.

When a person is filled with the Spirit, he is full of the graces and fruit of the Spirit (Galatians 5:22, 23). The works of the flesh are many. They arise from the evil heart of a man. But the fruit of the Spirit is one. It arises from the gracious presence of the Spirit of Christ in our hearts. The Spirit-filled man bears fruit with reference to God, to his fellowmen and toward himself. The fruit of the Spirit toward God is love, joy, and peace. The fruit of the Spirit toward men is longsuffering, gentleness and goodness. The fruit of the Spirit within is faith, meekness and temperance.

When a man is filled with the Spirit, I am sure it is safe to say he is filled with the desire of the Spirit. It is the office and work of God the Holy Spirit to glorify Christ. All who are filled with the Spirit are under the dominion of this great desire, that Christ may be glorified.

How?

We are commanded to be filled with the Spirit. That is our responsibility. So, this question must be answered. How can foul, sinful men and women, like you and me, be filled with the Holy Spirit? Just as the Spirit of God was poured out upon God's church on the Day of Pentecost, he must be poured into our hearts in the new birth by our dear Saviour, the Lord Jesus Christ (Titus 3:4-7).

We are filled with the Spirit as he fills us by his grace, shedding abroad in our hearts the love of God (Romans 5:5), constraining us to be aware Christ died for us, that we should not henceforth live unto ourselves but unto him who loved us and gave himself for us (2 Corinthians 5:14, 15).

To be filled with the Spirit is to believe on the Lord Jesus Christ. It is to trust our blessed Saviour. This is the promise of God in his Word. 'A new heart also will I give you, and a new spirit will I put within you: and I will take away the stony heart out of your flesh, and I will give you an heart of flesh. And I will put my spirit within you, and cause you to walk in my statues, and ye shall keep my judgments, and do them' (Ezekiel 36:26, 27). 'Nevertheless I tell you the truth; It is expedient for you that I go away: for if I go not away, the Comforter will not come unto you; but if I depart, I will send him unto you. And when he is come, he will reprove the world of sin, and of righteousness, and of judgment' (John 16:7-9).

The Spirit-filled life is the Christ-filled life. The Spirit-filled life is the faith-filled life. Believe on the Lord Jesus Christ and be 'filled with the Spirit'.

Chapter 62

'Giving Thanks'

Giving thanks always for all things unto God and the Father in the name of our Lord Jesus Christ.

(Ephesians 5:20)

I cannot imagine anything that should be of more interest to you than that which is set before us in Ephesians 5:20. I cannot imagine anyone not being interested in giving thanks. I cannot imagine any subject more practical and delightful. If you want to worship, honour and serve God, give thanks! If you want to help others, quit grumbling and give thanks! If you want to overcome depression, give thanks! Giving thanks is always good and in season. If we cannot always be singing with our lips, there should always be a song in our hearts. If we must, of necessity, pause from the outward expression of praise, we ought never to refrain from inwardly 'giving thanks'. There should always be a melody in the believer's heart, a melody of thanks, giving thanks to our God.

Our lives should be anointed with the precious oil of thankfulness. If our hearts grow cold we should warm them with the fire of gratitude. It is the duty of all men to give thanks unto God, but for us who have experienced his salvation, it is more than a mere duty; it is our privilege to be always 'giving thanks'.

Behold the wondrous love and grace of God in Christ Jesus. We have every reason imaginable for being a thankful people. Daily we are fed, upheld, protected and cared for in every way by the good hand of God's providence. Can we be so hardened as to withhold the praise of gratitude from our merciful Father? May God the Holy Spirit speak to our hearts under this blessed exhortation. 'Giving thanks always for all things unto God and the Father in the name of our Lord Jesus Christ.'

Privilege and duty

Giving thanks to God is a great privilege. It is the reasonable duty of believers. For a believer, every duty is a privilege. We do not force the children of God to do anything by holding over them the threats of the law. Thanksgiving is a duty but it can never be forced by law. This pleasant duty is forced only by the experience of grace. It rises from a heart overcome by the mercy, love and grace of God in Christ.

Giving thanks

Clearly there is something here for us to do. But what is it? What is required of us? Paul tells us our duty in two words, 'Giving thanks'. Thanksgiving is an expression of gratitude and the joyful celebration of divine goodness. We give thanks in our hearts, giving thanks to God for all he does to, for and with us. We are bound to show gratitude by our actions. Obedience is the sincerest form of giving thanks.

To perform our sometimes tiresome and laborious duties cheerfully is giving thanks to God. To bear pain and sickness patiently because it is the will of God is giving thanks to him. To sympathise with suffering saints for the love of Christ is to give thanks to God. To love the cause of God and defend it for Christ's sake is giving thanks to God. This is our duty. It is our privilege and it is most reasonable.

It is but a very small thing for us to give our poor thanks to our heavenly Father when we consider all he has done for us. He has given us life, breath and strength. He has saved us from wrath and sin by washing our souls in the blood of Christ. He has made us his children and heirs of eternal glory. It is most reasonable that we should all give thanks to him continually. This is something all of us can do. The poorest, weakest and least-gifted believer can give thanks. The smoking flax may give thanks that it is not quenched. The bruised reed can give thanks that it is not broken. Even the speechless mute can give thanks. His face can smile a psalm. The dying believer can give thanks, though he is too weak to speak.

Always

'Giving thanks' is what we are to do. But when are we to give thanks? We find the answer in our text, – 'Always'. We should give thanks to God at all times and in all circumstances (Psalms 145:2; 146:1, 2). The days of our lives should be full of praise to God. I am not talking about a pretence of giving thanks. I am not talking about putting on a smiley face and faking happiness. I am talking about something real. The believing heart should always be full of gratitude. No, I take that back. The believing heart is always full of gratitude. It is only the unbelieving heart that is not. My lips may not always be able to sing, but the heart of faith can.

When we awake in the morning, we ought to awake full of praise, for the dawn of another day wherein God's faithfulness shall be seen. When we lie down at night, our hearts should be full of gratitude for the mercies of God throughout the day. When we eat our bread, we should eat with thanksgiving. In the days of youth, we should thank God for godly parents. In our middle-age, we should thank God for strength, for household joys and the blessings of divine loving-kindness. In the mature days, when the head, like golden grain, bows with ripeness, the aged saint should begin the employment of heaven; he should always be giving thanks.

For all things

Another question arises. For what should we always be giving thanks? The answer is, 'For all things'. Now we come to the place where true faith is separated from carnal religion. Here the precious is separated from the vile and wheat from chaff. It is easy for me to tell you to give thanks in all things, but I have not always found it easy to practise what I preach. This I confess to my shame. Nevertheless, the believer's rule is, 'Giving thanks always for all things'.

Hear God's Word, 'Rejoice evermore. Pray without ceasing. In everything give thanks: for this is the will of God in Christ Jesus concerning you' (1 Thessalonians 5:16-18). The child of God should be thankful to God for all things, both in prosperity and in adversity. To give thanks sometimes is easy enough. Any mill will grind when the wind blows. We hardly need to be exhorted to give thanks when wine and riches increase. Anyone can give God thanks when the harvests are plentiful, the stalls are full, the bank account is padded and health is good. It is another thing to give God thanks in poverty, pain, sickness and sorrow.

We should give thanks, like Job, in times of adversity when health, family, wealth and friends have forsaken us. We should give thanks in times of temptation because his grace is sufficient still. When we are afflicted with the persecutions of men, we should still, like Paul and Silas, sing out the praises of God. We are to give thanks for all things, because 'this is the will of God in Christ Jesus concerning you'. 'Shall there be evil in a city, and the LORD hath not done it?' 'What? shall we receive good at the hand of God, and shall we not receive evil?'

We have our life and being from God (Psalms 100:3, 4; 139:14-16). We are preserved in life by God's gracious hand, day by day (Nehemiah 9:5, 6). Every daily blessing we receive is sanctified to our spiritual good by our God, when it is received with thanksgiving (Psalm 68:19; 1 Timothy 4:4).

Being the children of God, our hearts should be even more thankful for our many spiritual mercies and things that are eternal, than for our temporal benefits.

God has graciously given us the gospel and hearts to receive it. God has sent us his servants to teach us his truth. Every blessing of grace should fill our hearts with gratitude to God because they flow freely to us from him (Ephesians 1:3-14).

We have been chosen by God as the objects of his peculiar love, adopted into the family of heaven and redeemed by the blood of Christ. We have the absolute pardon and full forgiveness of sins by the substitutionary work of Christ. We have been called, born again, given faith in Christ by God the Holy Ghost, and have the promise of eternal life. In Christ, bankrupt sinners are the heirs of eternity!

Above all, we should say with the apostle, 'Thanks be unto God for his unspeakable gift'. Jesus Christ, our Saviour, is the greatest blessing of God's grace and the unspeakable gift of his love. 'For God so loved the world, that he gave his only begotten Son' (John 3:16). 'God commendeth his love toward us, in that, while we were yet sinners, Christ died for us' (Romans 5:8). Christ Jesus is given to us freely because God loves us. Christ is a suitable gift to meet the needs of sinners. The Lord Jesus Christ is a suitable gift, for in him we have all things (1 Corinthians 1:24-30). Christ is an unchangeable gift, never to be taken from us.

O my soul, give thanks always and for all things to God my Father in the name of my ever-blessed Saviour, the Lord Jesus Christ! We should never murmur and complain, but give thanks. All things are ours. Ingratitude is the child of unbelief, but thankfulness is born of faith. Let it be ours never to doubt, but be always thankful and believing. 'Be careful for nothing: but in every thing by prayer and supplication with thanksgiving let your requests be made known unto God' (Philippians 4:6). We should always be thankful, for whatsoever comes to us is the will of God in Christ Jesus our Mediator.

I would be toward God like John Bradford was toward Queen Mary. When he was reviled as a rebel, that saint and martyr said, 'I have no quarrel with the queen. If she release me, I will thank her. If she imprison me, I will thank her. If she burn me, I will thank her.' Augustine tells us the early saints, when they met, would never part company without saying, 'Deo Gratias'. 'Thanks be unto God.'

Unto God in the name of Christ

You will notice that our text has another word of instruction. To whom are we to be giving thanks? 'Giving thanks always for all things unto God and the Father'. God is our Creator, but he is more. He is our Father. God is the one who continually preserves us in Christ and has freely given us all things. How are we to give thanks? Paul tells us, 'In the name of our Lord Jesus Christ'. The Lord Jesus Christ has taught us to give thanks to the Father. In giving thanks to the Father we are simply following the example Christ has given us. The mercy, love, grace and glory of God is revealed to us in Christ. For this we give thanks. The mercies of God come to us as the result of Christ's death and resurrection. God will accept thanksgiving of such worms as we are only because Christ makes intercession for us.

Prerequisites

Before there can be any acceptable giving of thanks to God, some prerequisites, must be met. God will not accept man in his natural condition. Like the ploughing of the wicked, even the thanksgiving of a natural, sinful man is an abomination to God. Before God will accept even our worship, praise and thanksgiving, we must be washed in the Saviour's blood and renewed by his grace.

Before there is any thanksgiving, there must be a renewing of the heart by God. Let it be solemnly remembered, until he has a new heart, no man can give thanks always to God, through Jesus Christ,. The old heart is ungrateful. It is a putrid fountain. It cannot send forth sweet streams of thanksgiving. The heart of man is opposed to God; it cannot bless him in a way that he will accept. Before you can give thanks, 'Ye must be born again'. Before you can give thanks to God, there must be an acknowledgement of God; you must realise that he is. If God is not real to your heart, you will never give thanks to him. More than that, you must have a realisation of God's love. You must realise that all things come from God.

Before anyone will give thanks to God for all things, he must be reconciled to God. Before your soul will bless God, you must hear him say, 'I have blotted out, as a thick cloud, thy transgressions, and, as a cloud, thy sins'. Before God will accept your praise, you must be reconciled to him in all things.

We thank God that he is reconciled to his people by the blood of Christ. 'God was in Christ, reconciling the world unto himself.' It is only when our hearts are reconciled to God, being sprinkled by the blood of Christ, that we can or will give thanks to him continually. When we are reconciled to God's justice, we will thank him for his mercy, but not until then. When we are reconciled to God's righteousness, we will thank him for his Substitute, but not until then. You will never give thanks to God for anything until you reconcile yourself to the fact that you deserve nothing and have all in Christ.

When the Spirit of adoption in our hearts, cries, 'Abba, Father,' then we can give thanks to God. 'Behold, what manner of love the Father hath bestowed upon us, that we should be called the sons of God ... Beloved, now are we the sons of God' (1 John 3:1, 2).

One other thing is required before you and I will give thanks to God always and for all things. There must be a resignation of our hearts to God. I cannot give thanks to God for all things until I give all things to God! 'Not my will, but thine be done.'

My Jesus, as Thou wilt!
O may Thy will be mine!
Into Thy hand of love I would my all resign.
Through sorrow or through joy,
Conduct me as Thine own;
And help me still to say,
My Lord, Thy will be done.

Encouragements

I want to encourage you in this excellent duty, to be always giving thanks. Thanksgiving honours God. 'Whoso offereth praise glorifieth me' (Psalm 50:23). There can be no higher recommendation of any course of action to the believer than to tell him that it honours God.

Thanksgiving is a merciful preventive of many sins. Giving thanks will help to keep us from murmuring and complaining. It will keep our hearts from being hardened toward the providence of God. Thanksgiving will help to prevent unbelief. Giving thanks will, in great measure, be a cure for spiritual pride. 'Who maketh thee to differ from another? and what hast thou that thou didst not receive? now if thou didst receive it, why dost thou glory, as if thou hadst not received it?' (1 Corinthians 4:7).

Thanksgiving is a duty, but it is also a very helpful privilege. All those who give thanks always for all things to God will find it most profitable to their souls. If we give thanks to God continually, we will always keep him in remembrance. The grateful acknowledgement of God's mercy breeds in us a love for God (Psalm 116:1; 1 John 4:19). Giving thanks to God encourages our hope in God. By remembering what he has done in the past, we become more and more confident in hope of the future.

The day shall soon come when we will be able to truly give thanks to God always and for all things. Thanksgiving shall be the eternal employment of heaven. Let us begin now to give thanks, and we shall have a little of heaven upon the earth. 'By him therefore let us offer the sacrifice of praise to God continually, that is the fruit of our lips giving thanks to his name' (Hebrews 13:15).

Chapter 63

Doing The Will Of God

Wherefore be ye not unwise, but understanding what the will of the Lord is ... Finally, my brethren, be strong in the Lord, and the power of his might.

(Ephesians 5:17-6:10)

Many talk piously about seeking the will of God for their lives and act as if it is difficult to know the Lord's will. Yet, in all our relationships and responsibilities, the will of God is plainly revealed in the passage before us. It is not mysterious, 'super-spiritual', or difficult to discern. It is as plain as the nose on your face. The only question is this, will we or will we not do what God reveals his will to be?

The true believer, that person who is truly born of God, does what is right in the sight of God with a willing heart in all his earthly relationships. 'A wise man's heart is at his right hand' (Ecclesiastes 10:2). His heart rules his hand!

God's saints do not live perfectly, or even come close to doing so. We do not always do that which we know to be right, and when we do something that is right, sin defiles it. But in the tenor of his life, every believer follows Christ, obeys his Father, and does what is right, because God has put that which is right within him.

Righteousness imputed

In justification, righteousness is imputed to us. We have been made right in the eyes of God's holy law by the obedience and death of our Lord Jesus Christ as our Substitute. As God made Christ sin for us and imputed our sins to him, he has imputed Christ's righteousness to us, making us the righteousness of God in him. Redemption is righteousness performed by Christ's obedience, justice satisfied by Christ's death, and sin put away by Christ's sacrifice.

Righteousness imparted

In regeneration and sanctification, righteousness is imparted to us. In the new birth, God the Holy Spirit makes us partakers of the divine nature. He gives us the nature, the mind and the will of Christ. The old, sinful nature of flesh is still with us, but now Christ dwells within. That is imparted righteousness. God has put right within us. Righteousness reigns within every believer and makes every believer do that which is right with a willing heart.

In Ephesians 5:17-6:10 of the Holy Scriptures, God the Holy Ghost tells us six specific things that are the will of God for every chosen, blood-bought sinner, six things God would have us be in this evil world, six things he would have you and me do.

I am certain that those who do the will of God in common, ordinary relationships and responsibilities will also find and do the will of God in areas of specific calling in the service of Christ, his gospel, and his people. Those who do not do the will of God in these common affairs of life will not and cannot serve the cause of Christ in higher capacities.

Be filled

First, it is the will of God, the will of the Triune Jehovah, the will of God the Father, the will of God the Son and the will of God the Holy Ghost, that the people of his choice be filled with the Holy Spirit. He would have us give ourselves up to the dominion, rule and control of Christ our Lord by his Spirit. 'And be not drunk with wine, wherein is excess; but be filled with the Spirit' (v. 18).

The only way to live for God is to live by God. 'Ye must be born again.' You must believe on the Lord Jesus Christ. You must surrender yourself to the rule and reign of Jesus Christ as your Lord to be ruled, motivated and governed by his Spirit through the Word of God (Luke 14:25-33).

Awake, come to Christ, trust him and he will fill you with his Spirit (John 7:37-39). This filling of the Holy Spirit is not some ecstatic, emotional, unexplainable, senseless Pentecostal experience. It is the experience of every believer.

When you come to Christ, your life ceases to be ruled by sin, Satan and self. Now you walk in the Spirit, and mind the things of the Spirit (Romans 8:1-5). This is what happens in the new birth. This is what faith in Christ is; it is giving myself over to the Son of God, bowing to him as my Lord.

Yet this admonition is here given to us who are already believers, to people who are already born of God. Day by day, hour by hour, moment by moment we must come to Christ in faith, surrender to him as our Lord, and be filled with his

Spirit. Give yourself over to the rule of Christ, so that you are controlled by the Spirit (Mark 8:34-36; Romans 12:1, 2).

Be joyful

Second, it is the will of God for his people to be a joyful, singing people. 'Speaking to yourselves in psalms and hymns and spiritual songs, singing and making melody in your heart to the Lord' (v. 19).

O Spirit of God, give me grace to ever have a song of joyful praise in my heart to God! The Lord God would have us constantly rejoicing and promoting and inspiring joy in one another (Psalms 97:1, 12; 98:4; 105:3; Philippians 4:4-8).

Be thankful

Third, it is the will of God for his people to be thankful. 'Giving thanks always for all things unto God and the Father in the name of our Lord Jesus Christ' (v. 20).

'And let the peace of God rule in your hearts, to the which also ye are called in one body; and be ye thankful. Let the word of Christ dwell in you richly in all wisdom; teaching and admonishing one another in psalms and hymns and spiritual songs, singing with grace in your hearts to the Lord. And whatsoever ye do in word or deed, do all in the name of the Lord Jesus, giving thanks to God and the Father by him' (Colossians 3:15-17).

Be submissive

Fourth, it is the will of God that we be submissive, not only to him, but also to one another. 'Submitting yourselves one to another in the fear of God' (v. 21).

'If there be therefore any consolation in Christ, if any comfort of love, if any fellowship of the Spirit, if any bowels and mercies, Fulfil ye my joy, that ye be likeminded, having the same love, being of one accord, of one mind. Let nothing be done through strife or vainglory; but in lowliness of mind let each esteem other better than themselves. Look not every man on his own things, but every man also on the things of others. Let this mind be in you, which was also in Christ Jesus' (Philippians 2:1-5). Let each prefer the other and all strife will cease. But, as long as we insist upon having our way, as long as we esteem ourselves more highly than others, strife and division runs rampant.

Be good

Fifth, it is the will of God that we be good, be good to one another, be good to all and do good to all, in every relationship of life (vv. 5:22-6:9), as Paul shows here:

If you ladies would be good wives, you must and will 'submit yourselves unto your own husbands'. 'Wives, submit yourselves unto your own husbands, as unto the Lord. For the husband is the head of the wife, even as Christ is the head of the church: and he is the saviour of the body. Therefore as the church is subject unto Christ, so let the wives be to their own husbands in everything' (vv. 22-24).

Any woman who knows Christ, follows Christ, trusts Christ and is under the rule of Christ as her Lord, willingly submits to her husband in the Lord and submits to him as unto the Lord. What a beautiful woman such a woman is!

'Likewise, ye wives, be in subjection to your own husbands; that, if any obey not the word, they also may without the word be won by the conversation of the wives; While they behold your chaste conversation coupled with fear. Whose adorning let it not be that outward adorning of plaiting the hair, and of wearing of gold, or of putting on of apparel; But let it be the hidden man of the heart, in that which is not corruptible, even the ornament of a meek and quiet spirit, which is in the sight of God of great price. For after this manner in the old time the holy women also, who trusted in God, adorned themselves, being in subjection unto their own husbands: Even as Sara obeyed Abraham, calling him lord: whose daughters ye are, as long as ye do well, and are not afraid with any amazement' (1 Peter 3:1-6).

This submission is real. It is not in word only, or in outward deed. It is a matter of heart and spirit. It is every wife's responsibility to think well and speak well of her husband. If she thinks highly of him, her esteem of him is reflected in outward obedience. As the church makes the will of Christ her law, so the wife must make the will of her husband her law. A wife should have no will of her own, but to submit to the will of her husband.

'The husband is the head of the wife.' This is God's order. It does not change (1 Corinthians 11:3; 14:34, 35; 1 Timothy 2:11, 12). Wives, obey your husbands 'in the Lord'. Young ladies, do not marry out of the Lord. Do not marry any man to whom you cannot give this unreserved submission.

You men, the primary responsibility of every home rests upon you, upon the shoulders of the husband. Contrary to popular opinion, husbands make or break the home. The husband is the head of the household by God's design, decree and revelation. Every man is responsible under God to exercise the rule of his family. But, if you would have your wife's reverence and willing submission, you must win it by your unquestionable, selfless, committed love.

'Husbands, love your wives, even as Christ also loved the church, and gave himself for it; That he might sanctify and cleanse it with the washing of water by the word, That he might present it to himself a glorious church, not having spot, or wrinkle, or any such thing; but that it should be holy and without blemish. So ought men to love their wives as their own bodies. He that loveth his wife loveth himself. For no man ever yet hated his own flesh; but nourisheth and cherisheth it, even as the Lord the church: For we are members of his body, of his flesh, and of his bones. For this cause shall a man leave his father and mother, and shall be joined unto his wife, and they two shall be one flesh. This is a great mystery: but I speak concerning Christ and the church. Nevertheless let every one of you in particular so love his wife even as himself; and the wife see that she reverence her husband' (vv. 25-33).

How is a husband to love his wife? The answer is clear, 'as Christ loved the church'. Nourish her, provide for her, cherish her, comfort, protect and cheer her! Forsake everything for her (v. 31). Love is not a mere emotion. It is not merely a passionate feeling. Love is a matter of resolute, determined commitment. Love lays down its life for the good of its object!

Marriage is a permanent union of two into one! Close the divorce door! It is a union of lives and is the best of all earthly relationships. Marriage is that for which every mother and father should prepare their children. When your son gets married, cut the apron strings. When your daughter gets married, cut the apron strings.

It takes two things to make a marriage work. Every husband must love his wife as himself and every wife must see that she reverences her husband.

Paul says to you who are children, 'Children, obey your parents in the Lord: for this is right. Honour thy father and mother; (which is the first commandment with promise;) That it may be well with thee, and thou mayest live long on the earth' (6:1-3). 'Fathers, provoke not your children to wrath' (6:4). Mothers tend to be too lenient. Fathers tend to be too severe. But fathers have the primary responsibility of discipline. So, there is both a word of caution and a word of instruction. Do not alienate your children from you, from Christ, and from the gospel by unwise and unreasonable discipline. See to it that your children mind you, but do not be severe, demeaning, sharp-tempered and unforgiving. Do not place unreasonable restraints or unreasonable expectations upon them. Don't spoil them! But don't isolate them!

'Bring them up in the nurture and admonition of the Lord'. Teach your children the Word of God and the way of faith by precept, by example and by exposure!

Let every worker serve his employer with singleness of heart, doing service as to the Lord. 'Servants, be obedient to them that are your masters according to the flesh, with fear and trembling, in singleness of your heart, as unto Christ; Not with eyeservice, as menpleasers; but as the servants of Christ, doing the will of God from the heart; With good will doing service, as to the Lord, and not to men:

Knowing that whatsoever good thing any man doeth, the same shall he receive of the Lord, whether he be bond or free' (6:5-8).

Do what is right, for the glory of God, serving God in all things, and you will be blessed of God. 'Them that honour me I will honour' (1 Samuel 2:30). You honour Christ, and God will honour you! You do what is right, and God will take care of your needs.

Let every employer treat those who work for him fairly and honestly. 'And, ye masters, do the same things unto them, forbearing threatening: knowing that your Master also is in heaven; neither is there respect of persons with him' (6:9).

Be strong

Sixth, it is the will of God that you and I be strong. In all things seek grace and be strong in the Lord, doing the will of God for the glory of Christ. 'Finally, my brethren, be strong in the Lord, and in the power of his might' (6:10). We are altogether insufficient for these things, but God's grace is sufficient!

Everything here spoken of springs from and is done by faith in Christ. When Paul says, 'be strong', he is saying be empowered by the might of God's strength. Be strong is to acknowledge that you cannot do the things here declared to be the will of God by your own strength. To be strong is to look to Christ, to believe on the Son of God, to be filled with the Spirit of God, and be empowered to live for God and do the will of God. 'Trust in the LORD with all thine heart; and lean not unto thine own understanding. In all thy ways acknowledge him, and he shall direct thy paths' (Proverbs 3:5, 6).

Let us 'adorn the doctrine of God our Saviour in all things' (Titus 2:10).

Chapter 64

Three Things That Will Guarantee A Happy Home

Wives, submit yourselves unto your own husbands, as unto the Lord. For the husband is the head of the wife, even as Christ is the head of the church: and he is the saviour of the body. Therefore as the church is subject unto Christ, so *let* the wives *be* to their own husbands in everything. Husbands, love your wives, even as Christ also loved the church, and gave himself for it; That he might sanctify and cleanse it with the washing of water by the word, That he might present it to himself a glorious church, not having spot, or wrinkle, or any such thing; but that it should be holy and without blemish. So ought men to love their wives as their own bodies. He that loveth his wife loveth himself. For no man ever yet hated his own flesh; but nourisheth and cherisheth it, even as the Lord the church: For we are members of his body, of his flesh, and of his bones. For this cause shall a man leave his father and mother, and shall be joined unto his wife, and they two shall be one flesh. This is a great mystery: but I speak concerning Christ and the church. Nevertheless let every one of you in particular so love his wife even as himself; and the wife *see* that she reverence *her* husband. Children, obey your parents in the Lord: for this is right. Honour thy father and mother; (which is the first commandment with promise;) That it may be well with thee, and thou mayest live long on the earth. And, ye fathers, provoke not your children to wrath: but bring them up in the nurture and admonition of the Lord.

(Ephesians 5:22-6:4)

I cannot begin to enumerate all the blessings of divine mercy which I enjoy. Truly, the Lord God has been good to me. But I can tell you this, the Lord has graciously bestowed upon me the four rarest, richest, most honourable and most precious privileges a man can enjoy in this world.

God has revealed his Son in me. God has given me the privilege of being a part of a church family where the gospel of Christ is honoured. God has made me a preacher of the gospel. He has entrusted to my hands the gospel of his grace and the care of his people. And the Lord God has given me the blessed privilege of living in a happy home.

Would you be interested in three things that will guarantee a happy home? Some of you are older than I am and have been married longer than I have. But I am no novice. I have been preaching the gospel of the grace of God for almost 50 years; and I have enjoyed the benefits of a truly happy home for 48 years. I do not pretend to have all the answers to the many problems you may face in your home. But I do know that any problem you may have in your home will arise from one of three areas. I do not often make any guarantees but the Word of God and my experience as a pastor, a husband and a father have convinced me that there are three things that will guarantee a happy home.

I am talking to you who are believers. I am talking to you as men and women who recognise the authority of the Word of God. I am talking to you who know the saving grace of God in Christ, to you who submit yourselves to Jesus Christ as your Lord, to you who seek his glory and endeavour to live for his honour. This is what I want to press upon you, you can build your home for the glory of Christ. If you would do so, it will require deliberate effort on your part, but you can do it.

If we would build our homes for the glory of Christ, we must recognise and bow to the authority of the Word of God in our homes (2 Timothy 3:16). You must not allow social philosophy, human opinion or the custom of the day to govern your home. We must not allow the latest opinion poll to dictate our families' principles. The Word of God gives us plain, clear, unmistakable instruction in all areas of family life. Finances, sexual behaviour, child rearing and moral conduct are all plainly explained for God's people in the Bible. God tells us what is right, and what is wrong. If we are interested in building our homes for the glory of Christ, we must recognise and subject ourselves to the authority of God's Word.

If we would build our homes for the glory of Christ, we must get our priorities in order (Matthew 6:31-33). There are some things more important than a big brick house in the most elite part of town, the social class to which we belong, the clothes we wear, the accumulation of money and the recognition of men. It is positively wrong for believers to live for, and seek after, those things. Concerning ourselves and our families, our primary concern must be about our souls.

Seek the glory of God in all things. Make that your priority and you will not greatly err. See to it your family worships Christ. Do not allow anything to keep you or your children from worshipping the Lord our God. Seek the welfare of God's church. My family is not my primary concern, but rather God's family. Endeavour to promote the gospel of the grace of God. I do not suggest you rob your family of food and shelter. I do say it is more important for me to give myself, my time, my labour and my money for the furtherance of the gospel than it is for me to live in the lap of luxury. If we would build our homes for the glory of Christ, and have any real spiritual influence over our families, our priorities must be right.

If we would build our homes for the glory of Christ, we must live as believers in our homes. If we are truly the children of God, we are strangers and pilgrims in this world. We should be content with God's good providence, desiring neither more nor less than our heavenly Father is pleased to bestow upon us. If we are true believers, we will demonstrate love, patience, tenderness and self-denial in our homes. There is no place in our home life for anger, wrath, malice and selfishness. This is what I am saying, children of God, live as the children of God at home.

Here are three things that will guarantee a happy home. I guarantee you that wherever you find these three things, you will find a happy home. If you desire to have a happy home, you must seek these three things. This is what the Spirit of God tells us in Ephesians 5:22-6:4. A happy home begins with a loving husband at the head of it. A happy home requires a submissive, obedient, dedicated wife. In a happy home, the children must be respectful and obedient.

Loving husband

First, a happy home must begin with a loving husband at the head of it (Ephesians 5:23, 25, 28, 29). 'Husbands love your wives.' Yes, still today, a man must be the head of his house. It is not possible to have a happy home unless he is. God holds me responsible for my household. Before God, I am prophet, priest and king in my home. I am God's representative in my family. That is an awesome responsibility. I am the one responsible to provide for my family, to train my children, and to govern my household. Every husband must be the head of his family. The decisions of the family, the welfare of the family, and the government of the family rest on his shoulders alone. He must exercise headship in true love, ruling his house for the glory of God. Joshua said, 'As for me and my house, we will serve the LORD'.

What is my responsibility as the head of my house? There are certain things God requires of me, things which my family may reasonably expect of me. It is my responsibility to provide for my family (1 Timothy 5:8), and to protect them. It is my responsibility to teach my family and lead them in the worship of God. It is my responsibility to teach and train my children (Ephesians 6:4). I do so by instruction, example and by discipline. A loving father will see to it that his children obey him.

It is my responsibility to love my wife. How am I to love my wife? I am to love her 'as Christ also loved the church, and gave himself for it', to love her to such a degree that I prefer her happiness to my own happiness and her welfare to my own welfare. I am to lay down my life for her (Ephesians 5:25, 28, 29).

What do such responsibilities as these require a man to be? Three things are essential characteristics of true manliness. These three characteristics should be found in every man, especially in those who assume the responsibilities of a husband and father. No young lady in her right mind will marry a man who does not possess these three characteristics of true manhood.

First, as the head of his house a man must display firmness. Every woman wants and needs a man who is a real man. The woman is the weaker sex. God has made her with a natural need for a man upon whom she can lean and depend (Genesis 3:16). True manliness involves firmness, not harshness, not meanness, not brute force, but firmness. Second, as the head of his house a man must display dependability. Our wives need to be able to depend upon us. It is not possible for a woman to respect a man who is lazy and irresponsible. She needs to know that her husband will provide for her and the children. A woman cannot respect a man that she cannot count on. If you want the respect of your family, you must be responsible and dependable. Third, as the head of his house a man must display tenderness. Every real man is a gentle-man; tender, loving, kind and thoughtful. I cannot imagine any excuse for a man neglecting his wife. Women love affectionate words, thoughtful gestures and special attention, almost as much as men do. Men, learn to be thoughtful, caring and tender about your wife's needs, her emotions, and her wishes. Dwell with your wife in knowledge and honour (1 Peter 3:7).

In your speech and in your actions be tender, thoughtful, loving and gentle. I am sure your wife will respond favourably. A truly happy home must begin with a loving husband at the head of it.

Submissive wife

A happy home requires a submissive, obedient and dedicated wife (Ephesians 5:22, 23; 1 Peter 3:1-6). By divine inspiration, the husband is commanded to love his wife, and by divine inspiration, the wife is commanded to reverence, submit to and obey her husband. This submission is real. It is not in word only, or in outward deed. It is a matter of heart and spirit. If you ladies would be good wives, you must and will 'submit yourselves unto your own husbands' (vv. 22-24). It is not difficult for a man to love his wife if she reverences him and submits to him; and it is not difficult for a woman to reverence and submit to her husband if he truly loves her.

This is not a matter of male supremacy and female inferiority. It is a matter of divine arrangement. Our president may or may not be a man who is superior to us, but by God's arrangement, he is in a position of authority over us. It is our duty to show him the proper reverence and obedience as our president. Even so, it is the responsibility of a wife to reverence and obey her husband as her head.

Your husband is in a God-ordained position of authority over you. To rebel against him is to rebel against God. To speak evil of him is to speak evil of God. To dishonour him is to dishonour God. No woman will ever find happiness in her home until she recognises her husband as her head, reverences him and submits to him as such.

There are three things that the Scriptures require of a good, faithful wife. These three things are exactly what every man wants and needs in his wife. Ladies, if you would be a real companion and helpmate to your husband, if you want a happy home, you must seek to fulfil these three areas of responsibility.

Every man wants and needs the reverence of his wife. Your husband needs to know that you truly respect and appreciate him. Ladies, speak well of your husbands. Praise them, honour them and encourage them with your speech. Do not ever belittle him, either in private or in public. Do not even do it in jest. If you will show your husband reverence, both in your speech and in your submissive obedience to his desires, it is very likely you will receive the love and tenderness you desire from him. I have never yet seen a woman who reverenced and obeyed her husband fail to have a happy home.

Every man wants and needs for his wife to be a faithful housewife (Titus 2:5). I do not mean that a woman must not work outside the home, or that she should have no outside interests. But the Word of God does teach that the primary, principle sphere of a wife's responsibility is to be in her home (Proverbs 31:10-31). Nothing pleases a man more than for his wife to keep a neat, clean house, spend some time preparing good meals and put forth some effort preparing special treats for him. If you want your husband to come home at night, give him a reason for doing so. Spend your days making your home and he may spend more of his evenings with you in it.

And every man needs for his wife to be content. A loving husband will give or do most anything within his ability to make his wife happy. But you ladies must learn to be content with what he is able to give and do. Do not ever nag him about what you do not have or what you wish you had. Don't ever compare him with other men. Learn to enjoy what God has given you. Be industrious, thrifty and content and your husband will love you for it. If you will learn to live within your means, so your husband does not have to work just to pay the creditors, it will make life much happier and more pleasant for both you and your husband.

Let me make just two comments here to both husbands and wives: First our families need us, much more than they need all the frills we may give them to pacify them. Second, do not build your home around your children. One day they will be grown and gone and it will be just the two of you again.

In order to have a happy home, you must have a loving husband at the head of it, and it must have a submissive, obedient and dedicated wife.

Obedient children

Third, in a truly happy home, the children must be respectful and obedient (Ephesians 6:1-4). It is not possible to have a happy home with unruly, disobedient, and disrespectful children. Neither the parents nor the children are happy in such a situation. It is the responsibility of children to honour and obey their parents. And it is the responsibility of parents to see to it that their children both honour and obey them. I know people say that it cannot be done, but God requires it, and it can be done. Start early, be consistent, firm and loving in your discipline, and your children will honour you and obey you. I recommend three things to you parents.

Be a loving but firm disciplinarian. If you love your children you will make them obey your word and wishes without argument or hesitation. God holds you responsible for your child's conduct (Proverbs 13:24; 19:18; 23:13, 14; 29:15-17).

Live before your children as you would have your children to live after you. Discipline is only effectual if it is enforced by example. There is more truth than error in the old proverb, 'Like father, like son; like mother, like daughter'.

In all things, seek your child's spiritual and eternal welfare above all earthly considerations. Provide your children with the best possible instruction in the gospel of Christ. Keep them under the sound of the gospel. Teach them to reverence God's Word and to respect God's servants. Commit your children to the Lord.

Do you want a happy home? Do you want to honour Christ in your home? You men and women can build happy homes together for the glory of Christ. Recognise the authority of the Word of God in your home. Get your priorities in order and live as believers in your home. May God give us grace and wisdom to do what is right and to do what is truly best for our children, for the glory of Christ.

Chapter 65

Christ Loved The Church

Husbands, love your wives, even as Christ also loved the church, and gave himself for it; That he might sanctify and cleanse it with the washing of water by the word, That he might present it to himself a glorious church, not having spot, or wrinkle, or any such thing; but that it should be holy and without blemish. So ought men to love their wives as their own bodies. He that loveth his wife loveth himself. For no man ever yet hated his own flesh; but nourisheth and cherisheth it, even as the Lord the church: For we are members of his body, of his flesh, and of his bones. For this cause shall a man leave his father and mother, and shall be joined unto his wife, and they two shall be one flesh. This is a great mystery: but I speak concerning Christ and the church. Nevertheless let every one of you in particular so love his wife even as himself; and the wife *see* that she reverence *her* husband.

(Ephesians 5:25-33)

Marriage union

What subject could be more precious to our souls than the marriage union of Christ and his church? We cannot be sufficiently thankful to God the Holy Ghost for this portion of Holy Scripture, which so fully explains this sweet, assuring, soul-comforting subject.

Were it not for that which God the Holy Ghost here tells us, no man would ever have imagined that the institution of marriage in the Garden of Eden was a shadow and picture of the everlasting union of Christ and his church. Yet that is precisely the doctrine of our text. Ephesians 5:25-33 gives us God's own explanation of that first marriage recorded in the second chapter of the Book of Genesis. Truly, 'this is a great mystery'.

When 'the LORD God said, it is not good that the man should be alone; I will make him an help meet for him' (Genesis 2:18), and then caused a deep sleep to fall upon Adam and formed Eve from one of Adam's ribs, he gave us a picture of our Saviour and his church, a picture of our union with our Redeemer, a picture of our Saviour's love for us and his utter devotion to us, and a picture of our union with him. What a delightful, instructive picture it is!

When Adam saw his wife, in all the perfection of beauty in which the Lord God created her and brought her to him, he called her bone of his bone and flesh of his flesh. Here God the Holy Ghost tells us that the reason he did so was because God's elect are one with the Lord Jesus Christ. When Adam called his divinely created bride, 'Woman, because she was taken out of Man', he had his eye upon the last Adam, Christ Jesus, and his church which was taken out of his side. And when Adam said, 'Therefore shall a man leave his father and his mother, and shall cleave unto his wife: and they shall be one flesh', he spoke prophetically of the incarnation of our blessed Saviour, by which he made himself bone of our bone and flesh of our flesh, that he might suffer and die for his beloved bride and make his beloved to be bone of his bone and flesh of his flesh, that we might 'dwell in him, and he in us, because he hath given us of his Spirit' (1 John 4:13). How wonderfully and vividly this portrays the fact that Christ loved the church!

We know Adam spoke prophetically of our Lord Jesus Christ because Adam had no father to leave.

Everlasting union

Obviously, the marriage of Christ and his church took place before the worlds were framed by the word of God. When Christ was brought forth and set up as the Head and Husband of his church, the church was brought forth and set up with him. There could not have been a head without a body. There could not have been a husband without a wife. Christ and his church, as Husband and wife, as Bridegroom and bride, are from everlasting married, and are from everlasting one. His delights were with us from everlasting (Proverbs 8:31; Hosea 2:19).

When the Lord God chose his elect, the church, in Christ before the foundation of the world, he chose her to be holy and without blame before him in love, as the Spirit of God tells us in Ephesians 1:4. When we were presented to Christ as his bride, the church, we were presented to him as Eve was presented to Adam, in the perfection of beauty, holy and without blame before him in love. From everlasting, she was as the King's daughter, all glorious within, dressed in clothing of wrought gold (Psalm 45:13). Though we fell into poverty and wretchedness by sin, when

Christ married her, his church was 'holy and without blame before him in love'. And now, being washed from her sins in his blood and born of his Spirit, every saved sinner, every believer, every member of his church is 'holy and without blame before him in love'. And such, the Spirit of God tells us in our text, we shall be when the Lord Jesus Christ comes to present his church to himself at the last day, 'a glorious church, not having spot, or wrinkle, or any such thing, but that it should be holy, and without blemish'.

Who can imagine the glories of that day, when the Lord Jesus brings his church home and presents us to himself, being fully prepared in body, soul and spirit for the everlasting enjoyment of our Lord in glory, 'holy and without blame before him in love'? In the perfection of his beauty we shall then enter with him into the marriage supper of the Lamb and be forever with the Lord! All because 'Christ also loved the church, and gave himself for it'.

In our text, Paul is showing us the various duties of husbands and wives. A wife must see that she reverences her husband. Paul says, 'Husbands, love your wives, even as Christ also loved the church, and gave himself for it'. Having mentioned the love of Christ, the apostle could not resist the impulse to speak of the details of Christ's love and the glorious church, which he has redeemed. I will follow his example. I would say with Paul, 'Husbands, love your wives'. The best argument I can produce to enforce that exhortation is the love of Christ for his church.

The love of Christ, what a theme this is! The apostle said that it is a love that passes knowledge. If it passes knowledge, how much more does it excel any description I can give of it. The heart can feel this love but the tongue can never describe it. If there is one subject I prefer above all others, this is it. 'Christ also loved the church, and gave himself for it.' It is a theme that altogether baffles me, and makes me feel ashamed of my feeble attempts to speak of it. The love of Christ is the most amazing thing in heaven or earth. If I had heard that Christ pitied us, I could understand that. When I read that he had mercy upon us, I could comprehend that. But it is written that he actually loves us! The love of one mortal for another mortal is easily understood. The love of the infinite Persons of the Godhead for one another, we can imagine. But what kind of love is this? The infinite, eternal, incomprehensible God loves poor, sinful, finite creatures. Who can grasp that? Miracle of miracles! He loved me and gave himself for me.

A comparison

Under the inspiration of the Holy Spirit, Paul makes a comparison that we could not dare to make had not the Holy Spirit himself drawn it. Paul compares the love of Christ for the church to the love of a husband for his wife. 'This is a great mystery: but I speak concerning Christ and the church.' This is a mystery too deep for human intellect to dive into. Its depths will overcome all human reason. This is a subject too sacred to think or speak of without the utmost solemnity of heart.

'Husbands, love your wives, even as Christ also loved the church and gave himself for it.' A parallel is drawn between poor mortals like us who occupy the position of husbands, and our glorious Lord, who is God over all and blessed forever. In marvellous condescension, the Son of God takes the church to be his holy bride. The Lord Jesus Christ is our heavenly Bridegroom, our Husband, utterly devoted to us in love. Let us now rejoice in the love he shows to us.

This is the lesson which the Holy Spirit here gives by the pen of the Apostle Paul. The Lord Jesus Christ freely and willingly gave himself for his people, so that he might present us to himself a glorious church.

The Saviour's love

The first thing our text tells us is that, 'Christ also loved the church'. Love must have an object and the love of Christ has an object. What is the church which Christ loved? There is much confusion concerning the meaning of the word 'church' as it is used in the Scriptures. Almost every religious denomination claims to be the true church. I will not enter into any arguments concerning those things; but I think that it is important for us to understand what Paul means in this verse by 'the church'. The word 'church' is used in four distinct ways in the New Testament.

It is applied to the whole body of God's elect. Paul says, 'Ye are come unto mount Sion, and unto the city of the living God, the heavenly Jerusalem, and to an innumerable company of angels, To the general assembly and church of the first born, which are written in heaven' (Hebrews 12:22, 23). All baptised believers in one place or district are called the church. We read, 'Saul was consenting unto his (Stephen's) death. And at that time there was a great persecution against the church which was at Jerusalem; and they were all scattered abroad throughout the regions of Judaea and Samaria, except the apostles' (Acts 8:1). Sometimes it is used to describe a small number of professing believers in a particular family. Paul spoke of Priscilla and Aquilla, and 'the church that is in their house' (Romans 16:5). The term church is even applied to the whole body of baptised people throughout the world, both good and bad. 'God hath set some in the church, first apostles, secondarily prophets, thirdly teachers … ' (1 Corinthians 12:28).

Before I go further, let me briefly tell you what Paul does not mean when he uses the word 'church'. When Paul speaks of the church, he is not talking about a material building. He is not talking about a religious denomination. In this verse, Paul is not even talking about all professed Christians. And though usually when Paul talks about the church, he is addressing one local congregation of believers, he is not here talking about any local assembly.

In this verse of Scripture the Apostle is talking about the whole body of God's elect. He is talking about Christ's entire mystical body, 'the general assembly and church of the first born'. This is the entire number of the redeemed, both in the Old Testament and the New, both on earth and in heaven. This is the church which is the body and bride of Christ.

All who are chosen, redeemed, justified, called, sanctified and glorified are in this church. All who repent and believe the gospel, all who love Christ, all who are clothed in his righteousness are members of this church. This is that hundred and forty-four thousand redeemed ones, who are saved out of great tribulation. This is the heavenly Jerusalem. This is the bride, the Lamb's wife.

Take a moment to recall what this church was by nature. The church which Christ loved was and is by nature as sinful as the rest of the human race. She fell with the rest of mankind in that great rebellion against God in the Garden. The sin of our father Adam was imputed to us, as it was to all other men. The consequences of sin were upon us, the same as the rest of mankind. We were radically depraved, inclined to every form of evil. We were under the sentence of death and the curse of the law. There was nothing in us, but sin, deception, blasphemy and filth.

Remember that between the brightest saint in heaven and the blackest sinner in hell, there is no difference except that which Christ has made. We 'were by nature the children of wrath, even as others'.

What is more, we were all defiled by our own transgressions. Perhaps we did not all fall into the same vices; but we all possessed the same lusts. When we read the black catalogue of human sin, we are made to weep, for 'such were some of you'.

Perhaps you say, 'But why did God make us a part of Christ's church? He could have made a church of the holy angels. He could have found better men.' That is certain. But we answer, 'Even so, Father, for so it seemed good in thy sight'. We had no dowry to bring to our Saviour. We were impure. We had no beauty to attract his favour. Everything about us should have repelled his love. We were polluted in blood. Yet eternal love says, 'Deliver him from going down to the pit: I have found a ransom'.

Look at the church of Christ, even as you see her visibly in the world. Even in her regenerate state, she speaks the truth when she says, 'I am black … as the tents of Kedar'. She is so often unbelieving and ready to murmur at God. She is torn with strife, schisms and divisions. She is marred with envying, backbitings, suspicion and bitterness. How she is marred with pride, heresy and self-confidence.

Yet, for all of this, it is written, 'Christ also loved the church'. Who can imagine such love as this! I will not attempt to describe its fulness. Let me just give you some marks of Christ's love for his church. Children of God, do not attempt to understand; just bathe your souls in it.

Christ loved the church particularly. We thank God that we have learned to love the doctrines of distinguishing love and grace. Predestination, election and discrimination are not hard words for us to pronounce. We love to read this text and put the emphasis where God puts it: 'Christ also loved the church, and gave himself for it'. Only for it! Specifically for it! He did not love the world. 'Christ also loved the church, and gave himself for it.' He did not give himself for the world, but for the church. 'Christ loved the church and gave himself for it.'

That is a plain, clear, unmistakable declaration of limited atonement. Christ loved the church. Christ gave himself for the church. Christ died for the church that he might, by his sin-atoning death, save the church of his elect. The Lord Jesus Christ died with a specific people in view, a people who had been set apart by the Triune God for salvation before the foundation of the world. Christ did not merely render them salvable, but he guaranteed that they would all be saved.

In our text Paul compares the love of Christ to the love of a husband for his wife. Surely, no one would suggest that a man is to love all women as he loves his wife! Our loving Redeemer does not love all the world as he loves his church. He says, 'I have loved thee with an everlasting love'. That means, 'I have loved thee with a special, peculiar, distinguishing love'.

Christ loved his church eternally. The love of Christ did not begin when we believed, nor when he died, nor even when he came into the world. No! The love of Christ has no beginning. It is eternal. Nor shall it have an end. It is everlasting.

Christ loved his church unselfishly. The Lord loves us, not for what good he can get from us, or with us. He loves us for what he is able to bestow upon us. His is the strongest love that ever was, for he has loved ugliness until he changed it into beauty. He loved this sinner, until he changed him into a saint.

I cannot explain it, but I know it to be a truth of God's Word. Christ even loves his church with a love of complete complacency, satisfaction and delight all the time! Child of God, let this truth ravish your heart. Our Redeemer delights in us as the object of his love. It is written, 'Thou shalt be called Hephzibah', that is, 'My delight is in her'.

Look out upon God's creation. Would you choose a bird or a beast of the field as the object of your deepest love? Yet the Son of God has set his heart upon such worms as we are!

Christ loved his church with an intense love of sympathy. He is bone of our bone and flesh of our flesh; he is touched with the feeling of our infirmity.

The love of Christ for his church is a love of sweet communion. O blessed thought, the Son of God delights to dwell with his people. He reveals himself to us as he does not reveal himself to the world.

The love of Christ for his church is a constant and enduring love. 'Having loved his own which were in the world, he loved them unto the end.' No changes can attend Jehovah's love! His love is perfect and knows no change!

One more thing I must say before leaving this part of my subject. There is a blessed, everlasting union of love between the Lord Jesus Christ and his church. 'For this cause shall a man leave his father and mother, and shall be joined unto his wife, and they two shall be one flesh. This is a great mystery: but I speak concerning Christ and the church' (Ephesians 5:31, 32).

Union is the essence of the marriage bond and we are one with Christ. Since we are one with Christ, we must be eternally with him. If his members perish, he will be bereaved. If his members perish, he will not be perfect. If his members perish, he will never see the fulness of his body and be satisfied.

Are we one with him? Then we may boldly say, 'Who shall separate us?' 'The Lord, the God of Israel, saith that he hateth putting away.'

The Saviour's sacrifice

Second, look at our dear Saviour's sacrifice of love. 'Christ also loved the church, and gave himself for it.' Since the church was not fit for Christ by nature, he resolved to make her so by grace. He could not be in communion with sin. Therefore, the sin must be purged away. Perfect holiness must be accomplished for that one who is the bride of God's dear Son. How shall this be accomplished? He 'gave himself for it'.

Had the Saviour given up his crown, his royalty, his glory to come down to the earth for a while, that would have been a great mercy. Had he given up the happiness of his Father's house for a season, that would have been great grace. But that is not enough. He not only left his Father's house and parted with his crown, but he gave himself.

The Lord Jesus Christ gave himself for us in the covenant of grace before the world began. We were espoused and betrothed unto Christ before the foundation of the world as his chosen bride. He gave himself to us in covenant agreement. 'I will sow her unto me in the earth; and I will have mercy upon her that had not obtained mercy; and I will say unto them which were not my people, Thou art my people; and they shall say, Thou art my God' (Hosea 2:23).

He gave himself as our kinsman Redeemer before we ever fell. He gave himself as our loving Provider and Protector in the years of our wandering (Hosea 2:8). Though we were in the arms of another, we belonged to Christ; and he had given himself as our Head and Husband. He resolved to win our hearts to himself.

In the fulness of time, he came and gave himself in the incarnation. The angels have never ceased to wonder at this great mystery of godliness, 'God was manifest in the flesh'. He took our total nature upon himself in everything, except sin. He was one with us. He gave himself through his earthly life for us. He gave us a perfect righteousness in his life, and a perfect example to follow. He loved us freely that God might be glorified in our salvation.

In due time, having accomplished perfect righteousness for us, Christ gave himself into the hands of death to satisfy the justice of God, to pay the penalty due to our sins, when, at last, he who knew no sin was made sin for us. 'In due time, Christ died for the ungodly.'

Behold your Bridegroom, forsaken of God for you! He was made sin and a curse for you. Behold, he died for you and for me. He says, 'I have bought you with the silver of my sweat and the gold of my blood, and you are mine'.

But that is not all. In the time of love, the blessed Saviour spread his skirt of love over you and gave himself in the new birth to you. He sought you out. He found you naked, polluted in your own blood, spread his skirt over you, and said, 'Live', and live you do! He came to the auction block of polluted humanity and gave himself for you. He is still giving himself for you.

Christ is our Intercessor and he will not hold his peace until all his ransomed ones are with him. He will not be satisfied until we are all crowned with his own glory. He will not rest until all his church is seated with him upon his throne. All that Jesus Christ is, he gives to his church.

What shall we do in response to such a loving Husband? We should be filled with the deepest gratitude and render unto him entire obedience. Let us see that we reverence our Husband and seek to be like our glorious Head.

Chapter 66

Union With Christ

For we are members of his body, of his flesh, and of his bones. For this cause shall a man leave his father and mother, and shall be joined unto his wife, and they two shall be one flesh. This is a great mystery: but I speak concerning Christ and the church.

(Ephesians 5:30-32)

'We are members of his body, of his flesh, and of his bones.' Having made that statement, the Apostle Paul says, 'This is a great mystery'. I do not hesitate to say that this text is one of the most wonderful and meaningful statements to be found in the pages of Inspiration. It sets forth the mystery of mysteries, the very substance of the most lofty doctrine of Divine Revelation: the living, loving, and lasting union of Christ and his church.

Most assuredly, we shall never, at least not in this world, fathom the depths of this great sea. This is a text that must not be looked upon with the eyes of cold, theological orthodoxy. That might make us content to say, 'Yes, that is a great and important truth', and then leave it. This is manna from heaven. It is to be tasted, eaten, digested and lived upon day by day, hour by hour, moment by moment. This is a text to take to your closet and there turn it over in the meditation of your heart. Get alone with your heavenly Husband and worship. Then, in your heart, you shall rejoice in such blessed realities as tongue can never utter.

Even now, I ask you to pray for that frame of mind that is suitable to think upon such a subject. Come, like Mary, and sit at the Saviour's feet, leaving the cares of the day behind you. Drink in the love of Christ which is like 'wines on the lees well refined', that is to be found in this inspired declaration. 'We are members of his body, of his flesh, and of his bones.' This is the children's bread. It belongs only to God's dear children. It is Israel's manna. This is like the stream that flowed from Israel's smitten Rock. It flows neither for Edom, nor for Amalek, but for the chosen seed. If you are not joined to Christ by a living faith, all I have to say will be but sounding brass and tinkling cymbal. It is said concerning the members of Christ alone, 'We are members of his body, of his flesh, and of his bones'.

To whom it may concern

Look back to the beginning of the epistle and you will see who the Apostle is addressing when he says 'we'. That little word 'we' is like the door of Noah's ark. It shuts us in or it shuts us out. Does it shut you out or in? The Apostle wrote these words to those of whom it is written, 'Blessed be the God and Father of our Lord Jesus Christ, who hath blessed us with all spiritual blessings in heavenly places in Christ: According as he hath chosen us in him before the foundation of the world, that we should be holy and without blame before him in love: Having predestinated us unto the adoption of children by Jesus Christ to himself, according to the good pleasure of his will, To the praise of the glory of his grace, wherein he hath made us accepted in the beloved. In whom we have redemption through his blood, the forgiveness of sins, according to the riches of his grace' (Ephesians 1:3-7).

Is this all doctrinal theory with you or is it a blessed reality of life? What is the ground of your confidence before God? Do you trust the Lord Jesus Christ? Is he to you 'wisdom, and righteousness, and sanctification, and redemption?' If so, God has chosen you. Christ has redeemed you. You are born of God. You are accepted in the Beloved. Among all those spiritual blessings, none is sweeter or more blessed than this fact, this fact that is beyond all question, this fact of undoubted assurance, you are one with him. Of all whom the Lord God has chosen, the Spirit of God says, 'We are members of his body, of his flesh, and of his bones'.

The mystery

What is this great mystery? 'We are members of his body, of his flesh, and of his bones.' The incarnation of our Lord is called by the Apostle the great mystery of godliness. This mystery is the great mystery of grace. 'We are members of his body.' Since Paul himself calls this a mystery, I think that Charles Hodge is correct in stating that, 'Any explanation which dispels that mystery, and makes the doctrine taught perfectly intelligible, must be false'. Realising the impossibility of fully answering my question, I will simply give a few precious truths that are plainly revealed in the Book of God.

'We are members of his body, of his flesh, and of his bones.' As you read those words, recall the events that are recorded in the second chapter of Genesis verse 23. There is, I think, a distinct allusion here to the creation of Eve. The very words of Adam are quoted by the Apostle Paul. Mentally, we are conducted to that scene in the Garden of Eden, when the first man gazed upon the first woman, who was created to be his companion and helpmeet. 'And Adam said, This is now bone of my bones, and flesh of my flesh: she shall be called Woman, because she was taken out of Man' (Genesis 2:23). What did Adam mean when he used those words? It is certain the Great Husband of our souls must mean the same thing, only in an emphatically spiritual sense.

A similarity of nature

The first thing evident in these words is that there is a similarity of nature between Christ and his church. When Adam looked at Eve, he did not regard her as a stranger, as a creature of a different mind and nature. He said, 'She is bone of my bones and flesh of my flesh'. One meaning of those words is that she was of the same nature and race as Adam himself. There is a very blessed spiritual truth here.

The Lord Jesus Christ has taken upon himself our nature. We rejoice to declare that Christ himself is 'God over all, God blessed for ever', that he is the eternal Son of the eternal Father, that he 'thought it not robbery to be equal with God'. We worship our Redeemer as the sovereign Creator. 'All things were made by him; and without him was not any thing made that was made.' He is very God of very God. Yet, the joy of our salvation is this: because of the Saviour's great love for us, the Lord Jesus Christ, the Son of God, took our nature into union with himself.

'For both he that sanctifieth and they who are sanctified are all one: for which cause he is not ashamed to call them brethren ... For verily he took not on him the nature of angels; but he took on him the seed of Abraham. Wherefore in all things it behoved him to be made like unto his brethren, that he might be a merciful and faithful high priest in things pertaining to God, to make reconciliation for the sins of the people' (Hebrews 2:11, 16, 17).

The very nature that we have upon this earth, once was carried about among us by Christ Jesus, and is now seated upon the throne of glory. Remember, Christ is not man deified, and he is not God humanized. He is perfectly God, and at the same time perfectly man. He is the God-man. He is our blessed Kinsman-Redeemer.

It is necessary that the Redeemer be God, or else he could not satisfy infinite holiness, justice and wrath. It is necessary that he be man, because man who sinned must be punished.

Dwell upon this thought for a moment: Christ Jesus is a man, like unto his brethren in all things, sin alone excepted. He was born of the virgin as a man. He was cared for like any baby. He knew the depressions of our nature. He was tempted in all points like as we are. He knew all the pains of our nature; poverty, hunger, thirst, sorrow, reproach, slander and treachery. Christ Jesus was tossed on the stormy sea. For him the ground brought forth briars and thistles. He suffered, he ate, he laboured, he rested, he wept and he rejoiced, just as we do.

But mark this one glorious exception. 'He … knew no sin.' He had no taint of original sin. He had no spot of actual transgression. Yet he who knew no sin was made sin for us, else, he could never have been justly punished for sin as our Substitute. As a real man, our Lord died in our place, was buried, and is now ascended into heaven. There is a man in glory. He is exalted above all things, bone of our bone, and flesh of our flesh. Since there is a man in heaven, like unto myself, there is hope for me.

Now, by the mighty operation of God, my brother, my sister, as he has made your nature his, his nature is yours. 'Whereby are given unto us exceeding great and precious promises: that by these ye might be partakers of the divine nature, having escaped the corruption that is in the world through lust' (2 Peter 1:4).

We were carnal, sold under sin, but Christ has made us spiritual by divine creation. 'Therefore, if any man be in Christ, he is a new creature: old things are passed away; behold, all things are become new' (2 Corinthians 5:17). The new birth is nothing less than Christ himself being formed in you. It is the sovereign creation of the life of Christ in you. Now, as spiritual, you have a new, divine nature. You cry out to God in prayer, as did our Saviour when he was here. Your meat and drink is to do the will of your Father. In agony of soul, you strive against sin. Your heart beats with love for God. Your life is marked by one goal. You long for God's glory above all else. You cannot be satisfied until you awake in the likeness of him after whose image you are created. What a blessed truth! 'We are members of his body, of his flesh, and of his bones.' He bares our nature in heaven and we bare his nature upon the earth. We live in Christ and Christ lives in us.

An intimate relationship

These words imply an intimate relationship. It seems unlikely to me that Adam would have said, 'She is bone of my bones, and flesh of my flesh', if he had thought

Eve would disappear, or become the wife of another. Eve was Adam's helpmeet, joined to him in the bonds of intimate communion. Therefore, he did not simply say, 'She is of the same bone and flesh as I am', but 'She is bone of my bones, and flesh of my flesh'. They were one.

There is no relationship upon the earth that is nearer or more blessed than marriage. It is a relationship of love, joy and peace. It is the divinely ordained union of man and woman that is dissolved only by death. Now, think of this. You women, as is your relationship to your husband, you men, as is your relationship to your wife, such is the relationship that exists between you as a believer and the Son of God, the Lord Jesus Christ. This is the nearest, dearest, closest, most intense, most intimate relationship which can be imagined.

This is a more intimate relationship than that of parents and children. Parents may forget their children and fail to have compassion upon them but Jehovah shall never neglect his wife. Children, at least when they are small, cannot enter into the thoughts and feelings of their parents but the wife communes with her husband. She is one with him and she knows his cares and sorrows, his joys and delights. His very will is made known to her. Children are born and raised for separation from their parents, to live on their own, with their own husbands and wives; but husband and wife are united for life.

Children of God, we can never explain, or even understand, this deep mystery; our souls are wed to the Son of God. 'Let him kiss me with the kisses of his mouth: for thy love is better than wine.' He espoused us as his bride before the world began. He redeemed us for himself. He prepared for us our wedding garments, and allured us into the wilderness and won our hearts, and has taken us into union with himself. Blessed be God; my Maker, my Redeemer, my King is my Husband! 'We are members of his body, of his flesh, and of his bones.' Is this the kind of relationship you have with Christ? Are you wed to him?

A mysterious origin

I clearly see a deeper meaning than this in our text. These words certainly declare a mysterious origin. Though Adam was unconscious when Eve was created, it seems clear from his statement that he knew Eve's origin was within himself. Whether Adam knew it or not, Christ knows right well the origin of his spouse. He knew where his bride came from. The mark is still in his side. From the side of the second Adam, a new Eve was born, the mother of all living.

Our Lord said, 'Except a corn of wheat fall into the ground and die, it abideth alone: but if it die, it bringeth forth much fruit' (John 12:24). Had Jesus Christ not suffered and died, he would have been made to abide alone. But, by his sufferings and death the church is born into the world.

What is this church which has its origin in the death of Christ? It is the church which is made up of all the people of God, all the redeemed of Christ, all believers, all who love the name of Christ. It is not all professing Christians, or all religious people, or any denomination, but the church which is his body; bone of his bones and flesh of his flesh. This church springs from Christ, as Levi sprang from the loins of Abraham. This church lives upon Christ. This is the church 'that cometh up from the wilderness, leaning upon her beloved'. She is ravished with Christ's love. She leans upon him for all her hope. Her desire is toward her Beloved. She is set as a seal upon the Saviour's arm, and loved with a love stronger than death.

Are you a member of this church? Only those who thus have their origin in Christ are 'members of his body, of his flesh, and of his bones'.

A loving possession

I must also call your attention to the fact that these words imply a loving possession. Adam said, 'She is bone of my bones and flesh of my flesh'. She belongs to me. Now, let this thought dance through your soul, you belong to Christ. 'Ye are not your own … ye are bought with a price.'

For many a year we willingly, gladly, laid in the arms of another, but we belonged to Christ like Gomer belonged to Hosea. Christ redeemed us by price and by power. Let him alone have our love. Set your heart upon your Husband. Realise his possession of your entire being. O God, give me grace to live only and always for him! Do you belong to Christ? If so, 'we are members of his body, of his flesh, and of his bones.

A vital union

There is a vital union between Christ and his church. When Paul shows our union with Christ by using the picture of the husband and wife relationship, he used a very blessed picture, but he knew there was something more. He shows us here that the church is even more closely related to Christ than is a wife to her husband. In a mysterious sense they are one but in reality they are separate individuals. However, Christ and his church are in reality one in the closest sense imaginable, indescribably closer than the mind of man upon earth can imagine. 'We are members of his body, of his flesh, and of his bones'. This is not just unity; it is identity. What a mystery; I am one with Christ!

What does this mean? It means that Christ must have his church, and that we must have Christ. Having chosen to become our Mediator, Christ cannot be complete without his church. Paul says of the church, 'which is his body, the fulness of him that filleth all in all'.

Such a statement as this could not be imagined, were it not given by inspiration. The church is the fulness of Christ. We are essential to his mediatorial glory. Without his fulness, he would not be full!

The Saviour must have his saved ones. The Redeemer must have his redeemed ones. The Sanctifier must have his sanctified ones. The King must have his subjects. The Shepherd must have his sheep. The Head must have his body.

When I say there is a vital union between us and Christ, I mean we cannot do without him. 'Whom have I in heaven but thee? and there is none upon earth that I desire beside thee' (Psalm 73:25).

How is it that we are one with Christ? We are one with him eternally. For as long as Christ has been my Saviour, I have been his, one with him from everlasting! We have been one with him secretly from everlasting, and become one with him manifestly when called by his grace. Are you one with Christ? 'We are members of his body, of his flesh, and of his bones'.

Things secured

What does our union with Christ secure for us? This much is certain: Our union with Christ secures our safety. Our beloved Head is in heaven. As long as my head is above water, his feet can never drown. Our Lord says, 'Because I live, ye shall live also'. 'I give unto them eternal life, and they shall never perish.'

If my security were dependent upon me, I know I should surely be soon lost. But our life is Christ and he can never perish. Therefore, we must be secure.

If we are members of his body, of his flesh, and of his bones, then he will one day present us to himself 'not having spot, or wrinkle, or any such thing'. Soon, oh, blessed thought, soon he shall appear, and we shall be like him, for we shall see him as he is.

We shall share in all the glory of Christ. His glory he will not give to another. But we are one with him and we shall have his glory. Does he have perfect holiness? Then we shall. Does he enjoy perfect rest? Then we shall. Does he sit upon a throne? Then we shall. Does he wear a crown? Then we shall. Does he have perfect joy? Then we shall. Is he triumphant? Then we shall be. Is he the heir of all things? Then we are, too. Is he great? Then we shall be. John Kent wrote,

'Twixt Jesus and the chosen race,
Subsists a bond of sovereign grace,
That hell, with its infernal train,
Shall ne'er dissolve, nor rend in vain.

Hail sacred union, firm and strong!
How great the grace! How sweet the song!
That worms of earth should ever be
One with incarnate Deity!

One in the tomb when He arose,
One when He triumphed o'er His foes,
One when in heaven He took His seat,
While seraphs sang all hell's defeat.

This sacred tie forbids our fears,
For all He is, or has is ours;
With Him, our Head, we stand or fall,
Our Life, our Surety, and our All!

I have not begun to scratch the surface of this vast aspect of grace! Our union with Christ is eternal. Our union with our Saviour was not altered by our fall in Adam. Our union with the Lord Jesus preserved us through all our days of rebellion and unbelief. The prodigal son was just as much his father's son in the far country, where he wasted his life in riotous living, as he was before he left the father's house, and as he was when he came home. Our union with Christ is always the same.

Do you know the truth of Paul's words? 'We are members of his body, of his flesh, and of his bones.' Do you have this living, loving, lasting union with Christ? If you do, child of God, rejoice! Your Bridegroom is coming! When he does, he will present us to himself, 'A glorious church, not having spot, or wrinkle, or any such thing … holy and without blemish … before him in love'. 'So, shall we ever be with the Lord. Wherefore, comfort one another with these words.'

Chapter 67

A Call To War

Finally, my brethren, be strong in the Lord, and in the power of his might. Put on the whole armour of God, that ye may be able to stand against the wiles of the devil. For we wrestle not against flesh and blood, but against principalities, against powers, against the rulers of the darkness of this world, against spiritual wickedness in high *places*. Wherefore take unto you the whole armour of God, that ye may be able to withstand in the evil day, and having done all, to stand. Stand therefore, having your loins girt about with truth, and having on the breastplate of righteousness; And your feet shod with the preparation of the gospel of peace; Above all, taking the shield of faith, wherewith ye shall be able to quench all the fiery darts of the wicked. And take the helmet of salvation, and the sword of the Spirit, which is the Word of God: Praying always with all prayer and supplication in the Spirit, and watching thereunto with all perseverance and supplication for all saints; And for me, that utterance may be given unto me, that I may open my mouth boldly, to make known the mystery of the gospel, For which I am an ambassador in bonds: that therein I may speak boldly, as I ought to speak.

(Ephesians 6:10-20)

I once heard Bro. Rolfe Barnard tell the story of a young man back in 1940. He received a registered letter from the government of the United States informing him that he was to appear on Monday afternoon at one o'clock at an address on Park Avenue in New York City, New York. The only thing he knew of on Park Avenue was the world famous, luxurious Waldorf Astoria Hotel, which occupies the block between 49th and 50th Streets in Midtown Manhattan. Needless to say, he was curious and excited to think he had been selected by the United States

Government to some event at the famous hotel. His excitement caused him to forget that the United States had just passed the Selective Service Act – the Draft. When he got to the address he was given, he found a small room beside the famous hotel and realised he was being drafted into the army, as the nation prepared for war.

That is a pretty good picture of what commonly happens when sinners first come to Christ. They have been told all their lives that faith in Christ is the end of all trouble, the cure for all care and the beginning of a life filled with nothing but happiness, joy, peace and tranquillity. But, as soon as a sinner enters in by the Door, as soon as he goes in by the Gate called Strait, he discovers he has entered into a war, a war from which there is no release, as long as we live in this world.

When I call you to come to Christ, when I call upon you to believe on the Lord Jesus Christ, when I call you to faith in Christ, I'm calling you to enlist under the banner of the Son of God. It is 'A Call To War'.

Militant and triumphant

The old writers used to talk about 'the church triumphant' when referring to God's saints in Heaven, and 'the church militant' when referring to God's saints still in this world. The church triumphant is made up of those saints, those members of Christ's church, whose victory is won, whose battle is over, who are at rest with Christ. The church militant is made up of all God's saints on earth; men and women who are always at war, at war with the world, the flesh and the devil.

The church of God is not a social club. It is not a religious society. The church of Christ is an army at war. Everyone who is truly a part of the church has enlisted as a soldier in the ranks of King Jesus. So long as you and I are in this world, we will be involved in a holy warfare, if we follow Christ. There is no truce with Satan. There is no peace with sin. There is no treaty with the ungodly. The saints in heaven, seated at the side of the King, are the church triumphant. We who are yet on earth are the church militant, always at war. This passage is, 'A Call To War'.

Always at war

Our Saviour said, 'I came not to send peace, but a sword' (Matthew 10:34). His church, the church of God, was born in persecution, martyrdom, suffering, imprisonment, bloodshed and death. It was so all through Christ's life upon this earth and his earthly life ended by execution, put to death by the hands of his enemies. It was so in the lives of the apostles. Many of them died as martyrs. It was so in the story of the early Christian church. Throughout the first century the church endured unspeakable persecution.

Nothing has changed. That persecution has continued. It is true that today the open physical persecution of the church is limited to certain areas of the world. But it is none the less cruel and relentless in its ever-growing hatred of Christ and his church. Though, in this part of the world, we are now free from physical persecution, we are not free from our warfare. As a Spartan was born for war, so a believer is born into conflict. His destiny is to be assailed and it is his duty to attack. Every child of God in this world is to be like David, who is described as running to meet Goliath. We have a King to serve, the King of kings. We have a cause to defend, we are set for the defence of the gospel. We have a Captain over us, the Captain of our salvation. Him we must follow. We have a kingdom to establish, the kingdom of heaven. We have an enemy to overthrow, the prince of the power of the air. We have a banner to raise, the banner of the cross. And we are assured that victory shall be ours, because 'the gates of hell shall not prevail against' the army of God.

Paul's conclusion

Paul is bringing his letter to a close. He has spoken of the great purpose of God in Christ, the blessedness of a believer's high calling, and the life that follows the call of God. The standards have been set. The standards for personal life, life in the church, life in the home and life in the world have been plainly set forth. Now, he reminds us that such a life cannot be lived without a constant spiritual battle. The intensity of this battle becomes more and more evident in our experience of grace. Therefore, Paul concludes this epistle with this note of urgency, giving 'A Call To War'. Why is this call so urgent? Because the church has enemies that are hell-bent on its destruction. Those enemies must be stedfastly resisted and positively opposed by all who name the name of Christ. It is the responsibility of every believer to behave as a soldier of Jesus Christ; opposing the world, the flesh and the devil; opposing Balaam, Baal, Babylon and antichrist; furthering the kingdom of Christ in the strength of God by the gospel.

In this final word of exhortation, the believer is portrayed as a soldier in an army of which Christ is the Head and Captain. The Apostle gives his exhortation in four points in these verses.

Our sobering admonition

First, we must give heed to our sobering admonition. 'Finally, my brethren, be strong in the Lord, and in the power of his might. Put on the whole armour of God, that ye may be able to stand against the wiles of the devil' (vv. 10, 11).

'Finally', Paul here urges us to begin in the Lord and end in the Lord. He says, 'be strong in the Lord, and in the power of his might'.

Robert Hawker wrote, 'He that begins in the Lord's strength, will be sure to find strength all the way in his warfare. And there never was an instance of a child of God being finally defeated, that did so. The armies in heaven overcame by the blood of the Lamb (Revelation 12:11). And the Church upon earth is said to be more than Conquerors, through him that loveth them. (Romans 8:37).'

The paramount necessity for a soldier is to be stout-hearted and well-armed. Therefore, Paul gives us this admonition to be courageous for Christ's cause.

As the soldiers of Christ, believers must be strong and courageous. Christianity is not child's play. It is high time that we stand as men for the cause of our King. Let a man be ever so well armed outwardly, it will do him little good if he has a coward's heart. Every soldier must have strength of heart. He must have strength to serve in whatever capacity it is required of him, and strength to face his enemy in battle. He must have strength to suffer. This is strength given only by God the Holy Ghost. Christ is our Strength!

Paul is not talking about physical strength, mental strength or even moral strength. He is talking about spiritual, God-given strength of heart and soul. We must 'be strong in the Lord, and in the power of his might'. If we would live for God, if we would honour God, if we would serve the cause of God; his glory, his gospel and his people, we must get our strength from him, from 'the power of his might', in the vigour of his force.

Do not dismiss this admonition hastily. If God the Holy Spirit has regenerated you, if he has given you faith in Christ, you cannot be a stranger to this holy warfare. If we would wage a good warfare, we must know where our strength lies. It is not in tears, in brokenness of heart, in repentance, in resolutions, in our skills and abilities, or in anything of our own, it is in Christ alone!

We have no strength in ourselves. 'Our natural courage', Matthew Henry wrote, 'is perfect cowardice, and our natural strength is perfect weakness; but all our sufficiency is of God'. We must be constantly supplied with God's almighty power. Apart from him we can do nothing. But with him we can testify, 'I can do all things through Christ which strengtheneth me' (Philippians 4:13). 'Our sufficiency is of God.' We have every reason to be courageous in the cause of Christ. The ground of our courage is not our strength, but the all-sufficient power of the omnipotent God! 'When I am weak, then am I strong.' Our strength is his righteousness, his blood, his grace and his intercession (Psalms 27:1; 37:39; 62:7; 71:16).

Next, the Apostle tells us we must 'put on the whole armour of God'. Courage is not enough. We must also be well armed. Being in a state of war, we must always be ready for battle. This is called the armour of God because he both prepares it and bestows it. It is a whole, complete and perfect armour. There is nothing wanting. It is armour of God's giving. Yet it is our responsibility to put it on. Here, God the Holy Ghost calls us to act in faith, to believe God, to trust Christ, and trusting Christ, he calls for us to make an all-out assault upon the very gates of hell!

There is good reason for this admonition. 'That ye may be able to stand against the wiles of the devil.' The arch-enemy of Christ and his people is Satan. His malice is directed against them. Having been cast out of heaven, he is filled with fury and envy, because he hath but 'a little season'. His purpose is to dethrone the Son of God and to destroy his kingdom. He walks about as a roaring lion, seeking whom he may devour. As we shall see, he has a powerful and well-organised army. It is this prince of darkness whom we must oppose.

Satan employs the strategy of deception in his rage against the souls of men. He mixes error with truth to make it appear plausible (Genesis 3:4, 5, 22). He will often quote Scripture in defence of his temptations (Matthew 4:6). He appears as an angel of light and transforms his ministers into the apostles of Christ (2 Corinthians 11:13, 14). He performs supernatural miracles in the name of God (2 Thessalonians 2:1-4, 9). He persuades people he does not really exist. He resides in places where he is not expected to be (Matthew 24:15; 2 Thessalonians 2:4). He promises people that good can be accomplished by wrongdoing (Luke 4:6, 7).

We must be aware of Satan's devices, lest he get an advantage of us. He does more harm in sheepskin than by roaring as a lion. Let us then put on the armour of God to stand against his strategy of deceit. Even now, let me assure you that as we stand our ground in the strength of Christ, clothed in his armour, Satan shall soon be bruised under our feet (Romans 16:20).

Our spiritual adversary

Second, mark our spiritual adversary. If a man would wage a wise and successful warfare, he must know his enemy. Therefore, Paul writes, 'For we wrestle not against flesh and blood, but against principalities, against powers, against the rulers of the darkness of this world, against spiritual wickedness in high places' (v. 12).

The combat for which we are to be prepared is not against ordinary human enemies. We are not fighting against frail, mortal men. We are fighting the prince of darkness. Our warfare is not with politicians, educationalists or scientists. It is with religion. Our warfare is not with brothels. It is with Babylon. Our warfare is not with communists. It is with self-righteousness. Our warfare is not with the state. It is with self! This warfare is a spiritual conflict between the Prince of Life and the prince of darkness. Our warfare is with the spiritual forces of evil, under allegiance to Satan himself. Our enemies are numerous and powerful. They are wicked and malicious. The combat we are in, though it is spiritual, is real hand to hand, face to face and toe to toe fighting.

Our sufficient armour

Third, the Apostle tells us about our sufficient armour. 'Wherefore take unto you the whole armour of God, that ye may be able to withstand in the evil day, and having done all, to stand. Stand therefore, having your loins girt about with truth, and having on the breastplate of righteousness; and your feet shod with the preparation of the gospel of peace; above all, taking the shield of faith, wherewith ye shall be able to quench the fiery darts of the wicked. And take the helmet of salvation, and the sword of the Spirit, which is the word of God' (vv. 13-17).

Paul repeats his exhortation to assume the whole armour of God and calls us to set ourselves in battle-array against the prince of darkness. It is the responsibility of the church to enter and overcome the domain of Satan. 'Go ye into all the world, and preach the gospel.' The gates of hell cannot stand against the attack of the kingdom of God by the gospel. Let us take the armour of God; and we shall be victorious, even in this evil day. We do not know when the day of severe trial will come, so let us be always ready. Having done all, let us stand (Psalms 41:2; 49:5).

We must stand armed. Here is the Christian in complete armour. This is the armour of God, the armour of light, the armour of righteousness. It has been well observed that in this list there is no armour for the back. If we turn our back upon the enemy we are exposed to danger. Let us resolve, by God's grace, not to give an inch, never to turn our backs to the enemy, but ever advance.

Paul uses the illustration of the Roman legionaries, the best-equipped soldiers of his day. He shows a clear reference to the Old Testament prophecies as well. 'And righteousness shall be the girdle of his loins, and faithfulness the girdle of his reins' (Isaiah 11:5). 'And he hath made my mouth like a sharp sword; in the shadow of his hand he hath hid me, and made me a polished shaft; in his quiver hath he hid me' (Isaiah 49:2). 'For he put on righteousness as a breastplate, and an helmet of salvation upon his head; and he put on the garments of vengeance for clothing, and was clad with zeal as a cloak' (Isaiah 59:17). Each of these is a prophecy of the work of our great Captain, the Lord Jesus Christ. Paul would have us follow him, into war and onward to victory. Stand therefore, and this is the way we must stand.

Our girdle
Truth must be the girdle of our loins. The loins are the seat of all bodily strength. Every soldier must have his belt, or military girdle. Without this, he might be mortally wounded.

It is truth, sincerity and candour which gives the believer strength. God desires truth, that is sincerity, in the inward parts. This was Paul's testimony, 'Our rejoicing is this, the testimony of our conscience, that in simplicity and godly sincerity, not with fleshly wisdom, but by the grace of God, we have had our conversation in the world' (2 Corinthians 1:12). Some understand this to be the doctrinal truth of the gospel. It holds us strong and protects us as a girdle does the loins. The gospel of Christ restrains from evil, as a girdle holds firm the body.

Our breastplate
Righteousness must be our breastplate. The breastplate secures the vital organs of the body. It shelters the heart. This is the righteousness of Christ. It repels the accusations of Satan, and secures us from wrath and condemnation.

Our Boots
Our feet must be secured with the gospel of peace. The shoes of the Roman soldier were boots of brass to protect his legs and feet from the traps of his enemies. The preparation of the gospel implies the firm and solid knowledge of the gospel. This is the ground upon which the soldier of Christ must stand. It is the gospel of peace. It declares the peace made by the blood of Christ. It brings peace between God and man, and makes men peaceable. It gives peace to distressed minds. As we stand upon the truth of the gospel the deceptive snares of Satan will do us no harm.

Our Shield
We must take the shield of faith to quench the fiery darts of the wicked. The shield is that protection the solder has to repel the spears and arrows of his enemies. Faith is our shield. Satan, that wicked one, assails us with fiery darts of temptations and threatenings of the law. But faith is our shield on every side. Faith is the evidence of things hoped for. It lays hold of the benefits of redemption. Perhaps it is best to interpret this of Christ, the object of faith. He is a Shield round about us.

Our Helmet
No soldier would go to war without protection for his head. Let us therefore take the helmet of salvation. A helmet holds the head erect and protects it. That is what

God's salvation does for us. In another place Paul calls it the hope of salvation. Satan tempts us to despair, but a good hope gives us courage, confidence and joy.

Our Sword

If we would invade and conquer the kingdom of darkness, we must carry with us the sword of the Spirit. The Word of God is compared to a sword because it has two edges; the law and the gospel. The law slays. The gospel gives life. The Bible is the sword of the Spirit. God is the author of it. He alone can make it powerful.

Our stedfast attitude

Fourth, in verses 18-20 we see what our stedfast attitude must be as we wage war against the world, the flesh and the devil. 'Praying always with all prayer and supplication in the Spirit, and watching thereunto with all perseverance and supplication for all saints; and for me that utterance may be given unto me, that I may open my mouth boldly, to make known the mystery of the gospel, for which I am an ambassador in bonds: that therein I may speak boldly, as I ought to speak' (vv. 18-20).

As our warfare is not carnal, but spiritual, we must be watchful in prayer. Pray constantly. Pray in the Spirit. Ask for specific things and pray with perseverance.

Pray for all the saints. We are all soldiers in the same army. We are all members of the same body. Pray for those you depend upon to minister to your soul's needs by the Word of God. Pray that God will give them doors of utterance and boldness to preach. Pray that the gospel may be effectual.

Rouse, then, soldiers, rally round the banner!
Ready, steady – Pass the word along;
Onward, forward, shout aloud Hosanna!
Christ is Captain of the mighty throng!

Chapter 68

'Be Strong In The Lord'

Finally, my brethren, be strong in the Lord, and in the power of his might. Put on the whole armour of God, that ye may be able to stand against the wiles of the devil. For we wrestle not against flesh and blood, but against principalities, against powers, against the rulers of the darkness of this world, against spiritual wickedness in high *places*.

(Ephesians 6:10-12)

The Apostle gives a stirring and powerful call to war. We are involved in a war, a holy war, a warfare raging in our souls and all around us, a warfare against our own flesh, against Satan, against hell, and against all spiritual wickedness. It is a warfare for which we have no sufficiency in ourselves. We are weak. Yet ours is a warfare from which there is no release in this world. We must find strength, a constant source of strength. That source, that strength is our Saviour, the Lord Jesus Christ.

First, Paul rouses our hearts to courage, looking to Christ for strength. 'Be strong in the Lord'. He would rally our hearts beneath the banner of our great Captain lest we should be put to flight by some sudden alarm or fear of danger.

It is as if Paul says, 'Trembling souls, though your enemies are strong, skilful, numerous and well-appointed, do not let them shake your courage'. 'Be strong in the Lord.' It is true, we are weak and few, but the Lord God is our strength. The weight of the battle lies on his shoulders, not upon our skill or strength. John Trapp, commenting on this admonition, wrote, 'Get God's arm, wherewith to wield his armour, and then you may do anything'.

Then, Paul comforts our hearts by assuring us that the ground of our courage is the almighty power of Christ, our mighty Captain. Paul is writing to you and me,

God's saints, who are always in the heat of battle. He urges us to begin in the Lord that we may end in the Lord. Never has a child of God been conquered and defeated by the powers of darkness. 'The armies in heaven', Robert Hawker reminds us, 'overcame by the blood of the Lamb (Revelation 12:11). And the church upon earth is said to be more than conquerors through him that loveth them (Romans 8:37)'.

Final word

It is important for us to realise the relation of this challenge to the rest of this epistle. Paul's word 'finally' does not imply that he just happened to think of one more word of instruction, which he would add to the rest. No. This is the apostle's final word regarding all that he has written in these six chapters of Inspiration. This is the conclusion he draws from all that has been said to this point. He had carefully described the blessed and eternal truths of the gospel God has revealed in his Son, the Lord Jesus Christ. Then he made specific application of all these gospel revelations to our lives as the saints of God in this world; in our homes, in church in business. He tells us to honour God in our day-by-day life and to be followers of God, imitators of Christ, walking in the Spirit. 'Submitting yourselves one to another in the fear of God' (Ephesians 5:21).

In this epistle, God the Holy Ghost has given each of us instruction concerning how to fill our station in life. There is a word for pastors and sheep, a word for husbands and wives, a word for parents and children, and there is a word for servants and masters. Like a wise general, Paul has arranged his soldiers and drawn them up in ranks, appointing to each his duty. Now he prepares us for battle. Paul was an experienced soldier. He knew what snares and traps there are to overcome. He knew what enemies are to be faced. He knew the Christian's life is constant war with sin, the world and Satan. He knew we would be tempted to give up in the face of formidable enemies. He knew conflict wearies men who love peace! He knew it wears one down, works on the mind, takes its toll on the body, and weighs heavily on the heart. Therefore, Paul concludes his epistle with this challenge: 'Finally, my brethren, be strong in the Lord and in the power of his might'.

Count the cost

Let all who would make a profession of faith in Christ, sit down first and count the cost. You must take up your cross and follow Christ into war. Christ is Captain of a mighty army. Children of God, we are soldiers enlisted beneath the banner of the cross. The fight is severe. The battle is long. The cause is noble. The victory is sure. Let us, therefore, 'be strong in the Lord'.

Paul's was now a prisoner in Rome. But how does this great man spend his time in prison? We do not find he wrote one invective word against those wicked men whose malice had placed him in bonds. We read of no dispatches to court to procure his freedom. He did not spend his time giving political advice. He said nothing about government conspiracies or secret societies. This faithful man was concerned only for Christ's glory, his gospel and his people. The great care of his heart was for the churches of Christ. He knew that soon he must die. Therefore, like a faithful steward, he laboured to set the house of God in order before his departure. He wrote many letters to the churches to help them to stand fast in the liberty wherewith Christ had made them free. Ephesians, Philippians, Colossians and Philemon are all Prison Epistles, written by Paul when a prisoner at Rome.

Paul was no sooner cast into prison than he began to preach. Even in prison, he attacked the gates of hell, and poor sinners were brought out of the bondage of Satan's prison. How good it was for Onesimus that Paul was sent to jail. When God sent Paul to Rome it was on an errand of mercy for Onesimus and many others. It looked as though Satan has won the day. Paul was in prison at last. But there he does his greatest work to destroy the kingdom of darkness. He had left the Ephesian elders at Miletus, never to see their faces again. But, before his departure to glory, he takes time to leave one last word with them, by which he would strengthen their hand to carry on this holy war.

The exhortation

Here is Paul's inspired exhortation to strength, 'Finally, my brethren, be strong in the Lord and in the power of his might'. It is necessary for the saints of God to be strong and resolute in the faith of the gospel, and in faithfulness to Christ, relying entirely upon the strength of the Lord.

It is true that the saints of God are to be humble, self-denying, submissive and patient. But we are not to be effeminate, timid or cowardly. Believers are to show firmness of mind, resolution, courage, strength and fortitude in all things. 'For God hath not given us the spirit of fear; but of power, and of love, and of a sound mind' (2 Timothy 1:7). Believers, above all men, must be men. 'Watch ye, stand fast in the faith, quit you like men, be strong' (1 Corinthians 16:13).

Charles Buck gives an excellent definition of the strength the apostle here calls for: 'Christian fortitude may be defined as that state of mind which arises from truth and confidence in God; enables us to stand collected and undisturbed in the time of difficulty and danger; and is an equal distance from rashness on the one hand, and pusillanimity (cowardliness) on the other'.

The strength Paul is talking about arises from faith in Christ. 'Behold, I lay in Zion a chief corner stone, elect, precious: and he that believeth on him shall not be confounded' (1 Peter 2:6). Those who live by faith must be strong and courageous concerning those things which are obviously the will of God. Let the child of God be convinced of the will of God, and he will be strong in submitting to it, strong in obeying it, strong in performing it.

If you and I would obey our God, we must be strong, courageous, resolute, determined and unshakable. I am not talking about strength we can muster. I am talking about strength only God can give. It is to be had only by faith in Christ, faith he alone gives and sustains. Yet, it is our responsibility to 'be strong in the Lord and in the power of his might'. We must never rely upon the resources of nature, but upon the power of his might, the vigour of life derived from his omnipotence and grace (Joshua 1:7; Isaiah 35:3, 4)

When our duty is set before us, we must undertake it in the strength of his grace with courage and determination for the honour of God, depending upon him who is our Strength. If God has called us to a work, he will carry us through it. But we must be strong, courageous, lest we be turned aside from God's revealed will. We must face opposition, even danger, with confident courage and strength. We must meet every difficulty 'strong in the Lord and in the power of his might'. William Gurnall said, 'It requires more prowess and greatness of spirit to obey God faithfully, than to command an army of men, to be a Christian than a captain'.

Our responsibilities are such as requires great boldness of faith and confidence in Christ to perform them. The believer must wage a constant and irreconcilable war against the lusts of his own heart. The believer must walk in a manner that is singularly opposed to this world. In this present evil world, we must live soberly, righteously and godly, adorning the doctrine of God our Saviour in all things. The child of God must persevere in his course to heaven, despite every difficulty, until the end of his life. Certainly, when we consider our own weakness, we must recognise that it takes great strength and courage to walk before God. The difficulties and dangers that lie in our way are more than we can bear in ourselves. There are many things to discourage us; our trials, temptations and afflictions. There are many things to alarm us. We have seen many better than ourselves fall and turn from Zion's way. More than that, our enemies are many and strong. The wicked of this world mock, deride and abuse us. Our own flesh is opposed to us. Satan constantly roars against us.

Truly, the righteous must be as bold as lions. We have great need of courage and strength. Let us take this exhortation to heart: 'Be strong in the Lord and in the power of his might'. Be courageous to do the will of God. Fortify your heart with the love of God. Establish your heart with the promises of the gospel. Strengthen your heart with the very power of God. For the glory and honour of God, let us take courage and be strong.

The exhibition

Next consider the exhibition of strength. We are told to be strong, that is, be strong and exhibit strength. We must be strong in the Lord ourselves. We must exhibit strength for the benefit of our brothers and sisters in Christ. It takes great strength of heart for a believer to bear all his afflictions with patience and firmness of heart. 'If thou faint in the day of adversity, thy strength is small' (Proverbs 24:10). When God sends us severe trials by his providence, we must be firm in faith, knowing that he can do no wrong. When we are required to suffer at the hands of men for Christ's sake, we must gladly bear our reproach (1 Peter 2:19-25).

Great strength is required for God's saints to maintain the spiritual warfare in which we are constantly engaged. Those who preach the gospel must be men of strength, courage, and boldness. They must declare the truth of God whether men will hear, or whether they will forbear. The saints of God are at war in this world; and we must face our enemies – principalities, powers, the rulers of the darkness of this world, spiritual wickedness in high places, ungodly, hell-inspired religion and doctrine – with unbending strength.

The last enemy we must face, death, is made to bow before the God-given strength of faith in Christ. We face death with confidence because Christ has abolished its power. We face death with courage because it is for us the door of hope. Death brings us into greater discoveries of the love of Christ and the glory of God. Death will be only once. For us it will be the birthday of an eternal world of bliss. God's saints are calm and bold, confident and strong in the hour of death because of the promise of resurrection glory. Hear what God says about his people and their enemies in the hour of death, 'Fear and dread shall fall upon them; by the greatness of thine arm they shall be as still as a stone; till thy people pass over, O LORD, till the people pass over, which thou hast purchased' (Exodus 15:16).

The excitements

There are many things that may serve as excitements to strength for God's elect. Having exhorted us to be strong, to be resolute, determined and courageous in our warfare, the apostle is careful to show us that our only hope of strength is in the Lord. 'Be strong in the Lord and in the power of his might.'

Be strong, because God has promised us his own almighty strength. 'Fear thou not; for I am with thee: be not dismayed; for I am thy God: I will strengthen thee; yea, I will help thee; yea, I will uphold thee with the right hand of my righteousness' (Isaiah 41:10). One of the names of our God is 'the Strength of Israel' (1 Samuel 15:29). We have no strength of our own to pray; but God will strengthen us by his Spirit (Romans 8:26). We have no strength in our trials, but our God gives us the strength of his presence to overcome them (1 Corinthians 10:13; Hebrews 13:5, 6). We who preach the gospel have no strength to serve God aright, but our sufficiency is of God (2 Corinthians 2:16, 17; 3:5). We are commanded to work out our own salvation with fear and trembling; but we have no strength of our own. 'It is God which worketh in you both to will and to do of his good pleasure.' It is true, we must persevere in the faith; but we are too weak, therefore we are kept by the power of God through faith (John 10:28-30, 17:11).

How does God strengthen us? He strengthens us by his power, by his grace, by his Spirit, by his presence, by his Word, and by his people. Let us rejoice to say of Christ our God, 'The LORD is my strength and song, and is become my salvation' (Psalm 118:14). Christ is our strength for righteousness, redemption, peace, sanctification, protection, preservation, obedience and he is our strength in judgment. 'O bless our God, ye people, and make the voice of his praise to be heard: Which holdeth our soul in life, and suffereth not our feet to be moved' (Psalm 66:8, 9). It is Christ who is the author and finisher of our faith and to him alone we must look for strength.

May God be pleased to make us strong in our day, as he did those great heroes of faith in the days of old! May he make us like Enoch to walk with God, like Noah to obey God, like Abraham to follow God, like Moses to lead God's people, like Joshua to serve God. May we defend God's honour like Elijah, fight God's enemies like David, dare to have a purpose true and dare to make it known, like Daniel. May he enable us to preach the gospel like Peter and Paul and to count nothing dear but the honour and will of God (Acts 20:24). May we be strong in the love of Christ unto the end like men such as Latimer, Ridley and Bradford. May we be like Christ himself to serve God at any cost, strong to do his will, strong to seek his honour and strong to serve his kingdom (Isaiah 50:5-7). Oh, my God, make me, this weak, sinful man, strong in the Lord and in the power of thy might, for Christ's sake!

Chapter 69

Our Warfare

Put on the whole armour of God, that ye may be able to stand against the wiles of the devil. For we wrestle not against flesh and blood, but against principalities, against powers, against the rulers of the darkness of this world, against spiritual wickedness in high *places.* Wherefore take unto you the whole armour of God, that ye may be able to withstand in the evil day, and having done all, to stand.

(Ephesians 6:11-13)

While we live in this world, we are a people at war, relentlessly at war. We must, therefore, seek the strength and courage of confident faith in Christ. In Ephesians 6:11-13, the Apostle shows us why such holy courage is required. It was the desire of this noble warrior, when he was about to retire from the field, to prepare his successors for the battle. The fight is on. We must be strong. Therefore, he says, 'Put on the whole armour of God, that ye may be able to stand against the wiles of the devil'.

Throughout this epistle Paul has stressed both the absolute sovereignty of God and the total responsibility of man in the matter of salvation. Salvation is the product of God's sovereign grace. Yet it is the gift of God to man's faith. These two things are beautifully combined in the close of this epistle. We must equip ourselves with a full suite of arms. It is our responsibility to put the armour on, and our responsibility to use it skilfully. The weapons are called 'the whole armour of God'. It is God who has forged them. It is God who gives them. Man is not able to employ them, not even for a moment, except by the power of God. The battle is the Lord's and the victory is the Lord's.

We are soldiers at war. We shall overcome. We will be triumphant. But our victory will be by 'the blood of the Lamb'. William Hendriksen made this observation. 'It is true that the counsel of God from eternity will never fail, but it is just as true that in that plan of God from eternity it was decided that victory will be given to those who overcome. Overcomers are conquerors, and in order to conquer, one must fight.'

Prepare for war

Paul's first word of direction is this: If we profess faith in Christ, we must prepare for war. 'Put on the whole armour of God, that ye may be able to stand against the wiles of the devil' (v. 11).

Our Saviour declared to his disciples, 'Think not that I am come to send peace on earth: I came not to send peace, but a sword' (Matthew 10:34). 'He that taketh not his cross, and followeth after me, is not worthy of me' (Matthew 10:38). 'If any man will come after me, let him deny himself, and take up his cross, and follow me' (Matthew 16:24).

The life of faith is the greatest fight on earth. The gospel trumpet has been sounded. Let those who would follow Christ prepare themselves to battle. No man goes to war without preparation. If he does, you will find him very soon, either slain or wounded on the battlefield or else hiding in a ditch. Here, Paul shows us how to prepare for war.

When a soldier prepares for war he puts on his armour. What is the armour we are to put on? The believer's armour is Christ himself. 'But put ye on the Lord Jesus Christ, and make not provision for the flesh, to fulfil the lusts thereof' (Romans 13:14). If we would be triumphant over the prince of darkness, we must be clothed with Christ in the armour of light.

Paul tells us to avoid our carnal lusts of rioting, drunkenness and wantonness. Perhaps you are thinking, 'Pastor, how am I to avoid the lusts of the flesh?' Put on Christ! Paul does not say, 'Put on sobriety, temperance and chastity', as the moral philosopher might. He says, 'Put ye on the Lord Jesus Christ'. Until Christ is put on, man is unarmed. It is not man's virtue and morality that repels Satan's temptations, but Christ. The believer's armour is the grace that God in Christ provides for all who trust him: the girdle of truth, the breastplate of righteousness, and the shield of faith.

Through the fall of our father Adam, all the race of mankind became naked and subject to the power of Satan. Finding us naked and unarmed, he takes us in the snare of sin and makes us his slaves, until God comes by almighty grace and delivers us from the kingdom of darkness. The unregenerate man is in a helpless condition before the fiend of hell who seeks to devour his soul. He is unfit to fight Christ's battle. A soul out of Christ is naked and vulnerable. He is destitute of all armour to defend himself and subject to being taken captive by Satan at his will (2 Timothy 2:14-26).

The unregenerate are children of darkness. They may be ever so wise in this world but they are ignorant of all things spiritual and ignorant of Satan, sin and the devices of hell. The man who is without Christ is impotent, as well as ignorant. Even if he knew his ruined condition and the evil purposes of Satan, he has no power to withstand the wicked one. The wicked have no power to cast off the yoke of their oppressor. The unregenerate are in a state of friendship with sin and Satan. All the unconverted are, in their heart, in league with Satan against God. Pity the poor soul who is in league with hell!

Let men pretend what they will. They may be very moral, very religious and very respected, but if they have no heart-faith in Christ they are at enmity against God. You are either a believer bowing to Christ the King, or you are a hater of God in arms against Christ our King. There is no in-between ground. There is no sitting on the fence.

Practical lessons

There are some very practical lessons for us here. We should never be surprised to see Satan's dominion over men made manifest. When Satan comes against a natural man and overthrows every moral restraint, it is no marvel. The man is unarmed. But when he comes against one of the weakest of God's saints, he can do no harm. Such a one is protected with the walls of salvation. All the fury of hell cannot break through the Bulwark of Zion (Isaiah 11:9; 65:25; Acts 28:6). You may rest assured that Satan will be in a rage wherever the gospel is preached. The preaching of the gospel is the battering ram of heaven that destroys the gates of hell.

When a man stands forth to preach the gospel, Satan will raise up opposition to him. But the gospel alone is the power of God unto salvation. The gospel shall prevail. One angel goes out to preach and another angel flies back with the report of victory. 'Babylon is fallen, is fallen.' It was by the gospel that the apostles turned the world upside-down. It is by the same gospel that the kingdoms of this world will become the kingdom of God's dear Son. Realising what a sad condition men and women are in by nature, we should be faithful and dedicated to declare the gospel of Jesus Christ.

I fear many a professor of religion will be found naked, unarmed, without Christ in the evil day. Paul's admonition has a ring of fervency about it. 'The servant of the Lord must not strive; but be gentle unto all men, apt to teach, patient, in meekness instructing those that oppose themselves; if God peradventure will give them repentance to the acknowledging of the truth; and that they may recover themselves out of the snare of the devil, who are taken captive by him at his will' (2 Timothy 2:24-26).

God's armour

The armour which we must put on is 'the whole armour of God'. We must not decide for ourselves what armour we will wear. The trash of your own whims will not do. It is not left up to the soldier to bring what weapons he pleases. He must take the armour of God. We are bound up to God's order. Those who employ what God has not appointed shall be called into account, even though they appear successful in their labours. The Lord God will say to them, 'Who hath required this at your hands?'

We dare not add anything to God's Word, or God's rule, or God's weaponry. His ways are above our ways. Read again the wars of Israel. God told them when and where to fight, who to fight, and what weapons to use. We, too, must submit to God's authority (2 Corinthians 10:3-5).

There are many who have added to God's armour. We must never be named among them. Papists add works, ceremonies and indulgences to the gospel. Protestants add law and sacraments to the gospel. Baptists add law-obedience, sabbath days, altars and religious entertainment to the gospel. We must build God's church with the gold, silver and precious stones of the gospel, not with the wood, hay and stubble of the flesh.

The armour God provides for us is whole, complete and entire. Nothing is lacking. God's armour and God's armour alone is suitable to fight his battles. It is complete, because it protects us on every side, serves us in every need and is sufficient to withstand every enemy.

This armour which God has graciously provided must be used. The Christian's armour is made to be worn. There will be no laying it down until our warfare is ended and our course is complete.

Not only must we use the armour that God has ordained, we must rely upon him for its success. God alone can and will make the weapons of our warfare effectual. Prayer is a weapon in God's arsenal but only God can make our prayers effectual. Faith is a weapon in Christ's cause but only Christ can make our faith fruitful. Hope is a helmet to protect us but only God can give us a good hope. Righteousness is our breastplate but it must be the righteousness that God gives in Christ. It is that prayer, that faith, that hope and that righteousness which is born of God that overcomes the world. Let us never be satisfied with any armour that is not of God. He has provided us with armour in Christ; he bestows it, and he alone makes it effectual.

The necessity

The Apostle also shows us the necessity for putting on the whole armour of God. 'That ye may be able to stand against the wiles of the devil.' Satan is a subtle and crafty foe. He is called the old serpent because the serpent is the most subtle of all creatures. The old serpent is a master-deceiver.

Satan shows his subtlety in choosing the most advantageous time to tempt us. He is always quick to bring temptations upon new converts. He tempts us severely when we are brought down with afflictions. Anytime a man undertakes a noble work for God's glory, Satan will assail him furiously. This is especially true regarding gospel preachers. When believers become weak through pride and self-contentment, Satan tempts them, as in the case of David and Peter.

Satan uses a very clever strategy against God's people. He mixes truth with error and quotes Scripture. He appears as an angel of light, fashions his ministers into apostles of Christ, makes them preachers of righteousness, and persuades men that he does not exist.

Satan uses those we might least suspect to turn us from God's gospel, God's Word, and God's will. Delilah did more harm to Samson than all the armies of the Philistines. Job's wife tried to poison his soul. Peter tried to keep the Lord Jesus from going up to Calvary. Agabus and the Apostle Paul's travelling companions tried to keep him from going up to Jerusalem. Preachers are the serpent's favourite targets, setting them off on false doctrine, and on novelties; trolling them with religious controversy and curiosities.

Satan assails the saints as a malicious and deceitful accuser. He aggravates us with our sins. He mocks our services, ridicules our faith and tries to divide brethren. He seeks to destroy our peace by always trying to keep us looking to ourselves.

Know our enemy

Having declared the necessity of the warfare, the Apostle Paul points out the enemy in verse 12. 'For we wrestle not against flesh and blood, but against principalities, against powers, against the rulers of the darkness of this world, against spiritual wickedness in high places.' The word Paul uses to describe this warfare is 'wrestle'. This is not an impersonal conflict. Every child of God is engaged in a personal battle unto death.

Paul says our enemies are not material, they are non-material. They are not visible, they are invisible. They are not physical, they are spiritual. Paul would be the first to declare the insignificance of material enemies. The church lived and prospered for over three hundred years under the most vicious and violent persecutions imaginable. Paul himself had experienced much violence from the force of physical enemies. He counted that but a light thing. To this man, physical warfare was hardly worth mentioning.

The real enemies he faced were unseen. They were not flesh and blood, but 'principalities and powers'. These are the enemies we must face. Our enemies are not mere frail men of 'flesh and blood'. The enemies of our souls are spiritual. Satan and the hosts of angels who followed him in rebellion are opposed to us. They are mightier and smarter than we are, and are expert in every form of religion. They are enemies who are hell-bent on our destruction, the destruction of our souls, the destruction of God's church and the destruction of our cause; the glory of God, the furtherance of the gospel, the building of God's kingdom.

Therefore, we must be valiant warriors. And, if we would be valiant warriors, if we would prevail over our foes, we must 'put on the whole armour of God'. Let us be well prepared. Be of good courage. Rely upon the strength of our God. The striving is long. The battle is hard. But victory shall be ours. Christ, our mighty Captain, our omnipotent Man of War, has conquered Satan already. Therefore, we need not flinch to oppose him (John 12:31; Colossians 2:6-15).

Meet the enemy

Next, Paul says we must go out and meet the enemy in the field. 'Wherefore take unto you the whole armour of God, that ye may be able to withstand in the evil day, and having done all, to stand' (v. 13).

Those who go to war in Christ's armour do so with deliberate purpose. Being clothed in the whole armour of God you are now able to meet the evil one.

The church as a whole should be on the attack, constantly assaulting the gates of hell with the gospel. God's promise to his church is just as true as it was in the days of Joshua. 'Every place that the sole of your foot shall tread upon, that have I given unto you, as I said unto Moses … There shall not any man be able to stand before thee all the days of thy life: as I was with Moses, so I will be with thee: I will not fail thee, nor forsake thee. Be strong and of a good courage' (Joshua 1:3, 5, 6). The gates of hell shall not prevail against the assault of God's church. Compare those passages with Hebrews 13:5, 6. 'Let your conversation be without covetousness; and be content with such things as ye have: for he hath said, I will never leave thee, nor forsake thee. So that we may boldly say, The Lord is my helper, and I will not fear what man shall do unto me.'

We have the promise of God's presence and his power. Let us therefore be strong, courageous and valiant in the cause of Christ. Let us also be found faithful, even in the heat of the battle; faithful to God's cause, faithful to God's glory, faithful to God's gospel, and faithful to God's people.

The church as a whole and each individual believer, must go out against Satan, the prince of darkness. The church is only as strong as her individual members.

Having done all, in this evil day, let us, like true soldiers, stand, earnestly contending for the faith. The day has come of which Paul warned. Sin and iniquity abound, error and heresy are received as truth, persecutions arise and the love of many waxes cold. So, stand fast. If need be, like Athanasius, stand alone. Withstand the course of ease and pleasure, and every temptation to quit your post. Withstand error, every heresy and every distraction from the gospel.

Stand firmly upon Christ as the only foundation of your soul before God. His blood is your only cleansing. His righteousness is your only covering. His forgiveness is your only hope. His power is your only strength.

Stand in the plain truth of Holy Scripture. 'Having your loins girt about with truth.' Satan will try to entangle you with obscure Scripture texts. He will try to entrap you with mysterious questions and make mysterious prophecies a snare to your soul. Stand resolutely upon God's rich grace in Christ.

In the last part of verse 13, Paul gives us a word of assurance, 'Having done all – or overcome all, or accomplished all, or finished all – to stand'. Satan, with all his wits and wiles, shall never vanquish one soul that is clothed with Christ and armed with his grace. All the saints are sifted but they are all triumphant. Satan himself shall soon be bruised under the feet of God's elect (Romans 16:20).

Come now and enlist in the army of God under the banner of the cross. Believe on the Lord Jesus Christ. Wash your soul in his blood. Put on his garments, the garments of salvation. Go to war! Put on the whole armour of God – the girdle of truth, the breastplate of righteousness, the boots of grace, the shield of faith, the helmet of salvation, the sword of the spirit, the weapon of prayer – and go to war against hell, standing with your feet firmly planted on the Rock of God! Victory is sure! We are more than conquerors through him that loved us and gave himself for us. Christ made an end of sin, overcame the world and has conquered Satan. 'And the God of peace shall bruise Satan under your feet shortly. The grace of our Lord Jesus Christ be with you. Amen' (Romans 16:20). Preacher and hymn writer Joseph Irons wrote

> Let Zion's soldiers muster, round
> The cross, to meet the foe;
> The trumpet gives a certain sound,
> Go on, to conquer go!
>
> The trumpet says the Lord is nigh,
> Your strength in Him is found;
> He reigns victorious on high,
> This is the certain sound.
>
> The trumpet says the victory's won,
> For all the chosen race,
> Go on to glory and renown,
> And shout victorious grace!

Chapter 70

‘Girt About With Truth’

Stand therefore, having your loins girt about with truth, and having on the breastplate of righteousness.

(Ephesians 6:14)

In the sixth chapter of the Book of Ephesians, the Apostle Paul gives us a rousing call to war. The old soldier knew the battle would soon be over for him. He knew he would shortly join the ranks of the triumphant. For himself, it was delightful to anticipate the future. He wrote to Timothy, ‘The time of my departure is at hand. I have fought a good fight, I have finished my course, I have kept the faith: Henceforth there is laid up for me a crown of righteousness, which the Lord, the righteous judge, shall give me at that day: and not to me only, but unto all them also that love his appearing’ (2 Timothy 4:6-8).

However, this mighty leader in the army of heaven was concerned for those soldiers who must be left behind, into whose hands the battle would now fall. Therefore, he calls us to courage. In verse 12, he identifies the enemy and assures us that though the battle may be long and hard, victory is certain (Romans 16:20). He tells us we must be properly prepared for our warfare. We must take to ourselves ‘the whole armour of God’. In verses 10-17 of this chapter, he enumerates the various pieces of armour God has prepared for us. Those who go to war under the banner of the Lord of Hosts dare not do so in any armour except that which God has forged. Human strength, human wisdom and human devices are not suitable for our holy warfare. Therefore, Paul carefully shows us what the armour of God is, describing it piece by piece. This armour makes up a complete suit, furnishing the believer with everything he needs to go against his spiritual enemies.

In our text the Apostle tells us that we must take the field wearing the girdle of truth. 'Stand therefore, having your loins girt about with truth.' The soldier's girdle was a very important part of his armour. The girdle was a wide, heavy belt used to join the upper and lower pieces of armour. No part of the body was exposed. It was also a beautifully crafted part of his attire. It was an ornament as well as a weapon. The girdle was designed to give strength to the rest of the body. The soldier's girdle was not really a weapon at all but it is here listed first because the girdle (the belt) kept all the other pieces of armour together and gave the soldier in the field of battle both support and agility. It braced him up for conflict.

Paul's doctrine here is obvious. It is our responsibility to stand against the wiles of the devil and the only way to do so is by having our loins girt about with the truth of God. May God the Holy Spirit graciously gird us about with the truth, day by day, hour by hour, moment by moment; that we may be able to stand against the wiles of the devil.

Our responsibility

It is our responsibility to stand against Satan, resisting his temptations. Specifically, he tells us we must 'stand against the wiles of the devil' (v. 11). Do not be so foolish as to think lightly of this. Satan is real. His temptations are crafted with hellish skill. His influence is unrelenting and unrelentingly subtle. His power is beyond our imagination and his wiles; his methods, his strategy of assault, are crafty, subtle and hidden.

'Stand therefore.' In verse 13 this word 'stand' has the idea of 'standing triumphant and victorious when the war is over'. But here in verse 14, it speaks of our position in the field of war. This is a military expression. It is a word of command, implying the duty required of us. Plant your feet upon the Rock of God and stand.

Let there be no cowardly retreat or treacherous yielding to the methods of evil by which Satan seeks to devour. When a captain sees his men beginning to shrink in battle, or thinks they might be ready to flee, he charges them to stand. 'Stand like men, hold your ground, repel the enemy.' This is the sense of Paul's words here. Children of God, Satan must be stoutly resisted and never yielded to. For this we have the express command of God in Holy Scripture. 'Resist the devil, and he will flee from you' (James 4:7). 'Whom resist stedfast in the faith' (1 Peter 5:9).

To stand against Satan takes courage. That is what the girdle of truth gives, courage to stand in the heat of the battle.

Sometimes resisting Satan may cost us dear. The Apostle says, 'Ye have not yet resisted unto blood, striving against sin' (Hebrews 12:4). He implies by those words that such may be the case. Those who name the name of Christ carry his honour into the field with them. 'For Christ's sake' we must resist our adversary. Let us be like Job, who when Satan dared to say to God that Job served him for personal gain, was sorely tempted; in his family, his health, his wealth, his honour, and by his friends. Yet he stood firm, resisting Satan's assaults. He worshipped God and God gloried over Job before Satan saying, 'Still he holdeth fast his integrity' (Job 2:3).

It is our safety to stand against and resist Satan at all times. All the armour that is described here is for fighting. Yet all the armour here described is defensive, except for the sword of the Spirit. As long as we are opposing Satan, we are safe. But if we yield to him, we have no armour to secure us.

Those who enlist under the banner of the cross must burn their bridges behind them. This standing against Satan is but a part of our perseverance. 'The just shall live by faith: but if any man draw back, my soul shall have no pleasure in him' (Hebrews 10:38). The meaning of that text is just this: he that stands to his faith comes off with his life. He that recoils and runs from his colours, God will have no pleasure in him, except in the just execution of his wrath upon him.

Satan is such an enemy that the only way to deal with him is by resisting him. Though he roars like a lion he is a coward at heart. Believe this, Satan trembles in the presence of the faith of God's elect. Satan is an enemy that encroaches little by little. The Apostle says, 'Let not the sun go down upon your wrath: Neither give place to the devil' (Ephesians 4:26, 27). By that he implies that Satan gets the advantage of us little by little. Give in to one temptation and you open the door to others. Therefore, we must resist the devil at all times and in all things. Satan is an accusing enemy. When the devil accuses us, we must resist him by continually laying hold of Christ our Righteousness.

Not only must we stand against Satan, resisting his temptations; we must stand in our place. It is the soldier's responsibility to hold his station. Some have been executed for leaving their station, though they were successful. General MacArthur was a very successful soldier. But he was relieved of his duties because he refused to follow his commander's order. It is the believer's duty to stand in the particular place where God has set him. 'Let every man, wherein he is called, therein abide with God' (1 Corinthians 7:24).

We can do nothing acceptable to God, except in the place of our calling. I am sure Uzza had good intentions of keeping the ark of God, but God had not required it of him. If a man leaves his post without God's bidding, he also leaves the promise of God's protection. 'As a bird that wandereth from her nest, so is a man that wandereth from his place' (Proverbs 27:8).

God has a place for every man, woman and child in his kingdom to serve him. But no man has leave to choose his own place. Korah was punished in wrath for trying to usurp Moses' place in Israel. Saul's sacrifice was an abomination to God, because he tried to take the place of the priest. Peter was rebuked for his care about John's place. God requires no more of us than faithfulness in our place.

Let us, therefore, stand against Satan, resisting his temptations, standing faithfully at our post, standing faithfully in our work. How shall we stand? Paul tells us, 'Having your loins girt about with truth'.

Our strength

Our only strength against Satan is the truth of God. Our Lord said to Pilate, 'For this cause came I into the world, that I should bear witness unto the truth'. And Pilate said, 'What is truth?' Now you and I might ask a similar question concerning our text. What does Paul mean by 'truth'? Let us seek the answer from God, rather than going away in ignorance as Pilate did.

Three things are certainly implied in our text by this word 'truth'. Christ himself is the truth. The inspired volume of Sacred Scripture is the truth. The sincerity of heart is truth. It is not enough to have truth on our side, if we do not have truth in our hearts. Jehu was a great stickler against idolatry but he was a hypocrite at heart. We must have all three. We must have Christ to enlighten us in truth. We must have the Word of God to guide us in truth. We must have a new heart of sincerity to govern us in the truth.

Christ

Christ is the truth of God and we must have him and trust him as such. 'I am the way, the truth, and the life: no man cometh unto the Father but by me' (John 14:6). 'The law was given by Moses, but grace and truth came by Jesus Christ' (John 1:17). The Lord Jesus Christ is the truth of God. All truth is in him and comes from him. In order to have truth, we must have Christ.

Christ is the truth of all the types and shadows of the law. Those things that have now vanished away were but 'figures of the true' (Hebrews 9:24). Christ is the true bread, the true manna from heaven. He is the true brazen serpent to whom we look for healing from all our sins. He is the true rock of Israel, the foundation that supplies all our needs. Christ is the true ladder of Jacob, by which God comes to us and we come to God. Christ is the true ram that is sacrificed for us. Christ is the true Passover Lamb, by whose blood we are redeemed. Christ is the true High Priest over the house of God, who makes us accepted before God.

The Lord Jesus Christ taught the truth while he was here upon the earth. He taught us God's purpose of grace in redemption. He taught us the moral depravity and spiritual impotence of human nature, and the necessity of regeneration. He taught us the necessity of spiritual worship. He taught us the certainty of the resurrection and eternal judgment, and the bliss of eternal glory. In the life, death and resurrection of our Lord Jesus Christ, we have the full, final and complete revelation of the truth of God.

The glory of God is revealed in the face of Jesus Christ by the gospel. Christ is the Word of God, the express image of his person and the brightness of his glory. There is no knowledge of the God of truth except in his Son. Jesus Christ is the only Mediator by whom the God of glory is revealed to sinful men. If you have Christ, you have the truth. If you do not have Christ, there is no truth in you. The Lord Jesus Christ is a girdle for our loins to protect and defend us, and to strengthen us at all times.

Holy Scripture

Our minds must also be strengthened by the Word of God, which is truth. 'Wherefore gird up the loins of your mind.' Gird them up with the Word of God. This blessed Book is the Book of God. It is the inspired, inerrant, infallible Word of God. 'All Scripture is given by inspiration of God, and is profitable for doctrine, for reproof, for correction, for instruction in righteousness, that the man of God may be perfect, throughly furnished unto all good works' (2 Timothy 3:16, 17). The Holy Spirit was given upon the ascension of Christ to guide the apostles, infallibly, into all truth.

The Word of God is profitable for us in all its purposes. It is our only source of doctrine and our only rule for reproof. The Bible is our only book of discipline and is our only source of instruction in righteousness. The Word of God thoroughly supplies us with all we need for our spiritual warfare.

It seems to me that by 'truth' the apostle is here speaking of the doctrine of Christ in the Scriptures, the doctrine of the gospel. The truth of God is Substitution. The doctrine of God is the girdle of truth (Isaiah 5:27; Ephesians 1:13). The doctrine of God is the doctrine of man's utter ruin in sin, and of God's glorious sovereignty in salvation. It is the doctrine of Christ's substitutionary redemption (1 Corinthians 15:1-3; 2 Corinthians 5:21; Galatians 3:13, 14), and his sovereign Lordship by virtue of his death and resurrection.

We must have our hearts and minds strengthened with the girdle of truth. It is only by being men and women of understanding in the Scripture that we are established, strengthened and settled; that we may earnestly contend for the faith once delivered to the saints. Only as we know the Word of God, do we have strength to stand against the wiles of the devil.

When men know the truth of Christ, they are armed against false doctrine such as legalism, religious fables, doctrines of men, vain philosophy and every wind of doctrine (Ephesians 4:8-24). Only those who are settled in the truth are free to serve God. When you are established in the truth you will be bold to profess it, regardless of the consequences.

Sincerity

The saints of God must have their hearts girded about with sincerity, or truth in the heart. David said, 'Behold, thou desirest truth in the inward parts' (Psalm 51:6). This sincerity of heart is the exact opposite of hypocrisy. 'Let us draw near with a true heart' (Hebrews 10:22). 'Fear the LORD, and serve him in sincerity and in truth' (Joshua 24:14). We are to serve the Lord with the 'unleavened bread of sincerity and truth' (1 Corinthians 5:8).

Sincerity itself is nothing. We must have a godly sincerity, so that with our hearts we desire the will and glory of God. True worshippers worship God in the Spirit and in truth (John 4:23, 24). We must have truth of heart, if we would withstand the evil day. Truth of heart makes us willing to serve God and gives us strength to serve him. The person who loves God in truth, serves him, not for fear or reward, but because he loves him. It is the truth of the heart that God approves of, not the outward services. God looks on the heart. Man looks on the outward appearance.

The knowledge and belief of the truth is the first and indispensable qualification for a Christian soldier. To enter into this spiritual conflict ignorant or doubting, would be to enter battle blind and lame. As the girdle gives strength and freedom of action, and therefore confidence, so does the truth when spiritually apprehended and believed. Let no one imagine that he is prepared to withstand the assaults of the powers of darkness if his mind is stored with his own theories or with the speculations of others.

Nothing but the truth of God clearly understood and cordially embraced will enable us to keep our feet for a moment before the principalities and powers of spiritual wickedness in high places. Reason, tradition, speculative notions of religion and dead orthodoxy are a girdle of spider's web! Truth alone, abiding in the mind in the form of God-given knowledge, can give strength and confidence, even in the ordinary conflicts of the Christian life, much more in any really 'evil day'.

Putting on the girdle

The words 'having your loins girt about with truth' might better be translated 'gird yourselves with truth'. The Spirit of God here tells us that we must gird ourselves with truth. It is much the same as Paul's frequently given admonition to 'put on Christ'. I know that we can do so only as God the Holy Ghost gives us grace to do so, but this is something we are commanded to do. So, let me give you some directions for putting on the girdle of truth.

Christ is the truth of God which we must receive, put on, love and rejoice in. We must buy the truth and sell it not. Christ the truth is the rare jewel of heaven for which a man must give all things. We must worship God and walk in the truth, that means walk in Christ; by his power and after his example. Any doctrine that detracts from Christ, turns your attention away from Christ, or puts anything in the place of Christ is false doctrine.

The Word of God is the truth of God by which our hearts are established. Be like the Bereans who 'searched the scriptures daily, whether those things were so'. Do not receive anything by the mere persuasion of men, search the Scriptures. 'Study to shew thyself approved unto God, a workman that needeth not to be ashamed, rightly dividing the word of truth.' Do not enslave yourself to the judgment of any man, any denomination, any system or any creed, except, 'Thus saith the LORD'. Be careful in your attendance upon the ministry of the Word, and beware of curiosity for novel or mysterious doctrines.

Do not rest with a mere head knowledge of divine truth. Seek to know the truth by experience. Ask God to establish your heart in the truth by the instruction of the Holy Spirit. Be willing to put aside prejudice and learn the truth. 'Let every man be swift to hear, slow to speak, and slow to wrath.'

Live upon the truth you profess. Do you profess to believe in blood redemption? Then trust the blood alone to cover your sins. Do you say you believe in forgiveness? Then forgive others. Do you say that Christ is all? Then love Christ above all. Do you say you believe in God's sovereignty? Then trust him in all things. In ourselves we are weak, nothing but weakness, but God provides us with the girdle of truth.

Sincerity is the truth of God in the heart. If we would be sincere, let us have our hearts fixed upon God our Saviour. Have eyes for none but 'Jesus only'. Trust his providence, rely upon his grace, rest in his care, seek his glory. Meditate upon his own sincerity and faithfulness to you.

In this day, when many turn aside to the right hand and to the left, let us stand against the wiles of the devil. Stand for the truth and the honour of Christ. Stand in the place of your calling. 'Let us hold fast the profession of our faith without wavering; (for he is faithful that promised:)' (Hebrews 10:23). And when we have stood to the end of the battle, we will find that we stood only because Christ stood with us (2 Timothy 4:16-18).

Chapter 71

'The Breastplate Of Righteousness'

Stand therefore, having your loins girt about with truth, and having on the breastplate of righteousness.

(Ephesians 6:14)

The Apostle Paul is showing us how to make use of the armour God has graciously provided for us. The alarm has been sounded. A rousing call to battle has been issued. Our courage has been excited. The enemy has been identified. We have been assured of the victory. As Zion's soldiers, we have our marching orders. 'Wherefore, take unto you the whole armour of God, that you may be able to withstand in the evil day, and having done all, to stand.' In verse 14, God the Holy Ghost tells us how we are to stand.

In the confidence and courage of God-given faith, we have taken the field, relying upon the strength of the Almighty. Having our loins girt about with truth we are set in array against the gates of hell. The next word of instruction is our text, 'Stand … having on the breastplate of righteousness'.

The breastplate was a very important piece of armour for a Roman soldier. It extended from the base of the neck to the upper part of the thighs, covering all the vital organs of life; the heart, lungs, kidneys and abdomen. A soldier could survive many wounds to the arms or legs. But a wound in this area would be the sure forerunner of death. We can understand the breastplate was a vital piece of armour. It is not at all strange then that Paul should use the soldier's breastplate to represent the righteousness of Christ.

The righteousness of Christ is a breastplate to cover our souls and protect our hearts. Like the girdle of truth, the breastplate of righteousness is essential. These two pieces of armour are joined together in our text, as they were literally joined together when worn by a Roman soldier. The soldier's breastplate was buckled to his girdle. Both, together, are necessary.

Truth is a girdle for the loins of our soul. Having our loins girt about with truth, we are strengthened and protected. The girdle of truth gives us freedom to carry on the warfare committed to our hands. There is little danger of men being overcome by error who are firmly established in truth. But along with truth, there must be righteousness.

By every means available we must have our hearts established with the real, solid, substantial truths of the gospel, but that is not enough. We must also have the righteousness of Christ.

Believers are righteous

The righteousness of Christ is the security of our souls and the rule of our lives. This is what it is to have on 'the breastplate of righteousness'. He is truly holy who has the righteousness of Christ imputed to his account and infused into his soul. All such men live in and by the righteousness that is in Christ Jesus. Believers, regenerate men and women, are people who seek to live in the likeness of Christ, who is their Life. They are, as Jerome long ago described them, men and women 'in whose veins the blood of Christ is yet warm'. Believers were first called 'Christians' at Antioch (Acts 11:26), because they were then, and are now, men and women who are like Christ; followers of Christ and disciples of Christ.

We all know that God's people are righteous. The Lord Jesus Christ is made of God unto us righteousness. All who are born of God are made righteous by God in justification and in sanctification. Yet this righteousness is something that must be pursued by us. We are here called upon by the Spirit of God to put it on. 'Having on the breastplate of righteousness', we are to put it on as a part of 'the whole armour of God'. The righteousness of Christ is the believer's breastplate to guard us against the assaults of Satan, to secure us from all wrath and condemnation, and to make us fearless in doing the will of God.

The armour

Before we come to our text, I want to remind you that when Paul admonishes us to 'put on the whole armour of God', he is simply telling us to put on the Lord Jesus Christ. Christ in his person, offices and work is the entire armour of God for us. In these verses, the Apostle uses the various pieces of armour, by which ancient Roman soldiers were clad when they went into battle, as spiritual representations of the different branches of Christ's work for us. For example, the girdle of truth is the revelation of truth by Christ our Prophet. The breastplate of righteousness is the righteousness of Christ our Representative. The gospel of peace is the good news of Christ our High Priest. The shield of faith is the gift of Christ our ascended Lord. The helmet of salvation is the deliverance of Christ our mighty Saviour. The sword of the Spirit is the Word of God given by Christ our Mediator.

The breastplate

The first question which must be answered is this, what is this breastplate of righteousness? We must carefully avoid the mere mechanical interpretation of Scripture. We should not press the illustration of a soldier's armour too far. This is an allegory. Paul wants us to grasp the spiritual significance of his words. So, what is the righteousness Paul spoke of here?

Be sure you understand that Paul is not here talking about moral integrity or legal righteousness. The New English Bible, as it is called, translates the word 'righteousness' as 'integrity'. But the integrity of a man is not what Paul is talking about. Neither does he speak of the legal righteousness of the Mosaic law. These things can never repel the fiery darts of Satan. The things religious infidels call 'personal righteousness' and 'personal holiness' cannot resist the accusations of conscience, the whispers of despondency and the power of temptation; much less the severity of the law or the assaults of Satan.

Legal righteousness is that which God requires of man by the law. 'Moses describeth the righteousness which is of the law, That the man which doeth those things shall live by them' (Romans 10:5). If you would attain righteousness by your obedience to the law of God, if you would make yourself righteous. Three things are necessary. 1. You must render to God an absolutely perfect obedience to all the law. The whole law must be kept with the whole heart. The least defect, either in thought or deed, is the breach of all. 'For it is written, Cursed is everyone that continueth not in all things which are written in the book of the law to do them' (Galatians 3:10). 2. That perfect obedience must be perfectly performed by you personally and perpetually. 3. If the law is once broken in the slightest degree, it can never be mended, though a man live perfectly all the rest of his days.

But the Book of God declares, 'By the deeds of the law there shall no flesh be justified in his sight' (Romans 3:20). 'Knowing that a man is not justified by the works of the law, but by the faith of Jesus Christ, even we have believed in Jesus Christ, that we might be justified by the faith of Christ, and not by the works of the law: for by the works of the law shall no flesh be justified' (Galatians 2:16). We lost all hope of legal righteousness in the fall of our father Adam. By nature, we have no ability or desire to obey God's law.

No man living can be accepted by God on the grounds of legal obedience because all we do is tainted by sin. 'All are under sin; as it is written, there is none righteous, no, not one.' The most boastful philosopher among the Gentiles has nothing of which to boast before God. The most self-righteous Pharisee is nothing but a sinful mass of flesh before God. The holiest saint who ever lived can never stand accepted in any degree before God on his own merits.

Children of God, even our best righteousnesses are but filthy rags before God. David, the man after God's own heart said, 'Enter not into judgment with thy servant: for in thy sight shall no man living be justified' (Psalm 143:2).

Is the law therefore useless? No. The law is holy, and just and good for its purpose. But it was never intended as a means of acceptance with God. It was never intended to be a means of attaining righteousness or to be a rule of life. The law shows us our guilt. It restrains sin by threatening punishment. The law drives us away from Sinai to Calvary, away from Moses to Christ (Romans 10:4).

The righteousness which Paul calls our breastplate is the righteousness of Christ. This is the doctrine of the gospel, doctrine which all men by nature reject. They will not submit to the righteousness of Christ as their only righteousness and ground of acceptance with the Holy Lord God. 'They being ignorant of God's righteousness, and going about to establish their own righteousness, have not submitted themselves unto the righteousness of God. For Christ is the end of the law for righteousness to everyone that believeth' (Romans 10:3, 4).

As the disobedience of Adam made all his seed sinners, so the obedience of Christ makes all his seed righteous. The Lord Jesus Christ accomplished a perfect righteousness for us as a man, while he was here upon the earth. The Lamb of God died to satisfy the demands of justice against us because of sin. The Christ of God arose to glory to give repentance and the remission of sins to every believer.

The Scriptures everywhere declare this blessed, gospel doctrine of substitution. God requires from me a perfect obedience to his law and provides it in my Substitute. God requires the very man who sinned be infinitely punished and he punished our sins in our Substitute (Isaiah 53:4-11; Romans 3:24-26; 4:25-5:1, 10, 17-19; 2 Corinthians 5:17-21). The Substitutionary work of Christ is so perfect that God made his Son to be our sin, and he made us to be Christ's righteousness. If Christ were not made sin, it would have been most unjust for him to die. If we were not made righteous, it would be impossible for us to live. That is the doctrine of this Book.

In the new birth the sinner who trusts the Son of God, is made partaker of the divine nature (2 Peter 1:4), and the Lord Jesus Christ is formed in us (Galatians 4:19; Colossians 1:27). His righteousness is imparted to us and infused in us by the grace and power of God, making us new creatures in him (2 Corinthians 5:17).

The Puritan, William Gurnall, describes this righteousness imparted to us as 'a supernatural principle of life planted in the heart of every child of God by the powerful operation of the Holy Spirit'. This is one of those blessings of grace secured for us in the new covenant. 'A new heart also will I give you, and a new spirit will I put within you: and I will take away the stony heart out of your flesh, and I will give you an heart of flesh. And I will put my spirit within you, and cause you to walk in my statutes, and ye shall keep my judgments, and do them' (Ezekiel 36:26, 27). This is that principle of life created in us by the quickening power of God the Holy Spirit (Ephesians 2:8-10). This is that seed which cannot sin, which lives in every believer (1 John 3:9). This is the new man within us created in righteousness and true holiness. In the new birth righteousness becomes the principle by which the believer's life is governed.

This breastplate of righteousness, the righteousness by which we stand accepted with God, is the very same righteousness in which Christ himself, as our God-man Mediator, stands accepted with the Triune Jehovah (Isaiah 11:5; 59:16-21).

The comparison

Next, consider this question: Why is the righteousness of Christ compared to a breastplate? Here are three points of similarity.

The breastplate was designed to preserve the soldier's life and the righteousness of Christ preserves God's saints. His righteousness preserves us from Satan's fury and preserves us from divine judgment.

The breastplate was made for the soldier before he put it on. The righteousness of Christ was prepared for us by God himself. It was formed and moulded in the eternal covenant. It was made for God's elect at Calvary, and is put on every regenerate sinner in the new birth by the power and grace of God the Holy Spirit.

The breastplate made a soldier bold and fearless, knowing he could not now be easily harmed by his foes. The same is true of God's saints. We trust in the righteousness of Christ, and being secure in that; having the testimony of God in our hearts that we please him, redeemed and saved sinners are made bold and confident. 'The wicked flee when no man pursueth: but the righteous are bold as a lion' (Proverbs 28:1).

Our text speaks of us 'having on the breastplate', but in verse 11 the Apostle tells us to 'put on the whole armour of God' and this 'breastplate of righteousness', being part of that armour, we must put on. Time and again, we are told to put on the Lord Jesus Christ, to put on the new man, to put on righteousness. That is because we must daily seek Christ and rely upon his righteousness, daily seeking to be renewed in his grace and righteousness (Philippians 3:3-10).

By trusting

Then lastly, how do we put on the Lord Jesus Christ as the breastplate of righteousness? We must renounce all self-righteousness if we would have the righteousness of Christ and receive the righteousness of Christ by faith (Romans 5:1). We must rely upon the righteousness of Christ as our only righteousness, the only ground of acceptance before God. 'Stand therefore … having on the breastplate of righteousness.' That is what it is to live by faith. That is what it is to walk with God (Colossians 2:6). We stand against Satan, our accuser, and his temptations, trusting the righteousness of Christ our Saviour (Zechariah 3:1-9).

We stand against our own carnal nature, trusting Christ, the Lord our Righteousness. All we do is done with an eye of faith upon Christ, realising that our best works are but sin and filthy rags, and are acceptable to God only upon the righteousness of Christ (1 Corinthians 1:30, 31). In the day of judgment, when we stand before the Great White Throne, we shall stand firm; bold, confident and trusting in the righteousness of Christ.

Bold shall I stand in that great day,
For who aught to my charge shall lay,
While through Thy blood absolved I am
From sin's tremendous guilt and shame?

This is my joy, and this is the sum of all I write and preach. It was the sum and joy of all that my Saviour preached while he walked on the earth. 'I have preached righteousness in the great congregation: lo, I have not refrained my lips, O LORD, thou knowest. I have not hid thy righteousness within my heart; I have declared thy faithfulness and thy salvation: I have not concealed thy lovingkindness and thy truth from the great congregation' (Psalm 40:9, 10).

Chapter 72

The Shoes Of Gospel Peace

And your feet shall be shod with the preparation of the gospel of peace.
(Ephesians 6:15)

Over 500 years ago, Martin Luther nailed his famous Ninety-five Theses to the church door in Wittenberg, Germany, beginning the Protestant Reformation. Of all the reformers of that era, I probably have less in common with Luther theologically than many of the other men. But there are none of the reformers that I esteem more highly. Luther was bold, dogmatic, unrelenting; a manly, labouring pastor who didn't know the meaning of the words 'back-up' or 'back-off'. There was fire in his soul. He burned with passion. He did nothing by halves.

On one occasion, in great spiritual conflict in his soul with Satan, the conflict was so real it almost took on a physical manifestation. Suddenly, the fiery, passionate Martin Luther, in his great anger with Satan and his hellish assault against him, grabbed the inkwell on his desk and threw it at the devil, splattering ink all over the wall of his study. That wall stood with the ink stains on it for many years reminding those who saw it of how vivid the believer's spiritual conflict was in Luther's life.

It is that conflict Paul writes about in this sixth chapter of Ephesians. 'Finally, my brethren, be strong in the Lord, and in the power of his might. Put on the whole armour of God, that ye may be able to stand against the wiles of the devil. For we wrestle not against flesh and blood, but against principalities, against powers, against the rulers of the darkness of this world, against spiritual wickedness in high places. Wherefore take unto you the whole armour of God, that ye may be able to withstand in the evil day, and having done all, to stand. Stand therefore, having your loins girt about with truth, and having on the breastplate of righteousness; And your feet shod with the preparation of the gospel of peace; Above all, taking the shield of faith, wherewith ye shall be able to quench all the fiery darts of the wicked. And take the helmet of salvation, and the sword of the Spirit, which is the word of God' (Ephesians 6:10-17).

Every true believer is a soldier at war, enlisted in the army of Christ, beneath the banner of the cross. In this portion of Holy Scripture, the Apostle Paul is describing the believer's armour allegorically by alluding to the combat dress of the ancient Roman soldier. Each piece of the Roman soldier's armour is used to describe the spiritual weapons of our warfare. Verse 15 describes the shoes of gospel peace, 'And your feet shod with the preparation of the gospel of peace'.

We are, all the days of our lives in this world, engaged in a life and death conflict, in hand-to-hand combat, with the world, the flesh and the devil. If you go to war, you must be prepared and equipped with armour, the whole armour of God: the girdle of truth, the breastplate of righteousness and the shoes of gospel peace.

Paul's direction here, 'Stand therefore, having … your feet shod with the preparation of the gospel of peace', is an allusion to the boots worn by ancient warriors in battle. This, too, was an important part of the soldier's protection. Usually, the boots were made of brass and leather, with short nails extending from the soles. They covered the soldier's feet, ankles, and calves. These boots preserved the soldier's feet from the dangerous snares of the enemy. They secured his feet in marching and in standing his ground in battle.

What Paul teaches here is that we must have the gospel of peace to protect us, to aid us in our marches, and to enable us to stand firm in the day of conflict with our enemies. We are not to furnish ourselves, in any manner, with carnal weapons. But, having the preparation or foundation of the gospel under our feet, wearing shoes of gospel peace, we are ready to go on in our march through the world.

God's church is an army in motion (Matthew 28:18-20). The believer is a soldier on the march. Therefore, shoes are provided for his feet. He has the helmet of salvation for his head, because he is to be thoughtful. His heart is covered with the breastplate of righteousness, because he is a man of feeling. His whole nature is protected by the shield of faith, because he is called to perseverance. He has the Sword of the Spirit for his hand, with which to assail the foes. And he has the shoes of gospel peace for his feet, that he may march against the gates of hell and stand firm in the heat of battle.

We must never be passive, inanimate and motionless. God works in us to will and do of his good pleasure. His grace is the great power which secures our salvation. But his grace is also the motivation of life. Grace imparts a healthy life; and life rejoices in activity. The Lord God never intended for his people to be cold, dead statues. He means for us to have life, to have it more abundantly, to be full of life and energy. He has given us feet and he intends us to use them.

Satan cannot bear a man who serves God earnestly. He does damage to the kingdom of darkness. Therefore, he is constantly assailed by Apollyon, the dragon of hell. The devil will not leave him alone. The fiend of hell constantly seeks to destroy such a man. The prince of darkness will try, if he can, to injure the man's character, to interrupt his communion with God, to spoil the simplicity of his faith, to make him proud of what he is doing, or to make him despair of success. Satan will do anything to bruise the heels of those who march against him in the name of Christ. He tries in every way possible to trip us up. Because of all these dangers, mercy has provided gospel shoes for the believer's feet, shoes of the best kind. These are shoes that can be worn only by warriors who serve the Lord of Hosts.

The gospel does for the believer what the iron-spiked boots did for the Roman warrior. The gospel makes us ready to march, gives us a firm foothold and defends us against the snares of the devil.

The shoes

Every believer, every child of God, every soldier in Christ's army is prepared for battle with the gospel of peace as shoes for his feet. The gospel is good news of redemption by the blood of Christ. It is the message of hope, mercy and grace from the God of heaven to poor sinners. The gospel is full of blessings, any one of which would outweigh the world in value. The gospel is as free as it is full. It is everlasting and immutable. We can never think too much of the gospel or exaggerate its worth.

Paul takes from this choice gospel its most excellent essence: peace. From this peace, he tells us, shoes are prepared for the soldier of the cross. Being 'shod with the preparation of the gospel of peace', a man walks over the lion and the serpent unharmed. He walks over the burning coals of malice, slander and persecution untouched. What better shoes could our souls require? Gospel peace provides shoes suitable to the feet of every soldier and pilgrim who is marching to Zion.

The gospel proclaims the accomplishment of peace. When God created the first man Adam, there was a perfect love and peace between them. God was at peace with man. Man was at peace with God. They had sweet fellowship and communion with one another walking together in the Garden. But when Adam sinned, peace was broken. Immediately, a quarrel began. Ever since Adam rebelled against God there has been a quarrel between God and man.

This is a mutual and universal quarrel. All men by nature are at war with God. We were all 'children of wrath, even as others' (Ephesians 2:3). 'The carnal mind is enmity against God: for it is not subject to the law of God, neither indeed can be' (Romans 8:7). The apostle tells us we were alienated from God and enemies in our minds (Colossians 1:21). Every part of man's being is opposed to God (Romans 3:10-18). Man's understanding is opposed to God's wisdom. Man's heart is opposed to God's heart. His will is opposed to God's will, and his mind is opposed to God's mind.

Because man is at arms against God, so God in justice is opposed to every man. 'God is angry with the wicked every day ... He hath bent his bow, and made it ready. He hath also prepared for him the instruments of death' (Psalm 7:11-13).

God has set up the royal standard of his law in defiance of all the sons of Adam. 'The soul that sinneth, it shall die.' All men have rebelled against the crown of heaven. They are traitors to the dignity of God's own majesty. As such, God has taken the field against them with the fire and sword of divine vengeance.

At every place where sin sets its foot against God in the earth, there the wrath of God meets fallen man. As man is altogether sinful, so he is altogether cursed. Inside and outside, body and soul, man is the object of divine wrath by nature. God is so angry with man that it is written, even 'the sacrifice of the wicked is an abomination to the LORD' (Proverbs 15:8).

On God's part this is a righteous quarrel. He has every reason to be angry with man. Sin is the breach of God's will and the transgression of God's law. It is an affront to God's holiness and open rebellion against God's sovereignty. Sin is the assault of God's character and the attempt of man to rob God of his glory. It is man's attempt to rape the Almighty, shove him off his throne, and assassinate the God of Glory! Indeed, God has every reason to be angry with man. But on man's part the quarrel is altogether unrighteous and unreasonable. God has done nothing to deserve our enmity.

Unless this quarrel is taken up by a suitable daysman, by a satisfactory mediator, it will be an everlasting quarrel. Death brings an end to other feuds, but not to this one. Death brings the sinner into an endless state of misery and torment, where he goes on hating, cursing and blaspheming God; and God goes on hating, plaguing and punishing man eternally.

Such is man's condition by nature. He is under the sentence of wrath. But the gospel is the message of peace, proclaiming that God's own Son has accomplished peace for sinners! The guilty sinner is surrounded on every side with the flood of divine wrath. No help is to be seen, no hope is to be heard of until the gospel comes, like the dove bringing the olive branch of peace. In the gospel we are told that the tide is turned, the flood of wrath has now been dried up by Christ our Substitute, who was 'made a curse for us'.

Blessed be God, the Lord Jesus Christ, God's own dear Son, has intervened on our behalf. He took up the quarrel and made peace through the blood of his cross! God demanded righteousness. Christ gave it. He demanded blood. Christ gave it. God demanded death. Christ gave it.

Being the God-man, Christ our Mediator settled the quarrel. He satisfied divine justice and made our peace with God. 'God was in Christ, reconciling the world unto himself' (2 Corinthians 5:19). 'When we were enemies, we were reconciled to God by the death of his Son' (Romans 5:10).

Having satisfied God's anger against man, our Mediator takes away man's enmity against God by the gospel alone. Through the gospel, the Holy Spirit changes the rebel sinner's heart. In the gospel, Christ proclaims the terms of peace. The sinner must confess his guilt. He must throw down his weapons of warfare and surrender to mercy. He must sue for mercy at the throne of grace. He must believe the gospel. 'Therefore being justified by faith, we have peace with God' (Romans 5:1). Faith does not constitute or accomplish our justification and peace, but it does receive it.

The gospel gives us perfect peace of conscience. There is nothing which will so well prepare the saints for doing the Lord's bidding as peace of heart. A sense of perfect peace with God is the grandest thing in all the world to sustain God's soldiers. By the gospel we are assured that sin and guilt is gone, God is reconciled, and condemnation is lifted.

Let a man know his sins are forgiven for Christ's sake, that he is reconciled to God by the death of his Son, that between him and God there is no wall of separation and see what joy floods his soul. When we know God looks upon us as being cleansed from every speck of sin by the blood of Christ, that we are accepted in the Beloved and we are forever reconciled to God, then we can march through life without fear. 'There is no fear in love; but perfect love casteth out fear' (1 John 4:18). When a man is at peace with God, he has no reason to fear. 'If God be for us, who can be against us.'

We can march peacefully through the roughest places of our pilgrimage when we have communion with God. Communion brings peace. The promises of the gospel sustain us with great peace. Christ has promised to protect us, keep us, guide us, provide for us, and to never leave us. Christ has promised us a kingdom. Oh, weary pilgrims, look over the Book of promises once again and be at peace. For all the promises of God are in Christ Jesus, yea and amen.

When the gospel reconciles our hearts in all things to the heart of our Redeemer, then we have peace. We walk in peace only as we walk with God, having our feet shod with the gospel of peace. Let us walk in faith, trusting Christ for everything. Walk in joy, having all in him. Walk in peace, knowing his presence. Walk in thanksgiving, knowing his goodness. Walk in hope, relying upon his promise. 'The peace of God will keep your hearts and minds through Christ Jesus the Lord.'

'Rejoice in the Lord alway: and again I say, Rejoice. Let your moderation be known unto all men. The Lord is at hand. Be careful for nothing; but in everything by prayer and supplication with thanksgiving let your requests be made known unto God. And the peace of God, which passeth all understanding, shall keep your hearts and minds through Christ Jesus. Finally, brethren, whatsoever things are true, whatsoever things are honest, whatsoever things are just, whatsoever things are pure, whatsoever things are lovely, whatsoever things are of good report; if there be any virtue, and if there be any praise, think on these things' (Philippians 4:4-8).

The gospel is called the gospel of peace, because it also gives us peace with one another. There is in Christ Jesus a union between us and all believers, and we should walk in peace toward our brethren. In Christ all natural distinctions of race, sex and class are destroyed. There should be nothing to divide me in heart from any man in the kingdom of Christ. 'If it be possible, as much as lieth in you, live peaceably with all men' (Romans 12:18). 'Blessed are the peacemakers: for they shall be called the children of God' (Matthew 5:9).

Having described these shoes, let me say this: These were the shoes our Master wore; and these are the shoes he gives us to wear. 'Peace I leave with you, my peace I give unto you' (John 14:27). Christ always lived in communion with his Father, and sought the good of his brethren. He had for his enemies only prayers and tears. As peace kept him all the days of his life, so it will keep us. You never find him worried, disturbed or frustrated, because his feet were shod with peace.

The preparation

The gospel of peace was prepared by God himself. In the counsel of peace, before the world began, the Triune God resolved upon the most suitable way to accomplish peace for us. He made Christ the Mediator of peace. He agreed upon the terms of peace and in the fulness of time, he sent his Son to accomplish peace by his substitutionary work.

The wisdom of God could not have devised a method of salvation more advantageous to the exalting of his own glorious name and the happiness of his people than he has done by reconciling us to himself through Christ the Mediator. By the death of Christ, God displayed sin it its most hideous character. At Calvary, God displayed the fulness of his justice. At the cross, God displayed his own infinite holiness. Through the sacrifice of his Son, God gave the fullest possible display of his infinite love and mercy. Through the substitutionary work of Christ for our salvation, God destroyed every ground for human pride.

Having prepared peace for us, God proclaims peace to poor sinners by the gospel. But before any sinner will ever seek peace with God, God must prepare the heart of his elect to receive it. This is the difference between the true believer and the carnal professor. God destroys every false hope of peace. By the law he makes the sinner know his guilt. By the gospel he breaks the sinner's heart and crushes his rebellion in the revelation of Christ. Then he sends forth his Spirit as the messenger of peace to poor sinners.

The Lord God graciously prepares all his children for their pilgrimage to glory with the gospel of peace. The word 'preparation' here simply means to make ready and firmly establish, or to fix upon a firm foundation. God makes his servants, who must lead the way in Zion, ready to preach the gospel. Those who preach the gospel stand in the forefront of the battle. They must be established with a firm and solid knowledge of the gospel, ready to march through this world with peace.

The shoes' value

I rejoice to tell you that these gospel shoes fit perfectly. Many would give you the shoes of the law. With them there is much straining, tugging and pulling. When you get them on, they are too tight and give much pain. With the law, there is no peace. But for poor lame Mephibosheths, gospel shoes work miracles. They make us to leap and dance before God. This is an old shoe that is just suited for us. It helps our infirmities, heals the wounds of our sin, and strengthens our weak knees. Let me show you how comfortable these shoes are.

The preparation of the gospel of peace is a shoe that gives us a firm foothold. Habakkuk must have been singing of this shoe when he said, 'The Lord God is my strength, and he will make my feet like hinds' feet, and he will make me to walk upon mine high places' (Habakkuk 3:19). Nothing helps a man to stand fast in the Lord like the gospel of peace. Doctrinal error shall not overthrow him. Temptation shall not take him in its snare. Assaults will not move him. Fear will not make him flee.

Our shoes are driven into the eternal truths of God and they hold like anchors. Our creed is interwoven with personal experience, and we cannot deny it. We have nothing to do with an atonement that does not atone. Let others preach salvation by free-will if they please, we declare nothing but free-grace. Sovereignty, substitution and satisfaction are cleats in our shoes, nails in the soles of our gospel boots, that enable us to stand firm.

The shoes of which our text speaks are most suitable for marching. A sense of pardoned sin and reconciliation to God prepares us for anything and everything. When the burden of sin is gone, all other burdens are light.

These gospel shoes effectually preserve us in the King's highway. The way is sometimes rough and rugged. It is stained with the blood of pilgrims before us. It is a narrow way but the peace of the gospel keeps us in the way.

These gospel shoes are good for climbing, too. By the gospel we sometimes climb Mt. Tabor and behold Jesus only. Sometimes we go to the heights of Mt. Pisgah, and, by the gospel, we get a vision of the Glory Land that is soon to be revealed. How blessed are those hours when we can by the gospel ascend Hermon, and commune with God face to face. There God speaks to us as a man does with his familiar friend.

The heart that is prepared with the peace of the gospel has shoes suitable for running as well as climbing. When our hearts are assured by the gospel of peace with God, then do we run with patience the race that is set before us, and walk in peace through the dark valley.

These gospel shoes are also good for fighting. Being armed with the gospel of peace, we stand fast in the evil day. We withstand every accusation. We march stedfastly against every foe; the world, the flesh and the devil. And soon the promise shall come, 'The God of peace shall bruise Satan under your feet shortly'.

'Stand therefore having … your feet shod with the preparation of the gospel of peace.' Then, my friends, we shall be able to say with Paul, 'I am ready'. He is the strongest, ablest man in the world who has peace, 'the peace of God, which passeth all understanding' (Philippians 4:7). He is ready to work, ready to fight the good fight, ready to suffer, ready to preach, ready to die. May God the Holy Ghost put on you and me the shoes of the gospel of peace, for Christ's sake!

Chapter 73

The Shield Of Faith

Above all, taking the shield of faith, wherewith ye shall be able to quench all the fiery darts of the wicked.

(Ephesians 6:16)

Like the Spartans of old, every child of God is born a warrior. It is our destiny to be assaulted. It is our duty to attack. We are constantly engaged in defensive warfare. Satan is a relentless foe, assailing our souls day and night, sometimes openly, more often with great subtlety. We are required to earnestly defend the faith that was once delivered to the saints. We have to resist the wicked one and stand against the wiles of the devil. And having done all, still we must stand.

But that man is a poor excuse for a soldier who only defends. The Church of God is the army of Christ. That army is an offensive army, storming the gates of hell with the gospel. The Christian, the believer, the child of God, is a soldier who is on the march against the powers of darkness. Like David, he says, 'I come to thee in the name of the LORD of hosts, the God of the armies of Israel, whom thou hast defied' (1 Samuel 17:45). We wrestle not against flesh and blood, but against principalities and powers. The weapons of our warfare are not carnal, but spiritual, 'mighty through God to the pulling down of strong holds' (2 Corinthians 10:4). Onward, my brethren, onward we must go, attacking the castles of darkness, pulling down their strongholds, and driving the Canaanites from the land. What does our Captain say? 'Go ye into all the world, and preach the gospel to every creature' (Mark 16:15).

We must never forget these facts. We must never be found sleeping. The watchmen on the walls of Zion; gospel preachers, must never allow themselves the leisure of ease and rest. God's servants must be vigilant and alert. You who are Zion's soldiers must never become indifferent about your responsibility in the place assigned to you. Therefore, God the Holy Ghost, by the Apostle Paul gives a rousing call to arms in Ephesians 6:10-20. In order to properly prepare us for our daily warfare, this valiant and well-experienced soldier tells us the various pieces of armour which we must use, and how to use them; the girdle of truth, the breastplate of righteousness, and the shoes of gospel peace.

In verse 16, we are exhorted to arm ourselves with the shield of faith. 'Above all, taking the shield of faith, wherewith ye shall be able to quench all the fiery darts of the wicked.'

Faith is the grace of graces. It stands here in the midst of her companions: truth, righteousness, peace, salvation and revelation. It stands among them as the heart is in the midst of the body. It is like David when Samuel 'anointed him in the midst of his brethren'. When Paul comes to speak of faith, he seems to lift its head above all its fellows, giving it pre-eminence. 'Above all, taking the shield of faith.'

The grace of faith is like the shield of mighty men, by which mighty things are done, and by which the believer not only repels, but conquers the enemy.

Faith

First, let me say something about faith itself. I want to answer this very important question: what is the faith which serves the believer as a shield? We are living in a day when the souls of men are being deceived with many substitutes for 'the faith of God's elect'. Faith is more than a mere decision. It is more than a system of doctrine. It is more than a plan of salvation. What is the faith which is here commended to us? What is this shield of faith?

Frequently, God himself, the Triune Jehovah, the great object of faith, is represented as a shield for his people. As our God is the object of our faith, he is a shield to our souls. 'After these things the word of the LORD came unto Abram in a vision, saying, Fear not, Abram: I am thy shield, and thy exceeding great reward' (Genesis 15:1).

All the perfections of God; his power, faithfulness, truth and immutability encompass the saints as a shield. By faith, we lay hold of God's perfections to oppose the temptations of Satan.

As the love and favour of God are objects of faith, these are a shield for us as well. 'For thou, LORD, wilt bless the righteous; with favour wilt thou compass him as with a shield' (Psalm 5:12). 'For the LORD God is a sun and shield: the LORD will give grace and glory: no good thing will he withhold from them that walk uprightly' (Psalm 84:11).

The word 'faith' sometimes represents the doctrine of the gospel. It is the faith once delivered to the saints. The gospel of Christ, and the truths and promises of it are a shield to God's children. Our Lord Jesus Christ, the One we trust, is the whole of our faith. Christ is our Shield faith. By faith we hold up the Person, blood and righteousness of our Substitute against Satan's accusations. Christ is our shield of protection and security from the wrath of God, divine justice and eternal death.

Certainly, when we think of faith as a shield, we must not exclude these objects of faith. But in our text, Paul speaks of the grace of faith as the believer's shield. This is what we call saving or justifying faith. This is the grace which makes God's saints a match for the devil. Those who truly have this God-given, God-wrought faith as their shield are as sure of victory, as if they were now sitting upon the triumphal chariot in glory. John wrote, 'Ye have overcome the wicked one ... This is the victory that overcometh the world, even our faith' (1 John 2:13; 5:4). What is this faith, by which sinners receive God's salvation and triumph over the devil?

Satan has raised up many counterfeits by which he deceives the souls of many. When he cannot deceive with a counterfeit, he tries to bring us into despair with doubts. There are many who have no other hope of heaven than a mere historical faith. That is, they have received the historical facts of the gospel and agree with them, but this is not true faith. This is the faith of devils. The devils believe the same facts as most religionists. 'Thou believest that there is one God; thou doest well: the devils also believe, and tremble' (James 2:19).

Many take up a temporary faith under some influence of religion. This it is like seed on stony ground; received in a heart that is not prepared by Holy Spirit conviction and it soon withers away. Multitudes in our day are deceived by 'miracle faith'. They have either seen, or experienced some supernatural miracle, or at least think they have; and they believe, not upon the foundation of God's truth, but upon the basis of the miracle, like those who saw our Lord's miracles and those who ate the loaves and fish.

Another thing, saving faith is not a bare assent to the truths of the gospel. One of the greatest dangers of modern-day fundamentalism is that of presenting men with the truths of the gospel and persuading them to profess faith on the basis of their argument with those truths. They present men with 'four spiritual laws', 'the plan of salvation', or take them down 'the Romans road', then tell them they are born-again by agreeing with those truths. The poor, bewildered sinner, too ignorant to know better, is told simply to repeat a prayer with the 'soul-winner', then he is told he is saved. My soul rises with indignation against these butchers of souls!

It needs to be understood that justifying faith is not assurance. When Satan cannot deceive the soul with a false faith, he tries to destroy the comfort of faith by telling us that unless we have assurance, we do not have faith. Brethren, assurance is a great, comforting, desirable gift of grace. But many dear saints do not have assurance. Assurance is not faith. It is the fruit of faith. John wrote to them that believe on the name of the Son of God, that they might know that they had eternal life. The commandment is not, 'Be assured that your sins are forgiven, and that you are God's child'. The commandment is, 'Believe on the Lord Jesus Christ, and thou shalt be saved'. Faith is resting upon Christ crucified for the pardon of sin and everlasting life; upon the warrant of God's own promise.

The unique object of faith is Jesus Christ crucified. The only ground of faith upon which we have hope of eternal life is the substitutionary work of Christ (1 Corinthians 15:1-3). Faith believes that God is willing to pardon sin and trusts him to do so by Christ. We see that Christ has made a suitable payment to divine justice. Our faith is not merely in Christ as the Son of God, but as the bleeding, dying, sin-atoning, risen, accepted Substitute, who is the Son of God. There is no redemption, no pardon, no forgiveness without the shedding of blood. We trust him 'whom God hath set forth to be a propitiation through faith in his blood' (Romans 3:25).

There are, according to the Scriptures, three things essential to saving faith. First, before any man will ever trust Christ, he must have a knowledge of him. 'Faith cometh by hearing, and hearing by the word of God' (Romans 10:17). Man must know his need of Christ and he must know Christ's power to satisfy that need. Then, second, there must be an assent or agreement to God's testimony concerning his Son. Third, and only then, there is trust or confidence in Christ. This is resigning and committing the soul to Christ, trusting everything to his hands. Faith ventures on Christ and is commitment to Christ (Luke 14:25-33; John 2:23, 24).

Faith a shield

Second, why does the apostle compare faith to a shield? A shield is a piece of armour soldiers carried with them onto the battlefield when they were to engage the enemy. It defended them against the weapons of their foes. Faith is a necessary part of our armour in this world, our field of battle. All Christ's soldiers must carry this shield into the field against their enemy the devil. Faith is a shield to defend us against sin, Satan, the lusts of the flesh and the soul-assaulting allurements of the world. Let me give you just a few reasons why faith is compared to a shield.

Like a shield, faith protects every spiritual faculty of the believer. The helmet defends the head. The breastplate defends the breast. The shoes defend the feet, but the shield defends all. The shield of faith protects us against those temptations which Satan levels at the head. The deceiver tries to get us to doubt the truth of God concerning the eternal deity of Christ, the Trinity, the covenant of grace, the virgin birth, the incarnation, real substitution, the satisfaction of Christ, and the new nature of the believer, telling us that since we cannot understand them, they must not be true. The child of God humbly resists Satan's temptation, saying, 'I will trust the Word of God, rather than my own reason. What I cannot comprehend, I will nevertheless believe.'

Very often the fiend of hell strives to hit the believer's conscience with one of his fiery darts. He is a vicious and cruel enemy. He aims his assaults to wound and terrify the conscience of God's children. He reminds us of the evil of our sin, the wickedness of our hearts, and the infirmities of our flesh. How he delights to disturb the peace of God's saints. He raises Moses up and seeks to condemn in conscience those he can never condemn at the bar of God. But faith steps in like a shield and protects us from the malice of the old serpent. Faith responds to Satan's accusations, 'Christ died for sinners and I am a sinner, the worst of sinners, yet as Christ died to secure mercy for sinners, I throw myself upon the arms of mercy'. Hear the Word of God. 'If our heart condemn us, God is greater than our heart, and knoweth all things' (1 John 3:20).

The devil never tires. When one assault fails, he comes at us from another side. He tries to ensnare the affections of our hearts, or to deaden our fervent love to Christ. He will set the pleasures and profits of the world before us. 'If you will but compromise a little, look what you can have', he says. 'If you will leave off this point of conscience, look what you can gain.' If that does not work, he makes all the wealth, fame and honour of the world most appealing in order to turn our eyes away from Christ and the world to come.

As a shield enables the soldier to do mighty things in battle, so faith enables God's saints to do mighty things in their march to Zion. Faith enabled Abel to worship God in the teeth of opposition. Faith enabled Enoch to walk with God in a crooked and perverse generation. Faith enabled Noah to obey God when all the world rebelled against him. Faith enabled Abraham and Sarah to have a son in their old age. Faith enabled Abraham to sacrifice everything to the will of God. Faith enabled Moses to deny the pleasures of Egypt and to deliver Israel. Faith kept the harlot Rahab from perishing. Faith stopped the mouth of the lions for Daniel. Faith preserved the three Hebrew children in the fiery furnace.

Above all

Third, how is the shield of faith above the other pieces of our armour? 'Above all, taking the shield of faith.' The shield was prized by the ancient foot soldiers more than any piece of armour. They counted it a greater shame to lose their shield than to lose the field in battle. They esteemed it an honour to die with their shield in their hand. Once it is reported that as a young Spartan went off to war, his mother laid this charge upon him. 'See that you either bring your shield home with you, or that you are brought home on your shield.' She would rather see him dead, than come home having forsaken his shield.

Faith is above our other pieces of armour because faith quenches all the fiery darts of the wicked one. The assaults and temptations of Satan are called fiery darts, because they come suddenly, swiftly and in great numbers. They are like those poisonous darts which, if they even graze the skin, fill the body with fever. They are grievous and troublesome. They inflame the mind, exciting us to sin. They are like those arrows which are set on fire and shot into the city to burn it up. But faith quenches these fiery darts, by laying hold of the blood, righteousness, intercession and dominion of Christ the Lord. Faith is above the others, because faith in Christ tells us that everything we do for him is acceptable to our God. All we do is tainted with sin, but faith pleads the merits of Christ, doing all for his sake; and God accepts our work according to our faith.

Faith strengthens all other graces. When love is cold, faith enflames it with the love of Christ. When strength fails us, faith lays hold of Christ's strength. When sin besets us, faith establishes us with the righteousness of Christ. When we are doubtful, faith supports us with hope. When we fall under the assaults of Satan, faith picks us up. When we are despondent, faith restores our joy, when we are despairing, faith re-assures us. Faith may be hindered, but never entirely broken, or lost. Our Lord says, 'I have prayed for thee, that thy faith fail not' (Luke 22:32).

Do you have this shield of faith? True faith produces a heart love, heart submission and heart obedience to Christ. Those who have this faith constantly feel their need of Christ and constantly seek him and communion with him. Those who have this faith do not simply trust Christ in spiritual matters, we trust him in every detail of life. 'The just shall live by his faith.' If you have this shield of faith then take it with you always. It should be taken up every morning and carried with you through the day. Take it up at home, at work and when you come to the house of God. Take it with you to the hospital bed and to the house of mourning. Take it with you everywhere, ever anticipating Christ's appearance and his glory.

Chapter 74

‘The Helmet Of Salvation’

And take the helmet of salvation.

(Ephesians 6:17)

The soldiers of Christ must ‘take the helmet of salvation’. If we were not soldiers, we would not need armour. But being soldiers, we need to be covered from head to foot with armour that has been proved. Being a soldier during a time of war, is not a very pleasant occupation. It is one thing to enlist in the army when there is no prospect of people actually going to war. It is something else to enlist when you know you will soon be on the battlefield. The flesh is naturally opposed to warfare. When the battle is hot and long, we are all tempted to desert our colours. That we have no abiding city here is a truth we all know. Yet most of us try to make the earth as comfortable for ourselves as if it were our abiding residence. We are all soldiers in a battle. We know that. Yet we often think we can be friends of the world and the friends of God at the same time.

Often I meet with brothers and sisters in Christ who are very troubled. They are having struggles with lusts, temptations and sins they never met with before. That is not at all surprising. When you united with God’s saints, under the banner of the cross, you did not sheathe your sword. You drew it out against the enemy. Perhaps it would be better when people joined the church, if we did not congratulate them, as though the victory were won. It might be better to give them a word of preparation. Maybe we should, even then, sound the trumpet. When you take up the banner of the cross, you may be assured, the enemy will begin to march against you. The fight has just begun.

Always at war

Remember, brothers and sisters in Christ, we are soldiers at all times. We ought to sit, even at our table, as a soldier sits, ever ready for battle. We should go out into the world as a soldier goes out to battle. Having put your armour on, never take it off. If you do, in some unguarded moment, you may meet with serious wounds. We are marching as soldiers in the enemy's country. We are engaged in battle against one who will never make a truce. Be sure you know who your enemies are: the world, the flesh and the devil. Right up to the river's edge, the conflict must be waged. The ground must be taken foot by foot, inch by inch. Not one step may be taken on this side of Jordan without conflict and strife. Once you are on the other side, you can lay aside your sword and take up your palm branch. There you can take off your helmet and wear your crown. When we have entered the Land of Promise, our hands shall no longer learn war. Our hearts will learn the music of peace, rest and victory. But until then, we are at war. If you would wear the Saviour's crown, you must carry his cross. If you would win the victory, you must fight the enemy. If you would win the prize, you must run the race.

Hope is our helmet

With this in mind, the Apostle tells us we must 'take the helmet of salvation'. The helmet was a cap of thick leather, or brass, extending from the base of the neck over the soldier's forehead. On the top there was an ornament and coat of arms. The purpose of a helmet was to protect the head from blows from an axe or sword.

What Paul here calls 'salvation', in 1 Thessalonians 5:8, he calls 'the hope of salvation'. Like the soldier's helmet, a well-founded hope of salvation will preserve us in this day of spiritual conflict. It will give us confidence and guard us against the blows of the enemy. A 'good hope' of salvation defends the soul from attacks by the world, assaults of our proud flesh and Satan's fiery darts. Soldiers do not fight well without a hope of victory and the soldier of Christ cannot contend well with his foes without the hope of final salvation, a 'good hope through grace' (2 Thessalonians 2:16). The knowledge and assured hope of salvation and eternal glory by Christ will sustain the believer throughout his warfare upon the earth. If we have the hope of eternal life as the anchor of our souls, what have we to dread?

Isaiah 59

In all that Paul urges in Ephesians 6:10-20, he is telling us that as the soldiers of Christ in this world, as in all other things, we must follow the example of our Lord Jesus Christ, the Captain of our salvation. In Isaiah 59:16-19, the prophet of God gives us the example Paul urges us to follow. 'And he – the Son of God, our Saviour, the Lord Jesus Christ – saw that there was no man, and wondered that there was no intercessor: therefore his arm brought salvation unto him; and his righteousness, it sustained him. For he put on righteousness as a breastplate, and an helmet of salvation upon his head; and he put on the garments of vengeance for clothing, and was clad with zeal as a cloke. According to their deeds, accordingly he will repay, fury to his adversaries, recompence to his enemies; to the islands he will repay recompence. So shall they fear the name of the LORD from the west, and his glory from the rising of the sun. When the enemy shall come in like a flood, the Spirit of the LORD shall lift up a standard against him'.

As the enemy comes in like a flood, may the Spirit of God lift up the banner of the cross, 'Jesus Christ and him crucified', in our hearts against him!

Our helmet

What is our helmet? I want to show you the answer to this question from the Word of God. The Apostle is drawing attention to the head and brain; the understanding, and mind of the heaven-born soul. He has dealt with the feelings and sensibilities, the emotions and desires of the believer already. We have seen how the enemy attacks at those points. Now we must be careful to protected the head as well.

Some seem satisfied to protect their feelings and emotions. I know that is needful; but it is not sufficient. The emotions of the heart and the understanding of the head cannot be separated. Both heart and head are vital and must be protected. By all means, get the breastplate of righteousness and the shield of faith, but do not overlook your head. Get understanding, too. When Paul speaks of the helmet of salvation he is speaking of our entire attitude toward God's salvation.

Gospel doctrine

We must have a sound doctrinal understanding of salvation. It is true that doctrinal knowledge is not in itself salvation. But without a doctrinal knowledge of salvation there is no salvation. Our doctrinal knowledge may be in the simplest form, but it is necessary. Faith without knowledge is mere superstition. See to it your heart burns with fervent love. But see to it that your head is established with knowledge also. This was Paul's exhortation to young Timothy. 'For God hath not given us the Spirit of fear; but of power, and of love, and of a sound mind' (2 Timothy 1:7).

I make no apology for being a doctrinal preacher. It is the responsibility of every gospel preacher to feed his congregation with sound doctrine. God's promise to the church in the New Testament was this, 'I will give you pastors according to mine heart, which shall feed you with knowledge and understanding' (Jeremiah 3:15). In most places, when men seek a pastor, they seek everything in him except a man with the God-given ability to feed their souls with the Word of God. Most congregations want a man who is good at working with young people, or good to visit, or good at counselling. But as for sound, thorough and consistent exposition of sacred Scripture, they care little. It is the business of a pastor to preach. The only way for him to feed his congregation is to spend his time in prayer, meditation and study of the Scriptures. Every gospel preacher must give himself to this work! This is the work of the ministry (1 Timothy 4:13-16).

The doctrine by which I feed your souls is the doctrine of the gospel. This is the message of the Bible. From the beginning to the end, the Word of God is designed to show men the necessity and way of salvation by Christ. No matter what our subject is, no matter what our text is, we are to preach the gospel to men.

We must maintain God's absolute sovereignty, and continually set before men their depravity, inability and condemnation. We rejoice to encourage the hope of sinners with the message of unconditional, personal, eternal election. Our hearts rejoice to declare that Christ has accomplished the salvation of his people by an effectual redemption and to make men see there is no possibility of salvation without the omnipotent calling of the Holy Spirit. We delight to comfort those who trust the Saviour with truths of our final perseverance and preservation in the faith by the power of God. We assure poor, needy sinners with the promise of God that, 'Whosoever believeth that Jesus is the Christ is born of God' (1 John 5:1).

In a word, we make all men to know that man is a sinful, condemned, rebellious, hell-deserving creature, while God is glorious in mercy. We say 'salvation is of the Lord'. Our salvation was purposed in eternity, accomplished at Calvary, applied in time, and shall be perfected in glory by the three Persons of the Holy Trinity.

Shall we apologize for this? Never! This is the message of Scripture. 'Then he said unto them, O fools, and slow of heart to believe all that the prophets have spoken: Ought not Christ to have suffered these things, and to enter into his glory? And beginning at Moses and all the prophets, he expounded unto them in all the scriptures the things concerning himself' (Luke 24:25-27).

This is the message God uses to save sinners, comfort and edify the saints, and magnify the name of Christ (Acts 20:26, 27; 1 Corinthians 2:2). For us who know it best, there is no message so sweet, comforting, joyful, edifying and refreshing as the old, old story of the gospel. When the saints of God have a good understanding in the gospel, it will give them a sound mind and serve them like a soldier's helmet. It will protect from attacks of scepticism and all the assaults of heresy. A sound knowledge of the gospel will protect from those times of personal unbelief and from the vain philosophies of men. A knowledge of gospel doctrine will protect you from every false gospel and the doctrines of men that are contrary to the truth.

We do not need to study what the various cults believe. We need to study the gospel of Christ. Then when we see heresy, we will know it. The best way to prove that a stick is crooked is to lay a straight one beside it.

Good hope

The best way to interpret scripture is to compare scripture with scripture. If you compare our text, 'And take the helmet of salvation', with 1 Thessalonians 5:8, 9, you will see that Paul is talking about the believer's hope. 'But let us, who are of the day, be sober, putting on the breastplate of faith and love; and for an helmet, the hope of salvation. For God hath not appointed us to wrath, but to obtain salvation by our Lord Jesus Christ.' Hope in this context is the desire and expectation of eternal salvation. The soldier fights with confidence because he has a good hope of victory. Fight on, saints of God, Christ gives us hope, a 'good hope through grace', a sure hope. Like Jeremiah, our troubles will be many; but the Lord is our portion forever; and we may safely hope in him (Lamentations 3:21-26).

Get the silly notion out of your head that there is something magical about Christianity that will keep you from all the problems of life. As long as we are in this world, we will have trouble, tribulation and sorrow. But we do not despair. We have hope in Christ, both sure and stedfast. We hope in God's covenant mercies, the Saviour's eternal love, Christ's unfailing faithfulness and in the Lord's saving goodness. We hope and patiently wait for the salvation of the Lord.

Three tenses

It is true that our salvation was finished from the foundation of the world by the purpose of God, obtained at Calvary by Christ's precious blood, and is accomplished in us in regeneration by the Spirit's omnipotent mercy. Yet there are three tenses of salvation. One, we have been saved. We were chosen in Christ before the foundation of the world, redeemed by Christ at Calvary, and regenerated by Christ in the new birth. Two, we are being saved. We are not yet made perfect. And, three, there is for us a future tense of salvation. The day is coming when we shall be perfectly conformed to the image of our Saviour. It is the hope of this salvation Paul speaks of as 'the helmet of salvation'.

Do not allow your troubles that come from all directions to overwhelm you. Christ is ours. Christ is coming and we have the hope of salvation by him, in him, and with him. Our Lord told us there would be wars and rumours of wars, sorrow and great tribulation. But he said, 'Watch and pray' and 'faint not'. Take 'for an helmet, the hope of salvation' (1 Thessalonians 5:8). The King is coming riding upon the clouds of glory, victory is sure.

Our troubles will be many, but 'our light affliction, which is but for a moment, worketh for us a far more exceeding and eternal weight of glory' (2 Corinthians 4:17). 'But the God of all grace, who hath called us unto his eternal glory by Christ Jesus, after that ye have suffered a while, make you perfect, stablish, strengthen, settle you' (1 Peter 5:10). After we have suffered a while, Christ will come!

John told us of the many beasts of persecution; of military power, economic power, religious power and earthly catastrophes that would afflict the church in all ages. But he also said we have hope. 'Behold, he cometh.' Let us be 'looking for that blessed hope, and the glorious appearing of the great God and our Saviour Jesus Christ' (Titus 2:13).

Assurance

When Paul tells us to 'take the helmet of salvation', he means also we should seek an assured knowledge of our interests in Christ, who is our Salvation. There is an assurance which we must denounce. It is a carnal, hypocritical assurance. There are multitudes who perish in their sins with a presumptuous assurance that they are saved, yet without any warrant from the Word of God. I endeavour to shatter to pieces the false, carnal assurance of religious professors. But the children of God should seek a confident assurance of their interest in Christ.

I know there are some of God's true people who do not enjoy the blessedness of assurance. Assurance and salvation are not the same thing. A man is saved by faith in Christ, no matter how weak and trembling that faith may be. Assurance is often wrongly sought through works and emotions, as a result many lack the comfort, joy and confidence of settled assurance built on gospel understanding.

The helmet is usually the last piece of armour a soldier puts on and assurance is sometimes one of the last graces that a believer obtains. First, there must be the breastplate of righteousness, the shield of faith, the girdle of truth, and the shoes of gospel peace. Then comes the helmet of an assured salvation.

Like salvation, assurance is a gift of God's grace. If you would have it, you must seek it from him. Assurance comes to us by a living union with Christ and a stedfast faith in his Word. Being united to Christ by faith and living upon him as our hope of salvation, we learn to trust him (Colossians 2:6). Spirit of God, give us grace to walk and war by faith alone, trusting Christ alone and we will have this assurance. Our Saviour promised, 'My sheep hear my voice, and I know them, and they follow me: And I give unto them eternal life; and they shall never perish' (John 10:27, 28). The reason many of God's people lack assurance is that they do not stedfastly look to Christ. We look at Christ with one eye and with the other at our sins, our failures and our corruptions. Christ alone must be our assurance.

When Paul says, 'Take the helmet of salvation', he means for us to confidently trust the Saviour. Trust his righteousness, the merits of his blood and the promises of his Word. Trust his power, his goodness and his grace. 'The helmet of salvation' is a sound understanding of the gospel. It is the hope of salvation by Christ and it is the assurance of our personal interest in Christ our Saviour.

Our need

Why do we need this helmet? As soldiers we are engaged in warfare and we must have the helmet of salvation to protect and defend us against the blows of our enemies. An assured hope of salvation protects us from every form of attack.

The world allures us with the charms of vanity, pleasure, fame and fortune. But if we are assured of our interest in Christ and eternal glory by him, we will not be much inclined to forsake our eternal inheritance for this perishing world.

Our own sinful flesh attempts to destroy us. But an assured hope in Christ subdues the power of the flesh and keeps it from overcoming us. 'Greater is he that is in you, than he that is in the world' (1 John 4:4). Our sinful lusts rise up, but we deny them, saying Christ has conquered you. Our pride rises up, but we beat it down as a traitor against Christ. Our old corruptions erupt in our hearts to make us despair of salvation. We weep over them but deny them a hearing and refuse to let Satan raise Moses up against us, saying Christ has forgiven me through his blood.

Satan comes against us in great fury, but we overcome him with an assured hope in Christ. When he tempts us to sin, our helmet protects us. When he assails us with inconsistencies or errors, we are protected by our helmet. When he accuses us of sin and threatens us with the law, we repel his blows, taking the helmet of salvation, we say, 'I am in Christ, I trust him alone, and for me there is no possibility of condemnation'.

Those who have an assured hope of salvation in Christ are most actively engaged in serving him. We fight on with confidence, 'Looking unto Jesus the author and finisher of our faith', confident that victory is ours. Even as he looked not at the cross and shame, but at the joy and victory he would accomplish, so we look not at our troubles, but at our triumph. Those who have for a helmet the assured hope of salvation face the last struggle of death with confidence. Hope holds the head of faith erect and strong when Jordan swells before God's saints.

Someone once wrote, 'The least degree of faith takes away the sting of death, because it takes away the guilt; but the full assurance of faith breaks the very teeth and jaws of death, by taking away the fear and dread of it'.

These were Samuel Rutherford's words on his death bed, 'O that all my brethren did know what a Master I have served, and what peace I have this day! I shall sleep in Christ, and when I awake, I shall be satisfied with his likeness.'

On his death bed Richard Baxter said, 'I bless God I have gotten a well-grounded assurance of my eternal happiness, and great peace and comfort within'. In his dying moments someone asked him how he was doing. The old saint said, 'Almost well'.

Put it on

Perhaps you are asking, 'How am I to take the helmet and put it on?' Here are only a few brief words of instruction:

Faithfully attend the ministry of the Word. It is through the reading and preaching of the Word of God that you can obtain a sound understanding of gospel doctrine.

Study Christ. The more you know of Christ's glorious Person and his saving fulness, his everlasting love and his covenant mercy, his sovereign majesty and his amazing grace, the more you will be inclined to trust him.

Spend much time in private worship, praise, meditation and prayer, and trust Christ completely. Trust him at all times and in all things. Live upon his merits, and take him at his Word.

Take your helmet, the helmet of salvation. Go forth to the conflict. In the holy confidence of faith, serve your Master. Patiently wait for your salvation. Courage, my brother, it is near. Courage my sister, Christ is coming! Courage children of God, victory is sure! 'Stand still, and see the salvation of the LORD.'

Chapter 75

Take The Sword

And take … the sword of the Spirit.

(Ephesians 6:17)

'Take the sword.' – Take the sword! That is the command of God in Ephesians 6:17 to all who are his. It is not enough to be resisting, we must conquer. We are not merely to defend our ground; we are to assail the enemy. We take the helmet to protect our head and we take the sword to attack the enemy. Ours is a stern conflict. We must stand and withstand, assail and conquer. Therefore, we must take unto ourselves the whole armour of God.

No compromise

The defence of Zion's walls, the defence of our souls, our assault on the gates of hell and our conquest over the world, the flesh, and the devil must be obtained by fighting a stern, relentless, determined war. Many try compromise. But for faithful souls compromise is out of the question. With regard to spiritual matters – the truth of God, the glory of God, and the Word of God – we must be like Moses in Pharaoh's court. Stand your ground, feet firmly planted and refuse to compromise on the slightest point.

The language of deceit is not suitable for a blood-bought tongue. Our adversary, the devil, is the father of lies. Those who are with him understand the craftiness of deception but God's saints abhor it. If we discuss terms of peace and attempt to gain something by compliance, we have entered a course of shame and disgrace. Our Saviour, our Captain, has not sent us out to offer concessions to the enemy.

Men tell us and our flesh tells us, 'Yield a little and the world will accept you. If your doctrine were a little more lax, not quite so sharp, if you just were not so dogmatic, you would not meet with so much opposition.'

But we have no such instruction from our Commander, Christ the Lord. When peace is made, he will make it. There can be no peace for the ungodly until they surrender to our mighty Commander, whose name is the Prince of Peace, King of Kings and Lord of Lords. The Mighty God says, 'Take the Sword'.

We can never hope to gain anything in this warfare by being neutral, or seeking a truce. We are not to cease from our conflict and try to appease or even make ourselves more appealing to our Lord's enemies. In the kingdom of God, compromise is treason! 'Take the sword.' There is no time for philosophical talk and intellectual debate. The word thunders out, 'Take the sword'. Our Captain's voice is a clarion trumpet sound, 'Take the sword'.

We are not obedient to our text unless with clear, sharp and decisive resolve, we take 'the sword of the Spirit, which is the word of God'. We must march over the gates of hell and up to the gates of the city Beautiful with our sword in hand.

God the Holy Spirit here teaches us that the inspired Word of God is a sword, mighty through the power of God, by which the enemies of Christ are slain. This is the last piece of armour named by the Apostle Paul in this chapter. It should be noted this is the only offensive weapon named. We are to use the sword of the Spirit, and that only, as our weapon of offence. We need to know how to handle this mighty two-edged sword, and be determined to substitute nothing in its place. Let our Commander's voice ring in our ears and inspire our souls for the conflict. 'Take the sword, take the sword, and go forth to battle.'

What is the sword?

What is the Sword of the Spirit? The answer is plainly given in our text: 'The sword of the Spirit, which is the word of God'. The Holy Spirit has a sword. The Spirit of God is as quiet as the dew, as tender as anointing oil, as soft as the evening breeze, as peaceful as the dove. Yet he has a sword. This sword is unlike all others. With this sword he both kills and makes alive. He bears not the sword in vain. Of him it may be said, 'The LORD is a man of war: the LORD is his name.'

Christ the Living Word

The essential, living Word of God is our Lord Jesus Christ, God's eternal Son. Christ is the full, complete revelation of God to men. He is the embodiment of the divine Revelation. We have this plainly stated in several passages of Scripture.

'In the beginning was the Word, and the Word was with God, and the Word was God' (John 1:1).

'The Word of God is quick, and powerful, and sharper than any twoedged sword, piercing even to the dividing asunder of soul and spirit, and of the joints and marrow, and is a discerner of the thoughts and intents of the heart. Neither is there any creature that is not manifest in his sight: but all things are naked and opened unto the eyes of him with whom we have to do' (Hebrews 4:12, 13).

'And he was clothed with a vesture dipped in blood: and his name is called The Word of God' (Revelation 19:13).

The written Word

These passages all speak of our great Saviour, the Lord Jesus Christ, the Son of God. But he is not the 'word of God' spoken of in our text. Here Paul is talking about the written, or declared Word, that goes forth out of the Saviour's mouth. 'And out of his mouth goeth a sharp twoedged sword, that with it he should smite the nations' (Revelation 19:15). I want you to note several things about this 'sword of the Spirit, which is the word of God'.

The Holy Scriptures are undoubtedly the Word of God. By the Scriptures, I mean the Old and the New Testaments. The Scriptures are called the sword of the Spirit because he is the author of the Book. The Holy Spirit revealed the mind of God to holy men whom he chose. He spoke the word to their hearts and made them think as he thinks and write what he would have them write. All that they spoke and wrote, under his influence, was spoken and written as the very Word of God.

God did not give his prophets and apostles a theme to write on, according to their own abilities. They were secretaries who wrote infallibly what he dictated. This is the claim of those men who wrote the Scriptures. 'All Scripture is given by inspiration of God' (2 Timothy 3:16). That is, the Word of God came as truly and immediately from the heart and mind of God, as our breath comes from our bodies. 'Holy men of God spake as they were moved – or carried along – by the Holy Ghost' (2 Peter 1:21).

We do not have to depend only on the testimony of those who penned the Scriptures. There is abundant evidence that the Bible is the very voice of God written out on paper. The very substance of the Scriptures demonstrates their divine origin. There are many historical statements in the Bible that could not have been known except by revelation. The account of the creation must have been revealed. The everlasting decrees of God must have been revealed. The covenant of eternal grace is a matter of revelation alone.

The honest integrity and simplicity of those men who recorded the Scriptures in recording the faults and failures of themselves and their dearest friends and companions shows their divine origin. Find me a volume anywhere that is written by a man that records the faults of that man, his family, or his friends, without making excuse for them. Noah's drunkenness is stated plainly. Abraham's sin is not covered. Moses revealed his own faults and the idolatry of his brother, and the sin of his sister are not omitted. David, the man after God's own heart, is set before us not only in his greatness, but also in his shame.

The same spirit is demonstrated throughout the gospels, the book of Acts, and the epistles. The absolute and perfect fulfilment of the prophecies of the Old Testament are an undeniable proof of their divine origin. The intricate details of Christ's Person, his birth, his life and his sufferings are plainly set forth in the Old Testament. The many things with reference to the nation of Israel were prophesied long before they took place. Their bondage in Egypt and the day of their deliverance. The exact period of their Babylonian captivity. Their rejection of the Messiah, and their utter ruin.

The doctrinal portions of Scripture have a positive stamp of divine inspiration. The nature and character of God is a matter known only by revelation. The Trinity of the Divine Persons could not be known, but by revelation. The truths of the gospel could have no source, but the mind of God.

The substance of Scripture demands a belief in their divine origin. Their perfect unity compels us to say this is the Word of God. The books of the Old and New Testaments are sixty-six in number. They were written over a period of four thousand years, by a great variety of men. Yet they all contain the same message, declaring to men that the holy and just God is merciful to sinful men, and saves them by the substitutionary work of his own Son. In a word, the message of the Bible is this, 'In due time, Christ died for the ungodly'.

Another evidence of inspiration is the effects of the Bible upon men. The Word of God searches the heart and pierces the conscience. It tells a man things about himself no one could know but the man himself. It tells us things about ourselves we do not know. The Word of God powerfully convinces men of sin, righteousness and judgment yet it has the power to comfort and raise the souls of men.

The Bible is the Word of God and alone is the sword of the Spirit. As the Word of God, it is absolutely complete and sufficient. 'God, who at sundry times and in divers manners spake in time past unto the fathers by the prophets, hath in these last days spoken unto us by his Son' (Hebrews 1:1, 2). The Word of God, which was completed with the writings of the apostles of Christ himself, is God's full revelation. The Bible is sufficient in itself for all things. It makes us wise unto salvation, showing us the way of faith. It is our doctrinal creed, our book of discipline and our only rule of faith and practice. The Word of God is the only sword employed by the Holy Spirit for the salvation of men and the edification of the saints. Many today have stooped to cheap tricks and entertainment to imitate the accomplishment of what they think the gospel cannot do. The church is the pillar and ground of the truth. It is our business to declare to men the Word of God. We dare not construct a new word from God. We need no further revelation, no vision, no authority but, 'Thus saith the LORD'.

Why the sword of the Spirit?

Why is the Word of God called the sword of the Spirit? The Word of God, in the hand of the Spirit, wounds terribly and makes the heart of man to bleed. Some of you can remember how you were cut Sunday after Sunday, week after week, by this mighty sword. The mighty sword pursued you, until finally your heart was pierced and you were slain. Then, he that killed made you alive. Still the Word is a sword. How it pierces. How it hacks away at the flesh. How it cuts our pride. How it demolishes our idols.

The Word of God is a sharp two-edged sword. John Gill said, 'The Word of God is compared to a sword, for its two edges: the law and the gospel. The one convicts of sin and cuts it to the heart, and the other cuts down all the goodliness of man.' With one swing of the sword, the law of God slays the sinner. The demands of the law are holy and perfect. Every man has broken the law, is without excuse and is under the sentence of condemnation.

The Word of God is the sword of the Spirit. It is the Holy Spirit alone who can instruct us in the proper use of this weapon. No one can handle the sword of the Spirit correctly unless he is taught of God. The saints of God know the voice of God by instinct, for the Spirit dwells in them. The Spirit takes the things of Christ and shows them to us. He teaches us such things as are written in the Book of God.

The Spirit of God alone makes this sword powerful and effectual. When the Holy Spirit makes the Word of God effectual to the hearts of men then we can say with Paul, 'The weapons of our warfare are not carnal, but mighty through God to the pulling down of strong holds' (2 Corinthians 10:4). We have seen giants slain by this sword and we yet expect to see others slain. This sword is the product of the Spirit of God and he preserves it. 'The word of the Lord endureth for ever. And this is the word which by the gospel is preached unto you' (1 Peter 1:25).

Who is to wield it?

Who must take the sword of the Spirit? This is a charge given to every child of God. 'Take the sword of the Spirit, which is the word of God'. This is a charge given to every gospel church. Take 'the sword of the Spirit, which is the word of God'. This is a charge given to every preacher of the gospel. Take 'the sword of the Spirit, which is the word of God'. The Lord God, who chose us and called us to the work of the gospel, has laid down the method of our ministry and the weapons of our warfare. All carnal weapons we must carefully avoid such as human reason, human eloquence, deceit and trickery. The only weapon of our warfare is the Word of God. Reverence it. Study it. Pray over it. Meditate upon it. Preach it tenderly, powerfully, persuasively, fully and boldly. In preaching the Word of God, we must insist upon the foundation doctrine of the Word, the doctrine of Christ, continually. I wish preachers would quit trying to be brilliant. Oh, that preachers would in simplicity declare the Word of God. Just declare, man's ruin by the fall, redemption by the blood of Christ, regeneration by the Holy Spirit, and the absolute Lordship and sovereignty of Christ.

How?

How are we to use this mighty weapon? We must use it against all our enemies. When Satan would tempt us, we repel him with 'thus saith the LORD'. When our lusts rage within us, we fight them off with 'it is written'. When heresies are propounded we put them down by 'God hath spoken'. When doubts arise, we hear the Word of God. When afflictions come we listen to the voice of God in his Word.

We must use the sword of the Spirit to invade the kingdom of darkness. This alone will convince men of sin. This alone will reprove men with righteousness. This alone will persuade men of justice satisfied. It is by the Word of God that sinners are slain.

See that you reverence your Bible. Believe your Bible. It is the Word of God. All things stand or fall according to what is written in this sacred volume. Obey your Bible. Pray for the power of the Holy Spirit to accompany the ministry of the Word. Take unto you 'the sword of the Spirit, which is the word of God'. Soon we shall overcome by this mighty weapon. 'They overcame him by the blood of the Lamb, and by the word of their testimony' (Revelation 12:11). In that great day, our Lord shall judge men by every word that proceeds from the mouth of God.

Chapter 76

Praying In The Spirit

Praying always with all prayer and supplication in the Spirit, and watching thereunto with all perseverance and supplication for all saints; And for me, that utterance may be given unto me, that I may open my mouth boldly, to make known the mystery of the gospel, For which I am an ambassador in bonds: that therein I may speak boldly, as I ought to speak.

(Ephesians 6:18-20)

Prayer

What is prayer? When and how are we to pray? Do we have any reason to expect God to hear our prayers? I hope the Lord will enable me to answer those questions for you in a practical way. I am not going to give you any set formulas for prayer. Nor will I try to establish a certain time for you to pray. The Pharisee made long prayers with a definite formula and in a formal posture. He prayed long, prayed frequently and prayed publicly, but God did not hear him. Whereas, the poor publican offered to God one, short, humble prayer, trusting in the merits of Christ, and the God of all grace heard him.

Prayer Defined

It is very difficult to give a definition of true prayer. It has been called the breath of a newborn soul. It is characterised by confession, faith, intercession, request and praise. But all of these things come short. Perhaps I can best describe it by first pointing out some mistaken notions about prayer.

Prayer is more than a ritual performed at given times. It is more than repeating something someone has written, and more than asking and receiving. True prayer might be defined in this way: it is the believing, submissive heart worshipping God and seeking his will. Prayer is an act not of the body, but of the heart. It is an act but it is more than an act. It is a spirit of faith, confidence and submission.

Last statement

The Apostle comes to his last statement with regard to what we as God's people have to do in this matter of our spiritual warfare against Satan and the hosts of evil.

The New Testament plainly teaches us that because we are the children of God we must expect attacks upon us by the powers of darkness, such as we have never known or realised before. But, thank God, we are not only told we will have to wrestle and fight with our enemy, we are also told how to do so successfully. Paul has assured us of the final triumph of the kingdom of Christ over the kingdom of darkness. He has described for us each piece of armour. Now he concludes his exhortations by instructing us in this matter of prayer.

What is the meaning of this final exhortation? What relationship does this praying in the Spirit have with what Paul has been saying up to this point? It is this: praying in the Spirit is something we must do, and keep on doing, in order to rightly use our armour. This is to be our prevailing attitude and work throughout the days of our warfare with the world, the flesh and the devil. Paul is saying, 'Take these pieces of armour and put them on. Put them on carefully and use them in the way I have described. In addition to that, always at all times, and in every circumstance keep on praying in the Spirit'. One of our hymns expresses Paul's meaning nicely:

Stand up, stand up for Jesus,
Stand in His strength alone;
The arm of flesh will fail you,
You dare not trust your own:
Put on the gospel armour,
Each piece put on with prayer,
Where duty calls, or danger,
Be never wanting there.

What Paul teaches us in these verses is that everything we have to do as God's people in this world must be done in the spirit and attitude of prayer. It strikes me that Paul had a very specific reason for ending this particular epistle with an exhortation to prayer. Perhaps above all other books in the New Testament, the epistle to the Ephesians is devoted to doctrine. This is a book full of the deepest mysteries and most profound theology to be found anywhere in the Bible. The great principles which govern the life of every individual believer and the life of the church as a whole are clearly taught in these six chapters. It is interesting to observe therefore, as he comes to his closing remarks, that they form an exhortation about prayer. It appears to me Paul is telling us praying in the Spirit is the most important aspects of a believer's life. Praying in the Spirit is the secret source of a believer's strength. Perhaps this is the thing of greatest importance if it is properly understood.

When?

The first question that we are confronted with is this: When are we to pray? The apostle says, 'Praying always'. What prominence does this matter of prayer have in our lives? This is a question I address to us all. I ask it of the humble and unlearned. I ask it of the well-educated and knowledgeable. I ask it of the preacher and the hearer. Do we know anything of real prayer? If so, what is the place of prayer in our daily lives?

Let me say at the outset that in the New Testament it is assumed that all true believers are people of prayer. It is true, our attitude toward prayer may vary. The strength and liveliness of prayer may at times be hindered. The confidence and joy of prayer may be interrupted for a season. But all believers pray. Prayer is the breath of the heaven-born soul. Prayer is the cry of the newborn babe in grace. Frequently, we hear of a person who is described as 'a praying Christian'. But there is no such thing as a Christian who does not pray. We grow in prayer, just as we grow in faith. All God's people pray.

In our text Paul does not admonish us to pray, but to pray always. Our Lord said to his disciples, 'When ye pray', assuming that they would pray. The wicked, the unbelieving, the hypocrite, the Pharisee, the religionist all say prayers; but the children of God pray. Prayer is not just a mark of strong faith; prayer is a mark of faith, period! All of God's children pray. What convinced God's church that Saul of Tarsus had been truly converted was this statement, 'Behold, he prayeth'. Prayer is the longing, the panting, of our souls after God.

When Paul admonishes us to pray always, he is telling us that the armour which God has provided for us cannot be used except in fellowship and communion with God. The armour and the spiritual application of it must always be conceived of in a vital and living manner. Every single piece is utterly useless, unless always and at all times we are in a living relationship to God, and receiving strength and power from him. To put it another way, the Apostle is telling us that even orthodoxy is not enough. We must be orthodox, but we need God's power. There is nothing so tragic as dead orthodoxy. Prayer is more important than mere religious knowledge and understanding. The ultimate test of my real knowledge and understanding of the Scriptures is my attitude to prayer. The more I know God, the more I seek him.

Paul's admonition is this: the children of God in this world should always pray. Our Lord taught us 'men ought always to pray and not to faint'. By his own example, he has shown us the value of prayer. Time and time again we see the Lord Jesus coming apart to pray. He spent entire nights in prayer. He rose up early before the dawn to pray. Surely, we who are but mortal men and women should learn from the Saviour's example the value of prayer. When Paul says, 'Praying always', I think he has three things specifically in mind.

The apostle means we ought to pray as often as we have opportunity. We ought to pray at all times and under all circumstances. Our prayers may be oral, or they may be silent. They may be lengthy or brief. Every blessing and every trial, every joy and every sorrow, every pain and every relief, every temptation and every deliverance, should supply an occasion and bring us before the Lord in prayer.

For another thing, Paul is showing us the necessity of walking by faith (Proverbs 3:5, 6). When he says, 'Pray without ceasing', he is telling us to live in the constant awareness of our dependence upon God's grace, strength and wisdom. We are dependent upon our God for the necessities of life. We are dependent upon him for our entire salvation, and our sanctification. In all things we must be looking unto Jesus, the Author and Finisher of our faith.

The Apostle Paul is showing us the necessity of seeking the Lord. Prayer is seeking God. When Paul tells us to be 'praying always', he is saying make prayer our way of life. Seek his grace, his will, his wisdom, his guidance, his presence, his power and his glory, always. When Paul urges us to pray always, I think he has in mind the idea of constantly waiting upon the Lord. 'Wait on the LORD: be of good courage, and he shall strengthen thine heart: wait, I say, on the LORD' (Psalm 27:14). 'Truly, my soul waiteth upon God: from him cometh my salvation … My soul, wait thou only upon God; for my expectation is from him' (Psalm 62:1, 5). Waiting upon the Lord is not a passive state of indifference. It is watching, looking, expecting and anticipating at all times the accomplishment of God's promise and purpose, without tense anxiety and fear (Philippians 4:5-7).

How are we to pray?

How are we to pray? The Apostle assumes that all of God's people will pray. He teaches us to pray always. Now he shows us how. 'With all prayer and supplication in the Spirit, and watching thereunto with all perseverance and supplication.'

Certain prayers that are clearly opposed to Paul's language in this verse. You will notice that the language Paul is using is full of life, vitality, energy, fervency and zeal. Any prayer not marked, at least in measure, by these things is contrary to the spirit of our text. Vain repetitions are not praying. Cold, heartless, formal prayers are to be avoided. Frequently, men will ask us to 'say a prayer'. I dare say that 'saying a prayer' is near-kin to blasphemy. Any prayer that calls attention to ourselves, except as sinners in need of mercy, is contrary to the spirit of our text.

Paul encourages us to constantly employ every form and aspect of prayer. I do not think he is limiting us to either private or public prayer in this verse. He is telling us how we should pray, both in private and in public. We should employ 'all prayer and supplication'. All of our praying should be marked by reverent adoration, praise, worship and thanksgiving. We should come to God in reverence confessing our sin. We should come before him with adoration for his glorious Person. We should come before the Lord with praise for his blessings in Christ. We should come before the Triune God to worship him with joy because of our knowledge of him. We should make thanksgiving a great part of our praying, because of God's bountiful goodness to us. Prayer arises from our sense of need, so we make supplication to the Lord. We ought to freely pour out to the Lord the needs of our hearts and ask him to supply those needs (Hebrews 4:16).

Above all else, we must pray in the spirit. This is the thing that is emphasised over and over again in the New Testament, praying in the spirit. This is the real essence, the very life of prayer (Ephesians 2:18; Romans 8:23-26; Jude 20). If we ever truly pray, we pray in a spiritual way, with fervency of heart, by the assistance of the Holy Spirit. This means that the Holy Spirit creates the prayer within us. He directs the prayer, and empowers us to offer it. Praying in the spirit is praying according to the will of God. It is praying with freedom, ease, and liberty before God. Praying in the spirit always results in true worship. When we pray in the spirit, we lay hold of God.

Such prayers may be no more than sighs and groans of the heart which tongue cannot utter. They may be just brief ejaculations of the heart. They may be well ordered petitions. They may be private. They may be public. But they are always powerful and prevailing with God. Paul tells us. 'Watching thereunto with all perseverance and supplication.' Let your prayers be marked by expectancy. Persevere in prayer. Keep on making your supplication to the Lord. 'Men ought always to pray and not to faint.' In this way, we put on the whole armour of God. In this way, we are prepared for war. To keep your armour bright, attend to it with care, walking in your Captain's sight, and watching unto prayer.

What?

The last question for our consideration is this. What should the children of God pray for? Our prayers should be specific. We should have a definite goal in mind when we go to God in prayer. The Apostle tells us we should pray 'for all saints; and for me that utterance may be given unto me, that I may open my mouth boldly, to make known the mystery of the gospel, for which I am an ambassador in bonds: that therein I may speak boldly, as I ought to speak'.

Far too often, I fear, our prayers are selfish. We pray for our children, our families, our church and our country. Paul says that prayer is to be made for all saints. Let us pray for ourselves but do not make self the centre of prayer. We must pray for all of God's saints. We are all members of one body. We all have the same enemy, and we all have the same trials and temptations.

Whenever I undergo some trial, some sorrow or adversity, it should cause me to pray for my brethren because there are others who are facing the very same problem (Hebrews 13:1-5). This mutual caring for one another increases the love, joy, peace and strength of Christ's kingdom upon the earth.

Paul tells us we should pray for the successful ministry of the gospel. Pray for those who preach the gospel; they are, after all, only men. Pray that God will give his servants both boldness and power. Pray for the power of the Spirit of God to attend the ministry of the Word, that the mystery of the gospel might be revealed.

Let us make the disciples' request our own. 'Lord, teach us to pray' (Luke 11:1). Pray always. Seek every opportunity for prayer. Live in dependence upon the Lord, seeking him in all things. Pray with importunity, like the Syrophenician woman, and wait upon our God with expectation.

May it please God the Holy Spirit to make us men and women of prayer. In all things, may this be our desire, let God be magnified.

Chapter 77

Pray For Me

Praying always with all prayer and supplication in the Spirit, and watching thereunto with all perseverance and supplication for all saints; And for me, that utterance may be given unto me, that I may open my mouth boldly, to make known the mystery of the gospel. For which I am an ambassador in bonds: that therein I may speak boldly, as I ought to speak. But that ye also may know my affairs, *and* how I do, Tychicus, a beloved brother and faithful minister in the Lord, shall make known to you all things: Whom I have sent unto you for the same purpose, that ye might know our affairs, and *that* he might comfort your hearts. Peace *be* to the brethren, and love with faith, from God the Father and the Lord Jesus Christ. Grace *be* with all them that love our Lord Jesus Christ in sincerity. Amen.

(Ephesians 6:18-24)

How often have you said to someone, 'Pray for me'? How often have you heard that request from a sick friend, a troubled soul, or a heavy heart? How often I have asked others to 'pray for me'. But what are we asking when we say to someone, 'Pray for me'? What are our friends asking of us, when they say to us, 'Pray for me'? Let me show you the example of one man, the Apostle Paul. As much as possible, I want to use Paul's words in Ephesians 6:18-24 as my own words. This was his request and it is mine also.

Acts 20

Paul was a devoted, zealous preacher of the gospel. He was determined to seize every opportunity to spread the gospel through the world, using every means at his disposal.

He visited Ephesus briefly on his first missionary journey (Acts 18:18-21). On his third missionary journey, the Apostle returned to Ephesus for three years. By the preaching of the gospel, he was used by God the Holy Ghost to persuade many in that huge, pagan city to turn from their idols to the living God, trusting our Lord Jesus Christ (Acts 19, 20). The church God raised up there was dear to Paul, and Paul was dear to that congregation.

Toward the end of his third missionary journey, Paul stopped by Miletus, and there the elders of the Ephesian congregation came to visit their cherished minister. Just before parting, Paul gave his friends a solemn charge, commending them and the church they served 'to God and the Word of his grace'.

'And from Miletus he sent to Ephesus, and called the elders of the church. And when they were come to him, he said unto them, Ye know, from the first day that I came into Asia, after what manner I have been with you at all seasons, Serving the Lord with all humility of mind, and with many tears, and temptations, which befell me by the lying in wait of the Jews: And how I kept back nothing that was profitable unto you, but have shewed you, and have taught you publickly, and from house to house, Testifying both to the Jews, and also to the Greeks, repentance toward God, and faith toward our Lord Jesus Christ. And now, behold, I go bound in the spirit unto Jerusalem, not knowing the things that shall befall me there: Save that the Holy Ghost witnesseth in every city, saying that bonds and afflictions abide me. But none of these things move me, neither count I my life dear unto myself, so that I might finish my course with joy, and the ministry, which I have received of the Lord Jesus, to testify the gospel of the grace of God. And now, behold, I know that ye all, among whom I have gone preaching the kingdom of God, shall see my face no more. Wherefore I take you to record this day, that I am pure from the blood of all men. For I have not shunned to declare unto you all the counsel of God. Take heed therefore unto yourselves, and to all the flock, over the which the Holy Ghost hath made you overseers, to feed the church of God, which he hath purchased with his own blood. For I know this, that after my departing shall grievous wolves enter in among you, not sparing the flock. Also of your own selves shall men arise, speaking perverse things, to draw away disciples after them. Therefore watch, and remember, that by the space of three years I ceased not to warn every one night and day with tears. And now, brethren, I commend you to God, and to the word of his grace, which is able to build you up, and to give you an inheritance among all them which are sanctified' (Acts 20:17-32).

'And when he had thus spoken, he kneeled down, and prayed with them all. And they all wept sore, and fell on Paul's neck, and kissed him, Sorrowing most of all for the words which he spake, that they should see his face no more. And they accompanied him unto the ship' (Acts 20:36-38).

Acts 21

Taking leave of his Ephesian brethren, Paul left for Jerusalem. Finding believers in Syria, he tarried with them for seven days. There, the brethren, being concerned for Paul, begged him not to proceed to Jerusalem. But he would not be deterred. Then at Caesarea, a certain prophet named Agabus came to Paul with a message from God, telling him plainly what would happen if he went to preach the gospel at Jerusalem.

'And as we tarried there many days, there came down from Judaea a certain prophet, named Agabus. And when he was come unto us, he took Paul's girdle, and bound his own hands and feet, and said, Thus saith the Holy Ghost, So shall the Jews at Jerusalem bind the man that owneth this girdle, and shall deliver him into the hands of the Gentiles. And when we heard these things, both we, and they of that place, besought him not to go up to Jerusalem. Then Paul answered, What mean ye to weep and to break mine heart? for I am ready not to be bound only, but also to die at Jerusalem for the name of the Lord Jesus. And when he would not be persuaded, we ceased, saying, The will of the Lord be done' (Acts 21:10-14).

A final request

What a remarkable, self-denying, self-sacrificing man Paul was! What an example he set for all who would walk in his steps! O Spirit of God, make me such a preacher! Make me such a faithful servant!

When we get to Ephesians 6, all that had been prophesied in Acts 20 and 21 concerning this man has come to pass. Now, as he comes to the end of his epistle to his dear friends at Ephesus, Paul has one final word, one final request. He says, 'Brethren, pray for me'.

He was now in prison at Rome. He knew, as he had told them, he would never again see his beloved brethren at Ephesus upon the earth. The old soldier knew that he was soon going to be required to lay down his life for the gospel's sake. He wrote this epistle to strengthen them and us in the great truths of the gospel, to establish us in the love of Christ, to unify God's saints in the bonds of peace, to exhort us to godly conduct, and to encourage us in our spiritual warfare.

Now, he must conclude his epistle. In doing so, I can only imagine the thoughts that must have rushed through his mind. These would be the last words that these brethren would have from him. What should he say? What would be most beneficial to the church he was leaving behind at Ephesus? What would most effectually secure the church's adherence to the gospel and loyalty to Christ? With those thoughts in mind, the Apostle expressed the great desire of his soul to the brethren at Ephesus in the words of our text here in Ephesians 6:18-24.

God's true servants labour in the Word for the glory of Christ, for the furtherance of the gospel, and for the edification of the church. Knowing their own weaknesses, their own sin, and their utter inability to do the work God has put in their hands, they need and desire the prayers of God's people on their behalf. This is what Paul asked, and this is what I ask as a pastor – pray for me.

Regarding the present

As a pastor, I ask that my people pray for me regarding the present, that I may make known the mystery of the gospel. 'And for me, that utterance may be given unto me, that I may open my mouth boldly, to make known the mystery of the gospel. For which I am an ambassador in bonds: that therein I may speak boldly, as I ought to speak' (vv. 19, 20). I want to be found faithful unto death preaching the gospel of Christ.

This was the matter of eminent concern to the Apostle Paul. He requested an interest in the prayers of God's saints for this cause – that he might make known the mystery of the gospel. All other matters were secondary to this. Paul did not ask the saints to pray for his imprisonment, his physical infirmities or his reproach. He did not ask that he might be freed from his bonds. He was willing to endure anything so that he might preach the gospel (Acts 21:11-13).

Paul desired prayer be made for him to preach the gospel with boldness. Even in prison, he considered himself to be an ambassador. He was sent of God with a message to declare. He wanted a door of utterance that he might have opportunity to preach. He wanted boldness and blunt assertiveness, to preach the gospel regardless of personal cost. This is the one thing I desire. That I may preach the gospel, that I may 'make known the mystery of the gospel'.

These three things I hold to be of highest importance.

I want to know the gospel

'Moreover, brethren, I declare unto you the gospel which I preached unto you, which also ye have received, and wherein ye stand; By which also ye are saved, if ye keep in memory what I preached unto you, unless ye have believed in vain. For I delivered unto you first of all that which I also received, how that Christ died for our sins according to the scriptures; And that he was buried, and that he rose again the third day according to the scriptures' (1 Corinthians 15:1-4).

'For I am not ashamed of the gospel of Christ: for it is the power of God unto salvation to everyone that believeth; to the Jew first, and also to the Greek. For therein is the righteousness of God revealed from faith to faith: as it is written, The just shall live by faith. For the wrath of God is revealed from heaven against all ungodliness and unrighteousness of men, who hold the truth in unrighteousness' (Romans 1:16-18). It is the gospel of God. It is the gospel promised in the Scriptures. It is the gospel concerning God's Son.

I want to be saved by the gospel

I want to preach the gospel (1 Corinthians 9:16). I want God to give me a door of utterance, and I want to preach with bold simplicity. We must not be bound by ambition, human pride, men or customs and traditions.

Someone may say, why are these things so important? It is important for just this reason – most people today have never heard the gospel! Today's gospel emphasises what the sinner does for God, rather than what God does for the sinner. Today's gospel emphasises heaven and hell, rather than the real issues of Christ and sin. Today's gospel is a message to the head, not to the heart, and today's gospel calls on men to stand up and be counted, while the gospel of God calls on men to bow down and worship.

I want to make known to men everywhere the mystery of the gospel, that is the mystery of God's salvation through a Substitute. So, as Paul asked his brethren, I ask this one thing of those who hear me. I ask nothing more. Pray for me. God has sent me into this world with a message. I am an ambassador of God. Pray that I may have a door of utterance. Pray that I may be bold in preaching. Pray that I may preach the gospel and every time I preach God will give me his message to deliver.

Regarding the future

When I am gone, when my work is done, it is my earnest prayer that God will graciously send another pastor, another preacher, who will be faithful to the gospel for the comfort of the hearts of his people. 'But that ye also may know my affairs, and how I do, Tychicus, a beloved brother and faithful minister in the Lord, shall make known to you all things: Whom I have sent unto you for the same purpose, that ye might know our affairs, and that he might comfort your hearts' (vv. 21, 22).

Paul's self-denial was remarkable. He had great personal needs. But his concern was for the church he was leaving behind. Therefore, he sent Tychicus to minister to his beloved brethren. If a man is a true pastor, his chief concern is for the church of Christ and the ministry of the gospel. Paul sent Tychicus with the highest possible recommendation. Tychicus was a beloved brother and a faithful minister. He came to comfort the saints.

You will notice that there was no hint of jealousy between these men. What tender concern this local church had for the man by whom God had taught them the gospel! What tender concern Paul had for this congregation. These two things characterise any God-called pastor: First, he is a brother of a tender, loving heart. Second, he is faithful to God, to the gospel, to the souls of men and to his calling.

Those who are called of God to this holy work have noble desires which motivate them. They seek the glory of God. They declare unto men the mystery of God and they seek to comfort the saints of God.

Your blessedness

I have one other desire that is expressed in our text. I want you to know and enjoy all the blessings of God in Christ. 'Peace be to the brethren, and love with faith, from God the Father and the Lord Jesus Christ. Grace be with all them that love our Lord Jesus Christ in sincerity. Amen.' (vv. 23, 24). I pray that our God will continue to heap on you all the blessings of his goodness and grace in Christ Jesus.

I want you to enjoy peace. May God assure your hearts of peace in Christ. May God govern your hearts with peace. May God give you peace with one another. Such peace is always intimately connected with your attitude toward those who labour in the gospel for your souls. 'And we beseech you, brethren, to know them which labour among you, and are over you in the Lord, and admonish you; And to esteem them very highly in love for their work's sake. And be at peace among yourselves' (1 Thessalonians 5:12, 13).

I want you to be filled with love. May God grant to you a fuller knowledge and assurance of his love in Christ. May He cause you to love Christ, to love the gospel, and to love one another. I pray that God will establish in your hearts this divine character of love. Without it there is no true, saving faith.

I want you to grow in faith and confident assurance, 'the full assurance of faith'. May it please our God to grant to you his constant, free, unmerited grace in Christ. Grace brings faith. Faith brings love. Love brings peace, and all these come to us from God our Father through our Lord Jesus Christ.

Brethren, pray for me, that I may be faithful to seek the glory of Christ, that I may be faithful to preach the gospel, that I may finish my course with honour to the glory of Christ (2 Timothy 4:1-18).

Index Of Bible Verses

Old Testament

Psalms

Proverbs

Ecclesiastes

Index Of Bible Verses

New Testament

www.ingramcontent.com/pod-product-compliance
Lightning Source LLC
Chambersburg PA
CBHW020457100426
42812CB00024B/2686

* 9 7 8 1 9 0 8 4 7 5 3 1 2 *